AMERICAN FOREIGN
RELATIONS
1973

A DOCUMENTARY RECORD

COUNCIL ON FOREIGN RELATIONS BOOKS

Founded in 1921, the Council on Foreign Relations, Inc. is a non-profit and non-partisan organization of individuals devoted to the promotion of a better and wider understanding of international affairs through the free interchange of ideas. The membership of the Council, which numbers about 1,600, is made up of men and women throughout the United States elected by the Board of Directors on the basis of an estimate of their special interest, experience and involvement in international affairs and their standing in their own communities. The Council does not take any position on questions of foreign policy, and no person is authorized to speak for the Council on such matters. The Council has no affiliation with and receives no funding from any part of the United States government.

The Council conducts a meetings program to provide its members an opportunity to talk with invited guests who have special experience, expertise or involvement in international affairs, and conducts a studies program of research directed to political, economic and strategic problems related to United States foreign policy. Since 1922 the Council has published the quarterly journal, *Foreign Affairs*. From time to time the Council also publishes books and monographs which in the judgment of the Committee on Studies of the Council's Board of Directors are responsible treatments of significant international topics worthy of presentation to the public. The individual authors of articles in *Foreign Affairs* and of Council books and monographs are solely responsible for all statements of fact and expressions of opinion contained in them.

AMERICAN FOREIGN RELATIONS 1973
A DOCUMENTARY RECORD

Continuing the Series
DOCUMENTS ON AMERICAN FOREIGN RELATIONS

Edited by RICHARD P. STEBBINS and ELAINE P. ADAM

A Council on Foreign Relations Book
Published by
New York University Press • New York • 1976

PREFACE

This volume combines a narrative account of America's foreign relations during 1973 with a presentation of some of the major documents reflecting the country's international experience in that critical year. On the narrative side, the volume continues—albeit on a somewhat reduced scale—the series of annual foreign policy surveys initiated by the Council on Foreign Relations in 1931 and issued with some regularity, under the title of *The United States in World Affairs*, until the inception of the present series in 1971. Concurrently, the documentary content of the volume continues the service provided for more than three decades by the *Documents on American Foreign Relations* series, initiated by the World Peace Foundation in 1939 and carried forward by the Council on Foreign Relations from 1952 through 1970. The fusion of narrative and documentation, commenced on a trial basis with the inauguration of the present series in 1971, is designed to provide a single, comprehensive, and authoritative record of American foreign policy as it develops through the bicentennial decade and beyond.

The need of a coherent presentation of the tangled international history of 1973 has appeared to be best served by a preliminary review of the year's highlights which is followed by 30 broadly chronological chapters, each comprising an editorial summary together with a selection of pertinent documentary material. Editorial treatment of the documents, which are presented in most instances in their authoritative official texts, has been limited mainly to the correction of obvious errors of redaction, the insertion within square brackets of needed supplementary details, and the elucidation of any remaining obscurities through explanatory footnotes. Publications referred to by abbreviated titles are fully identified in the Appendix, which lists the principal sources found useful in the preparation of the volume. All dates refer to the year 1973 unless another year is specified.

The editorial procedure described above admittedly requires the exercise of a high degree of individual judgment and demands all possible impartiality and objectivity in the handling of controversial material. While hopeful that the volume will not be found wanting in this respect, the editors wish to emphasize that the editorial viewpoint is of necessity a personal one and in no way reflects the outlook of the Council on Foreign Relations or any of its officers and directors, members, or staff.

Among their immediate associates, the editors would wish to note their special indebtedness to Grace Darling Griffin, Publications Manager, and Janet Rigney, Librarian, of the Council on Foreign Relations, and to Despina Papazoglou, Associate

Managing Editor, and other friends at NYU Press. They are also indebted to various official agencies which have provided documentary material, and to *The New York Times* for permission to reprint texts or excerpts of documents appearing in its pages. As always, the editors themselves are responsible both for the choice and presentation of the documents and for the form and content of the editorial matter.

R.P.S.
E.P.A.

April 30, 1976

CONTENTS

INTRODUCING 1973   **1**

1. The Second Term Begins   **5**

(1) "A New Era of Peace": Second Inaugural Address of President Richard M. Nixon, January 20, 1973   8

2. Indochina: The "Peace With Honor"   **13**

(2) Assurances to Saigon: Letter from President Nixon to President Nguyen Van Thieu of the Republic of Vietnam, January 5, 1973   19

(3) "Peace With Honor": Radio-Television address by President Nixon on the initialing of the Vietnam Agreement, January 23, 1973   20

(4) Significance of the Agreement: News conference statement by Dr. Henry A. Kissinger, Assistant to the President for National Security Affairs, January 24, 1973 (Excerpt)   23

(5) Agreement on Ending the War and Restoring Peace in Vietnam, signed in Paris and entered into force January 27, 1973   39

(6) Dr. Kissinger Goes to Hanoi: Joint Communiqué issued by the United States and the Democratic Republic of Vietnam, February 14, 1973   52

(7) The International Conference on Vietnam, Paris, February 26-March 2, 1973   54

    (a) Views of the United States: Statement to the Conference by Secretary of State William P. Rogers, February 26, 1973   54
    (b) Act of the International Conference on Vietnam, signed at Paris and entered into force March 2, 1973   58

(8) Visit of President Thieu to the United States: Joint Communiqué of President Nixon and President Thieu on their meetings at the Western White House, San Clemente, April 2-3, 1973   63

(9)   Complaints of Violations of the Cease-fire: United States Note Verbale tr͟nsmitted April 20, 1973 for delivery to participants in the International Conference on Vietnam   67

3. Deepening the China Dialogue   75

(10) "U.S.-China Relations: Progress Toward Normalization": Address by Marshall Green, Assistant Secretary of State for East Asian and Pacific Affairs, before the Sulgrave Club, Washington, February 20, 1973   77

(11) Dr. Kissinger's Meetings with Chinese Leaders in Peking, February 15-19, 1973   82

    (a) Communiqué issued by the United States and the People's Republic of China, February 22, 1973   82

    (b) News conference statement by Dr. Kissinger, February 22, 1973 (Excerpt)   83

(12) Establishment of a United States Liaison Office in Peking: News conference statement by President Nixon, March 15, 1973   86

4. Reshaping Foreign Economic Policy   89

(13) The Second Devaluation of the Dollar: Statement by Secretary of the Treasury George P. Shultz, February 12, 1973   94

(14) The Proposed Trade Reform Act: Message from President Nixon to the Congress, April 10, 1973   99

5. Latin American Preoccupations   117

(15) Eighth Annual Meeting of the Inter-American Economic and Social Council (IA-ECOSOC), Bogotá, January 29-February 9, 1973   121

    (a) Message from President Nixon to the Chairman of the meeting, made public February 1, 1973   121

(16) The Cuba Hijacking Agreement, February 15, 1973   122

(a) Memorandum of Understanding on Hijacking of Aircraft and Vessels and Other Offenses, accepted by the United States and Cuba and entered into force February 15, 1973   122

(b) Significance of the Agreement: News conference comments by Secretary of State Rogers, February 15, 1973   124

(17) Meetings of the United Nations Security Council in Panama, March 15-21, 1973   126

(a) Views of the United States: Statement by Ambassador John A. Scali, United States Representative to the Council, March 20, 1973   126

(b) Draft Resolution on the Panama Canal, vetoed by the United States March 21, 1973   134

(c) Explanation of the United States Position: Statement by Ambassador Scali to the Council, March 21, 1973   136

(18) Third Regular Session of the General Assembly of the Organization of American States (OAS), Washington, April 4-15, 1973   139

(a) Views of the United States: Statement by Secretary of State Rogers in Plenary Session, April 6, 1973   139

6. African Perplexities   **149**

(19) "The Realities of United States-Africa Relations": Address by David D. Newsom, Assistant Secretary of State for African Affairs, before the Royal Commonwealth Society, London, March 14, 1973   152

7. Middle East Anxieties   **163**

(20) "Encouraging a Negotiating Process in the Middle East": Address by Joseph J. Sisco, Assistant Secretary of State for Near Eastern and South Asian Affairs, May 7, 1973   168

8. Launching the "Year of Europe"   **177**

(21) "The Year of Europe": Address by Dr. Kissinger

before the Annual Meeting of the Associated Press
Editors, New York, April 23, 1973   181

9. "Something Is Rotten . . ."   **191**

(22)   "United States Foreign Policy for the 1970's
—Shaping a Durable Peace": Remarks by Presi-
dent Nixon on transmitting his Fourth Annual
Report to Congress on United States Foreign
Policy, May 3, 1973   197

(23)   Armed Forces Day, 1973: Address by President
Nixon at Norfolk Naval Base, Norfolk, Virginia,
May 19, 1973   200

10. Development, Food, and Energy Problems (I)   **207**

(24)   The Foreign Assistance Program: Message from
President Nixon to the Congress, May 1, 1973   210

(25)   Drought Relief and Rehabilitation Needs in West
and Central Africa: Statement by Assistant
Secretary Newsom before the Subcommittee on
African Affairs of the Committee on Foreign
Relations, United States Senate, June 15, 1973   214

(26)   International Ramifications of the Energy Situation: Statement by William J. Casey, Under Secretary of State for Economic Affairs, before the
Committee on Interior and Insular Affairs, United
States Senate, May 1, 1973   217

(27)   The Organization for Economic Cooperation and
Development (OECD): Meeting of the Council at
Ministerial Level, Paris, June 6-8, 1973   224

       (a) Final Communiqué   224

11. Diplomatic Occasions, June 1973   **229**

(28)   The Central Treaty Organization (CENTO): Twentieth Session of the Council of Ministers, Tehran,
June 10-11, 1973   231

       (a) Views of the United States: Statement by

Secretary of State Rogers, Head of the United
States Observer Delegation, June 10, 1973   232
(b) Final Communiqué, June 11, 1973   234

(29) The North Atlantic Treaty Organization (NATO):
Ministerial Session of the North Atlantic Council,
Copenhagen, June 14-15, 1973   236

(a) Final Communiqué   236

(30) Reaffirmation of the Paris Agreement on Vietnam,
June 13, 1973   239

(a) Joint Communiqué of the Parties to the
Agreement, signed in Paris June 13, 1973   239
(b) News conference statement by Dr. Kissinger,
Paris, June 13, 1973   247

12. Brezhnev Comes to America   **251**

(31) Agreement on Negotiating Principles for Strategic
Arms Limitation, June 21, 1973   256

(a) News conference statement by Dr. Kissinger,
June 21, 1973   256
(b) "Basic Principles of Negotiations on the Further Limitation of Strategic Offensive Arms,"
signed at Washington and entered into force
June 21, 1973   262

(32) Agreement on Prevention of Nuclear War, June
22, 1973   263

(a) News conference statement by Dr. Kissinger,
June 22, 1973   263
(b) "Agreement on the Prevention of Nuclear
War," signed at Washington and entered into
force June 22, 1973   266

(33) Review of the Visit, June 24-25, 1973   269

(a) News conference statement by Dr. Kissinger,
San Clemente, June 25, 1973   269
(b) Joint United States-Soviet Communiqué,
dated June 24 and released June 25, 1973   273

13. Promoting Détente in Europe   **285**

(34) Preparatory Consultations Relating to Central

Europe, Vienna, January 31-June 28, 1973   290

    (a) Nineteen-country Communiqué issued at Vienna June 28, 1973   290

(35) Conference on Security and Cooperation in Europe (CSCE): First Stage, Helsinki, June 3-7, 1973   291

    (a) Views of the United States: Statement by Secretary of State Rogers to the Conference, July 5, 1973   291

    (b) Communiqué on the First Stage of the Conference, July 7, 1973   297

14. Japan and The Pacific   **299**

(36) Ninth Meeting of the Joint United States-Japan Committee on Trade and Economic Affairs, Tokyo, July 16-17, 1973   303

    (a) The Framework of American-Japanese Relations: Opening statement by Secretary of State Rogers, July 16, 1973   303

(37) Meeting of President Nixon and Prime Minister Kakuei Tanaka, Washington, July 31-August 1, 1973: Joint Communiqué issued at the conclusion of the talks, August 1, 1973   312

15. Middle East Storm Signals   **317**

(38) A New Initiative in the Security Council   320

    (a) Proposals for a New Departure: Statement by Ambassador Scali to the Security Council, June 14, 1973   320

    (b) Draft Resolution vetoed by the United States July 26, 1973   325

    (c) Statement by Ambassador Scali to the Security Council, August 15, 1973   326

(39) Interception by Israel of a Lebanese Airliner, August 10, 1973   330

    (a) Statement by Ambassador Scali to the Security Council, August 14, 1973   330

    (b) Condemnation of Israel: Security Council

Resolution 337 (1973), adopted August 15, 1973   332

(c) Statement by Ambassador Scali to the Security Council, August 15, 1973   333

16. Ending Combat in Indochina   **335**

(40) Rejection of the "Cambodia Rider": Message from President Nixon to the House of Representatives, returning without approval the Second Supplemental Appropriation Act of 1973 (H.R. 7447), June 27, 1973   340

(41) Legislative-Executive Compromise, July 1, 1973   342

(a) Second Supplemental Appropriations Act, 1973: Public Law 93-50, approved July 1, 1973 (Excerpt)   342
(b) Joint Resolution Making Continuing Appropriations for the Fiscal Year 1974: Public Law 93-52, approved July 1, 1973 (Excerpts)   343
(c) Statement by President Nixon on signing the two bills, July 1, 1973   343

(42) Implementation of the Cutoff   344

(a) Letter from President Nixon to the Speaker of the House of Representatives and the Majority Leader of the Senate, August 3, 1973   344
(b) Termination of United States Combat Activity in Cambodia: Statement by Gerald L. Warren, Deputy White House Press Secretary, August 15, 1973   345

17. Change in Foggy Bottom   **349**

(43) Resignation of Secretary Rogers and Nomination of Dr. Kissinger: News conference announcement by President Nixon, August 22, 1973   354

(44) Views of the Secretary-designate: News conference statement by Dr. Kissinger, San Clemente, August 23, 1973   356

(45) "A Just Consensus, a Stable Order, a Durable Peace": Address by Secretary Kissinger at the 28th Regular Session of the United Nations General Assembly, September 24, 1973   359

(46) Current Diplomatic Business: News conference
statement by Secretary Kissinger, New York, September 26, 1973 (Excerpt)   366

18. Southeast Asian Adjustments   **371**

(47) Construction of Airfields in South Vietnam:
United States Note delivered to the Embassy of the
Democratic Republic of Vietnam (DRV) at Paris
September 10, 1973   374

(48) Completion of Internal Political Agreement in
Laos: United States Government statement, September 14, 1973, and letter from President Nixon
to Prime Minister Souvanna Phouma   375

(49) The South-East Asia Treaty Organization: Press
statement issued at the conclusion of the 18th annual meeting of the SEATO Council, New York,
September 28, 1973   376

19. Meetings on Trade and Money   **379**

(50) The General Agreement on Tariffs and Trade
(GATT): Meeting of the Contracting Parties at
Ministerial Level, Tokyo, September 12-14, 1973   383

(a) Presentation of United States Views: Statement by Secretary of the Treasury Shultz to the
Contracting Parties, September 12, 1973   383
(b) Guidelines for Multilateral Trade Negotiations: The "Declaration of Tokyo," approved by the Contracting Parties September
14, 1973   391

(51) The International Bank for Reconstruction and
Development (IBRD) and the International Monetary Fund (IMF): Annual meeting of the Boards
of Governors, Nairobi, September 24-28, 1973   394

(a) An Outline for Monetary Reform: Report to
the Board of Governors of the International
Monetary Fund by Ali Wardhana, Chairman
of the Committee on Reform of the International Monetary System and Related
Issues, September 24, 1973   394

(b) Views of the United States: Statement to the Boards of Governors by Secretary of the Treasury Shultz, September 25, 1973 396

20. "New Era" in the Americas?   407

(52) The Coup in Chile: Statement by Jack B. Kubisch, Assistant Secretary of State for Inter-American Affairs, before the Subcommittee on Inter-American Affairs of the Committee on Foreign Affairs, House of Representatives, September 20, 1973 412

(53) "A Western Hemisphere Relationship of Cooperation": Toast by Secretary Kissinger at a luncheon honoring Latin American delegations to the General Assembly, New York, October 5, 1973 415

21. Congress, Trade Reform, and Détente   419

(54) National Legislative Goals: Message of President Nixon to the Congress, September 10, 1973 (Excerpts) 424

(55) Status of Trade Reform Legislation: Statement by President Nixon, October 4, 1973 432

(56) "Moral Purpose and Policy Choices": Address by Secretary of State Kissinger before the Third Pacem in Terris Conference, sponsored by the Center for the Study of Democratic Institutions, Washington, October 8, 1973 433

22. The Guns of October   443

(57) The Responsibilities of the United Nations: Statement by Ambassador Scali to the Security Council regarding the situation in the Middle East, October 8, 1973 453

(58) Emergency Security Assistance for Israel and Cambodia: Message from President Nixon to the Congress, October 19, 1973 455

(59) First U.N. Cease-fire Resolution, October 22, 1973 457

(a) Statement of Ambassador Scali to the Security Council, October 21, 1973 457

(b) Security Council Resolution 338 (1973), adopted October 22, 1973 459

(60) Second U.N. Cease-fire Resolution, October 23, 1973 459

(a) Security Council Resolution 339 (1973), adopted October 23, 1973 459

(b) Statement of Ambassador Scali to the Security Council, October 23, 1973 (Excerpt) 460

(61) Request for Soviet and American Forces: Statement of Ambassador Scali to the Security Council, October 24, 1973 461

(62) Significance of the Military Alert: News conference comments by Secretary Kissinger, October 25, 1973 (Excerpts) 463

(63) Third U.N. Cease-fire Resolution, October 25, 1973 469

(a) Statement of Ambassador Scali to the Security Council, October 25, 1973 469

(b) Security Council Resolution 340 (1973), adopted October 25, 1973 469

(64) Views of President Nixon: News conference statement, October 26, 1973 470

(65) Establishment of the U.N. Emergency Force (UNEF), October 27, 1973 472

(a) Plans for the Force: Report of Secretary-General Kurt Waldheim to the Security Council, October 27, 1973 472

(b) Security Council Resolution 341 (1973), adopted October 27, 1973 475

(c) Statement of Ambassador Scali to the Council, October 27, 1973 476

(66) Further Action by the Security Council, November 1-2, 1973 477

(a) Statement by Security Council President Peter Jankowitsch of Austria, November 2, 1973 477

(b) Statement of Ambassador Scali to the Council, November 2, 1973 478

23. Restricting Presidential War Powers **481**

(67) The War Powers Resolution: House Joint Reso-

lution 542, 93rd Congress, passed by the Senate October 10 and by the House of Representatives October 12, 1973   484

(68)   Veto of the War Powers Resolution: Message from President Nixon to the House of Representatives, returning House Joint Resolution 542 without his approval, October 24, 1973   490

(69)   Enactment of the War Powers Resolution over the President's Veto: White House statement, November 7, 1973   494

24. Development, Food, and Energy Problems (II)   **495**

(70)   "A Comprehensive Development Policy for the United States": Address by Under Secretary of State Casey before the Overseas Development Council, October 25, 1973   501

(71)   Funds for the International Development Association and the Asian Development Bank: Message from President Nixon to the Congress, October 31, 1973   510

(72)   "A Comprehensive Approach to Worldwide Problems of Food Shortages and Malnutrition": Statement by Maurice J. Williams, Acting Administrator of the Agency for International Development (AID) and the President's Special Relief Coordinator for Major Disasters Abroad, October 5, 1973   514

(73)   "The Energy Emergency": Radio-Television address by President Nixon, November 7, 1973   520

25. Starting the Diplomatic Shuttle   **529**

(74)   Egyptian-Israeli Disengagement Agreement: Letter from Secretary Kissinger to Secretary-General Waldheim, November 9, 1973   534

(75)   Visit to the People's Republic of China, November 10-14, 1973: Joint Communiqué issued in Washington and Peking, November 14, 1973   535

(76)   "Where We Stand": News conference statement by Secretary Kissinger, November 21, 1973   537

26. No Peace for Indochina   **541**

(77)   Admonition to North Vietnam: United States Note
       delivered to the Embassy of the Democratic Re-
       public of Vietnam at Paris, October 26, 1973   543

(78)   The Crisis of the Khmer Republic: Statement by
       Ambassador W. Tapley Bennett, Jr., United States
       Deputy Permanent Representative, to the United
       Nations General Assembly, December 5, 1973 (Ex-
       cerpts)   545

27. Atlantic Dialogue, Part Two   **551**

(79)   Conference on Mutual Reduction of Forces and
       Armaments and Associated Measures in Central
       Europe, Opened in Vienna October 30, 1973   557

       (a) Statement to the Conference by Ambassador
            Stanley H. Resor, Chairman of the United
            States Delegation, October 31, 1973   557

(80)   Ministerial Session of the North Atlantic Council,
       Brussels, December 10-11, 1973   563

       (a) Final Communiqué   563

(81)   "The United States and a Unifying Europe—The
       Necessity for Partnership": Address by Secretary
       of State Kissinger before the Pilgrims of Great
       Britain, London, December 12, 1973   566

28. Breathing Spell at the United Nations   **577**

(82)   Criticism of United States Policy toward Southern
       Rhodesia: General Assembly Resolution 3116 (XX-
       VIII), December 12, 1973   583

(83)   Convention on the Prevention and Punishment of
       Crimes Against Internationally Protected Persons,
       Including Diplomatic Agents, adopted by the
       General Assembly December 14, 1973   586

       (a) General Assembly Resolution 3166 (XXVIII),
            December 14, 1973, with text of the Con-
            vention   586

       (b) Views of the United States: Statement by Am-
            bassador Bennett in Plenary Session, Decem-
            ber 14, 1973   594

(84) Conference on the Law of the Sea: General
      Assembly Resolution 3067 (XXVIII), November
      16, 1973   598

29. Geneva Conference on the Middle East   **603**

(85) Opening Sessions of the Conference, December
      21-22, 1973   608

      (a) Statement of Secretary Kissinger to the Con-
          ference, December 21, 1973   608
      (b) Remarks by Secretary Kissinger on Leaving
          Geneva, December 22, 1973   613

30. Into the Unknown   **615**

(86) Foreign Policy Highlights of 1973: News con-
      ference statement by Secretary Kissinger, Decem-
      ber 27, 1973   618

APPENDIX: PRINCIPAL SOURCES   **627**

INDEX   **631**

MAP: THE MIDDLE EAST WAR THEATER, 1967-1973   **165**

INTRODUCING 1973

NINETEEN SEVENTY-THREE will be remembered as the year when flames of war, checked temporarily in Indochina, erupted with redoubled fury in the Middle East; when a world long menaced by a deteriorating environment and threats of large-scale famine was suddenly engulfed in the reality of a global energy crisis; and when the United States was shaken to its roots by the disclosures of misconduct in high places conventionally referred to as the Watergate scandals.

American recollection will undoubtedly remain primarily focused upon the domestic tribulations which, by the end of 1973, had all but crippled the administration of President Richard M. Nixon, reversing the national judgment that had returned the 37th President to office with 60.7 percent of the vote in the election of November 7, 1972. Yet 1973 was equally studded with major international occurrences, among which the conclusion of the Vietnam war and the outbreak of renewed warfare between the Arab states and Israel were perhaps the most portentous. Events accompanying the Israeli-Arab conflict, in particular, cast doubt not only upon the much-advertised détente between Washington and Moscow but also upon America's relations with its European partners and Japan, not to mention its increasingly precarious situation with respect to the international energy balance.

Likewise deserving mention among the year's significant events were the advancement of the dramatic, ultimately abortive American plan for a "new Atlantic Charter" to memorialize the so-called "Year of Europe"; the visit to the United States of Leonid I. Brezhnev, General Secretary of the Communist Party of the Soviet Union; the opening of a long-awaited Conference on Security and Cooperation in Europe, of East-West talks on Mutual Reduction of Forces and Armaments and Associated Measures in Central Europe, of the "Tokyo Round" of multilateral negotiations on international trade, and of the Third United Nations Conference on the Law of the Sea; the assumption by Dr.

1

Henry A. Kissinger, the President's long-time Assistant for National Security Affairs, of the added position of Secretary of State, held thus far in the Nixon administration by William P. Rogers; the passage by Congress of legislation barring any further U.S. combat operations in Indochina, and severely restricting the exercise of the presidential war powers; a worldwide alert of U.S. military forces in a threatened confrontation with the Soviet Union over the Middle East; and the onset of a global economic crisis whose lingering effects would be apparent well beyond the middle of the decade.

As with other recent years, 1973 was also punctuated by such dismaying occurrences as the killing by Palestinian terrorists of American and Belgian diplomats in Khartoum, and of innocent travelers at the international airports of Athens and Rome. Although American pressure helped secure approval by the United Nations of a convention directed against terrorist attacks on diplomats and other internationally protected persons, the world organization remained deaf to American pleas for more effective measures to curb the export of terrorism affecting private individuals.

Important changes of government also took place in some of the countries of greatest interest to the United States. Especially notable were the events in Chile, where the controversial "Popular Unity" government of President Salvador Allende Gossens was overthrown in a military coup that resulted in Allende's death and in the installation of a harshly repressive military regime. In Argentina, a seven-year period of military rule was ended with the return to supreme power of former President Juan Domingo Perón, the one-time populist dictator overthrown in 1955. In Thailand, too, a military-dominated regime was removed from office, in this instance by a student revolt; whereas in Afghanistan another former dictator, General Sardar Muhammad Daud, established himself as President after deposing the former monarch, King Muhammad Zahir Shah, during the latter's absence from the country.

Unscheduled changes of regime occurred in Europe as well. Greece's unpopular George Papadopoulos, who had led a military coup in 1967 and was installed as President in June 1973, was overthrown in November in a further coup whose moving spirit was identified as Brigadier General Dimitrios Ioannides, the head of the military police. Admiral Luis Carrero Blanco, the second highest official in the Spanish Government led by General Francisco Franco, was assassinated on December 20, presumably by Basque nationalists, and succeeded by Carlos Arias Navarro, the first civilian to hold such office under the Franco regime.

Amid such changes, the foreign relations of the United States appeared on the whole to be progressing favorably during the earlier months of 1973, when the conclusion of peace settlements in Vietnam and Laos was followed by promising new initiatives in monetary and trade policy, while the rhythm of détente was maintained by a Kissinger visit to the People's Republic of China and by the Brezhnev visit to the United States in June. By summer, however, a definite loss of momentum was becoming evident as the Vietnam peace arrangements became increasingly frayed, Congress refused to finance any further combat activity in Indochina, and France and other European governments stiffened their resistance to Dr. Kissinger's plan for an Atlantic declaration. By autumn, the situation had turned sharply downward with the outbreak of war in the Middle East, the actions of the principal oil-producing countries in raising prices and embargoing deliveries to countries friendly to Israel, and the accompanying strains in U.S. relations with allied as well as Arab and Communist governments. Processes of recovery, facilitated by an Egyptian-Israeli military disengagement agreement and the opening of the Geneva Conference on the Middle East, were only beginning to operate as the year ended.

On the domestic front, meanwhile, it had been downhill practically all the way, for the trial of the original Watergate burglars in January had initiated a process of disclosure that soon reached into the highest echelons of government. As early as April 30, the mounting indications of White House involvement in electoral misconduct and subsequent "cover-up" operations had forced the President to part with two of his closest associates, H. R. Haldeman and John D. Ehrlichman. By May, Mr. Nixon's own role was being critically scrutinized in the special Senate hearings chaired by Democratic Senator Sam J. Ervin, Jr., of North Carolina. The subsequent discovery of the White House tapes, with the resultant legal and constitutional dispute over their availability to Watergate investigators, led directly to the famous "Saturday night massacre" of October 20, when Special Prosecutor Archibald Cox was dismissed by presidential order and Attorney General Elliot L. Richardson resigned together with his Deputy, William D. Ruckelshaus. The impact of these events, occurring at or near the climax of the Middle East crisis, was accentuated by the parallel difficulties of Vice-President Spiro T. Agnew, who resigned on October 10 under a threat of criminal prosecution growing out of well-documented financial irregularities before and since his accession to the vice-presidency.

The influence of these developments upon the conduct of American foreign policy eludes precise measurement. In the somewhat abstract view of Secretary of State Kissinger, the task of foreign policy was complicated, and long-term dangers were created, "to the degree that the authority of those who have the responsibility for conducting foreign policy is being drawn into question by whatever process."[1] President Nixon himself invariably deprecated the preoccupation with Watergate as a contemptible distraction from the great issues of international policy. ". . . Let others wallow in Watergate, we are going to do our job," he declared on one occasion.[2] "Let others spend their time dealing with the murky, small, unimportant, vicious little things," he said again in toasting Japan's Prime Minister, Kakuei Tanaka. "We have spent our time and will spend our time building a better world."[3]

Inevitably, however, the President's own behavior in the conduct of his office showed traces of the strain induced by the Watergate investigations. Even more remarkable than the stridency of some of his comments on world affairs was his avoidance of direct participation in the discussion preceding the worldwide alert of U.S. military forces at the climax of the Middle East crisis, an event that coincided with one of the significant peaks in the Watergate fever chart.[4] Beyond these purely personal manifestations, the gradual deflation of presidential prestige undoubtedly favored the successful moves in Congress to call a halt to combat operations in Indochina and subject the exercise of presidential war powers to unprecedented restriction. Although it would be futile to try to establish a mechanical correlation between Watergate developments and foreign policy moves, the Watergate story remains an inescapable if not decisive factor in the evolution of American foreign relations during 1973.

[1]News conference, Dec. 6, in *Bulletin*, vol. 69 (1973), p. 759.
[2]Remarks of July 20, in *Presidential Documents*, vol. 9 (1973), p. 917.
[3]Remarks of Aug. 1, in same, p. 943.
[4]Cf. Chapter 21.

1. THE SECOND TERM BEGINS

The impact of Watergate was all the more devastating because it intruded so intemperately upon the euphoric mood in which the Nixon administration began its second term of office on January 20, 1973. That occasion had been one that the reelected President had every reason to hail, not only as a stunning personal vindication but as a moment of genuine national triumph. The war in Vietnam, whose honorable conclusion Mr. Nixon had so often promised over the years that had elapsed since his bid for the Republican Party nomination in 1968, at last was visibly ending in the wake of a final spasm of airborne violence, the "Christmas bombing" of Hanoi and Haiphong at the end of 1972. The near-revolutionary protest movement that had so disturbed the Johnson and early Nixon administrations had largely subsided. The voters' recent rejection of the Democratic presidential ticket led by Senator George S. McGovern suggested widespread acceptance of the President's pragmatic, unideological, rather self-contented approach in both domestic and foreign policy.

The first Nixon term, in 1969-73, had been primarily a period of adjustment to the mood of national retrenchment that followed the exertions of the quarter-century after World War II. The "Nixon Doctrine," proclaimed at Guam on July 25, 1969,[1] had helped to rationalize a hoped-for redistribution of responsibilities in which the United States could expect more strenuous effort from its allies and friends and would demand proportionately less of itself. In addition, the waning of the crusading "cold war" spirit had encouraged a vastly different relationship with the leading Communist powers. In two epochal journeys in the months preceding the 1972 election, the President had opened up a channel of com-

[1]*Documents, 1968-69*, pp. 329-34.

5

munication with the People's Republic of China and markedly strengthened the hopes for continued "peaceful coexistence" with the Soviet Union, the world's most formidable military power outside the United States itself. These well-publicized achievements outweighed, for many Americans, the growing hostility of much of the "third world," the well-nigh universal condemnation of America's war in Vietnam, the persistence of a formidable international arms race, and the occasional discomfiture of allies and friends by peculiarities in the style or substance of American foreign policy.

Although the average American voter was less alert to foreign policy subtleties than to the day-to-day reality of racial tensions, soaring crime rates, and remorseless inflation, the choice of Mr. Nixon for a second term had shown that his attitude in regard to domestic affairs was also widely acceptable. Nixon voters, by and large, had appeared loath to accept the doctrine that America had lost its moral bearings and was floundering in a morass of self-indulgence, violence, and illegality. They seemed, however, to appreciate the President's manifest sympathy for the more favored sections of the community, and patently approved his efforts to limit the Federal Government's role in dealing with the problems of American society.

Reluctant to adopt a tragic view of the current national situation, the majority of Mr. Nixon's electoral supporters had seemed to be unaffected by newspaper and television reports that linked the "bugging" of the Democratic National Committee headquarters in Washington's Watergate complex, originally discovered June 17, 1972, with persons prominent in the Committee to Reelect the President and in the White House executive offices. It would later become known that President Nixon himself, though seemingly without foreknowledge of the eavesdropping stunt devised by lesser functionaries, had been deeply involved in the subsequent "cover-up" effort and had gone to considerable lengths in trying to divert the ensuing criminal investigation from sensitive areas of his administration. Thus far, however, most Nixon partisans had been content to rely upon the reiterated assurance that "the White House has had no involvement whatever in this particular incident." [2] Thanks largely to the effective work of presidential Counsel John W. Dean, 3rd, and others, the trial of the Watergate burglars and their immediate associates that began in Judge John J. Sirica's Washington courtroom on January 8, 1973, two months after the election, appeared unlikely to result in any repercussions that could impair the prospects of the new administration.

[2] News conference, June 22, in *Public Papers, 1972*, p. 691.

Precisely how the President intended to translate his recent electoral victory into national policy had remained a matter of widespread speculation in the weeks that preceded his second inaugural. The general scope of his ideas, likes, and dislikes was of course well known, and political and public interest had tended to center on his reputed plans for tightening the Executive Branch and furthering the already formidabie concentration of power within the Executive Office of the President, where H.R. Haldeman held sway as White House Chief of Staff and John D. Ehrlichman, as Assistant to the President for Domestic Affairs, was acquiring an authority second only to that already wielded by Dr. Kissinger in the National Security area. Among leading cabinet officers, it was known that Mr. Rogers was continuing as Secretary of State, in spite of an unresolved jurisdictional problem involving the line of demarcation between his department's responsibilities and those of the President's Assistant for National Security Affairs. Elliot L. Richardson was succeeding Melvin R. Laird at Defense, and George P. Shultz had already succeeded John B. Connally as Secretary of the Treasury and the government's leading authority in the economic area. Richard Helms, Director of Central Intelligence since 1966, had recently been named Ambassador to Iran, and was being succeeded at CIA by Dr. James R. Schlesinger, previously the Chairman of the Atomic Energy Commission; while George Bush, the erstwhile U.S. Representative to the United Nations, was becoming Chairman of the Republican National Committee and would be replaced in New York by television newsman John A. Scali.

So far as substantive policy was concerned, there were already indications that some of the rigors associated with the Vietnam war period would soon be relaxed. An important economic policy move was the termination on January 11, 1973, of the mandatory wage and price controls imposed in 1971 at the height of a Vietnam-engendered economic crisis.[3] A parallel move, already in the making and announced on January 27 to coincide with the signature of the Vietnam peace agreement, was the ending of the military draft which had been in effect with one brief interval since 1940. This move would fulfill the President's 1968 commitment to institute an all-volunteer defense establishment as soon as the Vietnam emergency was ended.

Mr. Nixon had also expressed a desire to impart a sense of "vitality" and "excitement" to his second term, and the buoyantly optimistic tone of the inaugural address which he read on the Capitol steps on January 20 (**Document 1**) was wholly consistent with this intention. Characteristic of his way of thinking were the

[3]Cf. *AFR, 1971*, pp. 576-82.

perception of foreign and domestic affairs as interdependent, indissolubly related objects of national concern; the preeminent importance which he assigned to foreign affairs within this framework; and the simultaneous enunciation of far-reaching goals ("a peace which can endure for generations to come") and of a low-keyed, even revisionist approach to their pursuit ("the time has come to turn away from the condescending policies of paternalism . . . . let us encourage individuals at home and nations abroad to do more for themselves, to decide more for themselves")—a precept which, incidentally, would be only intermittently followed by the American Government in the ensuing months. Ironically as parts of the address must read in the light of later knowledge, it still offers a classic statement of some of the guiding ideals—as well as the practical limitations—of American foreign policy at a significant turning point in its evolution.

(1) "A New Era of Peace": Second Inaugural Address of President Richard M. Nixon, January 20, 1973.[4]

Mr. Vice President, Mr. Speaker, Mr. Chief Justice, Senator Cook, Mrs. Eisenhower,[5] and my fellow citizens of this great and good country we share together:

When we met here 4 years ago,[6] America was bleak in spirit, depressed by the prospect of seemingly endless war abroad and of destructive conflict at home.

As we meet here today, we stand on the threshold of a new era of peace in the world.

The central question before us is: How shall we use that peace?

Let us resolve that this era we are about to enter will not be what other postwar periods have so often been: a time of retreat and isolation that leads to stagnation at home and invites new danger abroad.

Let us resolve that this will be what it can become: a time of great responsibilities greatly borne, in which we renew the spirit and the promise of America as we enter our third century as a Nation.

This past year saw far-reaching results from our new policies for peace. By continuing to revitalize our traditional friendships, and by our missions to Peking and to Moscow, we were able to establish the base for a new and more durable pattern of relationships among the nations of the world. Because of America's bold initiatives, 1972 will be long remembered as the year of the greatest

[4]Text from *Presidential Documents*, vol. 9 (1973), pp. 33-6.
[5]Vice-President Spiro T. Agnew, Speaker Carl Albert, Chief Justice Warren E. Burger, Senator Marlow W. Cook, Mrs. Dwight D. Eisenhower.
[6]*Documents, 1968-69*, pp. 38-43.

progress since the end of World War II toward a lasting peace in the world.

The peace we seek in the world is not the flimsy peace which is merely an interlude between wars, but a peace which can endure for generations to come.

It is important that we understand both the necessity and the limitations of America's role in maintaining that peace.

Unless we in America work to preserve the peace, there will be no peace.

Unless we in America work to preserve freedom, there will be no freedom.

But let us clearly understand the new nature of America's role, as a result of the new policies we have adopted over these past 4 years.

We shall respect our treaty commitments.

We shall support vigorously the principle that no country has the right to impose its will or rule on another by force.

We shall continue, in this era of negotiation, to work for the limitation of nuclear arms and to reduce the danger of confrontation between the great powers.

We shall do our share in defending peace and freedom in the world. But we shall expect others to do their share.

The time has passed when America will make every other nation's conflict our own, or make every other nation's future our responsibility, or presume to tell the people of other nations how to manage their own affairs.

Just as we respect the right of each nation to determine its own future, we also recognize the responsibility of each nation to secure its own future.

Just as America's role is indispensable in preserving the world's peace, so is each nation's role indispensable in preserving its own peace.

Together with the rest of the world, let us resolve to move forward from the beginnings we have made. Let us continue to bring down the walls of hostility which have divided the world for too long, and to build in their place bridges of understanding—so that despite profound differences between systems of government, the people of the world can be friends.

Let us build a structure of peace in the world in which the weak are as safe as the strong, in which each respects the right of the other to live by a different system, in which those who would influence others will do so by the strength of their ideas and not by the force of their arms.

Let us accept that high responsibility not as a burden, but gladly—gladly because the chance to build such a peace is the noblest endeavor in which a nation can engage; gladly also because only if we act greatly in meeting our responsibilities abroad will we remain a great Nation, and only if we remain a great Nation will we act greatly in meeting our challenges at home.

We have the chance today to do more than ever before in our history to make life better in America—to ensure better education, better health, better housing, better transportation, a cleaner environment—to restore respect for law, to make our communities more livable—and to ensure the God-given right of every American to full and equal opportunity.

Because the range of our needs is so great, because the reach of our opportunities is so great, let us be bold in our determination to meet those needs in new ways.

Just as building a structure of peace abroad has required turning away from old policies that have failed, so building a new era of progress at home requires turning away from old policies that have failed.

Abroad, the shift from old policies to new has not been a retreat from our responsibilities, but a better way to peace.

And at home, the shift from old policies to new will not be a retreat from our responsibilities, but a better way to progress.

Abroad and at home, the key to those new responsibilities lies in the placing and the division of responsibility. We have lived too long with the consequences of attempting to gather all power and responsibility in Washington.

Abroad and at home, the time has come to turn away from the condescending policies of paternalism—of "Washington knows best."

A person can be expected to act responsibly only if he has responsibility. This is human nature. So let us encourage individuals at home and nations abroad to do more for themselves, to decide more for themselves. Let us locate responsibility in more places. And let us measure what we will do for others by what they will do for themselves.

That is why today I offer no promise of a purely governmental solution for every problem. We have lived too long with that false promise. In trusting too much in government, we have asked of it more than it can deliver. This leads only to inflated expectations, to reduced individual effort, and to a disappointment and frustration that erode confidence both in what government can do and in what people can do.

Government must learn to take less from people so that people can do more for themselves.

Let us remember that America was built not by government, but by people—not by welfare, but by work—not by shirking responsibility, but by seeking responsibility.

In our own lives, let each of us ask—not just what will government do for me, but what can I do for myself?

In the challenges we face together, let each of us ask—not just how can government help, but how can I help?

Your National Government has a great and vital role to play. And I pledge to you that where this Government should act, we will act boldly and we will lead boldly. But just as important is the role that each and every one of us must play, as an individual and as a member of his own community.

From this day forward, let each of us make a solemn commitment in his own heart: to bear his responsibility, to do his part, to live his ideals—so that together, we can see the dawn of a new age of progress for America, and together, as we celebrate our 200th anniversary as a nation, we can do so proud in the fulfillment of our promise to ourselves and to the world.

As America's longest and most difficult war comes to an end, let us again learn to debate our differences with civility and decency. And let each of us reach out for that one precious quality government cannot provide—a new level of respect for the rights and feelings of one another, a new level of respect for the individual human dignity which is the cherished birthright of every American.

Above all else, the time has come for us to renew our faith in ourselves and in America.

In recent years, that faith has been challenged.

Our children have been taught to be ashamed of their country, ashamed of their parents, ashamed of America's record at home and its role in the world.

At every turn we have been beset by those who find everything wrong with America and little that is right. But I am confident that this will not be the judgment of history on these remarkable times in which we are privileged to live.

America's record in this century has been unparalleled in the world's history for its responsibility, for its generosity, for its creativity, and for its progress.

Let us be proud that our system has produced and provided more freedom and more abundance, more widely shared, than any system in the history of the world.

Let us be proud that in each of the four wars in which we have been engaged in this century, including the one we are now bringing to an end, we have fought not for our selfish advantage, but to help others resist aggression.

And let us be proud that by our bold, new initiatives, by our steadfastness for peace with honor, we have made a breakthrough toward creating in the world what the world has not known before—a structure of peace that can last, not merely for our time, but for generations to come.

We are embarking here today on an era that presents challenges as great as those any nation, or any generation, has ever faced. We shall answer to God, to history, to our conscience for the way in which we use these years.

As I stand in this place, so hallowed by history, I think of others who have stood here before me. I think of the dreams they had for America and I think of how each recognized that he needed help far beyond himself in order to make those dreams come true.

Today I ask your prayers that in the years ahead I may have God's help in making decisions that are right for America and I pray for your help so that together we may be worthy of our challenge.

Let us pledge together to make these next 4 years the best 4 years in America's history, so that on its 200th birthday America will be as young and as vital as when it began, and as bright a beacon of hope for all the world.

Let us go forward from here confident in hope, strong in our faith in one another, sustained by our faith in God who created us, and striving always to serve His purpose.

2. INDOCHINA: THE "PEACE WITH HONOR"

The negotiation of a formal agreement to end the decades-old conflict in Vietnam will certainly be ranked among the major diplomatic achievements of the Nixon administration, notwithstanding the fact that the resultant peace arrangements proved largely illusory and dissolved completely within a period of fifteen months. Ideally, a peace agreement among the United States, the Democratic Republic of (North) Vietnam, the Republic of (South) Vietnam, and the insurgent "Provisional Revolutionary Government of the Republic of South Vietnam" should have marked the climax of President Nixon's first term, rather than the opening event of his second. It had been twelve days before the November 7 election, on October 26, 1972, that Dr. Kissinger had voiced the administration's belief that peace was "at hand" as the result of the secret negotiations he had conducted with Special Adviser Le Duc Tho and other North Vietnamese representatives since the summer of 1969.[1] But though the main outlines of a peace agreement could already be made public at that time, the task of filling in the details and securing the acquiescence of the various parties had required almost another three months.

In the course of that period, the United States had exerted extremely heavy pressure not only upon North Vietnam, which was subjected to an unprecedented series of bombing attacks over an eleven-day period in late December 1972, but also upon the Saigon government led by President Nguyen Van Thieu, who took a highly critical view of the proposed agreement and insisted that it conferred unfair and potentially fatal advantages upon his Communist adversaries. Especially serious, in President Thieu's eyes, were the

---

[1]*AFR, 1972,* p. 285. For more detailed discussion see especially *Nixon Report, 1973,* pp. 42-74, and Kalb, *Kissinger,* pp. 418-22 and 430-31.

absence of any clear provision requiring the withdrawal of upward of 145,000 North Vietnamese troops then deployed in South Vietnam; the lack of any clear-cut affirmation of the sovereignty of the Saigon government in the area south of the Demilitarized Zone (DMZ) between North and South Vietnam; and the provision for far-reaching Communist participation in South Vietnam's political processes under the aegis of a tripartite "National Council of National Reconciliation and Concord."

Though President Nixon had been willing to pass along these objections to the North Vietnamese, the American leader had taken the view that rather than quibbling over details, South Vietnam would be well advised to accept the proposed terms and to rely on the support of the United States in ensuring that they were faithfully complied with. In a secret letter addressed to President Thieu on November 14, 1972 (and made public at the time of the Saigon government's final collapse on April 30, 1975), Mr. Nixon had offered the South Vietnamese leader "my absolute assurance that if Hanoi fails to abide by the terms of this agreement it is my intention to take swift and severe retaliatory action."[2] Ignoring a vigorous domestic argument about the limits of the presidential war powers, the American chief executive renewed his assurances in a further letter to his South Vietnamese opposite on January 5, 1973 (**Document 2**). "Should you decide . . . to go with us," the President reiterated, "you have my assurance of continued assistance in the post-settlement period and that we will respond with full force should the settlement be violated by North Vietnam." These assurances, however, were never communicated to the American Congress, which held a rather different view about the advisability of further military action in Indochina and later passed legislation prohibiting any U.S. combat activities in that part of the world after August 15, 1973.[3]

Equally unknown to Congress and the public were any understandings that might be under discussion with the North Vietnamese in regard to U.S. aid in reconstructing their devastated country. Months earlier, at a time when a peace agreement still appeared remote, President Nixon had indicated that Hanoi might ultimately receive as much as $2.5 billion in American aid as part of a $7.5 billion, five-year regional reconstruction program after peace was concluded.[4] But no such figure appeared in the draft peace terms, Article 21 of which stated merely that "In pursuance of its traditional policy, the United States will contribute to healing

---

[2] *New York Times*, May 1, 1972, quoted in *AFR, 1972*, p. 276.
[3] Cf. Chapter 16.
[4] *Nixon Report, 1972*, p. 119.

the wounds of war and to postwar reconstruction of the Democratic Republic of Viet-Nam and throughout Indochina." "The definition of any particular sum," said Dr. Kissinger in a commentary on the peace terms, "will have to await the discussions which will take place after the agreements are in force."[5]

All the more surprising, therefore, were Hanoi's subsequent assertions that President Nixon, in a written communication dated February 1, 1973, had promised to provide the DRV with $3.25 billion in reconstruction assistance, entirely free of any political conditions.[6] In the absence of confirmation from the American side, such a pledge in the terms alleged would seem to run counter to all that is known of the Nixon administration's diplomatic outlook and practice. A more trustworthy reflection of the President's own attitude was to appear in his "State of the World" report released in May 1973. "We will not provide aid to the Democratic Republic of Vietnam if it violates the [Paris] Agreement," Mr. Nixon declared at that time. "Hanoi cannot expect to receive our economic assistance while pursuing its goals through military pressure."[7]

President Nixon said nothing of such technicalities in the broadcast speech on January 23 (Document 3) in which he announced that all remaining obstacles had at long last been overcome and that an agreement consistent with the American concept of "peace with honor" had been initialed in Paris earlier that day by Dr. Kissinger and Le Duc Tho. Elucidated more fully at a Kissinger news conference on January 24 (Document 4), the "Agreement on Ending the War and Restoring Peace in Vietnam" and its accompanying protocols were duly signed in Paris on January 27, with Secretary of State Rogers representing the United States. In addition to an immediate cease-fire in place, the main agreement (Document 5) called for a withdrawal of U.S. and allied military forces from South Vietnam within 60 days; the return of captured military personnel and foreign civilians within the same period; reorganization of South Vietnam's political life under the auspices of the "National Council of National Reconciliation and Concord"; peaceful reunification of Vietnam, on a step-by-step basis, by mutual agreement between Hanoi and Saigon; establishment of joint and international military commissions to superintend the execution of the agreement, and the convening within 30 days of an international conference to guarantee its provisions; withdrawal of

---

[5]News conference, Jan. 24, in *Presidential Documents*, vol. 9 (1973), p. 72.
[6]Leslie H. Gelb, in *New York Times*, Feb. 2 and 3, 1976; see further same, Mar. 27 and Apr. 17, 1976, and Chapter 16 below.
[7]*Nixon Report, 1973*, p. 62.

foreign military forces from Cambodia and Laos; and a U.S. contribution "to healing the wounds of war and to postwar reconstruction of the Democratic Republic of Vietnam and throughout Indochina."

In signing the relevant papers, the United States officially made known its expectation "that this Agreement will usher in an era of reconciliation with the Democratic Republic of Vietnam as with all the peoples of Indochina." The task of seeking a reconciliation with the notoriously hostile North Vietnamese regime was promptly initiated by Dr. Kissinger, who stopped over in Hanoi for three days on February 10-13 in the course of a Far Eastern journey that also took him to Thailand, Laos, mainland China,[8] and Japan. In Hanoi, both sides agreed on the importance of scrupulous implementation of the Paris agreement and the need for a "new relationship" between North Vietnam and the United States. Among the announced results of the visit (Document 6) was the establishment of a Joint Economic Commission to develop their bilateral economic relations and, presumably, make plans for the disbursement of the expected U.S. aid.

Another auspicious development was the conclusion on February 21, after many months of tedious negotiation, of an agreement on a cease-fire and a political reconciliation in nearby Laos. For years the nominally neutral, U.S.-supported Royal Laotian Government headed by Prince Souvanna Phouma had been attempting, with diminishing success, to cope with a Communist-led insurgent movement which was backed by North Vietnam and nominally led by the Prime Minister's half brother, Prince Souphanouvong. Under the agreement concluded February 21—technically not an international agreement, but an internal accord between the "Vientiane Government side" and the Pathet Lao or "Patriotic Forces side"—an immediate cease-fire was to be followed within 30 days by the establishment of a Provisional Government of National Union and a National Consultative Political Council, both set up on a tripartite basis not unlike that envisaged for South Vietnam. A further 60 days would then elapse before the required withdrawal of the estimated 40,000 to 60,000 North Vietnamese troops in Laos and the dissolution of U.S.-organized "Special Forces" in the country.[9]

No parallel cease-fire appeared to be in prospect in Cambodia, where the U.S.-supported "Khmer Republic" government of

[8]See further Chapter 3.
[9]English texts of the agreement, differing considerably in detail, appear in *New York Times*, Feb. 22, 1973; *Keesing's*, pp. 25843-4; and *Foreign Affairs Reports* (New Delhi), Sept. 1973, pp. 215-19. For further developments cf. Chapters 16 and 18.

President Lon Nol was under attack by forces nominally loyal to Prince Norodom Sihanouk, the ousted Chief of State, and aided by some 25,000 North Vietnamese troops. Although the Phnom Penh government announced a suspension of offensive operations immediately following the Paris agreement, and the United States temporarily suspended the air combat missions it had been flying in support of government forces, these gestures were ignored by the Communist "Khmer Rouge" and related elements, which already menaced the capital and continued to strengthen their positions even after U.S. bombing was resumed soon afterward. In the view of official Washington, the continuance of large-scale operations in agreement with the Cambodian Government was in no way inconsistent with the Paris agreement, but actually offered the best available means of obtaining compliance with its provisions.[10]

South Vietnam itself remained well short of complete pacification as the time for the projected international conference approached. Scattered fighting was still occurring, and the 1,160-member International Commission of Control and Supervision (ICCS), composed of representatives of Canada, Hungary, Indonesia, and Poland, had encountered considerable operational difficulties, many of them attributable to delays in organizing the four-party Joint Military Commission (JMC) made up of North and South Vietnam, the United States, and the Provisional Revolutionary Government.

Addressing the twelve-party International Conference on Vietnam as it opened in Paris on February 26 (**Document 7a**), Secretary of State Rogers particularly emphasized the need of strict respect for all the provisions of the Paris agreement, including those relating to the cessation of military activities in Laos and Cambodia. Mitchell Sharp, Canadian Secretary of State for External Affairs, went further and stated that Canada would actually withdraw from membership in the ICCS unless proper conditions for its functioning could be created. Completing their somewhat half-hearted deliberations on March 2 with the signature of the "Act of the Conference" or "Act of Paris" (**Document 7b**), the participating governments acknowledged the sanctity of the Paris agreement and its protocols and agreed in general terms that they would consult or reconvene if circumstances should so dictate.

Developments in the weeks that followed the Paris conference continued somewhat disappointing to those who had supposed the January 27 agreement marked the termination of the conflict over Indochina. In spite of growing doubts about the intentions of the

---

[10]Rogers statement to Senate Foreign Relations Committee, Apr. 30, in *Bulletin*, vol. 68 (1973), pp. 652-5. For further developments cf. Chapter 16.

respective Vietnamese parties, some further progress was registered
as the military observation teams began to carry out inspections in
the countryside. The withdrawal of U.S. troops and the release of
the remaining U.S. prisoners of war were completed on March 28
(although some 1,300 military personnel and civilians remained
unaccounted for); and talks about a political settlement in South
Vietnam were initiated in Paris by representatives of the Saigon and
Provisional Revolutionary governments.

Yet by April 2, when President Thieu arrived at San Clemente
for a two-day conference with President Nixon, the two leaders
once again were giving voice to "great concern" about what were
described in their communiqué (**Document 8**) as "infiltrations of
men and weapons in sizeable numbers from North Vietnam into
South Vietnam in violation of the Agreement on Ending the War."
Presumably recalling President Nixon's earlier, secret assurances,
the two leaders expressed a joint opinion "that actions which
would threaten the basis of the Agreement would call for appropriately vigorous reactions."

It was North Vietnam, however, that seized the role of public ac-
cuser in a diplomatic note addressed on April 16 to all participants
in the recent Paris conference. According to Hanoi's assertions, the
United States and South Vietnam were already guilty of multiple
and massive violations of the cease-fire agreement. In a heavily
documented counterblast transmitted April 20 (**Document 9**), the
United States dismissed the North Vietnamese charges as "utterly
groundless." "The main obstruction to peace," the American note
insisted, "consists of military activities carried out by the
Democratic Republic of Vietnam and forces under its control in
South Vietnam, Laos and Cambodia in direct and inexcusable contravention of the Agreement on Ending the War and Restoring
Peace in Vietnam and of the Agreement on the Restoration of
Peace and Reconciliation in Laos." By way of a response to such
provocations, the United States announced the suspension of its
mine clearance operations in North Vietnamese waters, resumed
the conduct of reconnaissance flights over North Vietnam by
pilotless aircraft, and discontinued its participation in the economic
talks which had been initiated with North Vietnamese representatives in Paris. The outlook for permanent peace in Southeast Asia
no longer seemed very bright, in spite of plans for another round of
talks between Dr. Kissinger and Le Duc Tho.[11]

[11]See further Chapters 11 and 16.

(2)   Assurances to Saigon: Letter from President Nixon to
President Nguyen Van Thieu of the Republic of Vietnam,
January 5, 1973.[12]

January 5, 1973

Dear Mr. President:

This will acknowledge your letter of December 20, 1972.

There is nothing substantial that I can add to my many previous messages, including my December 17 letter,[13] which clearly stated my opinions and intentions. With respect to the question of North Vietnamese troops, we will again present your views to the Communists as we have done vigorously at every other opportunity in the negotiations. The result is certain to be once more the rejection of our position. We have explained to you repeatedly why we believe the problem of North Vietnamese troops is manageable under the agreement, and I see no reason to repeat all the arguments.

We will proceed next week in Paris along the lines that General Haig[14] explained to you. Accordingly, if the North Vietnamese meet our concerns on the two outstanding substantive issues in the agreement, concerning the DMZ and the method of signing and if we can arrange acceptable supervisory machinery, we will proceed to conclude the settlement. The gravest consequence would then ensue if your government chose to reject the agreement and split off from the United States. As I said in my December 17 letter, "I am convinced that your refusal to join us would be an invitation to disaster—to the loss of all that we together have fought for over the past decade. It would be inexcusable above all because we will have lost a just and honorable alternative."

As we enter this new round of talks, I hope that our countries will now show a united front. It is imperative for our common objectives that your government take no further actions that complicate our task and would make more difficult the acceptance of the settlement by all parties. We will keep you informed of the negotiations in Paris through daily briefings of Ambassador [Pham Dang] Lam.

I can only repeat what I have so often said: The best guarantee for the survival of South Vietnam is the unity of our two countries which would be gravely jeopardized if you persist in your present

---

[12]Released Apr. 30, 1975; text from *New York Times*, May 1, 1975.
[13]President Nixon's letter of Dec. 17, 1972 has not been published.
[14]Maj. Gen. Alexander M. Haig, Jr., Deputy Assistant to the President for National Security Affairs; cf. *AFR, 1972*, p. 277.

course. The actions of our Congress since its return have clearly borne out the many warnings we have made.

Should you decide, as I trust you will, to go with us, you have my assurance of continued assistance in the post-settlement period and that we will respond with full force should the settlement be violated by North Vietnam. So once more I conclude with an appeal to you to close ranks with us.

Sincerely,

RICHARD NIXON

His Excellency
Nguyen Van Thieu
President of the Republic of Vietnam
Saigon.

(3)   "Peace With Honor": Radio-television address by President Nixon on the initialing of the Vietnam Agreement, January 23, 1973.[15]

Good evening. I have asked for this radio and television time tonight for the purpose of announcing that we today have concluded an agreement to end the war and bring peace with honor in Vietnam and in Southeast Asia.

The following statement is being issued at this moment in Washington and Hanoi:

At 12:30 Paris time today [Tuesday], January 23, 1973, the Agreement on Ending the War and Restoring Peace in Vietnam[16] was initialed by Dr. Henry Kissinger on behalf of the United States, and Special Adviser Le Duc Tho on behalf of the Democratic Republic of Vietnam.

The agreement will be formally signed by the parties participating in the Paris Conference on Vietnam on January 27, 1973, at the International Conference Center in Paris.

The cease-fire will take effect at 2400 Greenwich Mean Time, January 27, 1973. The United States and the Democratic Republic of Vietnam express the hope that this agreement will insure stable peace in Vietnam and contribute to the preservation of lasting peace in Indochina and Southeast Asia.

---

[15]Text from *Presidential Documents*, vol. 9 (1973), pp. 43-5.
[16]Document 5.

That concludes the formal statement.

Throughout the years of negotiations, we have insisted on peace with honor. In my addresses to the Nation from this room of January 25 and May 8, [1972][17] I set forth the goals that we considered essential for peace with honor.

In the settlement that has now been agreed to, all the conditions that I laid down then have been met. A cease-fire, internationally supervised, will begin at 7 p.m., this Saturday, January 27, Washington time. Within 60 days from this Saturday, all Americans held prisoners of war throughout Indochina will be released. There will be the fullest possible accounting for all of those who are missing in action.

During the same 60-day period, all American forces will be withdrawn from South Vietnam.

The people of South Vietnam have been guaranteed the right to determine their own future, without outside interference.

By joint agreement, the full text of the agreement and the protocols to carry it out,[18] will be issued tomorrow.

Throughout these negotiations we have been in the closest consultation with President Thieu and other representatives of the Republic of Vietnam. This settlement meets the goals and has the full support of President Thieu and the Government of the Republic of Vietnam, as well as that of our other allies who are affected.

The United States will continue to recognize the Government of the Republic of Vietnam as the sole legitimate government of South Vietnam.

We shall continue to aid South Vietnam within the terms of the agreement and we shall support efforts by the people of South Vietnam to settle their problems peacefully among themselves.

We must recognize that ending the war is only the first step toward building the peace. All parties must now see to it that this is a peace that lasts, and also a peace that heals, and a peace that not only ends the war in Southeast Asia, but contributes to the prospects of peace in the whole world.

This will mean that the terms of the agreement must be scrupulously adhered to. We shall do everything the agreement requires of us and we shall expect the other parties to do everything it requires of them. We shall also expect other interested nations to help insure that the agreement is carried out and peace is maintained.

As this long and very difficult war ends, I would like to address a

---

[17]*AFR, 1972*, pp. 239-45 and 257-61.
[18]See note 27 to Document 4.

few special words to each of those who have been parties in the conflict.

First, to the people and Government of South Vietnam: By your courage, by your sacrifice, you have won the precious right to determine your own future and you have developed the strength to defend that right. We look forward to working with you in the future, friends in peace as we have been allies in war.

To the leaders of North Vietnam: As we have ended the war through negotiations, let us now build a peace of reconciliation. For our part, we are prepared to make a major effort to help achieve that goal. But just as reciprocity was needed to end the war, so, too, will it be needed to build and strengthen the peace.

To the other major powers that have been involved even indirectly: Now is the time for mutual restraint so that the peace we have achieved can last.

And finally, to all of you who are listening, the American people: Your steadfastness in supporting our insistence on peace with honor has made peace with honor possible. I know that you would not have wanted that peace jeopardized. With our secret negotiations at the sensitive stage they were in during this recent period, for me to have discussed publicly our efforts to secure peace would not only have violated our understanding with North Vietnam, it would have seriously harmed and possibly destroyed the chances for peace. Therefore, I know that you now can understand why, during these past several weeks, I have not made any public statements about those efforts.

The important thing was not to talk about peace, but to get peace and to get the right kind of peace. This we have done.

Now that we have achieved an honorable agreement, let us be proud that America did not settle for a peace that would have betrayed our allies, that would have abandoned our prisoners of war, or that would have ended the war for us but would have continued the war for the 50 million people of Indochina. Let us be proud of the 2½ million young Americans who served in Vietnam, who served with honor and distinction in one of the most selfless enterprises in the history of nations. And let us be proud of those who sacrificed, who gave their lives so that the people of South Vietnam might live in freedom and so that the world might live in peace.

In particular, I would like to say a word to some of the bravest people I have ever met—the wives, the children, the families of our prisoners of war and the missing in action. When others called on us to settle on any terms, you had the courage to stand for the right kind of peace so that those who died and those who suffered would not have died and suffered in vain, and so that where this generation knew war, the next generation would know peace. Nothing means more to me at this moment than the fact that your long vigil is coming to an end.

Just yesterday, a great American, who once occupied this office, died. In his life President [Lyndon B.] Johnson endured the vilification of those who sought to portray him as a man of war. But there was nothing he cared about more deeply than achieving a lasting peace in the world.

I remember the last time I talked with him. It was just the day after New Year's. He spoke then of his concern with bringing peace, with making it the right kind of peace, and I was grateful that he once again expressed his support for my efforts to gain such a peace. No one would have welcomed this peace more than he.

And I know he would join me in asking for those who died and for those who live, let us consecrate this moment by resolving together to make the peace we have achieved a peace that will last.

Thank you and good evening.

(4) Significance of the Agreement: News conference statement by Dr. Henry A. Kissinger, Assistant to the President for National Security Affairs, January 24, 1973.[19]

(Excerpt)

DR. KISSINGER. Ladies and gentlemen, the President last evening presented the outlines of the agreement[20] and by common agreement between us and the North Vietnamese we have today released the texts.[21] And I am here to explain, to go over briefly what these texts contain, and how we got there, what we have tried to achieve in recent months and where we expect to go from here.

Let me begin by going through the agreement, which you have read.

PROVISIONS OF THE AGREEMENT

Chapter I: Vietnamese National Rights

The agreement, as you know, is in nine chapters. The first affirms the independence, sovereignty, unity and territorial integrity,

[19]Text from *Presidential Documents*, vol. 9 (1973), pp. 64-70.
[20]Document 3.
[21]Document 5.

as recognized by the 1954 Geneva Agreements on Vietnam,[22] agreements which established two zones, divided by a military demarcation line.

Chapter II: Cease-fire and Withdrawal

Chapter II deals with the cease-fire. The cease-fire will go into effect at 7 o'clock Washington time on Saturday night [January 27]. The principal provisions of Chapter II deal with permitted acts during the cease-fire and with what the obligations of the various parties are with respect to the cease-fire.

Chapter II also deals with the withdrawal of American and all other foreign forces from Vietnam within a period of 60 days. And it specifies the forces that have to be withdrawn. These are in effect all military personnel and all civilian personnel dealing with combat operations. We are permitted to retain economic advisers and civilian technicians serving in certain of the military branches.

Chapter II further deals with the provisions for resupply and for the introduction of outside forces. There is a flat prohibition against the introduction of any military force into South Vietnam from outside of South Vietnam, which is to say that whatever forces may be in South Vietnam from outside South Vietnam, specifically North Vietnamese forces, cannot receive reinforcements, replacements, or any other form of augmentation by any means whatsoever. With respect to military equipment, both sides are permitted to replace all existing military equipment on a one-to-one basis under international supervision and control.

There will be established, as I will explain when I discuss the protocols, for each side, three legitimate points of entry through which all replacement equipment has to move. These legitimate points of entry will be under international supervision.

Chapter III: Return of POW's

Chapter III deals with the return of captured military personnel and foreign civilians as well as with the question of civilian detainees within South Vietnam.

This, as you know, throughout the negotiations, presented enormous difficulties for us. We insisted throughout that the question

[22]Full texts in *American Foreign Policy, 1950-1955*, pp. 750-67 and 785-7; partial text in *Documents, 1954*, pp. 283-302 and 311-14.

of American prisoners of war and of American civilians captured throughout Indochina should be separated from the issue of Vietnamese civilian personnel detained—partly because of the enormous difficulty of classifying the Vietnamese civilian personnel by categories of who was detained for reasons of the civil war and who was detained for criminal activities, and secondly, because it was foreseeable that negotiations about the release of civilian detainees would be complex and difficult and because we did not want to have the issue of American personnel mixed up with the issues of civilian personnel in South Vietnam.

This turned out to be one of the thorniest issues, that was settled at some point and kept reappearing throughout the negotiations. It was one of the difficulties we had during the December negotiations.[23]

As you can see from the agreement, the return of American military personnel and captured civilians is separated in terms of obligation, and in terms of the time frame, from the return of Vietnamese civilian personnel.

The return of American personnel and the accounting of missing in action is unconditional and will take place within the same time frame as the American withdrawal.

The issue of Vietnamese civilian personnel will be negotiated between the two Vietnamese parties over a period of 3 months, and as the agreement says, they will do their utmost to resolve this question within the 3 month period.

So I repeat, the issue is separated, both in terms of obligation and in terms of the relevant time frame from the return of American prisoners, which is unconditional.

We expect that American prisoners will be released at intervals of 2 weeks or fifteen days in roughly equal installments. We have been told that no American prisoners are held in Cambodia. American prisoners held in Laos and North Vietnam will be returned to us in Hanoi. They will be received by American medical evacuation teams and flown on American airplanes from Hanoi to places of our own choice, probably Vientiane.

There will be international supervision of both this provision and of the provision for the missing in action. And all American prisoners will, of course, be released, within 60 days of the signing of the agreement. The signing will take place on January 27, in two installments, the significance of which I will explain to you when I have run through the provisions of the agreement and the associated protocols.

[23]Cf. *AFR, 1972*, pp. 292-9.

Chapter IV: Self-determination for South Vietnam

Chapter IV of the agreement deals with the right of the South Vietnamese people to self-determination. Its first provision contains a joint statement by the United States and North Vietnam in which those two countries jointly recognize the South Vietnamese people's right to self-determination, in which those two countries jointly affirm that the South Vietnamese people shall decide for themselves the political system that they shall choose and jointly affirm that no foreign country shall impose any political tendency on the South Vietnamese people.

The other principal provisions of the agreement are that in implementing the South Vietnamese people's right to self-determination, the two South Vietnamese parties will decide, will agree among each other, on free elections, for offices to be decided by the two parties, at a time to be decided by the two parties. These elections will be supervised and organized first by an institution which has the title of National Council for National Reconciliation and Concord, whose members will be equally appointed by the two sides, which will operate on the principle of unanimity, and which will come into being after negotiation between the two parties, who are obligated by this agreement to do their utmost to bring this institution into being within 90 days.

Leaving aside the technical jargon, the significance of this part of the agreement is that the United States has consistently maintained that we would not impose any political solution on the people of South Vietnam. The United States has consistently maintained that we would not impose a coalition government or a disguised coalition government on the people of South Vietnam.

If you examine the provisions of this chapter, you will see, first, that the existing government in Saigon can remain in office; secondly, that the political future of South Vietnam depends on agreement between the South Vietnamese parties and not on an agreement that the United States has imposed on these parties; thirdly, that the nature of this political evolution, the timing of this political evolution, is left to the South Vietnamese parties, and that the organ that is created to see to it that the elections that are organized will be conducted properly, is one in which each of the South Vietnamese parties has a veto.

The other significant provision of this agreement is the requirement that the South Vietnamese parties will bring about a reduction of their armed forces, and that the forces being reduced will be demobilized.

Chapter V: Reunification and the DMZ

The next chapter deals with the reunification of Vietnam and the relationship between North and South Vietnam. In the many negotiations that I have conducted over recent weeks, not the least arduous was the negotiation conducted with the ladies and gentlemen of the press, who constantly raised issues with respect to sovereignty, the existence of South Vietnam as a political entity, and other matters of this kind. I will return to this issue at the end when I sum up the agreement, but it is obvious that there is no dispute in the agreement between the parties that there is an entity called South Vietnam, and that the future unity of Vietnam, as it comes about, will be decided by negotiation between North and South Vietnam, that it will not be achieved by military force, indeed, that the use of military force with respect to bringing about unification, or any other form of coercion, is impermissible according to the terms of this agreement.

Secondly, there are specific provisions in this chapter with respect to the Demilitarized Zone. There is a repetition of the agreement of 1954 which makes the demarcation line along the 17th Parallel provisional, which means pending reunification. There is a specific provision that both North and South Vietnam shall respect the Demilitarized Zone on either side of the provisional military demarcation line, and there is another provision that indicates that among the subjects that can be negotiated will be modalities of civilian movement across the demarcation line, which makes it clear that military movement across the Demilitarized Zone is in all circumstances prohibited.

Now, this may be an appropriate point to explain what our position has been with respect to the DMZ. There has been a great deal of discussion about the issue of sovereignty and about the issue of legitimacy, which is to say which government is in control of South Vietnam, and, finally, about why we laid such great stress on the issue of the Demilitarized Zone.

We had to place stress on the issue of the Demilitarized Zone because the provisions of the agreement with respect to infiltration, with respect to replacement, with respect to any of the military provisions, would have made no sense whatsoever if there was not some demarcation line that defined where South Vietnam began. If we had accepted the proposition that would have in effect eroded the Demilitarized Zone, then the provisions of the agreement with respect to restrictions about the introduction of men and materiel into South Vietnam would have been unilateral restrictions applying only to the United States and only to our allies. Therefore, if there was to be any meaning to the separation of military and political issues, if there was to be any permanence to the military provisions that had been negotiated, then it was essential that there was a definition of where the obligations of this agreement began. As you can see from the text of the agreement, the principles that we defended were essentially achieved.

Chapters VI and VII: International Machinery; Laos and Cambodia

Chapter VI deals with the international machinery, and we will discuss that when I talk about the associated protocols of the agreement.

Chapter VII deals with Laos and Cambodia. Now, the problem of Laos and Cambodia has two parts. One part concerns those obligations which can be undertaken by the parties signing the agreement—that is to say, the three Vietnamese parties and the United States—those measures that they can take which affect the situation in Laos and Cambodia.

A second part of the situation in Laos has to concern the nature of the civil conflict that is taking place within Laos and Cambodia and the solution of which, of course, must involve as well the two Laotian parties and the innumerable Cambodian factions.

Let me talk about the provisions of the agreement with respect to Laos and Cambodia and our firm expectations as to the future in Laos and Cambodia.

The provisions of the agreement with respect to Laos and Cambodia reaffirm, as an obligation to all the parties, the provisions of the 1954 agreement on Cambodia[24] and of the 1962 agreement on Laos,[25] which affirm the neutrality and right to self-determination of those two countries. They are, therefore, consistent with our basic position with respect also to South Vietnam.

In terms of the immediate conflict, the provisions of the agreement specifically prohibit the use of Laos and Cambodia for military and any other operations against any of the signatories of the Paris Agreement or against any other country. In other words, there is a flat prohibition against the use of base areas in Laos and Cambodia.

There is a flat prohibition against the use of Laos and Cambodia

---

[24]Full text in *American Foreign Policy, 1950-1955*, pp. 767-75; partial text in *Documents, 1954*, pp. 307-10.
[25]*Documents, 1962*, pp. 284-94.

for infiltration into Vietnam or, for that matter, into any other country.

Finally, there is a requirement that all foreign troops be withdrawn from Laos and Cambodia, and it is clearly understood that North Vietnamese troops are considered foreign with respect to Laos and Cambodia.

Now, as to the conflict within these countries which could not be formally settled in an agreement which is not signed by the parties of that conflict, let me make this statement, without elaborating it: It is our firm expectation that within a short period of time there will be a formal cease-fire in Laos which, in turn, will lead to a withdrawal of all foreign forces from Laos and, of course, to the end of the use of Laos as a corridor of infiltration.

Secondly, the situation in Cambodia, as those of you who have studied it will know, is somewhat more complex because there are several parties headquartered in different countries. Therefore, we can say about Cambodia that it is our expectation that a *de facto* cease-fire will come into being over a period of time relevant to the execution of this agreement.

Our side will take the appropriate measures to indicate that it will not attempt to change the situation by force. We have reason to believe that our position is clearly understood by all concerned parties, and I will not go beyond this in my statement.

Chapters VIII and IX: Normalizing Relations; Implementation

Chapter VIII deals with the relationship between the United States and the Democratic Republic of Vietnam.

As I have said in my briefings on October 26 and on December 16,[26] and as the President affirmed on many occasions, the last time in his speech last evening, the United States is seeking a peace that heals. We have had many armistices in Indochina. We want a peace that will last.

And, therefore, it is our firm intention in our relationship to the Democratic Republic of Vietnam to move from hostility to normalization, and from normalization to conciliation and cooperation. And we believe that under conditions of peace we can contribute throughout Indochina to a realization of the humane aspirations of all the people of Indochina. And we will, in that spirit, perform our traditional role of helping people realize these aspirations in peace.

[26]*AFR, 1972*, pp. 285-99.

Chapter IX of the agreement is the usual implementing provision.

So much for the agreement.

PROVISIONS OF THE PROTOCOLS

Prisoners of War

Now, let me say a word about the protocols.[27] There are four protocols or implementing instruments to the agreement: on the return of American prisoners, on the implementation and institution of an international control commission, on the regulations with respect to the cease-fire and the implementation and institution of a joint military commission among the concerned parties, and a protocol about the deactivation and removal of mines.

I have given you the relevant provisions of the protocol concerning the return of prisoners. They will be returned at periodic intervals in Hanoi to American authorities and not to American private groups. They will be picked up by American airplanes, except for prisoners held in the southern part of South Vietnam, which will be released at designated points in the South, again, to American authorities.

We will receive on Saturday, the day of the signing of the agreement, a list of all American prisoners held throughout Indochina. And both parties, that is to say, all parties have an obligation to assist each other in obtaining information about the prisoners, missing in action, and about the location of graves of American personnel throughout Indochina.

The International Commission has the right to visit the last place of detention of the prisoners, as well as the place from which they are released.

International Commission of Control and Supervision [ICCS]

Now, to the International Control Commission. You will remember that one of the reasons for the impasse in December was the difficulty of agreeing with the North Vietnamese about the size of the International Commission, its function, or the location of its teams.

On this occasion, there is no point in rehashing all the differences. It is, however, useful to point out that at that time the proposal of the North Vietnamese was that the International Con-

---

[27]For details of the protocols see note 31 on p. 39 below.

trol Commission have a membership of 250, no organic logistics or communication, dependent entirely for its authority to move on the party it was supposed to be investigating; and over half of its personnel were supposed to be located in Saigon, which is not the place where most of the infiltration that we were concerned with was likely to take place.

We have distributed to you an outline of the basic structure of this Commission. Briefly stated, its total number is 1,160, drawn from Canada, Hungary, Indonesia, and Poland. It has a headquarters in Saigon. It has seven regional teams, 26 teams based in localities throughout Vietnam which were chosen either because forces were in contact there or because we estimated that these were the areas where the violations of the cease-fire were most probable.

There are 12 teams at border crossing points. There are seven teams that are set aside for points of entry, which have yet to be chosen, for the replacement of military equipment. That is for Article 7 of the agreement. There will be three on each side and there will be no legitimate point of entry into South Vietnam other than those three points. The other border and coastal teams are there simply to make certain that no other entry occurs, and any other entry is by definition illegal. There has to be no other demonstration except the fact that it occurred.

This leaves one team free for use, in particular, at the discretion of the Commission. And, of course, the seven teams that are being used for the return of the prisoners can be used at the discretion of the Commission after the prisoners are returned.

There is one reinforced team located at the Demilitarized Zone and its responsibility extends along the entire Demilitarized Zone. It is in fact a team and a half. It is 50 percent larger than a normal border team and it represents one of the many compromises that were made, between our insistence on two teams and their insistence on one team. By a brilliant stroke, we settled on a team and a half. [*Laughter*]

With respect to the operation of the International Commission, it is supposed to operate on the principle of unanimity, which is to say that its reports, if they are Commission reports, have to have the approval of all four members. However, each member is permitted to submit his own opinion, so that as a practical matter any member of the Commission can make a finding of a violation and submit a report, in the first instance to the parties.

The International Commission will report for the time being to the four parties to the agreement. An international conference will take place, we expect, at the Foreign Ministers' level within a month of signing the agreement. [28]

[28]See Document 7.

That international conference will establish a relationship between the International Commission and itself, or any other international body that is mutually agreed upon, so that the International Commission is not only reporting to the parties that it is investigating. But, for the time being, until the international conference has met, there was no other practical group to which the International Commission could report.

Cease-fire and Joint Military Commissions

In addition to this international group, there are two other institutions that are supposed to supervise the cease-fire. There is, first of all, an institution called the Four-Party Joint Military Commission, which is composed of ourselves and the three Vietnamese parties, which is located in the same place as the International Commission, charged with roughly the same functions, but, as a practical matter, it is supposed to conduct the preliminary investigations, its disagreements are automatically referred to the International Commission, and, moreover, any party can request the International Commission to conduct an investigation regardless of what the Four-Party Commission does and regardless of whether the Four-Party Commission has completed its investigation or not.

After the United States has completed its withdrawal, the Four-Party Military Commission will be transformed into a Two-Party Commission composed of the two South Vietnamese parties. The total number of supervisory personnel, therefore, will be in the neighborhood of 4,500 during the period that the Four-Party Commission is in existence, and in the neighborhood of about 3,000 after the Four-Party Commission ceases operating and the Two-Party Commission comes into being.

Deactivation and Removal of Mines

Finally, there is a protocol concerning the removal and deactivation of mines which is self-explanatory and simply explains—discusses the relationship between our efforts and the efforts of the DRV [Democratic Republic of Vietnam] concerning the removal and deactivation of mines which is one of the obligations we have undertaken in the agreement.

SIGNING THE DOCUMENTS

Now, let me point out one other problem. On Saturday, January 27, the Secretary of State on behalf of the United States, will sign the agreement bringing the cease-fire and all the other provisions of the agreement and the protocols into force. He will sign in the morning a document involving four parties, and in the afternoon a document between us and the Democratic Republic of Vietnam. These documents are identical, except that the preamble differs in both cases.

The reason for this somewhat convoluted procedure is that, while the agreement provides that the two South Vietnamese parties should settle their disputes in an atmosphere of national reconciliation and concord, I think it is safe to say that they have not yet quite reached that point, indeed, that they have not yet been prepared to recognize each other's existence.

This being the case, it was necessary to devise one document in which neither of the South Vietnamese parties was mentioned by name and, therefore, no other party could be mentioned by name, on the principle of equality. So the four-party document, the document that will have four signatures, can be read with great care and you will not know until you get to the signature page whom exactly it applies to. It refers only to the parties participating in the Paris Conference, which are, of course, well known to the parties participating in the Paris Conference. [*Laughter*]

It will be signed on two separate pages. The United States and the GVN [Government of (the Republic of) Vietnam] are signing on one page and the Democratic Republic of Vietnam and its ally are signing on a separate page. And this procedure has aged us all by several years. [*Laughter*]

Then there is another document which will be signed by the Secretary of State and the Foreign Minister of the Democratic Republic of Vietnam in the afternoon. That document, in its operative provisions, is word for word the same as the document which will be signed in the morning, and which contains the obligations to which the two South Vietnamese parties are obligated.

It differs from that document only in the preamble and in its concluding paragraph. In the preamble it says the United States, with the concurrence of the Government of the Republic of Vietnam, and the DRV, with the concurrence of the Provisional

Revolutionary Government, and the rest is the same, and then the concluding paragraph has the same adaptation. That document, of course, is not signed by either Saigon or its opponent and, therefore, their obligations are derived from the four-party document.

I do not want to take any time in going into the abstruse legalisms. I simply wanted to explain to you why there were two different signature ceremonies, and why, when we handed out the text of the agreement, we appended to the document which contains the legal obligations which apply to everybody—namely, the four parties—why we appended another section that contained a different preamble and a different implementing paragraph which is going to be signed by the Secretary of State and the Foreign Minister of the Democratic Republic of Vietnam.

This will be true with respect to the agreement and three of the protocols. The fourth protocol, regarding the removal of mines, applies only to the United States and the Democratic Republic of Vietnam and, therefore, we are in the happy position of having to sign only one document.

SUMMARY OF THE NEGOTIATIONS

Now, then let me summarize for you how we got to this point, and some of the aspects of the agreement that we consider significant, and then I will answer your questions.

As you know, when I met with this group on December 16, we had to report that the negotiations in Paris seemed to have reached a stalemate. We had not agreed at that time, although we didn't say so on the—we could not find a formula to take into account the conflicting views with respect to signing. There were disagreements with respect to the DMZ and with the associated aspects of what identity South Vietnam was to have in the agreement.

There was a total deadlock with respect to the protocols, which I summed up in the December 16 press conference. The North Vietnamese approach to international control and ours were so totally at variance that it seemed impossible at that point to come to any satisfactory conclusion. And there began to be even some concern that the separation which we thought we had achieved in October between the release of our prisoners and the question of civilian prisoners in South Vietnam was breaking down.

When we reassembled on January 8, we did not do so in the most cordial atmosphere that I remember. However, by the morning of January 9, it became apparent that both sides were determined to make a serious effort to break the deadlock in negotiations. And we adopted a mode of procedure by which issues in the agreement and issues of principle with respect to the protocols were discussed at meetings between Special Adviser Le Duc Tho and myself, while concurrently an American team headed by Ambassador Sullivan and a Vietnamese team headed by Vice Minister Thach[29] would work on the implementation of the principles as they applied to the protocols.

For example, the Special Adviser and I might agree on the principle of border control posts and their number, but then the problem of how to locate them, according to what criteria, and with what mode of operation presented enormous difficulties.

Let me on this occasion also point out that these negotiations required the closest cooperation throughout our Government, between the White House and the State Department, between all the elements of our team, and that, therefore, the usual speculation of who did what to whom is really extraordinarily misplaced.

Without a cooperative effort by everybody, we could not have achieved what we have presented last night and this morning.

The Special Adviser and I then spent the week, first on working out the unresolved issues in the agreement, and then the unresolved issues with respect to the protocols, and finally, the surrounding circumstances of schedules and procedures.

Ambassador Sullivan remained behind to draft the implementing provisions of the agreements that had been achieved during the week. The Special Adviser and I remained in close contact.

So by the time we met again yesterday, the issues that remained were very few, indeed, were settled relatively rapidly. And I may on this occasion also point out that while the North Vietnamese are the most difficult people to negotiate with that I have ever encountered when they do not want to settle, they are also the most effective that I have dealt with when they finally decide to settle. So that we have gone through peaks and valleys in these negotiations of extraordinary intensity.

Now then, let me sum up where this agreement has left us, first, with respect to what we said we would try to achieve, then with respect to some of its significance, and, finally, with respect to the future.

First, when I met this group on October 26 and delivered myself of some epigrammatic phrases, we obviously did not want to give a complete checklist and we did not want to release the agreement as it then stood, because it did not seem to us desirable to provide a checklist against which both sides would then have to measure success and failure in terms of their prestige.

---

[29]William H. Sullivan, Deputy Assistant Secretary of State for East Asian and Pacific Affairs, and Nguyen Co Thach, Vice Minister for Foreign Affairs.

At that time, too, we did not say that it had always been foreseen that there would be another three or four days of negotiation after this tentative agreement had been reached. The reason why we asked for another negotiation was because it seemed to us at that point that for a variety of reasons, which I explained then and again on December 16, those issues could not be settled within the time frame that the North Vietnamese expected.

It is now a matter of history, and it is, therefore, not essential to go into a debate of on what we based this judgment. But that was the reason why the agreement was not signed on October 31, and not any of the speculations that have been so much in print and on television.

Now, what did we say on October 26 we wanted to achieve? We said, first of all, that we wanted to make sure that the control machinery would be in place at the time of the cease-fire. We did this because we had information that there were plans by the other side to mount a major offensive to coincide with the signing of the cease-fire agreement.

This objective has been achieved by the fact that the protocols will be signed on the same day as the agreement, by the fact that the International Control Commission and the Four-Party Military Commission will meet within 24 hours of the agreement going into effect, or no later than Monday morning, Saigon time, that the regional teams of the International Control Commission will be in place 48 hours thereafter, and that all other teams will be in place within 15 and a maximum of 30 days after that.

Second, we said that we wanted to compress the time interval between the cease-fires we expected in Laos and Cambodia and the cease-fire in Vietnam.

For reasons which I have explained to you, we cannot be as specific about the cease-fires in Laos and Cambodia as we can about the agreements that are being signed on Saturday, but we can say with confidence that the formal cease-fire in Laos will go into effect in a considerably shorter period of time than was envisaged in October, and since the cease-fire in Cambodia depends to some extent on developments in Laos, we expect the same to be true there.

We said that certain linguistic ambiguities should be removed. The linguistic ambiguities were produced by the somewhat extraordinary negotiating procedure whereby a change in the English text did not always produce a correlative change in the Vietnamese text. All the linguistic ambiguities to which we referred in October have, in fact, been removed. At that time I mentioned only one, and therefore I am free to recall it.

I pointed out that the United States position had consistently been a rejection of the imposition of a coalition government on the people of South Vietnam. I said then that the National Council of Reconciliation was not a coalition government, nor was it conceived as a coalition government.

The Vietnamese language text, however, permitted an interpretation of the words "administrative structure" as applied to the National Council of Reconciliation which would have lent itself to the interpretation that it came close or was identical with a coalition government.

You will find that in the text of this agreement the words "administrative structure" no longer exist and therefore this particular, shall we say, ambiguity has been removed.

I pointed out in October that we had to find a procedure for signing which would be acceptable to all the parties for whom obligations were involved. This has been achieved.

I pointed out on October 26 that we would seek greater precision with respect to certain obligations particularly, without spelling them out, as they applied to the Demilitarized Zone and to the obligations with respect to Laos and Cambodia. That, too, has been achieved.

And I pointed out in December that we were looking for some means, some expression, which would make clear that the two parts of Vietnam would live in peace with each other and that neither side would impose its solution on the other by force.

This is now explicitly provided, and we have achieved formulations in which in a number of paragraphs, such as Article 14, 18(e) and 20, there are specific references to the sovereignty of South Vietnam.

There are specific references, moreover, to the same thing in Article 6 and Article 11 of the ICCS protocol. There are specific references to the right of the South Vietnamese people to self-determination.

And, therefore, we believe that we have achieved the substantial adaptations that we asked for on October 26. We did not increase our demands after October 26 and we substantially achieved the clarifications which we sought.

Now then, it is obvious that a war that has lasted for 10 years will have many elements that cannot be completely satisfactory to all the parties concerned. And in the two periods where the North Vietnamese were working with dedication and seriousness on a conclusion, the period in October and the period after we resumed talks on January 8, it was always clear that a lasting peace could come about only if neither side sought to achieve everything that it had wanted; indeed, that stability depended on the relative satisfaction and therefore on the relative dissatisfaction of all of the parties concerned. And therefore, it is also clear that whether this agreement brings a lasting peace or not depends not only on its provisions but also on the spirit in which it is implemented.

It will be our challenge in the future to move the controversies that could not be stilled by any one document from the level of military conflict to the level of postive human aspirations, and to absorb the enormous talents and dedication of the people of Indochina in tasks of construction rather than in tasks of destruction.

We will make a major effort to move to create a framework where we hope in a short time the animosities and the hatred and the suffering of this period will be seen as aspects of the past, and where the debates concern differences of opinion as to how to achieve positive goals.

Of course, the hatreds will not rapidly disappear, and, of course, people who have fought for 25 years will not easily give up their objectives, but also people who have suffered for 25 years may at last come to know that they can achieve their real satisfaction by other and less brutal means.

The President said yesterday that we have to remain vigilant, and so we shall, but we shall also dedicate ourselves to positive efforts. And as for us at home, it should be clear by now that no one in this war has had a monopoly of moral insight. And now that at last we have achieved an agreement in which the United States did not prescribe the political future to its allies, an agreement which should preserve the dignity and the self-respect of all of the parties, together with healing the wounds in Indochina we can begin to heal the wounds in America.

Now, I will be glad to answer any questions.[30]

*   *   *

---

[30]The remainder of the news conference appears in *Presidential Documents, loc. cit.*, pp. 70-74, and *Bulletin*, vol. 68 (1973), pp. 164-9.

*(5)   Agreement on Ending the War and Restoring Peace in Viet-
       nam, signed in Paris and entered into force January 27,
       1973.*[31]

AGREEMENT ON ENDING THE WAR AND RESTORING PEACE IN
VIET-NAM

The Parties participating in the Paris Conference on Viet-Nam,

With a view to ending the war and restoring peace in Viet-Nam
on the basis of respect for the Vietnamese people's fundamental
national rights and the South Vietnamese people's right to self-
determination, and to contributing to the consolidation of peace in
Asia and the world,

Have agreed on the following provisions and undertake to
respect and to implement them:

Chapter I

THE VIETNAMESE PEOPLE'S FUNDAMENTAL NATIONAL RIGHTS

Article 1

The United States and all other countries respect the in-

---

[31]Text from TIAS 7542 (24 UST 4-23). Printed here is the full text of the agreement as signed by the four parties, minus the three accompanying protocols
"Concerning the Return of Captured Military Personnel and Foreign Civilians
and Captured and Detained Vietnamese Civilian Personnel" (24 UST 24-33);
"Concerning the Cease-fire in South Viet-Nam and the Joint Military Commissions" (24 UST 35-52); and "Concerning the International Commission of Control and Supervision" (24 UST 53-66).

As noted in Document 4, a second text with a slightly different preamble and
one additional protocol was prepared for signature by the United States and the
Democratic Republic of Vietnam. In the text of the main agreement (24 UST
115-32), as well as in the protocols, the opening phrase which appears in the
four-party agreement and its protocols (*viz.*, "The Parties participating in the
Paris Conference on Viet-Nam") is replaced by the following:

"The Government of the United States of America, with the concurrence of the
Government of the Republic of Vietnam,

"The Government of the Democratic Republic of Viet-Nam, with the concurrence
of the Provisional Revolutionary Government of the Republic of South Viet-
Nam,". Attached to the two-party agreement, in addition to counterparts of the
three protocols listed above (24 UST 138-78), is a fourth (first) protocol "Concerning the Removal, Permanent Deactivation, or Destruction of Mines in the
Territorial Waters, Ports, Harbors, and Waterways of the Democratic Republic of
Viet-Nam" (24 UST 133-7).

Unofficial texts of the agreements and protocols appear in *Presidential
Documents*, vol. 9 (1973), pp. 51-64, and *Bulletin*, vol. 68 (1973), pp. 174-88.

dependence, sovereignty, unity, and territorial integrity of Viet-Nam as recognized by the 1954 Geneva Agreements on Viet-Nam.[32]

Chapter II

CESSATION OF HOSTILITIES — WITHDRAWAL OF TROOPS

Article 2

A cease-fire shall be observed throughout South Viet-Nam as of 2400 hours G.M.T. [Greenwich Mean Time], on January 27, 1973.

At the same hour, the United States will stop all its military activities against the territory of the Democratic Republic of Viet-Nam by ground, air and naval forces, wherever they may be based, and end the mining of the territorial waters, ports, harbors, and waterways of the Democratic Republic of Viet-Nam. The United States will remove, permanently deactivate or destroy all the mines in the territorial waters, ports, harbors, and waterways of North Viet-Nam as soon as this Agreement goes into effect.

The complete cessation of hostilities mentioned in this Article shall be durable and without limit of time.

Article 3

The parties undertake to maintain the cease-fire and to ensure a lasting and stable peace.

As soon as the cease-fire goes into effect:

(a) The United States forces and those of the other foreign countries allied with the United States and the Republic of Viet-Nam shall remain in-place pending the implementation of the plan of troop withdrawal. The Four-Party Joint Military Commission described in Article 16 shall determine the modalities.

(b) The armed forces of the two South Vietnamese parties shall remain in-place. The Two-Party Joint Military Commission described in Article 17 shall determine the areas controlled by each party and the modalities of stationing.

(c) The regular forces of all services and arms and the irregular forces of the parties in South Viet-Nam shall stop all offensive activities against each other and shall strictly abide by the following stipulations:

[32]Cf. note 22 above.
[33]7:00 P.M., Eastern Standard Time.

— All acts of force on the ground, in the air, and on the sea shall be prohibited;

— All hostile acts, terrorism and reprisals by both sides will be banned.

Article 4

The United States will not continue its military involvement or intervene in the internal affairs of South Viet-Nam.

Article 5

Within sixty days of the signing of this Agreement, there will be a total withdrawal from South Viet-Nam of troops, military advisers, and military personnel, including technical military personnel and military personnel associated with the pacification program, armaments, munitions, and war material of the United States and those of the other foreign countries mentioned in Article 3 (a). Advisers from the above-mentioned countries to all paramilitary organizations and the police force will also be withdrawn within the same period of time.

Article 6

The dismantlement of all military bases in South Viet-Nam of the United States and of the other foreign countries mentioned in Article 3 (a) shall be completed within sixty days of the signing of this Agreement.

Article 7

From the enforcement of the cease-fire to the formation of the government provided for in Article 9 (b) and 14 of this Agreement, the two South Vietnamese parties shall not accept the introduction of troops, military advisers, and military personnel including technical military personnel, armaments, munitions, and war material into South Viet-Nam.

The two South Vietnamese parties shall be permitted to make periodic replacement of armaments, munitions and war material which have been destroyed, damaged, worn out or used up after the cease-fire, on the basis of piece-for-piece, of the same characteristics and properties, under the supervision of the Joint Military Commission of the two South Vietnamese parties and of the International Commission of Control and Supervision.

Chapter III

THE RETURN OF CAPTURED MILITARY PERSONNEL AND FOREIGN CIVILIANS, AND CAPTURED AND DETAINED VIETNAMESE CIVILIAN PERSONNEL

Article 8

(a) The return of captured military personnel and foreign civilians of the parties shall be carried out simultaneously with and completed not later than the same day as the troop withdrawal mentioned in Article 5. The parties shall exchange complete lists of the above-mentioned captured military personnel and foreign civilians on the day of the signing of this Agreement.

(b) The parties shall help each other to get information about those military personnel and foreign civilians of the parties missing in action, to determine the location and take care of the graves of the dead so as to facilitate the exhumation and repatriation of the remains, and to take any such other measures as may be required to get information about those still considered missing in action.

(c) The question of the return of Vietnamese civilian personnel captured and detained in South Viet-Nam will be resolved by the two South Vietnamese parties on the basis of the principles of Article 21 (b) of the Agreement on the Cessation of Hostilities in Viet-Nam of July 20, 1954.[34] The two South Vietnamese parties will do so in a spirit of national reconciliation and concord, with a view to ending hatred and enmity, in order to ease suffering and to reunite families. The two South Vietnamese parties will do their utmost to resolve this question within ninety days after the cease-fire comes into effect.

Chapter IV

THE EXERCISE OF THE SOUTH VIETNAMESE PEOPLE'S RIGHT TO SELF-DETERMINATION

Article 9

The Government of the United States of America and the Government of the Democratic Republic of Viet-Nam undertake to

---

[34]Article 21 (b) reads: "The term 'civilian internees' is understood to mean all persons who, having in any way contributed to the political and armed struggle between the two parties, have been arrested for that reason and have been kept in detention by either party during the period of hostilities."

respect the following principles for the exercise of the South Vietnamese people's right to self-determination:

(a) The South Vietnamese people's right to self-determination is sacred, inalienable, and shall be respected by all countries.

(b) The South Vietnamese people shall decide themselves the political future of South Viet-Nam through genuinely free and democratic general elections under international supervision.

(c) Foreign countries shall not impose any political tendency or personality on the South Vietnamese people.

Article 10

The two South Vietnamese parties undertake to respect the cease-fire and maintain peace in South Viet-Nam, settle all matters of contention through negotiations, and avoid all armed conflict.

Article 11

Immediately after the cease-fire, the two South Vietnamese parties will:

— achieve national reconciliation and concord, end hatred and enmity, prohibit all acts of reprisal and discrimination against individuals or organizations that have collaborated with one side or the other;

— ensure the democratic liberties of the people: personal freedom, freedom of speech, freedom of the press, freedom of meeting, freedom of organization, freedom of political activities, freedom of belief, freedom of movement, freedom of residence, freedom of work, right to property ownership, and right to free enterprise.

Article 12

(a) Immediately after the cease-fire, the two South Vietnamese parties shall hold consultations in a spirit of national reconciliation and concord, mutual respect, and mutual non-elimination to set up a National Council of National Reconciliation and Concord of three equal segments. The Council shall operate on the principle of unanimity. After the National Council of National Reconciliation and Concord has assumed its functions, the two South Vietnamese parties will consult about the formation of councils at lower levels. The two South Vietnamese parties shall sign an agreement on the internal matters of South Viet-Nam as soon as possible and do their utmost to accomplish this within ninety days after the cease-fire comes into effect, in keeping with the South Vietnamese people's aspirations for peace, independence and democracy.

(b) The National Council of National Reconciliation and Concord shall have the task of promoting the two South Vietnamese parties' implementation of this Agreement, achievement of national reconciliation and concord and ensurance of democratic liberties. The National Council of National Reconciliation and Concord will organize the free and democratic general elections provided for in Article 9 (b) and decide the procedures and modalities of these general elections. The institutions for which the general elections are to be held will be agreed upon through consultations between the two South Vietnamese parties. The National Council of National Reconciliation and Concord will also decide the procedures and modalities of such local elections as the two South Vietnamese parties agree upon.

Article 13

The question of Vietnamese armed forces in South Viet-Nam shall be settled by the two South Vietnamese parties in a spirit of national reconciliation and concord, equality and mutual respect, without foreign interference, in accordance with the postwar situation. Among the questions to be discussed by the two South Vietnamese parties are steps to reduce their military effectives and to demobilize the troops being reduced. The two South Vietnamese parties will accomplish this as soon as possible.

Article 14

South Viet-Nam will pursue a foreign policy of peace and independence. It will be prepared to establish relations with all countries irrespective of their political and social systems on the basis of mutual respect for independence and sovereignty and accept economic and technical aid from any country with no political conditions attached. The acceptance of military aid by South Viet-Nam in the future shall come under the authority of the government set up after the general elections in South Viet-Nam provided for in Article 9 (b).

Chapter V

THE REUNIFICATION OF VIET-NAM AND THE RELATIONSHIP BETWEEN NORTH AND SOUTH VIET-NAM

Article 15

The reunification of Viet-Nam shall be carried out step by step through peaceful means on the basis of discussions and agreements between North and South Viet-Nam, without coercion or annexation by either party, and without foreign interference. The time for reunification will be agreed upon by North and South Viet-Nam.

Pending reunification:

(a) The military demarcation line between the two zones at the 17th parallel is only provisional and not a political or territorial boundary, as provided for in paragraph 6 of the Final Declaration of the 1954 Geneva Conference.[35]

(b) North and South Viet-Nam shall respect the Demilitarized Zone on either side of the Provisional Military Demarcation Line.

(c) North and South Viet-Nam shall promptly start negotiations with a view to reestablishing normal relations in various fields. Among the questions to be negotiated are the modalities of civilian movement across the Provisional Military Demarcation Line.

(d) North and South Viet-Nam shall not join any military alliance or military bloc and shall not allow foreign powers to maintain military bases, troops, military advisers, and military personnel on their respective territories, as stipulated in the 1954 Geneva Agreements on Viet-Nam.

---

[35]Paragraph 6 reads: "The Conference recognizes that the essential purpose of the agreement relating to Viet-Nam is to settle military questions with a view to ending hostilities and that the military demarcation line is provisional and should not in any way be interpreted as constituting a political or territorial boundary. The Conference expresses its conviction that the execution of the provisions set out in the present declaration and in the agreement on the cessation of hostilities creates the necessary basis for the achievement in the near future of a political settlement in Viet-Nam."

Chapter VI

THE JOINT MILITARY COMMISSIONS,
THE INTERNATIONAL COMMISSION
OF CONTROL AND SUPERVISION,
THE INTERNATIONAL CONFERENCE

Article 16

(a) The Parties participating in the Paris Conference on Viet-Nam shall immediately designate representatives to form a Four-Party Joint Military Commission with the task of ensuring joint action by the parties in implementing the following provisions of this Agreement:

— The first paragraph of Article 2, regarding the enforcement of the cease-fire throughout South Viet-Nam;
— Article 3 (a), regarding the cease-fire by U.S. forces and those of the other foreign countries referred to in that Article;
— Article 3 (c), regarding the cease-fire between all parties in South Viet-Nam;
— Article 5, regarding the withdrawal from South Viet-Nam of U.S. troops and those of the other foreign countries mentioned in Article 3 (a);
— Article 6, regarding the dismantlement of military bases in South Viet-Nam of the United States and those of the other foreign countries mentioned in Article 3 (a);
— Article 8 (a), regarding the return of captured military personnel and foreign civilians of the parties;
— Article 8 (b), regarding the mutual assistance of the parties in getting information about those military personnel and foreign civilians of the parties missing in action.

(b) The Four-Party Joint Military Commission shall operate in accordance with the principle of consultations and unanimity. Disagreements shall be referred to the International Commission of Control and Supervision.

(c) The Four-Party Joint Military Commission shall begin operating immediately after the signing of this Agreement and end its activities in sixty days, after the completion of the withdrawal of U.S. troops and those of the other foreign countries mentioned in Article 3 (a) and the completion of the return of captured military personnel and foreign civilians of the parties.

(d) The four parties shall agree immediately on the organization, the working procedure, means of activity, and expenditures of the Four-Party Joint Military Commission.

Article 17

(a) The two South Vietnamese parties shall immediately designate representatives to form a Two-Party Joint Military Commission with the task of ensuring joint action by the two South Vietnamese parties in implementing the following provisions of this Agreement:

— The first paragraph of Article 2, regarding the enforcement of the cease-fire throughout South Viet-Nam, when the Four-Party Joint Military Commission has ended its activities;
— Article 3 (b), regarding the cease-fire between the two South Vietnamese parties;
— Article 3 (c), regarding the cease-fire between all parties in South Viet-Nam, when the Four-Party Joint Military Commission has ended its activities;
— Article 7, regarding the prohibition of the introduction of troops into South Viet-Nam and all other provisions of this Article;
— Article 8 (c), regarding the question of the return of Vietnamese civilian personnel captured and detained in South Viet-Nam;
— Article 13, regarding the reduction of the military effectives of the two South Vietnamese parties and the demobilization of the troops being reduced.

(b) Disagreements shall be referred to the International Commission of Control and Supervision.
(c) After the signing of this Agreement, the Two-Party Joint Military Commission shall agree immediately on the measures and organization aimed at enforcing the cease-fire and preserving peace in South Viet-Nam.

Article 18

(a) After the signing of this Agreement, an International Commission of Control and Supervision shall be established immediately.
(b) Until the International Conference provided for in Article 19 makes definitive arrangements, the International Commission of Control and Supervision will report to the four parties on matters

concerning the control and supervision of the implementation of the following provisions of this Agreement:

— The first paragraph of Article 2, regarding the enforcement of the cease-fire throughout South Viet-Nam;
— Article 3 (a), regarding the cease-fire by U.S. forces and those of the other foreign countries referred to in that Article;
— Article 3 (c), regarding the cease-fire between all the parties in South Viet-Nam;
— Article 5, regarding the withdrawal from South Viet-Nam of U.S. troops and those of the other foreign countries mentioned in Article 3 (a);
— Article 6, regarding the dismantlement of military bases in South Viet-Nam of the United States and those of the other foreign countries mentioned in Article 3 (a);
— Article 8 (a), regarding the return of captured military personnel and foreign civilians of the parties.

The International Commission of Control and Supervision shall form control teams for carrying out its tasks. The four parties shall agree immediately on the location and operation of these teams. The parties will facilitate their operation.

(c) Until the International Conference makes definitive arrangements, the International Commission of Control and Supervision will report to the two South Vietnamese parties on matters concerning the control and supervision of the implementation of the following provisions of this Agreement:

— The first paragraph of Article 2, regarding the enforcement of the cease-fire throughout South Viet-Nam, when the Four-Party Joint Military Commission has ended its activities;
— Article 3 (b), regarding the cease-fire between the two South Vietnamese parties;
— Article 3 (c), regarding the cease-fire between all parties in South Viet-Nam, when the Four-Party Joint Military Commission has ended its activities;
— Article 7, regarding the prohibition of the introduction of troops into South Viet-Nam and all other provisions of this Article;
— Article 8 (c), regarding the question of the return of Vietnamese civilian personnel captured and detained in South Viet-Nam;
— Article 9 (b), regarding the free and democratic general elections in South Viet-Nam;
— Article 13, regarding the reduction of the military ef-

fectives of the two South Vietnamese parties and the demobilization of the troops being reduced.

The International Commission of Control and Supervision shall form control teams for carrying out its tasks. The two South Vietnamese parties shall agree immediately on the location and operation of these teams. The two South Vietnamese parties will facilitate their operation.

(d) The International Commission of Control and Supervision shall be composed of representatives of four countries: Canada, Hungary, Indonesia and Poland. The chairmanship of this Commission will rotate among the members for specific periods to be determined by the Commission.

(e) The International Commission of Control and Supervision shall carry out its tasks in accordance with the principle of respect for the sovereignty of South Viet-Nam.

(f) The International Commission of Control and Supervision shall operate in accordance with the principle of consultations and unanimity.

(g) The International Commission of Control and Supervision shall begin operating when a cease-fire comes into force in Viet-Nam. As regards the provisions in Article 18 (b) concerning the four parties, the International Commission of Control and Supervision shall end its activities when the Commissions's tasks of control and supervision regarding these provisions have been fulfilled. As regards the provisions in Article 18 (c) concerning the two South Vietnamese parties, the International Commission of Control and Supervision shall end its activities on the request of the government formed after the general elections in South Viet-Nam provided for in Article 9 (b).

(h) The four parties shall agree immediately on the organization, means of activity, and expenditures of the International Commission of Control and Supervision. The relationship between the International Commission and the International Conference will be agreed upon by the International Commission and the International Conference.

Article 19

The parties agree on the convening of an International Conference within thirty days of the signing of this Agreement to acknowledge the signed agreements; to guarantee the ending of the war, the maintenance of peace in Viet-Nam, the respect of the Vietnamese people's fundamental national rights, and the South Vietnamese people's right to self-determination; and to contribute to and guarantee peace in Indochina.

The United States and the Democratic Republic of Viet-Nam, on behalf of the parties participating in the Paris Conference on Viet-Nam, will propose to the following parties that they participate in this International Conference: the People's Republic of China, the Republic of France, the Union of Soviet Socialist Republics, the United Kingdom, the four countries of the International Commission of Control and Supervision, and the Secretary General of the United Nations, together with the parties participating in the Paris Conference on Viet-Nam.

Chapter VII

REGARDING CAMBODIA AND LAOS

Article 20

(a) The parties participating in the Paris Conference on Viet-Nam shall strictly respect the 1954 Geneva Agreements on Cambodia[36] and the 1962 Geneva Agreements on Laos,[37] which recognized the Cambodian and the Lao peoples' fundamental national rights, i.e., the independence, sovereignty, unity, and territorial integrity of these countries. The parties shall respect the neutrality of Cambodia and Laos.

The parties participating in the Paris Conference on Viet-Nam undertake to refrain from using the territory of Cambodia and the territory of Laos to encroach on the sovereignty and security of one another and of other countries.

(b) Foreign countries shall put an end to all military activities in Cambodia and Laos, totally withdraw from and refrain from reintroducing into these two countries troops, military advisers and military personnel, armaments, munitions and war material.

(c) The internal affairs of Cambodia and Laos shall be settled by the people of each of these countries without foreign interference.

(d) The problems existing between the Indochinese countries shall be settled by the Indochinese parties on the basis of respect for each other's independence, sovereignty, and territorial integrity, and non-interference in each other's internal affairs.

[36]Cf. note 24 above.
[37]*Documents, 1962*, pp. 284-94.

Chapter VIII

THE RELATIONSHIP BETWEEN THE UNITED STATES AND THE DEMOCRATIC REPUBLIC OF VIET-NAM

Article 21

The United States anticipates that this Agreement will usher in an era of reconciliation with the Democratic Republic of Viet-Nam as with all the peoples of Indochina. In pursuance of its traditional policy, the United States will contribute to healing the wounds of war and to postwar reconstruction of the Democratic Republic of Viet-Nam and throughout Indochina.

Article 22

The ending of the war, the restoration of peace in Viet-Nam, and the strict implementation of this Agreement will create conditions for establishing a new, equal and mutually beneficial relationship between the United States and the Democratic Republic of Viet-Nam on the basis of respect for each other's independence and sovereignty, and non-interference in each other's internal affairs. At the same time this will ensure stable peace in Viet-Nam and contribute to the preservation of lasting peace in Indochina and Southeast Asia.

Chapter IX

OTHER PROVISIONS

Article 23

This Agreement shall enter into force upon signature by plenipotentiary representatives of the parties participating in the Paris Conference on Viet-Nam. All the parties concerned shall strictly implement this Agreement and its Protocols.[38]

Done in Paris this twenty-seventh day of January, one thousand nine hundred and seventy-three, in English and Vietnamese. The English and Vietnamese texts are official and equally authentic.

---

[38]For the protocols see note 31.

FOR THE GOVERNMENT OF THE
UNITED STATES OF AMERICA:

(*Signed*):

William P. Rogers
Secretary of State

FOR THE GOVERNMENT OF THE
REPUBLIC OF VIET-NAM:

(*Signed*):

Tran Van Lam
Minister for Foreign Affairs

FOR THE GOVERNMENT OF THE
DEMOCRATIC REPUBLIC
OF VIET-NAM:

(*Signed*):

Nguyen Duy Trinh
Minister for Foreign Affairs

FOR THE PROVISIONAL
REVOLUTIONARY GOVERNMENT
OF THE REPUBLIC
OF SOUTH VIET-NAM:

(*Signed*):

Nguyen Thi Binh
Minister for Foreign Affairs

(6)   Dr. Kissinger Goes to Hanoi: Joint communiqué issued by the United States and the Democratic Republic of Vietnam, February 14, 1973.[39]

Dr. Henry A. Kissinger, Assistant to the President of the United States, arrived in Hanoi on February 10, 1973, and left Hanoi on February 13, 1973. He was accompanied by Mr. Herbert G. Klein, Director of Communications for the Executive Branch, Ambassador William H. Sullivan, Deputy Assistant Secretary of State, and other American officials.

During his stay in Hanoi, Dr. Henry A. Kissinger was received by Premier Pham Van Dong, Special Advisor Le Duc Tho, and Vice Premier Nguyen Duy Trinh. The DRVN [Democratic Republic of Vietnam] side and the U.S. side had frank, serious, and constructive exchanges of views on the implementation of the agreement on ending the war and restoring peace in Vietnam which was signed in Paris on January 27, 1973,[40] as well as post-war relations between the Democratic Republic of Vietnam and the United States, and other subjects of mutual concern. Special Advisor Le Duc Tho and Dr. Kissinger also held discussions in a continuation of their meetings which took place in Paris during the past four years. In addition to these working sessions, Dr. Kissinger and his party visited a number of points of interest in Hanoi.

The two sides carefully reviewed the implementation of the Paris

[39]Text from *Presidential Documents*, vol. 9 (1973), pp. 141-2.
[40]Document 5.

Agreement on Vietnam in the recent period. They discussed various imperative measures which should be taken to improve and expedite the implementation of the agreement, and also agreed that they would continue to have periodic exchanges of views in order to ensure that the agreement and its protocols are strictly and scrupulously implemented, as the signatories have undertaken.

The two sides welcomed the discussions between the two South Vietnamese parties for the purpose of carrying out the provisions concerning self-determination in South Vietnam, in accordance with the stipulations of the Paris Agreement on Vietnam.

The Democratic Republic of Vietnam and the United States declared that the full and scrupulous implementation of the Paris Agreement on Vietnam would positively contribute to the cause of peace in Indochina and Southeast Asia on the basis of strict respect for the independence and neutrality of the countries in this region.

The two sides reaffirmed that the problems existing between the Indochinese countries should be settled by the Indochinese parties on the basis of respect for each other's independence, sovereignty, and territorial integrity, and non-interference in each other's internal affairs. They welcomed the negotiations between the parties in Laos, which are intended to produce a peaceful settlement in that country.

The two sides exchanged views on the manner in which the United States will contribute to healing the wounds of war and to post-war economic reconstruction in North Vietnam. They agreed to establish a DRVN-U.S. Joint Economic Commission. This Commission, which will be composed of an equal number of representatives from each side, will be charged with the task of developing the economic relations between the Democratic Republic of Vietnam and the United States.

The two sides also exchanged views on the convening of [the] International Conference on Vietnam, as provided for in Article 19 of the Paris Agreement on Vietnam. They will continue their consultations with the other participants in the conference so as to prepare the ground for a successful meeting.

The two sides considered the post-war relationship between the Democratic Republic of Vietnam and the United States, and examined concrete steps which can be taken to normalize the relations between the two countries. They agreed on certain general principles which should govern their mutual relations:

—All provisions of the Paris Agreement on Vietnam and its protocols should be fully and scrupulously implemented.

—The Democratic Republic of Vietnam and the United States should strive for a new relationship based on respect for each other's independence and sovereignty, non-interference in each other's internal affairs, equality and mutual benefit.

—The normalization of the relations between the Democratic Republic of Vietnam and the United States will help to ensure stable peace in Vietnam and contribute to the cause of peace in Indochina and Southeast Asia.

Dr. Kissinger and his party expressed warm appreciation for the hospitality extended by the Democratic Republic of Vietnam. Both sides hope that this visit will mark the beginning of new bilateral relations.

(7) The International Conference on Vietnam, Paris, February 26-March 2, 1973.

(a) Views of the United States: Statement to the Conference by Secretary of State William P. Rogers, February 26, 1973.[41]

Minister Schumann:[42] Your government has untiringly offered generous hospitality and assistance throughout the long and difficult period of our negotiations. For that, we are grateful to you. It is both fitting and meaningful that we should gather in Paris, where we have for so many years labored to bring an end to conflict that has resulted in so many casualties—so much devastation. Now we are assembled in a historically significant effort to underwrite and solidify the peace that has finally been achieved. The instruments of peace before us have been welcomed enthusiastically throughout the world. That is because they hold out promise that an era of reconciliation in Southeast Asia has truly begun.

For its part, the United States intends to do its utmost to insure that the work of our conference is pursued in a spirit of conciliation and good will. This conference at the foreign ministers level presents an opportunity for concerted and constructive international action unparalleled in recent history.

I think it is appropriate as we begin our discussions to consider for a moment our fundamental objective. Certainly we will espouse different points of view during the next several days. But common goals and aspirations motivate us to concentrate on a single objective: peace. After all, is peace not the reason we are here today in spite of differences that may exist among some of us? Is it not that

---

[41]Text from *Bulletin*, vol. 68 (1973), pp. 337-9.
[42]Maurice Schumann, French Minister for Foreign Affairs.

objective which causes people all over the world to focus their attention with such hope on this conference?

We represent a wide spectrum of nations and peoples assembled in conference seeking to give meaning to the most elusive of man's aims: that of living together peacefully. We are gathered here today with a mandate, if you will, from people all over the world. If we are to succeed—and my government is totally committed to success—we must be willing to work together, to pool our intellects, our abilities, and our resources. Above all, we will be required to focus our attention on the future rather than on the past. Recriminations about the past, point and counter point, attack and counterattack, are instruments of conflict. We are here to seek reconciliation and concord. This is not a conference on how or why a war was fought; this is a conference on how peace should be waged.

It goes without saying that peace in Indochina is vital to tranquillity throughout the world. Those of us who have suffered great human losses in Indochina have agreed to transform the sinews of war into sinews of peace. In order to succeed, the help of the other parties at this conference will be needed—your help and unflagging cooperation in the cause of peace will be needed. This is what this conference is all about.

We should not be surprised that the attention of the world is centered on this conference. The opportunity given to us and the responsibilities weighing on us are formidable. The agreement signed in this room on January 27[43] was not merely a cease-fire agreement, but an agreement on ending the war and restoring peace.

It took the first essential step without which peace would have remained merely a distant goal. However, it recognized, by making provision for this conference, that continuing international cooperation and discipline is required if the beginnings of peace in Indochina are to be nurtured and channeled into an enduring reality.

This conference draws together the parties directly involved in the war in Viet-Nam along with others. The presence of each party here manifests an interest in and capability of making important contributions to a stable and lasting peace.

There is, I am confident, no disagreement that all of us maintain genuine interest in the avoidance of war and preservation of international peace and security. Here, now, collectively we have the opportunity to advance this shared interest by wholeheartedly en-

---

[43]Document 5.

dorsing and supporting the agreement in all of its aspects and by other means we can separately and collectively devise.

This conference has an unprecedented opportunity to act in a concerted and constructive manner to guarantee stability and security in Indochina.

The agreement uses the word "guarantee." I have been asked by some of my colleagues about the use of this word. What does "guarantee" mean? Does it mean the use of force if necessary? Certainly not force that results from the use of arms. But what about the force that comes from a common commitment to peace? If each party around this table endorses this agreement, supports this agreement, makes a total and unrestrained commitment to playing a responsible role in carrying out this agreement, then peace will be guaranteed.

Our *first* order of business then, I believe, is to recognize that the agreement and protocols constitute a major contribution to peace, self-determination, national independence, and friendly relations among states—and accordingly to acknowledge, approve, and support that agreement and those protocols.

Second, it is our view that this conference should exhort the parties signatory to the agreement and the protocols and all other nations as well—there are others indirectly involved—strictly to respect and observe all of the provisions of the agreement and the protocols.

Third, we should create a useful and meaningful relationship between the International Commission of Control and Supervision (ICCS) and the conference. This would permit the International Commission to keep the parties informed of important developments. It would enhance the stability of the peace and would give substance to the principle set forth in the agreement that the conference should guarantee the maintenance of the peace.

You may ask, Do the parties to this conference have a responsibility in the event of a violation which threatens the peace, the independence or the right of the South Vietnamese people to self-determination? It would seem to me that we do have such a responsibility. We have a responsibility, I believe, individually and jointly, to consult with each other to determine the necessary remedial measures.

Certainly, after such consideration, if it is determined by six or more of us that this is the case and that peace is in jeopardy, then the right and responsibility to reconvene this conference should exist. Otherwise, how could we ever apply our combined authority? Otherwise, would not the reports and views of the ICCS be empty and meaningless gestures?

We all hope that reconvening this conference will never be

necessary. Certainly, there is no reason to set up or create any elaborate machinery or standby body to deal with such a contingency, which in all probability will never arise. However, I believe a simple mechanism for reconvening must exist. So our *fourth* order of business, it seems to me, is to create such a standby mechanism or procedure.

The conference also has before it the question of what it can do to assist in bringing a stable peace to Laos and Cambodia, recognizing that the durability of peace in any one state of Indochina depends in part on ending the fighting and keeping the peace throughout the area. This also is a challenge we must address.

Specifically, article 19 of the Viet-Nam agreement provides that the international conference shall contribute to and guarantee peace in Indochina, which, of course, includes Laos and Cambodia.

What can we do to contribute to peace in Laos and Cambodia? First, we can endorse and support the terms of the cease-fire that has been entered into concerning Laos. I would not think that a reference by this conference to that effect would be opposed by any of the participants around this table. Second, we can undertake to encourage and support efforts to achieve an agreement in Cambodia.

But the most important thing we can do is to give full recognition and meaning to the single most important provision in the agreement relating to Laos and Cambodia. I refer to article 20 (b). The article says that foreign countries shall put an end to all military activities in Laos and Cambodia, totally withdraw from and refrain from reintroducing into these two countries troops, military advisers, and military personnel.

Why do I underscore the importance of this provision? Because if the provision is scrupulously observed then the problems that remain will be problems for indigenous populations to solve. Solutions to those problems, we are convinced, can and will be reached peacefully—and without delay.

Stated another way: The war continues in Cambodia and the cease-fire in Laos is not yet fully effective because of the presence of foreign forces in those countries.

Therefore, by endorsing the Paris agreement, we support article 20 (b) calling for the removal of all foreign forces from Laos and Cambodia. When this provision is honored the cease-fire agreement in Laos will be honored and peace will come to Cambodia. That, I believe, should be our *fifth* order of business.

Article 21 of the agreement provides that the United States will contribute to reconstruction throughout Indochina. Thus we have given our pledge to the principle of helping. In article 19 the agreement also deals with this international conference and states the hope that this conference will contribute to and guarantee peace in Indochina. To that end there is nothing that this conference could do that would be more concrete and meaningful than to assist in such a relief, rehabilitation, and reconstruction effort. Obviously the manner and extent of such contribution must rest with each party here represented. Certainly, some parties may not have the ability to make any meaningful contribution. Clearly, other nations not here represented will want to play a major role in any rehabilitation and reconstruction effort. And most important of all, any contribution, however made, must be made in full consultation with and respect for the sovereignty of the recipients and without any political consideration of any kind.

With these considerations in mind, the principle of assisting this war-torn area of the world toward rehabilitation and reconstruction we deem of great importance.

The suggestions I have outlined for this conference are not without their problems. But as I said earlier, we are prepared to listen, to share views and exchange ideas with each of the parties represented here. What is important is that we strive to put aside our differences, that we concentrate on our common goals and recognize that our obligations here transcend parochial interests. That is the challenge I believe we face. That is the challenge I believe we will meet.

(b) Act of the International Conference on Vietnam, signed at Paris and entered into force March 2, 1973.[44]

ACT
OF THE INTERNATIONAL CONFERENCE OF VIET-NAM

The Government of the United States of America;
The Government of the French Republic;
The Provisional Revolutionary Government of the Republic of
    South Viet-Nam;
The Government of the Hungarian People's Republic;
The Government of the Republic of Indonesia;
The Government of the Polish People's Republic;
The Government of the Democratic Republic of Viet-Nam;
The Government of the United Kingdom of Great Britain and
    Northern Ireland;

---

[44]TIAS 7568; 24 UST 486-91.

The Government of the Republic of Viet-Nam;
The Government of the Union of Soviet Socialist Republics;
The Government of Canada; and
The Government of the People's Republic of China;

In the presence of the Secretary-General of the United Nations;

With a view to acknowledging the signed Agreements; guaranteeing the ending of the war, the maintenance of peace in Viet-Nam, the respect of the Vietnamese people's fundamental national rights, and the South Vietnamese people's right to self-determination; and contributing to and guaranteeing peace in Indochina;

Have agreed on the following provisions, and undertake to respect and implement them;

Article 1

The Parties to this Act solemnly acknowledge, express their approval of, and support the Paris Agreement on Ending the War and Restoring Peace in Viet-Nam signed in Paris on January 27, 1973, and the four Protocols to the Agreement signed on the same date (hereinafter referred to respectively as the Agreement and the Protocols).[45]

Article 2

The Agreement responds to the aspirations and fundamental national rights of the Vietnamese people, *i.e.*, the independence, sovereignty, unity, and territorial integrity of Viet-Nam, to the right of the South Vietnamese people to self-determination, and to the earnest desire for peace shared by all countries in the world. The Agreement constitutes a major contribution to peace, self-determination, national independence, and the improvement of relations among countries. The Agreement and the Protocols should be strictly respected and scrupulously implemented.

Article 3

The Parties to this Act solemnly acknowledge the commitments by the parties to the Agreement and the Protocols to strictly respect and scrupulously implement the Agreement and the Protocols.

[45]Document 5. For the protocols see note 31.

Article 4

The Parties to this Act solemnly recognize and strictly respect the fundamental national rights of the Vietnamese people, *i.e.*, the independence, sovereignty, unity, and territorial integrity of Viet-Nam, as well as the right of the South Vietnamese people to self-determination. The Parties to this Act shall strictly respect the Agreement and the Protocols by refraining from any action at variance with their provisions.

Article 5

For the sake of a durable peace in Viet-Nam, the Parties to this Act call on all countries to strictly respect the fundamental national rights of the Vietnamese people, *i.e.*, the independence, sovereignty, unity, and territorial integrity of Viet-Nam and the right of the South Vietnamese people to self-determination and to strictly respect the Agreement and the Protocols by refraining from any action at variance with their provisions.

Article 6

(a) The four parties to the Agreement or the two South Vietnamese parties may, either individually or through joint action, inform the other Parties to this Act about the implementation of the Agreement and the Protocols. Since the reports and views submitted by the International Commission of Control and Supervision concerning the control and supervision of the implementation of those provisions of the Agreement and the Protocols which are within the tasks of the Commission will be sent to either the four parties signatory to the Agreement or to the two South Vietnamese parties, those parties shall be responsible, either individually or through joint action, for forwarding them promptly to the other Parties to this Act.

(b) The four parties to the Agreement or the two South Vietnamese parties shall also, either individually or through joint action, forward this information and these reports and views to the other participant in the International Conference on Viet-Nam for his information.

Article 7

(a) In the event of a violation of the Agreement or the Protocols which threatens the peace, the independence, sovereignty, unity, or territorial integrity of Viet-Nam, or the right of the South Vietnamese people to self-determination, the parties signatory to the Agreement and the Protocols shall, either individually or jointly, consult with the other Parties to this Act with a view to determining necessary remedial measures.

(b) The International Conference on Viet-Nam shall be reconvened upon a joint request by the Government of the United States of America and the Government of the Democratic Republic of Viet-Nam on behalf of the parties signatory to the Agreement or upon a request by six or more of the Parties to this Act.

Article 8

With a view to contributing to and guaranteeing peace in Indochina, the Parties to this Act acknowledge the commitment of the parties to the Agreement to respect the independence, sovereignty, unity, territorial integrity, and neutrality of Cambodia and Laos as stipulated in the Agreement, agree also to respect them and to refrain from any action at variance with them, and call on other countries to do the same.

Article 9

This Act shall enter into force upon signature by plenipotentiary representatives of all twelve Parties and shall be strictly implemented by all the Parties. Signature of this Act does not constitute recognition of any Party in any case in which it has not previously been accorded.

Done in twelve copies in Paris this second day of March, One Thousand Nine Hundred and Seventy-Three, in English, French, Russian, Vietnamese, and Chinese. All texts are equally authentic.

For the Government of the
United States of America
The Secretary of State

(*Signed*): WILLIAM P. ROGERS

For the Government of
the French Republic
The Minister for
Foreign Affairs

(*Signed*): MAURICE SCHUMANN

For the Provisional Revolutionary
Government of the
Republic of South Viet-Nam
The Minister for
Foreign Affairs

(*Signed*): NGUYEN THI BINH

For the Government of the
Hungarian People's Republic
The Minister for
Foreign Affairs

(*Signed*): JANOS PETER

For the Government of the
Republic of Indonesia
The Minister for
Foreign Affairs

(*Signed*): ADAM MALIK

For the Government of the
Polish People's Republic
The Minister for
Foreign Affairs

(*Signed*): STEFAN OLSZOWSKI

For the Government of the
Democratic Republic of Viet-Nam
The Minister for
Foreign Affairs

(*Signed*): NGUYEN DUY TRINH

For the Government of the
United Kingdom of Great Britain
and Northern Ireland
The Secretary of State
for Foreign and
Commonwealth Affairs

(*Signed*): ALEC DOUGLAS-HOME

For the Government of the
Republic of Viet-Nam
The Minister for
Foreign Affairs

(Signed): TRAN VAN LAM

For the Government of the
Union of Soviet Socialist Republics
The Minister for
Foreign Affairs

(Signed): ANDREI A. GROMYKO

For the Government
Canada
The Secretary of State for
External Affairs

(Signed): MITCHELL SHARP

For the Government of the
People's Republic of China
The Minister for
Foreign Affairs

[SEAL] *(Signed)*: CHI PENG-FEI

(8) *Visit of President Thieu to the United States: Joint communiqué of President Nixon and President Thieu on their meetings at the Western White House, San Clemente, April 2-3, 1973.*[46]

The President of the United States, Richard M. Nixon, and the President of the Republic of Vietnam, Nguyen Van Thieu, met for two days of discussions in San Clemente at the outset of President Thieu's official visit to the United States. Taking part in these discussions on the United States side were the Secretary of State, William P. Rogers; the Assistant to the President for National Security Affairs, Henry A. Kissinger; the Ambassador of the United States to the Republic of Vietnam, Ellsworth Bunker; the Ambassador-designate of the United States to the Republic of Viet-

[46]Text from *Presidential Documents*, vol. 9 (1973), pp. 328-31.

nam, Graham Martin; and other officials. On the side of the Republic of Vietnam the Minister for Foreign Affairs, Tran Van Lam; the Minister of Economy, Pham Kim Ngoc; the Minister of Finance, Ha Xuan Trung; the Special Assistant to the President for Foreign Affairs, Nguyen Phu Duc; the Vietnamese Ambassador to the United States, Tran Kim Phuong, and other officials also participated in the discussions.

The discussions were held in a very cordial atmosphere appropriate to the enduring relationship of friendship which exists between the governments of the Republic of Vietnam and the United States. The two Presidents discussed the course of U.S.-Vietnamese relations since their meeting at Midway Island on June 8, 1969[47] and the postwar relationship between the two countries. They reached full consensus in their views.

President Nixon and President Thieu reviewed the progress that has been made in economic, political and defense affairs in Vietnam since the Midway meeting. President Nixon expressed gratification with the proficiency of South Vietnam's armed forces and noted their effective and courageous performance in halting the invasion launched by North Vietnam on March 30, 1972. The President also expressed satisfaction with the development of political institutions and noted the political stability that has prevailed in South Vietnam in recent years. President Thieu reaffirmed his determination to assure social and political justice for the people of South Vietnam.

The two Presidents expressed their satisfaction at the conclusion of the Agreement on Ending the War and Restoring Peace in Vietnam,[48] as well as the Act of the International Conference on Vietnam[49] which endorsed this Agreement. They asserted the determination of their two governments to implement the provisions of the Agreement scrupulously. They also affirmed their strong expectation that the other parties signatory to the Agreement would do the same in order to establish a lasting peace in Vietnam. The two Presidents expressed their appreciation to the other members of the international community who helped in achieving the Agreement and particularly to the four member governments of the International Commission of Control and Supervision whose representatives are observing its implementation. They consider that the International Commission, acting in cooperation with the Four Parties to the Agreement, is an essential element in the structure of restoring peace to Vietnam and expressed their deter-

---

[47]*Documents, 1968-69*, pp. 261-7.

[48]Document 5.

[49]Document 7b.

mination to further encourage the most effective and objective possible supervision of the Agreement.

President Nixon informed President Thieu of his great interest in the meetings between representatives of the two South Vietnamese parties which are currently taking place in France in an effort to achieve an internal political settlement in South Vietnam. President Thieu said that his government is resolved at these meetings to achieve a settlement which will fully insure the right of self-determination by the South Vietnamese people in accordance with the Agreement on Ending the War. President Thieu expressed his earnest desire for a reconciliation among the South Vietnamese parties which will fulfill the hopes of the South Vietnamese people for peace, independence, and democracy.

Both Presidents, while acknowledging that progress was being made toward military and political settlements in South Vietnam, nevertheless viewed with great concern infiltrations of men and weapons in sizeable numbers from North Vietnam into South Vietnam in violation of the Agreement on Ending the War, and considered that actions which would threaten the basis of the Agreement would call for appropriately vigorous reactions. They expressed their conviction that all the provisions of the Agreement, including in particular those concerning military forces and military supplies, must be faithfully implemented if the cease-fire is to be preserved and the prospects for a peaceful settlement are to be assured. President Nixon stated in this connection that the United States views violations of any provision of the Agreement with great and continuing concern.

Both Presidents also agreed that there could be lasting peace in Vietnam only if there is peace in the neighboring countries. Accordingly they expressed their earnest interest in the achievement of a satisfactory implementation of the cease-fire agreement reached in Laos on February 21. They expressed their grave concern at the fact that Article 20 of the Agreement which calls for the unconditional withdrawal of all foreign forces from Laos and Cambodia has not been carried out. They agreed that this Article should be quickly implemented.

In assessing the prospects for peace throughout Indochina the two Presidents stressed the need for vigilance on the part of the governments in the Indochinese states against the possibility of renewed Communist aggression after the departure of United States ground forces from South Vietnam. They stressed the fact that this vigilance will require the continued political, economic, and military strength of the governments and nations menaced by any renewal of this aggressive threat. Because of their limited resources, the nations of the region will require external assistance to preserve the necessary social and economic stability for peaceful development.

In this context, President Thieu affirmed the determination of the Vietnamese people and the Government to forge ahead with the task of providing adequate and timely relief to war victims, reconstructing damaged social and economic infrastructures, and building a strong and viable economy, so that the Vietnamese nation can gradually shoulder a greater burden in the maintenance of peace and the achievement of economic progress for its people. The two Presidents agreed that in order to attain the stated economic goals as quickly as possible, the Republic of Vietnam will need greater external economic assistance in the initial years of the post war era. President Nixon reaffirmed his wholehearted support for the endeavors of post war rehabilitation, reconstruction and development of the Republic of Vietnam. He informed President Thieu of the United States intention to provide adequate and substantial economic assistance for the Republic of Vietnam during the remainder of this year and to seek Congressional authority for a level of funding for the next year sufficient to assure essential economic stability and rehabilitation for that country as it now moves from war to peace. He recognized that the economic development and self-sufficiency of South Vietnam depend to a significant extent on its ability to promote and attract foreign investment. He also expressed his intention to seek Congressional support for a longer range program for the economic development of South Vietnam now that the war has ended.[50]

The two Presidents expressed their earnest hope that other nations as well as international institutions will act promptly on a positive and concerted program of international assistance to the Republic of Vietnam. They also agreed that consultations should soon be held in this regard with all interested parties.

The two Presidents expressed hope that the implementation of the Agreement on Vietnam would permit a normalization of relations with all countries of Southeast Asia. They agreed that this step and a regional reconstruction program will increase the prospects of a lasting peace in the area.

President Nixon discussed the future security of South Vietnam in the context of the Nixon Doctrine. The President noted that the assumption by the Republic of Vietnam of the full manpower requirements for its own defense was fully in keeping with his doctrine. He affirmed that the United States for its part, expected to continue, in accordance with its Constitutional processes, to supply

[50]Cf. Document 24.

the Republic of Vietnam with the material means for its defense consistent with the Agreement on Ending the War.

President Thieu asked President Nixon to convey to the American people and particularly to families bereaved by the loss of loved ones, the deep and abiding appreciation of the people of South Vietnam for the sacrifices made on their behalf and the assistance given to the Republic of Vietnam in its long struggle to maintain its freedom and preserve its right of self-determination.

Prior to the departure of President Thieu for Washington to continue his official visit to the United States, both Presidents agreed that through the harsh experience of a tragic war and the sacrifices of their two peoples a close and constructive relationship between the American and the South Vietnamese people has been developed and strengthened. They affirmed their full confidence that this association would be preserved as the foundation of an honorable and lasting peace in Southeast Asia.

President Thieu expressed his gratitude for the warm hospitality extended to him and his party by President Nixon.

(9) Complaints of Violations of the Cease-fire: United States Note Verbale transmitted April 20, 1973 for delivery to participants in the International Conference on Vietnam.[51]

1. The Department of State of the United States of America presents its compliments to the Ministry of Foreign Affairs/Ministry of External Affairs of [Union of Soviet Socialist Republics, People's Republic of China, Great Britain, France, Republic of Vietnam, Democratic Republic of Vietnam, Hungary, Poland, Indonesia, Canada; and Secretary General of the U.N. Kurt Waldheim] and has the honor to refer to a note[52] dated April 16, 1973, transmitted by the Government of the Democratic Republic of Vietnam to the Government of the United States and, it is assumed, also to the other signatories of the Act of the International Conference on Vietnam.

2. In its Note, the Government of the Democratic Republic of Vietnam, on its own behalf and occasionally also in the name of the "Provisional Revolutionary Government", purports to describe the situation of South Vietnam and lodges charges against the Government of the United States and the Government of the Republic of Vietnam.

---

[51]Department of State Press Release 117, Apr. 24; text from *Bulletin*, vol. 68 (1973), pp. 599-603.
[52]Summary in *Keesing's*, p. 26018.

3. The United States rejects as utterly groundless the accusations of the Democratic Republic of Vietnam, and views this note as an ill-disguised attempt by the Democratic Republic of Vietnam to divert attention away from its own numerous and extremely serious violations of the ceasefire.

4. Contrary to the contentions listed in the note, it is abundantly clear that the main obstruction to peace consists of the military activities carried out by the Democratic Republic of Vietnam and forces under its control in South Vietnam, Laos and Cambodia in direct and inexcusable contravention of the Agreement on Ending the War and Restoring Peace in Vietnam[53] and of the Agreement on the Restoration of Peace and Reconciliation in Laos.[54]

5. Of extreme concern is the vast quantity of military equipment shipped clandestinely since January 28 from North Vietnam into South Vietnam without the least effort to observe Articles 7 and 20 of the Peace Agreement of January 27. Evidence is overwhelming of continued illegal movement of equipment and supplies out of North Vietnam into or through Laos and Cambodia and into South Vietnam for the use of the military forces opposing the legitimate governments of those countries. Included in the supplies reaching South Vietnam are over 400 tanks and armored vehicles, 300 artillery pieces of various types and vast quantities of ammunition, vehicles, etc. For example, from the time of the Vietnam ceasefire through April 18, 1973, over 27,000 short tons of military supplies have been moved through the demilitarized zone into South Vietnam. In the same period, over 26,000 short tons were moved from North Vietnam into Laos. Also during this period, we have detected over 17,000 military truck movements from North Vietnam into Laos and over 7,000 crossing the demilitarized zone into South Vietnam. None of the peace-keeping organs established by the Peace Agreement has been given the opportunity to monitor these shipments.

6. Evidence of an intention to persist in violations of Article 20 of the Agreement is the substantial effort being made to upgrade the road system within Laos and adjoining parts of South Vietnam. Bridge and drainage ditch construction have been observed on Route 7, the primary route into the Plain of Jars from North Vietnam and on Routes 4 and 4/7 which transit the northern plain in an east-west direction. Furthermore, there is evidence of continuing North Vietnamese efforts to construct a road from southern Laos into Quang Tri and Quang Ngai Provinces. This cross-border route is not close to any of the designated entry points and its only logical

[53]Document 5.
[54]Cf. above at note 9.

use could be as a clandestine supply highway into the central coastal regions of South Vietnam.

7. The Democratic Republic of Vietnam also has moved military personnel and military equipment in and through the demilitarized zone is direct violation of Articles 7 and 15 (B) of the Peace Agreement and of Article 7 of the Ceasefire Protocol.

8. In most serious violation of the Agreement, more than 30,000 North Vietnamese army personnel are known to have continued moving through Laos and Cambodia into South Vietnam after the ceasefire on January 28. These combat replacements have greatly increased the capability of North Vietnamese army units in the south. In addition there is evidence that new North Vietnamese army organizations, such as anti-aircraft artillery units, entered South Vietnam after January 28. For example, the Khe Sanh airfield complex has recently been ringed with SA—2 missiles, which clearly were not present prior to the ceasefire.

9. Not content with illegally building up its military potential, the Democratic Republic of Vietnam has since the ceasefire actually employed these and other forces under its command to launch attacks on hamlets, villages and Republic of Vietnam military positions throughout the country in unequivocal violation of the fundamental purpose of the Peace Agreement as embodied in Articles 2 and 3. The assaults have generally consisted of mortarings and shellings, frequently followed by ground attacks in an obvious effort to expand the area controlled by forces under North Vietnamese command. In some cases the assaults were of such intensity as to require withdrawal of government defending forces, for example, from positions at Hoang Hau near Hue, on the Cambodian border in Chau Duc Province and in Bac Lieu Province. Other beleaguered outposts long occupied by the Republic of Vietnam armed forces continue to hold out despite persistent harassment, such as at Tonle Cham in Tay Ninh, at Rach Bap in Binh Duong and in the Hong Ngu and Cai Cai districts of Kien Phong Province.

10. North Vietnamese forces, moreover, continue larger military offensives aimed at opening up new supply routes and expanding their control, such as in the Sa Huynh area of southern Quang Ngai Province.

11. Troops under the control of the Democratic Republic of Vietnam also have placed many mines in violation of Article 5 of the Ceasefire Protocol and have tried to interfere with resumed train service. Earlier this month, in Phu Yen Province, a mine was set under a train and a ground attack was launched on a track repair crew.

12. These forces, moreover, have fired mortars and artillery in-

discriminately into many cities, refugee camps and other centers of population, for example in Tan Chau and Phan Thiet, causing heavy civilian casualties. They have even mortared the team locations of the International Commission of Control and Supervision at Tri Ton and Hong Ngu.

13. In addition to widespread attacks on Republic of Vietnam territorial security forces, agents of the Democratic Republic of Vietnam have continued their acts of terrorism including assassinations, tossing grenades in public places, minings of public thoroughfares and widespread abductions.

14. Another serious impediment to peace is the record of the Democratic Republic of Vietnam and the "Provisional Revolutionary Government" of clear and calculated obstructionism in the Four Party Joint Military Commission. Both consistently refused to participate meaningfully in any Four Party Joint Military Commission investigation which would not benefit their cause. Accordingly, they blocked or prevented investigation of the downing of a CH—47 helicopter, of the Sa Huynh attack and the Khe Sanh missile installation, to cite only three representative examples.

15. The tactic to stall and obstruct was also clearly evident in the refusal to deploy fully to the field. The North Vietnamese deployed to only five of the seven regional headquarters, and their associates of the "Provisional Revolutionary Government" to only one. Deployment to sub-regional teams was minimal. The "Provisional Revolutionary Government" had less than one quarter of its authorized contingent functional at any one time.

16. Thus the Democratic Republic of Vietnam and the "Provisional Revolutionary Government" must bear the responsibility for failure of the Four Party Joint Military Commission to fulfill its assigned functions.

17. Of particular concern to the United States is the failure to date of the Democratic Republic of Vietnam to provide information about Americans missing in action in Indochina or those known to have died there, as required by Article 8 (B) of the Paris Agreement.

18. The charges levied against the United States by the Democratic Republic of Vietnam in its note, include the allegation that the United States gave "backing" to the Government of the Republic of Vietnam in failing to observe the ceasefire and thereby seriously violated Articles 2 and 3 of the Agreement on Ending the War and Restoring Peace in Vietnam. The entire charge is without foundation. The United States concentrated instead after January 28 on observing the terms of the Agreement scrupulously by withdrawing its own military forces from Vietnam and refraining from

participating in any hostilities in Vietnam. Any arms and military equipment provided to the Republic of Vietnam have been strictly in accordance with Article 7 of the Paris Agreement and Article 7 of the Ceasefire Protocol.

19. The Democratic Republic of Vietnam also alleges that the withdrawal of United States forces has been concluded in a manner at variance with Articles 5 and 6 of the Paris Agreement and accuses the United States of failing to withdraw its armaments and dismantle its bases as required by those Articles. Article 5, however, required withdrawal only of those armaments, munitions, and war material which the United States (or allies of the United States and the Republic of Vietnam) may have owned in South Vietnam at the date of or subsequent to the date of entry into force of the Agreement. It did not require the withdrawal from South Vietnam of any armaments which the United States, prior to the entry into force of the Agreement, no longer owned because of prior transfer. This was the meaning of the phrase "of the United States" in Article 5. The same phrase with the same meaning was used in Article 6 with respect to military bases to be dismantled. The United States has fully complied with these provisions. All military equipment and military base facilities formerly owned by the United States forces in South Vietnam which remained there after March 28, had been transferred to the Government of the Republic of Vietnam prior to January 27.

20. The referenced note makes the further charge that the United States has supplied arms, munitions, and war materials to the Republic of Vietnam in violation of the Agreement and its Ceasefire Protocol. This charge is simply without merit. Article 7 of the Agreement permits the South Vietnamese parties to replace, on a piece-for-piece basis, destroyed, damaged, worn out or used up armaments, munitions and war material. The United States and the Republic of Vietnam have established procedures for monitoring arms shipments, to ensure compliance with these restrictions, and records are being maintained which verify this compliance. Introduction of these replacements, as well as these records and procedures, are always open to inspection and observation of the International Commission of Control and Supervision and the Two Party Joint Military Commission. Introduction of these replacements has been restricted to those three points of entry that have been designated by the Republic of Vietnam under the terms of the Agreement.

21. The contention in the note of the Democratic Republic of Vietnam that the United States has left behind over 10,000 military personnel disguised as civilian advisers has no basis in fact and is undoubtedly an attempt to draw attention from the large numbers

of North Vietnamese armed forces in the South. The United States, in accordance with Article 5 of the Peace Agreement, has withdrawn its troops and its military and police advisers. There remain in South Vietnam only about 200 American military personnel, belonging to the Defense Attache Office, the Embassy Marine Security Guard and the team attempting to resolve the status of the missing in action. There are no military persons disguised as civilians. As publicly stated, the total number of official American personnel in South Vietnam is less than 9,000, the large majority of whom are filling logistics and maintenance functions which are soon to be taken over by the South Vietnamese.

22. Other Americans are performing the kinds of functions conducted by diplomatic, consular and AID [Agency for International Development] missions throughout the world. The purposes and functions of the personnel of the United States remaining in South Vietnam are fully known to the Government of the Democratic Republic of Vietnam and are completely in keeping with the January 27 Agreement.

23. The United States also is accused of violating Article 8 of the Act of Paris[55] by virtue of its military activities in Laos immediately after the conclusion of the ceasefire agreement between the Lao parties. United States military activities since the ceasefire have been very limited. They were conducted at the request of Prime Minister Souvanna Phouma. They were made necessary by, and were in direct response to, major and flagrant violations of that agreement by the North Vietnamese and Pathet Lao forces, specifically the post-ceasefire attacks at Pak Song on February 23 and Tha Vieng on April 13.

24. The Democratic Republic of Vietnam further alleges United States violation of the "independence, sovereignty, unity, territorial integrity and neutrality" of Cambodia by continuing to conduct military activities in that country. In fact, these activities are limited to air support operations in response to the continued military operations in Cambodia by the Democratic Republic of Vietnam, and were requested by the Khmer Republic itself. In late January, the Government of the Khmer Republic suspended all offensive operations and the United States likewise halted offensive air operations. However the reaction of the Democratic Republic of Vietnam and Cambodian forces under its control was a total military offensive, despite obligations assumed by the Democratic Republic of Vietnam in Article 20 of the Agreement and Article 8 of the Act of Paris. In order to induce compliance with those essential provisions, without which the entire Vietnam Agreement would

[55]Document 7b.

be endangered, the United States is giving air support to the Khmer forces.

25. With respect to allegations by the Democratic Republic of Vietnam concerning the continued detention of South Vietnamese civilians, the Government of the Republic of Vietnam will doubtless wish to rebut them, but the Government of the United States wishes to point out that the "Provisional Revolutionary Government" has offered to release only several hundred civilian prisoners despite the fact it has captured many thousands. This is an issue where reciprocity is clearly essential.

26. The allegation that the United States Government was deliberately delaying mine-clearing operations is patently false. The United States mine-clearing operation has progressed as rapidly as safety, available forces, weather and restrictions imposed by the Democratic Republic of Vietnam would allow. We have been able to adhere to our agreed schedule despite the loss of two helicopters. Every available United States mine counter-measures unit has been marshalled for this operation. In fact, a force significantly greater than that originally proposed by the United States and accepted by the Democratic Republic of Vietnam has been employed.

27. The fact that only a few mines have been observed to explode is completely understandable and not at all surprising. As has been carefully explained to the Democratic Republic of Vietnam representatives on numerous occasions, the mines have a variable neutralization capability that can be programmed and which has resulted in the neutralization of most of them by now. Nevertheless, adequate safety cannot be guaranteed unless all affected areas are methodically swept with proper equipment by highly trained personnel.

28. However, in view of the many serious violations of other provisions of the Agreement by the Democratic Republic of Vietnam, which have been discussed above, the United States has decided to suspend its mine clearance operations. This suspension is justified as a response to the numerous material breaches of the Agreement by the Democratic Republic of Vietnam in accordance with the rule of international law that a material breach of an international agreement by one party entitles the other party to suspend operation of the Agreement in whole or in part. This rule of customary international law is set forth in Article 60 of the 1969 Convention on the Law of Treaties.[56] The United States is, of course, prepared to resume mine clearance operations as soon as

[56]Vienna Convention on the Law of Treaties, signed for the U.S. on Apr. 24, 1970 and transmitted to the Senate Nov. 22, 1971 (Ex. L, 92-1) but not yet acted upon by that body as of the end of 1974.

the Democratic Republic of Vietnam begins to act in compliance
with its obligations under the Agreement.

29. The Government of the United States thus categorically
rejects the general and the specific charges that it has violated the
terms of the Agreement on Ending the War and Restoring Peace in
Vietnam. For its part, except as noted above, the Government of
the United States again affirms its intention to adhere to the terms
of the Agreement of January 27 and will exert its best efforts to
help bring about a lasting peace in Indochina. It calls on the
Democratic Republic of Vietnam and all other parties to the Final
Act of the International Conference on Vietnam to lend their support to this endeavor.

3. DEEPENING THE CHINA DIALOGUE

Apart from the Republic of Vietnam and some few other governments of strongly anti-Communist complexion, the outside world had generally shared America's optimistic assumption that the agreement on Vietnam would improve the climate of international relations and facilitate the solution of other international problems. The United States, it seemed, was ridding itself at last of an encumbrance that had clogged its diplomatic efforts for more than a decade. Once the Vietnamese slate had been wiped clean, it was assumed, the Nixon administration could address itself with renewed energy to some of the important foreign policy tasks of the second term—among them a consolidation of the détente with the Soviet Union, an amplification of the newly instituted dialogue with mainland China, a reaffirmation of historic ties with Europe and Japan, and a thorough reconstruction of the international trade and monetary system.

Even while the war in Indochina was still at its height, a resumption of contact between the United States and the People's Republic of China had been felt to lie in the interest of both parties, all the more so in view of the strained relationship prevailing between the latter power and the Soviet Union. President Nixon's visit to the China mainland in February 1972[1] had opened a year of striking progress in the development of bilateral relations in the fields of trade, people-to-people contact, and government-to-government communication. Marshall Green, the Assistant Secretary of State for East Asian and Pacific Affairs, assured the Sulgrave Club in a Washington address delivered just a year later **(Document 10)** that the mutual mistrust accumulated over more than two decades had been largely dispelled by the President's visit, and that differences in ideology were no longer a barrier to normal relations. Far from impeding the normalization process,

[1]*AFR, 1972*, pp. 302-17. For more detailed discussion cf. *Nixon Report, 1973*, pp. 16-25.

Mr. Green averred, the war in Vietnam had moved closer to settlement even as U.S.-Chinese relations improved, while even the sensitive Taiwan issue had been defused by the President's frank exposition of the American position. The United States, Mr. Green implied, continued to stand firm in its determination to maintain its diplomatic ties and defense obligations with President Chiang Kai-shek's Republic of China government on Taiwan; but it had also made clear to the Peking leadership that "with the prospect of a peaceful settlement in mind, our ultimate objective was the withdrawal of our forces and installations on Taiwan and . . . in the meantime we would progressively reduce our forces there as tension in the area diminished."

The apparent settlement of the war in Indochina was naturally regarded by both parties as an important step in this direction. In the eyes of the Chinese Communists, the Paris end-the-war agreement was "not only in conformity with the interests of the Vietnamese people and the American people but will also be conducive to the relaxation of tension in the Far East and Asia."[2] Dr. Kissinger, who spent four days in the People's Republic immediately following his February visit to Hanoi, expressed a similar view. "Last year," the Presidential Assistant told a news conference on his return to Washington (**Document 11b**), "our achievements consisted of setting out directions and indicating the roads that might be traveled. After the end of the war in Vietnam, and in these discussions in Peking, we were able to begin to travel some of these roads and to move from the attempt to eliminate the obstructions and the mistrust to some more concrete and positive achievements."

It was true that Dr. Kissinger's discussions with Premier Chou En-lai, Communist Party Chairman Mao Tse-tung, and other Chinese officials on February 15-19 resulted in no change in the situation regarding Taiwan, admittedly a crucial element in the Sino-American relationship. "The level of our troops in Taiwan," the Presidential Assistant later explained, "is not the subject of negotiation, but will be governed by the general considerations of the Nixon Doctrine with respect to danger in the area. There exists no immediate plan for any withdrawal, but there will be a periodic review."[3] What the two sides *had* agreed upon, according to the official communiqué (**Document 11a**), was that "the time was appropriate for accelerating the normalization of relations." In line with this observation, they had undertaken "to broaden their con-

---

[2]British Information Services, *Survey of Current Affairs*, vol. 3 (1973), p. 75.
[3]News conference, Feb. 22, in *Presidential Documents*, vol. 9 (1973), p. 171. For further details cf. Kalb, *Kissinger*, pp. 435-6.

tacts in all fields" and, more specifically, had "agreed on a concrete program of expanding trade as well as scientific, cultural and
other exchanges." (Some of the details were described in Dr.
Kissinger's news conference.) "To facilitate this process and to improve communications," it was further agreed "that in the near
future each side will establish a liaison office in the capital of the
other"—obviously a more efficient arrangement than the indirect
communications link established in 1972 by way of the two countries' embassies in Paris.[4]

Details of the new liaison arrangement were disclosed by
President Nixon in a news conference, held on March 15, that coincided with Peking's release of a CIA agent imprisoned since 1952 as
well as two American airmen shot down in 1965 and 1967. The U.S.
Liaison Office in Peking, the President reported **(Document 12)**,
would open about May 1 and would be headed by Ambassador
David K.E. Bruce, a lifelong Democrat who had held diplomatic
appointments under four Presidents and had served as Ambassador
to Britain, West Germany, and France as well as head of the U.S.
delegation to the Paris meetings on Vietnam. The choice of so
distinguished a diplomat and bipartisan symbol, President Nixon
explained, would serve to underline the fact that his visit to China
the year before had not been a "one-shot deal" but "the beginning,
we trust, of a longer journey, a journey in which we will have our
differences, but one in which the most populous nation in the world
and the United States of America can work together where their interests coincide for the cause of peace and better relations in the
Pacific and in the world." Peking's later choice of General Huang
Chen, an experienced diplomat and close friend of Chairman Mao,
to head the Chinese liaison office in the United States was
presumably motivated by similar reasoning.[5]

*(10) "U.S.-China Relations: Progress Toward Normalization":
Address by Marshall Green, Assistant Secretary of State for
East Asian and Pacific Affairs, before the Sulgrave Club,
Washington, February 20, 1973.[6]*

Just a year ago President Nixon set forth on his historic trip to
Peking. As a result of that decision and the talks the President held
with the leaders of China, new vistas have opened up in world

---

[4]*AFR, 1972*, p. 318.
[5]For later developments see Chapter 25 at note 8.
[6]Department of State Press Release 43; text from *Bulletin*, vol. 68 (1973), pp.
306-9.

diplomacy that augur well for the cause of peace. On this first anniversary, I would like to review with you the major accomplishments of the Peking summit, the progress we have made
since, and our hopes for the future in our efforts to improve
relations with the People's Republic of China [PRC].

At the conclusion of the President's visit to Peking, the United
States and the People's Republic of China issued a joint communique[7] in which the two sides expressed the belief that "the normalization of relations between the two countries" was "not only
in the interest of the Chinese and American peoples but also contributes to the relaxation of tension in Asia and the world." In support of this goal, we agreed to a number of specific means, such as
the development of people-to-people exchanges, expansion of
bilateral trade, and the improvement of communication at the
governmental level.

The distinction in the communique between means and ends is
clear. The President did not go to Peking to seek trade or exchanges or even communication for their own sake. Concern over
the state of relations between China and the United States did not
center on the absence of trade or exchanges or even communication, but on the state of our political relationship. The concern was that our relationship was not "normal"; and it was to
seek a normal relationship that the President went to Peking.

What do we mean by normalizing relations? Difficult as it may
be to achieve, it is a simple, commonsense concept relating to substance, not form. It is normal to trade. It is normal that countries
allow and encourage travel and exchanges of information and experience to broaden understanding between peoples. For any country to live in angry isolation is surely neither desirable nor normal.
But most important of all, "normal relations" means that countries, despite their differences, are able to discuss their problems
with a view toward resolving them or, if that is not possible, at least
to make them manageable until such time as they become soluble.

This is the relationship we have sought with the People's
Republic of China.

But before we could even hope to develop such a relationship,
certain obvious obstacles had to be addressed. The four principal
ones—regarded by many only a few years ago as in-
surmountable—were mutual mistrust, ideology, the war in Indochina, and Taiwan.

Of these, mutual mistrust was the most difficult and the most important to remove; for without an atmosphere of trust, a normal
relationship between nations is impossible. Our statements and par-

[7]*AFR, 1972*, pp. 307-11.

ticularly our actions in the months and years immediately preceding the summit—including the removal of existing barriers to trade, travel, and communication, the reduction of U.S. forces on the periphery of China in accordance with the Nixon doctrine—all contributed to building trust. But it was the President's visit to Peking last February which finally broke the logjam of twenty years of hostility and established an atmosphere of trust. The language of the communique issue at the end of the visit reflected that new atmosphere.

Ideology was perhaps a less serious obstacle. The passage of time and the shift away from bloc politics in the world had moderated the cold war. National interest had begun to outweigh rigid ideological or bloc considerations in the formulation of foreign policy on both sides. The summit both advanced and confirmed that trend. We both acknowledged our differences; indeed, the communique frankly spelled out those differences in what must be one of the most forthright declarations in diplomatic annals. Nevertheless we were able to agree that these differences need not prevent our two countries from conducting a normal relationship, settling disputes between us without resort to the threat or use of force. How nations structure themselves internally is less important to U.S. foreign policy than how they conduct themselves internationally. To the extent that other countries, including China, have come to share that view, the world has become safer from the danger of ideological confrontation and conflict.

The removal of ideology as an obstacle to normal relations helped make possible the removal of the Viet-Nam issue as an obstacle. For with the decline in the importance of ideology in foreign affairs, the war in Indochina became less a crusade on both sides and more simply a war in which the national interests of several countries were engaged. History provides ample evidence that crusades rarely end in a negotiated settlement. Dogma is not negotiable, and the best crusaders can hope for is a precarious truce. Policy positions, however, are negotiable, and reasonable men can find reasonable solutions.

We did not, of course, negotiate a settlement of the Viet-Nam conflict in Peking. But once the United States and China were able to agree, if only tacitly, that we could begin the process of improving relations without waiting for an end to the war, a settlement in Viet-Nam became more possible. We wanted peace, and there is ample evidence that China wanted peace.

The Taiwan problem was not resolved at the summit and will not be settled in bilateral talks between the United States and the People's Republic of China. The Chinese themselves—on both sides of the strait—must accomplish this; our interest is that any settlement be a peaceful one. But the opportunity the summit offered to restate our position clearly and remove any possible Chinese misunderstanding of our intentions certainly helped to defuse this emotional issue. By affirming that with the prospect of a peaceful settlement in mind, our ultimate objective was the withdrawal of our forces and installations on Taiwan and stating that in the meantime we would progressively reduce our forces there as tension in the area diminished, we made clear that we were not engaged in any plot to determine the status of Taiwan. As a result neither the issue itself nor our intention to maintain our diplomatic ties and defense obligations with the Republic of China constitutes a barrier to improvement in bilateral U.S.-P.R.C. relations.

Since the summit we have worked to build on the framework of the new relationship the President established, developing and expanding the three means agreed to in the Shanghai communique: trade, people-to-people contact, and government-to-government communication. Dr. Kissinger, as the President's special representative, has returned to Peking twice[8] to continue discussion of issues of mutual concern. We have established a point of contact in Paris, where our Ambassadors and the members of their staffs are able to meet on a practical day-to-day basis in accordance with the Shanghai communique understanding. In New York our two Missions to the United Nations have established a mutually useful relationship on matters relating to the work of that organization. The channels of communication are open and are being used not only to lessen the risk of confrontation through accident, miscalculation, or misunderstanding but to move positively to identify areas of common interest where cooperation in the cause of peace will be possible. This is the substance of normalization.

The development of trade, travel, and exchanges over the past year further reinforces the trend. The results, while not spectacular, have been encouraging. In December and January the Shenyang Acrobatic Troupe toured several cities in the United States, incidentally providing Chinese TV audiences for the first time with glimpses of New York City against a musical background of "Home on the Range." You may be less aware of two smaller but important visiting groups: a delegation of Chinese scientists and a group of Chinese physicians who came to the United States last fall to exchange information and renew contact with their American colleagues. On our side, over 1,000 Americans—including doctors, university professors, scientists, newsmen, and businessmen—visited China in the past year. These visits symbolize and give evidence of the improving relationship between the People's

---

[8]Same, p. 319, and Document 11.

Republic of China and the United States, but more important, they advance it.

Trade began slowly, but still the preliminary figures for the year and the projection for this year are impressive. Starting from a total two-way trade of less than $5 million in 1971, trade in 1972 climbed to about $100 million. In 1973, the estimate is that this figure will more than triple. In economic or world trade terms this may seem a modest figure. But China is not a major trading nation. As in the case of exchanges, the significance of growing trade lies in the contribution it makes to the goal of normal interaction between our two countries. To place our trade in this perspective, it is worth noting that should we succeed in increasing trade to the $350-400 million level this year or next, we may well become China's second-largest trading partner.

For the past year, we have been building on and seeking to strengthen the relationship established at the summit. But what about the future? We will continue to work to expand trade and exchanges, but our goal will be the real substance of a normal relationship between countries: the ability to deal with problems in a rational and pragmatic way, with due regard for the legitimate interests of all concerned.

Peking once saw us as an implacable enemy which sought to dominate various countries of East Asia and use them as a base from which to threaten the security of China. We in turn saw China as an expansionist power, a threat to its neighbors and to the stability and orderly growth of the region. Today our mutual perceptions are changing.

Here of course I am talking not about what will be necessarily, but what might be—and what ought to be. Much depends on what happens in the months ahead. Nations are, after all, ruled by men, and history is replete with examples of nations which have chosen to ignore their own national interest. But if China and the United States can continue to make progress toward a normal relationship and through that relationship contribute to a lasting peace in Asia, tension in the area will indeed significantly lessen and the prospects markedly improve for the development of a system of normal relationships among all the countries of the area.

As I look back now on the events of the past year, the President's visit to Peking assumes a significance far beyond its contribution to improved U.S.-China relations.

The example set by the President's trip to Peking changed men's minds; it also changed the policies of nations. The President's trip stimulated a series of movements toward détente. In Korea as in

Viet-Nam, adversaries have begun talking with one another.[9] Long-time antagonists who once confronted one another are now competing to show the world that they are at least as reasonable and flexible as their rivals. Summitry is now being practiced on an almost unprecedented scale—in part, perhaps the product of the jet age—and a new system of international relationships is becoming established in the world.

The President's trip to Peking was the catalyst; he set the example and made the seemingly impossible a reality. I daresay that it will be in these terms that history will assess the significance of his journey.

(11) Dr. Kissinger's Meetings with Chinese Leaders in Peking, February 15-19, 1973.

(a) Communiqué issued by the United States and the People's Republic of China, February 22, 1973.[10]

Dr. Henry A. Kissinger, Assistant to the U.S. President for National Security Affairs, visited the People's Republic of China from February 15 to February 19, 1973. He was accompanied by Herbert G. Klein, Alfred Le S. Jenkins, Richard T. Kennedy, John H. Holdridge, Winston Lord, Jonathan T. Howe, Richard Solomon, and Peter W. Rodman.

Chairman Mao Tsetung received Dr. Kissinger. Dr. Kissinger and members of his party held wide-ranging conversations with Premier Chou En-lai, Foreign Minister Chi Peng-fei, Vice Foreign Minister Chiao Kuan-hua, and other Chinese officials. Mr. Jenkins[11] held parallel talks on technical subjects with Assistant Foreign Minister Chang Wen-chin. All these talks were conducted in an unconstrained atmosphere and were earnest, frank and constructive.

The two sides reviewed the development of relations between the two countries in the year that has passed since President Nixon's visit to the People's Republic of China and other issues of mutual concern. They reaffirmed the principles of the Joint Communique issued at Shanghai in February 1972[12] and their joint commitment to bring about a normalization of relations. They held that the

---

[9]Cf. *AFR, 1972*, p. 340n.
[10]Text from *Presidential Documents*, vol. 9 (1973), pp. 169-70.
[11]Director for Asian Communist Affairs, Bureau of East Asian and Pacific Affairs, Department of State. (See further Document 12.)
[12]*AFR, 1972*, pp. 307-11.

progress that has been made during this period is beneficial to the people of their two countries.

The two sides agreed that the time was appropriate for accelerating the normalization of relations. To this end, they undertook to broaden their contacts in all fields. They agreed on a concrete program of expanding trade as well as scientific, cultural and other exchanges.

To facilitate this process and to improve communications it was agreed that in the near future each side will establish a liaison office in the capital of the other. Details will be worked out through existing channels.

The two sides agreed that normalization of relations between the United States and the People's Republic of China will contribute to the relaxation of tension in Asia and in the world.

Dr. Kissinger and his party expressed their deep appreciation for the warm hospitality extended to them.

(b) News conference statement by Dr. Kissinger, February 22, 1973.[13]

(Excerpt)

Ladies and gentlemen, I thought I would begin by making some remarks about my trip to the People's Republic of China, then take some questions on that, including the communiqué, and then perhaps make a few additional comments to the briefing that Ron has already given you on the Hanoi communiqué.[14]

To put this communiqué[15] into perspective and to elaborate on it for a bit, one should review the evolution of our China policy. When we first began our contacts with the People's Republic of China in 1969 through third parties, and in 1971 directly, the United States had not had any contact with the People's Republic in nearly 20 years, that is, no contact on a really substantial level.

Our early conversations were concerned primarily with building confidence, with explaining each other's position, with establishing channels of communication. Last year our achievements consisted of setting out directions and indicating the roads that might be traveled. After the end of the war in Vietnam, and in these discussions in Peking, we were able to begin to travel some of these

---

[13] Text from *Presidential Documents*, vol. 9 (1973), pp. 170-71.

[14] Document 6. Dr. Kissinger was introduced by Ronald L. Ziegler, Press Secretary to the President.

[15] Document 11a.

roads and to move from the attempt to eliminate the obstructions and the mistrust to some more concrete and positive achievements.

What happened in these meetings was really a continuation of possibilities that had been outlined during the President's visit and during the conversations between the President and Chairman Mao and Prime Minister Chou En-lai, except that now they took some more concrete form. As the communiqué points out, we reviewed the progress in Sino-American relations in great detail, and we reviewed the international situation in great detail.

We discussed the principles of the Shanghai communiqué,[16] particularly those that dealt with the desirability of normalization of relations, the desirability of reducing the danger of military conflict, the affirmation by both sides that neither would seek hegemony in the Pacific area, and each of them opposed the attempt of anyone else to achieve it, and that the relations between China and the United States would never be directed against any third country.

In that spirit, it was decided to accelerate the normalization of relations, to broaden contacts in all fields, and an initial concrete program for extending these contacts was developed.

Given this new range of contacts, it was decided that the existing channel in Paris was inadequate and that, therefore, each side would establish a liaison office in the capital of the other. This liaison office would handle trade as well as all other matters, except the strictly formal diplomatic aspects of the relationship, but it would cover the whole gamut of relationships. This liaison office will be established in the nearest future. Both sides will make proposals within the next few weeks to the other about their technical requirements, and henceforth it will be possible for the United States and the People's Republic of China to deal with each other in the capital of the other.

Now, in order to give some concrete expression to this desire for the normalization of relationships, it was agreed that a number of steps be taken.

First of all, the Chinese, as a sign of good will, have informed us that they would release, within the same time period as our withdrawal from Vietnam, the two military prisoners that they hold in China, Lieutenant Commander (Robert J.) Flynn and Major Philip (E.) Smith. They have been held in China since 1967 and 1965, respectively. They will be released within the next few weeks.

Prime Minister Chou En-lai also asked me to inform the President that the Chinese penal code provided for the periodic

[16]*AFR, 1972*, pp. 307-11.

review of the sentences of prisoners and that this provision would be applied in the case of John Downey.

The Chinese penal code provides for commutation of sentences on the basis of good behavior. We have been told that the behavior of Mr. Downey has been exemplary and that his case would be reviewed in the second half of this year.[17]

With respect to outstanding issues that have been discussed in other channels, it was agreed that the linked issue of United States private claims against the People's Republic of China and PRC blocked assets in the United States would be negotiated on a global basis in the immediate future. Discussions will begin on this subject between Secretary of State Rogers and the Chinese Foreign Minister next week when both are attending the International Conference on Vietnam in Paris, and we expect these negotiations to be concluded rapidly and in a comprehensive way, and we are certain that both sides are approaching them in a constructive spirit and in an attitude consistent with our intention to accelerate the improvement of our relations.

With respect to increased exchanges between the two countries, the Chinese have agreed to invite, during this year, the Philadelphia Symphony by the fall of 1973, a medical group during the spring, a scientific group during the summer, a group of elementary and high school teachers, again during the summer, and increased visits by Congressmen and Senators, as well as athletic teams, an amateur basketball team, and swimming and diving teams.

The People's Republic has agreed to send to the United States the archaeological exhibit from the Forbidden City, which will probably come here in 1974, a group of water conservation experts, insect hormone specialists, high energy physicists, and a gymnastic team.

When the liaison offices are established, possibility will exist for developing further contacts and accelerating this entire process.

The major point we want to make is this: Our contacts with the People's Republic of China have moved from hostility towards normalization. We both believe that it is essential for the peace of the world that the United States and the People's Republic of China act with a sense of responsibility in world affairs, that we are part of an international community in which all nations have a stake in preserving the peace, and that, therefore, as the Shanghai communiqué has already said and as was reaffirmed once again, the normalization of relations between the United States and the People's Republic is not directed against any other nation, but is

---

[17]Mr. Downey was released on Mar. 12 and Maj. Smith and Cmdr. Flynn on Mar. 15, 1973 (*Keesing's*, p. 25820).

part of a pattern that the President has pursued of building a structure of peace in which all nations can participate and in which all nations have a stake.

It remains for me only to say that we were received with extraordinary courtesy and that the discussions were conducted in what was always described as an unconstrained atmosphere.

Now I will take your questions on China and after that a few comments on North Vietnam.[18]

(12) Establishment of a United States Liaison Office in Perking: News conference statement by President Nixon, March 15, 1973.[19]

THE PRESIDENT. Ladies and gentlemen, I have an announcement with regard to our Liaison Office in Peking.

The office will open approximately on May 1, and Ambassador David [K. E.] Bruce will be the Chief of the Liaison Office. In the office will be approximately a total complement of 20 (30), of whom 10 will be at what we call the expert level; the others, of course, for the support level.

The two top assistants, top deputies to Ambassador Bruce—however, we should note, I call him Ambassador, but his title will be Chief of the Liaison Office—will be Mr. [Alfred leS] Jenkins from the State Department, who, as you know, is one of our top experts on Chinese-American relations in State; and Mr. [John H.] Holdridge from the NSC [National Security Council], who is the top man in the NSC advising in this area there.

We selected these two men because Mr. Jenkins and Mr. Holdridge not only are experts in Chinese—they are bilingual, incidentally, in both Chinese and American; they speak well; in fact I remember both assisted in translations when I have been there—but in addition to that, they are men who have from the beginning been participating in the new initiative between the People's Republic and the United States. They have accompanied me on my trip, and they have accompanied Dr. Kissinger on his trips.

A word about why Ambassador Bruce was selected. We called him out of retirement because I thought it was very important to appoint a man of great stature to this position. The Chinese accepted that view themselves, and we expect soon to hear from them

---

[18]The remainder of the news conference appears in *Presidential Documents*, vol. 9 (1973), pp. 171-5, and *Bulletin*, vol. 68 (1973), pp. 315-20.

[19]Text from *Presidential Documents*, vol. 9 (1973), pp. 271-2. The official announcement appears in same, p. 278, and in *Bulletin*, vol. 68 (1973), p. 414.

as to the appointment of the man they will have as his opposite number here in Washington. Another reason that I selected Ambassador Bruce was because of his great experience. All of you know that he has been Ambassador to Britain and Ambassador to Germany, Ambassador to France, and also headed our delegation in Paris in the Vietnam talks in 1971 and '72, in the early part of '72.[20]

A third reason, perhaps, has even greater significance. Many of you in this room were on the trip to China, and sometimes I suppose the feeling must have developed, "Well, this is a one-shot deal." I never considered it that, and all of you who reported on it did not consider it that. It was the beginning, we trust, of a longer journey, a journey in which we will have our differences, but one in which the most populous nation in the world and the United States of America can work together where their interests coincide for the cause of peace and better relations in the Pacific and in the world.

It is necessary that this be, therefore, a bipartisan enterprise in the highest sense of the word.

Mr. Bruce, as you know, while he has not been engaged in partisan politics, as such, is a Democrat. He has served four Presidents with equal distinction, Democratic Presidents as well as Republicans. And we believe that appointing him as head of the delegation indicates our intention that this initiative will continue in the future, whether the Presidency is occupied by a Democrat or a Republican. Of course, I am not making any predictions as to what will happen when I leave.

But that is the end of my announcement. We will now go to your questions. . . .

[20]Ambassador Bruce served as head of the U.S. delegation to the Paris meetings on Vietnam from July 1, 1970 to July 31, 1971.

4. RESHAPING FOREIGN ECONOMIC POLICY

While governments wrestled with the new situation in Southeast Asia, developments of comparable import had been occurring in the world's financial centers. The revolutionary transformation of the post-World War II international monetary system, initiated early in the decade with the suspension of dollar-gold convertibility by the United States in August 1971 and the 7.89 percent devaluation of the dollar in the Smithsonian Agreement of the following December,[1] was carried further with a second devaluation of the dollar, this time by 10 percent, on February 12, 1973. This move, in turn, helped stimulate a series of adjustments by other countries that ended in a general acceptance of "floating" exchange rates, which now were recognized for the first time as a respectable alternative to the traditional system of fixed parities maintained in concert with the International Monetary Fund (IMF).

The impetus to this second American devaluation was furnished by a renewal of heavy speculation against the dollar, in part the result of continued inflation in the United States and in part of widespread expectations of an upward revaluation of the West German and Japanese currencies. Attaining crisis proportions during the second week of February, the flight from the dollar precipitated intensive international consultations over the weekend of February 10-11 and led directly to the startling decisions announced by Secretary of the Treasury Shultz in Washington on Monday, February 12. In essence, the Secretary explained in a formal statement **(Document 13)** and accompanying news conference,[2] the

---

[1] *AFR, 1971*, pp. 577-82 and 604-9. The figure of 7.89 percent measures the reduction in the value of the dollar in terms of gold (from 1/35 oz. to 1/38 oz.); the more frequently cited figure of 8.57 percent measures the increase in the number of dollars per ounce of gold (from $35 to $38).

[2] News conference text in *Bulletin*, vol. 68 (1973), pp. 301-5. For more detailed discussion cf. *Nixon Report, 1973*, pp. 162-75.

President and his advisers had decided to make a virtue of necessity by using the crisis as an opportunity to forward the pursuit of several longstanding American objectives in the field of international trade and monetary affairs. Preeminent among these goals were (1) an acceleration of the improvement in the U.S. trade and payments position, "in a manner that will support our effort to achieve constructive reform of the monetary system"; (2) the laying of the legislative groundwork for "broad and outward-looking trade negotiations, paralleling our efforts to strengthen the monetary system"; and (3) the assurance of equitable treatment for American workers and businessmen in international trading relationships.

The opening move in this program, Secretary Shultz announced, would be a request to Congress to approve a further 10 percent reduction in the new par value of the dollar, established barely a twelvemonth earlier. As officially expressed in terms of the Special Drawing Rights (SDRs) of the International Monetary Fund, the dollar would step down from its current par value of 0.921053 SDR to a new parity of 0.828948 SDR. In terms of gold, the official price of an ounce of gold would increase from $38 to $42.222222.[3]

A particular objective of the change, Mr. Shultz noted, was to correct a "major payments imbalance" between the United States and Japan, one that the 16.88 percent revaluation of the yen at the time of the Smithsonian Agreement had failed to alleviate. As a contribution to this shared objective, he revealed, Japan had agreed to follow the example set earlier by Canada and the United Kingdom and would permit its currency to "float," without reference to its nominal par value, in the hope of bringing it into a more realistic relationship with other currencies. Switzerland and Italy also elected to "float" their currencies within the next day or two.

These actions failed, however, to produce the hoped-for return to stability in the world's financial markets. Within little more than a week, there began a further run on the dollar which, by the beginning of March, had precipitated what was widely regarded as the gravest international financial crisis of the entire postwar era. From March 2 onward, most official foreign exchange markets were closed as European Finance Ministers conferred in an atmosphere

---

[3]Official figures from *IMF Survey*, vol. 2 (1973), p. 53. The 10 percent figure measures the reduction in the value of the dollar in terms of SDRs and gold; the alternative figure, reflecting the increase in the number of dollars per SDR or other unit, amounts to 11.1 percent. The devaluation was officially effected by Public Law 93-110 of Sept. 21, 1973, and became effective for the IMF on Oct. 18, 1973 (same, p. 311).

of mounting hysteria. On Friday, March 9, the United States joined in a special meeting of the Finance Ministers and Central Bank Governors of fourteen industrial nations, convened in Paris by French Economy and Finance Minister Valéry Giscard d'Estaing. Unable to persuade the United States to promise it would support the dollar by intervening in the exchange markets, the participants nevertheless declared their collective determination (1) "to ensure jointly an orderly exchange rate system"; (2) to draft a set of interim measures that would enable the exchange markets to be reopened on Monday, March 19; and (3) to accelerate the work of basic monetary reform to which they were already committed as leading members of the IMF.[4]

Two "interim measures" that would be put into effect immediately were announced March 12 by the Finance Ministers of the nine-nation European Economic Community (EEC), and acknowledged by the larger, fourteen-nation group at a second Paris meeting four days later.[5] One was a new, 3 percent upward revaluation of West Germany's Deutsche mark (DM); the other, an agreement by six of the EEC members to "float" their currencies jointly, at the same time limiting possible fluctuations among themselves by staying within a maximum margin of 2.25 percent. Belgium, Denmark, France, West Germany, Luxembourg, and the Netherlands were the original participants in this arrangement, the so-called European "snake," which was later joined by Norway and Sweden. Abstaining from the arrangement were Ireland, Italy, and the United Kingdom, all of which expressed a hope of entering at a later date but did not in fact do so.

With the monetary situation temporarily stabilized by these arrangements, the United States could turn to two further elements in the comprehensive program announced by Secretary Shultz. One of these, the phasing out of various unpopular controls on foreign investment that had been instituted for balance-of-payments reasons during the 1960s, would be effected gradually and completed before the end of 1974. More urgent, as well as more controversial, was the President's announced determination to press for the enactment by Congress of comprehensive legislation in the field of international trade policy.

Three major purposes inspired the trade proposals that President Nixon submitted to the Congress with a lengthy message on April 10 (**Document 14**). First and foremost was the objective of improving the United States' capacity to compete with other

---

[4]Communiqué, Mar. 9, in *Bulletin*, vol. 68 (1973), p. 454.
[5]EEC communiqué, Mar. 12, in *New York Times*, Mar. 13, 1973; Paris communiqué, Mar. 16, in *Bulletin*, vol. 68 (1973), pp. 454-5.

nations in international trade, primarily by equipping the administration with appropriate authority to engage in intergovernmental trade negotiations, and secondarily by providing safeguards for American industries and workers who might be hurt by a change in trade patterns. A grant of broad negotiating authority would be indispensable if the United States was to participate effectively in the new round of multilateral trade negotiations that had been agreed upon at the time of the Smithsonian arrangements and was now scheduled to begin in September 1973 under the auspices of the General Agreement on Tariffs and Trade (GATT).[6] But any large-scale grant of discretionary authority to reduce tariffs and other barriers to trade was sure to be resisted by those of protectionist outlook in business, labor, and politics who felt that American interests were already threatened by overseas competition and that access to the American market, even on a reciprocal basis, should be restricted rather than broadened.

A second objective of the proposed trade legislation was to fulfill a commitment to the Soviet Government to restore the non-discriminatory or "most-favored-nation" (MFN) tariff treatment that Congress had withdrawn from all the Communist countries except Yugoslavia at the height of the Korean War in 1951.[7] Under the new conditions of the 1970s, continued discrimination against the U.S.S.R. had come to be regarded as a significant impediment to the growth of U.S.-Soviet trade, which was viewed by the two governments both as a desirable end in itself and as a central element in the broader political and military détente that both professed to be seeking. The obligation to accord MFN treatment to each other's exports had therefore been conspicuously written into the new U.S.-Soviet trade agreement which had been signed in Washington October 18, 1972, some five months after President Nixon's visit to the U.S.S.R., but which could not actually go into effect until this impediment was removed by Congress. Likewise contingent on a grant of MFN treatment to the Soviet Union was the settlement of the greater part of that country's lend-lease obligations to the United States, as set forth in a separate agreement signed at the same time.[8]

But though the authority to extend such treatment, under carefully specified conditions, was regarded by the Nixon administration as vital to the cause of détente, it was already evident that influential elements in Congress would be loath to concur at a

---

[6]For background see *AFR, 1972*, pp. 542-4, and see further Chapter 19.
[7]Poland had regained MFN status in 1960. For background cf. *AFR, 1972*, p. 123.
[8]Summaries of both agreements appear in same, pp. 121-7.

time when the U.S.S.R.'s restrictions on emigration by its own citizens, particularly those of Jewish background, had gained unfavorable notice throughout much of the world. Under the so-called Jackson-Mills-Vanik legislation, originally introduced in 1972 and named for Democratic Senator Henry M. Jackson of Washington and Democratic Representatives Wilbur Mills of Arkansas and Charles A. Vanik of Ohio, the administration would be expressly precluded from granting MFN status or trade credits to any Communist country that limited freedom of emigration. No fewer than 72 Senators had signified their support of this provision, which, if adopted, could completely block the execution of the administration's plans unless the Soviet Union were to change its emigration policy.[9]

Still another commitment which the President's trade proposals were designed to implement had been made as far back as October 31, 1969, when Mr. Nixon had told the Inter American Press Association in Washington that it was time "to press for a liberal system of generalized tariff preferences for all developing countries," and that the United States proposed to "seek adoption by all of the industrialized nations of [such] a scheme with broad product coverage and with no ceilings on preferential imports."[10] But though all other important industrial countries had since taken some action aimed at facilitating developing-country access to their markets, the American administration had not yet found a suitable opportunity to lay its own proposals before the Congress. Not until his message of April 10, 1973, almost three and one-half years after his original statement, did President Nixon offer specific proposals involving the initiation of a carefully circumscribed system of generalized trade preferences that would enable certain products of developing countries to benefit by duty-free treatment over a ten-year period.

Other problems of the developing countries, including their need for increased financial resources as well as the growing threat of famine in various overpopulated lands that seemed increasingly incapable of feeding themselves, would be the subject of later recommendations by the President and members of his administration. In the meantime, the trade message delineated a broad area for congressional action in matters of vital consequence to the United States and to its world position.

[9]For background cf. same, pp. 115-16; for further developments see Chapters 12 and 21.
[10]*Documents, 1968-69*, p. 433. For further background see *AFR, 1971*, pp. 616-17; same, *1972*, pp. 558-9. Other developing country problems are examined in Chapters 10 and 24 below.

(13) The Second Devaluation of the Dollar: Statement by Secretary of the Treasury George P. Shultz, February 12, 1973.[11]

The United States, as do other nations, recognizes the need to reform and strengthen the framework for international trade and investment. That framework must support our basic objective of enhancing the living standards of all nations. It must encourage the peaceful competition that underlies economic progress and efficiency. It must provide scope for each nation—while sharing in the mutual benefits of trade—to respect its own institutions and its own particular needs. It must incorporate the fundamental truth that prosperity of one nation should not be sought at the expense of another.

This great task of reform is not for one country alone, nor can it be achieved in a single step. We can take satisfaction in what has been accomplished on a cooperative basis since the actions announced on August 15, 1971, clearly signaled our recognition of the need for decisive change.[12]

—Intense negotiations established an important fact in December 1971: Mutual agreement can be reached on changes in the pattern of world exchange rates, including the parity of the U.S. dollar, in order to promote the agreed goal of a better balance in international trade and payments.[13]

—Monetary negotiations have been started by the "Committee of Twenty" on the premise that better ways must be found to prevent large payments imbalances which distort national economies, disturb financial markets, and threaten the free flow of trade.[14] The United States has made practical and specific proposals for international monetary reform.

—The groundwork is being laid for comprehensive trade negotiations.[15] Those negotiations should look beyond industrial tariffs to encompass also other barriers to the free flow of goods. They should assure fair competitive treatment of the products of all countries. They should also seek agreed ways of avoiding abrupt dislocations of workers and businesses.

---

[11]Department of the Treasury Press Release, Feb. 12; text from *Bulletin*, vol. 68 (1973), pp. 298-301. For a transcript of the accompanying news conference see same, pp. 301-5.
[12]*AFR, 1971*, pp. 577-82.
[13]Cf. same, pp. 607-9.
[14]Cf. same, *1972*, pp. 528-9.
[15]Cf. same, pp. 542-4.

In September 1972 the President told the financial leaders of the world that:

> The time has come for action across the entire front of international economic problems. Recurring monetary crises such as we have experienced all too often in the past decade, unfair currency alignments and trading arrangements which put the workers of one nation at a disadvantage with workers of another nation, great disparities in development that breed resentment, a monetary system that makes no provision for the realities of the present and the needs of the future—all these not only injure our economies; they also create political tensions that subvert the cause of peace.[16]

At the same meeting, I outlined the principles of a monetary system that would enable all nations, including the United States, to achieve and maintain overall balance in their international payments.[17] Those principles would promote prompt adjustment and would provide equitable treatment for all nations—large and small, rich and poor.

Yet in recent months we have seen disquieting signs. Our own trade has continued in serious deficit, weakening our external financial position. Other nations have been slow in eliminating their excessive surpluses, thereby contributing to uncertainty and instability. In recent days, currency disturbances have rocked world exchange markets. Under the pressure of events, some countries have responded with added restrictions, dangerously moving away from the basic objectives we seek.

Progress in the work of the Committee of Twenty has been too slow and should move with a greater sense of urgency. The time has come to give renewed impetus to our efforts in behalf of a stronger international economic order.

To that end, in consultation with our trading partners and in keeping with the basic principles of our proposals for monetary reform, we are taking a series of actions designed to achieve three interrelated purposes:

a. To speed improvement of our trade and payments position in a manner that will support our effort to achieve constructive reform of the monetary system;

b. To lay the legislative groundwork for broad and outward-

---

[16]Same, p. 531.
[17]Same, pp. 534-42.

looking trade negotiations, paralleling our efforts to strengthen the monetary system; and

c. To assure that American workers and American businessmen are treated equitably in our trading relationships.

For these purposes:

First, the President is requesting that the Congress authorize a further realignment of exchange rates. This objective will be sought by a formal 10 percent reduction in the par value of the dollar from 0.92106 SDR [special drawing rights] to the dollar to 0.82895 SDR to the dollar.

Although this action will, under the existing Articles of Agreement of the International Monetary Fund (IMF), result in a change in the official relationship of the dollar to gold, I should like to stress that this technical change has no practical significance. The market price of gold in recent years has diverged widely from the official price, and under these conditions gold has not been transferred to any significant degree among international monetary authorities. We remain strongly of the opinion that orderly arrangements must be negotiated to facilitate the continuing reduction of the role of gold in international monetary affairs.

Consultations with our leading trading partners in Europe assure me that the proposed change in the par value of the dollar is acceptable to them, and will therefore be effective immediately in exchange rates for the dollar in international markets. The dollar will decline in value by about 10 percent in terms of those currencies for which there is an effective par value; for example, the Deutsche mark and the French franc.

Japanese authorities have indicated that the yen will be permitted to float. Our firm expectation is that the yen will float into a relationship vis-a-vis other currencies consistent with achieving a balance of payments equilibrium not dependent upon significant government intervention.

These changes are intended to supplement and work in the same direction as the changes accomplished in the Smithsonian agreement of December 1971. They take into account recent developments and are designed to speed improvement in our trade and payments position. In particular, they are designed, together with appropriate trade liberalization, to correct the major payments imbalance between Japan and the United States which has persisted in the past year.

Other countries may also propose changes in their par values or central rates to the International Monetary Fund. We will suppport all changes that seem warranted on the basis of current and prospective payments imbalances, but plan to vote against any changes that are inappropriate.

We have learned that time must pass before new exchange relationships modify established patterns of trade and capital flows. However, there can be no doubt we have achieved a major improvement in the competitive position of American workers and American business.

The new exchange rates being established at this time represent a reasonable estimate of the relationships which—taken together with appropriate measures for the removal of existing trade and investment restraints—will in time move international economic relationships into sustainable equilibrium. We have, however, undertaken no obligations for the U.S. Government to intervene in foreign exchange markets.

Second, the President has decided to send shortly to the Congress proposals for comprehensive trade legislation.[18] Prior to submitting that legislation, intensive consultations will be held with Members of Congress, labor, agriculture, and business to assure that the legislation reflects our needs as fully as possible.

This legislation, among other things, should furnish the tools we need to:

i. Provide for lowering tariff and nontariff barriers to trade, assuming our trading partners are willing to participate fully with us in that process;

ii. Provide for raising tariffs when such action would contribute to arrangements assuring that American exports have fair access to foreign markets;

iii. Provide safeguards against the disruption of particular markets and production from rapid changes in foreign trade; and

iv. Protect our external position from large and persistent deficits.

In preparing this legislation, the President is particularly concerned that, however efficient our workers and businesses, and however exchange rates might be altered, American producers be treated fairly and that they have equitable access to foreign markets. Too often, we have been shut out by a web of administrative barriers and controls. Moreover, the rules governing trading relationships have, in many instances, become obsolete and, like our international monetary rules, need extensive reform.

We cannot be faced with insuperable barriers to our exports and yet simultaneously be expected to end our deficit.

At the same time, we must recognize that in some areas the

---

[18] Document 14.

United States, too, can be cited for its barriers to trade. The best way to deal with these barriers on both sides is to remove them. We shall bargain hard to that end. I am convinced the American workers and the American consumer will be the beneficiaries.

In proposing this legislation, the President recognizes that the choice we face will not lie between greater freedom and the status quo. Our trade position must be improved. If we cannot accomplish that objective in a framework of freer and fairer trade, the pressures to retreat inward will be intense.

We must avoid that risk, for it is the road to international recrimination, isolation, and autarky.

Third, in coordination with the Secretary of Commerce, we shall phase out the interest equalization tax and the controls of the Office of Foreign Direct Investment. Both controls will be terminated at the latest by December 31, 1974.

I am advised that the Federal Reserve Board will consider comparable steps for their Voluntary Foreign Credit Restraint Program.

The phasing out of these restraints is appropriate in view of the improvement which will be brought to our underlying payments position by the cumulative effect of the exchange rate changes, by continued success in curbing inflationary tendencies, and by the attractiveness of the U.S. economy for investors from abroad. The termination of the restraints on capital flows is appropriate in the light of our broad objective of reducing governmental controls on private transactions.

The measures I have announced today—the realignment of currency values, the proposed new trade legislation, and the termination of U.S. controls on capital movements—will serve to move our economy and the world economy closer to conditions of international equilibrium in a context of competitive freedom. They will accelerate the pace of successful monetary and trade reform.

They are not intended to, and cannot, substitute for effective management of our domestic economy. The discipline of budgetary and monetary restraint and effective wage-price stabilization must and will be pursued with full vigor. We have proposed a budget[19] which will avoid a revival of inflationary pressure in the United States. We again call upon the Congress, because of our international financial requirement as well as for the sake of

---

[19]President Nixon's budget message for the fiscal year 1974, transmitted Jan. 29, 1973 and printed in *Presidential Documents*, vol. 9 (1973), pp. 86-98, estimated budget receipts at $256 billion, budget outlays at $268.7 billion, and the resultant deficit at $12.7 billion.

economic stability at home, to assist in keeping Federal expenditures within the limits of the President's budget. We are continuing a strong system of price and wage controls. Recent international economic developments reemphasize the need to administer these controls in a way that will further reduce the rate of inflation. We are determined to do that.

The cooperation of our principal trading and financial partners in developing a joint solution to the acute difficulties of the last few days has been heartening. We now call upon them to join with us in moving more rapidly to a more efficient international monetary system and to a more equitable and freer world trading system[20] so that we can make adjustments in the future without crises and so that all of our people can enjoy the maximum benefits of exchange among us.

(14) The Proposed Trade Reform Act: Message from President Nixon to the Congress, April 10, 1973.[21]

To the Congress of the United States:

The Trade Reform Act of 1973, which I am today proposing to the Congress, calls for the most important changes in more than a decade in America's approach to world trade.

This legislation can mean more and better jobs for American workers.

It can help American consumers get more for their money.

It can mean expanding trade and expanding prosperity, for the United States and for our trading partners alike.

Most importantly, these proposals can help us reduce international tensions and strengthen the structure of peace.

The need for trade reform is urgent. The task of trade reform requires an effective, working partnership between the executive and legislative branches. The legislation I submit today has been developed in close consultation with the Congress and it envisions continuing cooperation after it is enacted. I urge the Congress to examine these proposals in a spirit of constructive partnership and to give them prompt and favorable consideration.

This legislation would help us to:

—Negotiate for a more open and equitable world trading system;

—Deal effectively with rapid increases in imports that disrupt domestic markets and displace American workers;

---

[20]See further Chapter 19.
[21]Text from *Presidential Documents*, vol. 9 (1973), pp. 343-55.

—Strengthen our ability to meet unfair competitive practices;

—Manage our trade policy more efficiently and use it more effectively to deal with special needs such as our balance of payments and inflation problems; and

—Take advantage of new trade opportunities while enhancing the contribution trade can make to the development of poorer countries.

STRENGTHENING THE STRUCTURE OF PEACE

The world is embarked today on a profound and historic movement away from confrontation and toward negotiation in resolving international differences. Increasingly in recent years, countries have come to see that the best way of advancing their own interests is by expanding peaceful contacts with other peoples. We have thus begun to erect a durable structure of peace in the world from which all nations can benefit and in which all nations have a stake.

This structure of peace cannot be strong, however, unless it encompasses international economic affairs. Our progress toward world peace and stability can be significantly undermined by economic conflicts which breed political tensions and weaken security ties. It is imperative, therefore, that we promptly turn our negotiating efforts to the task of resolving problems in the economic arena.

My trade reform proposals would equip us to meet this challenge. They would help us in creating a new economic order which both reflects and reinforces the progress we have made in political affairs. As I said to the Governors of the International Monetary Fund last September, our common goal should be to "set in place an economic structure that will help and not hinder the world's historic movement toward peace."[22]

TOWARD A NEW INTERNATIONAL ECONOMIC ORDER

The principal institutions which now govern the world economy date from the close of World War II. At that time, the United States enjoyed a dominant position. Our industrial and agricultural systems had emerged from the war virtually intact. Our substantial reserves enabled us to finance a major share of international recon-

[22]*AFR, 1972*, p. 530.

struction. We gave generously of our resources and our leadership in helping the world economy get back on track.

The result has been a quarter century of remarkable economic achievement—and profound economic change. In place of a splintered and shattered Europe stands a new and vibrant European Community. In place of a prostrate Japan stands one of the free world's strongest economies. In all parts of the world new economic patterns have developed and new economic energies have been released.

These successes have now brought the world into a very different period. America is no longer the sole, dominating economic power. The new era is one of growing economic interdependence, shared economic leadership, and dramatic economic change.

These sweeping transformations, however, have not been matched by sufficient change in our trading and monetary systems. The approaches which served us so well in the years following World War II have now become outmoded; they are simply no longer equal to the challenges of our time.

The result has been a growing sense of strain and stress in the international economy and even a resurgence of economic isolationism as some have sought to insulate themselves from change. If we are to make our new economic era a time of progress and prosperity for all the world's peoples, we must resist the impulse to turn inward and instead do all we can to see that our international economic arrangements are substantially improved.

MOMENTUM FOR CHANGE

The United States has already taken a number of actions to help build a new international economic order and to advance our interests within it.

—Our New Economic Policy, announced on August 15, 1971,[23] has helped to improve the performance of our domestic economy, reducing unemployment and inflation and thereby enhancing our competitive position.

—The realignment of currencies achieved under the Smithsonian Agreement of December 18, 1971,[24] and by the adjustments of recent weeks have also made American goods more competitive with foreign products in markets at home and abroad.

—Building on the Smithsonian Agreement, we have advanced

---

[23]Same, *1971*, pp. 577-82.
[24]Same, pp. 607-9.

far-reaching proposals for lasting reform in the world's monetary system.[25]

—We have concluded a trade agreement with the Soviet Union[26] that promises to strengthen the fabric of prosperity and peace.

—Opportunities for mutually beneficial trade are developing with the People's Republic of China.

—We have opened negotiations with the enlarged European Community and several of the countries with which it has concluded special trading agreements concerning compensation due us as a result of their new arrangements.

But despite all these efforts, underlying problems remain. We need basic trade reform, and we need it now. Our efforts to improve the world's monetary system, for example, will never meet with lasting success unless basic improvements are also achieved in the field of international trade.

BUILDING A FAIR AND OPEN TRADING WORLD

A wide variety of barriers to trade still distort the world's economic relations, harming our own interests and those of other countries.

—Quantitative barriers hamper trade in many commodities, including some of our potentially most profitable exports.

—Agricultural barriers limit and distort trade in farm products, with special damage to the American economy because of our comparative advantage in the agricultural field.

—Preferential trading arrangements have spread to include most of Western Europe, Africa and other countries bordering on the Mediterranean Sea.

—Non-tariff barriers have greatly proliferated as tariffs have declined.

These barriers to trade, in other countries and in ours, presently cost the United States several billion dollars a year in the form of higher consumer prices and the inefficient use of our resources. Even an economy as strong as ours can ill afford such losses.

Fortunately, our major trading partners have joined us in a commitment to broad, multilateral trade negotiations beginning this fall.[27] These negotiations will provide a unique opportunity for reducing trading barriers and expanding world trade.

It is in the best interest of every nation to sell to others the goods

[25]Cf. Chapter 19.
[26]*AFR, 1972*, pp. 121-7.
[27]Same, pp. 542-4; cf. Chapter 19.

it produces more efficiently and to purchase the goods which other nations produce more efficiently. If we can operate on this basis, then both the earnings of our workers and the buying power of our dollars can be significantly increased.

But while trade should be more open, it should also be more fair. This means, first, that the rules and practices of trade should be fair to all nations. Secondly, it means that the benefits of trade should be fairly distributed among American workers, farmers, businessmen and consumers alike and that trade should create no undue burdens for any of these groups.

I am confident that our free and vigorous American economy can more than hold its own in open world competition. But we must always insist that such competition take place under equitable rules.

THE URGENT NEED FOR ACTION

The key to success in our coming trade negotiations will be the negotiating authority the United States brings to the bargaining table. Unless our negotiators can speak for this country with sufficient authority, other nations will undoubtedly be cautious and non-commital—and the opportunity for change will be lost.

We must move promptly to provide our negotiators with the authority their task requires. Delay can only aggravate the strains we have already experienced. Disruptions in world financial markets, deficits in our trading balance, inflation in the international marketplace, and tensions in the diplomatic arena all argue for prompt and decisive action. So does the plight of those American workers and businesses who are damaged by rapidly rising imports or whose products face barriers in foreign markets.

For all of these reasons, I urge the Congress to act on my recommendations as expeditiously as possible. We face pressing problems here and now. We cannot wait until tomorrow to solve them.

PROVIDING NEW NEGOTIATING AUTHORITIES

Negotiators from other countries will bring to the coming round of trade discussions broad authority to alter their barriers to trade. Such authority makes them more effective bargainers; without such authority the hands of any negotiator would be severely tied.

Unfortunately, the President of the United States and those who negotiate at his direction do not now possess authorities comparable to those which other countries will bring to these bargaining sessions. Unless these authorities are provided, we will be badly hampered in our efforts to advance American interests and improve our trading system.

My proposed legislation therefore calls upon the Congress to delegate significant new negotiating authorities to the executive branch. For several decades now, both the Congress and the President have recognized that trade policy is one field in which such delegations are indispensable. This concept is clearly established; the questions which remain concern the degree of delegation which is appropriate and the conditions under which it should be carried out.

The legislation I submit today spells out only that degree of delegation which I believe is necessary and proper to advance the national interest. And just as we have consulted closely with the Congress in shaping this legislation, so the executive branch will consult closely with the Congress in exercising any negotiating authorities it receives. I invite the Congress to set up whatever mechanism it deems best for closer consultation and cooperation to ensure that its views are properly represented as trade negotiations go forward.

It is important that America speak authoritatively and with a single voice at the international bargaining table. But it is also important that many voices contribute as the American position is being shaped.

The proposed Trade Reform Act of 1973 would provide for the following new authorities:

First, I request authority to eliminate, reduce, or increase customs duties in the context of negotiated agreements. Although this authority is requested for a period of five years, it is my intention and my expectation that agreements can be concluded in a much shorter time. Last October, the member governments of the European Community expressed their hope that the coming round of trade negotiations will be concluded by 1975.[28] I endorse this timetable and our negotiators will cooperate fully in striving to meet it.

Secondly, I request a Congressional declaration favoring negotiations and agreements on non-tariff barriers. I am also asking that a new, optional procedure be created for obtaining the approval of the Congress for such agreements when that is appropriate. Currently both Houses of the Congress must take positive action before any such agreement requiring changes in domestic law becomes effective—a process which makes it difficult to achieve agreements since our trading partners know it is subject

---

[28]Communiqué of the Heads of State or Government of the countries of the enlarged Community (Paris, Oct. 20, 1972) in *Keesing's*, p. 25542.

to much uncertainty and delay. Under the new arrangement, the President would give notice to the Congress of his intention to use the procedure at least 90 days in advance of concluding an agreement in order to provide time for appropriate House and Senate Committees to consider the issues involved and to make their views known. After an agreement was negotiated, the President would submit that agreement and proposed implementing orders to the Congress. If neither House rejected them by a majority vote of all members within a period of 90 days, the agreement and implementing orders would then enter into effect.

Thirdly, I request advance authority to carry out mutually beneficial agreements concerning specific customs matters primarily involving valuation and the marking of goods by country of origin.

The authorities I outline in my proposed legislation would give our negotiators the leverage and the flexibility they need to reduce or eliminate foreign barriers to American products. These proposals would significantly strengthen America's bargaining position in the coming trade negotiations.

OBJECTIVES IN AGRICULTURAL TRADE

I am not requesting specific negotiating authority relating to agricultural trade. Barriers to such trade are either tariff or non-tariff in nature and can be dealt with under the general authorities I am requesting.

One of our major objectives in the coming negotiations is to provide for expansion in agricultural trade. The strength of American agriculture depends on the continued expansion of our world markets—especially for the major bulk commodities our farmers produce so efficiently. Even as we have been moving toward a great reliance on free market forces here at home under the Agricultural Act of 1970, so we seek to broaden the role of market forces on the international level by reducing and removing barriers to trade in farm products.

I am convinced that the concerns which all nations have for their farmers and consumers can be met most effectively if the market plays a far greater role in determining patterns of agricultural production and consumption. Movement in this direction can do much to help ensure adequate supplies of food and relieve pressure on consumer prices.

PROVIDING FOR IMPORT RELIEF

As other countries agree to reduce their trading barriers, we expect to reduce ours. The result will be expanding trade, creating more and better jobs for the American people and providing them with greater access to a wider variety of products from other countries.

It is true, of course, that reducing import barriers has on some occasions led to sudden surges in imports which have had disruptive effects on the domestic economy. It is important to note, however, that most severe problems caused by surging imports have not been related to the reduction of import barriers. Steps toward a more open trading order generally have a favorable rather than an unfavorable impact on domestic jobs.

Nevertheless, damaging import surges, whatever their cause, should be a matter of great concern to our people and our Government. I believe we should have effective instruments readily available to help avoid serious injury from imports and give American industries and workers time to adjust to increased imports in an orderly way. My proposed legislation outlines new measures for achieving these goals.

To begin with, I recommend a less restrictive test for invoking import restraints. Today, restraints are authorized only when the Tariff Commission finds that imports are the "major cause" of serious injury or threat thereof to a domestic industry, meaning that their impact must be larger than that of all other causes combined. Under my proposal, restraints would be authorized when import competition was the "primary cause" of such injury, meaning that it must only be the largest single cause. In addition, the present requirement that injury must result from a previous tariff concession would be dropped.

I also recommend a new method for determining whether imports actually are the primary cause of serious injury to domestic producers. Under my proposal, a finding of "market disruption" would constitute *prima facie* evidence of that fact. Market disruption would be defined as occurring when imports are substantial, are rising rapidly both absolutely and as a percentage of total domestic consumption, and are offered at prices substantially below those of competing domestic products.

My proposed legislation would give the President greater flexibility in providing appropriate relief from import problems—including orderly marketing agreements or higher tariffs or quotas. Restraints could be imposed for an initial period of five years and, at the discretion of the President, could be extended for an additional period of two years. In exceptional cases, restrictions could be extended even further after a two-year period and following a new investigation by the Tariff Commission.

IMPROVING ADJUSTMENT ASSISTANCE

Our responsibilities for easing the problems of displaced workers are not limited to those whose unemployment can be traced to imports. All displaced workers are entitled to adequate assistance while they seek new employment. Only if all workers believe they are getting a fair break can our economy adjust effectively to change.

I will therefore propose in a separate message to the Congress new legislation to improve our systems of unemployment insurance and compensation.[29] My proposals would set minimum Federal standards for benefit levels in State programs, ensuring that all workers covered by such programs are treated equitably, whatever the cause of their involuntary unemployment. In the meantime, until these standards become effective, I am recommending as a part of my trade reform proposals that we immediately establish benefit levels which meet these proposed general standards for workers displaced because of imports.

I further propose that until the new standards for unemployment insurance are in place, we make assistance for workers more readily available by dropping the present requirement that their unemployment must have been caused by prior tariff concessions and that imports must have been the "major cause" of injury. Instead, such assistance would be authorized if the Secretary of Labor determined that unemployment was substantially due to import-related causes. Workers unemployed because of imports would also have job training, job search allowances, employment services and relocation assistance available to them as permanent features of trade adjustment assistance.

In addition, I will submit to the Congress comprehensive pension reform legislation[30] which would help protect workers who lose their jobs against loss of pension benefits. This legislation will contain a mandatory vesting requirement which has been developed with older workers particularly in mind.

The proposed Trade Reform Act of 1973 would terminate the present program of adjustment assistance to individual firms. I recommend this action because I believe this program has been largely ineffective, discriminates among firms within a given industry and has needlessly subsidized some firms at the taxpayer's expense. Changing competitive conditions, after all, typically act not upon particular firms but upon an industry as a whole and I

[29]Message of Apr. 12, in *Presidential Documents*, vol. 9 (1973), pp. 368-72.
[30]Message of Apr. 11, in same, pp. 358-64.

have provided for entire industries under my import relief proposals.

DEALING WITH UNFAIR TRADE PRACTICES

The President of the United States possesses a variety of authorities to deal with unfair trade practices. Many of these authorities must now be modernized if we are to respond effectively and even-handedly to unfair import competition at home and to practices which unfairly prejudice our export opportunities abroad.

To cope with unfair competitive practices in our own markets, my proposed legislation would amend our antidumping and countervailing duty laws to provide for more expeditious investigations and decisions. It would make a number of procedural and other changes in these laws to guarantee their effective operation. The bill would also amend the current statute concerning patent infringement by subjecting cases involving imports to judicial proceedings similar to those which involve domestic infringement, and by providing for fair processes and effective action in the event of court delays. I also propose that the Federal Trade Commission Act be amended to strengthen our ability to deal with foreign producers whose cartel or monopoly practices raise prices in our market or otherwise harm our interest by restraining trade.

In addition, I ask for a revision and extension of my authority to raise barriers against countries which unreasonably or unjustifiably restrict our exports. Existing law provides such authority only under a complex array of conditions which vary according to the practices or exports involved. My proposed bill would simplify the authority and its use. I would prefer, of course, that other countries agree to remove such restrictions on their own, so that we should not have to use this authority. But I will consider using it whenever it becomes clear that our trading partners are unwilling to remove unreasonable or unjustifiable restrictions against our exports.

OTHER MAJOR PROVISIONS

Most-Favored-Nation Authority. My proposed legislation would grant the President authority to extend most-favored-nation treatment to any country when he deemed it in the national interest to do so. Under my proposal, however, any such extension to countries not now receiving most-favored-nation treatment could be vetoed by a majority vote of either the House or the Senate within a three-month period.

This new authority would enable us to carry out the trade

agreement we have negotiated with the Soviet Union and thereby ensure that country's repayment of its lend-lease debt. It would also enable us to fulfill our commitment to Romania[31] and to take advantage of opportunities to conclude beneficial agreements with other countries which do not now receive most-favored-nation treatment.

In the case of the Soviet Union, I recognize the deep concern which many in the Congress have expressed over the tax levied on Soviet citizens wishing to emigrate to new countries. However, I do not believe that a policy of denying most-favored-nation treatment to Soviet exports is a proper or even an effective way of dealing with this problem.

One of the most important elements of our trade agreement with the Soviet Union is the clause which calls upon each party to reduce exports of products which cause market disruptions in the other country. While I have no reason to doubt that the Soviet Union will meet its obligations under this clause if the need arises, we should still have authority to take unilateral action to prevent disruption if such action is warranted.

Because of the special way in which state-trading countries market their products abroad, I would recommend two modifications in the way we take such action. First, the Tariff Commission should only have to find "material injury" rather than "serious injury" from imports in order to impose appropriate restraints. Secondly, such restraints should apply only to exports from the offending country. These recommendations can simplify our laws relating to dumping actions by state-trading countries, eliminating the difficult and time-consuming problems associated with trying to reach a constructed value for their exports.

Balance of Payments Authority. Though it should only be used in exceptional circumstances, trade policy can sometimes be an effective supplementary tool for dealing with our international payments imbalances. I therefore request more flexible authority to raise or lower import restrictions on a temporary basis to help correct deficits or surpluses in our payments position. Such restraints could be applied to imports from all countries across the board or only to those countries which fail to correct a persistent and excessive surplus in their global payments position.

Anti-Inflation Authority. My trade recommendations also include a proposal I made on March 30th as a part of this Administration's effort to curb the rising cost of living.[32] I asked the Congress at that time to give the President new, permanent

[31]*AFR, 1972*, p. 168.
[32]*Presidential Documents*, vol. 9 (1973), p. 317.

authority to reduce certain import barriers temporarily and to a limited extent when he determined that such action was necessary to relieve inflationary pressures within the United States. I again urge prompt approval for this important weapon in our war against inflation.

Generalized Tariff Preferences. Another significant provision of my proposed bill would permit the United States to join with other developed countries, including Japan and the members of the European Community, in helping to improve the access of poorer nations to the markets of developed countries. Under this arrangement, certain products of developing nations would benefit from preferential treatment for a ten-year period, creating new export opportunities for such countries, raising their foreign exchange earnings, and permitting them to finance those higher levels of imports that are essential for more rapid economic growth.

This legislation would allow duty-free treatment for a broad range of manufactured and semi-manufactured products and for a selected list of agricultural and primary products which are now regulated only by tariffs. It is our intention to exclude certain import-sensitive products such as textile products, footwear, watches and certain steel products from such preferential treatment, along with products which are now subject to outstanding orders restricting imports. As is the case for the multilateral negotiations authority, public hearing procedures would be held before such preferences were granted and preferential imports would be subject to the import relief provisions which I have recommended above. Once a particular product from a given country became fully competitive, however, it would no longer qualify for special treatment.

The United States would grant such tariff preferences on the basis of international fair play. We would take into account the actions of other preference-granting countries and we would not grant preferences to countries which discriminate against our products in favor of goods from other industrialized nations unless those countries agreed to end such discrimination.

Permanent Management Authorities. To permit more efficient and more flexible management of American trade policy, I request permanent authority to make limited reductions in our tariffs as a form of compensation to other countries. Such compensation could be necessary in cases where we have raised certain barriers under the new import restraints discussed above and would provide an alternative in such cases to increased barriers against our exports.

I also request permanent authority to offer reductions in particular United States barriers as a means of obtaining significant advantages for American exports. These reductions would be strictly limited; they would involve tariff cuts of no more than 20 percent covering no more than two percent of total United States imports in any one year.

REFORMING INTERNATIONAL TRADING RULES

The coming multilateral trade negotiations will give us an excellent opportunity to reform and update the rules of international trade. There are several areas where we will seek such changes.

One important need concerns the use of trade policy in promoting equilibrium in the international payments system. We will seek rule changes to permit nations, in those exceptional cases where such measures are necessary, to increase or decrease trade barriers across the board as one means of helping to correct their payments imbalances. We will also seek a new rule allowing nations to impose import restrictions against individual countries which fail to take effective action to correct an excessive surplus in their balance of payments. This rule would parallel the authority I have requested to use American import restrictions to meet our own balance of payments problem.

A second area of concern is the need for a multilateral system for limiting imports to protect against disruptions caused by rapidly changing patterns of international trade. As I emphasized earlier, we need a more effective domestic procedure to meet such problems. But it is also important that new arrangements be developed at the international level to cope with disruptions caused by the accelerating pace of change in world trade.

We will therefore seek new international rules which would allow countries to gain time for adjustment by imposing import restrictions, without having to compensate their trading partners by simultaneously reducing barriers to other products. At the same time, the interests of exporting countries should be protected by providing that such safeguards will be phased out over a reasonable period of time.

PROMOTING EXPORT EXPANSION

As trade barriers are reduced around the world, American exports will increase substantially, enhancing the health of our entire economy.

Already our efforts to expand American exports have moved forward on many fronts. We have made our exports more competitive by realigning exchange rates. Since 1971, our new law permitting the establishment of Domestic International Sales Corporations has been helping American companies organize their export activities more effectively. The lending, guaranty and insurance authorities of the Export-Import Bank have been increased and operations have been extended to include a short-term discount loan facility. The Department of Commerce has reorganized its facilities for promoting exports and has expanded its services for exporters. The Department of State, in cooperation with the Department of Commerce, is giving increased emphasis to commercial service programs in our missions abroad.

In addition, I am today submitting separate legislation which would amend the Export Trade Act in order to clarify the legal framework in which associations of exporters can function. One amendment would make it clear that the act applies not only to the export of goods but also to certain kinds of services—architecture, construction, engineering, training and management consulting, for example. Another amendment would clarify the exemption of export associations from our domestic antitrust laws, while setting up clear information, disclosure and regulatory requirements to ensure that the public interest is fully protected.

In an era when more countries are seeking foreign contracts for entire industrial projects—including steps ranging from engineering studies through the supply of equipment and the construction of plants—it is essential that our laws concerning joint export activities allow us to meet our foreign competition on a fair and equal basis.

THE GROWTH OF INTERNATIONAL INVESTMENT

The rapid growth of international investment in recent years has raised new questions and new challenges for businesses and governments. In our own country, for example, some people have feared that American investment abroad will result in a loss of American jobs. Our studies show, however, that such investment on balance has meant more and better jobs for American workers, has improved our balance of trade and our overall balance of payments, and has generally strengthened our economy. Moreover, I strongly believe that an open system for international investment, one which eliminates artificial incentives or impediments here and abroad, offers great promise for improved prosperity throughout the world.

It may well be that new rules and new mechanisms will be needed for international investment activities. It will take time, however, to develop them. And it is important that they be developed as much as possible on an international scale. If we restrict the ability of American firms to take advantage of investment opportunities abroad, we can only expect that foreign firms will seize these opportunities and prosper at our expense.

I therefore urge the Congress to refrain from enacting broad new changes in our laws governing direct foreign investment until we see what possibilities for multilateral agreements emerge.

It is in this context that we must also shape our system for taxing the foreign profits of American business. Our existing system permits American-controlled businesses in foreign countries to operate under the same tax burdens which apply to its foreign competitors in that country. I believe that system is fundamentally sound. We should not penalize American business by placing it at a disadvantage with respect to its foreign competitors.

American enterprises abroad now pay substantial foreign income taxes. In most cases, in fact, Americans do not invest abroad because of an attractive tax situation but because of attractive business opportunities. Our income taxes are not the cause of our trade problems and tax changes will not solve them.

The Congress exhaustively reviewed this entire matter in 1962 and the conclusion it reached then is still fundamentally sound: there is no reason that our tax credit and deferral provisions relating to overseas investment should be subjected to drastic surgery.

On the other hand, ten years of experience have demonstrated that in certain specialized cases American investment abroad can be subject to abuse. Some artificial incentives for such investment still exist, distorting the flow of capital and producing unnecessary hardship. In those cases where unusual tax advantages are offered to induce investment that might not otherwise occur, we should move to eliminate that inducement.

A number of foreign countries presently grant major tax inducements such as extended "holidays" from local taxes in order to attract investment from outside their borders. To curb such practices, I will ask the Congress to amend our tax laws so that earnings from new American investments which take advantage of such incentives will be taxed by the United States at the time they are earned—even though the earnings are not returned to this country. The only exception to this provision would come in cases where a bilateral tax treaty provided for such an exception under mutually advantageous conditions.

American companies sometimes make foreign investments specifically for the purpose of re-exporting products to the United States. This is the classic "runaway plant" situation. In cases where foreign subsidiaries of American companies have receipts from exports to the United States which exceed 25 percent of the subsidiaries' total receipts, I recommend that the earnings of those subsidiaries also be taxed at current American rates. This new rule would only apply, however, to new investments and to situations where lower taxes in the foreign country are a factor in the decision to invest. The rule would also provide for exceptions in those unusual cases where our national interest required a different result.

There are other situations in which American companies so design their foreign operations that the United States treasury bears the burden when they lose money and deduct it from their taxes. Yet when that same company makes money, a foreign treasury receives the benefit of taxes on its profits. I will ask the Congress to make appropriate changes in the rules which now allow this inequity to occur.

We have also found that taxing of mineral imports by United States companies from their foreign affiliates is subject to lengthy delays. I am therefore instructing the Department of the Treasury, in consultation with the Department of Justice and the companies concerned, to institute a procedure for determining inter-company prices and tax payments in advance. If a compliance program cannot be developed voluntarily, I shall ask for legislative authority to create one.

THE CHALLENGE OF CHANGE

Over the past year, this Administration has repeatedly emphasized the importance of bringing about a more equitable and open world trading system. We have encouraged other nations to join in negotiations to achieve this goal. The declaration of European leaders at their summit meeting last October demonstrates their dedication to the success of this effort. Japan, Canada and other nations share this dedication.

The momentum is there. Now we—in this country—must seize the moment if that momentum is to be sustained.

When the history of our time is written, this era will surely be described as one of profound change. That change has been particularly dramatic in the international economic arena.

The magnitude and pace of economic change confronts us today with policy questions of immense and immediate significance. Change can mean increased disruption and suffering, or it can mean increased well-being. It can bring new forms of deprivation and discrimination, or it can bring wider sharing of the benefits of progress. It can mean conflict between men and nations, or it can mean growing opportunities for fair and peaceful competition in which all parties can ultimately gain.

My proposed Trade Reform Act of 1973 is designed to ensure

that the inevitable changes of our time are beneficial changes—for our people and for people everywhere.

I urge the Congress to enact these proposals, so that we can help move our country and our world away from trade confrontation and toward trade negotiation, away from a period in which trade has been a source of international and domestic friction and into a new era in which trade among nations helps us to build a peaceful, more prosperous world.

RICHARD NIXON

The White House,
    April 10, 1973.

5. LATIN AMERICAN PREOCCUPATIONS

President Nixon's commitment to a system of generalized trade preferences for developing countries had originally been put forward in the context of a broad discussion of Latin American policy that had especially stressed the emergence of a "more mature partnership" between the United States and its hemispheric associates.[1] Initial experience with this new partnership had not, however, inclined the other American countries to be less critical of their northern neighbor and its policies. Occasions of grievance still abounded in both the economic and the political areas.

On the economic side, there still remained a deep resentment in Latin America of the United States' alleged indifference to Latin American needs—coupled, not altogether paradoxically, with hostility to the big U.S.-owned corporations which had become perhaps the most prominent feature of the U.S. presence in Latin America. Perennial criticism of Washington's performance in regard to development aid and the treatment of Latin American exports had cast the United States in the role of a perpetual defendant in inter-American forums. While occasionally admitting that its partners' complaints might have some substance,[2] those who spoke for the United States invariably asserted that matters were on the verge of decisive improvement. A typical example was President Nixon's message early in 1973 to the annual meeting of the Inter-American Economic and Social Council (IA-ECOSOC) in Bogotá (**Document 15a**), where Latin American delegates were preparing to call for a further reshaping of the inter-American institutional structure—already reorganized as recently as 1970[3]—in an attempt

---

[1]Remarks to the Inter American Press Association, Oct. 31, 1969, in *Documents, 1968-69*, pp. 429-38.
[2]E.g., *AFR, 1971*, pp. 463-72. For fuller discussion of Latin American relations cf. *Nixon Report, 1973*, pp. 115-30.
[3]Protocol of Amendment to the Charter of the Organization of American States, signed at Buenos Aires Feb. 27, 1967 and entered into force Feb. 27, 1970 (TIAS 6847; 21 UST 607); summary in *Documents, 1968-69*, pp. 399-401.

to make it more responsive to human and developmental needs.

The picture was complicated by the variegated pattern of relationships that prevailed between the United States and individual Latin American countries, in part reflecting ideological sympathies and antipathies and in part the congruence or—more often—the conflict of specific national interests. Relations with conservative Latin American governments, like the military-backed regime in Brazil, were generally cordial; those with left-wing regimes, especially those of Communist tendency and those that nationalized U.S. property without due compensation, were just the opposite. Given the revolutionary temper prevailing in most parts of Latin America, this basic U.S. identification with conservative causes and factions contributed to what was fast becoming the virtual isolation of the United States within the American Hemisphere.

Especially vexatious was the situation with respect to Cuba, now well into its second decade under the regime of Premier Fidel Castro.[4] During the 1960s, the Havana government's admitted Communist ties and revolutionary activities directed against other American governments had brought about its virtual exclusion from the inter-American system and the imposition of a diplomatic and economic boycott by the Organization of American States (OAS). More recently, however, a number of Latin American countries had reestablished bilateral relations with Cuba and, in addition, had shown an interest in promoting its readmission to the inter-American family. The United States, thus far, had firmly resisted this trend, although it did avail itself of the opportunity to eliminate one source of friction by negotiating, during the winter of 1972-73, a specialized bilateral agreement whereby both countries undertook to deal severely with hijackers of each other's aircraft or vessels **(Document 16a)**. But Secretary Rogers, in announcing this arrangement on February 15, 1973 **(Document 16b)**, took care to state that this attempt "to deal with a very difficult problem in a practical way" did not foreshadow any change in over-all U.S. policy on the Cuban problem.

Two other Latin American governments with which the United States enjoyed less than ideal relations were the "Popular Unity" administration of President Salvador Allende Gossens in Chile and the personalistic regime of Brigadier General Omar Torrijos Herrera in Panama. Washington's disapprobation of Chile's leftward slide, apparent even before Allende's election in 1970, had become particularly acute since the uncompensated expropriation of U.S.-owned copper companies by the Chilean Government in

[4]For background cf. *AFR, 1971*, pp. 474-81.

1971.[5] By early 1973, the equal or greater hostility to the Allende regime of the U.S.-based International Telephone and Telegraph Corporation (ITT)—including its attempts to enlist official U.S. aid in blocking Allende's accession and subsequent exercise of power—was in the process of being brought to light by the U.S. Senate Subcommittee on Multinational Corporations, chaired by Senator Frank Church of Idaho.[6] That the Central Intelligence Agency and other U.S. Government organs might also have been involved in anti-Allende activities was already suspected by some, but would not be publicly confirmed till later in the decade.[7]

Washington's difficulties with Panama were not primarily ideological in character, but stemmed directly from the latter country's dissatisfaction over the desultory pace of the bilateral negotiations, initiated as far back as 1964, with a view to the revision or replacement of the 1903 treaty governing the status of the Panama Canal and the Canal Zone.[8] To reinforce its demand for far-reaching modifications of the existing treaty relationship, the Torrijos government had increasingly sought support from outside the Western Hemisphere, and it scored a major success early in 1973 in persuading the U.N. Security Council to forsake its regular premises in New York and hold a series of meetings in Panama City. The assault on U.S. policies that would foreseeably characterize the occasion would go forward under an agenda item titled "measures for the maintenance and strengthening of international peace and security in Latin America in conformity with the provisions and principles of the Charter."[9] The U.S. delegation to the U.N., while making clear its view that the proposed trip was unnecessary if not downright frivolous, refrained from formally opposing it.

Between March 15 and March 21, accordingly, the Security Council met ten times in Panama City in what quickly became a broad-based demonstration of sympathy for Panama and an equally wide-ranging attack on the imperialistic policies and practices ascribed to the United States. In a lengthy counterstatement delivered as the debate neared its end on March 20, Ambassador

[5]Same, pp. 481-6; cf. also *Bulletin*, vol. 68 (1973), pp. 366-7.
[6]U.S. Senate, 93d Cong., 1st sess., Committee on Foreign Relations, *Multilateral Corporations and United States Foreign Policy: Hearings* before the Subcommittee on Multinational Corporations on the International Telephone and Telegraph Company and Chile, 1970-71 (Washington:GPO, 1973).
[7]Cf. Chapter 20 at notes 9-14.
[8]For background cf. *AFR, 1971*, pp. 487-93.
[9]Security Council Resolution 325 (1973), Jan. 26, adopted without objection; details in *UN Monthly Chronicle*, vol. 10 (Feb. 1973), pp. 3-12, and *Bulletin*, vol. 68 (1973), pp. 242-5.

John A. Scali, the new U.S. Representative, offered a detailed defense of U.S. policies in the hemisphere and implied that the situation between the United States and Panama was one that could much better be handled without the interposition of the Security Council (**Document 17a**). Next day, March 21, Ambassador Scali cast the third U.S. veto in Security Council history to defeat an eight-power draft resolution (**Document 17b**) that urged the United States and Panama to conclude a new treaty without delay. Thirteen of the Security Council's fifteen members were nevertheless recorded in favor of this moderately phrased resolution, while the fourteenth, the United Kingdom, abstained. The basic objection, Mr. Scali explained (**Document 17c**), was the resolution's one-sided nature and the fact that it dealt with a matter already under negotiation between Panama and the United States. Unwilling to conclude its stay in Panama City without some positive achievement, the Security Council then adopted—with France, the United Kingdom, and the United States abstaining—a resolution that was obviously inspired by the ITT disclosures and deprecated attempts at "coercion" of Latin American countries by either "enterprises" or "states."[10]

A more conventional forum for discussion of inter-American questions was the General Assembly of the Organization of American States (OAS), which held its Third Regular Session in Washington on April 4-15 and listened to a voluminous exposition of U.S. views on current issues by Secretary of State Rogers (**Document 18a**). The most noteworthy results of this comparatively undramatic Assembly session were (1) the establishment of a special committee, as previously recommended by IA-ECOSOC, to study the inter-American system and propose measures for restructuring it; and (2) the adoption of a declaration of inter-American principles, which, as always, emphasized nonintervention and self-determination of peoples but also stressed the more novel concept of "plurality of ideologies" as one of the presuppositions of regional solidarity.[11]

Respect for Latin American diversity, together with the need for "realism, frankness, and mutual respect," were to be much emphasized by Secretary Rogers during a subsequent tour of Latin America[12] that would include a seat at the inauguration on May 25 of President Héctor J. Cámpora, the hand-picked candidate of ex-

[10]Resolution 330 (1973), Mar. 21, adopted by a vote of 12-0-3 (U.S.). For details on the Panama meetings see *UN Monthly Chronicle*, vol. 10 (Apr. 1973), pp. 15-58, and *U.S. Participation, 1973*, pp. 20-21.
[11]Texts in *Bulletin*, vol. 68 (1973), pp. 684-6; for other actions cf. *Keesing's*, pp. 26251-2.
[12]*Bulletin*, vol. 68 (1973), pp. 903-27.

President Perón and the victor in Argentina's recent presidential elections, as that country's first civilian chief executive since 1966. How genuine was the United States' acceptance of political diversity in Latin America, particularly where left-wing regimes were involved, was a question that would be further debated later in the year.[13]

(15) Eighth Annual Meeting of the Inter-American Economic and Social Council (IA-ECOSOC), Bogotá, January 29-February 9, 1973.

(a) Message from President Nixon to the Chairman of the Meeting, made public February 1, 1973.[14]

DEAR MR. CHAIRMAN: You and your distinguished colleagues in the Inter-American Economic and Social Council have my very warm greetings and best wishes as you begin your examination of the problems of hemispheric cooperation for development in today's world. While this examination cannot be completed in a few days or weeks, the meetings in Bogotá offer an opportunity to make a highly constructive beginning.

The most promising bases for hemispheric cooperation, of course, will be those areas where the interests of our nations already converge. The distinguished Chairman of CIAP [Inter-American Committee on the Alliance for Progress], Dr. Carlos Sanz de Santamaría, has challenged us to seek out these areas of convergence. His words, coming from a thoughtful man who was dedicated himself to the cause of inter-American cooperation, deserve a constructive response.

The Government of the United States looks forward to active participation in this endeavor. I have instructed Charles Meyer, the U.S. representative, and members of his delegation to work closely with you in developing new means of cooperation in this period of global and regional readjustment. I will read the report of your deliberations with interest, confident that they will enhance our ability to reinforce points of common interest while patiently working to reconcile any differences.

I have been impressed by the increasing ability of the countries of Latin America to marshal resources for their own development and to contribute to the development of other Latin American nations.

---

[13]See further Chapter 20 at note 5.
[14]Text from *Bulletin*, vol. 68 (1973), p. 275. Addressed to Rodrigo Llorent Martínez, Minister of Finance of Colombia and Chairman of the meeting, the message was read by Assistant Secretary of State Charles A. Meyer as head of the U.S. delegation.

Though the economic position of the United States has changed, we intend to fulfill our pledge to support your efforts to achieve economic and social development in the hemisphere. You can be sure, too, that my government will consult closely with yours as new international monetary and trade negotiations get underway. It is important that your views as well as ours contribute to shaping the new world order in these areas.

We all realize that we are at the beginning of an historic process—one in which the main elements of the inter-American system are already at work. The General Assembly of the OAS in April will provide us with another invaluable opportunity to help make the system more responsive to our shared needs and aspirations. You can be sure that the United States will continue its commitment to peace and progress in our hemisphere—and that inter-American cooperation will receive priority attention in my Administration over the next four years.

>Sincerely,

>>>>RICHARD NIXON.

(16)   The Cuba Hijacking Agreement, February 15, 1973.

(a)   Memorandum of Understanding on Hijacking of Aircraft and Vessels and Other Offenses, accepted by the United States and Cuba and entered into force February 15, 1973.[15]

The Government of the United States of America and the Government of the Republic of Cuba, on the bases of equality and strict reciprocity, agree:

FIRST: Any person who hereafter seizes, removes, appropriates or diverts from its normal route or activities an aircraft or vessel registered under the laws of one of the parties and brings it to the territory of the other party shall be considered to have committed an offense and therefore shall either be returned to the party of registry of the aircraft or vessel to be tried by the courts of that party in conformity with its laws or be brought before the courts of the party whose territory he reached for trial in conformity with its

---

[15]TIAS 7579 (24 UST 737-9). In the absence of diplomatic relations between the U.S. and Cuba, the Memorandum of Understanding was incorporated in a simultaneous exchange of notes in Washington between the Department of State and the Embassy of Czechoslovakia, as representative of Cuban interests in the U.S., and in Havana between the Embassy of Switzerland, as representative of U.S. interests in Cuba, and the Cuban Ministry of Foreign Relations.

laws for the offense punishable by the most severe penalty according to the circumstances and the seriousness of the acts to which this Article refers. In addition, the party whose territory is reached by the aircraft or vessel shall take all necessary steps to facilitate without delay the continuation of the journey of the passengers and crew innocent of the hijacking of the aircraft or vessel in question, with their belongings, as well as the journey of the aircraft or vessel itself with all goods carried with it, including any funds obtained by extortion or other illegal means, or the return of the foregoing to the territory of the first party; likewise, it shall take all steps to protect the physical integrity of the aircraft or vessel and all goods, carried with it, including any funds obtained by extortion or other illegal means, and the physical integrity of the passengers and crew innocent of the hijacking, and their belongings, while they are in its territory as a consequence of or in connection with the acts to which this Article refers.

In the event that the offenses referred to above are not punishable under the laws existing in the country to which the persons committing them arrived, the party in question shall be obligated, except in the case of minor offenses, to return the persons who have committed such acts, in accordance with the applicable legal procedures, to the territory of the other party to be tried by its courts in conformity with its laws.

SECOND: Each party shall try with a view to severe punishment in accordance with its laws any person who, within its territory, hereafter conspires to promote, or promotes, or prepares, or directs, or forms part of an expedition which from its territory or any other place carries out acts of violence or depredation against aircraft or vessels of any kind or registration coming from or going to the territory of the other party or who, within its territory, hereafter conspires to promote, or promotes, or prepares, or directs, or forms part of an expedition which from its territory or any other place carries out such acts or other similar unlawful acts in the territory of the other party.

THIRD: Each party shall apply strictly its own laws to any national of the other party who, coming from the territory of the other party, enters its territory, violating its laws as well as national and international requirements pertaining to immigration, health, customs and the like.

FOURTH: The party in whose territory the perpetrators of the acts described in Article FIRST arrive may take into consideration any extenuating or mitigating circumstances in those cases in which the persons responsible for the acts were being sought for strictly political reasons and were in real and imminent danger of death without a viable alternative for leaving the country, provided there was no financial extortion or physical injury to the members of the crew, passengers, or other persons in connection with the hijacking.

FINAL PROVISIONS:

This Agreement may be amended or expanded by decision of the parties.

This Agreement shall be in force for five years and may be renewed for an equal term by express decision of the parties.

Either party may inform the other of its decision to terminate this Agreement at any time while it is in force by written denunciation submitted six months in advance.

This Agreement shall enter into force on the date agreed by the parties.

DONE in English and Spanish texts which are equally authentic.

(b) Significance of the Agreement: News conference comments by Secretary of State Rogers, February 15, 1973.[16]

I am very pleased to announce that the United States and Cuba have reached agreement on hijacking. At 11:30 today I exchanged diplomatic notes containing the text of this agreement with Mr. [Jaroslav] Zantovsky, the Chargé d'Affaires of the Embassy of Czechoslovakia, which represents Cuban interests in this country. This exchange, and a similar exchange of notes which took place simultaneously in Havana between the Ambassador of Switzerland, representing the United States, and the Cuban Minister of Foreign Affairs, constitute the agreement of both governments to the terms of a Memorandum of Understanding on Hijacking of Aircraft and Vessels and Other Offenses.

Under the terms of this agreement, each government undertakes to prosecute hijackers in its own courts or to return them to the other country for prosecution. Thus, there will be no safe haven for hijackers in Cuba or the United States. This agreement applies to air piracy, to similar serious offenses involving vessels and other serious crimes. Since all of these crimes are already punishable under U.S. law, no change in the U.S. law will be necessary to carry out this agreement.

I also want to emphasize that nothing in this agreement is inconsistent with the traditional and strongly felt American view of the right to emigrate freely, nor does it constitute a change in our overall policy toward Cuba.

We believe that this agreement represents a significant step for-

[16]Text from *Bulletin*, vol. 68 (1973), pp. 249 and 251-2.

ward in our worldwide efforts to put an end to the problem of hijacking.

I want to pay particular tribute to the Swiss Government and to its Ambassador in Havana [Silvio Masnata] for their role in negotiating the agreement in our behalf.

* * *

Q. On the Cuban agreement, do you regard the agreement in any way as providing a basis for an improvement of relations with Cuba? And I wanted to ask, if I could, a second question. And that is, don't you believe that this will act as a psychological deterrent to any Cubans who might be thinking of escaping the island and coming to this country—in other words, political refugees?

A. As to the first part of your question, this does not foreshadow a change of policies as far as the United States is concerned toward Cuba. It is an attempt to deal with a very difficult problem in a practical way. And I think it does do that. And the Cuban Government, in these discussions that I have conducted indirectly through the Swiss now for three months, I think has been constructive and very businesslike. And we were able to reach this agreement, which I think is a good one for all concerned, without any major difficulties.

On the second point, what this agreement does is to make it clear that hijackers of aircraft or vessels cannot escape the laws of our country—and Cuba now has said the same thing: cannot escape the laws of Cuba—by claiming the right of asylum. This does not affect the right of asylum. The right of asylum continues to be a very sacred right and one that we will continue to honor.

What it does mean is that you cannot commit major crimes on the way to asylum. You can't endanger the lives of many other people in order to reach the place of asylum. And if you do that, then you have to bear the consequences of the laws. This agreement that we have made with Cuba does not require any additional laws on the part of the United States. It does mean that we will enforce the laws vigorously, and we will expect Cuba to do the same thing.

Q. Sir, what role did the airline pilots have in this negotiation or this agreement, and how valuable was that role to you?

A. Well, they did not have any role in it, and we did not want them to have a role, and I don't think that they felt they should play a role. This was a negotiation between Cuba and the United States conducted through the Swiss.

Insofar as our attitude is concerned, it made a great difference because the airline pilots made it clear that they were fed up with the situation and were going to take drastic action. And we were too. So we have consulted with them, and I think they are very pleased at the outcome.

As you know, there have been in the area of a hundred hijackings to Cuba in the last few years. And they endanger the lives of not only the passengers but the crew. So we have worked very closely with the airline pilots in efforts to solve the problem. But I wouldn't want to convey the thought that they have been involved in the negotiations as such.

(17) Meetings of the United Nations Security Council in Panama, March 15-21, 1973.

(a) Views of the United States: Statement by Ambassador John A. Scali, United States Representative to the Council, March 20, 1973.[17]

I join previous speakers to express my gratitude to the President, the Government, and the people of Panama for the admirable organization of this meeting by the Panamanian Government and for the welcome and hospitality that we have received here. It is indeed an exhilarating experience to see the determination, dedication, and devotion of the Panamanian people which is evident in the bustling economic activity, reflected most visibly in the pace of construction we see around us.

"Consideration of measures for the maintenance and strengthening of international peace and security in Latin America in conformity with the provisions and principles of the Charter"—that is the agenda item. For more than a century, the nations of Latin America have demonstrated an enviable and unparalleled record in achieving and maintaining international peace and security on this continent. They not only have avoided major international conflicts within the hemisphere but have also created a viable framework for the peaceful resolution of their differences. Latin American statesmen have eloquently set forth principles of international consultation and conciliation springing from the idea and view that international conflict in this area can and must be resolved peacefully. Many of these principles have found their way into the United Nations Charter and into the practice of the United Nations.

We note with particular pleasure the active role played by the people and leaders of our host country, Panama, who have been in the forefront of the development of the inter-American system since the founding of their country. In fact, the first seeds of pan-Americanism were planted here by Simón Bolívar, at the Panama Congress of 1826.

Mr. President,[18] the United States sets great store by its close and fruitful association with the countries of Latin America. We fully share their deep and genuine concern for the continuation of peace, prosperity, political stability, and economic and social development in this hemisphere.

The countries of this region were among the original supporters of the United Nations and have remained among the most faithful and dedicated of its members. All of us recognize their role in the United Nations and their contributions to international peace and security. Many Latin American countries have participated directly in U.N. peacekeeping operations, operations which go to the heart of this organization's purposes. All have contributed in many ways to the resolution of disputes among nations and of the problems confronting the world. We are all aware of the high competence of Latin American jurists in the field of international law and the unwavering support in this hemisphere for the sanctity of solemn treaty obligations even as the search for constructive change continues.

It is in fact the absence of truly threatening international issues within the Latin American area which led my government to question the necessity of our meeting away from U.N. Headquarters at this time. Our delegation expressed the views of the United States very clearly. Meetings of the Security Council, whether at Headquarters or away, should be based on its primary charter responsibility to maintain international peace and security.

While the Charter of the United Nations confers this responsibility on the Security Council, it also provides—indeed, in article 33, it specifically enumerates—many ways to resolve international issues before such matters are brought directly before the Council. A look at the efforts now underway with regard to nearly all the major problem areas of the world underscores this wide variety of channels, both inside and outside the United Nations, which can be used to achieve the charter goal of practicing tolerance and living together in peace with one another as good neighbors:

—The United States and the Soviet Union have undertaken with each other to do their utmost to avoid military confrontation and to respect the sovereign equality of all countries.

—The United States and the People's Republic of China have

---

[18] Juan Antonio Tack, Minister for Foreign Affairs of Panama.

undertaken to broaden the understanding between their peoples, and this process has taken new strides in recent weeks.

—The United States, together with other parties to the Viet-Nam conflict, has arrived at a cease-fire agreement for Viet-Nam, and other interested nations have pledged in Paris their full support and cooperation in strengthening peace in Indochina.

—In Europe, the United States is participating in preliminary discussions in Helsinki and Vienna aimed at specific and practical improvements in East-West relations.

These have all been due in large measure to the wise and imaginative leadership of our President, Richard Nixon, as he pursues his great goal of a generation of peace for all mankind.

Because of his diplomatic initiatives, his courage to try new approaches, the world is on the threshold of cooperation and friendship among nations undreamed of just a few years ago.

The Unique Inter-American Community

In looking back at what has been achieved, and forward to what remains to be done, one is struck by the variety of means, the wealth of institutions, and the host of relationships which can be turned to positive effect.

In this hemisphere our peoples over a period of 50 years have established relationships that, in our view, make us a unique community. There are of course a number of bilateral questions in this hemisphere that remain unresolved—many have been mentioned at this table—but progress is being made in many of these through patient negotiations. For instance, the United States and Panama have been seeking—through negotiation—a new status for the Panama Canal which would bring it into harmony with contemporary political realities.

With respect to multilateral relationships in this hemisphere, the regional institutions and arrangements we have developed and the broad and deep contacts joining our governments and our citizens have grown into what is now known as the inter-American system. That system is characterized not only by formal institutions but also by a sense of solidarity and a community of common interests and objectives on which we seek to build a lasting foundation for truly effective inter-American cooperation. We have a common faith in the benefits of freedom, the importance of the individual, the power of reason, and the rule of law. The conclusion that the inter-American system is indeed a foundation of some permanence is supported by the significant intellectual, economic, security, and political ties which further draw us together.

A system that is both progressive and evolving, and is notable for its continuing usefulness to its membership, is a system which is also able to accommodate diversities. The most obvious of these are the different cultural backgrounds, economic conditions, and political institutions which remind us that we are individual nations as well as members of a hemisphere community.

The Organization of American States is the keystone of the inter-American system. The OAS exists as a regional organization within the meaning of chapter VIII of the United Nations Charter. It is also the oldest international organization of its kind in the world, dating from 1890. It has grown from an institution concerned primarily with commercial affairs into an organization devoted to the peace and security of the hemisphere. It is also deeply involved in the region's economic and social development, educational, scientific, and cultural cooperation, human rights, juridical affairs, and technical assistance and training, to mention but a few. As it has grown, it has increased its capacity to achieve its essential purposes; these are to strengthen the peace and security of the continent, to prevent possible causes of difficulty, and to insure the peaceful settlement of disputes. It also provides for common action on the part of the member states in the event of aggression. It assists in the search for solutions to political, juridical, and economic problems when they arise among the members, and in the area of development it is concerned with the promotion of cooperative social and economic action.

The United States has also warmly supported the many activities of the United Nations in the area of economic and social development in Latin America. However, for most of the 1960's, the U.S. Government was the major external contributor of assistance to Latin America in seeking its economic and social development. As we agreed to do at Punta del Este in 1961,[19] the United States provided over $10 billion for the development of the American republics during the period 1961-72. We kept our promised word.

In the past few years, the countries of Latin America have increased their reliance upon the major multilateral lending institutions for the bulk of their official external capital assistance. In recognition of this situation, the United States has channeled an increasing proportion of its loan funds to Latin America through multilateral institutions, particularly the Inter-American Development ment Bank. In December of last year, for example, the United

[19]Declaration to the Peoples of America, Aug. 17, 1961, in *Documents, 1961*, pp. 433-5.

States formally signed the replenishment agreement under which it agreed to provide $1 billion to the Fund for Special Operations of the Bank.[20] The total flow of U.S. funds through all channels, bilateral and multilateral, has never been higher.

As a result, the total assistance received by Latin America from all sources is going up steadily. The United States has given special and increasing attention to the economic and social concerns of the hemisphere. Total lending commitments by AID, the Inter-American Development Bank, and the World Bank to Latin America in 1972 more than doubled those of 1964.

The United States has had a long and cordial relationship with the independent nations of this hemisphere. Recognizing the principle of sovereign equality and respect for the right of states to pursue their own development, the United States is building a constantly evolving relationship with Latin America, a relationship which we trust will become even more cordial and mutually beneficial.

Issues Before Other U.N. Bodies

Mr. President, I would like to reflect briefly regarding the U.S. position on some other issues which have been raised in statements before the Council.

The United States has always been, and continues to be, a strong advocate of the Latin American nuclear-free zone. We signed Protocol II of the Treaty for the Prohibition of Nuclear Weapons in Latin America (Treaty of Tlatelolco) on April 1, 1968. The protocol went into effect for the United States on May 12, 1971.[21] By these actions, the United States pledged itself to respect the denuclearized status of Latin America, not to contribute to any violation of the treaty, and not to use or threaten to use nuclear weapons against any of the contracting parties.

The question of permanent sovereignty over natural resources is currently an active item in the U.N., specifically in the ECOSOC [Economic and Social Council] Committee on Natural Resources and the Seabed Committee. We do not question the principle of "permanent sovereignty." However, at the same time we wish to point out that we do not believe that complex issue is properly before this Council. In accepting the principle of permanent sovereignty we strongly reaffirm our support for the principles of

---

[20]For background cf. *AFR, 1972*, p. 558.
[21]Same, *1971*, pp. 456-62.

U.N. General Assembly Resolution 1803,[22] including, inter alia, the observance in good faith of foreign investment agreements, the payment of appropriate compensation for nationalized property as required by international law, and the recognition of arbitration or international adjudication.

Similarly, we believe that the question of multinational corporations, which has been raised in different contexts, should not be brought before this Council. It is presently under discussion in several other more appropriate U.N. bodies. A group of eminent individuals, appointed by the Secretary General under ECOSOC Resolution 1721 of July 28, 1972, is studying the impact of multinational corporations. UNCTAD [United Nations Conference on Trade and Development] is doing a study of the restrictive business practices of multinational corporations. Finally, ILO [International Labor Organization] is looking into the relationships of activities of such corporations to social policy. We fail to see what the Security Council can effectively accomplish in this particular field.

We happen to share the judgment of the ECOSOC resolution that these corporations "are frequently effective agents for the transfer of technology as well as capital to developing countries." No country has to welcome or even accept foreign investment. And if it does so, it of course may establish its own rules. However, it also has the obligation, in that case, to abide by those rules, to compensate the investor for retroactive changes in the rules, or in the case of expropriation or nationalization of private property, to make adequate provision for just compensation as required by international law.

Negotiation of New Panama Canal Treaty

And now I come to discuss U.S. relations with Panama. Our close and mutually beneficial friendship has a long history, characterized, to be sure, by occasional differences and friction. But the bonds linking our two peoples continue strong and vibrant.

We rejoice in the progress achieved by Panama; it has been striking. Over the past four years the economy has been growing at a rate of 7-8 percent, one of the highest rates of growth in the world.

Outside help has contributed to this rate of growth, but there has also been a high level of labor and investment by the dedicated

[22]Resolution 1803 (XVII), Dec. 14, 1962, reaffirming permanent sovereignty over natural resources.

Panamanian people. My country is happy that it was able in 1972 to disburse in various ways approximately $227 million, with direct effect, and stimulate the Panamanian economy. In fact, our loans and grants to Panama represent the highest per capita level of U.S. assistance anywhere in the world, in part because of our friendship but mostly because Panama has demonstrated a high capacity to program and utilize financial assistance effectively.

We believe that all mankind has been well served by the Panama Canal since its completion nearly 60 years ago. During those years it has never been closed, and it has been transited by an ever-increasing number of ships carrying cargo to and from all parts of the world.

Although the 1903 treaty[23] still governs the basic relationship between the United States and Panama concerning the canal, that relationship was significantly revised, as well as reaffirmed, in the treaties of 1936 and 1955.[24] On both occasions the United States relinquished important rights and provided important new benefits for Panama.

In 1964, recognizing that a comprehensive modernization of our relationship should be undertaken, the United States began negotiations with Panama with three essential objectives in view,[25] which remain valid today:

1. The canal should be available to the world's commercial vessels on an equal basis at reasonable cost.

2. So that the canal should serve world commerce efficiently, the United States should have the right to provide additional canal capacity.

3. The canal should continue to be operated and defended by the United States for an extended but specified period of time.

It was recognized then, as it is today, that these objectives would require the conclusion of a new treaty or treaties to replace the 1903 treaty and its amendments. By 1967 three draft treaties had been negotiated and agreed to by the two negotiating teams. At that time the Panamanian Government did not move to ratify the treaties, but in October of 1970 requested the United States to renew

[23]Isthmian Canal Convention, signed at Washington Nov. 18, 1903 and entered into force Feb. 26, 1904 (Department of State Treaty Series, 431).
[24]General Treaty of Friendship and Cooperation, signed at Washington Mar. 2, 1936 and entered into force July 27, 1939 (same, 945); Treaty of Mutual Understanding and Cooperation, signed at Panamá Jan. 25, 1955 and entered into force Aug. 23, 1955 (TIAS 3297; 6 UST 2273).
[25]Cf. *Documents, 1964*, pp. 312-14.

negotiations. The United States agreed to do so, and negotiations were in fact renewed in June 1971, when the Panamanian negotiating team arrived in Washington.

During the intensive negotiations which followed, the United States has fully recognized that the relationship originally defined in the 1903 treaty needs to be brought into line with the realities of the world today as well as with the mutual interests of both countries.

The United States is ready to conclude a new treaty promptly. At the same time, we believe it necessary that the United States continue to be responsible for the operation and defense of the canal for an additional specified period of time, the length of which is one of many issues to be negotiated.

As a result of the persistent efforts made by both sides, significant progress has been made in the treaty talks toward reaching mutual understanding on major principles.

Mr. President, I would like to make clear that the United States, no less than others who have spoken at this table, supports Panama's just aspirations. The U.S. negotiators, cognizant of those aspirations, have already recognized that:

1. The 1903 canal treaty should be replaced by a new modern treaty.
2. Any new canal treaty should be of fixed duration, rejecting the concept of perpetuity.
3. Panama should have returned to it a substantial territory now part of the Canal Zone, with arrangement for use of other areas. Those other areas would be the minimum required for U.S. operations and defense of the canal and would be integrated into the legal, economic, social, and cultural life of Panama on a timetable to be agreed upon.
4. Panama should exercise its jurisdiction in the canal area pursuant to a mutually agreed timetable.
5. Panama should receive substantially increased annual payments for the use of its territory relating to the canal.

Accordingly, those who attack the 1903 Treaty are attacking a phantom foe, a nonexistent enemy. The 1903 treaty has already been revised significantly to Panama's advantage. We were on the verge of changing it a third time in 1967, and we are ready to change it again—to write a new treaty—when negotiations continue in the spirit of friendship and cooperation that should be the hallmark of Panama-U.S. relations.

We recognize that much remains to be settled; yet we believe the above points represent a substantial foundation of important principles and are confident that with continued good will by reasonable men on both sides, and some patience, a mutually satisfactory treaty can result.

Mr. President, in reviewing the relationships among the 532 million active and dynamic people residing in this hemisphere, it would be incorrect to leave the impression there are no problems or no issues needing attention. Obviously there are, as there are anywhere. But we know that both the good will and the diplomatic machinery already exist within the area to resolve these problems.

The question then arises as to what contribution the Council can make at this meeting and what the Council will carry back to United Nations Headquarters as a result of its meeting in Latin America.

For Latin American issues, as for issues in other parts of the world, the members of the Council must look to what this body can actually accomplish, the consistency of their proposed actions with the provisions of the charter, and their impact on the chances of resolving existing differences.

For the Council to take a partisan stand or reflect only a parochial viewpoint would risk undermining the processes of bilateral and regional diplomacy which have served this hemisphere so well.

For the Council to pronounce itself on a wider range of issues not directly concerned with the maintenance of international peace and security risks diluting the results already achieved in other United Nations organs and would make many question the seriousness of the Council's purpose in holding its meeting here.

We have been engaged in discussion since March 15, Mr. President, and much of what has been said is valuable, constructive, and informative. That in itself is a positive element. But this series of meetings can be productive, Mr. President, in other ways. Tomorrow evening we should be able to adjourn to return to New York and say that our deliberations have contributed renewed vigor to the effective, realistic, and harmonious search for the realization of the objectives of the United Nations, not only in Latin America but everywhere. If we can do that, Mr. President, then these meetings will have been a success.

(b) Draft Resolution on the Panama Canal, vetoed by the United States March 21, 1973.[26]

---

[26]U.N. document S/10931/Rev. 1, Mar. 21, 1973; text from Security Council, *Official Records: 28th Year, Supplement for Jan., Feb. and Mar. 1973*, pp. 57-8. The draft resolution was defeated by a vote of 13-1 (U.S.)-1 (U.K.).

Guinea, India, Indonesia, Kenya, Panama, Peru, Sudan and Yugoslavia: revised draft resolution

[*Original: English*]
[*21 March 1973*]

The Security Council,

Having considered the question of the Panama Canal under the item entitled "Consideration of measures for the maintenance and strengthening of international peace and security in Latin America in conformity with the provisions and principles of the Charter",

Recalling that it is a purpose of the United Nations to bring about, in conformity with the principles of justice and international law, adjustment or settlement of international disputes or situations which might lead to a breach of the peace,

Bearing in mind that the Republic of Panama is sovereign over its territory and that the free and fruitful exercise of sovereignty by peoples and nations over their natural resources should be fostered through mutual respect among States, based on their sovereign equality,[27]

Having heard the statements made before it by the representatives of the members of the Council, by Latin American Ministers for Foreign Affairs and by representatives of other States and organizations specially invited,

1. *Takes note* that the Government of the Republic of Panama and the United States of America in the Joint Declaration signed before the Council of the Organization of American States, acting provisionally as Organ of Consultation, on 3 April 1964,[28] agreed to reach a just and fair agreement, with a view to the prompt elimination of the causes of conflict between them;

2. *Takes note* also of the willingness shown by the Governments of the United States of America and the Republic of Panama to establish in a formal instrument agreements on the abrogation of the 1903 convention on the Isthmian Canal and its amendments and to conclude a new, just and fair treaty concerning the present Panama Canal which would fulfil Panama's legitimate aspirations and guarantee full respect for Panama's effective sovereignty over all of its territory;

3. *Urges* the Governments of the United States of America and the Republic of Panama to continue negotiations in a high spirit of

---

[27]See General Assembly resolutions 1514 (XV), 1803 (XVII) and 3016 (XXVII). [Footnote in original.]

[28]*Documents, 1964*, p. 311. [A footnote in the original refers to *Bulletin*, vol. 50 (1964), p. 656.]

friendship, mutual respect and co-operation and to conclude without delay a new treaty aimed at the prompt elimination of the causes of conflict between them;

4. *Decides* to keep the question under consideration.

(c) Explanation of the United States Position: Statement by Ambassador Scali to the Council, March 21, 1973.[29]

Despite the fact that the Representative of Panama[30] has expressed himself numerous times before this Council over the past week on the Panama Canal, he chose to deliver another litany this afternoon on the Panamanian version of history and the actual situation today. I have no intention of subjecting the distinguished members of this Council to a statement of similar length.

However, he continues to stress the convention of 1903. In fact we have heard a great deal in recent days of how the Isthmian Canal Convention was imposed on the people of Panama. Let us put the facts of the situation in the Security Council record. After the convention of 1903 was signed, it was sent to Panama for ratification. After ratification by the Panamanian Government, the treaty was sent around the country for consideration by the various elected municipal councils. The ratification of the treaty with the United States was overwhelmingly approved by these elected councils, with unanimous expressions of approval of the treaty. So much for the imposition of a treaty.

Now, in 70 years' time the views of the Government and people of Panama have changed with respect to the arrangements of 1903. That is not surprising. The views of the Government and people of the United States of America have also changed with respect to the treaty of 1903. That is what our two governments are negotiating about—to work out new arrangements to meet the just aspirations of Panama and the legitimate interests of the United States.

I believe, Mr. President, it is useful to clarify for the record this historical aspect of our relationship.

We regret having had to cast a negative vote on this resolution, because there is so much in it with which we could agree. But our negative vote should have come as no surprise to our host, the Republic of Panama, in view of the repeated exchanges of views that we have had about this meeting and about how it might end—and I am referring not only to discussions during this Security Council meeting but also to those that took place even before the Republic of Panama had pressed its campaign to have this meeting take place on its territory.

In those discussions the United States made clear its serious con-

---

[29]USUN Press Release 26, Mar. 22; text from *Bulletin*, vol. 68 (1973), pp. 495-6.
[30]Aquilino Boyd, Permanent Representative of Panama to the U.N.

cern that a meeting designed to put pressure on one party to an on-going bilateral negotiation could make those negotiations more difficult and impair the utility of this major organ of the United Nations. Up to the moment of our departure for Panama, we continued to receive assurances that everything would be done to maintain an atmosphere of moderation and restraint. I regret to say that while this proved true of the situation outside this chamber—and for this I wish to express our appreciation to our host—it has not been true of some of the statements made here.

Members of this Council should know that my delegation has made strenuous and repeated efforts in friendly conversations with our Panamanian hosts to arrive at a mutually acceptable form for a resolution but this very sincere effort has been rejected. I wish the members of the Council to know, however, that we were and are prepared to acknowledge the just aspirations of the Republic of Panama, for we do recognize those aspirations, along with the interests of the United States.

I have said that we regret having had to cast a negative vote on the Panamanian resolution because there is so much in it with which we could agree. As I have made clear, we agree with the Republic of Panama on the need to replace the 1903 convention by a totally new instrument reflecting a new spirit, we agree that such a new instrument should not run in perpetuity but should have a fixed term, and we agree on the progressive integration into the legal, economic, social, and cultural life of Panama of even those areas used for the operation and defense of the canal.

Why, then, when there is so much in it with which we agree, did we not vote in favor of the resolution or, as we were urged, at least abstain? Essentially, for two reasons.

First and foremost, as I have repeatedly pointed out both in public and in private, it is because all these matters are in process of bilateral negotiations. We do not consider it helpful or appropriate for the Security Council to adopt a resolution dealing with matters of substance in a continuing negotiation—and I may note that the Foreign Minister of Panama has himself spoken of the negotiations as continuing and not as having been broken off. Indeed, as many members know, we have only recently made certain new approaches to the Government of Panama. We believe it would be a disservice to the negotiations and an improper use of the Security Council if bilateral negotiations were subjected to this kind of outside pressure.

I am not, of course, suggesting here that those who cast affirmative votes on the resolution intended to exert any improper influence, but this is how the resolution would have been perceived in many quarters.

The Panamanian resolution, in our view, is unbalanced and incomplete and is therefore subject to serious misinterpretation. Further, the resolution is cast in the form of sweeping generalities, when we know that the real difficulties lie in the application of these generalities. Although it is true that the United States and Panama have reached common understanding over a number of important general principles, differences over some principles and many matters of detail remain. Finally, the present resolution addresses the points of interest to Panama but ignores those legitimate interests important to the United States.

The Panama Canal is not a work of nature or—as some have tried to put it—a natural resource. The canal is a very complex enterprise, and the working-out of a new regime for it cannot be accomplished by the wave of a hand or the quick stroke of a pen. It requires thoughtful and meticulous negotiation to achieve a fair reconciliation of interests. We have been and are prepared for such a negotiation. But the resolution that was just voted upon oversimplifies the issue to the point where it could have rendered a disservice.

This brings me back to what I said at the beginning of my intervention. It has been clear from the first mention of the idea that holding a Security Council meeting here to focus on this problem could complicate the process of negotiation. The United States is disappointed that others failed to appreciate this risk when lending their support to this meeting. Surely it should have been made obvious that the new treaty which we sincerely wish to negotiate with Panama must be acceptable to our Congress and people, as well as the Government and people of Panama.

Finally, I would respectfully suggest that we all assess with great care the nature and outcome of this meeting so as to avoid any repetition of a course of action that could prove damaging to the role and reputation of the Security Council. It would be most unfortunate if the Security Council were to be transformed into a small replica of the General Assembly, thereby impairing its capacity to deal effectively with specific issues affecting peace and security.

The U.S. delegation will not be leaving Panama in a spirit of rancor, far from it. Our friendship for Panama, for the people of Panama and of Latin America in general, is too deep for that. We continue to be willing to adjust any differences peacefully and in a spirit of give-and-take. We are, specifically, prepared to continue the negotiations and to carry them forward with good will and seriousness at whatever time the Government of Panama chooses. We believe that both Panama and the United States are destined by geography and common ideals to cooperate for their mutual advantage and to protect the interests of world commerce transiting the canal. That will continue to be the policy of the United States, and I am confident that in the end we shall reach an accord which both governments can firmly support and which will strengthen the close bonds of friendship between our peoples.

(18) Third Regular Session of the General Assembly of the Organization of American States (OAS), Washington, April 4-15, 1973.

(a) Views of the United States: Statement by Secretary of State Rogers in Plenary Session, April 6, 1973.[31]

This year marks the 25th anniversary of the signing of the Charter of the Organization of American States.[32] Twenty-five years is perhaps a short period in the life of nations which have enjoyed over a century and a half of productive relations.

We all are aware, nevertheless, how profoundly the world has changed in those 25 years. The hostilities and rigidities that characterized international relations then are being left behind. This restructuring of world politics has been accompanied by an even more profound change in the world economy. Europe and Japan have recovered economically. Many nations in the developing world—including nations in Latin America—have achieved both substantial economic growth and self-confidence.

These are changes which have an effect on all members of this organization. My nation has been deeply involved in many of them. The nations of Latin America have broadened their global economic and political involvement. Today more than ever, we are all influenced by the broad currents of world development.

It was in this context that in 1969 President Nixon enunciated a new U.S. policy for Latin America.[33] That policy reflected the changes in global and hemispheric relations which had already begun. It anticipated other changes in global economics and politics to come. As the President described it in his foreign policy report last year, the policy reflected four positive themes:

—A wider sharing of ideas and responsibility in hemispheric collaboration;

---

[31]Department of State Press Release 102, Apr. 6; text from *Bulletin*, vol. 68 (1973), pp. 675-81.
[32]Signed at Bogotá Apr. 30, 1948, and entered into force Dec. 31, 1951 (TIAS 2361; 2 UST 2394); text in *Documents, 1948*, pp. 484-502.
[33]Cf. note 1 above.

—A mature U.S. response to political diversity and nationalism;

—A practical and concrete U.S. contribution to economic and social development;

—A humanitarian concern for the quality of life in the hemisphere.[34]

That policy is in keeping with our desire for continued close association with the hemisphere and with the less intrusive international role we have adopted and the people of the United States have endorsed. It is a policy which reflects Latin America's claim and capacity to a greater voice in hemispheric affairs. It is a policy which acknowledges the diversity of the hemisphere even as it provides a framework for hemispheric collaboration. It is a policy which assumes the interdependence of the Americas and the involvement of the Americas in global affairs.

It is a policy, we are convinced, that outlines a constructive approach to sound relations. With progress made toward a more peaceful world generally, we are now in a position to give our relations with you more consistent attention. Over the next four years:

—We will continue to work closely with you on the many issues before the global community in which the United States and Latin America might develop convergent interests.

—We will concentrate within the hemisphere on building upon areas of cooperation.

—We will maintain our support of your efforts to bring a better life to your citizens, channeling the bulk of our assistance through multilateral institutions while at the same time seeking to expand Latin America's access to trade and investment opportunities.

—We will approach our bilateral dealings on the basis of how you conduct relations with us and not how you structure your societies internally.

Trade and Monetary Matters

Close cooperation between us on global issues could be particularly constructive. Many of the opportunities and challenges before us can no longer be met in the hemisphere alone.

[34]*Nixon Report, 1972*, pp. 90-100.

Solutions must be found in the world community. On many such issues, U.S. and Latin American interests tend to converge. On some they coincide.

Latin America and the United States can, in particular, be of assistance to each other in improving the world monetary and trading systems to assure that trade and capital move with a minimum of restrictions and that all nations share equitably in an expanding world economy.

President Nixon will shortly be proposing to Congress broad new trade legislation which will include the authority we need to carry out a policy of expanded and more equitable world trade in the talks which start this fall.[35] During those talks we believe that U.S. and Latin American delegations should establish a system of liaison, for we believe we share a number of common purposes which we can promote together. We should, for example, be able to cooperate on a number of concrete issues:

—We both will want to reduce barriers to agricultural trade. Latin America relies on agriculture for over half of its export earnings. The United States, unique among industrialized nations, exports 31 percent of its crop. The removal of restrictive practices against agricultural exports would benefit us all.

—We share an interest in the elimination of preferential arrangements which discriminate against one group of developing countries in favor of another or in favor of a few industrialized countries. Such exclusive arrangements have already prejudiced some exports from this hemisphere. Their extension will prejudice others. Neither Latin America nor the United States wants a Western Hemisphere trading bloc, nor have we ever found any bloc system to be a beneficial approach to our roles in international trade.

—We would all benefit from a reduction or elimination of administrative barriers which are used to artificially impede the growth of imports.

I should add that it is important that the GATT [General Agreement on Tariffs and Trade] session be a time of serious negotiations and not of confrontation. We will approach it this way and will seek to insure that the needs of developing countries are taken fully into account. We recognize of course that the countries of Latin America will share many trade interests in these talks with other developing nations. We also know that the concerns of

---

[35]Document 14. For the opening of the "Tokyo Round" of multilateral trade negotiations see Chapter 19.

developed and developing nations—and of you and of us—will diverge at some points. But it is essential that these differences not be allowed to deteriorate into the kind of sterile disputes that characterized the last meeting of UNCTAD [United Nations Conference on Trade and Development].[36] Latin American countries could provide leadership at the GATT session by encouraging all states to concentrate upon the achievement of concrete economic results and to avoid political issues more appropriate to other forums.

The trade negotiations must, of course, take place in a single forum, the GATT. But we believe joint participation there could be made more effective through further discussion among us on trade issues in the Special Committee for Consultation and Negotiations.

As the recent meeting of the Finance Ministers of the Committee of Twenty has shown, the United States and the states of Latin America also share a number of convergent interests in world monetary talks.[37] We worked closely with Argentina, Brazil, and Mexico in those talks and expect to continue to work with the nations of Latin America to seek a monetary system that will:

—Foster balance of payments adjustments by all countries, surplus and deficit, large and small;

—Make special drawing rights the principal reserve instrument and the common denominator in the system; and

—Recognize the interdependence of domestic and international economic policies, including the critical role of inflation control.

Law of the Sea

Law of the sea is another international issue where we can cooperate to achieve constructive results. Speaking in 1970 on the law of the sea, President Nixon said that if it is not modernized by common action, unilateral actions and international conflict are inevitable.[38] Three years have further confirmed that we must reach an international agreement.

Nations in Latin America, as elsewhere in the world, have adopted diverse stands on many of the issues involved. This diversity reflects such factors as whether or not they are coastal states, whether they have a large or small continental shelf, whether they

[36]Cf. *AFR, 1972*, pp. 477-8 and 556-7.
[37]Cf. Chapter 19.
[38]Statement of May 23, 1970, in *Documents, 1970*, pp. 331-3.

possess significant maritime interests, whether they have extensive or limited resources adjacent to their coasts. But while interests are diverse we earnestly hope that all the nations of the world, including most especially those of this hemisphere, can concur that each nation's interests ultimately can only be protected by international agreement. And we hope that we all will be prepared to make the accommodations necessary to build a broadly based international agreement.

In our opinion an international consensus is emerging on many of the issues involved. Certainly it is our hope that most states would be able at an early date to agree on:

1. A broad coastal state economic jurisdiction, beyond a 12-mile territorial sea, in which freedom of navigation and overflight would continue;
2. The right of free transit through and over international straits;
3. An international agreement including machinery for the deep seabed area and international standards together with compulsory settlement of disputes for areas under coastal state economic jurisdiction.

Some states of the hemisphere favor a territorial sea broader than 12 miles. However, we hope that the common interest in freedom of navigation and a common recognition of the economic and security needs of coastal states and the international community would lead all of us to agreement on a 12-mile territorial sea. We then could concentrate on the extent and nature of a coastal state economic jurisdiction which would accommodate the interests of all states.

If this is the case, we believe that it should be possible for the nations of this hemisphere to make a major contribution to an agreement which can be widely accepted, which will benefit us all, and which will eliminate present and potential conflicts. As we approach the Law of the Sea Conference we would hope to intensify our consultations with each of you to help advance the international consensus we believe is emerging.[39]

Terrorism

The inter-American system has often led the international community in devising agreed approaches to common problems. The

[39]See further Chapter 28 at note 23.

OAS convention on acts of terrorism of international significance[40] was the first important international effort to prevent and punish crimes of violence against the representatives of states and international organizations. The U.S. Senate has approved the convention, and we will be in a position to deposit our instrument of ratification as soon as implementing legislation is passed by our Congress. We hope other signatory nations will act promptly to ratify it and that the OAS members who have not yet signed will be able to lend their support.

Having led the way in arriving at an international approach to confronting terrorism, the Americas, we hope, can now actively cooperate in similar efforts to provide a broader international consensus. We see three areas where we can exert constructive leadership together:

—By making civil aviation safer by agreeing at this summer's civil aviation conference to deny refuge to those who commit terrorist acts against international civil aviation;[41]

—By protecting diplomats through opening for signature at the next U.N. General Assembly a convention based on the draft articles submitted by the International Law Commission;[42] and

—By thwarting the spread of terrorism through assuring that the ad hoc U.N. committee recommends to the next U.N. General Assembly an international convention providing for extradition or punishment in cases of international terrorism.[43]

I hope our delegations could all be instructed to work together toward these aims.

Mr. President, I would like to turn now to two areas in which cooperation within the hemisphere itself remains important. I refer to inter-American cooperation for development and to the status of inter-American institutions.

We are well aware how central economic relationships are to the health of our cooperation. In programs directed to the hemisphere we will continue our support for efforts to bring a better life to the citizens of your countries.

---

[40]Convention to Prevent and Punish the Acts of Terrorism Taking the Form of Crimes Against Persons and Related Extortion That Are of International Significance, approved by the OAS General Assembly Feb. 2, 1971 and entered into force for ratifying states Oct. 16, 1973 (*AFR, 1971*, pp. 437-41); approved by the Senate June 12, 1972 but not yet ratified by the U.S. as of early 1976.

[41]For the negative result of the conference cf. *AFR, 1972*, p. 516.

[42]Cf. Document 83.

[43]Cf. *AFR, 1972*, p. 515 and Chapter 28 at notes 20-21.

Cooperation for Development

In recent years I believe we all have come to the conclusion that development demands a comprehensive approach which includes dimensions other than official assistance. We now are specifically directing our own efforts to insure that all aspects of the development process are taken into account. Thus, I have asked our new Under Secretary for Economic Affairs[44] to coordinate a comprehensive development policy—including development assistance, international investment, debt relief, trade expansion, and population growth—so that the United States may better support a more rapid per capita economic growth in the developing world.

We concur in the view expressed in the recent meeting of the Inter-American Economic and Social Council that expanded trade can be the most important element in this process. In fact, the document that emerged from the Bogotá meeting contained many important ideas which we support; we regret that in the last day or two of its development a number of contentious proposals were added even though they would make the result unacceptable to us.

Particularly because of our support for accelerated development in Latin America, we will also include in the trade bill we are submitting to Congress next week a request for authority to extend generalized tariff preferences for developing countries. It is important to note that while it was necessary for us to delay action on generalized tariff preferences, our imports from Latin America nevertheless have been growing substantially for a number of years and last year rose by 18 percent.

I am not now in a position to describe to you the details of the trade bill until it is presented to our Congress next week.[45] However, I will be pleased to make myself available, together with the Under Secretary for Economic Affairs, to describe to you all aspects of the legislative proposal.

Foreign private investment can also make a major contribution to development. The United States benefited from it during our own development, and we expect increasing European and Japanese investment in our economy over the next few years. Today, as never before, other countries in this hemisphere which seek such investment can also draw it not only from the United States but also from Europe and Japan.

Countries must of course decide for themselves whether they want to attract such investment; and they will of course set for themselves the rules under which the investor operates. But foreign

[44]William J. Casey; cf. Document 70.
[45]Cf. Document 14.

investors should be able to rely on that determination. Because we believe private capital can be a major contribution to development and because we know it will move freely only if there is confidence that agreements will be observed, we will continue to insist on just compensation in cases of nationalization in accordance with the policy announced last January.[46] At the same time, the U.S. Government is committed to the pacific settlement of disputes by the procedures set forth in article 24 of the charter and will cooperate fully with any government that wishes to solve a problem on fair terms that respect the interests of both sides. In most cases, various procedures are possible, but the point of departure for any solution is good-faith negotiation in a spirit of compromise.

Grant and loan assistance also continues to have an important role in development. We intend to carry out our bilateral and multilateral assistance commitments. Thus, we are proceeding this spring with a request to Congress for the next installment of $693 million in our contribution to the replenishment of the Inter-American Development Bank.

Though it is unrealistic to project increases, we will make every effort to maintain our total assistance flows to Latin America at their present levels.

Perhaps the most easily controlled variable in accelerating the growth of per capita income is the rate of population increase. Latin America's population is still expanding at approximately 2.8 percent per year, the highest rate in the world. Thus, despite the fact that the area's gross product has recently been expanding at over 6 percent a year, increases in population have cut the per capita gains to just over 3 percent. This is an area where we believe more rapid progress can be made.

Not all nations of the hemisphere share our deep concern for the effects of too rapid population growth. But we can all be pleased that the former Foreign Secretary of Mexico, Dr. Carrillo Flores, will be the Executive Director of the United Nations World Population Year in 1974. And we were encouraged to see that at the recent meeting of Latin American Ministers of Health agreement was reached that governments should provide family planning services and information wherever national policies permit.

Inter-American Relations

The changes that have taken place in global economics and politics have also brought us to a new period in inter-American

[46]Nixon statement, Jan. 19, 1972, in *AFR, 1972*, pp. 559-63.

relations. In the immediate future we will all be reassessing the multilateral structures through which they are conducted.

In this connection some of you see an anomaly in the static nature of our relations with Cuba at a time when we are moving in such positive directions with Moscow and Peking. There is an anomaly, but we believe it lies in Cuba's attitudes, not in U.S. policy. The dramatic progress in our relations with China and the U.S.S.R. could not come about except as a result of mutuality. Thus far, we perceive no change in Cuba's basic position. At a time when the world is putting enmity behind it, Cuba continues to place an antagonistic and interventionist attitude at the center of its policy. Its military ties remain.

Though there have been shifts in Cuba's behavior in the hemisphere, the changes do not seem to us to reflect a modification of its basic policies toward other American states. We are aware that while many in this Organization take a similar view others have a different opinion. But we have so far seen no evidence of change in Cuban policies sufficient to convince us that the OAS economic and diplomatic measures toward Cuba should be altered.

For all these reasons our policies toward Cuba remain unchanged, as does our commitment to act only in concert with the other members of the OAS.

Indeed, our intention is to work in concert with the OAS wherever possible. That is why we attach significance to the important items 9 and 10 on our agenda. Those items, proposed by the Secretary General of this Organization and by the distinguished Foreign Minister of Venezuela,[47] reflect a desire to move away from the unproductive atmosphere which has recently been too frequent and to move toward means of working for common purposes. This is also evident in the mission undertaken by the Chairman of CIAP [Inter-American Committee on the Alliance for Progress].[48]

As we seek together to expand our collaboration and minimize contention between us, we are prepared to work with all member states to improve the OAS. We will study carefully any suggestions made here or in the committee which may be established. And we will have suggestions of our own.[49]

But ultimately the success of this or any other organization will be defined not by its structure but by the attitudes brought to it by its membership. Thus, in examining the OAS we will in fact be studying the "spirit of the hemisphere." The United States does

[47]Galo Plaza Lasso (Ecuador) and Arístides Calvani Silva.

[48]Carlos Sanz de Santamaría (Colombia).

[49]For the work of the Special Committee established by the Assembly see Chapter 20 at notes 3-4.

not believe that this spirit implies an obligation to agree on all issues. But it does believe that the spirit must take into account certain realities: the reality that many issues cannot be resolved within the inter-American framework; the reality that there are practical limits to U.S. commitments; the reality that most problems within a country must be solved by the country itself; that a beneficial, cooperative relationship among nations requires mutual respect. The United States respects every nation here represented. We will work cooperatively with each nation in this Organization on the basis of mutuality. The United States believes that the spirit that brings us together in this room must rest on the proposition that honest differences can and should be negotiated. It is the attitude of cooperation, accommodation, and reciprocal adjustment that has made our association fruitful in the past; it is an attitude that can enable us to reap new benefits in the future.

The United States thus welcomes the opportunity to enter into a constructive review of hemispheric relations. We see 1973 as a year of building. Now that the world is a safer place, there are energies, talents, and resources that can now be turned to other purposes. Latin America will have a high place on our agenda. I will participate personally in this effort and expect in the next few months to fulfill my longstanding desire to visit Latin America to exchange points of view with many of you in your own capitals.[50] In taking that trip I will be motivated by a constructive desire to make our association as firm, as realistic, and as equitable as friends can make it.

This meeting of the OAS General Assembly could have a decisive influence on the future of our community. If that influence is to be constructive, we should concentrate on areas where our interests converge. If we do, we will find it easier to resolve those issues on which we have differences. Over the years our community has shown both flexibility and imagination in meeting the changed demands of changing times. It is the hope of my government that this meeting, and what follows it, will reaffirm and strengthen the ties between us so that we can continue to realize the benefits that derive from our association in this significant Organization of American States.

[50]Cf. note 12.

6. AFRICAN PERPLEXITIES

Africa was another developing area whose problems often intruded on American attention, despite the fact that U.S. interests there were markedly less extensive than in Latin America. Though Washington frankly preferred where possible to limit direct American involvement to the economic sphere and leave the political initiative to others,[1] it strenuously rejected the charge that it was "neglecting" Africa or giving it a "low priority." "Out of the conflicting pressures for policies and resources upon and within a major nation," said David D. Newsom, the Assistant Secretary of State for African Affairs, in one of his frequent surveys of the American interest in the continent (**Document 19**), "the United States seeks to respect Africa's independence, to be responsive to Africa's needs, and to stand ready realistically to be helpful in furthering trends of change." Observers of the African scene had ample opportunity to weigh the consequences of this limited-involvement policy, particularly in the Southern African tangles that had become the constant concern of the Security Council and other U.N. bodies.

Two well-defined attitudes governed the American approach to African issues, Mr. Newsom explained in the address already quoted. One was an abhorrence of racial discrimination; the other, an opposition to the use of force as an instrument of political change. Among persons outside the U.S. Government, however, there were some who experienced difficulty in reconciling two attitudes which, although they sounded equally virtuous in the abstract, occasionally tended to cancel one another out in practice. In proclaiming its detestation of racial discrimination, the United States was at one with the vast majority of the world's governments, most of which were unsparing in their condemnation of the policies and practices of the white-dominated regimes in South Africa, Namibia (South West Africa), and Southern Rhodesia

[1]Cf. *Nixon Report, 1971*, pp. 114-21 (*AFR, 1971*, pp. 380-85). For fuller discussion see *Nixon Report, 1973*, pp. 153-60.

149

(Zimbabwe)—the self-governing British colony that had declared itself independent in 1965—as well as the Portuguese "overseas provinces" of Mozambique, Angola, and Portuguese Guinea or "Guinea-Bissau." At the same time, however, America's opposition to the use of force and violence in dealing with African problems had tried the patience of many of these same governments, particularly in the independent "black African" countries which had for years been urging stronger measures to complete the "liberation" of their continent.

Violence, as a practical matter, had been a fact of life in Southern Africa ever since the commencement in the early 1960s of armed insurgencies or "national liberation struggles" in the various Portuguese African territories. In Portuguese Guinea (Guinea-Bissau), the so-called African Independence Party of Guinea and Cape Verde (PAIGC) led by Amilcar Cabral had been conspicuously successful and, by late 1972, had appeared to be on the verge of formally declaring the territory's independence. This final step, however, was delayed by Cabral's assassination, allegedly by Portuguese agents, in Conakry (Guinea) on January 20, 1973, with the result that formal proclamation of the "State of Guinea-Bissau" did not take place until September 24, 1973. Reports of Portuguese atrocities—invariably denied by the responsible Portuguese authorities—were also received from Mozambique, where insurgent forces of the Mozambique Liberation Front (Frelimo) had been active for a dozen years. International opinion would be much exercised in the course of 1973 by reports of a Portuguese armed attack against the Mozambique village of Wiriyamu on December 16, 1972, in which over 400 villagers were alleged to have been killed.[2]

Southern Rhodesia, despite its government's frankly discriminatory racial policies, had remained peaceful until the closing days of 1972, when incidents of violence began to occur in the form of land-mine explosions in northern border areas and terrorist attacks on remote farmsteads. One consequence of these occurrences was the loan by South Africa of some armed police units to assist Rhodesian authorities in keeping order; another, the closing on January 9, 1973, of Rhodesia's border with its northern neighbor, Zambia, pending assurances from that black-ruled country that it would no longer permit terrorists to operate against Rhodesia from its territory. Although Zambia refused to give the required assurances, it defied its neighbor at considerable risk in view of its dependence on Rhodesian transit facilities for its copper exports. The situation prompted the U.N. Security Council to meet

[2]*Keesing's*, pp. 26099-104.

on several occasions during February and March to urge assistance for Zambia[3] —and also (with Britain and the United States abstaining) to demand the withdrawal of South African armed forces from Rhodesia, renew its denunciations of the illegal Rhodesian regime, and reiterate its demand that Britain reassert its authority and enable the people of "Zimbabwe" to exercise their right to self-determination and independence.[4]

The United States' own policy on the Rhodesian issue had incurred sharp disapproval from anticolonial governments, primarily because of the action of Congress in 1971 in invalidating a ban on the import of Rhodesian chrome ore and other strategic minerals, originally imposed by the Johnson administration in compliance with the program of economic sanctions decreed by the U.N. Security Council.[5] Already condemned by both the Security Council and the General Assembly, the American stand was again debated by the Security Council in May 1973 in connection with a report on the sanctions program which noted that such violations were both flagrant and widespread. A nine-power draft resolution which expressed grave concern at the violations and requested the repeal of any legislation permitting them was adopted on May 22 by 12 votes to 0, with France, the United Kingdom, and the United States abstaining.[6] A second, seven-power resolution that called for a partial extension of the sanctions program to South Africa, Mozambique, and Angola also drew eleven favorable votes but was vetoed by both the United Kingdom and the United States, while Austria and France abstained.[7] "In our view," said Ambassador Scali as he cast the second veto of his brief U.N. career, "to pass a resolution which is clearly unenforceable would seriously damage the reputation and credibility of the United Nations and further erode public confidence in the United Nations ability to act in a meaningful way."[8]

Aspects of the Rhodesian problem would continue to confront the United Nations at intervals throughout 1973, as would other African controversies which failed to move measurably closer to

[3]Resolutions 327 (1973), Feb. 2, adopted by a vote of 14-0-1 (U.S.S.R.), and 329 (1973), Mar. 10, adopted unanimously.
[4]Resolutions 326 (1973), Feb. 2, and 328 (1973), Mar. 10, both adopted by votes of 13-0-2 (U.K., U.S.). For details see *UN Monthly Chronicle*, vol. 10 (Feb. 1973), pp. 13-29; (Mar. 1973), pp. 3-9; (Apr. 1973), pp. 3-15; also *U.S. Participation, 1973*, pp. 209-11.
[5]For background cf. *AFR, 1971*, pp. 412-29; same, *1972*, pp. 394-405.
[6]Resolution 333 (1973), May 22, adopted by a vote of 12-0-3 (U.S.).
[7]U.N. document S/10928, May 17; failed of adoption by a vote of 11-2 (U.S.)-2. For details see *UN Monthly Chronicle*, vol. 10 (June 1973), pp. 3-20; *Bulletin*, vol. 69 (1973), pp. 40-43; *U.S. Participation, 1973*, pp. 211-13.
[8]Same, p. 213. For the previous veto cf. Document 17.

solution during these months. Hopes for a fruitful discussion with South Africa concerning its intentions in Namibia gained little encouragement from Secretary-General Kurt Waldheim's report to the Security Council on the preliminary contacts he had established with that body's approval in 1972. Although South Africa talked of possible self-determination for Namibia in not more than ten years, Mr. Waldheim advised the Council on April 30, its failure to provide a "complete and unequivocal" clarification of its policies raised a question as to whether the contacts should be continued at all.[9]

Events in the Sudan, where the U.S. Ambassador and two other ranking diplomats were murdered by "Black September" terrorists on March 2, belong more properly to the history of the Arab-Israel conflict than to that of Africa's struggle for political maturity, and will be noted in the next chapter. A more authentically African occasion was the dinner held at the White House on May 15 in honor of the Emperor Haile Selassie I, the 81-year-old monarch whom President Nixon described in his toast as "not only the revered leader of Ethiopia" but also "the acknowledged leader of Africa" and, indeed, "the senior statesman of the world."[10] The mutual encomiums exchanged by these two heads of state, at a time when famine and cholera (unknown to them) were spreading in Ethiopia and when the Watergate miasma was increasingly poisoning the American atmosphere, would have sounded doubly ironic could it have been foreseen that both leaders would be compelled to forsake their respective offices before the world was many months older.

(19) The Realities of United States-Africa Relations": Address by David D. Newsom, Assistant Secretary of State for African Affairs, before the Royal Commonwealth Society, London, March 14, 1973.[11]

The Commonwealth is probably the world's largest and most significant undefined organization. Similarly the relationship between the United States and the Commonwealth is undefined and, in some ways, special.

As a member of the first staff of the American Embassy in

[9]U.N. document S/10921, Apr. 30, 1973. For background cf. *AFR, 1972*, pp. 392-3, and see further *UN Monthly Chronicle*, vol. 10 (May 1973), pp. 39-40 and 59-60, and *U.S. Participation, 1973*, pp. 203-4. Further discussion of African affairs will be found in Chapter 28 at notes 9-18.

[10]*Presidential Documents*, vol. 9 (1973), pp. 673-4.

[11]Text from *Bulletin*, vol. 68 (1973), pp. 456-61.

Karachi in 1947, I was in at the beginning of the new Commonwealth. I have followed its fascinating history since then. I, together with many of my fellow countrymen, have admired the unique contribution that the Commonwealth and the ties between members of the Commonwealth have made to the history of this last quarter century.

Today I wish to speak to you about the relationship of the United States to Africa. It is most appropriate that I do so in this Commonwealth atmosphere since this relationship involves not only key African members of the Commonwealth but also a whole series of questions posed for Africa by the association of the United Kingdom with the Common Market.

The U.S. relationship to Africa is both old and new. It has been both romantic and realistic. It has been both positive and negative.

Central to our relationship to Africa is the ethnic tie, the enforced migration to America of slaves, largely from the west African areas of Nigeria, Dahomey, Togo, and Ghana.

One of the most neglected realities of American history is the fact that our nation started out as a multiracial society. Nearly one-fifth of the persons living in America before the American Revolution were of African descent. The census of 1790, virtually the first national act required of the Federal Government by the new Constitution, counted 3,929,000 persons, of whom 757,000 were black, including some 60,000 freemen and 697,000 slaves.

The enormous waves of immigrants from Europe in the 19th century and the early 20th century tended to diminish the proportion of all of the original groups in the total population, but persons of African descent still form about 11 percent of our population. In their search for their roots in Africa, and for their identity as Afro-Americans, and in their contribution to our own and world culture lie much of the dynamism of my country's link with Africa.

The existence of our own civil rights problems means, also, that the complex issues of southern Africa are seen, whether rightly or wrongly, as mirrors or extensions of our own racial difficulties. There is consequently among both blacks and whites a special attention to these problems. There exists, not unnaturally, the same divergence of opinion toward these problems that one finds toward our own domestic issues.

The black community's interest in Africa goes back to the early 19th century when freed slaves, with the help of white contributions, formed the American Colonization Society to found settlements in west Africa which eventually became the Republic of Liberia. Still today, the nation of Liberia, while not tied to the United States in any political way, remains a special symbol of our links with Africa.

The 19th century saw the romantic period. Americans followed with fascination and admiration the adventures of European missionaries and explorers making their way into "the dark continent." Henry M. Stanley's exploits brought the African scene closer to home. The first U.S. missionary activities in black Africa began in the early 1800's in Liberia and Sierra Leone.

American trade with Africa began in the very early days of our Republic as clipper ships from Massachusetts rounded the Cape of Good Hope seeking spices and timber in east Africa and beyond. We signed a treaty with Zanzibar and Muscat in 1832.

African Expectations of the United States

As political movements began in Africa in the 20th century, their leaders found special interest in the history of the American colonies—if you will forgive me—in their struggle for freedom. The writings of Paine, Jefferson, and others struck responsive chords. Some of the dissimilarities were overlooked and the similarities seized upon.

Many of the political leaders in independent Africa were educated in the United States—Nkrumah of Ghana, Banda of Malawi, and Azikiwe of Nigeria.

The result of these ties was that African nations entered their independence with great expectations of the United States.

With knowledge of the Marshall plan still fresh in the minds of many African leaders, there was expectation that the United States would provide massive assistance to Africa.

With an awareness of the writings of the early Americans and of Lincoln, there was the expectation that we would take the lead in supporting the struggle for independence in Africa. Strong sentiments on existing independence movements were expressed frequently in the United States, giving further support to this expectation.

A knowledge of the power and wealth of the United States fed expectation of a degree of influence that could, if it wished, change the internal policies of African governments and right the wrongs of colonialism and apartheid.

Each of these positive expectations had, in a sense, a reverse side.

The fact that Africans identified with America's support for independence fed concern among expatriates and former colonial powers that we were out to replace them.

Natural rivalries of commercial competition served further to feed these anxieties about our intention.

The image of the wealth of the United States held by some Africans served to create apprehensions regarding the exercise of that wealth. The United States became feared—and envied.

The impressions of U.S. influence, sparked by such books as "The Invisible Government," gave rise to fears and allegations of U.S. political manipulation. The CIA became an ogre and a symbol.

Bases of U.S. Policies Toward Africa

The last few years have been spent getting the United States and its relationship with Africa in focus. Particularly has this been true during the past four years, when, in the words of President Nixon, we have sought a relationship of candor:[12]

Africa's friends must find a new tone of candor in their essential dialogue with the Continent. All too often over the past decade the United States and others have been guilty of telling proud young nations, in misguided condescension, only what we thought they wanted to hear. But I know from many talks with Africans, including two trips to the Continent in 1957 and 1967, that Africa's new leaders are pragmatic and practical as well as proud, realistic as well as idealistic. It will be a test of diplomacy for all concerned to face squarely common problems and differences of view. The United States will do all it can to establish this new dialogue.

Our policies toward Africa rest, to start with, on a clear definition of U.S. interests in Africa.

First, there is the historic and ethnic interest in Africa. While in many ways the black groups in America still concentrate almost totally on domestic issues and have not yet developed a visibly effective constituency for Africa, the interest is there. No American policy toward Africa can ignore this deep and growing interest in a meaningful relationship to the continent by so large a group of our citizens.

Secondly, and closely tied to the first, is the keen interest in the humanity of Africa on the part of blacks and many whites. Whether it be a problem of famine or war or a problem of human rights, the American policymaker is continually made conscious of the strong empathy which exists toward Africa.

More traditional diplomatic and economic interests also exist. As

[12]*Nixon Report, 1970*, p. 90.

a major power, we desire effective diplomatic access to the governments of Africa, representing as they do almost one-third of the members of the United Nations. In full recognition of the sensitive nationalism of the newly independent nations, we desire fair opportunities for trade and investment.

The United States does not desire—even if it had the capabilities and resources to do so—to replace the former colonial powers in trade and economic relations with the African nations. We appreciate and wish to be responsive to the desire of the African nations to diversify their economic relations. We continue to believe, however, that the traditional ties of language, education, and business that link these nations with the metropole nations in Europe are important to both partners, and to the extent each desires to retain them, they should be encouraged.

The question frequently is raised, particularly on this side of the Atlantic, of the U.S. military interest in Africa. We count this a lesser interest. We have two remaining military communications stations in Africa which we shall presumably need until technology makes them unnecessary. We recognize the importance to Europe of the cape route; we do not, however, give this interest priority over other more direct concerns in Africa.

Response to African Interests and Concerns

The pursuit of the interests of any nation in Africa requires, also, an understanding of African interests and concerns. No policies are going to be effective which fail to take these into account and to seek in some measure to be responsive.

From my own frequent travels in Africa and my own discussions with African leaders, I would define African interests as three: nationbuilding and true sovereignty, survival and development, and a resolution of the inequities of southern Africa.

American policies seek meaningful responses to each of these African concerns.

There is the strongest desire among Africans to build the nations inherited from the colonial era, with boundaries fixed by that era, and with institutions compatible with the customs and traditions of the peoples. We recognize that there have been and will be changes in the institutions left behind by the colonial powers. We accept that there will be variety in forms of government and philosophies and that we can deal with nations, regardless of their institutions, on a basis of mutual respect and common interest.

We recognize that Africans do not wish to be pawns in a great-power conflict. We accept their relations with all nations. We ask only that they be true to their nonalignment in the balanced treatment and understanding they give to all. We do not accept that there can be a double standard according to which the United States can be condemned for certain actions while other nations are not. Neither do we accept that African nations can turn blind eyes to human disaster within their own continent while seeking the condemnation of others.

In an African Continent understandably sensitive on the issue of sovereignty, we Americans have had a special myth to overcome: the myth of manipulation. I hope that this is dead. I hope that we have been able to convince the African governments that we are not involved in any way in seeking to determine how they are governed or by whom.

African leaders understandably are preoccupied with critical economic problems. Many search for the resources needed for development. Others, less fortunate, search for the resources needed for survival. Sixteen of the poorest countries of the world are in Africa.

I will not deny that the response to Africa's economic needs has presented us with some very difficult problems. As I pointed out, African expectations of what we might provide were high. We have not come up to those expectations.

Assistance, Investment, and Trade

As Americans, however, coming late into the scene in Africa, we feel that we have made a substantial and meaningful contribution to African development. Bilateral assistance, both that given directly in country programs and that provided on a regional basis, has been maintained at approximately the same level through the past 10 years: about $350 million per year. If one adds another $200 million provided annually through international institutions such as the United Nations Development Program and the World Bank, the U.S. contribution represents about 20 percent of all aid going to Africa.

In attempting to assert their independence from the developed countries, which are the major suppliers of traditional aid, the African countries are seeking increased control over investment and assured market conditions for their primary commodities. As a major supplier of foreign investment and consumer of primary products, the United States has an important interest in these matters as well. With each side looking at these matters from its own perspective, however, there is not always an identity of perceived national interests.

The United States strongly believes that private foreign investment, as a carrier of technology, of trade opportunities, and of capital itself, and as a mobilizer of domestic resources, in turn becomes a major factor in promoting economic development. Another factor is the increasing need of the United States for energy sources and other primary resources, an important share of which will come from Africa.

Yet the terms on which private capital will accept investment risk in African countries at times conflict with the strong desire of the African nations for a greater share in both the equity and management of investment projects.

Terms such as "Africanization" and "nationalization" frighten some investors. They are considered to be political necessities in many parts of Africa. Fortunately, the result, so far in Africa, has been in most cases a sincere effort to find, through negotiations, ways to meet the needs and respected rights of both parties. I detect in American business a greater recognition of the desire of a number of African states for participation in investment. I detect in many African countries a greater recognition of the important and beneficial role played by the private foreign investor. I hope both trends continue.

African countries such as Ghana and the Ivory Coast, with a heavy dependence upon single agricultural commodities, have pressed for international commodity agreements, particularly in coffee and cocoa. They have received strong support from Latin America.

The United States played a leading role in negotiating the first International Coffee Agreement in 1962[13] and has played a leading role in supporting that agreement. For most of its period, the agreement operated in the interests of both producers and consumers, since it was designed to meet the particular circumstances which obtained at that time. On cocoa, we were active participants in the long series of negotiations which led to conclusion of an agreement last fall.[14] We did not sign it, however, because we believe it is seriously flawed and may not achieve its purpose of stabilizing cocoa prices and earnings.

With regard to commodity trade in general, we see a growing need for attacks on the underlying problems and for new approaches which are not trade restrictive, but trade creating in nature. We will, however, continue to consider proposals for traditional commodity agreements on a case-by-case basis.

Next year will be the year of a renegotiation of the Yaounde Con-

[13]Done at New York Sept. 28, 1962 and entered into force for the U.S. July 1 - Dec. 27, 1963 (TIAS 5505; 14 UST 1911).
[14]International Cocoa Agreement, open for signature Nov. 15, 1972 - Jan. 15, 1973 and entered provisionally into force June 30, 1973.

vention linking the European Community to Africa.[15] Already consultations have started on how the Anglophone countries will fit into the older arrangements. Both trade and aid are involved. The United States recognizes the importance of the Yaounde Convention to the African signatories. At the same time, we strongly oppose the system of special and reverse tariff preferences which forms a part of the present agreements. In this we are not alone. Canada and Japan oppose these reverse preferences, and we note that African countries increasingly are questioning their desirability.

While our trade with Africa does not compare with more traditional suppliers and markets, we strongly believe that Africa will benefit if it is open to all on a nondiscriminatory basis. This, too, is a critical and difficult element in our response to Africa's economic needs.

U.S. Approach to Southern African Issues

This leaves our response to the third African preoccupation—the complex issues of southern Africa. These issues pose very special problems for the Commonwealth, as they do for us.

The American attitude toward this area is clear. It was defined in President Nixon's foreign policy report of 1972 in these words:[16]

As I have repeatedly made clear, I share the conviction that the United States cannot be indifferent to racial policies which violate our national ideals and constitute a direct affront to American citizens. As a nation, we cherish and have worked arduously toward the goal of equality of opportunity for all Americans. It is incumbent on us to support and encourage these concepts abroad, and to do what we can to forestall violence across international frontiers.

In our approach to the issues of southern Africa, we proceed on several premises. First, in this day and age, the influence of any nation, however powerful, in the internal affairs of another is severely limited. The idea that the United States by any action—including the use of economic and military force, if that were realistic—could bring about fundamental changes in another

[15]Signed at Yaoundé, Cameroon, July 20, 1963 and renewed July 29, 1969 for the period ending Jan. 31, 1975.
[16]*Nixon Report, 1972*, p. 105; for comment cf. *AFR, 1972*, pp. 381-2.

society is without foundation. We certainly cannot do it in southern Africa. If change comes, it must come primarily from within.

Secondly, the United States cannot pursue policies which simply accept the situation in southern Africa as it is, or contribute to its perpetuation, nor those which endorse violence as a means to change. Consequently, we conscientiously pursue an arms embargo policy toward all sides in both South Africa and the Portuguese territories. We exercise restraint in our commercial and government-financing activities in both.

Thirdly, we believe that if we are to contribute meaningfully to change in the area, it is not through the pressure of isolation but through keeping open the doors of communication with all elements of the population, particularly in South Africa. If peaceful change is to come, in our view, it will come through a general recognition of the unacceptability of present policies in those areas brought about by continuing contact with the world outside.

Certain special problems arise.

One commonly held idea in the United States is that official insistence on the withdrawal of our private investment in South Africa would bring effective pressure for change. We do not think so. Our investment represents only 16 percent of the total foreign investment in South Africa. It is closely interlinked with South African interests. It is doubtful that it could be repatriated, even if we decreed it. It is not only our view, but also that of many black South Africans, that it is far better to encourage those firms which are there to lead the way to upgrading the work and social conditions of the nonwhite labor force. This we do.

Rhodesia, as you all well know, represents a special case. Except for the symbolically significant but economically insignificant breach of Rhodesian sanctions by the action of our Congress, we fully support the economic sanctions against Rhodesia and believe they are having an effect. We are deeply conscious of the grave problem the Rhodesian situation presents for our British friends. We hope that your patience will yet find a way of getting black and white in Rhodesia together for a workable solution.

The United Nations is another special situation. The problems of southern Africa are discussed frequently at the United Nations, and action is sought increasingly that exceeds the ability of the organization to implement.

While sympathetic with the objectives of many of the resolutions, the United States does not find that it can support what it considers unworkable resolutions, sometimes based on unfair judgments. Such resolutions also frequently raise questions of precedents and budget which further prevent our support. By the simple vote, we sometimes appear to be anti-African when the issues are far more complex.

The United States does welcome and support those efforts which emerge within the United Nations to bring about discussions between the parties directly concerned with these problems.

Such an effort is that undertaken by Secretary General Waldheim on Namibia. An effort was implied in the vote in December in the Security Council on the Portuguese territories,[17] but has yet to come to fruition. In our view, whatever the fate of the liberation approach, talks must ultimately come between those involved in the problem. However frail may be the chances, we hope ways can be found to start.

To the nations of the Commonwealth, as to the United States, the African Continent has a special significance. In that continent are the last hard-core problems of achieving self-determination, problems which have both built and divided the Commonwealth. In that continent lie continuing problems of human dignity and human rights, of such great concern to all our peoples.

I should like to assure you today that the United States recognizes these problems and the need for their solution. The United States is neither "neglecting" Africa nor giving it a "low priority." Out of the conflicting pressures for policies and resources upon and within a major nation, the United States seeks to respect Africa's independence, to be responsive to Africa's needs, and to stand ready realistically to be helpful in furthering trends of change.

[17] *AFR, 1972*, pp. 393-4.

7. MIDDLE EAST ANXIETIES

If Africa still remained at the periphery of U.S. policy interests, the problems of the Middle East, in contrast, stood near the center of American preoccupation. Events of the quarter-century since the birth of independent Israel in 1948 had highlighted the area's unique significance to American interests, from an economic and military as well as a political standpoint.

American solicitude for Israel, as a friendly democracy surrounded by hostile Arab neighbors, had in recent years been increasingly tempered by other cares, particularly since the Six-day War of June 1967 and the Israeli occupation of huge tracts of Arab territory beyond the previous armistice lines. Intent upon maintaining an uninterrupted flow of Middle Eastern oil, so necessary to the life of its industrialized partners and, increasingly, to its own as well, the United States was also conscious of a danger that any renewal of hostilities in the region could involve it in a military confrontation with the U.S.S.R., the self-appointed patron of the Arab states and their principal source of up-to-date military equipment. This dangerous possibility, in Washington's view, had still to be taken into account despite the broadly worded pledges of mutual restraint that had been exchanged by the leaders of the two governments on the occasion of President Nixon's Soviet visit in May 1972.[1]

The only real solution to this complex of problems, in the American view, would be the establishment of a just and lasting peace between Israel and its Arab neighbors; and the furtherance of such a peace had stood out as the primary goal of American policy in the region even before the 1967 war. The basic principles to be observed in any peace settlement had been laid down by the U.N. Security Council in its celebrated Resolution 242 of November 22, 1967,[2] and the task of promoting discussion among the parties to

[1]"Basic Principles of Mutual Relations Between the United States of America and the Union of Soviet Socialist Republics," May 29, 1972, in *AFR, 1972*, pp. 75-8.
[2]*Documents, 1967*, pp. 169-70.

this end had been entrusted to Ambassador Gunnar V. Jarring of Sweden as Special Representative of the U.N. Secretary-General. But since the views and objectives of the belligerents were so wide apart that no direct discussion among them had proved possible over a period that now exceeded five years, the United States had also made an effort to interest them in an alternative, "step-by-step" approach that would promote the same ultimate end but would concentrate on trying to solve one problem at a time.

Initiated as far back as 1970, this American effort had produced at least one solid achievement in the establishment of a *de facto* cease-fire between Israel and the United Arab Republic (Egypt) in the summer of that year. Much subsequent discussion had been devoted to the possibility of a further agreement encompassing a reopening of the Suez Canal, which had been sabotaged by Egypt in 1967, and a partial withdrawal of Israeli military forces from the occupied Sinai Peninsula.[3] Such an agreement was well worth pursuing, said Joseph J. Sisco, the Assistant Secretary of State for Middle Eastern and South Asian Affairs, in reviewing the essential features of the Arab-Israeli problem in a speech delivered May 7, 1973 (**Document 20**). Unless the movement toward peaceful settlement was maintained, this authority warned, there was a danger that the situation would deteriorate once again and that still another failure would have to be entered in what had already become a "tragic catalogue of lost opportunities."

There was no need for Mr. Sisco to document his description of the current state of affairs in the Middle East as "a situation that every rational person knows in his innermost thoughts is not normal, not stable, and not durable." The risks and heartbreaks inseparable from the five-and-one-half-year-old situation of "no war, no peace" that prevailed between Israel and the Arab belligerents—which included various Palestinian commando and terrorist groups as well as the governments of Egypt, Jordan, Lebanon, and Syria—had been written in blood for all to see. Such earlier atrocities as the killing of eleven Israeli athletes at the Olympic Games in Munich on September 11, 1972[4] had been followed during early 1973 by new incidents of terrorism and violence that pointed up not only the irreconcilable hostility of Israel's Palestinian foes but also the increasing harshness of Israel's response to terrorist harassment.

Three incidents in particular had caused worldwide shudders in the early months of 1973, though only the first had occurred in

---

[3]*Documents, 1970*, pp. 131-41; *AFR, 1971*, pp. 203-11; same, *1972*, pp. 198-206. For fuller discussion cf. *Nixon Report, 1973*, pp. 132-42.
[4]*AFR, 1972*, pp. 206-9.

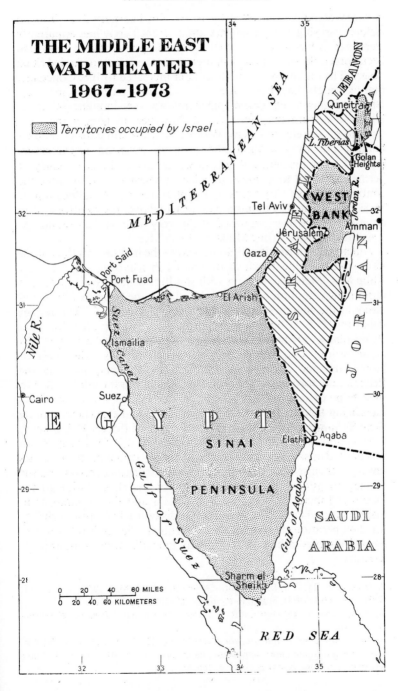

THE MIDDLE EAST
WAR THEATER
1967–1973

Territories occupied by Israel

territory actually controlled by Israel. On February 21, a Libyan airliner carrying 113 passengers and a French crew had apparently wandered off course on a flight from Tripoli to Cairo, and had been forced down by Israeli fighters over the Israeli-occupied Sinai desert. The initial loss of 106 lives later increased to 108. Conceding that its pilots had been overzealous in this particular instance, Israel promised *ex gratia* payments to the families of those killed—a gesture that quite failed, however, to temper the stern reproof of Secretary-General Waldheim or the still harsher rebukes handed out by the International Civil Aviation Organization (ICAO).[5] The incident did not, however, affect the U.S. policy of permitting Israel to acquire sufficient modern arms to balance the continuing Soviet shipments to Egypt and Syria. An allocation of 36 Skyhawk and 48 Phantom jets for Israel over the next four years appears to have been promised at this very time on the occasion of a visit from Israeli Prime Minister Golda Meir.[6]

American and Belgian diplomats were the innocent victims of the next violent incident, which originated in Khartoum on March 1 while Mrs. Meir was visiting with the President in Washington. A diplomatic reception being held that day at the Saudi Arabian Embassy in the Sudanese capital in honor of George C. Moore, the departing U.S. Counsellor of Embassy, was invaded by eight Palestinians, affiliated with the "Black September" terrorist organization, who seized the persons of the host, the guest of honor, the new U.S. Ambassador, Cleo A. Noel, Jr., and the Belgian and Jordanian Chargés d'Affaires. The intruders failed in their hope of securing the release of specified groups of terrorists then being held in Jordan, West Germany, and elsewhere, among them Sirhan B. Sirhan, the convicted slayer of Robert F. Kennedy. "We cannot and will not give in to blackmail," President Nixon was quoted as saying. Foiled in their primary demand, the terrorists revenged themselves by killing their two American captives and the Belgian by gunfire in the early evening of March 2. Although the Palestine Liberation Organization (PLO) and the *al-Fatah* commando group headed by Yasir Arafat disavowed any responsibility for the operation, the Sudanese Government claimed to know better and imposed a ban on Palestinian guerrilla organizations in its territory.[7]

[5]*Keesing's*, pp. 25757-8; *UN Monthly Chronicle*, vol. 10 (Mar. 1973), p. 29; (Apr. 1973), p. 99; (July 1973), p. 105; *Bulletin*, vol. 68 (1973), pp. 369-70.
[6]Kalb, *Kissinger*, p. 451; Edward R. F. Sheehan in *Foreign Policy*, No. 22 (Spring 1976), p. 10.
[7]*Keesing's*, pp. 25805-6; *Bulletin*, vol. 68 (1973), pp. 353-5. The eight terrorists were later sentenced to life imprisonment and handed over to the PLO by the Sudanese Government in June 1974 (*Keesing's*, p. 26603).

Capitulation to terrorist demands, in the opinion of President Nixon and most other governmental authorities, could only encourage further outrages; yet a refusal to yield to blackmail, as in the Khartoum case, seemed scarcely to discourage new terrorist actions. Between April 9 and April 14, other groups of Arab terrorists attempted to blow up the Israeli Ambassador's residence in Nicosia, Cyprus, and to attack an Israeli airliner preparing to load passengers at Nicosia airport; Israeli commandos, in what was described as a retaliatory raid on Beirut on April 10, killed three of the top *al-Fatah* and PLO leaders, together with several members of other Palestinian organizations; and Arabic-speaking gunmen blew up two oil storage tanks at the Sidon (Lebanon) terminal of the U.S.-owned Trans-Arabian Pipeline Company.[8]

Unlike the other incidents, the Israeli raid on Beirut was a governmental action and prompted a Lebanese complaint to the U.N. Security Council, which met no fewer than seven times before adopting on April 21 a modified Anglo-French resolution that condemned Israel's "repeated military attacks" against Lebanon and called upon it to "desist forthwith." Although the resolution implied awareness of other recent incidents and broadly condemned "all acts of violence which endanger or take innocent lives,"[9] the United States abstained from voting on the ground that even though the text reflected some progress, it still fell short of "evenhanded condemnation of all forms of violence." China, Guinea, and the U.S.S.R., on the other hand, took a diametrically opposite view and abstained in protest against the resolution's comparative leniency toward Israel.

The Security Council took two further actions during this same series of meetings. It authorized a routine warning, sure to be disregarded by Israel, against the holding of a contemplated anniversary parade whose route would pass through both the Israeli and the Jordanian sectors of Jerusalem.[10] And it requested Secretary-General Waldheim to prepare a comprehensive review of U.N. efforts pertaining to the Middle East since 1967, as a basis for possible future discussion by the Council.[11] Responding to this request, the Secretary-General four weeks later submitted what he himself described as a record of "great efforts but little

---

[8]Same, p. 25868.
[9]Resolution 332 (1973), Apr. 21, adopted by a vote of 11-0-4 (U.S.). For details see *UN Monthly Chronicle*, vol. 10 (May 1973), pp. 3-38; *Bulletin*, vol. 68 (1973), pp. 656-60; *U.S. Participation, 1973*, pp. 3-4.
[10]*UN Monthly Chronicle*, vol. 10 (May 1973), p. 39.
[11]Resolution 331 (1973), Apr. 20, adopted without vote; details in same, pp. 3, 32-3, and 38.

progress.''[12] If the diplomatic impasse in the Middle East continued, the State Department's Bureau of Intelligence and Research observed in a May 31 memorandum to Secretary Rogers, Egyptian patience might soon be exhausted and a "resumption of hostilities by autumn" would become "a better than even bet.''[13]

(20) "Encouraging a Negotiating Process in the Middle East": Address by Joseph J. Sisco, Assistant Secretary of State for Near Eastern and South Asian Affairs, May 7, 1973.[14]

In this 25th year of Israel's independence, much is being said—and rightly so—about the accomplishments of this remarkable state and its remarkable people. The Second World War accelerated the striving of many people for national independence and changed the map of our world in ways few could have imagined when that war began. In one sense, Israel is simply one of the many young states that have swelled the membership of the United Nations from 51 when it was originally founded to 132 today.

But in another sense, Israel is unique among the new states of the world. There were many, well before the beginning of this century, who did envisage its creation; and for millennia, before the phenomenon of the modern nation-state appeared on the historical scene, Jews everywhere kept alive the vision of their nationhood.

In our century, out of the horrors of the holocaust, the vision of those generations of men and women was transformed into the reality of the State of Israel. Israel could not have come into being and survived had it not been for the indomitable will of its people for existence and independence. At the same time, on this 25th anniversary, it is fitting to recall also the role of others. First, the partition decision and subsequent admission of Israel to United Nations membership were an important part of the juridical foundations of the state. The United Nations itself is only three years older than the State of Israel, and their histories have been intertwined for the past quarter of a century—occasionally for better and, particularly in recent years, too often for worse. Secondly, while Israel

[12]U.N. document S/10929, May 18, in U.N. Security Council, *Official Records: 28th Year, Supplement for Apr., May and June 1973*, pp. 37-53.
[13]Extract from the report of the Select Committee on Intelligence, U.S. House of Representatives, Jan. 1976, in *Village Voice* (New York), Feb. 16, 1976, p. 78. For further developments see Chapter 15.
[14]Department of State Press Release 135; text from *Bulletin*, vol. 68 (1973), pp. 844-8. The address was delivered at a celebration of the 25th anniversary of Israel sponsored by the American Israel Public Affairs Committee and the Jewish Community Council of Greater Washington.

with some justification has often felt it stood alone, the support of other nations—above all, the United States—has been indispensable at critical moments to Israel's creation, growth, and survival. That support draws in the first instance on the help and faith of the Diaspora, but its base is far broader than that.

As these opening remarks suggest, I believe this is an occasion for standing back from the preoccupations of the moment, from the crises and headlines and tragedies and hopes of today—a time for a sober look at the past 25 years to see what lessons they teach us for the next 25.

First, Israel had to feel strong and secure and confident of its survival before it could think about tomorrow and the day after tomorrow. Israel lived so many of its first 25 years with an abiding sense of insecurity that some have not yet become accustomed to the fact that Israel today is strong, is secure, and is confident of its survival. Moreover, there is no doubt that the support of the United States, both material and moral, has made a major contribution to the strength of Israel. That support and that strength have been a principal deterrent to renewed hostilities in the area. I am confident that the United States will remain steadfast in its support for Israel's security.

Foreign Minister [Abba S.] Eban has recently alluded to Israel's strength in this way:

It is of course a fact that we are still the target of perils and threats, but it is also a fact that Israel is, in the last resort, a strong and solid reality. Strong and solid in its capacities of defense; strong in the inspiration of its heritage and faith; strong in its economic resources; strong in the support that it receives from the Jewish people; strong in its science and learning; strong in the overall balance of its links with governments and peoples across the world. True, all these elements of strength and solidity are relative and not absolute, but they are impressive in relation to the resources and capacity of all our adversaries.

At the same time, I believe it is appropriate here to express a few words of caution to our Israeli friends—words expressed in the spirit of friendship and mutual confidence between us which permits us to speak frankly and without suspicions of ulterior motives. I would suggest that while Israel's strength must be maintained, the next 25 years present a corollary challenge. Again, I want to borrow the words of Israel's Foreign Minister:

. . . A confident and balanced national style is perfectly reconcilable with an alert security consciousness and a rational and firm political line. The problem is how to put the emphasis on freedom, tolerance, equality, social justice, spiritual and intellectual creativity and human brotherhood, as the salient characteristics of a strong and confident Israeli society . . .

There is a second point regarding the past 25 years which I believe is worth making, and this relates to both Israel and its Arab neighbors. For most of the past 25 years, both have held seemingly irreconcilable perceptions of what their respective national interests required with respect to the other. Before 1967 the Arab world, with few exceptions, was unanimous in believing that its national interest required the elimination of the State of Israel. Before 1967 Israel believed its national interest required, above all, Arab recognition of its sovereignty and its right to exist in peace and was prepared to accept something like the armistice lines of 1949 as its recognized international boundaries. Since 1967, while there are still Arab voices calling for the disappearance of Israel, there are many others in the Arab world who now perceive their national interest as compatible with the existence of a sovereign Israel, though within the former armistice lines. I believe that for most Arabs, Israel's existence is no longer the principal issue; and this is a major positive element in the Middle East today. Unfortunately, while the gap on the question of existence and coexistence of Israel has narrowed, the gap on the question of borders has widened. Since 1967, while Israelis have not agreed among themselves on what the boundaries of the state should be, they are generally agreed that those boundaries should be substantially different from the armistice lines. Sadat,[15] in turn, insists that there can be no changes in his borders. "Not an inch of territory," he repeats time and again.

Myths Which Obscure the Realities

Third, the vision of both sides has often been clouded by myths of the past which have persisted in obscuring the realities of the present:

—Before 1967 each side's perception of the other was compounded, in part at least, of myth. To the Arabs, Israel did not exist as a dynamic evolving reality. It was "occupied Palestine" and referred to as such. Arabs tended to think of Israel and its society as frozen in the patterns of 1947, as a state which would be made to disappear someday, leaving no trace on the land. Israel was seen as

[15]Anwar al-Sadat, President of the Arab Republic of Egypt (previously the United Arab Republic) since Sept. 28, 1970.

on the verge of collapse from internal decay, an artificial entity propped up by others which would not withstand the tide of history.

—The Israeli counterpart of this myth before 1967 was its perception of a monolithic Arab world, strife torn and backward. All Arabs were perceived as essentially the same, and there was little understanding of the sense of a Palestine-Arab identity in the Middle East which distinguished the Palestinian Arabs from the Arabs of Lebanon or Syria or Transjordan or the peninsula.

—In the aftermath of the 1967 war, the increasing interaction of Arabs and Israelis in Gaza, in the occupied West Bank, and across the Jordan River began a process of breaking down these myths which each had held of the other. This is an essentially healthy process and one of the positive byproducts of that war.

But other myths have arisen and persist:

—There is the myth, now accepted as reality in much of the Arab world, that the six-day war was the result of unprovoked Israeli aggression.

—There is the myth, believed still by many even though now discounted by some Arab leaders, that units of the U.S. Air Force participated on Israel's side in the six-day war. This myth has recently arisen in a new form in the "big lie" charging that the CIA and the American Embassy in Beirut were parties to the recent Israeli raid in Lebanon.

—On the Israeli side, there is the myth that the six-day war was the result of a calculated Arab plan to launch a war of destruction against Israel. In my view, the most plausible explanation is that the six-day war resulted from improvised actions and reactions by each side. Combined with each side's perception and suspicion of the other's intentions, the cumulative weight of these actions and reactions made inevitable a war neither side deliberately sought at that time.

—Next, there is the myth that security is solely a function of the physical location of territorial boundaries. As Foreign Minister Eban said recently, much more eloquently than I can:

The question of boundaries is one of the components of peace and not its sole condition. The balance of forces, the spirit and resourcefulness of our defenders, the application of science to the reinforcement of the economy, the strength of our international ties, these are all factors of equal weight. Without them our security would be undermined, no matter what boundaries we were to establish. The problem is not merely how to define our own historic rights, but how to bring them into harmony with the rights of others and with our own right to peace.

—Another myth, of which we have heard much lately in the Arab world, is that peace can be achieved by going to war. Certainly the lessons of the last three wars between Arabs and Israelis prove just the opposite.

—Finally, there is the myth that peace can be made by proxy; that powers not party to the conflict, acting independently or through the United Nations, can somehow substitute for negotiations between the parties themselves. This has not been the case in any of the successful negotiations of international disputes in recent history, and the Middle East is no exception. The United Nations and outside powers can play a responsible role in encouraging the parties to get a negotiating process started, but they cannot be part of the process itself. When they seek to substitute their views for the positions of the parties directly concerned or openly advocate the positions of one party, they do not further progress, they inhibit it.

A History of Lost Opportunities

All of this suggests a fourth lesson, and I believe it is the principal lesson to be learned from the past. The history of the Arab-Israeli problem is a history of lost opportunities. So often opportunities have slipped through the fingers of those concerned—slipped through their fingers just when they thought they could grasp them. At such moments, the opportunities were all the more precious because they seemed near enough to be seen but too far off to be tasted.

Perhaps the greatest opportunity came after the six-day war in 1967. In November of that year the United Nations Security Council was able to agree unanimously on a set of principles, embodied in its Resolution 242[16] and accepted by the principal parties to the conflict, which laid a new foundation for a peaceful settlement:

—First, the Security Council did not label one side or the other as an aggressor in the 1967 war. Rather than looking backward and seeking to apportion blame, it looked forward and sought to build a better future.

—Second, the Security Council did not call for unconditional Israeli withdrawal to the armistice lines as had been the case at the time of the 1956 war in Sinai. Rather, it called for "withdrawal . . .

[16]*Documents, 1967*, pp. 169-70; cf. above at note 2.

from territories occupied" in the 1967 war as part of a package settlement in which the parties would agree to respect each other's right to live in peace within secure and recognized boundaries. The Security Council resolution established principles. It did not establish borders or define precisely the obligations of peace and security.

—Third, the United Nations recognized that a settlement could not be imposed from outside. Instead, it established the principle that peace should be based upon agreement between the parties to the conflict.

These were principles for which the United States fought hard and successfully in the deliberations of the United Nations. They remain the essential framework for peace in the area, and if the Security Council departs from these principles any future prospects for negotiation between the parties will have been seriously jeopardized.

Why have so many opportunities been missed, at great costs in lives and resources, since the adoption of the November 1967 Security Council resolution? If we had the complete answer to that question, perhaps our efforts in the cause of Middle East peace would have been more successful over the years. But I do believe I know part of the answer, and it is this: Neither side, Arab or Israeli, has collectively defined its goals in terms of what economists like to call the "opportunity costs" of achieving those goals; in other words, in terms of what it is willing to forgo in the process. To be sure, there are Arabs who still say today: We want peace but only when Israel as a Jewish state is no more. There are Israelis who say: We want peace but only if we can also keep the occupied territories.

But these are statements of individuals or political groupings, not the positions of governments. There is no broadly agreed consensus on either side as to what the acceptable tradeoffs might be. States seem to follow the patterns of human nature—the desire to have it both ways, to have their cake and eat it too, to keep their options open.

In this sixth year since 1967 of no war and no peace, I believe it is time for the parties to begin to choose options, to establish priorities, to decide what is most important and what it will cost, and to decide whether it is worth the price. I do not say that this or any other opportunity that may come along is the last one in history, but I do believe that the cost of each missed opportunity in the Middle East is becoming progressively higher than the previous one.

Complexities in the Pursuit of Peace

As we stand back and view the Middle East in the perspective of time, what do we see today? We see a situation that every rational person knows in his innermost thoughts is not normal, not stable, and not durable. True, the world has lived with many such situations, and when the balance of power is properly maintained, such situations can last for a surprisingly long time. But need they? And isn't the cost in the end often greater than it would have been if both sides had seized the opportunities and taken the risks necessary to resolve conflicts sooner?

We have a 33-month-old cease-fire in the context of the reduced likelihood of a Soviet-American confrontation. However, the cycle of violence continues and has taken an appalling toll of life. The victims have included many innocent and uninvolved civilians— Olympic athletes, airline passengers, dedicated diplomats, recently a foreign national in Beirut, and countless others in Israel, in the Arab world, and elsewhere.

The Security Council on April 21 took a small step forward in facing up to this pressing problem. The resolution which was passed,[17] while very far from the balanced outcome we sought, condemned terrorist violence for the first time. For the first time, the Security Council has recognized that terrorism is part of the problem and not simply an irrelevant byproduct. The question now is: Where do we go from here? How do we at long last begin to build on the framework for peace contained in Security Council Resolution 242, on the cease-fire along the Suez Canal negotiated by the United States, on the stability in Jordan and the efforts to find a new stability in Lebanon, on the widely shared desire to develop further the mutually beneficial relations between high-energy-consuming countries and the oil-producing nations of the Middle East?

In this connection, there has been much speculation of late as to whether the so-called energy crisis is going to lead to changes in our Middle East policy. In my view, this is the wrong way to pose the question. The question is whether our policy of seeking to promote a peaceful settlement is going to succeed, so that there will be no temptation for some to seek to politicize the energy problem, to their own detriment as much as to the detriment of others.

For its part, the United States is continuing to press the search for answers. The present "no war, no peace" situation is unstable and unsatisfactory. As a beginning, it would be well to build on the present cease-fire. There should be a cease-fire on inflammatory rhetoric; a cease-fire on public statements of ultimate and rigid

[17]Cf. above at note 9.

positions; a cease-fire on violence of all kinds from whatever source. Just as we called on the parties in 1970, on the eve of the U.S.-initiated cease-fire, to stop shooting and start talking, today we urge they stop shouting and start listening.

We need—the world badly needs—a period of calm and quiet diplomacy in the Middle East. For our part, we began that process during what President Nixon has described as his Middle East month. We had useful discussions with the leaders of Jordan and Israel and with a senior adviser to the President of Egypt.[18] That continuing process has been complicated by the recent kaleidoscope of violent events, but it has not been stopped. We intend to carry it forward through diplomatic channels. We intend to continue urging on the parties the need for getting negotiations started and to continue exploring with them ways to do this. The principal parties concerned have said they want to keep the doors of diplomacy open. We intend to take them at their word.

It would not be realistic to think, after so many years of effort, that there lurks somewhere, waiting to be discovered, a magic formula which would suddenly solve the Arab-Israeli problem in a single dramatic stroke. A way must be found in the first instance to reconcile Egyptian sovereignty and Israeli security needs. In our judgment, the chasm on an overall settlement is too broad to bridge in one jump. But practical step-by-step progress is feasible, beginning with negotiations on an agreement for some Israeli withdrawal in Sinai, the reopening of the Suez Canal, and an extended cease-fire. I am convinced an interim Suez Canal agreement would not and should not become an end in itself, but would lead to increasingly productive negotiations on the larger issues. These also include the Jordanian-Israeli aspects of the settlement and the need to meet the legitimate concerns of the Palestinians. It is in the context of such active negotiations between the parties that the United States can be most helpful.

The President has said we will give high priority to moving the Middle East situation toward a settlement. Since we set that course four years ago, we have had some notable successes as well as some temporary setbacks. We see no reason to change course or diminish our efforts. I can assure you we do not intend to do so. Opportunities for diplomacy still prevail in 1973. Israel needs peace, its neighbors need peace, and the world needs peace. I would hope that we will not look back several years hence and conclude that the present period was another in the tragic catalogue of lost opportunities.

[18]President Nixon received King Hussein of Jordan on Feb. 6; Hafez Ismail, National Security Adviser to President Sadat, on Feb. 23; and Prime Minister Meir on Mar. 1 (*Presidential Documents*, vol. 9 [1973], pp. 126-8, 189, and 212-14).

8. LAUNCHING THE "YEAR OF EUROPE"

In contrast to the ceaseless demands of the Middle East, the imperative rquirements of the Indochina situation and the continuing claims of big-power diplomacy, the problems of the Atlantic world had been viewed by President Nixon's administration as something that could to some extent be set aside while more urgent matters were dealt with. If 1971 and 1972 had of necessity been devoted primarily to concluding the war in Vietnam and laying a basis for improved relations with the U.S.S.R. and China, 1973, the "Year of Europe," might all the more fittingly be dedicated to straightening out America's relationship with older allies and friends.

An intensified concern with Europe seemed doubly indicated because a number of important trends in the affairs of the Atlantic nations had been moving toward a point of early decision. The enlargement of the European Communities from a membership of six to nine, accomplished through the accession of Denmark, Ireland, and the United Kingdom to Community membership on January 1, 1973, had brought important modifications in the internal balance of the Atlantic grouping and affected the position and outlook of its members on both sides of the ocean. Transatlantic tensions over trade and financial policy, accumulating over a period of years, were approaching what might be a decisive showdown in the forthcoming negotiations for reform of the international monetary system and a far-reaching review of international trade rules.

The questions of European security likewise called for urgent reexamination in light of the shift in both political and military relationships that had accompanied the progress of East-West détente. The most serious obstacle to a direct discussion of security questions by Communist and Western governments had been

[1]For more detailed discussion cf. *Nixon Report, 1973*, pp. 76-93, and Kalb, *Kissinger*, pp. 426-30.

eliminated with the agreement on the status of Berlin concluded by the Big Four occupation powers in 1971 and placed in force in June 1972.[2] Preliminary discussions looking toward a Conference on Security and Cooperation in Europe (CSCE) had been under way in Helsinki since November 22, 1972, with 34 governments, including the United States and Canada, participating. Balancing this Soviet-inspired project, a Western proposal looking toward the discussion of Mutual and Balanced Force Reductions (MBFR) in Central Europe was also under examination by selected members of the North Atlantic Treaty Organization (NATO) and the Soviet-directed Warsaw Pact. These countries had begun preliminary talks in Vienna on January 31, 1973.[3]

These harbingers of a new European era had sharpened the perennial debate about the ways of ensuring the military defense of Western Europe, and about the appropriate form and extent of U.S. participation in that endeavor. Influential members of the U.S. Senate, headed by Democratic Majority Leader Mike Mansfield of Montana, had for years been urging a substantial reduction in the approximately 300,000 U.S. troops that were currently being maintained in Europe, the bulk of them under NATO command in Germany.[4] Only by extraordinary and repeated efforts had the Nixon administration been able to head off such initiatives and renew its periodic assurance to the other NATO members "that given a similar approach by our Allies, we will maintain and improve our forces in Europe and will not reduce them unless there is reciprocal action from our adversaries."[5] The recent commencement of East-West talks, and the continuing pressure of its overseas forces on the United States' balance of payments, ensured that this question would remain much to the fore in 1973.

While gratified by the United States' declared intention to take more systematic notice of their problems, the governments of Western Europe could not be certain that any specific proposals that might be developed in Washington would be entirely to their liking. A good deal of controversy and tension had surrounded European-American relations, particularly in the economic area, for several years past. President Nixon, thus far in 1973, had said little of America's current intentions, apart from a somewhat

[2]Quadripartite Agreement on Berlin, signed Sept. 3, 1971 and entered into force June 3, 1972 (TIAS 7551; 24 UST 283); see *AFR, 1971*, pp. 162-70; same, *1972*, pp. 158-62.

[3]For background cf. *AFR, 1971*, pp. 148-9 and 170-74; same, *1972*, pp. 147-55 and 174-84; also Chapter 13 at note 5.

[4]For background cf. *AFR, 1971*, pp. 148-54 and 170-73.

[5]E.g., *AFR, 1971*, p. 179; same, *1972*, p. 178.

ominous reference to "this period when we can either become competitors in a constructive way or where we can engage in economic confrontation that could lead to bitterness and which would hurt us both."[6] It had remained for Dr. Kissinger, the architect of the Vietnam peace settlement and of the new relationships with mainland China and the U.S.S.R., to provide the first public indications of the way the United States envisaged its "new relationship" with "the new Europe."

The most noted feature of Dr. Kissinger's maiden speech on European policy—an address to the annual meeting of the Associated Press Editors in New York on April 23 (**Document 21**)—was his call for something he termed "a new Atlantic charter," apparently a sort of "blueprint" setting common goals for the future that would be worked out in advance of a visit to Europe that President Nixon proposed to undertake toward the end of 1973. Of deeper significance than the procedural and literary aspects of this plan, however, was Dr. Kissinger's apparent conception of the "new relationship" between Europe and the United States that the document was supposed to bring into being—a relationship, incidentally, in which it appeared that Japan and Canada would also be called upon to play a significant part. It was the philosophical basis of the plan, more than its precise form or the circumstances of its enunciation, that recalled to many observers President Kennedy's proposal of 1962 with regard to an Atlantic "Declaration of Interdependence."[7]

Dr. Kissinger's proposal, like President Kennedy's, was destined to exert a profound influence on Western political thinking, even though doomed to fall short of detailed implementation. At bottom, it seemed to involve another application of the celebrated Nixon-Kissinger theory of "linkage," whereby any concessions made by one party in one area should be matched by other concessions by other parties in other areas. What the presidential assistant appeared to be saying, in simplest terms, was that the United States would continue to be helpful in Europe's defense if Europe, on its side, would be more helpful to the United States in economic and diplomatic matters. A "revitalized Atlantic partnership," as Dr. Kissinger appeared to view the matter, would evidently require some considerable revision of European attitudes in the direction of a greater "spirit of reciprocity."

While thoroughly understandable from an American point of view, such an approach was perhaps less perfectly attuned to the attitudes that currently prevailed in Western Europe. To European

---

[6]News conference, Jan. 31, in *Presidential Documents*, vol. 9 (1973), p. 107.
[7]*Documents, 1962*, pp. 225-6.

eyes, the old-established notion of "Atlantic partnership" had been increasingly obscured of late years by the vision of European construction that had inspired the recent enlargement of the Communities. Only six months previously, on October 19-20, 1972, the heads of state and government of "the nine" had met in Paris at a Community "summit" whose chief result had been a declared intent "to transform before the end of the present decade the whole complex of their relations into a European union."[8] Such a plan, to the European mind, had rather more to recommend it than the signature of some new and mysterious contract with the United States.

West German Chancellor Willy Brandt was the first allied leader to visit the United States in the aftermath of the Kissinger speech. (He had been preceded in February by Britain's Prime Minister Edward Heath, and in April by Italy's Giulio Andreotti.)[9] In Washington on May 1-2, the German leader did not commit himself to the details of the Kissinger plan, although he assured the President that his government would be prepared to take part in "an open and comprehensive discussion concerning the nature of a balanced partnership between the uniting Western Europe and the United States."[10] But France, under the influence of President Georges Pompidou and Foreign Minister Michel Jobert, had shown itself far less inclined to favor American initiatives. No formal communiqué was issued, and there was no public reference to the "new Atlantic charter," when President Pompidou, accompanied by Messrs. Jobert and Giscard d'Estaing, held a two-day meeting with President Nixon, Dr. Kissinger, and Secretary Shultz in Reykjavik, Iceland, on May 31-June 1.[11] M. Jobert, in particular, would continue to stand out as a keen opponent of American-inspired "Atlanticist" concepts.

From the standpoint of the general public, meanwhile, the notion of a "new Atlantic charter" had rapidly been lost to sight amid an avalanche of new developments relating in part to Watergate and in part to various phases of the East-West relationship.

---

[8]*Keesing's*, p. 25541.
[9]*Presidential Documents*, vol. 9 (1973), pp. 112-16, 385-6, and 388-9; also in *Bulletin*, vol. 68 (1973), pp. 269-74 and 603-6.
[10]Joint statement, May 2, in *Presidential Documents*, vol. 9 (1973), p. 447.
[11]Details in same, pp. 719-25; for further developments see Chapter 17 at note 12.

(21) *"The Year of Europe": Address by Dr. Kissinger before the*
annual meeting of the Associated Press Editors, New York,
April 23, 1973.[12]

This year has been called the year of Europe, but not because
Europe was less important in 1972 or in 1969. The alliance between
the United States and Europe has been the cornerstone of all postwar foreign policy. It provided the political framework for
American engagements in Europe and marked the definitive end of
U.S. isolationism. It insured the sense of security that allowed
Europe to recover from the devastation of the war. It reconciled
former enemies. It was the stimulus for an unprecedented endeavor
in European unity and the principal means to forge the common
policies that safeguarded Western security in an era of prolonged
tension and confrontation. Our values, our goals, and our basic interests are most closely identified with those of Europe.

Nineteen seventy-three is the year of Europe because the era that
was shaped by decisions of a generation ago is ending. The success
of those policies has produced new realities that require new approaches:

—The revival of western Europe is an established fact, as is
the historic success of its movement toward economic
unification.

—The East-West strategic military balance has shifted from
American preponderance to near-equality, bringing with it the
necessity for a new understanding of the requirements of our
common security.

—Other areas of the world have grown in importance. Japan
has emerged as a major power center. In many fields, "Atlantic" solutions to be viable must include Japan.

—We are in a period of relaxation of tensions. But as the rigid
divisions of the past two decades diminish, new assertions of
national identity and national rivalry emerge.

—Problems have arisen, unforeseen a generation ago, which
require new types of cooperative action. Insuring the supply of
energy for industrialized nations is an example.

These factors have produced a dramatic transformation of the
psychological climate in the West—a change which is the most
profound current challenge to Western statesmanship. In Europe, a
new generation to whom war and its dislocations are not personal
experiences takes stability for granted. But it is less committed to

[12]Text from *Bulletin*, vol. 68 (1973), pp. 593-8.

the unity that made peace possible and to the effort required to maintain it. In the United States, decades of global burdens have fostered, and the frustrations of the war in Southeast Asia have accentuated, a reluctance to sustain global involvements on the basis of preponderant American responsibility.

Inevitably this period of transition will have its strains. There have been complaints in America that Europe ignores its wider responsibilities in pursuing economic self-interest too one-sidedly and that Europe is not carrying its fair share of the burden of the common defense. There have been complaints in Europe that America is out to divide Europe economically, or to desert Europe militarily, or to bypass Europe diplomatically. Europeans appeal to the United States to accept their independence and their occasionally severe criticism of us in the name of Atlantic unity, while at the same time they ask for a veto on our independent policies—also in the name of Atlantic unity.

Our challenge is whether a unity forged by a common perception of danger can draw new purpose from shared positive aspirations.

If we permit the Atlantic partnership to atrophy, or to erode through neglect, carelessness, or mistrust, we risk what has been achieved and we shall miss our historic opportunity for even greater achievement.

In the forties and fifties the task was economic reconstruction and security against the danger of attack; the West responded with courage and imagination. Today the need is to make the Atlantic relationship as dynamic a force in building a new structure of peace, less geared to crisis and more conscious of opportunities, drawing its inspirations from its goals rather than its fears. The Atlantic nations must join in a fresh act of creation equal to that undertaken by the postwar generation of leaders of Europe and America.

This is why the President is embarking on a personal and direct approach to the leaders of western Europe. In his discussions with the heads of government of Britain, Italy, the Federal Republic of Germany, and France, the Secretary General of NATO, and other European leaders, it is the President's purpose to lay the basis for a new era of creativity in the West.

His approach will be to deal with Atlantic problems comprehensively. The political, military, and economic issues in Atlantic relations are linked by reality, not by our choice nor for the tactical purpose of trading one off against the other. The solutions will not be worthy of the opportunity if left to technicians. They must be addressed at the highest level.

In 1972 the President transformed relations with our adversaries to lighten the burdens of fear and suspicion.

In 1973 we can gain the same sense of historical achievement by reinvigorating shared ideals and common purposes with our friends.

The United States proposes to its Atlantic partners that by the time the President travels to Europe toward the end of the year we will have worked out a new Atlantic charter setting the goals for the future, a blueprint that:

—Builds on the past without becoming its prisoner.
—Deals with the problems our success has created.
—Creates for the Atlantic nations a new relationship in whose progress Japan can share.

We ask our friends in Europe, Canada, and ultimately Japan to join us in this effort.

This is what we mean by the year of Europe.

Problems in Atlantic Relationships

The problems in Atlantic relationships are real. They have arisen in part because during the fifties and sixties the Atlantic community organized itself in different ways in the many different dimensions of its common enterprise.

—In economic relations the European Community has increasingly stressed its regional personality; the United States at the same time must act as part of, and be responsible for, a wider international trade and monetary system. We must reconcile these two perspectives.

—In our collective defense we are still organized on the principle of unity and integration, but in radically different strategic conditions. The full implications of this change have yet to be faced.

—Diplomacy is the subject of frequent consultations but is essentially being conducted by traditional nation-states. The United States has global interests and responsibilities. Our European allies have regional interests. These are not necessarily in conflict, but in the new era neither are they automatically identical.

In short, we deal with each other regionally and even competitively on an integrated basis in defense, and as nation-states in diplomacy. When the various collective institutions were rudimentary, the potential inconsistency in their modes of operation was not a problem. But after a generation of evolution and with the new weight and strength of our allies, the various parts of the construction are not always in harmony and sometimes obstruct each other.

If we want to foster unity we can no longer ignore these problems. The Atlantic nations must find a solution for the management of their diversity to serve the common objectives which underlie their unity. We can no longer afford to pursue national or regional self-interest without a unifying framework. We cannot hold together if each country or region asserts its autonomy whenever it is to its benefit and invokes unity to curtail the independence of others.

We must strike a new balance between self-interest and the common interest. We must identify interests and positive values beyond security in order to engage once again the commitment of peoples and parliaments. We need a shared view of the world we seek to build.

Agenda for the Future

Economic

No element of American postwar policy has been more consistent than our support of European unity. We encouraged it at every turn. We knew that a united Europe would be a more independent partner. But we assumed, perhaps too uncritically, that our common interests would be assured by our long history of cooperation. We expected that political unity would follow economic integration and that a unified Europe working cooperatively would ease many of our international burdens.

It is clear that many of these expectations are not being fulfilled.

We and Europe have benefited from European economic integration. Increased trade within Europe has stimulated the growth of European economies and the expansion of trade in both directions across the Atlantic.

But we cannot ignore the fact that Europe's economic success and its transformation from a recipient of our aid to a strong competitor has produced a certain amount of friction. There have been turbulence and a sense of rivalry in international monetary relations.

In trade, the natural economic weight of a market of 250 million people has pressed other states to seek special arrangements to protect their access to it. The prospect of a closed trading system embracing the European Community and a growing number of other nations in Europe, the Mediterranean, and Africa appears to be at the expense of the United States and other nations which are excluded. In agriculture, where the United States has a comparative advantage, we are particularly concerned that Community protective policies may restrict access for our products.

This divergence comes at a time when we are experiencing a chronic and growing deficit in our balance of payments and protectionist pressures of our own. Europeans in turn question our investment policies and doubt our continued commitment to their economic unity.

The gradual accumulation of sometimes petty, sometimes major, economic disputes must be ended and be replaced by a determined commitment on both sides of the Atlantic to find cooperative solutions.

The United States will continue to support the unification of Europe. We have no intention of destroying what we worked so hard to help build. For us, European unity is what it has always been: not an end in itself but a means to the strengthening of the West. We shall continue to support European unity as a component of a larger Atlantic partnership.

This year we begin comprehensive trade negotiations with Europe as well as with Japan. We shall also continue to press the effort to reform the monetary system so that it promotes stability rather than constant disruptions. A new equilibrium must be achieved in trade and monetary relations.[13]

We see these negotiations as a historic opportunity for positive achievement. They must engage the top political leaders, for they require above all a commitment of political will. If they are left solely to the experts the inevitable competitiveness of economic interests will dominate the debate. The influence of pressure groups and special interests will become pervasive. There will be no overriding sense of direction. There will be no framework for the generous solutions or mutual concessions essential to preserve a vital Atlantic partnership.

It is the responsibility of national leaders to insure that economic negotiations serve larger political purposes. They must recognize that economic rivalry, if carried on without restraint, will in the end damage other relationships.

The United States intends to adopt a broad political approach that does justice to our overriding political interest in an open and balanced trading order with both Europe and Japan. This is the spirit of the President's trade bill[14] and of his speech to the International Monetary Fund last year.[15] It will guide our strategy in the trade and monetary talks. We see these negotiations not as a test of strength, but as a test of joint statesmanship.

[13]Cf. Chapter 19.
[14]Cf. Document 14.
[15]AFR, 1972, pp. 529-34.

Defense

Atlantic unity has always come most naturally in the field of defense. For many years the military threats to Europe were unambiguous, the requirements to meet them were generally agreed on both sides of the Atlantic, and America's responsibility was preeminent and obvious. Today we remain united on the objective of collective defense, but we face the new challenge of maintaining it under radically changed strategic conditions and with the new opportunity of enhancing our security through negotiated reductions of forces.

The West no longer holds the nuclear predominance that permitted it in the fifties and sixties to rely almost solely on a strategy of massive nuclear retaliation. Because under conditions of nuclear parity such a strategy invites mutual suicide, the alliance must have other choices. The collective ability to resist attack in western Europe by means of flexible responses has become central to a rational strategy and crucial to the maintenance of peace. For this reason, the United States has maintained substantial conventional forces in Europe and our NATO allies have embarked on a significant effort to modernize and improve their own military establishments.

While the Atlantic alliance is committed to a strategy of flexible response in principle, the requirements of flexibility are complex and expensive. Flexibility by its nature requires sensitivity to new conditions and continual consultation among the allies to respond to changing circumstances. And we must give substance to the defense posture that our strategy defines. Flexible response cannot be simply a slogan wrapped around the defense structure that emerges from lowest-common-denominator compromises driven by domestic considerations. It must be seen by ourselves and by potential adversaries as a credible, substantial, and rational posture of defense.

A great deal remains to be accomplished to give reality to the goal of flexible response:

—There are deficiencies in important areas of our conventional defense.
—There are still unresolved issues in our doctrine; for example, on the crucial question of the role of tactical nuclear weapons.
—There are anomalies in NATO deployments as well as in its logistics structure.

To maintain the military balance that has insured stability in Europe for 25 years, the alliance has no choice but to address these needs and to reach an agreement on our defense requirements. This task is all the more difficult because the lessening of tensions has given new impetus to arguments that it is safe to begin reducing forces unilaterally. And unbridled economic competition can sap the impulse for common defense. All governments of the Western alliance face a major challenge in educating their peoples to the realities of security in the 1970's.

The President has asked me to state that America remains committed to doing its fair share in Atlantic defense. He is adamantly opposed to unilateral withdrawals of U.S. forces from Europe. But we owe to our peoples a rational defense posture, at the safest minimum size and cost, with burdens equitably shared. This is what the President believes must result from the dialogue with our allies in 1973.

When this is achieved, the necessary American forces will be maintained in Europe, not simply as a hostage to trigger our nuclear weapons but as an essential contribution to an agreed and intelligible structure of Western defense. This, too, will enable us to engage our adversaries intelligently in negotiations for mutual balanced reductions.

In the next few weeks the United States will present to NATO the product of our own preparations for the negotiations on mutual balanced force reductions which will begin this year.[16] We hope that it will be a contribution to a broader dialogue on security. Our approach is designed not from the point of view of special American interests, but of general alliance interests. Our position will reflect the President's view that these negotiations are not a subterfuge to withdraw U.S. forces regardless of consequences. No formula for reductions is defensible, whatever its domestic appeal or political rationale, if it undermines security.

Our objective in the dialogue on defense is a new consensus on security, addressed to new conditions and to the hopeful new possibilities of effective arms limitations.

Diplomacy

We have entered a truly remarkable period of East-West diplomacy. The last two years have produced an agreement on Berlin,[17] a treaty between West Germany and the U.S.S.R.,[18] a strategic arms limitation agreement,[19] the beginning of negotiations

---

[16]Cf. Chapter 13 at note 5.

[17]Cf. note 2 above.

[18]Text in *Documents, 1970*, pp. 105-6; see further *AFR, 1971*, p. 164; same, *1972*, p. 148.

[19]Same, pp. 90-101.

on a European Security Conference and on mutual balanced force reductions,[20] and a series of significant practical bilateral agreements between Western and Eastern countries, including a dramatic change in bilateral relations between the United States and the U.S.S.R.[21] These were not isolated actions, but steps on a course charted in 1969 and carried forward as a collective effort. Our approach to détente stressed that negotiations had to be concrete, not atmospheric, and that concessions should be reciprocal. We expect to carry forward the policy of relaxation of tensions on this basis.

Yet this very success has created its own problems. There is an increasing uneasiness—all the more insidious for rarely being made explicit—that superpower diplomacy might sacrifice the interests of traditional allies and other friends. Where our allies' interests have been affected by our bilateral negotiations, as in the talks on the limitation of strategic arms, we have been scrupulous in consulting them; where our allies are directly involved, as in the negotiations on mutual balanced force reductions, our approach is to proceed jointly on the basis of agreed positions. Yet some of our friends in Europe have seemed unwilling to accord America the same trust in our motives as they received from us or to grant us the same tactical flexibility that they employed in pursuit of their own policies. The United States is now often taken to task for flexibility where we used to be criticized for rigidity.

All of this underlines the necessity to articulate a clear set of common objectives together with our allies. Once that is accomplished, it will be quite feasible, indeed desirable, for the several allies to pursue these goals with considerable tactical flexibility. If we agree on common objectives it will become a technical question whether a particular measure is pursued in a particular forum or whether to proceed bilaterally or multilaterally. Then those allies who seek reassurances of America's commitment will find it not in verbal reaffirmations of loyalty, but in an agreed framework of purpose.

We do not need to agree on all policies. In many areas of the world our approaches will differ, especially outside of Europe. But we do require an understanding of what should be done jointly and of the limits we should impose on the scope of our autonomy.

We have no intention of buying an illusory tranquillity at the expense of our friends. The United States will never knowingly sacrifice the interests of others. But the perception of common interests is not automatic; it requires constant redefinition. The relaxation of tensions to which we are committed makes allied

[20]Cf. above at note 3.
[21]*AFR, 1972*, pp. 114-27.

cohesion indispensable yet more difficult. We must insure that the momentum of détente is maintained by common objectives rather than by drift, escapism, or complacency.

America's Contribution

The agenda I have outlined here is not an American prescription, but an appeal for a joint effort of creativity. The historic opportunity for this generation is to build a new structure of international relations for the decades ahead. A revitalized Atlantic partnership is indispensable for it. The United States is prepared to make its contribution:

—We will continue to support European unity. Based on the principles of partnership, we will make concessions to its further growth. We will expect to be met in a spirit of reciprocity.

—We will not disengage from our solemn commitments to our allies. We will maintain our forces and not withdraw from Europe unilaterally. In turn, we expect from each ally a fair share of the common effort for the common defense.

—We shall continue to pursue the relaxation of tensions with our adversaries on the basis of concrete negotiations in the common interest. We welcome the participation of our friends in a constructive East-West dialogue.

—We will never consciously injure the interests of our friends in Europe or in Asia. We expect in return that their policies will take seriously our interests and our responsibilities.

—We are prepared to work cooperatively on new common problems we face. Energy, for example, raises the challenging issues of assurance of supply, impact of oil revenues on international currency stability, the nature of common political and strategic interests, and long-range relations of oil-consuming to oil-producing countries.[22] This could be an area of competition; it should be an area of collaboration.

—Just as Europe's autonomy is not an end in itself, so the Atlantic community cannot be an exclusive club. Japan must be a principal partner in our common enterprise.

We hope that our friends in Europe will meet us in this spirit. We have before us the example of the great accomplishments of the past decades and the opportunity to match and dwarf them. This is the task ahead. This is how, in the 1970's, the Atlantic nations can truly serve our peoples and the cause of peace.

[22]Cf. Document 26.

9. "SOMETHING IS ROTTEN . . ."

Since the conclusion of his initial year in office, it had been President Nixon's custom to submit to Congress and the nation an annual report on the progress of America's foreign relations and the ramifications of its current foreign policy. Prepared under the supervision of Dr. Kissinger's National Security Council staff and published under the general title of *U.S. Foreign Policy for the 1970's*,[1] these "State of the World" reports quite naturally cast a favorable light on the administration's achievements but also offered an invaluable analysis of the country's international situation as seen by its highest authorities. In their well-rounded examination of the military and economic as well as the political aspects of the national foreign relations, they tended to overshadow the more detailed reports on State Department activities made public since 1971 by Secretary Rogers.[2]

The fourth of President Nixon's "State of the World" reports, subtitled *Shaping a Durable Peace*, appeared on May 3, 1973, approximately three months later than usual. Such a delay was not abnormal in the complex, increasingly congested world of the 1970s. But though the content of this prestigious document contained no hint that anything was amiss in the American situation, it made its appearance at a moment of national stress in which both foreign and domestic affairs were inescapably involved. Since early in the spring, successive revelations bearing upon the Watergate scandal and associated "White House horrors" had cast a deepening shadow upon the presidential office and, not least, upon the chief executive himself.

The conviction of the original Watergate culprits by Judge Sirica's court on January 30 had failed to end the speculation about possible higher-level involvement in the Watergate break-in and other improper campaign activities, including the possible mis-

[1]See Appendix under *Nixon Report*.
[2]See Appendix under *Rogers Report*.

191

handling of campaign finances by persons high up in the Nixon organization. Judge Sirica himself suggested, shortly after the conclusion of the Watergate trial, that the full story had not yet come out and that a Senate select committee being set up under the chairmanship of Democratic Senator Sam J. Ervin, Jr., of North Carolina might be more successful in getting to the bottom of the matter.

That the records of the Nixon administration abounded in still undisclosed anomalies became increasingly evident over the next few weeks. A *Time* magazine story, initially denied but later substantially confirmed by the White House, described the wiretapping, under circumstances of questionable legality, of various officials and journalists in a campaign against security leaks initiated early in 1969. Hearings on the designation of L. Patrick Gray, 3rd, to succeed the late J. Edgar Hoover as Director of the Federal Bureau of Investigation (FBI) produced new indications that normal law-enforcement procedures had been short-circuited in the Watergate case, and ultimately led to Mr. Gray's resignation as Acting FBI Director. Judge Sirica, on March 23, made public a letter from convicted Watergate defendant James W. McCord, Jr., in which the latter flatly asserted that perjury had been committed at the trial and that the defendants had been under political pressure to plead guilty and protect the "higher-ups."

The potential gravity of the situation would seem to have been first brought home to President Nixon on March 21, when presidential Counsel John Dean directed his attention to the "cancer" that was developing within the presidency and could result in the indictment of prominent White House figures as well as that of John N. Mitchell, the former Attorney-General and later director of the Committee for the Reelection of the President. Any White House hope of "stonewalling" the investigation was undercut soon afterward by the decision of Mr. Dean and Jeb Stuart Magruder, Mr. Mitchell's deputy at the reelection committee, to tell what they knew to Federal prosecutors. By April 17, President Nixon was advising the press that in view of "serious charges" that had come to his attention, he had on March 21 begun "intensive new inquiries into this whole matter." "Real progress" had been made "in finding the truth," the President stated. The judicial process was moving ahead, and he would aid it "in all appropriate ways."[3]

Mr. Nixon's personal position deteriorated further over the next fortnight, primarily as the result of disclosures concerning the so-called White House "plumbers," the special investigations unit set up at the President's direction in June 1971 at a time when the top

[3]*Presidential Documents*, vol. 9 (1973), p. 387.

secret "Pentagon Papers" made available by Dr. Daniel Ellsberg were being published in *The New York Times* and other newspapers. Directed by Egil Krogh, Jr., in collaboration with David R. Young, Jr., and operating under the general direction of John D. Ehrlichman, this group had planned and supervised the burglary carried out on the night of September 3-4, 1971, at the Beverly Hills office of Dr. Ellsberg's psychiatrist, Dr. Lewis J. Fielding, with the participation of E. Howard Hunt, Jr., G. Gordon Liddy, and other CIA-connected individuals who were subsequently involved in the Watergate break-in. Now, in 1973, Dr. Ellsberg and an associate, Anthony J. Russo, Jr., were on trial in the Los Angeles courtroom of Federal Judge W. Matthew Byrne, Jr., on charges growing out of the Pentagon Papers disclosure. Belatedly advised of the Fielding burglary, Judge Byrne on April 27 revealed the story in open court and ordered an investigation of possible violations of the defendants' rights.

President Nixon, in a nationally televised discussion of Watergate on April 30,[4] just a few hours before his scheduled meeting with Chancellor Brandt, conceded for the first time that there had been "an effort to conceal the facts both from the public, from you, and from me." Ultimate responsibility for the Watergate incident was his, the President admitted, although he insisted that he personally had been too intent on "bringing peace to America, peace to the world" to involve himself directly in 1972 campaign operations. In what he described as a necessary move in the restoration of public confidence, Mr. Nixon revealed that he had gone so far as to accept the resignations of Messrs. Haldeman and Ehrlichman—"two of the finest public servants it has been my privilege to know"—though "with no implication whatever of personal wrongdoing on their part." Attorney-General Richard G. Kleindienst was also stepping aside, the President disclosed, because of his close association with some of those involved in the case; and Mr. Dean had "also resigned." Defense Secretary Elliot Richardson would now take over the Justice Department, Mr. Nixon revealed, and would be authorized to name a special prosecutor for Watergate matters.[5] The Watergate affair, the President stated in conclusion, had been claiming far too much of his own time and attention, and would not be permitted to en-

---

[4]Same, pp. 433-8.

[5]CIA Director Schlesinger was later named to succeed Richardson as Secretary of Defense, and was himself succeeded at CIA by William E. Colby, previously Deputy CIA Director for Operations. In June, the White House further disclosed that Mr. Ehrlichman's functions would be taken over by former Defense Secretary Melvin R. Laird as Counsellor to the President, while Mr. Haldeman's responsibilities would be assumed by General Alexander M. Haig, Jr., as Assistant to the President.

croach further on the discharge of his official responsibilities.
"There is vital work to be done toward our goal of a lasting structure of peace in the world—work that cannot wait, work that I
must do."

The diplomatic challenges to be faced in the coming weeks and
months were analyzed more fully in the "State of the World" report made public three days later, on Thursday, May 3, 1973. "We
cannot rest on our laurels now," Mr. Nixon insisted in the remarks
he recorded for radio broadcast as the report was released
(Document 22). "1973 and the years to come will test whether we
will go forward into a new era of international relations, or whether
we will go backward into preoccupation with ourselves, thus
allowing the world to slip back into its age-old patterns of conflict."

Not quite buried in the President's 234-page treatise was a frank
acknowledgment that the three-month-old peace in Vietnam which
had been so praised in January still remained "fragile"; that compliance with the cease-fire had been "spotty"; and that Hanoi, not
content with sending troops and military supplies into South Viet-
nam in "blatant" disregard of the cease-fire, continued its military
activities in Laos and Cambodia as well. "Whether this is a prelude
to another offensive is not clear," the President stated. "What is
clear is that it must cease. We have told Hanoi, privately and
publicly, that we will not tolerate violation of the Agreement."[6]

The President also had a word of warning against the tendency to
national complacency. "Detente is not the same as lasting peace,"
he wrote. "And peace does not guarantee tranquility or mean the
end of contention. The world will hold perils for as far ahead as we
can see." And yet, he suggested, the record of the past four years
gave grounds for abundant satisfaction, when measured against
"the challenges we faced and the goals we set. . . . During the next
four years—with the help of others—we shall continue building an
international structure which could silence the sounds of war for
the remainder of this century."[7]

However confident his expectations for the long-term future, the
President's hopes of putting Watergate behind him were swiftly
frustrated as new sensations succeeded one another with
frightening rapidity. On May 4, a Federal grand jury in Orlando,
Florida, indicted alleged "dirty tricks" specialist Donald H. Segretti in connection with an attempted "smear" of two aspirants to the

[6]*Nixon Report, 1973*, p. 65; see also Chapter 2 at note 7.
[7]Same, pp. 233-4.

1972 Democratic presidential nomination.[8] On May 10, another Federal grand jury in New York indicted two former Nixon cabinet officers and 1972 campaign functionaries, former Attorney-General Mitchell and former Secretary of Commerce Maurice Stans, on charges of fraud, conspiracy, and obstruction of justice in the handling of an unreported $200,000 campaign contribution made by financier Robert Vesco while his activities were under investigation by the Securities and Exchange Commission.[9]

Other blows rained down upon the administration with the backfiring of its efforts to ensure conviction and exemplary punishment in the Pentagon Papers case. Dr. Ellsberg and his co-defendant were unconditionally freed on May 11 when Judge Byrne dismissed the charges against them, citing numerous prosecution irregularities including the withholding of certain evidence obtained by wiretapping of a third party. New problems were to arise for President Nixon and for Dr. Kissinger, whose noninvolvement in any administration improprieties had thus far been thought axiomatic, by reason of the discovery of the missing wiretap evidence in Mr. Ehrlichman's White House safe. Included in this cache, it was disclosed on May 14, were records of FBI wiretapping of the telephones of four newsmen and thirteen government employees between May 1969 and February 1971 "in an effort to pinpoint responsibility for leaks of highly sensitive and classified information which, in the opinion of those charged with conducting our foreign policy, were compromising the nation's effectiveness in negotiations and other dealings with foreign powers."[10]

Further disclosures about the taps, the legality and utility of which have since been variously estimated, was to indicate that the targets included several members of Dr. Kissinger's own National Security Council staff, notably Dr. Morton H. Halperin, whose telephone was still being tapped months after he left government service. Dr. Kissinger, avowing that he had been greatly concerned about the leakage of classified information—some of it un-

[8]Sentenced in Nov. 1973 to six months' imprisonment after pleading guilty to charges of distributing illegal campaign literature, Segretti later became the chief prosecution witness against Dwight L. Chapin, his White House supervisor and the President's former appointments secretary. Chapin, in turn, was ultimately sentenced to 18 months' imprisonment following his conviction of lying to a Federal grand jury investigating Segretti's activities, but was released on parole on Apr. 2, 1976.
[9]Both defendants pleaded innocent and were subsequently acquitted, though Mitchell, together with Haldeman, Ehrlichman, and former Assistant Attorney General Robert C. Mardian, was later found guilty of conspiracy, obstruction of justice, and perjury in the Watergate cover-up trial that ended January 1, 1975.
[10]Statement by Acting FBI Director William D. Ruckelshaus, May 14, in *New York Times*, May 15, 1973.

doubtedly relating to such ultrasecret matters as the clandestine U.S. bombing of parts of neutral Cambodia—readily confirmed that he had been shown summaries of some of the taps, although he indicated that he had not requested or specifically approved them in advance.[11] Persistent questioning of this disclaimer by persons with knowledge of the matter was to haunt its author at various times in 1973 and later.

The raising of national security issues had meanwhile added a new dimension to the Watergate investigation, which entered a potentially climactic phase with the opening of the televised Senate hearings on May 17 and the induction of Professor Archibald Cox as Watergate Special Prosecutor. National security had also gained new prominence in President Nixon's public utterances, among them a noteworthy address at Norfolk Naval Base on Armed Forces Day, May 19 (**Document 23**). Never one to underrate the animosity of his critics, the chief executive now seemed to place even heavier reliance on those who sympathized most audibly with his concern for a "strong America"; his unwillingness to let the United States become "the second strongest nation in the world"; his disinclination to "start running now" in Southeast Asia or anywhere else; and his insistence that North Vietnam desist from a course of action which, he intimated, now threatened "systematically" to destroy the peace settlement reached in Paris.

Appeals to patriotism, however, no longer sufficed to shore up Mr. Nixon's shaken position. May 22 brought still another Nixon statement which dealt both with Watergate and with the various "national security" activities that had become entangled with the case—with the result, the President asserted, that further sensitive national security information was now in danger of being compromised. Repeating his categorical denial of any personal involvement in the Watergate burglary, the cover-up, the Fielding break-in, or any other improper activities, the President now offered a circumstantial if still incomplete account of his recollections of the 1969 wiretaps; of the abortive 1970 "Huston plan" for expanded domestic intelligence operations; of the establishment of the Special Investigations Unit (plumbers) in 1971; and of his attempts in 1972 and subsequently to promote the Watergate investigation while, at the same time, avoiding the exposure of "national security" operations undertaken either by the plumbers or by the CIA. The only restriction placed on the Watergate investigation, said Mr. Nixon in an assertion that he would explicitly retract a few days before his resignation in August 1973, had been designed "to ensure that the investigation of the break-in not ex-

[11]*New York Times*, May 15, 1973; see further Chapter 17 at note 8.

pose either an unrelated covert operation of the CIA or the activities of the White House investigations unit.''[12]

New evidence of presidential agitation was offered at a reception
for returned prisoners of war that took place at the State Department on May 24.[13] Repeating much of what he had said at Norfolk,
Mr. Nixon added an emotional plea for the respect of diplomatic
confidentiality. "And let me say," he declared in obvious reference
to the Ellsberg case, "I think it is time in this country to quit
making national heroes of those who steal secrets and publish them
in the newspapers." By proving that they could "tough it
through," the President asserted, the members of his audience had
helped to "reinstill faith where there was doubt before," and to ensure that America, as the richest and strongest country in the
world, would continue to "face up to our world responsibilities"
and to exhibit "the faith, the patriotism, the willingness to lead in
this critical period." Left unexamined was the question how far
other nations, under existing circumstances, would be disposed to
follow an American lead if one were given.

(22) *"United States Foreign Policy for the 1970's—Shaping a
Durable Peace": Remarks by President Nixon on trans-
mitting his Fourth Annual Report to Congress on United
States Foreign Policy, May 3, 1973.*[14]

Good evening.
The year 1972 was a time of more dramatic progress toward a
lasting peace in the world than any other year since the end of
World War II. But as encouraging as that progress was, we cannot
rest on our laurels now.

1973 and the years to come will test whether America will go

---

[12]*Presidential Documents*, vol. 9 (1973), pp. 693-8. The "unrelated covert operation
of the CIA," at first assumed to have been related to the "Bay of Pigs" invasion of
Cuba in 1961, was subsequently shown to have involved the "laundering" of campaign funds in Mexico prior to their use in financing clandestine activities. In a statement released Aug. 5, 1974, President Nixon contradicted his May 22 assertion in
the following terms: "The June 23 [1972] tapes clearly show . . . that at the time I
gave those instructions I also discussed the political aspects of the situation, and that
I was aware of the advantages this course of action would have with respect to
limiting possible public exposure of involvement by persons connected with the
reelection committee" (*Presidential Documents*, vol. 10[1974], pp. 1008-9).
[13]*Presidential Documents*, vol. 9 (1973), pp. 702-7; excerpts in *Bulletin*, vol. 68
(1973), pp. 930-36.
[14]Text from *Presidential Documents*, vol. 9 (1973), pp. 449-50.

forward into a new era of international relations, or whether we will go backward into preoccupation with ourselves, thus allowing the world to slip back into its age-old patterns of conflict.

If we meet this test, the rewards can be great. If we do not, a priceless opportunity may be tragically lost.

It is against this background of hope and danger that I have today submitted to the Congress my fourth annual report on United States foreign policy.[15] Tonight I want to share with you some highlights of that report.

Since the time of my last foreign policy review,[16] we have witnessed historic achievements on a number of fronts. After more than two decades of hostility and isolation, we have begun an entirely new relationship with the People's Republic of China when I visited Peking last year.[17]

Travel, exchanges, and trade between our two countries are accelerating. This month we shall open liaison offices in each other's capitals, headed by distinguished senior diplomats.[18]

The United States and the Soviet Union have taken a decisive turn away from the confrontation of the past quarter century. At our meeting last May, the Soviet leaders and I established a set of basic principles to govern our relations.[19]

We signed a series of cooperative agreements, and we laid the foundation for major increases in trade.[20] Most importantly, we reached an unprecedented agreement limiting the nuclear arsenals that have haunted the world for a generation.[21]

In the early months of 1973, intensive negotiations and a decisive military policy brought us at last to a just settlement of the long and costly war in Vietnam.[22] We achieved our fundamental objectives—a cease-fire, the return of our prisoners, a commitment to account for those missing in action, the honorable withdrawal of our forces, and the right of the people of South Vietnam to determine their own political future.

But the peace in Vietnam and the parallel peace in Laos remain fragile because of North Vietnam's continued violations of the peace agreement. A cease-fire still has not been reached in Cambodia. We earnestly hope these problems can be solved at the conference table.[23] We will not turn our back on our friends and allies

[15]*Nixon Report, 1973* (for full citation see Appendix).
[16]*Nixon Report, 1972*; cf. *AFR, 1972*, pp. 11-15.
[17]Same, pp. 307-18.
[18]Cf. Document 12.
[19]*AFR, 1972*, pp. 75-8.
[20]Same, pp. 66-75.
[21]Same, pp. 90-101.
[22]Cf. Chapter 2.
[23]Cf. Document 30.

while Hanoi makes a mockery of its promise to help keep the peace.

During recent months, with less fanfare than in negotiations with our adversaries, but with no less dedication, we have also been working closely with our Atlantic and Pacific partners. In addition, we have moved toward major reform of the international economic system, although the process of readjustment is still marked by crises.

We have continued to share more responsibilities with our friends under the Nixon Doctrine. In sum, recalling the challenges we faced and the goals we set at the outset of this Administration, all Americans can take satisfaction in the record of the recent past.

But our progress in the early 1970's has been more marked in reducing tensions than in restructuring partnerships. That is why we must make 1973 not only the "Year of Europe," as some have called it, but also the year of renewal for all of America's alliances and friendships.

In this spirit, we shall cooperate with our European friends to forge even stronger partnerships, cemented by a new articulation of the goals we share.[24]

There will be the closest collaboration on such major issues as the mutual and balanced reduction of forces in Europe, the European Security Conference, and the current round of strategic arms limitation talks. Before the end of the year, I will visit our Atlantic allies.

We shall also continue to attach the highest priority to our relations with our major Pacific ally, Japan. Prime Minister [Kakuei] Tanaka will visit the United States this summer for talks on this subject.[25]

We shall work with all concerned nations to create a stable monetary system and to promote freer trade. To make this possible, I again urge the Congress to pass promptly the crucial trade legislation I submitted last month.[26]

We are also seeking in 1973 to further the positive momentum in our relations with the Soviet Union. I look forward to welcoming the Soviet leadership to this country later in the year.[27]

Dr. Kissinger leaves tonight for Moscow to prepare for that visit.[28] New U.S.-Soviet talks are already underway aiming for further agreements on controlling nuclear weapons.

We shall also continue this year to build our promising new relationship with the People's Republic of China.

[24]Cf. Chapter 8.
[25]Cf. Document 37.
[26]Document 14.
[27]Cf. Document 33.
[28]Cf. note 1 to Chapter 12.

We shall pay particular attention to our neighbors in this hemisphere. Secretary Rogers is soon to embark on a trip to Latin America,[29] and I look forward to a similar journey myself during my second term.

We shall do our part with others to reduce tensions and increase opportunity in such areas as the Middle East, South Asia, and Africa.

We shall continue building new partnerships of shared responsibilities with all our friends around the globe. Approval of the foreign aid bill which I sent to the Congress this week[30] will be fundamental to this effort.

Our policy in the world for the next 4 years can be summarized quite simply:

Where peace is newly planted, we shall work to make it thrive.

Where bridges have been built, we shall work to make them stronger.

Where friendships have endured, we shall work to make them grow.

We shall keep America strong, involved in the world, meeting the responsibilities which no other free nation is able to meet in building a structure of peace.

I said upon taking office more than 4 years ago that a nation could aspire to no higher honor than the title of peacemaker.[31] America has done much to earn that title since then. Let us resolve to do still more in the years ahead.

Thank you, and good evening.

(23) Armed Forces Day, 1973: Address by President Nixon at Norfolk Naval Base, Norfolk, Virginia, May 19, 1973.[32]

Admiral [Douglas C.] Plate, Governor [Linwood] Holton, Members of the Congressional Delegation, and all of the distinguished guests here on the platform, and all of the distinguished people in this audience today on Armed Forces Day:

Beginning on a personal note, let me say that this is a very proud day for Mrs. Nixon, for me, for America, and for the State of Virginia.

As you might imagine, there were a number of suggestions made by the Defense Department as to where the President should go on

---

[29]Cf. Chapter 5 at note 12.

[30]Cf. Document 24.

[31]*Documents, 1968-69*, p. 39.

[32]Text from *Presidential Documents*, vol. 9 (1973), pp. 685-90.

Armed Forces Day. We selected Norfolk, Virginia, for reasons that all of you understand, and the State of Virginia, it seems to me, is a very appropriate place for us to celebrate this day, because it was at Yorktown, just a few miles from here, that the Armed Forces of the then very young country, the new United States, won the final victory that secured American independence. That happened in Virginia.

It was on this soil, and in the waters offshore, that some of the most epic battles of the War Between the States were waged. It was from this great port of Norfolk that fighting ships of the United States Navy have sailed the seas to the wars in crises of this century, most recently when ships like the *Independence*, which is behind us here, the *Newport News*, both of which served in the Gulf of Tonkin, and when the *Guam* joined the 6th Fleet during the Jordanian crisis 3 years ago.

Virginia has proudly been the home of some of America's greatest military commanders, from Washington to Robert E. Lee to the late "Sunny Jim" Vandergrift of the Marines who was buried with the highest honors at Arlington just a few days ago.

And Virginia today has the distinction of having more of its Senators and Representatives serving on the two Armed Services Committees in Congress than any State of this Union except one. That delegation includes four members who are with us today: Senator [Harry F.] Byrd [Jr.], Senator [William Lloyd] Scott, Congressman [Robert W.] Daniel, and Congressman Bill Whitehurst.

You can see why Governor Holton always speaks with such pride of Virginia's great tradition in the field of the Armed Services.

Now, what does Armed Forces Day mean? Let us think now not just in terms of this ship, not just in terms of the men and women who are serving here in our Armed Forces, but in terms of America and the world, for the rulebook says that—I speak as one who many years ago was in the Navy. As a matter of fact, I had what I, looking back, found was a very, rather subordinate position. I was a lieutenant junior grade, and if you think a lieutenant junior grade is important, ask a Navy chief and he will tell you how unimportant he is.

Well, the rulebook says that the men and women who wear the uniform of our country are supposed to salute the Commander in Chief, and, of course, anyone who is elected President of the United States is the Commander in Chief. But on this day, I, as your Commander in Chief, salute you, each and every American who serves in our Army, our Navy, our Air Force, our Marine Corps, and our Coast Guard. Your courage, your steadfastness are the backbone of America's influence for peace around the world.

And I speak for all of America today—that is one of the great privileges of being President of this country—I speak for all of our fellow Americans when I say we owe you, those who serve in our Armed Forces, a debt of gratitude we can never fully repay.

For the first time in 12 years, we can observe Armed Forces Day with all of our fighting forces home from Vietnam and all of our courageous prisoners of war set free and here, back home in America.

There was and will continue to be for years to come much controversy about this longest war in America's history, but historians will record in the end that no military organization ever took on a more selfless task and completed it more honorably than the Armed Forces of the United States have done in the defense of 17 million people of South Vietnam. It was an honorable task, and they did it well, and we owe them a debt for how well they did it.

So today we pay a special, heartfelt tribute to all who made this achievement possible:

—to the more than 2 million men and women now serving in uniform;
—to the millions of veterans who have returned to civilian life;
—to those missing in action and those magnificent men who "toughed it out" in enemy prison camps; and above all
—to the memory of those who gave their lives for their country.

Today, we are thankful, too, for the strengths and the sacrifices of America's military families. And today we are reminded and we do remind those young Americans who are completing their high school or college education—and I speak to all of you all over the country, as you complete your high school or college education this spring—let me say to you the profession of serving this country in the new volunteer armed force of the 1970's offers a career in which any young man or woman can find great pride and satisfaction; be proud to wear the uniform of the United States of America.

Over the past several years, the chances for peace have grown immeasurably stronger, not only in Southeast Asia, but all over the world. We have brought this long war in Vietnam to an end. After a generation of hostility, the United States has opened a new relationship with the leaders of one-fourth of all the people who live in the world, the People's Republic of China. We have negotiated far-reaching agreements with our longtime adversary the Soviet Union, including the first limitation of strategic nuclear arms. We have begun revitalizing our Atlantic partnership with Western Europe and our Pacific partnership with Japan.

In the explosive Middle East, we averted a major crisis in 1970. We have helped to establish a cease-fire which is now well into its third year.

There are still enormously difficult problems there and in other parts of the world, but we have come a long way over these past 5 years toward building a structure of peace in the world—much further simply than ending a long war, but building a structure that will avoid other wars, and that is what every American wants and that is what we are working toward today.

I know that some might interpret the achievements I have just mentioned as the result of diplomacy, diplomacy from the President and the Secretary of State and others who have responsibility. But that interpretation would be incomplete.

The positions that a head of state or a diplomat puts forward at the conference table are only as good as the national strength that stands behind those positions.

So it has been the respect of other countries for our military strength that has been vital to our many negotiating successes during the past 4 years. And that same military strength helps secure our own security and that of our friends as we go forward with them in building new partnerships.

What I am saying to you today is that a large share of the credit for America's progress toward building a structure of peace in the world goes to you, the men and women in uniform. You are the peace forces of the United States, because without you, we couldn't have made the progress we have made. They would not have respected us, and without strength, we would not have the respect which leads to progress. Let's keep that strength and never let it down, because our further hopes for peace also rely on you.

This year, the year 1973, we face a series of negotiations even more significant than those of the year 1972, negotiations that will help to determine the future of international peace and cooperation for the rest of this century and beyond.

Every time I see an audience like this, I look at everybody—the older people, particularly the people that I see over here in wheelchairs, and also the young people, those that are so young, with all of their years ahead—and my greatest hope is, make this country a better country for them in the future, make this world a more peaceful world for them.

That is what leadership is all about. That is what we are dedicated to here today.

In just a few weeks, as you know, General Secretary Brezhnev of the Soviet Union will be in this country for a summit conference to build on the new negotiations that we have made in United States-Soviet relations in Moscow 1 year ago. We are ready to join with the Soviet leaders in efforts to seek additional ways to limit strategic nuclear arms, to expand mutually advantageous trade, and, together with our allies, to work toward mutual and balanced reductions of the level of armed forces in Central Europe.[33]

We are moving, as I have already indicated, toward normalization of our relations with the People's Republic of China, now that our two nations are opening permanent liaison offices in Peking and in Washington.

We are committed to wide-ranging talks with our friends in Europe and in Japan, with particular emphasis on placing the international economy on a more secure and equitable footing.

Because all of that is at stake in the critical period ahead, we must reject the well-intentioned but misguided suggestions that, because of the progress we have made toward peace, this is the time to slash America's defenses by billions of dollars.

There could be no more certain formula for failure in the negotiations that I have just talked about, no more dangerous invitation for other powers to break the peace, than for us to send the President of the United States to the conference table as the head of the second strongest nation in the world. Let that never happen in the United States of America.

Let me put it quite bluntly, particularly in the presence of my colleagues from the House and the Senate, those distinguished Virginians who presently serve there and who happen to be also on the Armed Services Committees. Often when votes come up, as to whether America will be strong enough to keep its commitments or be so weak that it will not command respect in the world, those who vote to cut our arms are said to be for peace and those who vote for strength are said to be for war.

I want to put it right on the line today, bluntly: A vote for a weak America is a vote against peace. A vote for a strong America is a vote for peace, because a strong America will always keep the peace.

If the United States were to cut back unilaterally in the strength of our Armed Forces without obtaining reciprocal actions or commitments in return, that action—and I speak with measured tones—that action of unilaterally cutting our strength before we have a mutual agreement with the other side to cut theirs as well will completely torpedo the chances for any successful negotiations, and those who vote to cut that strength will be destroying the chances, the best chance we have had since World War II, to build an era of peace. And so support those men and women who have the courage in the Congress to vote for a strong

[33]Cf. Chapter 12.

America, rather than to vote for a weak America. We need a strong America if we are going to have peace.

Let me turn to that area of the world in which we need that strength so much—Southeast Asia.

After the long ordeal we have been through, I can realize how so many Americans say, "We want to do no more"—just 100 days after the cease-fire agreements were signed in Paris.[34] These agreements which preserve both the honor of the United States and the freedom of South Vietnam were achieved in principle through a combination of diplomacy and strength. They can only be maintained and upheld through that same combination—diplomacy and strength.

Now so far there has been considerable progress in carrying out the provisions of the peace agreement that we signed just 100 days ago in Paris. Our troops, our prisoners are home, violence in South Vietnam is declining, the cease-fire has been extended to Laos.

But compliance with the agreement is still gravely deficient in many respects. The cooperation which North Vietnam promised to give us in making a full accounting for Americans listed as missing in action has not been satisfactory. And I can assure you that we must and will insist that this promise, this pledge, this solemn agreement be kept, because just as America never broke faith with our prisoners of war, I can assure you today we will not break faith with those who are reported missing in action. They must all be accounted for by the North Vietnamese.

North Vietnam, as you have probably read, has also persisted in violations of the Paris agreements. They have, for example, refused to withdraw thousands of troops from Cambodia and Laos. They have poured huge amounts of military equipment into these areas and into South Vietnam.[35] And I say to you, my friends, today, it would be a crime against the memory of those Americans who made the ultimate sacrifice for peace in Indochina, a serious blow to this country's ability to lead constructively elsewhere in the world, for us to stand by and permit the peace settlement that we reached in Paris to be systematically destroyed by violations such as this.

That is why we are continuing to take the necessary measures to insist that all parties to the agreement keep their word, live up to their obligations. A peace agreement that is only a piece of paper is something that we are not interested in.

We want a peace agreement that is adhered to. We are adhering to the agreement. We expect the other side to adhere to that agreement.

[34]Document 5.
[35]Cf. Document 9.

It should be clearly understood by everyone concerned in this country and abroad, that our policy is not aimed at continuing the war in Vietnam or renewing the war that has been ended. Rather the aim of our policy is to preserve and strengthen the peace, a peace which we achieved at great cost in the past, which holds such promise in the future.

During the homecoming ceremonies for our returning prisoners of war several weeks ago, you may recall that one of the men had a small American flag which he had made while he was in prison. He carried it out to freedom with him. His name was Major Robert Pell, United States Air Force. When his turn came to speak, he held up that small flag and said, "We never lost faith in the American people, and we knew these colors wouldn't run."

We can be proud today that all during the long struggle in Vietnam, these colors—and there they are, see them there, gloriously flying in the wind—these colors didn't run from America's commitment to freedom and peace in the world. And let us resolve today, they are not going to start running now, not in Southeast Asia, not anywhere around the globe, wherever people put their trust in America.

I have seen virtually all of the world—not to every country but to most of them. I have seen hundreds of millions of people—young people like those I see here today, as well as their parents. And as I see them, I know that the hopes for all the people in the world—not just the 200 million Americans, but of 3 billion people in the world—the hopes of all the world's children for peace—they rest right here and nowhere else. They rest in our hands, in America's hands, and believe me, those hopes rest in good hands, in good hands.

And that whole world today is watching to see whether the Star-Spangled Banner still waves over the land of the free and the home of the brave. Well, together let us prove that it does. Let us so conduct ourselves at home that we truly remain the land of the free. And let us so meet our responsibilities in the world as to show that we are still, more than ever, the home of the brave.

And then we can look to the future with confidence that Armed Forces Day in the years to come will be not only a day of pride but also a day of peace for America and for all the people of the world.

10. DEVELOPMENT, FOOD, AND ENERGY PROBLEMS (I)

One area where there was an obvious need for sustained, creative American leadership was the relationship between the United States—or, more broadly, the 24 industrialized nations composing the Organization for Economic Cooperation and Development (OECD)—and the several dozen poorer countries within whose boundaries was concentrated the greater part of twentieth-century humanity. With the postwar retreat of colonialism and the tempering of East-West political competition for the allegiance of the "third world," economic factors had increasingly emerged as the decisive aspect of this "North-South" relationship, as it was often called. As has been suggested in earlier chapters of this record, the United States and the other advanced countries were being confronted year by year with ever more vehement demands from their poorer neighbors for a really decisive attack on the problems of economic underdevelopment and maldistribution of the world's goods.

One widely recognized aspect of this problem, the question of developing-country export earnings, had inspired the proposal in President Nixon's trade message of April 10[1] that Congress authorize a system of generalized trade preferences giving certain developing-country products duty-free access to the American market. Measures of a more familiar type were recommended, "with a special sense of urgency," in the President's annual request for funds to support the foreign aid program, submitted to Congress on May 1 (**Document 24**). In recognition of the demonstrated hostility of many legislators to a program which, in one form or another, had been operating for more than three decades, Mr. Nixon insisted that his recommendations for the fiscal year ending June 30, 1974 represented "the absolute minimum prudent investment which the United States can afford to make if we wish

---

[1]Document 14. For general background see especially *AFR, 1972*, pp. 555-71; also Document 70 below.

to help create a peaceful and prosperous world." Of a recommended allotment totaling $2.9 billion, only $1 billion would in any
case be allocated to development assistance (plus a further billion
recommended for the following fiscal year). The remaining $1.9
billion proposed for fiscal 1974 comprised $1,277 million for
military aid and $632 million for reconstruction in Indochina—the
question of possible assistance to North Vietnam being left in
abeyance pending further study of Hanoi's intentions regarding
cease-fire implementation.[2]

Absent from the presidential message was any special reference
to the problems of global food production and distribution, which,
not many years earlier, had occasioned widespread fears of impending mass starvation in developing countries where food supplies lagged perilously behind population growth. Though temporarily assuaged by the availability of the new agricultural
techniques comprising the so-called "Green Revolution," such
fears were once again reviving as the 1970s advanced. Aside from
the somewhat disappointing results of the "Green Revolution" to
date, developments during 1972—including widespread crop
failures, massive Soviet grain purchases in the United States and
elsewhere,[3] and skyrocketing increases in food costs—had abruptly
focused attention on the limitations of the global food economy
even in advanced countries. By 1973, the world was awakening to
famine as a present reality as awareness grew that mass starvation
was even then occurring in the Sahelian or Sahara border region of
West and Central Africa. (Less publicized were the famine conditions prevailing in parts of Ethiopia as well.) The Sahel emergency, described by Assistant Secretary of State Newsom in an appearance before a congressional subcommittee on June 15
(Document 25), was to be alleviated in the course of the year with
the help of a large-scale international relief effort. In the meantime,
it was beginning to inspire a somewhat more coherent international
approach to the whole problem of world food resources.[4]

Still another aspect of global economic relations that was
reaching a critical stage by early 1973 was the problem of world
energy resources—more particularly, the problem created for the
industrial world by its dependence on petroleum supplies controlled by members of the twelve-year-old Organization of
Petroleum Exporting Countries (OPEC). The rising price of OPEC
oil, together with the producer nations' demand for increased con-

---

[2]For action on the fiscal year 1974 aid program cf. Document 54 and Chapter 24 at
note 4.
[3]Cf. AFR, 1972, pp. 116-17.
[4]For further developments see Chapter 24 at note 6.

trol of production and marketing, had already caused uneasiness in consuming countries; and still greater difficulties could be confidently predicted in light of their steadily increasing energy requirements.[5] Even the United States could be vitally affected by such trends, despite its relatively slighter dependence on imported oil. President Nixon, in a message sent to Congress on April 18,[6] had recommended a number of steps to help avert the threat of "a genuine energy crisis," primarily through the development of new energy sources, conservation, and international cooperation in research and development. International aspects of the energy situation were more exhaustively examined by Under Secretary of State for Economic Affairs William J. Casey in a May 1 congressional appearance (**Document 26**) that painted in the background of the global energy crisis which would actually develop with unexpected rapidity a few months later.[7]

Rising fuel costs had played a significant part in the continuing increase in American domestic price levels, which had gained new impetus with the termination of wage and price controls at the beginning of 1973. Domestic inflation, in turn, had further undermined the exchange position of the dollar even in the brief period since the February devaluation. It was President Pompidou who caustically referred to a "third devaluation" of the dollar as exchange rates slumped and the unofficial gold price soared to levels well above $100 per ounce.

Renewed demands that the United States support the value of its currency through intervention in the foreign exchange markets were heard from various quarters when Secretary of the Treasury Shultz and other economic leaders of the industrial world assembled in Paris on June 6-8 for the annual ministerial meeting of the OECD Council. Once again, however, the American delegate successfully resisted the pressure of his ministerial colleagues. The communiqué made public at the conclusion of the meeting (**Document 27**) said merely that the fight against inflation was "a matter of common interest and a common obligation" and that OECD members acknowledged "the need to maintain the orderly functioning of foreign exchange markets" pending the forthcoming reform of the international monetary system.

Other points emphasized by the OECD Council at its ministerial-level meeting were the importance of the forthcoming multilateral trade negotiations, and the need for better cooperation with developing countries; mutual cooperation on energy policies; and

[5]For background cf. *AFR, 1972*, pp. 519-21.
[6]*Presidential Documents*, vol. 9 (1973), pp. 389-406; excerpts in *Bulletin*, vol. 68 (1973), pp. 561-6.
[7]For later developments cf. Chapter 24 at note 8.

increased attention to the qualitative aspects of economic growth. More incisive comment on some of these questions would have to await the new round of trade negotiations, now scheduled to open in Tokyo in September, and the annual meeting of the Boards of Governors of the International Bank and Monetary Fund, which would be held in Nairobi, Kenya, later in that month. These two meetings, it was generally agreed, would mark an epoch in the evolution of the entire postwar world economy.[8]

(24) The Foreign Assistance Program: Message from President Nixon to the Congress, May 1, 1973.[9]

To the Congress of the United States:

One of the most important building blocks in erecting a durable structure of peace is the foreign assistance program of the United States. Today, in submitting my proposed Foreign Assistance Act of 1973, I urge the Congress to act on it with a special sense of urgency so that we may continue the important progress we have made toward achieving peace during the past year.

Perhaps the most persuasive reason for a strong foreign assistance program was set forth by President Roosevelt in the days shortly before World War II,[10] when Britain needed help. "Suppose my neighbor's home catches fire," he said, "and I have a length of garden hose four or five hundred feet away. If he can take my garden hose and connect it up with his hydrant, I may help him to put out his fire."

Implicit in Roosevelt's analogy was the mutual benefit of giving assistance, for if the fire in question spread, both neighbors would be in danger. Those clear and simple assumptions underlaid our wartime assistance to our European allies and our post-war policy toward the nations of the Western Hemisphere.

Today, we see the wisdom of this policy on every hand. Western Europe is now a bulwark of freedom in the Atlantic Alliance. In the Pacific, Japan has emerged as a major economic power. The remarkable vigor and talents of her people and the dynamic efficiency of her industry are making significant and increasing contributions to other countries, so that Japan itself now plays an extremely important role in working toward a lasting peace in the Pacific.

In recent years, as we have sought a new definition of American

---

[8]Cf. Chapter 19.
[9]Text from *Presidential Documents*, vol. 9 (1973), pp. 438-40.
[10]Press conference, Dec. 17, 1940.

leadership in the world, assistance to other nations has remained a key part of our foreign policy. Under the Nixon Doctrine of shared responsibilities, we have tried to stimulate greater efforts by others. We want them to take on an increasing commitment to provide for their own defenses, their security and their economic development. Most importantly, we hope they will assume greater responsibility for making the decisions which shape their future.

We must not, however, try to shift the full weight of these responsibilities too quickly. A balance must be struck between doing too much ourselves and thus discouraging self-reliance, and doing too little to help others make the most of their limited resources. The latter course would spell defeat for the promising progress of many developing nations, destroy their growing self-confidence, and increase the likelihood of international instability. Thus it is critical that we provide a level of foreign assistance that will help to assure our friends safe passage through this period of transition and development.

The sums I am requesting in the Foreign Assistance Act of 1973 represent the absolute minimum prudent investment which the United States can afford to make if we wish to help create a peaceful and prosperous world. Altogether, authorizations under this bill amount to $2.9 billion for economic and military assistance in the coming fiscal year. During the current fiscal year, some $2.6 billion has been appropriated for such purposes under the strictures of a continuing resolution passed by the Congress.[11]

This new Foreign Assistance Act has several fundamental objectives:

—To help the developing countries achieve a greater measure of self-reliance in their struggle against hunger, disease and poverty;
—To respond swiftly to the ravages of natural disasters;
—To assist friendly governments in building and maintaining the military capability to protect their independence and security;
—And to help South Vietnam, Cambodia, and Laos begin the task of rehabilitating and reconstructing their war-torn countries.

Let us look more closely at each of these objectives.

DEVELOPMENT ASSISTANCE

Hunger, poverty and disease are still widespread among developing countries, despite their significant progress of recent

[11]Cf. *AFR, 1972*, pp. 557-8.

years. Their economic growth—averaging some 5.5 percent a year over the last decade—as well as rapid improvements in agricultural methods and in health care have not yet overcome many deep-seated problems in their societies. Their current needs represent a moral challenge to all mankind.

In providing assistance, however, we should not mislead ourselves into thinking that we act out of pure altruism. Successful development by friendly nations is important to us both economically and politically. Economically, many of the developing countries have energy resources and raw materials which the world will need to share in coming years. They also could represent larger markets for our exports. Politically, we cannot achieve some of our goals without their support. Moreover, if essential needs of any people go entirely unsatisfied, their frustrations only breed violence and international instability. Thus we should recognize that we assist them out of self-interest as well as humanitarian motives.

While development progress as a result of our aid has been less visible than some would like, I believe it is essential for us to persevere in this effort. I am therefore asking Congress to authorize some $1 billion for development assistance programs during fiscal year 1974 and approximately the same amount for fiscal year 1975.

EMERGENCY AID

America's fund of goodwill in the world is substantial, precisely because we have traditionally given substance to our concern and compassion for others. In times of major disaster, American assistance has frequently provided the margin of difference between life and death for thousands. Our aid to victims of disasters—such as the earthquake in Peru and floods in the Philippines—has earned us a reputation for caring about our fellowman.

No nation is more generous in such circumstances. And the American people respond with open hearts to those who suffer such hardship. I am therefore asking the Congress to authorize such amounts as may be needed to meet emergency requirements for relief assistance in the case of major disasters.

SECURITY ASSISTANCE

Security assistance has been a cornerstone of U.S. foreign policy throughout the last quarter century. Countries whose security we consider important to our own national interest frequently face military challenges, often prompted by third countries. In order to maintain a stable international order, it is important that these threatened countries not only be economically developed but also be able to defend themselves, primarily through their own resources.

The United States can rightly claim a number of successes in this regard during recent years. Our programs to help South Vietnam and South Korea build capable forces of their own, for instance, have permitted us to withdraw all of our forces—over 500,000 men—from South Vietnam and 20,000 men from South Korea.

It is unrealistic to think we can provide all of the money or manpower that might be needed for the security of friendly nations. Nor do our allies want such aid; they prefer to rely on their own resources.

We can and should, however, share our experience, counsel and technical resources to help them develop adequate strength of their own. It is for this reason that I ask the Congress to authorize $652 million in grant military assistance, $525 million in foreign military sales credits, and $100 million in supporting assistance funds for fiscal year 1974.

This year's foreign aid bill includes for the first time separate authority for a foreign military education and training program. We want to strengthen this program so that we can help friendly governments better understand our policies, while they develop a greater sense of self-reliance and professional capability in their own military services.

AID FOR INDOCHINA

The signing of cease-fire agreements in Vietnam and Laos marks the beginning of a trend toward a peaceful environment in Indochina. This change will permit us to turn our attention to the considerable post-war needs of Southeast Asia. To ignore these needs would be to risk the enormous investment we have made in the freedom and independence of the countries of Southeast Asia.

The legislation I am presenting today would authorize the continuation of our economic assistance to South Vietnam, Laos and Cambodia and would provide for a sound beginning in the process of rehabilitation and reconstruction there. I anticipate other nations will join in this effort, as they have elsewhere, to solidify the foundations for a new era of reconciliation and progress in Southeast Asia.

Relief assistance for refugees of the war in Southeast Asia is vital to this effort. These refugees number in the hundreds of thousands. In addition to their resettlement, this Administration proposes a major effort to help restore essential community services in areas which have suffered because of the war.

In this bill, I ask the Congress to authorize $632 million for the reconstruction effort in Indochina in fiscal year 1974.

My present request does not include any assistance for North Vietnam. It is my hope'that all parties will soon adhere fully to the Paris agreements.[12] If and when that occurs, I believe that American assistance for reconstruction and development of both South and North Vietnam would represent a sound investment in confirming the peace.

Representatives of the United States have recently been holding discussions with representatives of the Government of North Vietnam to assess economic conditions there and to consider possible forms of United States economic assistance. This assessment has now been suspended, pending clarification of North Vietnam's intentions regarding implementation of the cease-fire. Once Hanoi abandons its military efforts and the assessment is complete, the question of aid for North Vietnam will receive my personal review and will be a subject for Congressional approval.

For a quarter century, America has borne a great burden in the service of freedom in the world. As a result of our efforts, in which we have been joined by increasing numbers of free world nations, the foundation has been laid for a structure of world peace. Our military forces have left Vietnam with honor, our prisoners have returned to their families, and there is a cease-fire in Vietnam and Laos, although still imperfectly observed.

Our foreign assistance program responds to the needs of others as well as our own national needs—neither of which we can afford to ignore.

For our own sake—and for the sake of world peace—I ask the Congress to give these recommendations prompt and favorable consideration.

RICHARD NIXON

The White House,
   May 1, 1973.

(25) Drought Relief and Rehabilitation Needs in West and Central Africa: Statement by Assistant Secretary Newsom before the Subcommittee on African Affairs of the Committee on Foreign Relations, United States Senate, June 15, 1973.[13]

---

[12]Document 5.
[13]Text from *Bulletin*, vol. 68 (1973), pp. 77-9.

I am most grateful for the opportunity to discuss the disastrous effect of the worst drought in this century in several west and central African states, a geographic zone called the Sahel. The disaster has not had the dramatically sudden impact of an earthquake, a tidal wave, or a flood but it is nonetheless a true disaster; famine and misery face millions of persons. Because the effects of the drought have been creeping, world attention has not focused on it until recently.

The countries thus far most seriously affected are Mauritania, Senegal, Mali, Upper Volta, Niger, and Chad. Neighboring states have been hurt as well but to a lesser extent. We enjoy excellent relations with all of these governments. Over a period of years, we have worked with them on the problems of their economic development. Trust and confidence mark these efforts.

Several years of unusual dryness capped by a severe drought this past year have brought large expanses in this region to the edge of disaster.

On November 2, 1972, we drew the attention of high-level authorities of our own government to the seriousness of the problem which was developing, and later that month interagency efforts began to deal with the problem. Our response, which my colleague Don Brown [Donald S. Brown, Deputy Assistant Administrator, Bureau for Africa, Agency for International Development] will present in detail, springs from fundamental humanitarian considerations as well as our friendly relations with these admirable people. What many Americans do not realize is that from the earliest Middle Ages until the coming of the European colonizers this area of Africa was the home of great kingdoms which flourished on world trade. In the fourth century A.D. the Kingdom of Ghana, which spread into the Sahel zone, was already a rich and powerful state. In the Middle Ages, the University of Timbuktu in the Kingdom of Mali was renowned as one of the world's great centers of learning. Tides of history shift and modern history left these kingdoms behind, so that poverty and illiteracy predominate today and the countries stricken by this drought are, under the best of circumstances, among the economically poorest in the world by all the usual standards of judgment such as gross national product and per capita annual income. The latter would scarcely average $100. They remain, however, proud and self-reliant people.

Approximately 25 million people inhabit the six countries which I have mentioned above. Most of the population is rural and has been affected by the drought. Farmers, herders, and nomads have seen their crops fail, forage disappear, wells dry up, and their livestock suffer and, in serious proportion, die. The way of life for millions has been severely dislocated. It is clear from all reports that hunger and malnutrition are widespread and will grow. The drought has thus struck heavily at the resource base of these nations. Moreover, commercial crops such as peanuts in Senegal and cotton in Mali have been greatly reduced. Thus, the local food base has been greatly diminished, exports have fallen, foreign exchange reserves reduced, and the entire productive framework weakened.

Preoccupying as well to the area's leaders is a grave fiscal threat: Tax collections based on agriculture have dropped drastically. In some instances it has been necessary simply to waive tax obligations of the hard-hit farmers and herders. This will have serious repercussions on the total economy of each of these countries.

There has been an energetic response from the donor community. U.S. efforts to provide food and other forms of assistance have thus far surpassed $20 million. The European Community has had a more important role, a leadership role, which is appropriate in view of the many ties which it has with the region. Also participating are the U.S.S.R., the People's Republic of China, Saudi Arabia, Japan, several neighboring African nations, and others. U.N. Secretary General Waldheim, deeply concerned by the situation, designated Director General [Addeke H.] Boerma of the FAO [Food and Agriculture Organization] to coordinate donor activities and has appealed to the United States and other donors for more help.

Recipient governments have been deeply grateful for U.S. assistance thus far rendered. For example, the Senegalese Government has publicly acknowledged its thanks. Ambassadors from the area, who are here today, have told me personally of their gratitude. And President Diori [Hamani] of Niger has written President Nixon stating in part:

> . . . I wish to express to you, on behalf of my government, that of the people of Niger and of myself personally, our profound gratitude for the extent, effectiveness and speed of the various forms of assistance which the United States has willingly given Niger for the relief of its suffering people.
>
> Since the nutritional equilibrium in Niger can hardly be reestablished before October, we must continue to rely on international cooperation, notably that of the friendly government of the United States.

While the foregoing may appear to be an impressive response to a human tragedy, it is not enough. The next few weeks are critical, as the rainy season begins in this area and the need to plant crops recurs. The farmers must be strong enough to plant, tend, and eventually harvest their crops. In many areas the able-bodied must be returned to their normal settlements to carry out the planting. Feeding assistance must continue through the rainy season until harvests begin in September and October, and thereafter a major rehabilitation effort must be undertaken. Herds must be reconstituted, grazing areas restored, water sources reestablished, and a dispirited population encouraged to go on.

To review rehabilitation needs of the months and years ahead, the United Nations has called for a conference in Geneva at the end of June. From this meeting and from the needs which we will identify through the efforts of our missions in the Sahel we will define our proper role in a multidonor program. And at the same time we participate in rehabilitation we will encourage other donors to join with us in a long-range attack on the basic problem of the desertification of the Sahelian zone. From the present tragedy we hope to seize an initiative which will demonstrate our interest in coping with the natural problems of man living in the arid lands of the Sahel.

Parenthetically, Mr. Chairman,[14] I think this crisis and the need for a comprehensive response—short-term emergency feeding, medium-term rehabilitation, and long-range preventative measures to help overcome human and natural deficiencies—point up the merits of a functional approach on a regional basis to a major human problem. This approach is, as I understand it, one of the key objectives of the amendments to the Foreign Assistance Act which have been tabled by a majority of the membership of the House Foreign Affairs Committee. I heartily endorse this objective.

Before concluding, I would like to stress that the drought crisis and our response is not just an effort to help friends who have turned to us in their misfortunes but it is also a demonstration that we, the richest people of the earth, can extend a helping hand to the poorest. We need your committee's sympathetic support in meeting the responsibilities which this crisis places on us today and in the future.[15]

(26) International Ramifications of the Energy Situation: Statement by William J. Casey, Under Secretary of State for Economic Affairs, before the Committee on Interior and Insular Affairs, United States Senate, May 1, 1973.[16]

---

[14]Senator Hubert H. Humphrey (Democrat of Minnesota).

[15]For later developments cf. Chapter 24 at note 6.

[16]Text from *Bulletin*, vol. 68 (1973), pp. 702-6.

I appreciate the opportunity to testify today on this key question of our future energy supplies. The President's energy message[17] has set forward a comprehensive program to deal with many problems stemming from our increasing dependence on supplies from abroad. This committee has also done valuable work in studying the problem and in recommending courses of action. In many respects the conclusions you and the administration have reached are similar.

As the committee well knows, the international aspects of the problem are immense and pose very difficult questions in political relationships as well as in the economic area of supply and price, balance of payments, and trade relationships. The administration is currently exploring the options available for meeting these problems. It is my purpose in my statement and in my responses to the committee's questions to indicate some of the issues confronting us in our consideration of the international ramifications of our energy situation.

We have to assess the likelihood of emergencies and shortages of supply and what should be done about them. We have to find the most effective ways of cooperating with other countries on research and development to develop additional sources of energy. What is to be done? Several things are clear. If the United States is to have the option of limiting our future dependence on energy, particularly oil, imported from overseas sources, then we must first of all rebuild our domestic capacity to supply the larger share of our requirements. The President's program has recommended actions—deregulation of new gas, accelerated offshore exploration, development of our rich Alaskan resource, greater reliance on coal, and tax incentives for domestic exploration—which should help us meet that goal if implemented in a timely manner. Many of these steps will require legislative action, which we hope this committee will help be realized. At the same time, major efforts must be made to reduce the rate of growth in consumption, which is basic to the problem, and to develop new and cleaner sources of energy. The administration intends to develop programs vigorously in these areas in a balanced manner.

The steps we take in these fields cannot, however, eliminate the necessity over the shorter run to import increasingly significant amounts of energy. Our oil imports have already climbed to 30 percent of our total oil consumption. They will continue to increase at a rate of approximately 1 million barrels per day, or over 5 percent of consumption, each year until new domestic production can be developed. With not much new production expected from Canada

[17]Cf. above at note 6.

and Venezuela, the greater part of these necessary imports will come from the countries of Africa and the Middle East. I have attached a table which shows the projected sources and costs of our imports. We believe the President's program has established the ways in which these imports can be managed with maximum possible security and with minimum possible disruption to our domestic market and cost to our consumers while still giving encouragement to our domestic raw material and refining industries.

The balance of payments cost of these imports will be considerable. Even if our imports stabilize in the latter part of this decade at a level which we find acceptable, the annual cost may be as high as $20 billion. It obviously will take a concerted effort to expand our trade sufficiently to help meet bills of this magnitude. On the opposite side of this coin will be the growing revenues of the OPEC states, not all of which can be invested profitably in their own economies. Their excess revenues and their monetary reserves will be very large by 1980, not necessarily a large quantity when viewed against the larger liquid reserves of the world monetary system but nonetheless one which world institutions will have to accommodate in a manner which provides monetary stability and sound investment opportunities.

U.S. OIL IMPORT PROGRAM

Source	1972 (1,000 barrels/day)	1980 (1,000 barrels/day)	1980 Cost (cif)[a] (billions $)	
			Case I	Case II
Canada	1,200	1,000	1.5	1.8
Latin America	2,300	3,000	4.5	5.4
Asia	200	500	.7	.9
West Africa	300	1,000	1.5	1.8
North Africa	200	500	.7	.9
Middle East	500	3,000–6,000[b]	4.5–9.0	5.5–11.0
	4,700	9,000–12,000[b]	13.4–17.9	16.3–21.8

Figures rounded

[a]Costs based on (I) present high range import cost of $4/bbl, and (II) estimated $5/bbl.

[b]Range of imports will depend on degree to which trends in rates of increase of imports are reduced.

Changes in Oil Supply Relationships

The relationships between suppliers and consumers of energy—between oil exporters and importers—are undergoing major and rapid changes which our own increasing imports are compounding. Our emergence as the world's single most important importer of petroleum is destabilizing at this time of transition, and our importing colleagues consequently have every wish to see us take the steps necessary to limit our growth in imports. We alone among the major importing nations have a number of options open to us other than continued increases of imports. Our options are not, however, true choices. For if we do not accept them, if we simply continue to let our imports grow, we will only contribute to a further destabilization in world energy supply relationships, to greater increases in prices, and to the possibility of damaging and cutthroat competition with our friends and our allies for available energy supplies. In this context, the President's recommendations for expanding the production and variety of U.S. domestic energy resources are deliberate, positive efforts to ease the impact of the entry of our burgeoning demand into the world oil market.

The members of this committee are well aware of the scope and importance of the changes taking place in international oil supply relationships. The OPEC nations are pursuing a course, in which they have been very successful in recent years, designed to increase their revenues and their control over the oil-producing concessions and much of the marketing. The international oil companies, once so dominant in assuring a steady flow of supplies and a flexibility capable of meeting emergencies, have lost much of their freedom of action and their ability to make the important decisions on price and supply. The importing governments have to face higher costs, as well as a continued tightness of supply due to the incremental rates of growth in their demand.

OPEC nations, however, also have important internal and external problems and a real interest in cooperating with consuming nations. All of these producers require the technological, economic, and political cooperation of the developed consumer nations if they are to develop lasting benefits for their future generations during this favored period in their histories. Excessive price rises could, however, create instability which would affect producers as well and bring substitute fuels into the market quicker.

In these circumstances, it is hardly surprising that the energy-importing nations have become anxious over the security and cost of their vital oil supplies. They are also keenly interested in generating the necessary exports to pay for their increasing imports and have often sought to do so by means of bilateral arrangements with the oil-exporting governments. The result has been an increasing trend toward balkanization of the oil market. While there may be advantages to individual governments pursuing their ends through bilateral agreements, and this approach may even have some appeal in the abstract, we are concerned that it can have very harmful effects in a market so heavily influenced by the decisions of a very small number of suppliers. In short, each country seems capable of obtaining its own supply security only at the expense of its neighbor's increased insecurity. The possibility of a dangerous and divisive struggle among oil-importing nations for oil supplies and export markets is real and is made more so by the degree to which we continue to increase our own imports.

Steps taken now to increase our domestic supplies, develop new ones, or use existing supplies more efficiently will ease the problem.

International Consultations

Equally important is the necessity for the importing nations to take cooperative steps which will help avoid the sort of cutthroat competition among themselves which could harm everyone's interests. In accordance with the President's directive in the energy message, the Department of State intends to pursue this course vigorously in the coming months, building on the numerous exchanges we have already had with major importing governments. All major consumer nations now appear to favor some form of increased cooperation. The nature and limits of this generalized desire for cooperation vary, however, when specific alternatives are considered.

A high degree of consensus exists for three concepts: the necessity to avoid disruption of relations with OPEC countries, cooperate on development of new sources of energy, and increase protective security measures, which include import sharing with other consumer nations. Most major consumers favor expanding the range of energy supplies through the development of alternative sources, although some have a preference for bilateral arrangements with us on research and development rather than use of a multilateral framework and some want to focus primarily on longrun aspects of this type of cooperation. Increased security measures, such as emergency oil-sharing arrangements and enhanced storage capacity, also have wide support. Discussions are now underway to consider expanding, along the lines of the existing OECD European oil apportionment plan for time of emergency, an apportionment plan to include the United States and other non-European members.

However, we should not minimize the issues we face in considering cooperative measures. Among the points on which we will need to reach our own decisions and then agreement with OECD members are such questions as:

—Is the United States prepared to enter into binding arrangements for equitable import sharing during emergencies?
—Is the United States prepared if necessary to undertake rationing or consider other measures which could be taken to cope with a supply emergency under a sharing agreement?
—Is the United States prepared to share proprietary or government technological information in cooperative research projects?
—Is the United States prepared to establish a compulsory oil stockpile program?

The U.S. Government through the Department of State must continue to consult closely at a high level with all major consuming and producing nations to insure adequate supplies of energy at reasonable prices. The Department of State has been so proceeding as the record will clearly show. I plan next month to follow up the consultations initiated last year by Mr. Irwin [John N. Irwin II, then Deputy Secretary of State] with the 23 OECD countries.[18] Particular focus will be devoted to emergency procedures in the event of oil supply shortages and in the research and development of new forms and supplies of energy. An energy survey team composed of Japanese Government officials is in this country at the present time and has consulted with both the executive and legislative branches of government, as well as with private industry. We expect a visit from Common Market energy officials late next month. These consultations and this coordination are not designed for confrontation with producing countries, which would only increase the instability of the energy market. On the contrary, this government, as do other consuming nations, seeks closest consultation and cooperation with those nations endowed with excess supplies of energy. Prince Saud and Minister of Petroleum [Ahmad Zaki] Yamani of Saudi Arabia were in Washington last month discussing these problems at the highest level of government, both executive and legislative, as well as with industry. Deputy Secretary [Kenneth] Rush was in Tehran last week not only to confer with the

[18]New Zealand became the 24th OECD member on May 29, 1973; cf. Document 27.

Shah on Middle East problems but also to meet with all our Chiefs of Mission in the area.

Thanks to the remarkable efforts of private industry, the United States survived the oil crises which developed after World War I and World War II, when shortages were predicted by experts. Now the world is fortunate indeed to have available for development and production more than adequate petroleum reserves to last into the next century. Global reserves of gas are also immense and only await efficient development and production; for example approximately 10 billion cubic feet of gas is flared daily in the Persian Gulf. The Department of State will play its full role in seeking and developing the essential cooperation among nations to make this energy available to the international market at reasonable cost.

Cooperation in Energy Technologies

I might point out that there is now a reasonable amount of international cooperation in energy technologies on which we can build a more comprehensive R. & D. [research and development] program. For example, we have had longstanding cooperative programs with a number of countries in the nuclear reactor field. We have been cooperating with Poland in coal technology. We have programs with Japan and Italy in geothermal energy and with Germany in magnetohydrodynamics. In March of this year we agreed to cooperate with the Soviet Union in a number of energy technologies—thermal and hydro power stations, power transmission technology, magnetohydrodynamics, and solar and geothermal energy. We have suggested that the NATO Committee on the Challenges of Modern Society undertake programs in solar and geothermal energy.

Our task now is to enlarge and expand the scope and scale of international R. & D. cooperation. We intend to do so with a sharp focus on our priorities. In weaving the existing programs into a broader fabric of cooperation there are a number of factors we will want to keep in mind. Cooperation implies mutual interest, mutual needs, mutual goals, and mutual benefits. Unless other countries also benefit substantially through cooperation with the United States, there would be no incentive or advantage for them to join forces with us. The reverse is, of course, also true. We will also wish to pay particular attention to international cooperation at an industrial level. Experience has shown that as technologies approach a commercial stage, cooperation at a government-to-government level becomes more difficult. Cooperation at the industrial level is therefore especially pertinent to those technologies that might provide nearer term solutions to the energy question, and we will be exploring with industry possible mechanisms for assuring and accelerating such cooperation.

The principal foreign policy implication of our becoming a major importer of oil and gas is contained in the word "interdependence." Our natural resources, whether fossil fuels or ores, however immense, are finite. We must learn to use them efficiently. We must learn to conserve. But above all, we must recognize that we live on an increasingly interdependent planet and must work in harmony and cooperation with all others, regardless of political, economic, and cultural differences. This calls for even greater attention to basic programs pursued by this government, such as the reduction of trade barriers, the development of monetary stability, and above all, the generation of a generation of peace, which not only would conserve invaluable human resources but also prevent the grossest waste of the irreplaceable natural resources which have taken eons to make.

(27) The Organization for Economic Cooperation and Development (OECD): Meeting of the Council at Ministerial Level, Paris, June 6-8, 1973.

(a) Final Communiqué.[19]

The Council of the OECD met at Ministerial level in Paris on 6th, 7th and 8th June, 1973, under the Chairmanship of Mr. Gregorio Lopez Bravo, Minister for Foreign Affairs of Spain. Ministers welcomed the accession of New Zealand to the Convention on the Organisation,[20] which took place on 29th May.

International Economic Situation

Ministers welcomed the recovery in the level of economic activity and the expansion of world trade during the past year. However, they expressed their concern at the persistence and accentuation of inflationary pressures and emphasised that under existing conditions their Governments attach high priority in economic policies to reducing the rate of price increases. They noted action already taken to deal with inflation. They agreed on the need to prevent the emergence of excessive demand pressures, and, in the light of their

---

[19]Text from *OECD Observer*, No. 65 (Aug. 1973), pp. 3-4.
[20]Signed at Paris Dec. 14, 1960 and entered into force Sept. 30, 1961 (TIAS 4891; 12 UST 1728); text in *Documents, 1960*, pp. 332-42.

individual situations, to take vigorous anti-inflationary measures in other fields.

Ministers recognised that the rate of price increases and the spread of inflation from country to country make the fight against inflation a matter of common interest and a common obligation. They therefore agreed on the need for Member countries jointly to reinforce their actions in this field, so as to render more effective the measures which they are taking or may introduce.

The Council directed the Organisation to continue to examine the national and international factors supporting inflation, and the effects of inflation on the economies of Member countries; to review the anti-inflationary actions of Member countries; and to encourage all Member countries to persevere in the policies, individual or concerted, needed to restore suitable price stability.

Despite recent movements in the foreign exchange markets, Ministers took the view that the exchange rate relationships established between Member countries in February and March last[21] are realistic and generally appropriate to achieve a more satisfactory pattern of international payments. They expressed the firm determination of their Governments to follow the policies needed to this end, and will continue to consult each other closely thereon. Member Governments emphasised the need to maintain the orderly functioning of foreign exchange markets during the transitional period before the reform, on a stable and lasting basis, of the international monetary system.

Ministers stressed the urgency of completing the work necessary for this reform.

Long-Term International Monetary, Trade and Investment Issues

Ministers agreed on the urgent need for their Governments to pursue in the appropriate international forums the efforts initiated last year on international monetary reform, multilateral trade negotiations and international investment issues. They recognised that these subjects are interrelated. They look forward to early agreement on major elements of the monetary reform referred to above. They are confident that their Governments' preparations, domestic as well as multilateral, will enable active comprehensive negotiations on trade to be launched at the Tokyo meeting of the GATT.[22] They instructed the Executive Committee in Special Session to press forward with its work on international investment, including multinational enterprises, and other issues, described by its Chairman in his oral report. Ministers emphasised that all these

[21]Cf. Chapter 4.
[22]Cf. Document 50.

subjects form part of an overall effort to adapt the international economic system to new needs and opportunities, to the mutual advantage of all. They also reaffirmed the role of the OECD in keeping the overall objectives of this effort in view and in contributing to the understanding and the will necessary to the success of specific negotiations.

Policies for Co-operation with Developing Countries

Ministers reviewed the main aspects of economic co-operation with developing countries. They noted with concern the unevenness in the economic and social development of these countries and, in a number of them, the persistence of widespread unemployment, the inadequate growth of agricultural production, insufficient food supplies and heavy indebtedness. They noted also that the flow of financial resources to developing countries including official development assistance—in spite of substantial progress on the part of some OECD Members—has remained practically stationary in relation to gross national product over recent years.

Ministers expressed their support for the Organisation's efforts to apply increasingly an integrated approach in the work of its various committees on development matters, taking account of the aims of the International Development Strategy for the United Nations Second Development Decade.[23] They noted in particular that the Development Assistance Committee will continue to seek further progress in the volume and quality of aid, including a better adjustment of the terms to the requirements of individual recipients and, as stressed by several Ministers, further measures of untying,[24] as well as in adapting the forms of aid to the need to fight unemployment and poverty. Ministers invited the Trade Committee to pursue its consideration of means to expand the exports of developing countries, in particular through improved commodity trade and the Generalised System of Preferences. Ministers stressed that the need to secure additional benefits for the international trade of these countries would also be an important consideration in the forthcoming multilateral trade negotiations.

Energy policies

Ministers reviewed the progress which has been made in the Organisation's assessment of long-term energy problems.

---

[23]U.N. General Assembly Resolution 2626 (XXV), Oct. 24, 1970; excerpts in *Documents, 1970*, pp. 324-31.

[24]*AFR, 1971*, p. 575 n. 9.

Recognising that adequate energy supplies are of vital importance to Member countries, they stated their determination to intensify co-operation within OECD on energy policies.

Work on Qualitative Aspects of Economic Growth

Ministers expressed satisfaction with the progress of the Organisation's work on qualitative aspects of economic growth. The OECD has paid increasing attention to this subject since 1970, in order to assist Member countries in formulating policies which give fuller consideration to the various aspects of social well-being. They noted the recent adoption of a list of social concerns common to most Member countries which will serve as a basis for further work on social indicators. Ministers also stressed the need to give environment policies due weight along with other major national objectives, and to propose concrete solutions to environmental problems of common international interest.

11. DIPLOMATIC OCCASIONS, JUNE 1973

The ministerial session of the OECD Council was first in a series of high-level diplomatic meetings that extended through June and into July. Secretary Rogers, barely returned from his tour in Latin America, left Washington for Tehran to serve as head of the U.S. observer delegation to the annual Council meeting of the Central Treaty Organization (CENTO) on June 10-11. From the Iranian capital, the Secretary of State doubled back to Copenhagen to represent the United States at the spring ministerial session of the North Atlantic Council on June 14-15. Dr. Kissinger, meanwhile, had renewed his Parisian contact with Le Duc Tho of North Vietnam, with whom he joined on June 13 in sponsoring a ceremonious reaffirmation, by the four parties most immediately concerned, of the January 27 agreements on Vietnam. The diplomatic spotlight next shifted to the United States for the visit of General Secretary Brezhnev on June 18-25, returning to Europe for the opening of the Conference on Security and Cooperation in Europe (CSCE) in Helsinki on July 3-5.[1]

Regional security in Western and Southern Asia remained the dominant concern at the twentieth session of the CENTO Council of Ministers, at which both the regional members (Iran, Pakistan, and Turkey), and the United Kingdom and the United States—the latter, officially, as an observer rather than a participant—were represented by their respective Foreign Ministers. Secretary Rogers, in a formal presentation of American views **(Document 20a)**, restated familiar CENTO doctrine with regard to the importance of maintaining strength and promoting regional cooperation. In emphasizing "the need to maintain vigilance in the region," the final communiqué released June 11 **(Document 20b)** spoke also of the importance of an early and equitable settlement of the differences between India and Pakistan and between the Arab states and Israel.

---

[1]For the Brezhnev visit and the Security Conference see Chapters 12 and 13 respectively.

The need to meet "continuing subversive threats in the region" might have been even more strongly stated had it been foreseen that the government of neutral Afghanistan would be overthrown on July 17 in a military coup that appeared likely to create fresh opportunities for the spread of Soviet influence in Southern Asia.

A more detailed agenda faced the Copenhagen meeting of the North Atlantic Council, the supreme organ of the Western alliance and one whose sphere of responsibility explicitly encompassed the promotion of East-West détente as well as the assurance of Western defense. Insisting, as always, that a sound military capability was a fundamental prerequisite for better relations with the East, the assembled Ministers reviewed the status of détente diplomacy with particular reference to the forthcoming inauguration of the European Security Conference and the expected commencement in October of East-West negotiations on Mutual and Balanced Force Reduction (MBFR). A highlight of the Council's final communiqué, made public June 15 (**Document 29a**), was a preliminary response to Dr. Kissinger's "Year of Europe" proposal relating to a "new Atlantic charter." Acknowledging that "profound changes . . . were taking place in every field of international activity," the Ministers agreed in general terms "that the time had come, without prejudice to continuing negotiations in other fora, for their Governments to examine in a spirit of solidarity and by a common effort their relationships in the light of these changes." The conduct of such an analysis was entrusted to NATO's permanent Council in Brussels.[2]

The Paris meeting on Vietnam on June 13 was a more unusual event that stemmed directly from the failure of the earlier Paris agreement of January 27 to bring peace to Vietnam or to the other countries of Indochina. As already indicated, the intervening months had been marked by repeated breaches of the cease-fire in South Vietnam, continued infiltration of men and material from North to South, and total lack of agreement between the two South Vietnamese parties not only at the local military level but also in the political talks being held outside Paris. Canada, dissatisfied with the operating conditions accorded the International Commission of Control and Supervision (ICCS), was already contemplating a withdrawal from that four-nation body, on which it would eventually be replaced by Iran. The United States, in addition to its repeated warnings to North Vietnam, had broken off economic talks with Hanoi's representatives in mid-April, and had also discontinued its mine-clearing operations in North Vietnamese waters.[3]

[2]For later developments see Chapter 17 at note 11.
[3]Cf. Chapter 2 and Documents 22-3.

A not dissimilar situation existed in Laos, where fighting had gradually subsided since the February 21 cease-fire but the projected negotiations between the Vientiane government and the Pathet Lao still seemed to be getting nowhere. In Cambodia, where there was not even the pretense of a cease-fire, intensified U.S. bombing during the spring had failed to stem the deterioration of the Lon Nol government's position, or to encourage negotiations with Prince Sihanouk's government-in-exile in Peking. Rising congressional opposition to the Cambodia bombing afforded the Nixon administration an added incentive to try to rescue the Paris settlement before it collapsed entirely.

American initiative had been responsible for the scheduling of the new round of talks between Dr. Kissinger and Le Duc Tho, which began in Paris on May 17-23, continued on June 6-9, and culminated on June 12-13 with the acceptance by all four of the parties immediately concerned—the United States and the Republic of Vietnam on one side, the Democratic Republic of Vietnam and the Provisional Revolutionary Government on the other—of detailed measures to restore and implement the cease-fire. What was involved, Dr. Kissinger explained at a news conference after the signing, was not a new agreement, but "an amplification and a consolidation of the original agreement." Drawn up in the form of a joint communiqué signed by the four parties **(Document 30a)** and a parallel communiqué signed only by Messrs. Kissinger and Tho, the June 13 accord called for strict respect and scrupulous implementation of all provisions of the original Paris agreement, including those relating to Cambodia and Laos and also those relating to economic discussions between the United States and North Vietnam.

Concluding his elucidation of the agreement and its significance **(Document 30b)**, Dr. Kissinger prudently observed that there was nothing automatic about the execution of its terms. "To the extent that this communique prescribes the specific obligations and reaffirms them, it can contribute to the consolidation of peace," he said. "But it is never words alone that produce peace; it is the combination of words, the intention and the consequences of performance."[4] Experience would soon confirm the radical insufficiency of the words so painstakingly drafted in Paris.

(28) The Central Treaty Organization (CENTO): Twentieth Session of the Council of Ministers, Tehran, June 10-11, 1973.

[4]*Presidential Documents*, vol. 9 (1973), p. 764. For later developments see Chapter 16.

(a) Views of the United States: Statement by Secretary of State Rogers, Head of the United States Observer Delegation, June 10, 1973.[5]

First I would like to join with my colleagues in expressing appreciation to His Imperial Majesty the Shahanshah for his inspiring message, to the Prime Minister [Amir Abbas Hoveyda] for his gracious words, and to the Secretary General [Nassir Assar] for the very excellent report that he has given us.

It is with pleasure that I return to Tehran and to another meeting with my colleagues of the CENTO Council of Ministers. Each visit to this country creates a lasting impression of the graciousness of Iranian hospitality, the vitality of the country, and the friendliness of its people.

Mr. Chairman,[6] the United States finds much of value in its association with the Central Treaty Organization, both as a regional organization and as a means of reinforcing the close and cordial bilateral ties we have with each of the member states.

It is true that the world in which CENTO was born differs substantially from the world of today. The phrase which dominated our thoughts in the 1950's was "cold war." The policy which guides us today is to substitute negotiation for confrontation and to achieve a generation of peace. The changes in the world scene, however, make CENTO no less relevant than before.

The attainment of that goal, the goal of peace, demands our unwavering attention and sustained effort. The search for peace must be universal. All countries, large and small, can contribute to the emerging global structure of peace. The United States is striving to maintain the momentum that has built up in recent years. In that connection, this meeting is particularly opportune for it provides an opportunity for an exchange of views on the eve of President Nixon's talk with General Secretary Brezhnev in Washington. We believe, as I know you do, that improved relations between the Soviet Union and the United States should contribute to the security and stability of the CENTO region.

I want to join particularly with my colleagues and especially with what Sir Alec [Douglas-Home] said about the necessity for maintaining our strength. At a time when the prospects for peace seem bright, at a time when the world is a much safer place than it was four years ago, a much more peaceful world than it was four years ago, it is vital to maintain our strength and our resolve. Certainly,

---

[5]Department of State Press Release 203, June 11; text from *Bulletin*, vol. 69 (1973), pp. 81-3.
[6]Abbas Ali Khalatbary, Minister for Foreign Affairs of Iran.

if there is any lesson we have learned in history, it is that military weakness, lack of resolve, is an invitation to aggression. And really, that is what this meeting is about, it seems to me.

I look forward to my discussions with you on the Arab-Israel conflict, too, because the situation in the Middle East remains tenuous and fragile—although we are approaching three years of cease-fire between Egypt and Israel. During the first months of this year we have vigorously pursued a series of diplomatic contacts with the parties concerned. We are convinced that what is required is the beginning of a serious and genuine negotiating process between the parties. It is within a negotiating framework that the United States believes it can be most helpful to the parties in achieving the agreement called for by the November 1967 resolution of the United Nations,[7] a resolution which neither endorsed nor precluded the pre-June 1967 lines as the final lines. The main question facing the parties is how to reconcile the principle of sovereignty on the one hand and the needs of security on the other. These are both legitimate and understandable concerns of the parties in the area. It is not unimportant that both sides remain committed to the Security Council Resolution 242, regardless of their differing interpretations. For this reason, the United States will do everything it can to help assure that the delicate balance of this resolution will be maintained throughout the current proceedings of the United Nations Security Council.

We continue to give full support to the resolution. We will continue to assist the parties in making progress toward peace—a peace that meets the legitimate concerns of all of the states and peoples of the area, including the Palestinians.

I think, Mr. Chairman, it is interesting that the Middle East seems to be the one area in the world where there is a major conflict where the parties have not been able to directly or indirectly discuss their differences. It is the only area in the world now remaining where no negotiations have been conducted, where the parties have not actually actively exchanged views. And we think there is no substitute for that process. We do not believe that there is anything the United Nations can do as a body to make the parties come to an agreement, reach a settlement. We think it is vitally important that the parties start a serious negotiating process of some kind.

In the Persian Gulf we see an area of vast dimension, great vitality, and substantial resources.[8] We look primarily to the states in the area to produce new patterns of regional cooperation and stability in the area of increasing importance to the free world. We

[7]Cf. Chapter 7 at note 2.
[8]For fuller discussion see *AFR, 1972*, pp. 222-8.

are greatly encouraged to see so many indications of regional cooperation. These new relationships can help build a solid foundation for the future prosperity and stability of all states and peoples in the gulf.

We pay particular tribute to Iran and His Imperial Majesty for the leadership he has taken in this area of the world, which is so important to peace and stability.

We believe that significant progress has been made toward reconciliation in South Asia in the aftermath of the Indo-Pakistan war. Pakistan, India, Bangladesh made considerable progress at Simla.[9] Such a negotiating process, we hope, will also lead to a solution of the delicate questions which have been raised here this morning of prisoners of war and detainees to the satisfaction of all concerned. It is from reconciliation among South Asians themselves and their respective efforts to economic development that a strong bulwark of security can be built.

We realize, too, that the transition from confrontation to negotiation and cooperation both in the CENTO area and other parts of the world will not be without new problems. Thus prudence dictates that we must remain vigilant and strong in legitimate defense of our respective interests.

Mr. Chairman, peace has many components. One of them assuredly is cooperation among countries. In few parts of the world has this been more apparent than in the CENTO region, where cooperation has become a habit. The substance of cooperation may have changed from time to time—as indeed it should if it is properly to reflect new developments and new interests—but the spirit underlying it has not. We in the United States enter these discussions with that spirit in mind and in the belief that CENTO today, facing changed circumstances, is more important than ever as an instrument of cooperation and as an instrument of peace.

(b) Final Communiqué, June 11, 1973.[10]

The Council of Ministers of the Central Treaty Organization (CENTO), which was inaugurated by the message of His Imperial Majesty the Shahanshah Aryamehr, read by His Excellency Mr. Amir Abbas Hoveyda, Prime Minister of Iran, held their 20th Session in Tehran on June 10 and 11, 1973.

The Delegations were led by:

His Excellency Mr. Abbas Ali Khalatbary
Minister for Foreign Affairs
Iran

[9]Same, p. 229.
[10]Department of State Press Release 208, June 14; text from *Bulletin*, vol. 69 (1973), pp. 83-4.

His Excellency Mr. Aziz Ahmed, H.PK., HQA., S.PK.
Minister of State for Defense and Foreign Affairs
Pakistan

His Excellency Mr. Umit Haluk Bayulken
Minister for Foreign Affairs
Turkey

The Right Honorable Sir Alec Douglas-Home, K.T., M.P.
Secretary of State for Foreign and Commonwealth Affairs
The United Kingdom

The Honorable William P. Rogers
Secretary of State
The United States

Following an address by the Prime Minister of Iran, opening statements were made by the leaders of the Delegations and the Secretary General of CENTO, expressing their appreciation of the Shahanshah's gracious message and the warm hospitality of the host country.

His Excellency Mr. A.A. Khalatbary, Minister of Foreign Affairs of Iran, presided at the session.

The Council of Ministers conducted a comprehensive review of the international situation, paying particular attention to the matters of interest to the CENTO area. The Ministers recognized the strength and vitality of political and economic development achieved by the member countries, the importance of peaceful and just settlement of disputes, and the need to maintain vigilance in the region.

The Ministers affirmed the vital importance they attach to the preservation of the independence and territorial integrity of each of the member states in this region.

The Ministers noted the success with which Pakistan was meeting the problems which faced her, following the conflict with India. They expressed the hope that lasting peace on the Subcontinent could be secured through a just settlement of differences between Pakistan and India and they reaffirmed their support for Security Council Resolution No. 307 of 21 December 1971.[11] In particular the Ministers urged the early release of prisoners of war.

The Ministers viewed with concern the continuing critical situation in the Middle East. They reaffirmed their support of Security Council Resolution No. 242 of 22 November 1967,[12] and welcomed efforts being made to resolve the Arab-Israel dispute along the lines of the Resolution.

[11]Demanding observance of the cease-fire; text in *AFR, 1971*, pp. 246-7.
[12]*Documents, 1967*, pp. 169-70; cf. Chapter 7 at note 2.

Considering the continuing subversive threats in the region, the Ministers expressed the determination of their Governments to meet such efforts with all the means at their disposal.

The Ministers viewed with favor current negotiations for the purpose of reducing armaments and fostering conditions for peace and stability in Europe. They expressed the hope that these negotiations would not fail to take into consideration the interests of the CENTO region.

In approving the report of the Military Committee, the Ministers noted the continuing improvement in cooperation among the armed forces of their countries.

The Ministers expressed satisfaction with the rapid economic development of the regional countries. In reviewing the report of the Economic Committee, they directed the Committee to consider ways of expanding its work with a view to strengthening and promoting economic cooperation in CENTO.

In concluding their review of the activities over the past year, the Ministers noted with satisfaction the annual report of the Secretary General. They reiterated their determination to continue to cooperate for peace, security and stability to promote further social and economic development in the CENTO region.

The Ministers accepted the invitation of the Government of the United States to hold the next session of the Council in May 1974 in Washington.[13]

(29) The North Atlantic Treaty Organization (NATO): Ministerial Session of the North Atlantic Council, Copenhagen, June 14-15, 1973.

(a) Final Communiqué.[14]

1. The North Atlantic Council met in Ministerial session in Copenhagen on 14th and 15th June.

2. Ministers underlined the essential contribution which the Alliance has rendered over the years to the maintenance of international peace and security. The progress being made toward better East/West relations and the reduction of tensions in Europe could not have been achieved without the unshakeable resolve of the West to defend itself and a sound military capability to do so. Ministers asserted that an effective defense system remained a fun-

[13]The Council's 21st Session was held in Washington on May 21-2, 1974; for documentation see *Bulletin*, vol. 70 (1974), pp. 637-41.

[14]Department of State Press Release 213, June 18; text from *Bulletin*, vol. 69 (1973), pp. 89-90.

damental prerequisite for further progress. Consequently, the Allies must continue to make the efforts necessary to ensure their defense and security.

3. Ministers reaffirmed the principles and objectives of the Alliance established a quarter of a century ago. They noted, however, the profound changes which were taking place in every field of international activity. With this in mind, Ministers decided that the time had come, without prejudice to continuing negotiations in other fora, for their Governments to examine in a spirit of solidarity and by a common effort their relationships in the light of these changes. They entrusted the Council in permanent session with this task. Ministers expressed full confidence that the Alliance would continue to be a vital force for maintaining peace, improving East/West relations, and promoting greater security and well-being.

4. Ministers considered the outcome of the Multilateral Talks in Helsinki in preparation for the Conference on Security and Cooperation in Europe [CSCE].[15] Recalling the purpose of their Governments in entering into these talks, Ministers were satisfied that it had been possible at Helsinki to agree on arrangements for this Conference which would ensure that their proposals were examined fully and in depth.

5. Ministers stressed the need for the Conference to be conducted with all due deliberation befitting the range, complexity and importance of the subjects to be discussed, including security; economic, scientific, technological and environmental cooperation; cooperation in humanitarian and other fields and, in particular, in the field of human contacts. They reaffirmed that constructive and specific results could be achieved only through a process of detailed and serious negotiations without artificial time limits. They felt that given these circumstances there were reasonable hopes that the Conference could produce satisfactory results. Consequently, they expressed their willingness to begin the first phase of the Conference in Helsinki on July 3rd.[16] They noted that a decision on the opening date for the second phase of the Conference remains to be taken and agreed to consult further on this matter.

6. Ministers representing countries which participate in NATO's integrated Defense Program noted with satisfaction that the initiative for mutual and balanced force reductions in Central Europe which they took at Reykjavik in 1968[17] has led to Multilateral Exploratory Talks in Vienna. The agreements reached

[15]Cf. Chapter 13 at note 1.
[16]Cf. Document 35.
[17]*Documents, 1968-69*, pp. 133-4.

there thus far[18] are useful steps forward. These Ministers expect negotiations on specific force reduction and associated measures in Central Europe to begin in October 1973 as previously agreed. They reaffirmed the importance they attach to the prompt fulfilment of this commitment.

7. In such negotiations, it will be the aim of the Allied Governments concerned, bearing in mind the indivisibility of the security of the Alliance, to secure step by step practical arrangements which ensure undiminished security for all parties at a lower level of forces in Central Europe. The readiness of the Warsaw Pact countries to contribute to balanced results would, together with a successful outcome of the parallel negotiations in CSCE, open the way to a more fruitful and stable relationship in Europe. These Ministers reaffirmed the conviction of their Governments that unilateral action on the part of countries of the Alliance to reduce or withdraw forces would undermine the negotiation of satisfactory agreements aimed at enhancing military stability.

8. These Ministers noted with approval the extent of agreement already reached within the Alliance in preparation for negotiations on mutual and balanced force reductions. They requested the Council in permanent session to continue this work and to develop further an Alliance program for the forthcoming negotiations.

9. Ministers expressed satisfaction that the negotiations between the United States and the USSR seeking permanent limitations on strategic offensive arms (SALT TWO) were being pursued.[19] They recognized the importance of this subject for the Alliance and reaffirmed the continuing need for close Allied consultation.

10. Ministers considered the latest developments in questions concerning Germany. They noted the conclusion of the legislative process in the Federal Republic of Germany approving the Treaty on the basis of relations between the Federal Republic of Germany and the German Democratic Republic of 21st December, 1972, whose signature Ministers welcomed at their last meeting.[20] They also noted the conclusion of the legislative process to empower the Government of the Federal Republic of Germany to apply for entry to the United Nations. They expressed the hope that relations between the two German States would develop steadily in a satisfactory manner, taking into account the special situation in Germany.

11. As regards Berlin, Ministers share the view that the strict observance and full application of the Quadripartite Agreement of 3rd September, 1971[21] constitute a condition for lasting detente and

---

[18]Cf. Chapter 13 at note 5.
[19]Cf. *AFR, 1972*, pp. 108-12.
[20]Same, p. 179.
[21]*AFR, 1971*, pp. 166-70.

stability in Europe. They noted the practical improvements in the Berlin situation which the Agreement has produced and were in agreement that the opportunities which it affords for the continuing well-being of the city should be fully utilized.

12. Ministers took note of the report on the situation in the Mediterranean prepared on their instructions by the Council in permanent session. They reiterated their concern at the developments in this area which could have dangerous consequences for the countries of the Alliance. They accordingly instructed the Council in permanent session to continue its consultations on this question and to report to them at their next meeting.

13. Ministers received with interest a report by the Conference of National Armaments Directors on steps to improve armaments cooperation. Noting that the need to collaborate in the areas of standardization, development and procurement has become more pressing, they instructed the Council in permanent session to take the necessary action.

14. Ministers representing countries which participate in NATO's Integrated Defense Program welcomed the reaffirmation by the United States that, given a similar approach by their Allies, they would maintain and improve their forces in Europe and not reduce them except in the context of an East/West Agreement. These Ministers also recalled their previous Agreement that member nations were entitled to bring to the attention of the Alliance any special problems arising from balance of payment problems resulting from military expenditures for collective defense, and that Alliance solidarity can be strengthened by cooperation between members to alleviate these problems. They noted that permanent representatives have been directed to study these issues and to offer whatever recommendations seemed appropriate.

15. The next Ministerial session of the North Atlantic Council will be held in Brussels, on 10th and 11th December, 1973.[22]

(30) Reaffirmation of the Paris Agreement on Vietnam, June 13, 1973.

(a) Joint Communiqué of the Parties to the Agreement, signed in Paris June 13, 1973.[23]

[22]Cf. Document 80.

[23]Text from TIAS 7674 (24 UST 1676-88). Like the original Paris agreement of Jan. 27, 1973 (Document 5), the communiqué of June 13 was prepared and signed in two separate versions: the four-party version printed here, and a second version with a slightly different preamble and conclusion which was signed only by Dr. Kissinger and Le Duc Tho. This second, two-party version is printed in 24 UST 1699-1711 and (in partial text) in *Presidential Documents*, vol. 9 (1973), pp. 761-2, and *Bulletin*, vol. 69 (1973), p. 53. The specific textual differences are pointed out in notes 24 and 26 below.

The Parties signatory to the Paris Agreement on Ending the War and Restoring Peace in Viet-Nam, signed on January 27, 1973,[24]

Considering that strict respect and scrupulous implementation of all provisions of the Agreement and its Protocols[25] by all the parties signatory to them are necessary to ensure the peace in Viet-Nam and contribute to the cause of peace in Indochina and Southeast Asia,

Have agreed on the following points (in the sequence of the relevant articles in the Agreement):

1. In conformity with Article 2 of the Agreement, the United States shall cease immediately, completely, and indefinitely aerial reconnaissance over the territory of the Democratic Republic of Viet-Nam.

2. In conformity with Article 2 of the Agreement and with the Protocol on Mine Clearance:

(a) The United States shall resume mine clearance operations within five days from the date of signature of this Joint Communique and shall successfully complete those operations within thirty days thereafter.

(b) The United States shall supply to the Democratic Republic of Viet-Nam means which are agreed to be adequate and sufficient for sweeping mines in rivers.

(c) The United States shall announce when the mine clearance in each main channel is completed and issue a final announcement when all the operations are completed.

3. In implementation of Article 2 of the Agreement, at 1200 hours, G.M.T., June 14, 1973, the High Commands of the two South Vietnamese parties shall issue identical orders to all regular and irregular armed forces and the armed police under their command, to strictly observe the cease-fire throughout South Viet-Nam beginning at 0400 hours, G.M.T., June 15, 1973, and scrupulously implement the Agreement and its Protocols.

---

[24]In the two-party communiqué, this paragraph is replaced by the following:

"From May 17 to May 23, from June 6 to June 9, and on June 12 and 13, 1973, Dr. Henry A. Kissinger, on behalf of the Government of the United States of America, and Mr. Le Duc Tho, on behalf of the Government of the Democratic Republic of Viet-Nam, reviewed the implementation of the Paris Agreement on Ending the War and Restoring Peace in Viet-Nam and its Protocols and discussed urgent measures to ensure the correct and strict implementation of the Agreement and its Protocols.

"The Government of the United States of America, with the concurrence of the Government of the Republic of Viet-Nam,

"The Government of the Democratic Republic of Viet-Nam, with the concurrence of the Provisional Revolutionary Government of the Republic of South Viet-Nam,".

[25]For the protocols, see note 31 to Document 5.

4. The two South Vietnamese parties shall strictly implement Articles 2 and 3 of the Protocol on the Cease-Fire in South Viet-Nam which read as follows:

"Article 2

(a) As soon as the cease-fire comes into force and until regulations are issued by the Joint Military Commissions, all ground, river, sea and air combat forces of the parties in South Viet-Nam shall remain in place; that is, in order to ensure a stable cease-fire, there shall be no major redeployments or movements that would extend each party's area of control or would result in contact between opposing armed forces and clashes which might take place.

(b) All regular and irregular armed forces and the armed police of the parties in South Viet-Nam shall observe the prohibition of the following acts:

(1) Armed patrols into areas controlled by opposing armed forces and flights by bomber and fighter aircraft of all types, except for unarmed flights for proficiency training and maintenance;

(2) Armed attacks against any person, either military or civilian, by any means whatsoever, including the use of small arms, mortars, artillery, bombing and strafing by airplanes and any other type of weapon or explosive device;

(3) All combat operations on the ground, on rivers, on the sea and in the air;

(4) All hostile acts, terrorism or reprisals; and

(5) All acts endangering lives or public or private property.

Article 3

(a) The above-mentioned prohibitions shall not hamper or restrict:

(1) Civilian supply, freedom of movement, freedom to work, and freedom of the people to engage in trade, and civilian communication and transportation between and among all areas in South Viet-Nam;

(2) The use by each party in areas under its control of military support elements, such as engineer and transportation units, in repair and construction of public facilities and the transportation and supplying of the population;

(3) Normal military proficiency training conducted by the parties in the areas under their respective control with due regard for public safety.

(b) The Joint Military Commissions shall immediately agree on corridors, routes, and other regulations governing the movement of military transport aircraft, military transport vehicles, and military transport vessels of all types of one party going through areas under the control of other parties."

5. The Two-Party Joint Military Commission shall immediately carry out its task pursuant to Article 3(b) of the Agreement to determine the areas controlled by each of the two South Vietnamese parties and the modalities of stationing. This task shall be completed as soon as possible. The Commission shall also immediately discuss the movements necessary to accomplish a return of the armed forces of the two South Vietnamese parties to the positions they occupied at the time the cease-fire entered into force on January 28, 1973.

6. Twenty-four hours after the cease-fire referred to in paragraph 3 enters into force, the commanders of the opposing armed forces at those places of direct contact shall meet to carry out the provisions of Article 4 of the Protocol on the Cease-Fire in South Viet-Nam with a view to reaching an agreement on temporary measures to avert conflict and to ensure supply and medical care for these armed forces.

7. In conformity with Article 7 of the Agreement:

(a) The two South Vietnamese parties shall not accept the introduction of troops, military advisers, and military personnel, including technical military personnel, into South Viet-Nam.

(b) The two South Vietnamese parties shall not accept the introduction of armaments, munitions, and war material into South Viet-Nam. However, the two South Vietnamese parties are permitted to make periodic replacement of armaments, munitions, and war material, as authorized by Article 7 of the Agreement, through designated points of entry and subject to supervision by the Two-Party Joint Military Commission and the International Commission of Control and Supervision.

In conformity with Article 15(b) of the Agreement regarding the respect of the Demilitarized Zone, military equipment may transit the Demilitarized Zone only if introduced into South Viet-Nam as replacements pursuant to Article 7 of the Agreement and through a designated point of entry.

(c) Twenty-four hours after the entry into force of the cease-fire referred to in paragraph 3, the Two-Party Joint Military Commission shall discuss the modalities for the supervision of the replacements of armaments, munitions, and war material permitted by Article 7 of the Agreement at the three points of entry already agreed upon for each party. Within fifteen days of the entry into force of the cease-fire referred to in paragraph 3, the two South Vietnamese parties shall also designate by agreement three additional points of entry for each party in the area controlled by that party.

8. In conformity with Article 8 of the Agreement:

(a) Any captured personnel covered by Article 8(a) of the Agreement who have not yet been returned shall be returned without delay, and in any event within no more than thirty days from the date of signature of this Joint Communique.

(b) All the provisions of the Agreement and the Protocol on the Return of Captured Personnel shall be scrupulously implemented. All Vietnamese civilian personnel covered by Article 8(c) of the Agreement and Article 7 of the Protocol on the Return of Captured Personnel shall be returned as soon as possible. The two South Vietnamese parties shall do their utmost to accomplish this within forty-five days from the date of signature of this Joint Communique.

(c) In conformity with Article 8 of the Protocol on the Return of Captured Personnel, all captured and detained personnel covered by that Protocol shall be treated humanely at all times. The two South Vietnamese parties shall immediately implement Article 9 of that Protocol and, within fifteen days from the date of signature of this Joint Communique, allow National Red Cross Societies they have agreed upon to visit all places where these personnel are held.

(d) The two South Vietnamese parties shall cooperate in obtaining information about missing persons and in determining the location of and in taking care of the graves of the dead.

(e) In conformity with Article 8(b) of the Agreement, the parties shall help each other to get information about those military personnel and foreign civilians of the parties missing in action, to determine the location and take care of the graves of the dead so as to facilitate the exhumation and repatriation of the remains, and to take any such other measures as may be required to get information about those still considered missing in action. For this purpose, frequent and regular liaison flights shall be made between Saigon and Hanoi.

9. The two South Vietnamese parties shall implement Article 11 of the Agreement, which reads as follows:

"Immediately after the cease-fire, the two South Vietnamese parties will:

—achieve national reconciliation and concord, end hatred and enmity, prohibit all acts of reprisal and discrimination against individuals or organizations that have collaborated with one side or the other;

—ensure the democratic liberties of the people: personal freedom, freedom of speech, freedom of the press, freedom of meeting, freedom of organization, freedom of political activities, freedom of belief, freedom of movement, freedom of residence, freedom of work, right to property ownership and right to free enterprise.''

10. Consistent with the principles for the exercise of the South Vietnamese people's right to self-determination stated in Chapter IV of the Agreement:

(a) The South Vietnamese people shall decide themselves the political future of South Viet-Nam through genuinely free and democratic general elections under international supervision.

(b) The National Council of National Reconciliation and Concord consisting of three equal segments shall be formed as soon as possible, in conformity with Article 12 of the Agreement.

The two South Vietnamese parties shall sign an agreement on the internal matters of South Viet-Nam as soon as possible, and shall do their utmost to accomplish this within forty-five days from the date of signature of this Joint Communique.

(c) The two South Vietnamese parties shall agree through consultations on the institutions for which the free and democratic general elections provided for in Article 9(b) of the Agreement will be held.

(d) The two South Vietnamese parties shall implement Article 13 of the Agreement, which reads as follows:

"The question of Vietnamese armed forces in South Viet-Nam shall be settled by the two South Vietnamese parties in a spirit of national reconciliation and concord, equality and mutual respect, without foreign interference, in accordance with the postwar situation. Among the questions to be discussed by the two South Vietnamese parties are steps to reduce their military effectives and to demobilize the troops being reduced. The two South Vietnamese parties will accomplish this as soon as possible.''

11. In implementation of Article 17 of the Agreement:

(a) All the provisions of Articles 16 and 17 of the Protocol on the Cease-Fire in South Viet-Nam shall immediately be implemented with respect to the Two-Party Joint Military Commission. That Commission shall also immediately be accorded the eleven points of privileges and immunities agreed upon by the Four-Party Joint

Military Commission. Frequent and regular liaison flights shall be made between Saigon and the headquarters of the Regional Two-Party Joint Military Commissions and other places in South Viet-Nam as required for the operations of the Two-Party Joint Military Commission. Frequent and regular liaison flights shall also be made between Saigon and Loc Ninh.

(b) The headquarters of the Central Two-Party Joint Military Commission shall be located in Saigon proper or at a place agreed upon by the two South Vietnamese parties where an area controlled by one of them adjoins an area controlled by the other. The locations of the headquarters of the Regional Two-Party Joint Military Commissions and of the teams of the Two-Party Joint Military Commission shall be determined by that Commission within fifteen days after the entry into force of the cease-fire referred to in paragraph 3. These locations may be changed at any time as determined by the Commission. The locations, except for teams at the points of entry, shall be selected from among those towns specified in Article 11(b) and (c) of the Protocol on the Cease-Fire in South Viet-Nam and those places where an area controlled by one South Vietnamese party adjoins an area controlled by the other, or at any other place agreed upon by the Commission.

(c) Once the privileges and immunities mentioned in paragraph 11(a) are accorded by both South Vietnamese parties, the Two-Party Joint Military Commission shall be fully staffed and its regional commissions and teams fully deployed within fifteen days after their locations have been determined.

(d) The Two-Party Joint Military Commission and the International Commission of Control and Supervision shall closely cooperate with and assist each other in carrying out their respective functions.

12. In conformity with Article 18 of the Agreement and Article 10 of the Protocol on the International Commission of Control and Supervision, the International Commission, including its teams, is allowed such movement for observation as is reasonably required for the proper exercise of its functions as stipulated in the Agreement. In carrying out these functions, the International Commission, including its teams, shall enjoy all necessary assistance and cooperation from the parties concerned. The two South Vietnamese parties shall issue the necessary instructions to their personnel and take all other necessary measures to ensure the safety of such movement.

13. Article 20 of the Agreement, regarding Cambodia and Laos, shall be scrupulously implemented.

14. In conformity with Article 21 of the Agreement, the United States-Democratic Republic of Viet-Nam Joint Economic Com-

mission shall resume its meetings four days from the date of signature of this Joint Communique and shall complete the first phase of its work within fifteen days thereafter.

Affirming that the parties concerned shall strictly respect and scrupulously implement all the provisions of the Paris Agreement, its Protocols, and this Joint Communique, the undersigned representatives of the parties signatory to the Paris Agreement have decided to issue this Joint Communique to record and publish the points on which they have agreed.[26]

Signed in Paris, June 13, 1973.

For the Government of the
United States of America:

(*Signed*):

Henry A. Kissinger
Assistant to the President
of the United States of
America

For the Government of the
Democratic Republic of
Viet-Nam:

(*Signed*):

Le Duc Tho
Representative of the
Government of the Democratic
Republic of Viet-Nam

For the Government of the
Republic of Viet-Nam:

(*Signed*):

Nguyen Luu Vien
Representative of the
Government of the
Republic of Viet-Nam

For the Provisional
Revolutionary Govern-
ment of
the Republic of South
Viet-Nam:

(*Signed*):

Nguyen Van Hieu
Minister of State of the
Provisional Revolutionary
Government of the
Republic
of South Viet-Nam

[26]In the two-party communiqué, this paragraph is replaced by the following:

"Affirming that the parties concerned shall strictly respect and scrupulously implement all the provisions of the Paris Agreement, its Protocols, this Joint Communique, and a Joint Communique in the same terms signed by representatives of the Government of the United States of America, the Government of the Republic of Viet-Nam, the Government of the Democratic Republic of Viet-Nam, and the Provisional Revolutionary Government of the Republic of South Viet-Nam [i.e., Document 30a], the representative of the United States of America, Dr. Henry A. Kissinger, and the representative of the Democratic Republic of Viet-Nam, Mr. Le Duc Tho, have decided to issue this Joint Communique to record and publish the points on which they have agreed."

(b) *News conference statement by Dr. Kissinger, Paris, June 13, 1973.*[27]

(Excerpt)

DR. KISSINGER. Ladies and gentlemen, first of all, I want to thank those of you who have been following me around in these many sessions in November, December, January, February, and now, for your patience, sometimes for risking your necks. I regret I haven't been able to be more communicative at the end of each session, but these negotiations are somewhat complex and involve many parties.

I understand that there has already been a previous briefing which went to the details, but let me say very briefly what we consider to be the significance of this communique, what is in the communique, and then I will take your questions.

As you know, during the course of March and April the United States became quite concerned about the manner in which the cease-fire agreement was being implemented. We were specifically concerned about the following points:

One, the inadequate implementation of the cease-fire.

Secondly, the continued infiltration into South Vietnam and the continued utilization of Laos and Cambodia as corridors for that infiltration.

Three, we were concerned about the inadequate accounting for the missing in action.

Fourth, we were concerned about the violations of the demilitarized zone.

Fifth, we were concerned about the inadequate cooperation with the International Control Commission and the slow staffing of the two-party Military Commission.

Sixth, we were concerned about the violations of Article 20 requiring the withdrawal of foreign troops from Laos and Cambodia.

Needless to say, the other side had its list of complaints, and in these circumstances, we proposed that Mr. Le Duc Tho and I meet again to review the implementation of the agreements that had been so painfully negotiated last fall.

There was a preliminary meeting between Ambassador Sullivan and Vice Minister Thach,[28] and then on May 17 Le Duc Tho and I met again and reached some preliminary conclusions. We were in

[27]*Presidential Documents*, vol. 9 (1973), pp. 762-3. For the continuation of the news conference see same, pp. 763-5.
[28]Cf. note 29 to Document 4.

daily contact with the Government of South Vietnam through its delegation here, and through our embassy in Saigon. We then sent Ambassador Sullivan to Saigon for further consultations. I returned here. The negotiations continued. There was a slight interruption last Saturday [June 9], and we reached a final conclusion today.

As far as the content of the joint communique is concerned, we believe that we have achieved a satisfactory conclusion of the points that were of principal concern to the United States. There is, as you know, to be issued a new order on the cease-fire, which is to go into effect roughly 36 hours from now, which we hope and expect will be implemented fully.

Second, there is a clear repetition of the prohibitions against the infiltration of personnel and materiel into South Vietnam, except as replacements under Article 7 of the original agreement and according to procedures agreed to by the two parties with reference to respect for the demilitarized zone and to the prohibition of transiting the demilitarized zone except in accordance with the replacement provisions of the agreement.

Under the provisions for missing in action, all sides have pledged that they would make major efforts to help each other to account for the missing in action throughout Indochina, and this is a matter which is of great concern to the United States.

The two-party Military Commission is to be fully staffed and special assurances have been given in paragraph 12 about cooperation with the International Control Commission by all the parties to grant them reasonable freedom of movement.

With respect to Laos and Cambodia, the communique says that the provisions of Article 20 are to be scrupulously observed, and there have been long discussions about the whole complex of issues raised by Laos and Cambodia. However, since the final results depend on the sovereign decision of other parties, we will not discuss this subject here, and we will leave it to the results and to events to testify to progress.

The other subject which has been discussed and which I have left separately is that of political evolution in South Vietnam. As you know, the United States has always taken the view that the political evolution of South Vietnam is to be decided by the South Vietnamese.

Therefore, the United States has always believed—and that is reflected in the communique—that the political future of South Vietnam should be determined by a process of free and democratic general elections. The other provisions regarding political evolution reaffirm what is said in Chapter IV of the cease-fire agreement.

Now, we have today signed the communique, ladies and gentlemen, and the history of Indochina is replete with agreements and joint declarations. I am not naive enough to pretend to you that the mere fact of having again agreed to certain words in itself guarantees peace, but I will also say that since all parties have worked so seriously for the last 3 weeks, we have every hope that they will match this effort with performance, and, therefore, there is fresh hope, and we hope a new spirit, in the implementation of the agreement, which in itself is maintained.

What was signed today is an amplification and a consolidation of the original agreement. It is not a new agreement. Now, the people of Indochina, and especially the peoples of Vietnam, have suffered conflicts for a generation, and our greatest ambition has been to end their suffering and to restore peace, and it is our hope that by what has been done today, a significant step has been taken in the consolidation of peace in Vietnam and in Indochina.

* * *

12. BREZHNEV COMES TO AMERICA

Through all the varied developments of early 1973, the American Government had maintained its continuing interest in the new relationship with the Soviet Union that had seemed to open so auspiciously with President Nixon's precedent-setting visit to that country in May 1972. Preparations for a return visit by General Secretary Brezhnev, the official head of the Societ Communist Party and by far the most prestigious member of the Soviet hierarchy, had been in process almost since the President's return to Washington the previous June.

No one imagined that a Brezhnev visit to the United States would lead to further "breakthroughs" on the scale of the major arms limitation agreements concluded during President Nixon's Soviet trip. But lesser agreements in a variety of technical areas were nearing completion as 1973 advanced; and it was hoped that a broad discussion of security problems by the two leaders would give fresh impetus to the ongoing Strategic Arms Limitation Talks (SALT) in Geneva as well as the prospective Vienna negotiations on Mutual and Balanced Force Reduction (MBFR) in Central Europe. In addition, as Dr. Kissinger noted following his return from a preparatory visit to the U.S.S.R. in May,[1] one of the "prime utilities" of such a meeting was the opportunity to engage in a general survey of the international situation that would help prevent "misunderstandings and avoidable tension" and assist the two parties in gearing their actions to the expectation of a lasting peace.[2]

For President Nixon, the visit would also afford a welcome respite from domestic pressures, which now included not only the

[1]Cf. joint U.S.-Soviet statement, May 9, in *Presidential Documents*, vol. 9 (1973), p. 657.
[2]Kissinger news conference, June 14, in *Presidential Documents*, vol. 9 (1973), pp. 771-3. For more detailed discussion of U.S.-Soviet relations and arms control issues see *Nixon Report, 1973*, pp. 26-39 and 194-208.

latent threat of Watergate but also the public grumbling engendered by a continuous rise in living costs which now exceeded an annual rate of 9 percent. Tacitly conceding the failure of the "Phase III" stabilization program initiated in January, which had featured the lifting of controls on prices and wages, the President on June 13 returned to the opposite tack by freezing most prices for up to 60 days while still another anti-inflation program was being developed.

On the Watergate front, meanwhile, the Ervin committee hearings were cutting closer and closer to the bone as the time for the Brezhnev visit drew closer. Two days before the Soviet leader's scheduled arrival on June 16, the committee heard Jeb Stuart Magruder admit his own complicity in the "bugging" and cover-up and, in addition, implicate such presidential associates as Mitchell, Dean, and Haldeman, although he emphasized that he knew of no personal involvement on the part of the President. Testimony by former White House Counsel Dean, who might be better informed on this point, was put off until after the Brezhnev visit.

Although it was already being suggested that the Watergate scandals might seriously weaken the President's hand in negotiating with the Soviet leader, Brezhnev himself had made clear before leaving Moscow that he would think it most improper to involve himself in any way in this domestic American issue. Nothing, in fact, could have exceeded the air of cordiality and good fellowship exuded by the General Secretary from the moment of his arrival at Andrew's Air Force Base on June 16 to his leavetaking from San Clemente and subsequent televised address to the American people on June 24.[3] With studied impartiality, the Soviet party boss projected his warmth and charm upon the members of both the executive and the legislative branches. Particularly noted was Brezhnev's performance as host at a Blair House luncheon on June 19 for the members of the Senate Foreign Relations Committee and selected Representatives, at which he voiced an eloquent plea for the extension to his country of most-favored-nation commercial treatment as an essential tool of the trade expansion desired by both parties.

In making this plea, the Soviet leader was well aware that the only serious obstacle to nondiscriminatory tariff treatment for his country was the dislike of Congress for Moscow's policy of restricting Jewish emigration. With a flurry of statistics that purported to minimize the scope of this problem, the Soviet leader

---

[3]For full documentation see *Presidential Documents*, vol. 9 (1973), pp. 787-800, 806-29, and 831-55, or *Bulletin*, vol. 69 (1973), pp. 113-75.

insisted that such a matter was far too trivial to be permitted to interfere with good relations between the two countries.[4] He made no definite commitments, on this or any other occasion during his trip. Yet Dr. Kissinger, for one, would seem to have been impressed by Brezhnev's repeated "statement . . . to both our executive and Members of Congress to the effect that Soviet domestic law and practice placed no obstacles in the way of emigration."[5] That Brezhnev had not been fully successful in persuading the Congress of his good faith would nevertheless become evident as the year advanced.

Like the Nixon visit to the U.S.S.R., the Soviet leader's sojourn in the United States was punctuated not only by banquets and receptions but by the almost daily publication of new bilateral agreements relating to cooperation in various specialized areas: agriculture, oceanography, transportation, education and culture, taxation, atomic energy, commercial relations, and air services.[6] The most important fruit of the visit, however, was a new pair of accords directed toward the curbing of the strategic arms race and toward exorcising the danger of an outbreak of nuclear war between the two powers. Both of the agreements concluded on these subjects were rooted in the SALT exchanges which had been going on since 1969, and which had already produced the 1971 Agreement on Measures to Reduce the Risk of Outbreak of Nuclear War[7] as well as the 1972 Treaty on the Limitation of Anti-Ballistic Missile Systems[8] and the Interim Agreement on Certain Measures with Respect to the Limitation of Strategic Offensive Arms,[9] which had for the first time established certain limits on the growth of the two powers' missile armories during the ensuing five-year period.

In concluding the Interim Agreement on strategic arms limitation, the United States and the Soviet Union had pledged themselves to continue active negotiations with a view to concluding a more complete agreement in this area as soon as possible, presumably within the five-year life of the Interim Agreement. Although the search for such an agreement had been duly initiated

[4]New York Times, June 20, 1973. For background cf. Chapter 4 at note 9.
[5]Statement to the Senate Finance Committee, Dec. 3, 1974, in Bulletin, vol. 71 (1974), p. 937. For later developments see Chapters 21 and 30.
[6]For details see Document 33b.
[7]Signed in Washington and entered into force Sept. 30, 1971 (TIAS 7186; 22 UST 1590); text in AFR, 1971, pp. 110-12.
[8]Signed in Moscow May 26, 1972 and entered into force Oct. 3, 1972 (TIAS 7503; 23 UST 3435); text in AFR, 1972, pp. 90-95.
[9]Signed in Moscow May 26, 1972 and entered into force Oct. 3, 1972 (TIAS 7504, 23 UST 3462); text in same, pp. 97-101.

with the opening of the second phase of the SALT talks (SALT II) in Geneva in the fall of 1972,[10] it had become evident by the spring of 1973 that there would be insufficient time to negotiate a comprehensive, permanent agreement in advance of the proposed summit meeting. Accordingly, as Dr. Kissinger explained to the press in one of his background briefings on summit developments **(Document 31a)**, it had been decided that the negotiating process might still be given a new impetus by a discussion at the summit plus an agreement on certain principles that could guide the negotiators in their further work. It was with this aim in view that Messrs. Nixon and Brezhnev affixed their signatures on June 21 to a document entitled "Basic Principles of Negotiations on the Further Limitation of Strategic Offensive Arms" **(Document 31b)**, in which they reaffirmed the good intentions that had inspired the 1972 agreement and promised serious efforts to work out "the provisions of the permanent agreement on more complete measures on the limitation of strategic offensive arms with the objective of signing it in 1974"—still well before the 1977 expiration date of the Interim Agreement.

A similar concept underlay the "Agreement on the Prevention of Nuclear War" **(Document 32b)** which the two leaders signed in Washington on June 22—with the intention, in Dr. Kissinger's words **(Document 32a)**, of laying down "certain principles of conduct" that would reflect their mutual awareness "that the principal problem was how to prevent a war and not how to conduct a war." In a series of clauses that admittedly amounted to no more than an unenforceable declaration of intent, the two countries accordingly agreed "to act in such a manner as to prevent the development of situations capable of causing a dangerous exacerbation of their relations, as to avoid military confrontations, and as to exclude the outbreak of nuclear war between them and between either of the Parties and other countries." Using language that would be poignantly recollected at the time of the Middle East crisis the following October, they also agreed "to proceed from the premise that each Party will refrain from the threat or use of force against the other Party, against the allies of the other Party and against other countries, in circumstances which may endanger international peace and security," and to consult urgently with one another should there arise any risk of nuclear war between them.

"A further milestone in the constructive development of their relations," said the official communiqué that concluded the formal phase of the summit meetings on June 24 **(Document 33b)**. Expressing their mutual satisfaction at "the current process of im-

[10]Same, pp. 108-10.

provement in the international situation" and at what they called the "new and favorable opportunities for reducing tensions, settling outstanding international issues, and creating a permanent structure of peace," the two sides were able to voice identical opinions on both Indochina and Europe. Admitting that they held divergent views on the Middle East, they nevertheless agreed that the situation there was one that warranted deep concern and called for urgent efforts to promote a settlement fair to all parties. In emphasizing the positive impact of their discussions, both on the U.S.-Soviet relationship and on international relations generally, the two parties "reaffirmed that the practice of consultation should continue," "agreed that further meetings at the highest level should be held regularly," and disclosed that President Nixon had agreed to pay a second visit to the U.S.S.R. in the following year.

"Of course," Dr. Kissinger cautioned in the last of his press briefings on the summit meetings (Document 33a), "history is replete with changes of course and we must be vigilant and prepared for such an occurrence." Nevertheless, he said, "it is the belief of the President that this period has a unique opportunity to create a new and more peaceful system." "We consider the summit as a further advance along that road," the presidential assistant explained—"that as these meetings become a regular feature of international life, and as we come to take them more and more for granted, the results will follow paths that will come to seem more and more natural, and we would consider that one of the best signs that a peaceful world is coming into being."

Whatever the intrinsic worth of the summit accomplishments, the maintenance of a sense of progress in the international realm was vitally important to an American administration whose standing in other respects continued to deteriorate from day to day. Even the issuance of the summit communiqué was overshadowed by the concurrent resumption of the Watergate hearings, now featuring testimony by John Dean that directly implicated the President in the cover-up operation and also drew attention for the first time to the administration's celebrated "enemies list" and other vagaries of the Nixon White House. In addition, the administration found itself in growing difficulty with the Congress, which had voted to cut off all funds for further bombing of Cambodia and, after failing to override a presidential veto of such a prohibition on June 27, succeeded in forcing a compromise that would compel the President to terminate all combat operations throughout Indochina by August 15.[11]

In the economic area, meanwhile, mounting feed-grain prices

---

[11]Cf. Chapter 16.

and a growing threat of domestic food shortages had prompted the sudden imposition by the administration, also on June 27, of temporary export controls on soybeans and cottonseed and their products as a means of conserving American supplies. This step caused lively repercussions in Europe and Japan, which had become heavily dependent on these American products and were further disconcerted when additional feedstuffs were placed under control a few days later. By July 4, moreover, the dollar had plunged to record lows on European exchanges, amid talk of a possible third devaluation or even a deferment of the trade talks scheduled for September. Such trends presented a less than auspicious background for the important decisions that had soon to be taken in the field of European and Atlantic policy.

(31) Agreement on Negotiating Principles for Strategic Arms Limitation, June 21, 1973.

(a) News conference statement by Dr. Kissinger, June 21, 1973.[12]

MR. ZIEGLER. As we mentioned to you this morning, President Nixon and General Secretary Brezhnev have reached agreement on the basic principles of negotiation of further limitation for strategic offensive arms. The final agreement of those principles was reached in the meeting yesterday evening.

Also, an agreement will be signed today between the United States and the Soviet Union on scientific and technical cooperation in the field of peaceful uses of atomic energy.[13] The signing of both of these matters will take place at 3:30 in the East Room, which we have already announced.

Before Dr. Kissinger briefs you on the matters I have just referred to, together with Ambassador [U. Alexis] Johnson,[14] I should tell you that the morning meeting between the President and General Secretary [at Camp David] lasted for slightly over an hour. It began at 11:30 and ended at 12:30. Dr. Kissinger participated in most of that meeting.

The President and General Secretary then took a brief break and resumed their meetings at 1:20 and are still meeting at this time and plan to return to Washington for the signing ceremony at 3:30. With that, I will present to you Dr. Kissinger.

[12]Text from *Presidential Documents*, vol. 9 (1973), pp. 813-15. Dr. Kissinger was introduced by Ronald L. Ziegler, Press Secretary to the President.
[13]See note 65 below.
[14]U.S. Representative and chief of the U.S. delegation to the SALT talks, succeeding Ambassador Gerard C. Smith.

DR. KISSINGER. Ladies and gentlemen, I will go over the agreement on SALT principles with you. Due to some misunderstanding between Camp David and my office here, the actual text[15] hasn't been distributed to you, but it will be at the end of the meeting. I thought that in order to explain it adequately, I would read to you each of the principles and then explain what they mean.

There is no need for you to take down the text itself, because we are going to distribute it right after the meeting, together with a fact sheet, and my apologies for not having gotten it to you before this briefing.

Let me first give you some background on the principles that have been agreed upon and what they are intended to achieve.

As you know, the second round of SALT started last November, and as you know also, our representative is Ambassador Johnson, who is here to help with the briefing.

The objective of these talks has been to consider a permanent agreement limiting offensive weapons to replace the interim agreement that was signed in Moscow last May [26] and which came into effect last October [3] to run for 5 years.[16]

Now, in negotiating a permanent agreement, one faces problems that are more complex than those in an interim agreement. The essence of the interim agreement was that both sides froze their offensive weapons at the levels they had achieved last May and, frankly, at the levels that were foreseeable over the terms of the interim agreement, for a period of 5 years.

And as you know, we have always rejected the argument that we had agreed to a numerical inferiority in the interim agreement precisely because there was no possibility of overcoming that numerical inferiority in the 5 years for which the interim agreement was designed.

On the other hand, when you are dealing with a permanent agreement, you are affecting the long-term strategic interests of both countries, and, therefore, numbers that are acceptable in an interim agreement will have a different connotation in a permanent agreement, and safeguards will have to be looked at in a different context.

Secondly, with respect to a permanent agreement, we now face the situation that the numerical arms race, quantitative arms race, has been, in some respects, eclipsed in significance by the qualitative arms race.

Throughout the 1960's, it was considered that the buildup was the greatest threat to the stability of the arms race and hence to in-

[15]Document 31b.
[16]AFR, 1972, pp. 97-101; for full reference see note 9 above.

ternational peace. In this period we have to consider as well that the improvement—refinement of arms—in terms of accuracy, in terms of throw-weight, in terms of multiple warheads can be profoundly unsettling to this strategic equation, even when the numbers on both sides are kept fairly constant.

And thirdly, when one is talking about a permanent agreement, one has to consider the question not only of limiting arms, but the objective of reducing arms. It was in this context that the negotiations started last November and have been conducted for the last 6 months.

The negotiations went through the usual phase of some exploratory discussions, followed by some more concrete proposals by both sides. However, we faced the situation in April, where it became clear that a comprehensive agreement of a permanent nature would require more time than the interval before the summit allowed, and, therefore, the President, General Secretary Brezhnev, in their communications with each other, decided that perhaps the approach of agreeing on some principles that could guide the negotiators, coupled with some full discussions while they were meeting in the United States, could give a new impetus to the talks on strategic arms limitation. This is what was done.

In the closest consultation with Ambassador Johnson and with the allies most concerned, we developed a set of principles on a preliminary basis, which we have further discussed since the General Secretary has arrived in the United States, and which led to the agreement which we are releasing today.

Now, since you don't have the text, I think the best thing I can do is read it, and then attempt to explain its significance—what we understand by it. It isn't very long. I see somebody is looking at his watch. [*Laughter*]

The preamble says, the President of the United States and the General Secretary of the Central Committee of the CPSU [Communist Party of the Soviet Union], having thoroughly considered the question of the further limitation of strategic arms, and the progress already achieved at the current negotiations, reaffirming their conviction that the earliest adoption of further limitation of strategic arms would be a major contribution in reducing the danger of an outbreak of nuclear war and in strengthening international peace and security, have agreed as follows.

The primary significance of the preamble is the emphasis that both leaders give to their conviction of the importance of the earliest adoption of further limitation of strategic arms, not only with respect to reducing the danger of the outbreak of nuclear war, but with respect to the strengthening of international peace in general and, therefore, the personal backing that they are giving to a sense of urgency in the conduct of these negotiations.

The first principle is as follows: The two sides will continue active negotiations in order to work out a permanent agreement on more complete measures on the limitation of strategic offensive arms, as well as their subsequent reduction, proceeding from the Basic Principles of Relations between the United States of America and the Union of Soviet Socialist Republics signed in Moscow, May 29, 1972,[17] and from the interim agreement between the United States and the U.S.S.R. of May 26, 1972.

Over the course of the next year, the two sides will make serious effort to work out the provisions of the permanent agreement on more complete measures on the limitation of strategic offensive arms with the objective of signing in 1974.

The first principle substantially speaks for itself. It commits both sides to accelerate their efforts, and it commits both sides to make a major effort to achieve an agreement in 1974, or during the course of 1974. The two leaders would not have made this formal statement if they did not believe that this goal was within reach and was attainable.

Therefore, it represents a commitment by both sides to bring about—to do their utmost to bring about a permanent agreement on the limitation of strategic arms during the course of next year. This agreement is to be based on the basic principles of international relations that were established last year in Moscow and on the interim agreement. However, the United States' position has been clear that the agreement has to be more comprehensive and that the numbers that last governed the interim agreement would not be the numbers of a permanent agreement.

The second principle is: New agreements on the limitation of strategic offensive armaments will be based on the principles of the American-Soviet documents adopted in Moscow in May 1972 and the agreements reached in Washington in June 1973; and in particular, both sides will be guided by the recognition of each other's equal security interests and by the recognition that efforts to obtain unilateral advantage, directly or indirectly, would be inconsistent with the strengthening of peaceful relations between the United States of America and the Union of Soviet Socialist Republics.

This article attempts to set out the basic guidelines in which the two sides will approach the negotiations. It makes it clear that neither side can attempt to achieve, through these negotiations, a unilateral advantage and secondly, that we have always maintained the position that we did not separate our security interests from those of our allies.

I must mention one other point with respect to the first principle, which is to say that both sides have agreed that the negotiations should include not only limitations on strategic arms, but measures for the reduction of strategic arms.

The third principle states: The limitations placed on strategic offensive weapons can apply both to their quantitative aspects as well as to their qualitative improvement.

This is one of the essential differences between SALT I and SALT II. SALT I concerned primarily exclusively the question of numerical limitation. SALT II will include, as well, qualitative restraint. That will involve discussions on MIRV's [Multiple Independently Targetable Reentry Vehicles], on throw-weight, and issues introduced by the other side with respect to specific types of armaments, for example, on airplanes.

The fourth principle states: Limitations on strategic offensive arms must be subject to adequate verification by national technical means, which is a familiar principle from the previous SALT discussions and which the negotiating record makes it clear that we include, also, the imperative that both sides will maintain practices which facilitate monitoring the agreement.

The fifth principle applies to the modernization of arms and states: The modernization and replacement of strategic offensive arms would be permitted under conditions which will be formulated in the agreements to be concluded.

The essence here is that on the one hand there will be some provision for modernization and replacement. On the other hand, it also makes clear that the modernization and replacement cannot take place except under agreed conditions that do not threaten the purposes of the agreement.

The sixth principle is: Pending the completion of a permanent agreement on more complete measures of strategic offensive arms limitation, both sides are prepared to reach agreements on separate measures to supplement the existing interim agreement of May 26, 1972.

The significance of this principle is that, with respect to some issues that are time-urgent, in which the interval between now and the time in 1974 when we expect the permanent agreement to be concluded, that this interval might have a major impact on the existing strategic situations, both sides have agreed that they would be prepared to negotiate supplementary or separate measures to the interim agreement which would probably be of shorter duration and which would, of course, be absorbed by the permanent agreement.

The seventh principle is a reaffirmation of the accidental war agreement, which is to say that each side will continue to take necessary organizational and technical measures for preventing accidental or unauthorized use of nuclear weapons under its control in accordance with the agreement of September 30, 1971, between the United States of America and the Union of Soviet Socialist Republics.[18]

To sum up, the statement of principles which will be signed today, first, formally commits the two principal leaders to the urgency of completing a permanent agreement and the relationship between international peace and security and the completion of such an agreement.

Secondly, it states a deadline for the completion of the agreement, in 1974.

Thirdly, it includes reductions as one of the objectives of the agreement and not simply limitation.

Fourth, it defines a permanent agreement as one that will limit the number of weapons systems as well as to limit their qualitative improvement and, therefore, opens a dimension to the negotiations that was not covered by SALT I.

And it defines some general principles as yardsticks against which the negotiators can measure progress.

Now, these principles have to be seen also in terms of the negotiating record at Geneva, where both sides are now discussing concrete proposals and where it is, therefore, perfectly clear what both sides mean by such phrases as "qualitative changes" and other phrases.

It must also be seen in the light of the extensive discussions that took place yesterday between the President and the General Secretary which dealt with how to give effect to these principles and how to move forward to these negotiations so that the timetable that has been set out in these principles can be realistically met.

These, then, are the principles which will guide our actions over the next year. We expect that they will be seen as a major step in developing a permanent agreement on the limitation of offensive weapons—the ultimate reduction—as a move toward bringing under control not only the pace of the arms race, but its nature and, therefore, will contribute to long-term prospects of peace.

Now I will be glad to answer any questions.[19]

[18]Same, *1971*, pp. 110-12; for full reference see note 7 above.
[19]For the remainder of the news conference see *Presidential Documents, loc. cit.*, pp. 815-17, or *Bulletin*, vol. 69 (1973), pp. 137-41.

(b) Basic Principles of Negotiations on the Further Limitation of Strategic Offensive Arms, signed at Washington and entered into force June 21, 1973.[20]

BASIC PRINCIPLES OF NEGOTIATIONS ON THE FURTHER LIMITATION OF STRATEGIC OFFENSIVE ARMS

The President of the United States of America, Richard Nixon, and the General Secretary of the Central Committee of the CPSU, L.I. Brezhnev,

Having thoroughly considered the question of the further limitation of strategic arms, and the progress already achieved in the current negotiations,

Reaffirming their conviction that the earliest adoption of further limitations of strategic arms would be a major contribution in reducing the danger of an outbreak of nuclear war and in strengthening international peace and security,

Have agreed as follows:

First. The two Sides will continue active negotiations in order to work out a permanent agreement on more complete measures on the limitation of strategic offensive arms, as well as their subsequent reduction, proceeding from the Basic Principles of Relations between the United States of America and the Union of Soviet Socialist Republics signed in Moscow on May 29, 1972,[21] and from the Interim Agreement between the United States of America and the Union of Soviet Socialist Republics of May 26, 1972 on Certain Measures with Respect to the Limitation of Strategic Offensive Arms.[22]

Over the course of the next year the two Sides will make serious efforts to work out the provisions of the permanent agreement on more complete measures on the limitation of strategic offensive arms with the objective of signing it in 1974.

Second. New agreements on the limitation of strategic offensive armaments will be based on the principles of the American-Soviet documents adopted in Moscow in May 1972 and the agreements reached in Washington in June 1973; and in particular, both Sides will be guided by the recognition of each other's equal security interests and by the recognition that efforts to obtain unilateral advantage, directly or indirectly, would be inconsistent with the strengthening of peaceful relations between the United States of America and the Union of Soviet Socialist Republics.

[20]TIAS 7653 (24 UST 1472).
[21]*AFR, 1972*, pp. 75-8.
[22]Same, pp. 97-101; for full reference see note 9 above.

Third. The limitations placed on strategic offensive weapons can apply both to their quantitative aspects as well as to their qualitative improvement.

Fourth. Limitations on strategic offensive arms must be subject to adequate verification by national technical means.

Fifth. The modernization and replacement of strategic offensive arms / would be permitted under conditions which will be formulated in the agreements to be concluded.

Sixth. Pending the completion of a permanent agreement on more complete measures of strategic offensive arms limitation, both Sides are prepared to reach agreements on separate measures to supplement the existing Interim Agreement of May 26, 1972.

Seventh. Each Side will continue to take necessary organizational and technical measures for preventing accidental or unauthorized use of nuclear weapons under its control in accordance with the Agreement of September 30, 1971 between the United States of America and the Union of Soviet Socialist Republics.[23]

Washington, June 21, 1973

FOR THE UNITED STATES
OF AMERICA:

FOR THE UNION OF SOVIET
SOCIALIST REPUBLICS:

(*Signed*): Richard Nixon

(*Signed*): L. Brezhnev

President of the United
States of America

General Secretary of the
Central Committee, CPSU

(32) Agreement on the Prevention of Nuclear War, June 22, 1973.

(a) News conference statement by Dr. Kissinger, June 22, 1973.[24]

DR. KISSINGER. Ladies and gentlemen, let me put this agreement first in its context, describe what it is seeking to achieve, and then go through its specific provisions, a little bit of its history, and then I will take your questions.

The principal goal of the foreign policy of this Administration ever since 1969 has been to set up what the President has called a structure of peace, by which we mean an international system less

---

[23]*AFR, 1971*, pp. 110-12; for full reference see note 7 above.
[24]Text from *Presidential Documents*, vol. 9 (1973), pp. 823-4.

geared to the management of crises, less conscious of constant eruptions of conflict, in which the principal participants operate with a consciousness of stability and permanence.

This requires that all of the nations operate with a sense of responsibility, and it puts a particular obligation on the two great nuclear powers that have the capacity to destroy mankind and whose conflicts have produced so many of the crises of the postwar period.

In achieving this objective, the United States has operated on many levels. We have always believed that it required adequate strength to deter aggression. But we also have believed that we have to move from the period of military confrontation to a period which is characterized more by restraints and, eventually, co-operation. In our dealings with the other great nuclear super-power, the President, from the day of his first inauguration, has emphasized that we wanted to move from confrontation to negotiation.

In those negotiations we have operated on many levels. We have attempted to remove specific causes of tension. We have attempted to forge specific instruments of cooperation. And finally, we have attempted to develop certain principles of conduct by which the two great nuclear countries could guide their expectations and by which both in relations to each other and in their relations to third countries, they could calm the atmosphere and replace purely military measures by a new attitude of a cooperative international system.

It is in this spirit that last year in Moscow the United States and the Soviet Union signed certain principles of conduct[25] which were described then as a roadmap on a road that no one was forced to travel, but that if we wanted to travel it, it was there for the two major countries.

I believe we have traveled on this road in the last year, and, therefore, it was decided to formalize some of these principles in an agreement, to extend them in some respects, particularly concerning consultation. The origin of the negotiation, as it turned out, was at the last session of the Moscow summit meeting when there were some general exchanges with respect to how to control nuclear weapons in a political and diplomatic sense, beyond the negotiations going on in strategic arms limitations.

These discussions were continued between the President and Foreign Minister [Andrei A.] Gromyko on the occasion of Gromyko's visit to the United States last October. They were continued in exchanges between the two leaders. There was some

[25] AFR, 1972, pp. 75-8.

discussion when I visited the Soviet Union in September of last year, and the discussions continued this spring and were extensively pursued in Zavidovo[26] and finally concluded here.

Throughout, the United States has held the view that any obligations with respect to international conduct that applied to the two great nuclear powers, also had to apply to their relations to other countries, and we have held the view which was shared by the Soviet leaders that the principal problem was how to prevent a war and not how to conduct a war.

Therefore, this is an agreement which is designed to regulate the relations of the two nuclear powers to each other and to other countries in time of peace. It is an attempt to prevent the outbreak of nuclear war. And to the extent that it contributes to this task, it can be a significant landmark in the relationships of the United States to the Soviet Union and in the relationships of the two great nuclear countries towards all other countries of the world.

Now, let me run through the articles,[27] which are largely self-explanatory. Article I states that it is an objective of both the policy of the United States and the policy of the Soviet Union to remove the danger of nuclear war and the use of nuclear weapons. This has been a consistent goal of American foreign policy, and is a goal shared by all of mankind.

Article II applies this objective to the general conduct of both sides, that is to say, the prevention of nuclear war presupposes the avoidance of situations capable of an exacerbation of relations, avoidance of military confrontation, and it is in that context that the outbreak of nuclear war can be excluded.

The second article states this more concretely, by elaborating that the prevention of nuclear war presupposes the avoidance of force or the use or threat of force by the two nuclear countries towards each other and towards other countries.

Article III is a general article that simply states that the two nuclear countries have to develop their relations with each other and with third countries in a way consistent with the purposes of this agreement, and it makes it clear that while it is a bilateral agreement, the obligations are multilateral.

Article IV states that in any situation in which the two great nuclear countries might find themselves in a nuclear confrontation, or in which either as a result of their policies toward each other or as the result of developments elsewhere in the world, there is a danger of a nuclear confrontation between them, or between them or any other country, they are obligated to consult with each other in order to avoid this risk.

[26] A Soviet guest house; cf. Kalb, *Kissinger*, p. 439.
[27] Document 32b.

Article V permits the consultation, that these consultations be communicated to the United Nations, and to other countries, a clause which we would, of course, apply to our allies.

Article VI makes clear that this agreement deals with the prevention of war, and that if it fails, the existing obligations in existing documents, treaties, and alliances will be maintained.

So, we see the basic significance of this agreement as a step, a significant step toward the prevention of nuclear war and the prevention of military conflict. It is a formal obligation that the two nuclear superpowers have taken towards each other, and equally importantly towards all other countries, to practice restraint in their diplomacy, to build a peace that is permanent, to pursue a policy whose dedication to stability and peace will become, as General Secretary Brezhnev said last night at the banquet,[28] irreversible.

Of course, anyone who has studied the history of the last 30 years must recognize that agreements are not always maintained, and that there is nothing self-enforcing about this document. However, if the two great nuclear countries continue to be animated by the spirit in which they have conducted their policy of the last 2 years, then this document could mark a landmark on the road toward the structure of peace of which the President has been speaking and can be seen as a step towards a new era of cooperation in the relations of all nations and of lifting from them increasingly the fear of nuclear war and of war in general.

Now I will be glad to answer your questions.[29]

(b) Agreement on the Prevention of Nuclear War, signed at Washington and entered into force June 22, 1973.[30]

AGREEMENT BETWEEN THE UNITED STATES OF AMERICA
AND THE UNION OF SOVIET SOCIALIST REPUBLICS ON
THE PREVENTION OF NUCLEAR WAR

The United States of America and the Union of Soviet Socialist Republics, hereinafter referred to as the Parties,

Guided by the objectives of strengthening world peace and international security,

Conscious that nuclear war would have devastating consequences for mankind,

---

[28]*Presidential Documents*, vol. 9 (1973), p. 819.
[29]For the remainder of the news conference see same, pp. 824-7, or *Bulletin*, vol. 69 (1973), pp. 142-7.
[30]TIAS 7654 (24 UST 1479).

Proceeding from the desire to bring about conditions in which the danger of an outbreak of nuclear war anywhere in the world would be reduced and ultimately eliminated,

Proceeding from their obligations under the Charter of the United Nations regarding the maintenance of peace, refraining from the threat or use of force, and the avoidance of war, and in conformity with the agreements to which either Party has subscribed,

Proceeding from the Basic Principles of Relations between the United States of America and the Union of Soviet Socialist Republics signed in Moscow on May 29, 1972,[31]

Reaffirming that the development of relations between the United States of America and the Union of Soviet Socialist Republics is not directed against other countries and their interests,

Have agreed as follows:

Article I

The United States and the Soviet Union agree that an objective of their policies is to remove the danger of nuclear war and of the use of nuclear weapons.

Accordingly, the Parties agree that they will act in such a manner as to prevent the development of situations capable of causing a dangerous exacerbation of their relations, as to avoid military confrontations, and as to exclude the outbreak of nuclear war between them and between either of the Parties and other countries.

Article II

The Parties agree, in accordance with Article I and to realize the objective stated in that Article, to proceed from the premise that each Party will refrain from the threat or use of force against the other Party, against the allies of the other Party and against other countries, in circumstances which may endanger international peace and security. The Parties agree that they will be guided by these considerations in the formulation of their foreign policies and in their actions in the field of international relations.

Article III

The Parties undertake to develop their relations with each other and with other countries in a way consistent with the purposes of this Agreement.

[31]*AFR, 1972*, pp. 75-8.

Article IV

If at any time relations between the Parties or between either Party and other countries appear to involve the risk of a nuclear conflict, or if relations between countries not parties to this Agreement appear to involve the risk of nuclear war between the United States of America and the Union of Soviet Socialist Republics or between either Party and other countries, the United States and the Soviet Union, acting in accordance with the provisions of this Agreement, shall immediately enter into urgent consultations with each other and make every effort to avert this risk.

Article V

Each Party shall be free to inform the Security Council of the United Nations, the Secretary General of the United Nations and the Governments of allied or other countries of the progress and outcome of consultations initiated in accordance with Article IV of this Agreeement.

Article VI

Nothing in this Agreement shall affect or impair:
(a) the inherent right of individual or collective self-defense as envisaged by Article 51 of the Charter of the United Nations,
(b) the provisions of the Charter of the United Nations, including those relating to the maintenance or restoration of international peace and security, and
(c) the obligations undertaken by either Party towards its allies or other countries in treaties, agreements, and other appropriate documents.

Article VII

This Agreement shall be of unlimited duration.

Article VIII

This Agreement shall enter into force upon signature.

DONE at Washington on June 22, 1973, in two copies, each in the English and Russian languages, both texts being equally authentic.

FOR THE UNITED STATES
OF AMERICA:

FOR THE UNION OF SOVIET
SOCIALIST REPUBLICS:

(*Signed*): Richard Nixon

(*Signed*): L. Brezhnev

President of the United
States of America

General Secretary of the
Central Committee, CPSU

(33) *Review of the Visit, June 24-25, 1973.*

(a) *News conference statement by Dr. Kissinger, San Clemente, June 25, 1973.*[32]

MR. ZIEGLER. You have the communique,[33] which is embargoed until 1 o'clock, eastern time, and 10 o'clock, Pacific time. Dr. Kissinger is here to discuss that with you and take your questions on the communique and also on the summit between the President and General Secretary.

For the statistics buffs in the press corps, the President and General Secretary spent a total of 47 hours together. They met in formal sessions with advisers or alone for 18¼ hours. In addition, the President and General Secretary were together 28¾ hours at informal gatherings, social functions, and signing ceremonies, and events of that sort.

Q. How much alone, face to face?

MR. ZIEGLER. Almost 10 hours—9½ hours.

DR. KISSINGER. Ladies and gentlemen, I will not go through the communique because I understand you have already had a chance to read it. Let me make a few general observations about the summit and how it fits into the general development of our foreign policy, and then I will take questions about the communique or any other part of the summit which you may wish to raise.

---

[32]Text from *Presidential Documents*, vol. 9 (1973), pp. 848-9. On R. L. Ziegler cf. note 12 above.

[33]Document 33b.

One good way of assessing the results of the summit is to compare last year's communique[34] with this year's communique.

Last year's communique spoke about the desirability of peaceful coexistence. It said: "Having considered various areas of bilateral U.S.-Soviet relations, the two Sides agreed that an improvement in relations is possible and desirable."

This year we say that: "Both Sides are convinced that the discussions they have just held represent a further milestone in the constructive development of their relations.

"Convinced that such a development of American-Soviet relations serves the interests of both of their peoples and all of mankind, it was decided to take further major steps to give these relations maximum stability and to turn the development of friendship and cooperation between their peoples into a permanent factor for worldwide peace."

In other words, what marks the turning point last year, in which the fact of peaceful coexistence required special affirmation and the possibility of improving relations between the United States and the Soviet Union was thought deserving of special note, and this year we are speaking of a continuing relationship.

As a result, as relations between the Soviet Union and the United States proceed along the course that was charted last May, and accelerated this June, we cannot expect that these meetings, which we have affirmed should become a regular part of U.S.-Soviet relationships, will produce a dramatic new departure. It is the strength of this relationship as it develops that the road is charted and that what we expect to see is a further evolution along a path which will be increasingly free of confrontations, and which will become increasingly a part of a stable international system. This is the context in which we see the U.S.-Soviet relationship.

If you look back over previous summit meetings between Soviet and American leaders, they almost invariably occurred in the shadow of some crisis, and they were inevitably directed to removing some source of tension and some cause of confrontation.

In May 1972 we still met in the shadow of the Vietnamese war and the recent decisions that had led to an expansion of military operations in Indochina.[35] But even then, before the first talk enunciated some common principles of conduct and affirmed the desirability of a long-term evolution toward a peaceful and ultimately cooperative relationship between the two states and the two peoples. These expectations were fulfilled over the course of the year, and, therefore, what this summit intended to do was to

---

[34]*AFR, 1972*, pp. 66-75.
[35]Cf. same, p. 60.

strengthen the cooperative bonds that had developed in particular areas, to give a new impetus to the key areas of negotiations, especially strategic arms limitations and mutual force reductions, and thirdly, to take the joint principles one step further by embodying them in a formal agreement designed to prevent war, and especially nuclear war.

There is nothing I can add to the particular agreements that are enumerated in the communique that deal with the cooperative relationships in various fields and that represent a continuation of a process that started last year.

I can only say from my personal experience in participating in many of these negotiations that what I told you ladies and gentlemen before the summit has been reinforced by the experience of the summit. Many of these agreements do not themselves take the attention and time of the top leaders, and it would be absurd to pretend to you that the General Secretary and the President sit down and discuss the details of the civil aviation agreement, but it is also true that the imminence of their meetings, and the fact that they have determined to give a symbolic expression to this relationship gives an impetus to negotiations that otherwise would drag on for months, and permits the quick resolution of particular issues which, if left to the expert level, could produce extended stalemate. And there is some significance in having the relationship develop on such a broad front, developing on both sides a commitment that is becoming increasingly difficult to reverse.

With respect to the other areas, I have talked to you at some length about the decisions with respect to strategic arms limitation talks. I think you can assume that in addition to what has been stated formally in the agreement on principles,[36] that the two leaders had extensive discussions as to how the process can be accelerated so that a meaningful agreement can be achieved consistent with the deadline that they have set themselves. Therefore, we believe, with considerable hope, that a permanent agreement limiting strategic offensive arms, which would be one of the historic achievements in the field of arms control, can and will be negotiated during the course of 1974.[37]

With respect to the mutual balanced force reductions, we told you before this summit conference that this was not the forum in which to negotiate the specifics. This is a matter of the profoundest concern to our allies, and it had never been intended to discuss the specifics, the specific schemes, at this meeting.

However, as those who have followed the discussions realize,

[36]Document 31b.
[37]For a preview of 1974 developments cf. *AFR, 1972*, pp. 128-9.

there had been some uncertainty about when these discussions would begin. Prior to the meeting, in the preparatory conferences in Vienna, the Soviet position had tied the openings of the MBFR conference to the ending of the European Security Conference. At this meeting, it was decided that the MBFR conference would begin unconditionally on October 30, and, of course, both leaders agreed that they would make a serious effort to deal with the question of armaments in Central Europe.[38]

The Indochina problem, which last year was a source of contention, has received a common expression in this document.

And finally, there has been the agreement on the prevention of nuclear war.[39] Now, I have seen several comments to the effect that it is nonbinding, that it is not self-enforcing, and no doubt I have contributed to this by comments that reflect my former professorial profession, so let me state our position: that no agreement in history has ever enforced itself. Every agreement in history that has been observed has depended either on the willingness of the parties to observe it or on the willingness of one or the other parties to enforce it, or on the rewards for compliance and the risks of noncompliance.

This agreement is no different from any other agreement in that respect. When great powers make an agreement with each other, they, of course, have the capability of not observing it unless the other side is prepared to draw extreme consequences. But the violation of this agreement would have serious consequences for the whole context of U.S.-Soviet relations, and, conversely, the observance of this agreement can mark, as I said on Friday,[40] a milestone in the achievement of self-restraint by the major countries, a self-restraint which is, by definition, the essence of peace and which we intend to observe, which we expect the Soviet Union to observe, and which can therefore provide the foundation for a new international relationship.

Of course, history is replete with changes of course and we must be vigilant and prepared for such an occurrence, but it is the belief of the President that this period has a unique opportunity to create a new and more peaceful system. It is an opportunity that has come about partly as a result of the enormity of the weapons that would be used in case of a conflict, partly by the depth of human aspiration towards peace, partly as a result of the complexities of a world in which the ideological expectations of any side have not been fully met.

---

[38]For further discussion see Chapter 13.
[39]Document 32b.
[40]Document 32a.

But whatever the reasons, we consider the summit as a further advance along that road, that as these meetings become a regular feature of international life, and as we come to take them more and more for granted, the results will follow paths that will come to seem more and more natural, and we would consider that one of the best signs that a peaceful world is coming into being.

So this is our assessment of the summit and I will be glad to answer any questions on this, or on what I have said, or on the communique, or anything else related to the summit.[41]

(b) Joint United States-Soviet Communiqué, dated June 24 and released June 25, 1973.[42]

At the invitation of the President of the United States, Richard Nixon, extended during his official visit to the USSR in May 1972, and in accordance with a subsequent agreement, General Secretary of the Central Committee of the Communist Party of the Soviet Union [CPSU], Mr. Leonid I. Brezhnev, paid an official visit to the United States from June 18 to June 25. Mr. Brezhnev was accompanied by A. A. Gromyko, Minister of Foreign Affairs of the USSR, Member of the Politbureau of the Central Committee, CPSU; N. S. Patolichev, Miniser of Foreign Trade; B. P. Bugayev, Minister of Civil Aviation; G. E. Tsukanov and A. M. Aleksandrov, Assistants to the General Secretary of the Central Committee, CPSU; L. I. Zamyatin, General Director of TASS [Telegraphic Agency of the Soviet Union]; E. I. Chazov, Deputy Minister of Public Health of the USSR; G. M. Korniyenko, Member of the Collegium of the Ministry of Foreign Affairs of the USSR; G. A. Arbatov, Director of the USA Institute of the Academy of Sciences of the USSR.

President Nixon and General Secretary Brezhnev held thorough and constructive discussions on the progress achieved in the development of US-Soviet relations and on a number of major international problems of mutual interest.

Also taking part in the conversations held in Washington, Camp David, and San Clemente, were:

On the American side William P. Rogers, Secretary of State: George P. Shultz, Secretary of the Treasury; Dr. Henry A. Kissinger, Assistant to the President for National Security Affairs.

[41]For the remainder of the news conference see *Presidential Documents, loc. cit.*, pp. 850-55, or *Bulletin*, vol. 69 (1973), pp. 149-57.
[42]Text from *Presidential Documents*, vol. 9 (1973), pp. 840-48. The communiqué was released at San Clemente.

On the Soviet side A. A. Gromyko, Minister of Foreign Affairs of the USSR, Member of the Politbureau of the Central Committee, CPSU; A. F. Dobrynin, Soviet Ambassador to the USA; N. S. Patolichev, Minister of Foreign Trade; B. P. Bugayev, Minister of Civil Aviation; A. M. Aleksandrov and G. E. Tsukanov, Assistants to the General Secretary of the Central Committee, CPSU; G. M. Korniyenko, Member of the Collegium of the Ministry of Foreign Affairs of the USSR.

I. THE GENERAL STATE OF US—SOVIET RELATIONS

Both Sides expressed their mutual satisfaction with the fact that the American-Soviet summit meeting in Moscow in May 1972 and the joint decisions taken there have resulted in a substantial advance in the strengthening of peaceful relations between the USA and the USSR and have created the basis for the further development of broad and mutually beneficial cooperation in various fields of mutual interest to the peoples of both countries and in the interests of all mankind. They noted their satisfaction with the mutual effort to implement strictly and fully the treaties and agreements concluded between the USA and the USSR, and to expand areas of cooperation.

They agreed that the process of reshaping relations between the USA and the USSR on the basis of peaceful coexistence and equal security as set forth in the Basic Principles of Relations Between the USA and the USSR signed in Moscow on May 29, 1972[43] is progressing in an encouraging manner. They emphasized the great importance that each Side attaches to these Basic Principles. They reaffirmed their commitment to the continued scrupulous implementation and to the enhancement of the effectiveness of each of the provisions of that document.

Both Sides noted with satisfaction that the outcome of the US-Soviet meeting in Moscow in May 1972 was welcomed by other States and by world opinion as an important contribution to strengthening peace and international security, to curbing the arms race and to developing businesslike cooperation among States with different social systems.

Both Sides viewed the return visit to the USA of the General Secretary of the Central Committee of the CPSU, L. I. Brezhnev, and the talks held during the visit as an expression of their mutual determination to continue the course toward a major improvement in US-Soviet relations.

[43]*AFR, 1972*, pp. 75-8.

Both Sides are convinced that the discussions they have just held represent a further milestone in the constructive development of their relations.

Convinced that such a development of American-Soviet relations serves the interests of both of their peoples and all of mankind, it was decided to take further major steps to give these relations maximum stability and to turn the development of friendship and cooperation between their peoples into a permanent factor for worldwide peace.

II. THE PREVENTION OF NUCLEAR WAR AND THE LIMITATION OF STRATEGIC ARMAMENTS

Issues related to the maintenance and strengthening of international peace were a central point of the talks between President Nixon and General Secretary Brezhnev.

Conscious of the exceptional importance for all mankind of taking effective measures to that end, they discussed ways in which both Sides could work toward removing the danger of war, and especially nuclear war, between the USA and the USSR and between either party and other countries. Consequently, in accordance with the Charter of the United Nations and the Basic Principles of Relations of May 29, 1972, it was decided to conclude an Agreement Between the USA and the USSR on the Prevention of Nuclear War. That Agreement[44] was signed by the President and the General Secretary on June 22, 1973. The text has been published separately.

The President and the General Secretary, in appraising this Agreement, believe that it constitutes a historical landmark in Soviet-American relations and substantially strengthens the foundations of international security as a whole. The United States and the Soviet Union state their readiness to consider additional ways of strengthening peace and removing forever the danger of war, and particularly nuclear war.

In the course of the meetings, intensive discussions were held on questions of strategic arms limitation. In this connection both Sides emphasized the fundamental importance of the Treaty on the Limitation of Anti-Ballistic Missile Systems[45] and the Interim Agreement on Certain Measures with Respect to the Limitation of Strategic Offensive Arms[46] signed between the USA and the USSR

---

[44]Document 32b.
[45]*AFR, 1972*, pp. 90-95; for full reference see note 8 above.
[46]Same, pp. 97-101; for full reference see note 9 above.

in May 1972 which, for the first time in history, place actual limits on the most modern and most formidable types of armaments.

Having exchanged views on the progress in the implementation of these agreements, both Sides reaffirmed their intention to carry them out and their readiness to move ahead jointly toward an agreement on the further limitation of strategic arms.

Both Sides noted that progress has been made in the negotiations that resumed in November 1972, and that the prospects for reaching a permanent agreement on more complete measures limiting strategic offensive armaments are favorable.

Both Sides agreed that the progress made in the limitation of strategic armaments is an exceedingly important contribution to the strengthening of US-Soviet relations and to world peace.

On the basis of their discussions, the President and the General Secretary signed on June 21, 1973, Basic Principles of Negotiations on the Further Limitation of Strategic Offensive Arms.[47] The text has been published separately.

The USA and the USSR attach great importance to joining with all States in the cause of strengthening peace, reducing the burden of armaments, and reaching agreements on arms limitation and disarmament measures.

Considering the important role which an effective international agreement with respect to chemical weapons would play, the two Sides agreed to continue their efforts to conclude such an agreement in cooperation with other countries.

The two Sides agree to make every effort to facilitate the work of the Committee on Disarmament which has been meeting in Geneva.[48] They will actively participate in negotiations aimed at working out new measures to curb and end the arms race. They reaffirm that the ultimate objective is general and complete disarmament, including nuclear disarmament, under strict international control. A world disarmament conference could play a role in this process at an appropriate time.

III. INTERNATIONAL QUESTIONS: THE REDUCTION OF TENSIONS AND STRENGTHENING OF INTERNATIONAL SECURITY

President Nixon and General Secretary Brezhnev reviewed major questions of the current international situation. They gave special attention to the developments which have occurred since the time

---

[47]Document 31b.
[48]For details see especially *Bulletin*, vol. 70 (1974), pp. 128-34, and Chapter 28 at note 8.

of the US-Soviet summit meeting in Moscow. It was noted with satisfaction that positive trends are developing in international relations toward the further relaxation of tensions and the strengthening of cooperative relations in the interests of peace. In the opinion of both Sides, the current process of improvement in the international situation creates new and favorable opportunities for reducing tensions, settling outstanding international issues, and creating a permanent structure of peace.

Indochina

The two Sides expressed their deep satisfaction at the conclusion of the Agreement on Ending the War and Restoring Peace in Vietnam,[49] and also at the results of the International Conference on Vietnam which approved and supported that Agreement.[50]

The two Sides are convinced that the conclusion of the Agreement on Ending the War and Restoring Peace in Vietnam, and the subsequent signing of the Agreement on Restoring Peace and Achieving National Concord in Laos,[51] meet the fundamental interests and aspirations of the peoples of Vietnam and Laos and open up a possibility for establishing a lasting peace in Indochina, based on respect for the independence, sovereignty, unity and territorial integrity of the countries of that area. Both Sides emphasized that these agreements must be strictly implemented.

They further stressed the need to bring an early end to the military conflict in Cambodia[52] in order to bring peace to the entire area of Indochina. They also reaffirmed their stand that the political futures of Vietnam, Laos, and Cambodia should be left to the respective peoples to determine, free from outside interference.

Europe

In the course of the talks both Sides noted with satisfaction that in Europe the process of relaxing tensions and developing cooperation is actively continuing and thereby contributing to international stability.

The two Sides expressed satisfaction with the further normalization of relations among European countries resulting from treaties and agreements signed in recent years, particularly between

[49]Document 5.
[50]Document 7.
[51]Cf. Chapter 2 at note 9.
[52]Cf. Chapter 11.

the USSR and the FRG [Federal Republic of Germany].[53] They also welcome the coming into force of the Quadripartite Agreement of September 3, 1971.[54] They share the conviction that strict observance of the treaties and agreements that have been concluded will contribute to the security and well-being of all parties concerned.

They also welcome the prospect of United Nations membership this year for the FRG and the GDR [German Democratic Republic] and recall, in this connection, that the USA, USSR, UK and France have signed the Quadripartite Declaration of November 9, 1972, on this subject.[55]

The USA and the USSR reaffirm their desire, guided by the appropriate provisions of the Joint US-USSR Communique adopted in Moscow in May 1972,[56] to continue their separate and joint contributions to strengthening peaceful relations in Europe. Both Sides affirm that ensuring a lasting peace in Europe is a paramount goal of their policies.

In this connection satisfaction was expressed with the fact that as a result of common efforts by many States, including the USA and the USSR, the preparatory work has been successfully completed for the Conference on Security and Cooperation in Europe, which will be convened on July 3, 1973.[57] The USA and the USSR hold the view that the Conference will enhance the possibilities for strengthening European security and developing cooperation among the participating States. The USA and the USSR will conduct their policies so as to realize the goals of the Conference and bring about a new era of good relations in this part of the world.

Reflecting their continued positive attitude toward the Conference, both Sides will make efforts to bring the Conference to a successful conclusion at the earliest possible time. Both Sides proceed from the assumption that progress in the work of the Conference will produce possibilities for completing it at the highest level.

The USA and the USSR believe that the goal of strengthening stability and security in Europe would be further advanced if the relaxation of political tensions were accompanied by a reduction of military tensions in Central Europe. In this respect they attach great importance to the negotiations on the mutual reduction of

[53]*Documents, 1970*, pp. 105-6; cf. Chapter 11 at note 20.
[54]Quadripartite Agreement on Berlin, in *AFR, 1971*, pp. 166-70; same, *1972*, pp. 160-62.
[55]Same, p. 176. The two German states were admitted to U.N. membership on September 18, 1973; cf. Chapter 28 at note 4.
[56]*AFR, 1972*, pp. 66-75.
[57]Cf. Document 35.

forces and armaments and associated measures in Central Europe which will begin on October 30, 1973.[58] Both Sides state their readiness to make, along with other States, their contribution to the achievement of mutually acceptable decisions on the substance of this problem, based on the strict observance of the principle of the undiminished security of any of the parties.

Middle East

The parties expressed their deep concern with the situation in the Middle East and exchanged opinions regarding ways of reaching a Middle East settlement.

Each of the parties set forth its position on this problem.

Both parties agreed to continue to exert their efforts to promote the quickest possible settlement in the Middle East. This settlement should be in accordance with the interests of all states in the area, be consistent with their independence and sovereignty and should take into due account the legitimate interests of the Palestinian people.[59]

IV. COMMERCIAL AND ECONOMIC RELATIONS

The President and the General Secretary thoroughly reviewed the status of and prospects for commercial and economic ties between the USA and the USSR. Both Sides noted with satisfaction the progress achieved in the past year in the normalization and development of commercial and economic relations between them.

They agreed that mutually advantageous cooperation and peaceful relations would be strengthened by the creation of a permanent foundation of economic relationships.

They recall with satisfaction the various agreements on trade and commercial relations signed in the past year. Both Sides note that American-Soviet trade has shown a substantial increase, and that there are favorable prospects for a continued rise in the exchange of goods over the coming years.

They believe that the two countries should aim at a total of 2-3 billion dollars of trade over the next three years. The Joint US-USSR Commercial Commission continues to provide a valuable mechanism to promote the broad-scale growth of economic relations. The two Sides noted with satisfaction that contacts be-

[58]Cf. Documents 34 and 79.
[59]Cf. Chapter 15.

tween American firms and their Soviet counterparts are continuing to expand.

Both sides confirmed their firm intention to proceed from their earlier understanding on measures directed at creating more favorable conditions for expanding commercial and other economic ties between the USA and the USSR.

It was noted that as a result of the Agreement Regarding Certain Maritime Matters signed in October 1972,[60] Soviet and American commercial ships have been calling more frequently at ports of the United States and the USSR, respectively, and since late May of this year a new regular passenger line has started operating between New York and Leningrad.

In the course of the current meeting, the two Sides signed a Protocol augmenting existing civil air relations between the USA and the USSR[61] providing for direct air services between Washington and Moscow and New York and Leningrad, increasing the frequency of flights and resolving other questions in the field of civil aviation.

In the context of reviewing prospects for further and more permanent economic cooperation, both Sides expressed themselves in favor of mutually advantageous long term projects. They discussed a number of specific projects involving the participation of American companies, including the delivery of Siberian natural gas to the United States. The President indicated that the USA encourages American firms to work out concrete proposals on these projects and will give serious and sympathetic consideration to proposals that are in the interest of both Sides.

To contribute to expanded commercial, cultural and technical relations between the USA and the USSR, the two Sides signed a tax convention[62] to avoid double taxation on income and eliminate, as much as possible, the need for citizens of one country to become involved in the tax system of the other.

A Protocol was also signed on the opening by the end of October 1973 of a Trade Representation of the USSR in Washington and a Commercial Office of the United States in Moscow.[63] In addition a

---

[60]TIAS 7513 (23 UST 3573); cf. *AFR, 1972*, p. 119.

[61]Protocol on Questions Relating to the Expansion of Air Services, signed June 23, 1973 (TIAS 7658; 24 UST 1506). Unofficial texts of this and all other bilateral agreements concluded during the Brezhnev visit will be found in the general documentation cited in note 3 above. All agreements entered into force on signature except for the tax convention cited in note 62.

[62]Convention on Matters of Taxation, signed June 20, 1973, subject to ratification. The convention was submitted to the U.S. Senate Sept. 19, 1973 (S. Ex. T, 93-1) but was not acted upon during the 93d Congress in 1973-4.

[63]Signed June 22, 1973 (TIAS 7657; 24 UST 1501).

Protocol was signed on questions related to establishing a US-Soviet Chamber of Commerce.[64] These agreements will facilitate the further development of commercial and economic ties between the USA and the USSR.

V. FURTHER PROGRESS IN OTHER FIELDS
OF BILATERAL COOPERATION

The two Sides reviewed the areas of bilateral cooperation in such fields as environmental protection, public health and medicine, exploration of outer space, and science and technology, established by the agreements signed in May 1972 and subsequently. They noted that those agreements are being satisfactorily carried out in practice in accordance with the programs as adopted.

In particular, a joint effort is under way to develop effective means to combat those diseases which are most widespread and dangerous for mankind: cancer, cardiovascular or infectious diseases and arthritis. The medical aspects of the environmental problems are also subjects of cooperative research.

Preparations for the joint space flight of the Apollo and Soyuz spacecraft are proceeding according to an agreed timetable. The joint flight of these spaceships for a rendezvous and docking mission, and mutual visits of American and Soviet astronauts in each other's spacecraft, are scheduled for July 1975.

Building on the foundation created in previous agreements, and recognizing the potential of both the USA and the USSR to undertake cooperative measures in current scientific and technological areas, new projects for fruitful joint efforts were identified and appropriate agreements were concluded.

Peaceful Uses of Atomic Energy

Bearing in mind the great importance of satisfying the growing energy demands in both countries and throughout the world, and recognizing that the development of highly efficient energy sources could contribute to the solution of this problem, the President and General Secretary signed an agreement to expand and strengthen cooperation in the fields of controlled nuclear fusion, fast breeder reactors, and research on the fundamental properties of matter.[65] A Joint Committee on Cooperation in the Peaceful Uses of Atomic

---

[64]Signed June 22, 1973 (TIAS 7656; 24 UST 1498).

[65]Agreement on Scientific and Technical Cooperation in the Field of Peaceful Uses of Atomic Energy, signed June 21, 1973 (TIAS 7655; 24 UST 1486).

Energy will be established to implement this agreement, which has a duration of ten years.

Agriculture

Recognizing the importance of agriculture in meeting mankind's requirement for food products and the role of science in modern agricultural production, the two Sides concluded an agreement providing for a broad exchange of scientific experience in agricultural research and development, and of information on agricultural economics.[66] A US-USSR Joint Committee on Agricultural Cooperation will be established to oversee joint programs to be carried out under the Agreement.

World Ocean Studies

Considering the unique capabilities and the major interest of both nations in the field of world ocean studies, and noting the extensive experience of US-USSR oceanographic cooperation, the two Sides have agreed to broaden their cooperation and have signed an agreement to this effect.[67] In so doing, they are convinced that the benefits from further development of cooperation in the field of oceanography will accrue not only bilaterally but also to all peoples of the world. A US-USSR Joint Committee on Cooperation in World Ocean Studies will be established to coordinate the implementation of cooperative programs.

Transportation

The two Sides agreed that there are opportunities for cooperation between the USA and the USSR in the solution of problems in the field of transportation. To permit expanded, mutually beneficial cooperation in this field, the two Sides concluded an agreement on this subject.[68] The USA and the USSR further agreed that a Joint Committee on Cooperation in Transportation would be established.

[66]Agreement on Cooperation in Agriculture, signed June 19, 1973 (TIAS 7650; 24 UST 1439).
[67]Agreement on Cooperation in Studies of World Oceans, signed June 19, 1973 (TIAS 7651; 24 UST 1452).
[68]Agreement on Cooperation in Transportation, signed June 19, 1973 (TIAS 7652; 24 UST 1463).

Contacts, Exchanges and Cooperation

Recognizing the general expansion of US-USSR bilateral relations and, in particular, the growing number of exchanges in the fields of science, technology, education and culture, and in other fields of mutual interest, the two Sides agreed to broaden the scope of these activities under a new General Agreement on Contacts, Exchanges, and Cooperation, with a duration of six years.[69] The two Sides agreed to this in the mutual belief that it will further promote better understanding between the peoples of the United States and the Soviet Union and will help to improve the general state of relations between the two countries.

Both Sides believe that the talks at the highest level, which were held in a frank and constructive spirit, were very valuable and made an important contribution to developing mutually advantageous relations between the USA and the USSR. In the view of both Sides, these talks will have a favorable impact on international relations.

They noted that the success of the discussions in the United States was facilitated by the continuing consultation and contacts as agreed in May 1972. They reaffirmed that the practice of consultation should continue. They agreed that further meetings at the highest level should be held regularly.

Having expressed his appreciation to President Nixon for the hospitality extended during the visit to the United States, General Secretary Brezhnev invited the President to visit the USSR in 1974. The invitation was accepted.[70]

June 24, 1973

RICHARD NIXON
President of the United States of America

L. I. BREZHNEV
General Secretary of the Central Committee, CPSU

[69]General Agreement on Contacts, Exchanges and Cooperation in Scientific, Technical, Educational, Cultural and Other Fields, signed June 19, 1973 (TIAS 7649; 24 UST 1395).
[70]President Nixon visited the U.S.S.R. on June 27-July 3, 1974. For the official communiqué see *Presidential Documents*, vol. 10 (1974), pp. 753-63, or *Bulletin*, vol. 71 (1974), pp. 185-91.

13. PROMOTING DÉTENTE IN EUROPE

A point of special interest in the communiqué that concluded the
Nixon-Brezhnev meetings[1] was its expression of mutual satisfaction
that "the process of relaxing tensions and developing cooperation"
in Europe was "actively continuing and thereby contributing to international stability." Particularly encouraging to the two leaders,
it appeared, had been the recent progress in connection with two
longstanding diplomatic endeavors: (1) the successful completion
of preparatory work for the Conference on Security and
Cooperation in Europe (CSCE), which was due to open in Helsinki
on July 3, 1973; and (2) a procedural agreement relating to the
proposed negotiations on "the mutual reduction of forces and armaments and associated measures in Central Europe," which were
now set to begin in Vienna on October 30, 1973.

Preliminary consultations with regard to the proposed European
security conference, which had been intermittently advocated by
the Soviet Union since as far back as 1954, had been initiated in
Helsinki in November 1972 and, by June 8, 1973, had resulted in
detailed agreement on the organization, agenda, and other
technical aspects of the meeting.[2] Thirty-five nations would participate, among them the United States and Canada together with
all significant European states except Albania, which had refused
to have anything to do with the project. In addition to questions
relating to European security in the strict sense, the agreed agenda
provided for detailed discussion of cooperation in economics,
science and technology, the environment, and various humanitarian and cultural endeavors.

It had also been agreed at Helsinki that the conference would
take place in three stages: a ceremonial opening stage, to be held at
Foreign Ministers' level in the Finnish capital beginning July 3; a

[1]Document 33b. For background discussion cf. *AFR, 1971*, pp. 135-89; same,
1972, pp. 147-62 and 173-84.
[2]Text of Final Recommendations in *Bulletin*, vol. 69 (1973), pp. 181-8.

second stage, involving detailed committee work, which would take place in Geneva; and a formal conclusion, which would again take place in Helsinki at a level to be determined by the participating states.[3] General Secretary Brezhnev, whose government had originally fathered the conference idea, was known to favor a ceremonial windup at summit level; and President Nixon had agreed in the course of his talks with the Soviet leader "that progress in the work of the Conference will produce possibilities for completing it at the highest level."[4]

Preparations for negotiations concerning mutual and balanced force reductions (MBFR) in Central Europe, as originally proposed by the West in 1968, were not quite so far advanced; but here, too, a considerable measure of agreement had been achieved by the nineteen NATO and Warsaw Pact governments whose representatives had been engaged in preparatory consultations in Vienna since January 31, 1973. After weeks of argument about the participation of such Soviet-bloc states as Bulgaria and Romania, it had been agreed on May 14 that the countries taking part in the talks would best be divided into two separate categories. The burden of decision-making would be shared by the seven governments from NATO (Belgium, Canada, West Germany, Luxembourg, the Netherlands, the United Kingdom, and the United States) and the four from the Warsaw group (Czechoslovakia, East Germany, Poland, and the U.S.S.R.) that actually had military forces in the Central European area. The eight remaining states (Denmark, Greece, Italy, Norway, and Turkey from the West; Bulgaria, Hungary, and Romania from the East) would, it was agreed, participate "with a special status," the question of Hungarian participation being left open to possible reexamination in view of the presence of Soviet military forces in that country.[5]

The actual date for the commencement of the MBFR negotiations was first disclosed in the Nixon-Brezhnev communiqué, in which the United States and the Soviet Union affirmed "their readiness to make, along with other States, their contribution to the achievement of mutually acceptable decisions . . . based on the strict observance of the principle of the undiminished security of any of the parties."[6] Formal confirmation that the negotiations would begin on October 30 in Vienna was offered by the nineteen-nation preparatory group as it wound up its own consultations on June 28 (**Document 34a**).

[3]Same.
[4]Document 33b.
[5]Record of plenary meeting, May 14, in *Documents on Disarmament, 1973*, pp. 252-5.
[6]Document 33b.

France, it will be noted, was not and had never been a participant in the MBFR project; and even the initials MBFR were now being rendered obsolete by the formal designation of the subject of the forthcoming negotiations as "mutual reduction of forces and armaments and associated measures in Central Europe." Although the word "balanced" was dropped by the Vienna consultants in deference to objections from the Warsaw Pact countries, the Western governments took the view that the principle of balance was safeguarded by a universal agreement that, in the words of the June 28 communiqué, "specific arrangements will have to be carefully worked out in scope and timing in such a way that they will in all respects and at every point conform to the principle of undiminished security for each party."[7]

While detailed discussion of European military questions would thus be postponed until the autumn, the European Security Conference that was to open in Helsinki on July 3 would be addressing itself to the much broader question of the kind of European order that should emerge in place of the partitioned, bitterly divided Europe of "cold war" days. It was a tribute to the ingenuity of the Helsinki consultants that they had managed to elaborate the framework of such a conference in spite of the persistence of radically opposed conceptions regarding its nature and aims. The Soviet Union had never disguised the fact that its objective in promoting the conference was to win general, formal acknowledgment of the new political patterns brought about since World War II by the imposition of Communist rule in Eastern and parts of Central Europe. The Western governments, while obviously not inclined to contest the reality of Communist rule in countries where it already existed, had taken the position that their acquiescence in the European *status quo* should at least be balanced by an expansion and liberalization of the various forms of peaceful East-West contact. This, however, was an idea that most Communist rulers found quite repugnant to their political precepts if not to their whole system of rule.

The depth of this divergence was evident beneath the harmonious trappings that clothed the formal opening of the Security Conference on July 3. To leave no doubt about the position of the Soviet Union, Foreign Minister Andrei A. Gromyko promptly laid before the assembled delegations a "Draft General Declaration on the Fundamentals of European Security and Principles of Relations among European States"[8] that faithfully reflected his govern-

[7]Stockholm International Peace Research Institute, *Force Reductions in Europe* (Stockholm: SIPRI, 1974), pp. 21-2. For the opening of the Vienna negotiations see Chapter 27 at note 3.
[8]Text in *Soviet News*, No. 5696 (1973), pp. 309-10.

ment's known predilections. The states participating in the conference, this Soviet document averred, must "regard the existing frontiers in Europe as inviolable now and in the future"; furthermore, they must at all times "respect the political, economic and cultural principles of other states"—a thesis that could severely handicap the unrestricted intercourse being advocated in the West. Insisting on the importance of avoiding unnecessary delays, Gromyko further declared that there was "every opportunity" for the entire work of the conference to be concluded before the end of 1973, and that, as Brezhnev had indicated previously, the concluding stage would most appropriately take place "at a summit level."[9]

Most of the non-Communist Foreign Ministers adopted a more cautious stance. Secretary of State Rogers, in his address to the conference on July 5 (**Document 35a**), suggested that it would be well to "proceed as expeditiously as possible, but without undue haste." "We do not want to complete our work merely restating familiar principles," Mr. Rogers warned. Such worthwhile precepts as the renunciation of force and the inviolability of frontiers must not become impediments to peaceful change, he added; nor ought the conference to underestimate the importance of "the lowering of barriers to the freer flow of people, information, and ideas among the participating states."

Any attempt at reconciling these divergent positions would obviously have to be left to the "working" phase of the conference. The communiqué that marked the close of the Helsinki stage on July 7 (**Document 35b**) announced that this second stage would begin in Geneva on September 18, and that its purpose would be to "pursue the study of questions on the agenda and . . . prepare drafts of declarations, recommendations, resolutions or any other final documents" on the basis of the proposals submitted. (Contrary to Soviet hopes, this second, Geneva stage was destined to continue until July 1975 before agreement could be reached on the lengthy Final Act that was eventually signed in Helsinki by Heads of Government and other "High Representatives" on August 1, 1975.)[10]

Secretary Rogers, his mission in Helsinki completed, devoted the next two days to a continuation of the "bridge-building" efforts in Eastern Europe that had been a central theme of American policy since the Kennedy and Johnson administrations. In 1972, the Secretary of State had signed bilateral consular conventions with Poland, Romania, and Hungary;[11] and a similar convention was

[9]Same, p. 308.
[10]*Bulletin*, vol. 73 (1975), pp. 323-50.
[11]Cf. *AFR, 1972*, pp. 163-73.

now concluded with Czechoslovakia as a highlight of the first visit to that country by an American Secretary of State.[12] The mere fact of such a visit testified to the improvement of U.S.-Czechoslovak relations since the dark days less than five years earlier when Czechoslovakia had been invaded and occupied by forces of the other Warsaw Pact countries.

These varied initiatives involving East-West relations within the European theater might ultimately redound to the benefit of both sides; but they had done little as yet to close the rift that already existed between the United States and its allies in Western Europe. Still to be faced, on both sides of the Atlantic, was the basic issue implicit in Dr. Kissinger's "Year of Europe" speech: Would the countries of Western Europe, in recognition of their continuing dependence on U.S. defense support, adopt a more accommodating attitude on the trade and monetary problems that still awaited resolution in the appropriate international forums?

Thus far, there had been little movement in Europe toward the drafting of the "new Atlantic charter" proposed by President Nixon's Assistant for National Security Affairs; nor did the advocates of a reduction of U.S. military forces in Europe seem willing to await the forthcoming negotiations in Vienna before attempting to implement their plans by legislative action. While the NATO countries endeavored to concert their strategy for the coming force reduction talks, administration spokesmen in Washington attempted to combat the renewed threat of a congressional cutback in the 300,000-man American force in Europe and the Mediterranean.[13] This was a problem that would continue to figure not only in the developing struggle between the executive and Congress but also in the evolving relationship between the United States, its Western allies, and the countries of the Soviet bloc.[14]

---

[12]Rogers statement, July 8, in *Bulletin*, vol. 69 (1973), pp. 188-9. Signed in Prague July 9, 1973, the convention was transmitted to the Senate Feb. 21, 1974 (Ex. A, 93-2), approved by a Senate vote of 78-0 on Sept. 30, 1974, and ratified by the President on Dec. 16, 1974, but had not entered into force as of early 1976.

[13]For administration statements to congressional committees during July 1973 see *Bulletin*, vol. 69 (1973), pp. 209-28 and 286-92.

[14]For further developments see Chapters 17 and 21.

(34)   Preparatory Consultations Relating to Central Europe, Vienna, January 31-June 28, 1973.

>   *(a)   Nineteen-country Communiqué issued at Vienna June 28, 1973.*[15]

1. Preparatory consultations relating to Central Europe took place in Vienna from January 31, 1973 to June 28, 1973. Participation in and procedures for these consultations were as set forth in the Record of the plenary meeting of May 14, 1973.[16]

2. In the course of these consultations, it was decided to hold negotiations on mutual reduction of forces and armaments and associated measures in Central Europe. The negotiations will take place in Vienna, and will begin on October 30, 1973. It was also agreed that participation in and procedures for the negotiations will be as set forth in the Record of the plenary meeting of May 14, 1973.

3. The participants in the consultations had a useful and constructive exchange of views on an agenda for the forthcoming negotiations. They agreed that during the negotiations, mutual reduction of forces and armaments and associated measures in Central Europe would be considered. It was agreed that the general objective of the negotiations will be to contribute to a more stable relationship and to the strengthening of peace and security in Europe. They agreed that, in the negotiations, an understanding should be reached to conduct them in such a way as to ensure the most effective and thorough approach to the consideration of the subject matter, with due regard to its complexity. They also agreed that specific arrangements will have to be carefully worked out in scope and timing in such a way that they will in all respects and at every point conform to the principle of undiminished security for each party. It was decided that in the course of the negotiations, any topic relevant to the subject matter may be introduced for negotiation by any of those states which will take the necessary decisions, without prejudice to the right of all participants to speak and to circulate papers on the subject matter. This exchange of views on an agenda will greatly facilitate the work of the forthcoming negotiations. During the negotiations, the question of establishing working bodies or working groups will be considered.

4. The participants expressed their gratitude to the Government of the Republic of Austria for the considerate assistance and facilities it provided during the consultations and for its agreement that the forthcoming negotiations can take place in Vienna.

[15]Text from *Bulletin*, vol. 69 (1973), p. 659.
[16]*Documents on Disarmament, 1973*, pp. 252-5; cf. above at note 5.

*(35)   Conference on Security and Cooperation in Europe (CSCE):
First Stage, Helsinki, July 3-7, 1973.*

*(a)   Views of the United States: Statement by Secretary of
State Rogers to the Conference, July 5, 1973.*[17]

I would like to join my colleagues in expressing the gratitude of
the U.S. Government to the Government of Finland for its many
and substantial contributions to bringing this conference into
being. This conference provides the nations represented here a
historic opportunity. But whether the conference itself achieves
historic importance depends on how we—the Foreign Ministers
here present and the 35 governments we represent—avail ourselves
of the opportunity.

I think it can be said that so far the meeting has met our expectations. We have gathered together in a friendly and constructive manner and have engaged in what we refer to as a general
debate—but a debate with very few differences. I am the 21st
speaker, and unless I missed something, each speaker who preceded
me spoke thoughtfully, respectfully of the viewpoints of others,
and without using contentious rhetoric. Maybe we should not list
this as an accomplishment, but we can say it's a relief.

But beyond the friendly climate which has prevailed throughout,
we made a decision of major dimensions at the outset—almost
routinely. After careful consideration by our governments, we
unanimously adopted the Final Recommendations of the Helsinki
Consultations.[18] This, in fact, is a remarkable document. It is not
merely a conference agenda. It contains a long list of agreed principles and includes a detailed and carefully drafted work program
designed to promote peaceful evolution in Europe for the years
ahead. This document is a commitment to find new and more
civilized ways of dealing with one another. I wish to underline the
point that the commitments we have made here are solemn
obligations to develop comprehensive and specific measures to advance our relationships in that spirit.

I think President [Urho K.] Kekkonen [of Finland] captured the
essence of our decision when he said, "Security is not gained by
erecting fences; security is gained by opening gates."

For a quarter century, division has been the dominant feature of
Europe. We all recognize that this conference must not confirm the
barriers that still divide Europe. Rather, by our support of the final
recommendations we have expressly undertaken to lower these

[17]Department of State Press Release 237, July 6; text from *Bulletin*, vol. 69 (1973),
pp. 177-81.
[18]Same, pp. 181-8; cf. above at note 2.

barriers. We have said coexistence is not enough. Indeed, the document to which we have agreed requires constructive change on a broad front in order that with the passage of time we can engage in many truly cooperative and mutually beneficial and peaceful relationships.

The decisive challenge of the conference, then, is: Can we follow through?

We have had some discussion here about the time frame for meeting the challenge. It seems to me that that decision can be reached later on. If we are successful—and I believe we can succeed—then scheduling will come easily. If we fail, the schedule will be of little importance.

Cynics have suggested that the objective of an international conference is to complete it. I am sure that does not represent the views of any nation here. This conference, I believe, should proceed as expeditiously as possible, but without undue haste. What we seek is progress. Progress results from practical steps. Practical steps are not easy to take, but they are essential because we do not want to complete our work merely restating familiar principles.

As previous speakers have noted, the conference comes at a propitious time. Many nations represented here have dramatically contributed to creating the conditions which have made this conference possible. Four and one-half years ago President Nixon pledged that the policy of the United States would be to move from confrontation to negotiation in all areas of the world. He acted promptly to carry out his policy, and as a result it is generally acknowledged that today we live in a much more peaceful world. This new climate for peace benefits all of mankind. But much more remains to be done.

The universal hope for a durable peace can be significantly strengthened by the nations participating in this conference; that is the hope that permeates this hall. We represent most of the world's developed nations. Our economies produce about 75 percent of the world's wealth, and together we account for approximately 85 percent of the world's military expenditures. Our long-range goal must be an act of common will to bring our enormous resources to bear on the common problems we face and on assisting others less fortunate. Moreover, it is now within our grasp to contribute to an improved world climate so that a reduction in the world's armaments is a definite possibility.

We are all conscious, as so many have said, that the two World Wars began in Europe. We have all learned lessons from those conflicts. The United States has learned from our experience that Europe's security is indivisible from our own. The presence of my delegation today symbolizes that fundamental fact—the fact, if you will, of our engagement in Europe.

Americans believe that during the last generation we have made a constructive and successful commitment to peace and stability in Europe. And today, on behalf of the Government of the United States, I want to underscore the firmness of our resolve both to continue that commitment and to strengthen our relationship with all of the states represented here.

Let me turn briefly to some of the specific issues with which the conference has agreed to deal.

Nothing is more important than the principle that states refrain from the use or threat of force. It is the keystone in the arch of a durable peace, and we have accepted it as a fundamental principle in relations between states.

This means, of course, that frontiers should not be violated by force or threats of force. At the same time, this does not rule out—and I emphasize, does not rule out—peaceful changes in frontiers if such changes are based on popular will and mutual agreement between states. Certainly no one could validly contend otherwise, for such contention would violate the twin principles of sovereignty and the right of self-determination.

Another principle which this conference has already endorsed is the principle of universal respect for the right of every country to independence and to its own internal development free of outside interference, irrespective of its political, economic, or social system. We have said in effect that a country must not be denied these rights for any reason. That is why we Foreign Ministers have mandated the committee that it must "express the determination of the participating States to respect and apply the principles equally and unreservedly in all aspects to their mutual relations and co-operation, in order to ensure to all participating States the benefits resulting from the application of these principles by all." There is nothing equivocal about that decision which we have made. And in international affairs strict observance of that mandate is of utmost importance.

Another important mandate in the document states that we should study ways in which problems arising between states can be resolved on a peaceful basis early on to avoid later conflict. The committee could achieve meaningful results in this area by carefully developing plans for early consultation and possibly mediation to avoid confrontation.

The committee is also enjoined to give specific meaning to the concept of reduction of tensions in the military sphere as set forth in paragraph 23 of the final recommendations. Thus we support:

1. Advance notification of major military maneuvers;
2. Exchanges of observers by invitation at military maneuvers under mutually acceptable conditions; and
3. The study of prior notification of major military movements.

We have given support to these measures because we believe greater confidence can result from sharing such military information so that the margin for surprise can be substantially reduced.

A fundamental aspect of our commitment is outlined in section III.[19] I refer of course to the lowering of barriers to the freer flow of people, information, and ideas among the participating states. This aspect of our work stems from the importance we attach to human rights and fundamental freedoms. There are few words which are so filled with meaning, so venerated by people everywhere. But section III could turn out to be a sad footnote in future history books unless the committee finds concrete ways to embody the concepts contained therein so that the everyday lives of people are favorably affected. I have in mind here, for example, proposals for arrangements that will permit the reunification of families, more regular visits between the members of divided families, new ways of sharing experiences in various fields of professional and intellectual endeavor, and promoting closer links between our young people. Our youth should learn more about one another and about other states and systems. The future development of our relations can only profit from their mutual understanding.

We have agreed here also to facilitate travel for personal or professional reasons. In several countries, as in our country, citizens are free to travel anywhere in the world without any restriction or interference. I recognize of course that each state has its own regulations. But the thrust of the mandate is to encourage—indeed, to exhort—states to lower barriers to travel and encourage human contacts that are so essential to understanding and mutual respect in today's world.

It will also be important to give specific content to our agreement to improve the circulation of and access to information transmitted by the various media and to improve the conditions under which journalists may exercise their profession in our countries. The right of people to know fully what is happening in the world is a basic human right and a basic requirement for understanding and knowledge.

---

[19]"Co-operation in Humanitarian and Other Fields."

We have also agreed to reduce the obstacles in the development of trade by examining specific measures, among other things, to facilitate business contacts and the exchange of information on commercial opportunities.

In addition to our work in this conference, we have recognized that the process of reconciliation must move forward on a broader front. In this connection it should be noted that the increasingly united European Community has a special contribution to make as it forges an economic and political union among member states whose past disputes were a frequent cause of war in Europe. And by building closer ties with individual East European nations, members of the Community and other West European nations are lowering the barriers that have too long divided Europe.

The United States will continue to work closely with its allies in the Atlantic alliance, which contributes not only to the security and independence of its members but is also seeking new ways to improve relations in Europe.

With the nations of eastern Europe the United States has opened a new era of improved relations. We are dealing with each country in eastern Europe separately—determining our policy in accordance with the specific policies and actions of each and looking forward to a wider and more constructive association with all the nations of the area.

The United States and the Soviet Union have a major contribution to make to a secure and cooperative Europe. Just as the confrontation between our two nations contributed to the division of postwar Europe, so the recent improvement in our relations is helping to bring Europe together again.

At the conclusion of their meeting in Washington last month President Nixon and General Secretary Brezhnev affirmed that "ensuring a lasting peace in Europe is a paramount goal of their policies."[20] The agreement they signed on prevention of nuclear war[21] is a landmark in Soviet-American relations and should have a favorable impact upon European security as well. And by setting forth basic principles for further limitation of strategic arms[22] and by entering into several other agreements involving mutual endeavors, the Soviet Union and the United States further contributed to the goal, held by all of us at this conference, of strengthening stability and security in Europe.

The United States is also gratified by the progress being made in discussions in various forums on the limitation of arms and ar-

[20]Document 33b.
[21]Document 32b.
[22]Document 31b.

maments. We are particularly pleased that many of us here have reached agreement that negotiations on the mutual reduction of armed forces and armaments and associated measures in central Europe will begin on October 30.[23] These talks will be proceeding in Vienna at the same time as the second stage of this conference is going forward in Geneva. The Vienna talks should complement our efforts in this conference to strengthen stability and security in Europe.

As the first phase of the conference draws to a close, it might be well briefly to outline what we hope can be achieved during the second phase. The conference should:

1. Elaborate, with precision, upon the agreed general principles in ways that relate directly and specifically to the problems of states participating in the conference;

2. Reach agreements on specific military matters including exchange of certain significant military information and appropriate exchange of observers in order to increase confidence and dispel suspicion;

3. Develop methods for early and peaceful settlement of disputes which might have the potential for confrontation between any of the participating states;

4. Advance proposals for reducing barriers to the growth of trade, increasing commercial exchanges, industrial cooperation, cooperation in the field of science and technology; and

5. Of paramount importance, work out specific and meaningful ways to facilitate human contacts, the freer dissemination of information, and the broadening of cultural and educational cooperation.

In the second phase we have to translate the results of our work into dynamic programs which would give specific meaning to the relationships that we seek, and the United States will submit concrete proposals for this purpose. Finally, during the process we must adhere in all of our dealings to the spirit of reconciliation. For it is this spirit which has raised all of our hopes for a new era of peace in Europe and throughout the world.

Our goal should be a continent in which no nation feels threatened, a continent open to the free flow of people and ideas, and a continent enriched rather than divided by political and cultural diversity. Such a Europe will not come about merely by wishing for it or by making declarations about it. Only time will tell whether we have accomplished anything or not, but one thing is

[23]Document 34a.

certain: We must proceed with great industry and diligence in the days ahead and must pursue our goal with patience, understanding, and determination through the years to come. If there is a consensus among us in that spirit, then we may be proud of the few days we spent together in this friendly city of Helsinki.

(b) Communiqué on the First Stage of the Conference, July 7, 1973.[24]

The first stage of the Conference on Security and Cooperation in Europe took place in Helsinki from 3 to 7 July 1973. In accordance with the agreement reached earlier, this stage of the Conference was held at Foreign Minister level.

The following states are participating in the conference: Austria, Belgium, Bulgaria, Canada, Cyprus, Czechoslovakia, Denmark, Finland, France, German Democratic Republic, Federal Republic of Germany, Greece, Holy See, Hungary, Iceland, Ireland, Italy, Liechtenstein, Luxembourg, Malta, Monaco, Netherlands, Norway, Poland, Portugal, Romania, San Marino, Spain, Sweden, Switzerland, Turkey, Union of Soviet Socialist Republics, United Kingdom, United States of America, Yugoslavia.

At the Inaugural Session of the Conference Dr. Urho Kekkonen, President of the Republic of Finland, made a speech of welcome. Dr. Kurt Waldheim, Secretary-General of the United Nations, also addressed the Conference.

The Ministers adopted the Final Recommendations of the Helsinki Consultations[25] which comprise the agenda and instructions of the working bodies of the Conference together with the rules of procedure and the other arrangements relating to the conduct of the Conference. The text of these final recommendations is available to the public.

The Ministers stated the views of their governments on essential problems relating to security and cooperation in Europe, and on the further work of the Conference.

The Foreign Ministers of several states submitted proposals on various questions relating to the agenda. Others announced the intention to submit proposals during the second stage of the Conference.

The Ministers examined the manner in which the Conference would acquaint itself with points of view expressed by non-participating states on the subject of various agenda items. This matter was in particular considered in connection with the request

---

[24]Department of State Press Release 238, July 9; text from *Bulletin*, vol. 69 (1973), p. 181.
[25]Same as note 2.

of Malta and Spain in favor of Algeria and Tunisia. This matter was also considered in relation to other non-participating states bordering the Mediterranean. No consensus was reached for the time being.

The Ministers decided that the second stage of the Conference will meet in Geneva on September 18, 1973, in order to pursue the study of the questions on the agenda and in order to prepare drafts of declarations, recommendations, resolutions or any other final documents on the basis of the proposals submitted during the first stage as well as those to be submitted.

The coordinating committee made up of representatives of participating states will assemble for its first meeting in Geneva on August 29, 1973, in order to prepare the organization of the second stage.

The Ministers expressed the determination of their governments to contribute to the success of the further work of the Conference.

The participants in the Conference expressed their profound gratitude to the Government of Finland for its hospitality and for the important contribution made by Finland to the preparation of the Conference on Security and Cooperation in Europe and to the conduct of the first stage.

14. JAPAN AND THE PACIFIC

In putting forward the concept of a "Year of Europe" in his address of April 23,[1] Dr. Kissinger had in no wise overlooked the importance of Japan, a country that was an ally of the United States in all but name and, though geographically remote from Europe, was obviously involved in many of the same problems. "In many fields, 'Atlantic' solutions to be viable must include Japan," the presidential assistant had stated in his April 23 address. ". . . Just as Europe's autonomy is not an end in itself, so the Atlantic community cannot be an exclusive club. Japan must be a principal partner in our common enterprise." A basic objective of the "new Atlantic charter," Dr. Kissinger had emphasized, was the creation for the Atlantic nations of "a new relationship in whose progress Japan can share."

Just how this new, trilateral association was to achieve concrete reality was specified neither in the Kissinger speech nor in the lengthier discussion of American-Japanese relations that appeared a few weeks later in President Nixon's "State of the World" report.[2] The general trend of Washington's thinking, at this period when Japanese-American relations were regaining stability after the "Nixon shocks" of 1971 and the subsequent change of leadership in Tokyo,[3] was nevertheless transparently clear. As with Europe, so with Japan, the United States believed that the important help it was giving its partner, particularly in defense matters, should be matched by heightened understanding and cooperation from the other side on political and, above all, on monetary and trade questions.

Other trends in the Pacific area were also pressing their claims upon American attention. Developments related to the "Nixon Doctrine," the opening to China, and the end of the Indochina war

---

[1]Document 21.
[2]*Nixon Report, 1973*, pp. 94-105; for brief quotation see Document 36a.
[3]For background see *AFR, 1971*, pp. 367-75; same, *1972*, pp. 328-40.

had set in motion what was obviously a long-term process of reduction of the American military power deployed for so many years in Southeast Asia, Taiwan, Okinawa, and South Korea. Concurrently, American military planners were displaying a heightened interest in the strategic possibilities of the U.S.-administered Trust Territory of the Pacific Islands (Micronesia), particularly the Mariana Islands extending northward from U.S.-owned Guam. With U.S.-Micronesian negotiations on the future of the trust territory at least temporarily stalled, American spokesmen jolted the U.N. Trusteeship Council in the spring of 1973 by pointing out that separate negotiations already being carried on with Marianas representatives might ultimately result in the detachment of those islands from the remainder of the territory and their endowment with a "commonwealth" status under U.S. sovereignty.[4]

Two other situations in the Pacific and Far East were being watched with more immediate attention. France, in spite of years of international denunciation and a formal order from the International Court of Justice,[5] was once again preparing to carry out a series of atmospheric nuclear tests at its South Pacific proving ground at Mururoa Atoll. Tests would actually begin on July 21, to the vehement indignation of Japan, Australia, and New Zealand and the annoyance of the United States and others.

In what might conceivably be viewed as a more hopeful development, the leaders of the rival Korean governments on June 23 had put forward separate proposals for overcoming the political impasse that had kept Korea divided since World War II and, among other effects, had prevented either government's acceptance into the United Nations. According to President Park Chung Hee, the increasingly authoritarian leader of the southern, anti-Communist Republic of Korea (ROK), a reasonable exit from this situation might now be found in a simultaneous entry into the United Nations by both Korean states, as had been arranged in the case of the two German governments. But President Kim Il Sung of the northern, Communist-ruled Democratic People's Republic of Korea (DPRK) immediately rejected this plan, insisting that Korean entry into the United Nations should be postponed until the two parts of Korea had formed a confederal state that could join the world body as a single nation.[6] Although the two plans differed

[4]Details in *UN Monthly Chronicle*, vol. 10 (July 1973), pp. 93-103; *Bulletin*, vol. 69 (1973), pp. 312-16; *U.S. Participation, 1973*, pp. 194-9.
[5]ICJ communiqué, June 22, in *UN Monthly Chronicle*, vol. 10 (July 1973), pp. 84-6.
[6]*Keesing's*, p. 26148. For U.N. action on Korea during 1973, cf. Chapter 28 at note 7.

radically in detail, they testified to a common recognition that conditions in East Asia were changing and that the rigid positions both sides had maintained in the past were no longer in tune with the times.

Such, in broad outline, were the conditions obtaining in the Pacific half of the world when Secretary of State Rogers, Secretary of Commerce Frederick B. Dent, and other high U.S. officials flew to Tokyo for the ninth meeting of the Joint United States-Japan Committee on Trade and Economic Affairs, held in the Japanese capital on July 16-17. (Secretary of the Treasury Shultz, Secretary of Agriculture Earl L. Butz, and Chairman of the Council of Economic Advisers Herbert Stein were prevented from attending by obligations relating to the preparation of a new domestic economic program.)

Addressing this body's first session to be held since the financial crises of 1971, Secretary Rogers offered a detailed analysis of the current world situation as seen in Washington, and of the particular demands it imposed upon the United States and Japan **(Document 36a)**. In touching on all of the significant issues that would be taken up in subsequent discussions, the Secretary offered what amounted to a preview of the formal communiqué that was issued at the close of the meeting.[7] At a joint news conference with Japanese Foreign Minister Masayoshi Ohira, Mr. Rogers later agreed that the discussions had been helpful in defining the new U.S.-Japanese relationship in a global context and that they offered an excellent point of departure for an already scheduled meeting between Prime Minister Kakuei Tanaka and President Nixon that was to take place in Washington at the end of July.[8]

While Secretary Rogers went on to South Korea for a three-day visit and a warm endorsement of President Park's new proposals,[9] other members of the U.S. delegation returned to Washington to find the President hospitalized with viral pneumonia and struggling to avert a fresh deterioration of his personal position. Not only had the nation's economic situation remained unsatisfactory, as Mr. Nixon had himself conceded in inaugurating on July 18 a complicated "Phase IV" economic program that would, admittedly, be powerless to prevent such evils as a further substantial rise in food prices.[10] A Watergate development of the utmost seriousness was threatening to undermine the very foundations of the President's claims of noninvolvement.

[7]*Bulletin*, vol. 69 (1973), pp. 246-9.
[8]Same, p. 249.
[9]Same, pp. 253-7.
[10]*Presidential Documents*, vol. 9 (1973), pp. 906-12.

It was on July 16 that testimony before the Senate Watergate committee had first disclosed to an incredulous world the Nixon practice, hitherto unknown even to some of the President's most intimate advisers, of recording confidential conversations and telephone calls on concealed tape machines. Immediately there had been demands from the Senate committee and from Special Prosecutor Cox for the surrender of material pertinent to the Watergate investigation. When the President, now discharged from hospital, demurred on constitutional grounds, the Special Prosecutor instituted legal proceedings with a view to obtaining records of nine specific meetings and conversations. Similar action was taken by the Senate committee. On July 31, Democratic Congressman Robert F. Drinan of Massachusetts introduced a formal resolution looking to the impeachment of the President under the procedures laid down by the Constitution.

July 31 was also the day Prime Minister Tanaka began his two-day round of talks with President Nixon in Washington. "Let others spend their time dealing with the small, murky, unimportant, vicious little things," said Mr. Nixon in toasting his Japanese guest the following evening. "We have spent our time and will spend our time building a better world."[11] A similar note of uplift sounded through the two leaders' formal communiqué (**Document 37**), which naturally avoided reference to American domestic matters but emphasized that the discussions, "held in an atmosphere of cordiality and trust, reflected in tone and content the breadth and closeness of relations between Japan and the United States." Noting that the relationship between the two countries "has an increasingly important global aspect and makes a significant contribution to the movement toward peaceful relations throughout the world," the two leaders refrained from comment on nuclear testing in the Pacific but voiced a highly favorable impression of current developments regarding China, Korea, and even Indochina.

President Nixon, in addition, pointed out to his guest "the desirability of a Declaration of Principles to guide future cooperation among the industrialized democracies"; and Prime Minister Tanaka, after listening to these explanations, "expressed his positive interest therein" and cautiously agreed that the two countries "would consult closely on the matter as preparations proceed toward a Declaration acceptable to all the countries concerned." In what might be interpreted as a reciprocal gesture, President Nixon expressed a belief that a way should be found for Japan—like mainland China—to be permanently represented on the U.N.

[11]Same, p. 943.

Security Council. In addition, he reconfirmed a standing invitation for the Japanese Emperor and Empress to visit the United States, and expressed the hope of accepting a Japanese invitation to visit Japan with Mrs. Nixon before the end of 1974. The realization of both these projects, however, would have to be left to Mr. Nixon's successor as a result of the mounting difficulties that were to sweep the 37th President from office in just over a year's time.

(36) Ninth Meeting of the Joint United States-Japan Committee on Trade and Economic Affairs, Tokyo, July 16-17, 1973.

(a) The Framework of American—Japanese Relations: Opening statement by Secretary of State Rogers, July 16, 1973.[12]

Earlier this year in his annual foreign policy report to Congress, President Nixon affirmed:[13]

> . . . the U.S.-Japanese alliance remains central to the foreign policies of both countries. We are two major powers of the free world, interdependent to an extraordinary degree for our prosperity and our security. The United States therefore places the highest possible value upon this partnership. . . .

The President thus summarized a partnership that has given us both more than either of us could reasonably have expected 20 years ago.

Our alliance has been a critical element in the evolution of the more peaceful and more cooperative Asia in which both our nations have a vital interest. The success of our association is apparent in the strength and vigor of Japanese democracy, in the phenomenal performance of Japanese industry and commerce, and in the respect and influence which your nation enjoys throughout the world. These are achievements of the Japanese people. But the United States is pleased to have contributed to their realization because we, too, are strengthened and enriched through them.

Today we face new challenges and new possibilities brought about by the success of our association. We do so at a time when many of the fears that characterized international relations for nearly a quarter century are receding. The United States has been

---

[12]Department of State Press Release 250, July 16; text from *Bulletin*, vol. 69 (1973), pp. 238-43. Further documentation on the meeting appears in same, pp. 237-8 and 243-52.

[13]*Nixon Report, 1973*, 96.

intimately involved in bringing about this most hopeful change. So has Japan. Thus, before turning directly to U.S.-Japanese relations, I would like to discuss with you briefly some aspects of our efforts to build a more cooperative and more secure global community.

Earlier this month at Helsinki, with 34 other Foreign Ministers from Europe and North America, I attended a ministerial meeting of the Conference on Security and Cooperation in Europe.[14] The meeting was carried out in a climate of restraint and conciliation which should help the subsequent phase of the conference in Geneva make a genuine contribution to European détente. Nevertheless, it was clear that there are substantial East-West differences on the conduct of relations between states and on freer movement of people, information, and ideas across Europe. Detailed agreement on these matters is necessary if the conference is to bring closer a more secure and cooperative Europe.

I might say at this point that we have noted with interest the suggestion of Prime Minister Tanaka to call a general conference of Asian and Pacific nations. As we look ahead, a conference aimed at developing the principles and the mechanisms through which interested nations can promote peace, cooperation, and the lowering of tensions in the area could be most useful.

It is also of importance that nations of NATO and of the Warsaw Pact are to meet formally in Vienna on October 30 to seek the reduction of their forces stationed in central Europe.[15] It is likely that such initial troop cuts will focus on the forces of the United States and the Soviet Union stationed in the area.

In the talks at Helsinki and in the upcoming talks at Geneva, the goal of the United States and its European allies has been to decrease tensions across the continent of Europe without in any way lessening European security. With our European allies, we are convinced that the strength of our NATO alliance provides an essential ingredient in the progress toward détente.

The security relationship betwen Japan and the United States has played an analogous role in Asia. The steps we both have taken with Moscow and Peking would have been impossible without our firm security ties. Future advance depends on their maintenance. The United States of course recognizes the constitutional and psychological limits on Japan's defense effort. We do feel that there is room for Japan to assume a greater share of the responsibility for the promotion of peace and stability in Asia. But in urging Japan to do so, we do not suggest that Japan should exceed those limits.

[14]Document 35.
[15]Document 34a.

We also recognize that frictions are inevitable when troops, even those of an ally, are stationed on foreign soil. These frictions can be magnified in times of détente. Thus, the United States has sought to minimize the possibilities for misunderstandings and tensions resulting from the stationing of troops in Japan. That is why we have undertaken—with the cooperation of the Japanese Government—to make adjustments in our base structure in the Kanto Plains and in Okinawa. And that is why we wish to study further with the Japanese Government ways in which we can continue to consolidate and rationalize our bases. Our objective is to retain an effective deterrent presence with as little potential for friction as possible.

The changes that have taken place in relations between the United States and China, and the United States and the Soviet Union, have contributed significantly to a more secure—a more cooperative—world. We recognize that the issues on which peace and cooperation depend cannot be settled between the United States and its adversaries alone. The contributions and collaboration of our allies are essential. And as we improve our relations with Moscow and Peking, we have done nothing and will do nothing which will harm our allies' interest or weaken our alliances.

Last month President Nixon and General Secretary Brezhnev took steps toward a more stable and secure international environment.[16] We hope that such meetings will become a regular feature of Soviet-American relations as both countries seek to minimize the potential for confrontation between them, replacing it with the network of cooperative relations on which firm peace depends.

The agreement the President and General Secretary signed on prevention of nuclear war[17] was of particular significance for Soviet-U.S. relations. It also should contribute substantially to reducing the threat of nuclear war throughout the world, without impairing our other obligations and commitments.

The situation in the Middle East was also discussed at the summit. Both parties expressed their concern, reviewed their positions on this complex issue, and agreed to continue to exert efforts to promote an early settlement. The Soviets and we agreed that a settlement should be in accordance with the interests of all states in the area, be consistent with their independence and sovereignty, and should take into account the legitimate interests of the Palestinian people. The United States is convinced that a just and lasting peace in the Middle East will come only through an active negotiating

[16] Documents 31-3.
[17] Document 32b.

process carried out directly or indirectly between the parties directly involved. Though progress in that direction has been disappointingly slow, the cease-fire continues in place, and we are hopeful that all parties will continue to exercise restraint. We recognize the risks inherent in the existing situation and are giving it our active attention.[18]

Relations between ourselves and the People's Republic of China continue their orderly evolution. In fact, trade has developed much more rapidly than expected, and two-way trade this year may reach $700 million—more than twice previous estimates. We expect further growth with resolution of the linked issues of U.S. private claims against the Chinese and Chinese assets frozen in the United States. Negotiations on these matters continue, but we are hopeful that final agreement can be reached at an early date.

We regard as of special significance the mutual commitments undertaken by China with Japan and with the United States to renounce ambitions of hegemony in Asia and to resist attempts by others to impose such hegemony.[19] The new relationship between ourselves and Peking has not caused us to diminish either our friendship with or determination to fulfill our commitments to the Republic of China.

Peace in Indochina remains a matter of great concern to us. While many problems are still to be resolved, the fighting and loss of life fortunately have dropped to a much lower level. The climate of negotiation is much improved.

In Viet-Nam the legacy of decades of hostility is difficult to overcome, but the two parties are talking directly. Similarly, in Laos military operations have almost ceased and the prospects for an early political settlement are promising. In Cambodia the situation is especially complex, but as President Nixon pledged last month,[20] we shall do everything possible to help bring about peace there.

The reduced hostilities in the area make it possible for us all to turn our attention to the essential task of reconstruction and development. We value Japan's cooperation in this effort. Your interest and counsel have been most helpful, and we look forward to continued close consultation with you. As you know, our own Congress, no less than the administration, has made it clear that it gives great importance to the cooperative contribution of other countries to postwar rehabilitation and development. The World Bank and the Asian Development Bank (ADB) are both investigating the possibility of forming an international aid donor's group for the

[18]Cf. Chapter 15.
[19]Cf. *AFR, 1972*, p. 309, and Document 75 below.
[20]Document 40.

area. Japan would be an essential participant in such a grouping. For our part, we hope we will be able to move ahead with the recovery and development assistance programs that can be a vital factor for peace in the area.

Finally, let me note our strong support for the constructive proposals President Park has put forward to further lower tensions on the Korean Peninsula.[21] We are pleased to note the solid support your government accorded these important initiatives. Our security commitments in Korea have contributed to an environment in which the Koreans were prepared to move toward more normal relations. We will continue firmly to live up to them.

Mr. Foreign Minister [Masayoshi Ohira], during the public session of our meeting, I expressed satisfaction at the progress we have made in restoring balance to our economic relationship.[22] I repeat that expression of satisfaction here. The Japanese Government has taken significant steps to carry out Prime Minister Tanaka's promise to President Nixon to ease the unsustainable imbalance in our trade. We place high value on this effort.

In 1972 the U.S. trade deficit was $4.1 billion. In the first five months of 1973, however, our trade deficit with Japan was reduced by almost 50 percent from the same period in 1972.

We hope this trend will continue for the rest of the year. We also expect there will be further improvement next year. But we both still have much to do.

Most of the progress to date is due to higher prices and increased Japanese commodity purchases. Further steps by Japan to remove import restrictions and to encourage a positive attitude toward imports will be necessary. U.S. businessmen must also use the opportunities now open to them in the Japanese market, but clearly the momentum is toward a balanced economic relationship, and we are pleased to hear again of your commitment to maintain that direction.

As I suggested this morning, this progress has freed us to focus greater attention on the issues which now head the global agenda: trade and monetary negotiations, formulation of international investment guidelines, environmental protection, assistance to the developing world, and energy matters. As we approach these multilateral matters, we do so with a deeper appreciation of the changed economic relationships among major countries—changes most dramatically underlined by the remarkable growth of your economy. The postwar economic order was built around the dominant economic position of the United States. Today no nation

---

[21]Cf. above at note 6.
[22]*Bulletin, loc. cit.*, pp. 237-8.

holds such overwhelming dominance. All nations are becoming increasingly interdependent.

On economic issues, constructive leadership must come from the developed democracies—particularly Japan, the United States, and the European Community. The industrialized democracies are, or soon will be, embarked on trade and monetary negotiations.

As we and our partners enter these negotiations it is of paramount importance that for the health and strength of us all, we think and act in terms of us all. If we lose sight of our common interests—of our interdependence—we will all suffer.

Thus, the United States has called for agreement on the general principles that will guide us as we seek to resolve the common issues we face.[23] Without a firm declaration of principles, technical matters could themselves become the focus of attention, obscuring the overriding interest we all have in cooperating rather than competing.

We believe the contribution of Japan is essential to the development of the principles which will guide cooperation among the industrial democracies. In proposing the articulation of a general statement of principles, the United States is less interested in procedures than in getting the dialogue started on the substance of our objectives. In the near future we will want to consult with you on the objectives and principles which should guide our discussions.

Let me now touch briefly on some of the matters where U.S.-Japanese cooperation can yield impressive benefits to both of us and to the world community.

In the multilateral trade negotiations which begin this fall,[24] Japan and the United States can find common ground in such propositions as these:

—That the negotiations should cover both industrial and agricultural products;
—That within a reasonable period tariffs should be eliminated or substantially reduced;
—That significant nontariff barriers will be eliminated, reduced, or—where appropriate—codified in an agreed set of rules;
—That there be negotiated a multilateral safeguard system to ease the adjustment to a more open trading system; and
—That the negotiations make significant progress toward the reduction of developed countries' barriers against the exports of the less developed countries.

[23]Cf. Document 21.
[24]Cf. Chapter 19.

I would note that we are making every effort to obtain early congressional approval of President Nixon's trade reform legislation, which is designed to allow the United States to contribute to the liberalization of global trade.[25]

Restructuring of the global trading system should go hand in hand with a compatible and fundamental reform of the world's monetary system.[26] We are agreed that monetary reform is essential. I am pleased that the United States has taken the lead in setting forth an integrated and comprehensive proposal as a focus of discussion. The United States hopes that with Japan and other nations we can work together in the Committee of Twenty to bring about early agreement on a system that will bring a new balance in monetary affairs, that will treat all countries evenhandedly, and that will achieve essential stability in results through widening [sic] prompt and effective adjustment of payments surpluses and deficits.

The United States believes that modernization of the international economic system would be incomplete without a careful examination of the principles and policies underlying international investment. To complement the trade and monetary negotiations we are taking an active part in discussions on international investment in the OECD Executive Committee in special session.[27] We hope that Japan will join us there in promoting broad international consensus on national policies affecting international investment. We believe that the objective of these understandings should be to avoid national policies that distort the flow of foreign investment, to insure the fair treatment of foreign investors, and to allow international capital to flow as freely as possible, yielding the maximum benefit to the world economy.

The United States understands the special concerns which derive from Japan's dependence on imported sources of energy. We, too, have a growing need to import fuels and thus place a priority on the expansion and strengthening of cooperation with Japan in energy matters. We believe that such cooperation with oil-importing nations can and must be carried out without prejudice to relations with the oil-producing nations.[28]

The United States believes cooperation among oil-importing nations should include:

—First, cooperation within the OECD to establish a mutually acceptable oil-sharing arrangement in situations of critical shortage.

[25]Cf. Chapter 12 at note 4.
[26]Cf. Chapter 19.
[27]Cf. Document 27.
[28]Cf. Document 26.

—Second, sharing of information on both private and governmental negotiations with oil-producing nations. This exchange of information can reduce the anxieties which sometimes develop over access to oil.

—Third, expansion of supply through joint projects between Japanese and American firms aimed at the development of new energy sources in Siberia and elsewhere. While the United States cannot direct the investment decisions of our private firms, we stand ready to encourage them to consider the possibility of common ventures with Japanese firms.

—Fourth, accelerating progress toward meeting our common energy needs by joining our technologies and knowledge in joint research and development projects. We remain interested in sharing with Japan U.S. technology for use in the construction of a multinational uranium enrichment plant. And we hope we can discuss a broad bilateral agreement with Japan to facilitate our cooperation in this vital field.

Protection of the environment is another area in which our two nations could do more to accomplish our mutual purposes. We are both seriously concerned with the problems of pollution. We both have the technology and the resources with which to attack environmental contamination more effectively. The conclusion of a written agreement on environmental cooperation could not only improve on our present cooperation in this field; it also could set a pattern for environmental relations between highly developed countries. The United States believes that such an agreement should harmonize environmental standards, not only to protect the global environment but also to minimize the economic distortions caused by pollution controls.

Mr. Minister, I know our colleagues here would agree that the more prosperous, secure, and cooperative world we desire may remain elusive if the developing world fails to achieve sustained economic growth. While the primary responsibility for sound development policies lies with the poorer nations, both Japan and the United States can make a useful contribution to their efforts to achieve a better life for their citizens.

We agree that our development assistance performances can and should be improved. This is the goal we have set for ourselves. We welcome your stated intention to increase the quantity and improve the quality of Japan's concessional assistance. In view of your balance of payments situation, we would welcome further untying of your aid. We are also pleased that Japan proposes to expand its assistance outside of Asia.

Foreign private investments can make a most important contribution to accelerated economic growth in the poorer nations. We can concur that for such investment to prosper, our private firms must be confident that should they be expropriated they will receive just and effective compensation. To promote confidence and to protect our investors, the United States remains interested in developing multilateral approaches to investment disputes, a matter we discussed at the last joint Cabinet session.[29] Japan's growing investment in the developing world suggests to us that we can work closely together to promote such multilateral approaches.

Before concluding, I would like to state that we fully understand your concern at our recent decision to restrict the export of soybeans and soybean products and various other commodities.[30] We are aware of your dependence on soy products. We are pleased that it was possible to exempt from controls about 14,000 tons grown for human consumption under contract to Japanese firms.

Our export restrictions were unavoidable if we were to exercise the kind of discipline over our economy that both you and we agree is essential. The foreign and domestic demand for soy and soy products was such that, at the time of our decision to control exports, outstanding contracts already exceeded available supplies for the current crop year. In the absence of controls, supplies would have been exhausted in August. The licensing system we adopted was the only equitable way to share this excessive demand. The situation regarding other products under control was comparable.

Despite the licensing, taking soybeans and soy meal together, a record equivalent of 18.8 million tons will be exported this crop year, compared to 15.4 million tons last year. Demand in the United States has remained almost stable—just under 20 million tons.

Your imports from the United States will exceed your earlier projections. Japan is expected to import from the United States 3.6 million tons, compared to almost 3.2 million tons last year.

The restrictions do not apply to the new crop whose harvest will begin in September. Thus we hope they will be of short duration. We currently estimate that this year's harvest will break all records, running about 24 percent above last year's production. We do not like to limit our most competitive exports, and you can be assured that controls will not last a day longer than is necessary.

Mr. Minister, I have set forth some areas we wish to explore in depth with our counterparts. You and your colleagues will no doubt have other suggestions. As we define and pursue our mutual interests in our conversations, I am sure we will be making a major

[29]Held in Washington Sept. 9-10, 1971; cf. *Bulletin*, vol. 65 (1971), pp. 346-54.
[30]Cf. Chapter 12.

contribution to the success of the summit meeting between President Nixon and Prime Minister Tanaka,[31] enabling our two nations to broaden and deepen the long association that is so essential to us both.

(37) Meeting of President Nixon and Prime Minister Kakuei Tanaka, Washington, July 31-August 1, 1973: Joint Communiqué issued at the conclusion of the talks, August 1, 1973.[32]

1. Prime Minister Tanaka and President Nixon met in Washington July 31 and August 1 for comprehensive and fruitful exploration of a wide variety of subjects of mutual interest.

2. The discussions of the two leaders, held in an atmosphere of cordiality and trust, reflected in tone and content the breadth and closeness of relations between Japan and the United States. The primary focus of this meeting was the many common goals which Japan and the United States share and the common commitment of the two nations to a new era in this friendly relationship. They emphasized the high value they place on the important role that each plays in the cause of world peace and prosperity and the strong desirability of proceeding together toward that common objective by cooperative efforts wherever possible around the globe.

3. The Prime Minister and the President confirmed the durable character of the friendly and cooperative relations between Japan and the United States, which are based on a common political philosophy of individual liberties and open societies, and a sense of interdependence. They noted especially that the relationship between their two countries has an increasingly important global aspect and makes significant contribution to the movement toward peaceful relations throughout the world.

4. Expressing their satisfaction with the continuous dialogue which has taken place at various levels on subjects of mutual interest since their meeting in Hawaii in September 1972,[33] the Prime Minister and the President reviewed developments in the international situation. They discussed the global trend toward detente, as evidenced by the progress of the dialogue between the United States and the Union of Soviet Socialist Republics, the forthcoming negotiations on the mutual reduction of forces and

[31]Document 37.
[32]Text from *Presidential Documents*, vol. 9 (1973), pp. 944-7. Further documentation appears in same, pp. 939-40 and 942-4, and in *Bulletin*, vol. 69 (1973), pp. 297-301.
[33]*AFR, 1972*, pp. 337-40.

armaments in Central Europe, the Conference on Security and Cooperation in Europe, the return of the People's Republic of China to the international community, and the signing of the Paris Agreements for a peace settlement in Indochina. They expressed the hope that this trend would lead to the peaceful settlement of disputes throughout the world.

5. The Prime Minister and the President agreed on the need to maintain continuous consultation on questions of mutual concern in the international political field. They expressed their satisfaction with progress made in the area of arms control and the avoidance of conflict, including the SALT agreements and the US-Soviet Agreement on the Prevention of Nuclear War.[34]

6. The Prime Minister and the President noted with satisfaction the normalization of relations between Japan and the People's Republic of China and the movement toward more normal relations between the United States and the People's Republic of China. They expressed their strong hope for a stable and lasting peace in Indochina through scrupulous implementation of the Paris Agreements. They reaffirmed their resolve to assist the rehabilitation of Indochina. They welcomed the new developments in the Korean Peninsula, and expressed the readiness of their Governments to contribute to the furtherance of peace and stability in that area. They pledged to continue to facilitate regional cooperation in Asia as an important contributing factor in securing a lasting peace throughout that part of the world.

7. The President pointed out the desirability of a Declaration of Principles to guide future cooperation among the industrialized democracies. The Prime Minister expressed his positive interest therein. The Prime Minister and the President agreed that Japan and the United States would consult closely on the matter as preparations proceed toward a Declaration acceptable to all the countries concerned.

8. The Prime Minister and the President recognized that the existing framework of international relations had been the basis for the recent trend toward the relaxation of tensions in Asia and reaffirmed that continued close and cooperative relations between the two countries under the Treaty of Mutual Cooperation and Security[35] are an important factor for the maintenance of stability in Asia. The President confirmed the intention of the United States to maintain an adequate level of deterrent forces in the region. The two leaders noted with satisfaction continuing efforts to ensure the smooth and effective implementation of the Treaty and concurred

[34]Document 32b.
[35]Signed at Washington Jan. 19, 1960 and entered into force June 23, 1960 (TIAS 4509; 11 UST 1632); text and related documents in *Documents, 1960*, pp. 425-31.

on the desirability of further steps to realign and consolidate the facilities and areas of the United States Forces in Japan.

9. Recognizing that the greatest transoceanic commerce between two nations in the history of mankind greatly enriches the lives of the peoples of Japan and the United States, the Prime Minister and the President pledged to ensure that this trade continues to grow and to contribute to the expansion and prosperity of the world economy as a whole and to the over-all relationship between the two countries. They reviewed with satisfaction the discussions at the July meeting in Tokyo of the Japan-US Joint Committee on Trade and Economic Affairs[36] on the measures Japan has taken in the fields of trade and investment, for which the President again expressed the appreciation of the United States; on the marked improvement in the trade imbalance between the two countries, and the intention of both Governments to pursue policies designed to maintain the momentum of this improvement; on promoting investment between the two countries; and on the United States intention to exert its best efforts to supply essential materials including agricultural products to Japan, which the President reaffirmed. The Prime Minister and the President confirmed the understanding reached in the above meeting that on the basis of recent economic developments, Japan and the United States could look forward to new perspectives in the development of their economic relations.

10. The Prime Minister and the President reaffirmed the importance which they attach to a successful conclusion of the multilateral negotiations in the trade and monetary fields. They endorsed the objective of achieving an open and equitable world trade and investment, and a reformed international monetary system, responsive to the needs of an increasingly interdependent world economy. They expressed their mutual satisfaction that the Ministerial meeting to launch the new round of multilateral trade negotiations would be held in Tokyo in September.[37] They emphasized the firm intention of their Governments to work for as wide agreement as possible on the principles of monetary reform at the annual meeting of the International Monetary Fund in Nairobi later in that month.[38] In both of these undertakings, they pledged their cooperative efforts to assure early and constructive results in concert with other countries of the world.

11. The Prime Minister and the President agreed to continue to coordinate efforts to ensure a stable supply of energy resources to meet the rapidly growing requirements of their peoples. In this con-

[36]Cf. Document 36a.
[37]Cf. Document 50.
[38]Cf. Document 51.

nection, they expressed their common intention to pursue just and harmonious relationships with the oil producing states; to examine the possibility of developing within the framework of the OECD, an arrangement on sharing oil in times of emergency; and greatly to expand the scope of cooperation for exploring and exploiting energy resources and for research and development of new energy sources.

12. The Prime Minister and the President affirmed the importance of close cooperation between the two Governments in securing a stable supply of enriched uranium, including cooperation in the necessary research and development. They agreed that the two Governments should exert their best efforts for the satisfactory realization of a Japan-US joint venture to that end. In this connection, the President announced that the United States Government had authorized a group of American companies to enter into a contract with a private Japanese party to conduct a joint study of the economic, legal, and technical factors involved in the construction of a uranium enrichment plant in the United States in which Japan might participate.

13. The Prime Minister and the President recognized that expanded programs for improved communication and understanding are vital to strengthening the relationship between the two countries. Noting the warm reception in the United States to the activities of the Japan Foundation, the Prime Minister announced that the Government of Japan will grant, through the Foundation, funds in the amount of $10 million to several American universities for institutional support of Japanese studies, including the endowment of chairs for this purpose. The President stated his intention to expand support for those United States cultural and educational projects which had been so productive in the past, and to ask the Congress in the near future to appropriate the funds remaining in the GARIOA[39] account to strengthen Japan-US cultural and educational exchanges.

14. The Prime Minister and the President expressed satisfaction with the growing cooperation between Japan and the United States in the field of environmental protection. They commended the cooperative programs now in progress which would enable the two countries to cope more effectively with air and water pollution and other environmental problems, including those connected with sewage disposal and photochemical air pollution. They confirmed that such cooperative programs would be instrumental in protecting the environment and devising antipollution measures in both countries.

[39]Government and Relief in Occupied Areas.

15. The Prime Minister and the President noted with satisfaction the achievements of the medical, scientific and technological cooperative programs developed during the last decade between the two countries. They agreed to make an overall review of cooperative relationships in such fields in light of the broader requirements of the coming decade.

16. The Prime Minister and the President, recognizing that the United Nations is making an important contribution to the furtherance of international cooperation and is an effective forum for collective consultations, agreed that Japan and the United States should cooperate fully in their efforts to help move the Organization in a constructive direction. The President expressed the belief that for the Security Council to fulfill its primary responsibility under the United Nations Charter for the maintenance of international peace and security, a way should be found to assure permanent representation in that Council for Japan, whose resources and influence are of major importance in world affairs. The Prime Minister expressed his appreciation for this statement.

17. The President reconfirmed the standing invitation to Their Majesties, the Emperor and Empress of Japan, to visit the United States and hoped that the visit would take place in the near future at a mutually convenient time. The Prime Minister expressed his deep appreciation for this invitation, and on his part conveyed an invitation from the Government of Japan to President and Mrs. Nixon to visit Japan. In accepting this invitation, the President voiced his sincere gratitude for the warm sentiments toward the United States symbolized by it. It is hoped that the President's visit to Japan, to be arranged through diplomatic channels, will take place at a mutually convenient time before the end of 1974.[40]

18. The Prime Minister was accompanied by Foreign Minister Masayoshi Ohira, Takeshi Yasukawa, Japanese Ambassador to the United States, and Kiyohiko Tsurumi, Deputy Vice Minister of Foreign Affairs. Also taking part in the conversations on the American side were William P. Rogers, Secretary of State, Dr. Henry A. Kissinger, Assistant to the President for National Security Affairs, and Robert S. Ingersoll, American Ambassador to Japan.

[40]President Ford paid an official visit to Japan between Nov. 18 and 22, 1974. The communiqué appears in *Presidential Documents*, vol. 10 (1974), pp. 1481-3, and *Bulletin*, vol. 71 (1974), pp. 874-5.

15. MIDDLE EAST STORM SIGNALS

The month that opened with a reaffirmation of Japanese-American friendship[1] continued with a number of more sensational occurrences. On August 5, a Palestinian terrorist attack in the transit lounge of the Athens airport caused four deaths and 55 injuries, inaugurating still another series of violent incidents and U.N. debates relating to the Middle East. Next day, August 6, the Nixon administration suffered another body blow with the disclosure that Vice-President Spiro T. Agnew, though seemingly uninvolved in the Watergate scandals, was under criminal investigation in connection with activities growing out of his pre-1969 career in Maryland politics. In Indochina, where the struggle among indigenous forces continued at various levels, U.S. combat activity was halted by Act of Congress with effect from August 15. One week later, on August 22, the President announced that Secretary of State Rogers was withdrawing from governmental duty and would be succeeded by Dr. Kissinger in the dual capacity of Secretary of State and Assistant to the President for National Security Affairs.

The Athens airport attack of August 5 was one of the grislier episodes in the familiar cycle of Palestinian terrorism and Israeli retaliation, exemplified earlier in 1973 by such occurrences as the April 10 raid on Beirut and the decision of the Security Council to request a comprehensive report on U.N. efforts in the Middle East since 1967.[2] With Secretary-General Waldheim's report in hand, the Security Council had begun on June 6 a general discussion of the Middle East that lasted through ten meetings and was suspended on June 14 with the understanding that the subject would be pursued at further meetings in July.[3] "The Council faces a great responsibility," declared Ambassador Scali in a statement

---

[1]Chapter 14.
[2]Cf. Chapter 7 at notes 11-12.
[3]*UN Monthly Chronicle*, vol. 10 (July 1973), pp. 3-58.

(Document 38a) that expressed American support for this arrangement and disavowed the "partisanship" imputed to the United States by earlier speakers. Referring to the critical importance of the Council's 1967 resolution—which, he pointed out, still represented the only agreed basis for an eventual peace settlement—the American delegate spoke in terms of stark alternatives. "We can by our actions wreck the basis for agreement which now exists with all its calculated ambiguities," he said, "or we can preserve that basis and try to move forward with renewed energy. My government strongly believes that we must take the latter course."

But still more terrorist incidents were to occur before the Council could resume its discussion. An Israeli air attaché, Colonel Yosef Alon, was shot dead by unidentified assailants in Washington early on July 1 in what the "Voice of Palestine" in Cairo exultantly described as "the first execution of an Israeli representative in the United States." On July 19, seventeen persons in an Athens hotel were temporarily held hostage by a Palestinian guerrilla of uncertain affiliation. On the 20th, in an action subsequently condemned by the PLO, a quintet of self-styled "Palestinian commandos and Japanese Red Army members" seized a Japanese airliner in flight from Amsterdam—losing one of their number in the process—and diverted it to the Persian Gulf area and later to the Libyan airport of Benghazi, where it was destroyed without further loss of life on July 24.[4]

These events could only accentuate the differences within the Security Council between the Communist and "third world" champions of the Arab-Palestinian cause and the United States, by this time virtually the sole upholder of the Israeli side of the scale. Yet seldom had a group of Security Council members gone so far in identification with the Arab viewpoint as did the seven nonaligned countries—Guinea, India, Indonesia, Panama, Peru, Sudan, and Yugoslavia—whose draft resolution became the focus of debate as the Security Council resumed its meetings on July 20. Deploring Israel's continued presence in the occupied territories, as well as its alleged lack of cooperation with the U.N. Special Representative, the resolution entered new and highly controversial ground in calling for respect not only for the rights of all states in the Mideast area but also for "the rights and legitimate aspirations of the Palestinians."

Unlike the General Assembly, the Security Council had not thus far concerned itself directly with the "rights and aspirations" of the Palestinians. The 1967 resolution, for example, had been silent

[4]*Keesing's*, pp. 26085-7.

about Palestinian rights and had merely mentioned "a just settlement of the refugee problem" as one of the requirements of a just and lasting peace. For the Israelis, talk of Palestinian "rights and aspirations" was scarcely distinguishable from advocacy of Israel's destruction. The American delegation, too, found this new draft resolution "highly partisan and unbalanced," and expressed a fear that its adoption would do "irrevocable and permanent damage" to the earlier, 1967 resolution—which, as Ambassador Scali again recalled, still represented "the only agreed . . . basis" for a peaceful settlement.

Misgivings of this nature, however, carried but little weight with the thirteen Security Council members who cast their votes in favor of the pending resolution (Document 38b) on July 26—or with China, which refused its participation only because it found the resolution insufficiently pro-Arab. The United States thus stood completely alone in casting the negative vote that prevented the adoption of the resolution—a vote that constituted the fifth American veto in the Security Council, and the second on the Middle East.[5] "Another opportunity lost," declared Ambassador Scali in a statement in "explanation of vote" (Document 38a) in which he suggested that recent experience confirmed the superior merits of the "step-by-step" diplomacy preferred by the United States. "Our vote today," he said, "was a carefully considered action calculated to move the United Nations away from empty judgments on the past and toward concrete positive results in the real world."

Unhappily, however, developments in the "real world" remained as little conducive to regional peace as did the debates in the United Nations. New links in the chain of violence were even now being forged with the Athens airport massacre already described—which also was formally disavowed by the PLO—and, on August 10, by Israel's interception in Lebanese airspace of a Lebanese airliner chartered to Iraq which was diverted to an Israeli military airport in an unsuccessful bid to secure the persons of George Habbash, the leader of the left-wing Popular Front for the Liberation of Palestine (PFLP), and other terrorist leaders.[6] Security Council condemnation of this Israeli action was prompt and unanimous.[7] "National and international efforts to control terrorism must go forward," Ambassador Scali told the Council on August 14 (Document 39a). "They must, however go forward within and not outside the law."

[5] Details in *UN Monthly Chronicle*, vol. 10 (Aug.-Sept. 1973), pp. 3-23; *U.S. Participation, 1973*, pp. 4-5.
[6] *Keesing's*, pp. 26085-6.
[7] Details in *UN Monthly Chronicle*, vol. 10 (Aug.-Sept. 1973), pp. 23-44; *U.S. Participation, 1973*, pp. 5-6.

Endorsing the Council's condemnation and solemn warning to Israel **(Document 39b)**, the U.S. Representative insisted none the less that his vote did not portend any change in U.S. Middle Eastern policy. It did, he said **(Document 39c)**, reflect the strong feelings of the American people about the need for a just peace in the Middle East, elimination of all forms of international terrorism—"whether they be by individuals, groups, or governments"—and maintenance of the rule of law, "in the international field as at home."

In its understandable preoccupation with the terrorist aspect of Middle East affairs, the world was paying insufficient heed to another series of developments that can be seen in retrospect to have been more directly related to the new round of full-scale hostilities that took place in the early autumn. Apparently disappointed in its hope that the United States would persuade the Israelis to relinquish the occupied lands, President Sadat's Egyptian government had been actively engaged in mending its tattered relationships with Saudi Arabia, with Syria, and with the Soviet Union. Moscow, perhaps unmindful of its obligations toward the United States, had responded with a marked step-up in its military shipments to Egypt and Syria, whose armament had by late summer reached a point where they could begin detailed planning for a new assault against Israel. Neither Israel nor the United States, however, could quite believe—until the blow fell—that the Arab governments were genuinely resolved to carry out the almost mortal attack they were to launch against their unloved neighbor on Saturday, October 6.[8]

(38) A New Initiative in the Security Council.

(a) Proposals for a New Departure: Statement by Ambassador Scali to the Security Council, June 14, 1973.[9]

My government views this meeting of the Council as a challenge and an opportunity. It is a challenge to deal responsibly with one of the most important—and one of the most difficult—of the problems facing the world community. It is an opportunity of a kind we have not had since November 1967, when the Council last met to review the whole problem of the Middle East. It is thus more than just an occasion to hear the complaints of one side against the other. It is an opportunity to create circumstances in which, at long

[8]Cf. note 13 to Chapter 7. For further developments see Chapter 22.
[9]USUN Press Release 57, June 14; text from *Bulletin*, vol. 69 (1973), pp. 269-72.

last, Arab and Israeli might engage in a genuine negotiating process.

In the more than 5½ years since the Council last dealt with the issue in a comprehensive manner, many words have been spoken and many resolutions passed. In some ways, the problem is more difficult today than it was 5½ years ago. Time has a way of giving an aura of permanence to what once seemed transitory. This meeting should be first of all, therefore, an opportunity to reaffirm that we do not consider the present situation in the Middle East either natural or permanent. We should leave no doubt that it is neither natural nor permanent.

Time also has a way of subtly altering how we perceive problems and their solutions. This meeting is therefore an opportunity as well to review our perceptions, to see whether they have changed over the past 5½ years. This meeting should be an opportunity, in short, to recapture the hope and to reaffirm the resolve which inspired the Council on November 22, 1967, to give its unanimous approval to Resolution 242.[10] That decision was recognized at the time as a landmark in the long history of this problem in the United Nations. It remains a landmark today.

Resolution 242 reflected the Council's view that the time had come to move expeditiously toward a just and lasting peace in the Middle East after three wars with their toll of human tragedy and devastation and their threat to world peace. The resolution recognized that such a peace must be based on a just settlement not only of the problems arising out of the hostilities of June 1967 but also of the underlying causes of the Arab-Israeli conflict as they have existed now for over a quarter of a century.

What were the essential elements with which we began the search for peace in 1967?

First, it is important to remember that the Council, in calling for a cease-fire to end the fighting in June 1967, did not address the question of who was responsible for the outbreak of that fighting. Nor did it call for unconditional Israeli withdrawal.

Second, it is important to remember the nature and essential elements of Resolution 242 as they were generally understood at the time. The resolution was the result of compromise by all concerned, and this means that any settlement based upon it must reflect that spirit of compromise. Resolution 242 did not define the terms of settlement. In the language of the resolution itself, it defined a set of "provisions and principles" which constitute a framework for the terms of a final settlement. It is only fair to note that the terms to be negotiated must therefore be consistent with

[10]*Documents, 1967*, pp. 169-70.

those provisions and principles—not just with some of them, but with all of them taken together. If the terms of a settlement do not meet that test, they cannot, in our view, form part of the just and lasting peace we seek. Too often one side or the other has sought to emphasize certain elements of Resolution 242 while ignoring others.

What are the main provisions and principles of Resolution 242?

First, it includes in its preamble "the inadmissibility of the acquisition of territory by war and the need to work for a just and lasting peace in which every State in the area can live in security." We accept this principle as important and significant.

Second, Resolution 242 affirms that peace should include the application of two coequal principles. One is "Withdrawal of Israeli armed forces from territories occupied" in the 1967 conflict. My government endorses that principle in the context of the resolution as a whole. But the principle of withdrawal cannot be separated from the next balancing paragraph, which affirms the principle of "Termination of all claims or states of belligerency and respect for and acknowledgement of the sovereignty, territorial integrity and political independence of every State in the area and their right to live in peace within secure and recognized boundaries free from threats or acts of force."

Third, Resolution 242 affirms the necessity for guaranteeing freedom of navigation and for guaranteeing the territorial inviolability and political independence of every state in the area. Clearly the specific measures by which these important interests of the parties are to be guaranteed must be part of the detailed terms of a final settlement. They must be part of the structure of peace.

Fourth, Resolution 242 affirms the necessity for achieving a just settlement of the refugee problem. That, too, must clearly be part of the structure of peace. My government has made clear on a number of occasions our view that no structure of peace in the Middle East can be just and lasting if it does not make provision for the legitimate aspirations of the Palestinians. In our view, it is for the parties to work out what this means in specific terms.

Finally, Resolution 242 calls for agreement. In the context of the resolution, this clearly means agreement between the parties concerned. Ambassador Jarring, to whom I wish to pay special tribute today, was subsequently selected to assist the parties to this end. My government has never seen how such agreement is possible without an ongoing, serious negotiating process, either direct or indirect, which engages the parties themselves. We believe each member of this Council should do everything possible to encourage the parties to engage in such a dialogue. The recess in these deliberations which now lies before us provides each and all of us with an opportunity to take stock and to consider what can be done to bring about forward movement.

In the days just passed, several speakers have attributed to the United States a certain partisanship in its view of the Arab-Israeli dispute. Perhaps in doing so these speakers were reflecting a certain partisanship of their own. In any case, I wish to dismiss these allegations without exception. Like my predecessors, I represent to the best of my ability the interest of the United States, and not those of any other single state. In the Middle East, the overriding interest of the United States is in peace—a peace that will end the fear and uncertainty of the past quarter century. The interest of the United States demands we press ahead to seek that peace—a peace that will allow Arab and Israeli alike to reside within secure and recognized boundaries. The United States urgently desires friendly and enduring relations with all countries of the Middle East.

In his recent report to Congress, President Nixon solemnly stated, ". . . I have said that no other crisis area of the world has greater importance or higher priority for the United States in the second term of my Administration."[11] Mr. President, that judgment and that resolve are unchanged.

Our determination to serve this interest has only been strengthened by the passage of time. The disappointments of the past have strengthened the imperative to seek peace. Neither the United States nor any other power or combination of powers can negotiate such a peace. Only the parties can do that. But let there be no doubt about our determination to contribute whatever we can to the creation of circumstances in which the parties can achieve peace and security through negotiations.

We note, as other speakers before us have done, that in today's world, security means more than territory, more than the hoarding of armaments, and more than merely the absence of belligerency. Security—real security for all the parties—depends on willingness to put aside bitter quarrels, prejudices, fears, and misapprehensions of the past and to look ahead positively to developing a broad range of mutual interests which gives each party a vested interest in preserving peace.

What are the key issues with which such negotiations must come to grips? In simplest terms they are the issues of sovereignty and security. The parties must find a way to reconcile the two. One aspect of this problem is the question of boundaries. There are many strongly held views about where final boundaries between Israel and its neighbors should be drawn. Resolution 242 has often been cited to support one view or another. But the fact is that

[11]*Nixon Report, 1973*, p. 134.

Resolution 242 is silent on the specific question of where the final border should be located. It neither endorses nor precludes—let me repeat, neither endorses nor precludes—the armistice lines which existed between Israel, Egypt, Jordan, and Syria on June 4, 1967, as the final secure and recognized boundaries. Everyone knew when Resolution 242 was approved that this was an area of ambiguity. This was part of the compromise to which I have referred.

The central message of Resolution 242 is that there should be a fundamental change in the nature of the relationship of the parties with each other, a change from belligerency to peace, from insecurity to security, from dispossession and despair to hope and dignity for the Palestinians. Let me say again: It seems clear to us—logically, politically, historically, realistically—that the question of agreement of final boundaries must be viewed in the context of the total thrust and intent of Resolution 242. This question must therefore be resolved as part of the process of reaching agreement on all the complex factors governing a new relationship among the parties to replace that defined in the 1949 armistice agreements.

Mr. President, I have recalled the history of our efforts in 1967 not to argue the past, but because I believe we need to restore our perspective as we look to the future. Many sincere efforts have been made, by Ambassador Jarring and by governments, including my own, to help the parties find a way to negotiate the detailed terms of a final peace agreement. Whatever may have been their merits, none succeeded. We are therefore left with Resolution 242 as the only basis thus far accepted by both sides, with regard both to substance and to procedure. The principal parties concerned have accepted that basis, each in its own way, and this is what makes it uniquely important.

The Council faces a great responsibility. We can by our actions wreck the basis for agreement which now exists with all its conscious ambiguities, or we can preserve that basis and try to move forward with renewed energy. My government strongly believes that we must take the latter course. We are prepared to support a fresh attempt by Ambassador Jarring based on his mandate in Security Council Resolution 242.

We will be guided by this approach in judging whatever proposals may ultimately be placed before us. We agree with those who have argued that the Council has a responsibility to help bring about the implementation of Resolution 242. Implementation requires agreement, and agreement requires a process of negotiation. This is what the Council must encourage and facilitate. Such a process, in our view, must involve a patient, practical, step-by-step approach. It could begin, as we have long favored, with an agreement on some Israeli withdrawal in Sinai and a reopening of the Suez Canal within the context of an extended cease-fire, as the first stage on the road to a final settlement. Such a first step would be firmly linked to a final agreed settlement. But whether a beginning is made in this or some other way is less important than that such a process be started without delay. I assure you that my government is fully prepared to do its part to facilitate and sustain objectively and fairly any such process of negotiation until the goal the Council set for itself over 5½ years ago is achieved. This we will do in the interests of true and lasting peace in the Middle East for all concerned in this and future generations.

(b) Draft Resolution vetoed by the United States July 26, 1973.[12]

Guinea, India, Indonesia, Kenya, Panama, Peru, Sudan and Yugoslavia: draft resolution

[*Original: English*]
[*24 July 1973*]

The Security Council,

Having examined comprehensively the current situation in the Middle East,

Having heard in this context the statements of the participants in this debate, including the Foreign Ministers of Egypt, Algeria, Chad, Guinea, Nigeria, Saudi Arabia, the Sudan and the United Republic of Tanzania,

Emphasizing its primary responsibility for the maintenance of international peace and security,

Emphasizing further that all Members of the United Nations are committed to respect the resolutions of the Security Council in accordance with the provisions of the Charter of the United Nations,

Reaffirming resolution 242 (1967) of 22 November 1967,[13]

Conscious that the rights of the Palestinians have to be safeguarded,

Taking note of the report of the Secretary-General [*S/10929*][14]

---

[12]U.N. document S/10974, July 24; text from Security Council, *Official Records: 28th Year, Supplement for July, Aug. and Sept. 1973*, pp. 20-21. The resolution was defeated by a vote of 13-1 (U.S.)-0, with China not participating.

[13]*Documents, 1967*, pp. 169-70.

[14]Cf. Chapter 7 at note 12.

which includes an account of the objective and determined efforts of his Special Representative since 1967,

1. *Deeply regrets* that the Secretary-General was unable to report any significant progress by him or by his Special Representative in carrying out the terms of resolution 242 (1967), and that nearly six years after its adoption a just and lasting peace in the Middle East has still not been achieved;

2. *Strongly deplores* Israel's continuing occupation of the territories occupied as a result of the 1967 conflict, contrary to the principles of the United Nations Charter;

3. *Expresses* serious concern at Israel's lack of co-operation with the Special Representative of the Secretary-General;

4. *Supports* the initiatives of the Special Representative of the Secretary-General taken in conformity with his mandate and contained in his aide-mémoire of 8 February 1971;[15]

5. *Expresses* its conviction that a just and peaceful solution to the problem of the Middle East can be achieved only on the basis of respect for national sovereignty, territorial integrity, the rights of all States in the area and for the rights and legitimate aspirations of the Palestinians;

6. *Declares* that in the occupied territories no changes which may obstruct a peaceful and final settlement or which may adversely affect the political and other fundamental rights of all the inhabitants in these territories should be introduced or recognized;

7. *Requests* the Secretary-General and his Special Representative to resume and to pursue their efforts to promote a just and peaceful solution of the Middle East problem;

8. *Decides* to afford the Secretary-General and his Special Representative all support and assistance for the discharge of their responsibilities;

9. *Calls upon* all parties concerned to extend full co-operation to the Secretary-General and his Special Representative;

10. *Decides* to remain seized of the problem and to meet again urgently whenever it becomes necessary.

(c) Statement by Ambassador Scali to the Security Council, July 26, 1973.[16]

The history of the Middle East problem is a history of lost opportunities. Today's action by the Council represents another opportunity missed. My delegation profoundly regrets that the Council has not achieved a result that would give impetus to realistic ef-

---

[15]Cf. *AFR, 1971*, p. 197.
[16]USUN Press Release 68, July 26; text from *Bulletin*, vol. 69 (1973), pp. 272-4.

forts to work toward peace and stability in the Middle East. The U.S. Government is committed without qualification to continue such efforts.

In my statement of June 14 before this Council[17] I said: "My government views this meeting of the Council as a challenge and an opportunity. It is a challenge to deal responsibly with one of the most important—and one of the most difficult—of the problems facing the world community." And I said later, "It is an opportunity to create circumstances in which, at long last, Arab and Israeli might engage in a genuine negotiating process."

Unhappily, the Council did not meet the challenge. It lost the opportunity. The resolution before us was highly partisan and unbalanced. Its adoption could only have added another obstacle to getting a serious negotiating process started between the parties. It would have contributed another impractical and cosmetic result invoking the unreal rather than the real world. It is our hope that one day the choice made will be meaningful and face up to the hard reality that the job of peace in the area—the procedures and its contents—must be assumed by the parties themselves in an unprejudiced way.

Unhappily, the draft resolution put to the vote today, instead of focusing on possibilities for efforts toward agreement between the parties and trying to encourage such efforts, concerned itself with moral judgments about the past. The past is too much with us. We have been looking backward to grievances rather than forward to solutions.

To put it most succinctly, if this resolution had passed, it would have changed fundamentally, it would have overturned Security Council Resolution 242. It would, in other words, have undermined the one agreed basis on which a settlement in the Middle East could be constructed. That is why my government felt compelled to veto the resolution.

As members of the Council are aware, my delegation did its utmost to avoid this result. We presented to the cosponsors a series of reasonable and carefully thought out amendments.[18] Had they been accepted, the Council would have taken a modest step forward rather than a confused step backward.

Our suggested amendments are known to the members of the Council, and I need not review them in detail here. One, however, bears special emphasis because it goes to the heart of the distortion which the resolution voted on today would have perpetrated if it had been accepted. Operative paragraph 2 of that resolution treats

[17]Document 38a.
[18]The proposed amendments were submitted informally to the cosponsors and were not issued as official documents of the Security Council.

in isolation the Israeli presence in territories occupied in the 1967 conflict. It speaks of "the" territories, ignoring the significance—recognized when Resolution 242 was passed—of the omission of this definite article, the word "the," from the text of Resolution 242. And it takes no notice of the other fundamental and inseparable elements of that resolution: that the ending of occupation must be in the context of peace between the parties, that it must be in the context of the right of all states in the area to live within secure and recognized boundaries, and that it must be on the basis of agreement between the parties. Operative paragraph 2 bears no relationship to the provisions and principles of Resolution 242. It would constitute an entirely different resolution, contrary to the entire concept of Resolution 242. Our proposed amendment reads as follows:

Deeply regrets the failure to reach agreement on a just and lasting peace, including Israeli withdrawal from territories occupied in the 1967 conflict and secure and recognized boundaries;

If accepted, our proposed amendment would have preserved the essence and balance of Resolution 242—agreement, peace, withdrawal, and secure and recognized boundaries—which, I submit, remain the only hope if ultimately there is to be a just and lasting peace in the Middle East.

To our regret, these proposals did not evoke the response, the careful consideration, we believe they merited. Some argued that the proposals came too late. I understand what that implies about tactical factors in the processes of the Security Council. But, my friends, I submit that if there is the will, it is never too late to work for peace and security. It is not too late now, and my delegation believes that, while this debate is ending, our responsibility to search for solutions to the Middle East problem continues.

The purpose of our amendments was to bring the eight-power resolution into some measure of conformity with the essential provisions of Security Council Resolution 242, which remains the only agreed—I repeat, agreed—basis for a peaceful solution. The resolution voted upon today would have done irrevocable and permanent damage to this landmark resolution of this Council—a resolution which admittedly is interpreted differently by the two sides and whose constructive ambiguity can only be resolved in the caldron of negotiations between the parties, not by fiat of this Council or a group of outside powers.

Casting a veto is never easy. It is a most serious decision—one we do not take lightly. However, the essence of statemanship is to take a longer view—to persevere in the tough task of peacemaking, to find ways toward a lasting peace—and not to seek to score political points which have no lasting value.

Mr. President,[19] all need not be lost. We note that the Secretary General has the agreement of the parties to consult with them in the area. He has the continued support of the United States for this renewed effort, and despite the differences revealed in our deliberations here today, there are no differences on this point. I believe we all agree with the Secretary General's stated intention to engage himself in the pursuit of peace in the Middle East. He needs no new mandate. Security Council Resolution 242 remains the basic framework.

Allow me to make one more general observation about the approach embodied in the draft resolution we have today rejected. I would earnestly urge those who share my delegation's profound desire for a stable Middle East to ponder the lesson of history—that step-by-step diplomacy most often leads in an orderly way to important results. The effort to get across a broad chasm of difference in one leap involves the risk of falling all the way to the bottom of the chasm.

In closing, I would like to comment on allegations about the ineffectiveness of the Security Council and the United Nations made by certain speakers in this Chamber yesterday. I do not concur for a moment with these counsels of despair. It is true that we have not yet found the institutional antidote to many of the ills of mankind. I, too, am deeply disappointed by the outcome of this debate. In past years of observing the United Nations, I have been disappointed many times. But there is also a record of U.N. successes on important issues. My government believes that through sincere, patient, and determined efforts by its members, the United Nations and in particular the Security Council can become more effective, can deal successfully with the complex and difficult problems that face us. Our vote today was a carefully considered action calculated to move the United Nations away from empty judgments on the past and toward concrete positive results in the real world. It is only through such positive results that we can restore the confidence of those who doubt the United Nations—the institution that still embodies some of the noblest aspirations of mankind.

[19]Sir Colin Crowe (United Kingdom).

(39) Interception by Israel of a Lebanese Airliner, August 10, 1973.

 (a) Statement by Ambassador Scali to the Security Council, August 14, 1973.[20]

The issue before us today is clear. In recent years the world has seen threats to the safety of civil aviation increase at an alarming rate. We must find ways to reduce and ultimately eliminate such threats to the free and peaceful use of the world's airways. Travel by air, as was travel by sea in an earlier age, must be insulated and protected from unlawful interference. It must no longer be a pawn in international conflicts.

In this latest incident, information from Lebanese and Israeli Government authorities has established that a civil airliner en route from Beirut to Baghdad with 76 passengers aboard was intercepted by Israeli fighter aircraft over Lebanese territory on August 10 and forced to land in Israel. There can be no doubt that such actions by their very nature place the lives of the innocent persons aboard an aircraft in danger.

The United States deplores this violation of Lebanese sovereignty. We deplore this violation of the United Nations Charter and of the rule of law in international civil aviation.

Fortunately, no lives were lost and no material damage was incurred in this latest incident. While this does not modify our concern, we strongly urge all parties to retain a sense of perspective and prevent this incident from leading to further reprisals and counterreprisals. It is high time to call a full stop to all such acts and related acts and threats of violence.

The Representative of Israel has explained that the purpose of his government's action in diverting the airliner was to apprehend individuals responsible for terrorist acts. My government has been second to none in its condemnation of international terrorism, in the search for new instruments of international law to counter terrorism, and in urging other governments to take a strong stand and effective measures against those who endanger and take innocent lives in the name of serving a political cause.[21] National and international efforts to control terrorism must go forward. They must, however, go forward within and not outside the law. The commitment to the rule of law in international affairs, including the field of international civil aviation, imposes certain restraints on the methods governments can use to protect themselves against

[20]USUN Press Release 69, Aug. 14; text from *Bulletin*, vol. 69 (1973), pp. 356-7.
[21]Cf. *AFR, 1972*, pp. 486-516.

those who operate outside the law. My government believes actions such as Israel's diversion of a civil airliner on August 10 are unjustified and likely only to bring about counteraction on an increasing scale. Resort to any type of aerial kidnaping seriously jeopardizes the lives and safety of innocent bystanders. The U.S. Government has made strenuous efforts in and outside the United Nations to reach international agreement on measures that would protect such "third parties" who have no connection to the political dispute giving rise to the use of armed force. We have also made strenuous efforts to improve the security of international civil aviation through multilateral agreements and will continue our efforts at the ICAO [International Civil Aviation Organization] meetings which convene in Rome later this month.[22] Such practices as diverting civil aircraft constitute highly dangerous precedents for the safe and reliable conduct of international relations, commerce, and travel.

Last April in this Council I observed:[23]

The cycle of violence in this part of the world is not only continuing but has taken on newer and uglier dimensions. To the shame of all mankind, acts of violence and terror, often striking down innocent people, are on the verge of becoming a routine footnote to the tragic and unresolved Arab-Israeli conflict.

Unhappily, events in the past few weeks provide no evidence to contradict this melancholy conclusion. We hardly need reminding that only a few weeks ago, two gunmen opened fire senselessly in the midst of a crowded international air terminal in Athens, murdering three innocent travelers and injuring dozens of innocent bystanders. Just weeks before that, a Japanese airliner was hijacked and destroyed, and its passengers subjected to harsh threats and extreme danger. Last February, 106 persons on a Libyan airliner were the tragic victims of this same pattern of violence and counterviolence.[24] We are all aware that this cycle is a reflection of the tensions and hatreds growing out of the unresolved Arab-Israeli dispute. We are all aware that the ultimate solution lies in a just and lasting settlement of that dispute on the basis of Security Council Resolution 242. Pending this much-desired solution, however, we all have an obligation to seek to prevent that dispute from moving up another uglier notch, to seek to prevent its taking an even higher toll of innocent lives.

[22]Same, p. 516.
[23]Statement of Apr. 17, in *Bulletin*, vol. 68 (1973), p. 657.
[24]Cf. Chapter 7 at note 5.

The United States has consistently joined other members of this
Council to express its grave concern over the threat to innocent
human lives resulting from hijacking and other unlawful or unwarranted interference with civil aviation. We would join again in
urging all states, all individuals, and all political groups in the area
to refrain from actions which could imperil the lives of innocent
people and the safety of international travel. There can be no double standard here. There must be one law for all.

The record of the United Nations in dealing with the overall
problem of international terrorism is not so far a record of which
we can be proud. However, the Security Council is meeting today
to deal with a specific complaint about a specific incident. It should
deal promptly with this complaint on the basis of the facts while
keeping in perspective the broader issues.

Our task now is to unite on a resolution to express the common
attitude of this world body toward the regrettable and deplorable
incident under discussion. Let us do so with the intention that the
decision we make will mark a turning point—where men and
women dedicated to peace, with their eyes fixed on the future, as
well as the present, determine that the fabric of international
society requires that they reject unlawful interference with civil
aviation, from whatever quarter and for whatever motive.

(b) Condemnation of Israel: Security Council Resolution 337 (1973), adopted August 15, 1973.[25]

The Security Council,
Having considered the agenda contained in document S/Agen-
da/1736,
Having noted the contents of the letter from the Permanent
Representative of Lebanon addressed to the President of the
Security Council (S/10983),
Having heard the statement of the representative of Lebanon
concerning the violation of Lebanon's sovereignty and territorial
integrity and the hijacking, by the Israeli air force, of a Lebanese
civilian airliner on lease to Iraqi Airways,
Gravely concerned that such an act carried out by Israel, a Mem-
ber of the United Nations, constitutes a serious interference with
international civil aviation and a violation of the Charter of the
United Nations,
Recognizing that such an act could jeopardize the lives and safety

---

[25]Text from Security Council, *Official Records: 28th Year, Resolutions and
Decisions 1973*, p. 10; adopted unanimously.

of passengers and crew and violates the provisions of international conventions safeguarding civil aviation,

Recalling its resolutions 262 (1968) of 31 December 1968[26] and 286 (1970) of 9 September 1970,[27]

1. *Condemns* the Government of Israel for violating Lebanon's sovereignty and territorial integrity and for the forcible diversion and seizure by the Israeli air force of a Lebanese airliner from Lebanon's air space;

2. *Considers* that these actions by Israel constitute a violation of the Lebanese-Israeli Armistice Agreement of 1949, the cease-fire resolutions of the Security Council of 1967, the provisions of the Charter of the United Nations, the international conventions on civil aviation and the principles of international law and morality;

3. *Calls* on the International Civil Aviation Organization to take due account of this resolution when considering adequate measures to safeguard international civil aviation against these actions;

4. *Calls* on Israel to desist from any and all acts that violate Lebanon's sovereignty and territorial integrity and endanger the safety of international civil aviation and solemnly warns Israel that, if such acts are repeated, the Council will consider taking adequate steps or measures to enforce its resolutions.

(c) *Statement by Ambassador Scali to the Security Council, August 15, 1973.*[28]

Our vote today is a continuation of our efforts to extend the rule of law. The United States has consistently joined other members of this Council to express its grave concern over the threat to the innocent resulting from hijacking and other unlawful or unwarranted interference with civil aviation. Our vote in no way represents a change in my government's views on the problems and possibilities for solution in the Middle East. Nor should it be interpreted as endorsing the principle of sanctions as a means of dealing with this problem.

The American people feel strongly about the need for a just peace in the Middle East. They feel strongly about the need to eliminate all forms of international terrorism whether they be by individuals, groups, or governments. They also feel strongly about the rule of law, in the international field as at home.

That is why I have on two occasions observed in this Council that the cycle of violence in the Middle East is not only continuing—to

---

[26]Condemning Israel for an attack on the Beirut international airport.

[27]Calling for legal steps against hijacking.

[28]USUN Press Release 70, Aug. 15; text from *Bulletin*, vol. 69 (1973), pp. 357-8.

the shame of us all—but has taken on newer and uglier dimensions:[29]

> To the shame of all mankind, acts of violence and terror, often striking down innocent people, are on the verge of becoming a routine footnote to the tragic and unresolved Arab-Israeli conflict.

> Today we have taken an important step toward the reaffirmation of the rule of law in international civil aviation. Let me repeat what I said in this chamber on Tuesday [August 15]:[30]

> National and international efforts to control terrorism must go forward. They must, however, go forward within and not outside the law.

The fact that this resolution confines itself to expressing the Council's condemnation of a specific incident should serve as no comfort to anyone contemplating illegal acts of violence or terrorism. Rather it is a warning to all members of the world community that the community will no longer tolerate illegal interference with one of the basic means of communication from any quarter. Should there be further instances of international lawlessness or terror, I most sincerely hope that this body will again demonstrate similar unity and determination. Nor should our vote be read to mean any commitment to any kind of specific measures. Terrorism, illegal violence, and threats to the innocent must stop. Humanity demands it. Our conscience demands it. We for our part will continue to oppose such actions whether by governments, individuals, or groups, regardless of nationality or of motivation.

Yesterday I called on this Council to unite on a resolution which would mark a turning point in our efforts to eliminate international lawlessness and terrorism. Only time can tell whether we have done so. I pray the answer will be yes.

[29]Cf. above at note 23.
[30]Document 39a.

16. ENDING COMBAT IN INDOCHINA

Whatever the nagging discomforts of the Middle East situation, the animosities and hatreds prevailing in that area did not involve American responsibilities to quite the same extent as did the play of hostile forces in the states of Indochina. Developments there had signally failed to justify the hopes invested in the January peace agreement and its subsequent reaffirmation.[1] Although the level of fighting in South Vietnam had dropped significantly of late, the Joint Military Commission had made no progress in implementing the military provisions of the cease-fire, and the political talks between Saigon and PRG representatives remained completely deadlocked. North Vietnam, moreover, had quite failed to live up to its obligations to provide the United States with information about the more than 1,300 Americans who were listed as missing in action, and to help repatriate the remains of those who had died in captivity.[2] Partly for this reason, plans for U.S. reconstruction aid to North Vietnam, briefly revived at the time of the Paris agreement of June 13, had once again miscarried.[3]

In Laos, the cease-fire in effect since February 21 had not prevented intermittent skirmishing, while representatives of the Vientiane government and the Pathet Lao continued their arguments about the distribution of portfolios in the future coalition regime and about the Pathet Lao's demand to station troops in the two capitals of Vientiane and Luang Prabang.[4]

The situation of Cambodia's ill-fated "Khmer Republic," meanwhile, had undergone a catastrophic deterioration as the in-

[1]Documents 5 and 30.
[2]Cf. U.S. note, July 29, in *Bulletin*, vol. 69 (1973), p. 306.
[3]According to Hanoi's later account (as described by Leslie H. Gelb in *The New York Times* of Feb. 3, 1976), a detailed agreement providing for $3.25 billion in U.S. grant aid over a five-year period was ready to be signed July 23 but was torpedoed when the U.S. "demanded political conditions," presumably relating to the status of Americans missing in action.
[4]*Keesing's*, pp. 26019-20 and 26091.

competent Lon Nol administration struggled to exercise at least the forms of authority within its shrinking area of control. In contrast to Vietnam and Laos, insurgent military pressure against the Cambodian capital had actually been stepped up from June 1 onward, in spite of continued heavy bombing by U.S. B-52's and F-111's; and any hope of cease-fire negotiations seemed blocked by stubborn disagreements about who should talk to whom. While the United States and the Lon Nol regime insisted that peace negotiations should be held directly between the Phnom Penh government and the insurgents, the exiled Prince Sihanouk had scorned to talk to the "clique of traitors" who had unseated him. His objective had been to institute direct talks between his government-in-exile and the United States. But since Washington had thus far eluded his solicitations, the former Cambodian Chief of State was now asserting that Dr. Kissinger would not be welcome even if he should belatedly attempt to establish contact.[5]

This sorry state of affairs could only deepen congressional dismay at the fact that heavy U.S. bombing still continued in this part of Indochina, long after the signature of a peace agreement and the withdrawal of U.S. ground troops. Undeterred by Defense Secretary Richardson's opinion that the bombing required no congressional authorization,[6] both House and Senate during May had adopted amendments to a current supplemental appropriation bill that purported to forbid the use of specified funds for such purposes during the balance of the fiscal year ending June 30. An amendment originated by Democratic Senator Thomas F. Eagleton of Missouri, cutting off all funds for the support of military action in, over, or from the shores of Cambodia or Laos, was included in this legislation as it was reported by a Senate-House conference committee on June 18, approved by a voice vote of the House on June 25, and affirmed by an 81 to 11 vote of the Senate on June 26, four days before the end of the fiscal year.[7]

Though this particular provision could have no effect beyond June 30, steps to enforce a similar prohibition even after that date had already been taken in both houses of Congress. In the Senate, a State Department authorization bill already passed by the House had been approved on June 14, by 67 votes to 15, following acceptance of an amendment by Senators Clifford P. Case (Republican of New Jersey) and Frank Church (Democrat of Idaho) that prohibited the use of appropriated funds for bombing,

[5]Same, p. 26186.

[6]*New York Times*, May 8, 1973; see also Rogers statement, May 8, in *Bulletin*, vol. 68 (1973), pp. 859-60.

[7]H.R. 7447, making supplemental appropriations for the fiscal year ending June 30, 1973, and for other purposes; details in *Keesing's*, p. 25944.

shelling, or ground combat anywhere in Indochina without specific congressional authorization.[8] In the House, a similar amendment was attached on July 26, by a vote of 240 to 172, to a joint resolution making continuing appropriations for the first three months of the new fiscal year beginning July 1.[9]

Thus far, the only piece of cutoff legislation to have actually reached the President's desk was the Second Supplemental Appropriation Act for the fiscal year 1973, which included the Eagleton amendment. Although this amendment applied only to the period ending June 30, 1973, there was every reason to apprehend that if permitted to become law, it would be followed by other provisions that would tie the President's hands for the indefinite future. Even the Senate Minority Leader, Republican Hugh Scott of Pennsylvania, had let it be known tht he could not support continued bombing in Cambodia after June 30.

Apparently hoping to nip the evil in the bud, President Nixon on June 27 returned the Second Supplemental Appropriation Act to Congress with a veto message (**Document 40**) in which he expressed his "grave concern" that the enactment of the "Cambodia rider" would "cripple or destroy the chances for an effective negotiated settlement in Cambodia." By virtually removing the Communist incentive to negotiate, the President warned, such a measure would "effectively reverse the momentum towards lasting peace in Indochina set in motion last January and renewed in the four-party communique signed in Paris on June 13." Furthermore, Mr. Nixon added, by calling in question the American commitment both to the Vietnam settlement and to many other settlements or agreements with other nations, such action would "seriously undermine the chances for a lasting peace in Indochina and jeopardize our efforts to create a stable, enduring structure of peace around the world."

But though an immediate attempt to override the presidential veto in the House fell short of a two-thirds majority (the vote to override was 241 to 173), antiwar leaders in the Senate gave notice that they would continue to fight for a cutoff until "the will of the people" prevailed. Faced with the prospect of still another constitutional crisis, as well as a blockage of the appropriations needed to carry on the government, the President on June 29 signaled his readiness to compromise. Instead of June 30, he intimated, the bombing could be halted on August 15, and congressional approval would be sought for any military action that might be needed after that date.

[8]*New York Times*, June 15, 1973. The amendment was later included in modified form as sec. 13 of the Department of State Appropriations Authorization Act of 1973 (Public Law 93-126, Oct. 18, 1973); cf. note 9 below.
[9]Adopted in modified form as sec. 108 of Public Law 93-52 (Document 41b).

This arrangement was promptly incorporated in both of the pending appropriation bills, which were then passed or repassed by Congress in time for presidential signature as the new fiscal year began on July 1. In virtually identical language, the relevant sections of the Second Supplemental Appropriation Act, 1973 **(Document 41a)** and of the Joint Resolution continuing appropriations for the first quarter of fiscal 1974 **(Document 41b)** stipulated that as from August 15, 1973, no appropriated funds could be used directly or indirectly to support combat activities by U.S. military forces "in or over or from off the shores of" North Vietnam, South Vietnam, Laos, or Cambodia.[10] In addition, both enactments barred the use of appropriated funds for reconstruction aid to North Vietnam.[11]

In a statement issued as he signed the two appropriation measures **(Document 41c)**, President Nixon voiced the unexpectedly optimistic opinion that while a "sudden" bombing halt such as Congress had originally demanded "would not have brought us the lasting peace that we all desire," a "stable Cambodian settlement" might still be attained, "so long as we maintain reasonable flexibility in our policies, and essential air support is not withdrawn unilaterally while delicate negotiations are still underway."

In the obvious hope of making the most effective use of the interval before air operations must cease, the United States had already embarked upon a major effort to shore up Cambodia's self-defense capability, under a joint program that was said by Secretary Rogers to comprise the following elements:

"(i) emergency increases in the levels of the Cambodian armed forces;

(ii) accelerated deliveries and distribution during the first two weeks in August of military equipment, especially aircraft and related spare parts, pursuant to the United States Military Assistance Program;

(iii) accelerated deliveries and distribution during this same period of food stuffs, medical supplies and other items for humanitarian relief of the Cambodian population.

---

[10]Similar prohibitions were later included in the Department of State Appropriations Authorization Act of 1973 (sec. 13, Public Law 93-126, Oct. 18, 1973); the Department of Defense Appropriation Authorization Act, 1974 (sec. 806, Public Law 93-155, Nov. 16, 1973); the Foreign Assistance Act of 1973 (secs. 30 and 37, Public Law 93-189, Dec. 17, 1973); and the Department of Defense Appropriation Act, 1974 (sec. 741, Public Law 93-238, Jan. 2, 1974).

[11]A similar prohibition was included in the Foreign Assistance and Related Agencies Appropriation Act, 1974 (sec. 111, Public Law 93-240, Jan. 2, 1974).

(iv) redeployment of Cambodian armed forces, and in some cases civilians whom those forces are protecting, from exposed positions to positions where they can defend themselves and be resupplied in the absence of United States combat air support on and after August 15, 1973.''[12]

But though the tempo of American bombing in Cambodia was sharply stepped up even as the aid deliveries were being accelerated, the situation of beleaguered Phnom Penh continued to deteriorate from day to day. A peace appeal launched July 6 by Long Boret, Foreign Minister in the Lon Nol government, was praised by the State Department but scorned by Prince Sihanouk's regime, which once again demanded total withdrawal by the "foreign imperialists and their lackeys" and the overthrow of the "band of traitors" in the Cambodian capital.[13] In Washington, the political ferment attendant on these events was further accentuated by the revelations that were just then coming to light with regard to the secret bombing of Cambodian territory by U.S. forces between March 1969 and May 1970, ostensibly with Sihanouk's tacit approval but with scant notice to congressional leaders and some deliberate deception of the press and public.[14]

To complete the administration's discomfiture, there seemed to be a possibility that military operations in Cambodia might have to be halted even before August 15 under a court order, obtained by Democratic Representative Elizabeth Holtzman of New York, which was currently pending before the Supreme Court.[15] "I want the Congress to be fully aware of the consequences of its action," said President Nixon, reverting to pessimism in a letter addressed on August 3 to the Speaker of the House and the Senate Majority Leader (**Document 42a**). Enumerating the potentially unfavorable effects of the bombing cutoff, the President nevertheless assured the Cambodian people of "all possible support permitted under the law," and added a word of warning to Hanoi that recalled his earlier assurances to President Thieu. North Vietnam, Mr. Nixon declared, "would be making a very dangerous error if it mistook the cessation of bombing in Cambodia for an invitation to fresh aggression or further violations of the Paris Agreements. The American people would respond to such aggression with appropriate action."

[12]Rogers affidavit, Aug. 2, in *Bulletin*, vol. 69 (1973), p. 305.
[13]Same, p. 257, and *Keesing's*, p. 26186.
[14]The facts are conveniently assembled in *Keesing's*, pp. 26166-7. President Nixon's defense of the action was included in his New Orleans address of Aug. 20 to the Veterans of Foreign Wars, cited in note 6 to Chapter 17.
[15]Cf. Rogers affidavit, Aug. 2, in *Bulletin*, vol. 69 (1973), pp. 304-6.

340   16. ENDING COMBAT IN INDOCHINA

Representative Holtzman's "end-the-war" injunction was subsequently voided by a U.S. Court of Appeals, and military operations in Cambodia continued right up to the August 15 deadline. The immediate threat to Phnom Penh had by then been eased as the insurgent forces, apparently starved for ammunition owing to a cessation of deliveries from North Vietnam and China, diverted their attention to areas north of the capital.

In a statement confirming the cessation of U.S. combat air operations (**Document 42b**), White House Deputy Press Secretary Gerald L. Warren once again affirmed the U.S. commitment to support the Khmer Republic and promote negotiation among the Khmer parties. He also repeated almost word for word the President's admonition to North Vietnam. "It should be clearly understood in Hanoi," he said, "that the President will work with Congress in order to take appropriate action if North Vietnam mounts an offensive which jeopardizes stability in Indochina and threatens to overturn the settlements reached after so much sacrifice by so many for so long." Hanoi, however, had by this time gained considerable experience in reading the signals from Washington, and was presumably aware that a Congress which had finally forced a halt to U.S. military involvement in Indochina would be exceedingly loath to authorize its resumption.[16]

(40) Rejection of the "Cambodia Rider": Message from President Nixon to the House of Representatives, returning without approval the Second Supplemental Appropriation Act of 1973 (H.R. 7447), June 27, 1973.[17]

To the House of Representatives:

I am returning today without my approval H.R. 7447, the Second Supplemental Appropriation Act of 1973.

I am doing so because of my grave concern that the enactment into law of the "Cambodia rider" to this bill would cripple or destroy the chances for an effective negotiated settlement in Cambodia and the withdrawal of all North Vietnamese troops, as required by Article 20 of the January 27 Vietnam agreement.[18]

After more than ten arduous years of suffering and sacrifice in Indochina, an equitable framework for peace was finally agreed to in Paris last January. We are now involved in concluding the last element of that settlement, a Cambodian settlement. It would be

---

[16]For further developments cf. Chapter 26.
[17]Text from *Presidential Documents*, vol. 9 (1973), pp. 861-2.
[18]Document 5.

nothing short of tragic if this great accomplishment, bought with the blood of so many Asians and Americans, were to be undone now by Congressional action.

The decision to veto is never easy, but in this case there is no other responsible course open to me. To understand this decision, we should all recognize what the full impact would be if we call a total halt to U.S. air operations in Cambodia, as now sought by the Congress:

—A total halt would virtually remove Communist incentive to negotiate and would thus seriously undercut ongoing diplomatic efforts to achieve a ceasefire in Cambodia. It would effectively reverse the momentum towards lasting peace in Indochina set in motion last January and renewed in the four-party communique signed in Paris on June 13.[19]

—The proposed halt would also gravely jeopardize the ability of the Cambodian armed forces to prevent a Communist military victory achieved with the assistance of outside forces and the installation of a Hanoi-controlled government in Phnom Penh.

—A Communist victory in Cambodia, in turn, would threaten the fragile balance of negotiated agreements, political alignments and military capabilities upon which the overall peace in Southeast Asia depends and on which my assessment of the acceptability of the Vietnam agreements was based.

—Finally, and with even more serious global implications, the legislatively imposed acceptance of the United States to Communist violations of the Paris agreements and the conquest of Cambodia by Communist forces would call into question our national commitment not only to the Vietnam settlement but to many other settlements or agreements we have reached or seek to reach with other nations. A serious blow to America's international credibility would have been struck—a blow that would be felt far beyond Indochina.

I cannot permit the initiation of a process which could demolish so substantially the progress which has been made, and the future relationships of the United States with other nations.

However, I must emphasize that the provisions of H.R. 7447, other than the "Cambodia rider," contain a number of appropriations that are essential to the continuity of governmental operations. It is critical that these appropriations be enacted immediately.

---

[19]Document 30.

By June 28, nine Government agencies will have exhausted their authority to pay the salaries and expenses of their employees. The disruptions that would be caused by a break in the continuity of government are serious and must be prevented. For example, it will be impossible to meet the payroll of the employees at the Social Security Administration, which will threaten to disrupt the flow of benefits to 25 million persons.

But an even greater disservice to the American people—and to all other peace loving people—would be the enactment of a measure which would seriously undermine the chances for a lasting peace in Indochina and jeopardize our efforts to create a stable, enduring structure of peace around the world. It is to prevent such a destructive development that I am returning H.R. 7447 without my approval.

RICHARD NIXON

The White House,
  June 27, 1973.

(41) Legislative-Executive Compromise, July 1, 1973.

(a) Second Supplemental Appropriation Act, 1973: Public Law 93-50, approved July 1, 1973.

(*Excerpts*)

*   *   *

TITLE III
GENERAL PROVISIONS

Sec. 301. No part of any appropriation contained in this Act shall remain available for obligation beyond the current fiscal year unless expressly so provided herein.

*   *   *

Sec. 304. No funds appropriated in this Act shall be expended to aid or assist in the reconstruction of the Democratic Republic of Vietnam (North Vietnam).

*   *   *

Sec. 307. None of the funds herein appropriated under this Act may be expended to support directly or indirectly combat activities in or over Cambodia, Laos, North Vietnam and South Vietnam by United States forces, and after August 15, 1973, no other funds heretofore appropriated under any other Act may be expended for such purpose.

(b) *Joint Resolution Making Continuing Appropriations for the Fiscal Year 1974: Public Law 93-52, approved July 1, 1973.*

(Excerpts)

* * *

Sec. 108. Notwithstanding any other provision of law, on or after August 15, 1973, no funds herein or heretofore appropriated may be obligated or expended to finance directly or indirectly combat activities by United States military forces in or over or from off the shores of North Vietnam, South Vietnam, Laos or Cambodia.

* * *

Sec. 110. Unless specifically authorized by Congress, none of the funds herein appropriated under this joint resolution or heretofore appropriated under any other Act may be expended for the purpose of providing assistance in the reconstruction or rehabilitation of the Democratic Republic of Vietnam (North Vietnam).

* * *

(c) *Statement by President Nixon on signing the two bills, July 1, 1973.*[20]

I have today signed H.R. 9055, the second supplemental appropriation for fiscal year 1973, and H.J. Res. 636, the continuing joint resolution.

Last week I was compelled to veto the original supplemental bill because of my grave concern that enactment of the rider then attached to it, calling for an immediate halt to all air activity over Cambodia, would have led to a destructive series of events. As I indicated then,[21] such a precipitous step would have crippled or

---

[20]Text from *Presidential Documents*, vol. 9 (1973), p. 881. The statement was released at San Clemente.

[21]Document 40.

destroyed the chances for achieving a negotiated settlement in Cambodia. The stability of Southeast Asia would have been threatened, and we would have suffered a tragic setback in our efforts to create a lasting structure of peace.

The conclusion of a responsible settlement in Indochina has been and remains a matter of the greatest urgency. All but one of the major elements of that peace are now in place, forged against the will of a determined enemy by the sacrifice and courage of countless men and women, by our perseverance in protracted negotiations, and by the effectiveness and the deterrent of American military power. The last remaining element of the peace in Southeast Asia is a stable Cambodian settlement. I believe that settlement can be secured so long as we maintain reasonable flexibility in our policies, and essential air support is not withdrawn unilaterally while delicate negotiations are still underway.

A sudden bombing halt, however, would not have brought us the lasting peace that we all desire. As President, charged by our Constitution with responsibility for conducting our foreign policy and negotiating an end to our conflicts, I will continue to take the responsible actions necessary to win that peace. Should further actions be required to that end later this year, I shall request the Congress to help us achieve our objectives.

(42) Implementation of the Cutoff.

(a) Letter from President Nixon to the Speaker of the House of Representatives and the Majority Leader of the Senate, August 3, 1973.[22]

Dear Mr. Speaker:

By legislative action the Congress has required an end to American bombing in Cambodia on August 15th.[23] The wording of the Cambodia rider is unmistakable; its intent is clear. The Congress has expressed its will in the form of law and the Administration will obey that law.

I cannot do so, however, without stating my grave personal reservations concerning the dangerous potential consequences of this measure. I would be remiss in my constitutional responsibilities if I did not warn of the hazards that lie in the path chosen by Congress.

---

[22]Text from *Presidential Documents*, vol. 9 (1973), p. 955. Identical letters were addressed to House Speaker Carl Albert and Senate Majority Leader Mike Mansfield.
[23]Documents 41a and 41b.

Since entering office in January of 1969, I have worked ceaselessly to secure an honorable peace in Southeast Asia. Thanks to the support of the American people and the gallantry of our fighting men and allies, a ceasefire agreement in Vietnam and a political settlement in Laos have already been achieved. The attainment of a settlement in Cambodia has been the unremitting effort of this Administration, and we have had every confidence of being able to achieve that goal. With the passage of the Congressional act, the incentive to negotiate a settlement in Cambodia has been undermined, and August 15 will accelerate this process.

This abandonment of a friend will have a profound impact in other countries, such as Thailand, which have relied on the constancy and determination of the United States, and I want the Congress to be fully aware of the consequences of its action. For my part, I assure America's allies that this Administration will do everything permitted by Congressional action to achieve a lasting peace in Indochina. In particular, I want the brave and beleaguered Cambodian people to know that the end to the bombing in Cambodia does not signal an abdication of America's determination to work for a lasting peace in Indochina. We will continue to provide all possible support permitted under the law. We will continue to work for a durable peace with all the legal means at our disposal.

I can only hope that the North Vietnamese will not draw the erroneous conclusion from this Congressional action that they are free to launch a military offensive in other areas in Indochina. North Vietnam would be making a very dangerous error if it mistook the cessation of bombing in Cambodia for an invitation to fresh aggression or further violations of the Paris Agreements. The American people would respond to such aggression with appropriate action.

I have sent an identical letter to the Majority Leader of the Senate.

Sincerely,

RICHARD NIXON

(b) Termination of United States Combat Activity in Cambodia: Statement by Gerald L. Warren, Deputy White House Press Secretary, August 15, 1973.[24]

As you know, the combat air operations by the United States aircraft have ceased in Cambodia, and in order clearly to explain our

[24]Text from *Presidential Documents*, vol. 9 (1973), p. 984.

position, the President's position, concerning this action and to avoid any misunderstanding by others, I would like to make the following points:

—As the President indicated in his letter to Congressional leaders on August 3, this Administration is terminating combat activity in Cambodia in compliance with a specific, direct, and binding instruction from the Congress. The President continues to hold grave reservations about the wisdom of this legislative action. He is concerned that by its action the Congress has eliminated an important incentive for a negotiated settlement in Cambodia, has weakened the security of Cambodia's neighbors in Southeast Asia, and has eroded the structure of peace in Indochina laid down in the agreements of January 27. Most importantly, this Congressional act undermines the prospects of world peace by raising doubts in the minds of both friends and adversaries concerning the resolve and capacity of the United States to stand by international agreements when they are violated by other parties.

—While noting the dangers of this legislative action, the President most reluctantly accepted the August 15 cutoff date as a necessary compromise to avoid a major disruption in United States Government operations and to allow the Khmer Republic more time to adjust to the new situation. You will recall that at the time the law was enacted, the President faced the alternative of accepting a June 30 cutoff date or halting all governmental operations through a veto of the appropriations bill to which this legislation was attached. To have terminated immediately all combat support for the Khmer Republic in the face of a massive enemy attack would have been an irresponsible act depriving the Cambodian Government of the essential time to prepare for the future. In the light of these extreme alternatives, the only viable course was to reluctantly accept the date of August 15.

—During the 6 weeks which have ensued, our combat air support coupled with Cambodian efforts to improve and strengthen their forces have left the Khmer Republic in better shape to defend itself. We hope that the government will be able to defend itself and to hold its own against the insurgents and their North Vietnamese sponsors.

—In the meantime, the United States will stand firmly with the Khmer Republic in facing the current challenge and will continue to provide the maximum amount of economic and military assistance permitted by present legal constraints.

—We continue strongly to support a cease-fire through

negotiations among the Khmer parties. An end to the fighting and respect for Cambodia's sovereignty and neutrality are our principal goals there. Despite the efforts of many interested parties and the good will of the Khmer Republic, the Communist side remains intransigently opposed to any compromise.

—I should also recall the President's warning in his August 3 letter that the leaders of North Vietnam would be making a very dangerous error if they mistook the cessation of United States combat activity in Cambodia for an invitation to pursue a policy of aggression in Southeast Asia. It should be clearly understood in Hanoi that the President will work with Congress in order to take appropriate action if North Vietnam mounts an offensive which jeopardizes stability in Indochina and threatens to overturn the settlements reached after so much sacrifice by so many for so long.

17. CHANGE IN FOGGY BOTTOM

Unsullied by the noxious ooze of Watergate, Secretary of State Rogers was almost equally without responsibility for that other classic debacle of the Nixon administration, the unraveling of the Indochina peace settlement. But Mr. Rogers had also faced his personal sea of troubles in the progressive takeover of his Department's responsibilities by Dr. Kissinger's White House office, a process that had begun early in President Nixon's first term and had gradually relegated the President's senior Cabinet officer to what was sometimes described as little more than a ceremonial role. By the end of the first term, according to Mr. Rogers' later statement, he personally had intended to return to private law practice, although he had been persuaded to "stay on for awhile" because of such pressing matters as "the closing phase of our involvement in Viet-Nam, an uncertain cease-fire in the Middle East, the initial phase of the Conference on Security and Cooperation in Europe and the need for immediate attention to our relations with NATO, CENTO, Japan, South Korea and our Latin American allies. . . ."[1]

Dr. Kissinger had also appeared to find the system of divided responsibility increasingly irksome, and is said to have seriously considered retiring from government service during the period that followed the Vietnam agreement.[2] Apparently thinking better of this plan, however, the President's Assistant for National Security Affairs had persevered in an active and expanding diplomatic role which, by the summer of 1973, had left the Middle East and Latin America as practically the only areas in which the initiative was at least nominally being left to the Department of State. Among the consequences of this trend, it is said, was the withholding from Secretary Rogers and other high officials of incoming intelligence relating to so vital a matter as the U.S.S.R.'s compliance with the

---

[1]Letter to the President, Aug. 16, in *Presidential Documents*, vol. 9 (1973), p. 1025.
[2]*New York Times*, Apr. 13, 1976.

1972 strategic arms agreements. According to testimony before the House Select Committee on Intelligence on December 17, 1975, one specific report dealing with Soviet missile silo construction was withheld in this way from June 9 until August 8, 1973.[3]

Early historians of the Nixon administration have been unanimous in identifying Dr. Kissinger himself as a prime mover in the reconstruction of foreign policy leadership that occurred later in August and, for the first time, placed the machinery of the National Security Council system and the State Department under unified direction. A weakened and perhaps reluctant President, according to this interpretation, had found himself unable to stand up to his Assistant's demands that he be given titular as well as factual responsibility throughout the foreign policy area. World conditions had, in any case, developed in such a way as to offer Mr. Rogers the possibility of dignified withdrawal. "Now that the United States has ended its long war in Indochina; that the cease-fire in the Middle East has had its third anniversary; that the first phase of the Conference on Security and Cooperation in Europe has ended satisfactorily; and that our relations with our allies as well as with the Soviet Union and the People's Republic of China are on a good basis I believe the time is right for a change," he wrote the President on August 16.[4]

President Nixon acknowledged the Rogers letter—with a tribute to the Secretary's "unwavering good spirits, good judgment and good sense"—on August 20,[5] a day when the chief executive himself was making headlines with a New Orleans address to the Veterans of Foreign Wars that combined a defense of the secret bombing of Cambodia with a denunciation of so-called "unilateral disarmers" and a reiteration of the familiar demand for a defense "second to none."[6] Public announcement of Mr. Rogers' impending departure, and of Dr. Kissinger's appointment as his successor, was reserved for a presidential news conference—the first in five months—that took place at San Clemente on August 22 and was otherwise entirely given over to Watergate matters. As well as replacing Mr. Rogers as Secretary of State, the President explained (**Document 43**), Dr. Kissinger would retain his position as Assistant to the President for National Security Affairs as a means of promoting closer coordination between the White House, the "National Security area," and the Department of State.

Some of Dr. Kissinger's own thoughts about the appointment were revealed at a news conference held in San Clemente the

[3]Same, Dec. 18, 1975.
[4]*Presidential Documents*, vol. 9 (1973), p. 1025.
[5]Same.
[6]Same, pp. 1007-14; excerpts in *Bulletin*, vol. 69 (1973), pp. 341-5.

following day. "There is no other country in the world," said the
German-born Secretary-designate, a one-time refugee from Nazi
racial persecution, "in which a man of my background could be
even considered for an office such as the one to which I have been
nominated, and that imposes on me a very grave responsibility
which I will pursue in the national interest."[7]

Reviewing some of his broad objectives as Secretary of State
(**Document 44**), Dr. Kissinger stressed the need for what he called
"a greater institutionalization of foreign policy" in order that the
foundations laid in President Nixon's first term might lead to "the
building of a more permanent structure . . . that we can pass on to
succeeding administrations so that the world will be a safer place
when they take over." As part of this endeavor, the Secretary-
designate expressed a keen desire "to work with the great
professionals in the Foreign Service," "to bring the Congress into a
close partnership in the development, planning, and execution of
our foreign policy," and "to conduct foreign policy in as open a
manner as is consistent with the goal which we all share, which is to
bring about a lasting peace."

Though President Nixon had expressed a hope that Senate
hearings on the nomination would be speedily concluded, Dr.
Kissinger's confirmation was delayed for nearly a month while his
credentials were being scrutinized by the Foreign Relations Committee chaired by Democratic Senator J. William Fulbright of
Arkansas. The eminent qualifications of the nominee in terms of
education and experience were questioned by no one, although
there were undertones of concern about the implications of the
"two hat" system that would combine the offices of Secretary of
State and Assistant for National Security Affairs. Much more
serious were the reservations that centered about the presidential
assistant's role in initiating the wiretapping of officials and
newsmen in the spring of 1969, when the administration had been
so concerned about security leaks relating to Cambodia and the
SALT negotiations.[8]

In the end, the Foreign Relations Committee spent more time
discussing this issue with Dr. Kissinger and other executive branch
witnesses than it devoted to any other single subject. Although the
committee became deeply concerned over "the pattern of casual
and arbitrary infringement of individual rights" that its inquiry
brought to light, it ultimately concluded, in carefully unen-
thusiastic phrasing, that the inquiry into Dr. Kissinger's role "did

[7]*Presidential Documents*, vol. 9 (1973), p. 1029.
[8]Cf. Chapter 9 at notes 10-11.

not constitute grounds to bar his confirmation as Secretary of State."[9] Approved September 19 by a committee vote of 16 to 1 (Democratic Senator George McGovern of South Dakota being the lone dissenter), the nomination was confirmed September 21 by a 78 to 7 vote of the full Senate. The nominee was then sworn in at the White House on Saturday, September 22, two days before a scheduled policy address as chief American spokesman at the 28th Regular Session of the U.N. General Assembly in New York.

An appearance by the Secretary of State before a body that could be considered the most representative organ of contemporary humanity afforded a natural opportunity for the enunciation of a philosophic view of world affairs as seen from an American viewpoint. Dr. Kissinger, who had already gained a reputation for lucid exposition of complex technical—especially military—issues, devoted his first address to tne United Nations (**Document 45**) to the world's imperative need for a broader, more idealistic focus. "Beyond the bilateral diplomacy, the pragmatic agreements, and dramatic steps of recent years," he said, "we envisage a comprehensive, institutionalized peace—a peace which this organization is uniquely suited to foster and to anchor in the hearts of men. . . ."

"Progress on the traditional agenda is not enough," the new Secretary insisted. "The more we succeed in solving political problems, the more other and perhaps deeper challenges emerge. . . .As the threat of war recedes, the problem of the quality of life takes on more urgent significance"—and he proceeded to enumerate a whole series of areas in which international cooperation would henceforth be indispensable: the environment, food supplies, energy, trade and monetary affairs, the exploration of the seabed. His most specific proposal—that a World Food Conference be organized under U.N. auspices in 1974—gained added significance from the broader context in which he seemingly envisaged it. "From hesitant cooperation born of necessity," Dr. Kissinger summarized, it was time to move "to genuine collective effort based on common purpose."

Secretary Kissinger's U.N. address appeared to spring from much the same intellectual sources as his April 23 proposal regarding a "new Atlantic Declaration of Principles" or "new Atlantic charter," to be completed by the nations of Western Europe and North America in advance of a contemplated European visit by President Nixon.[10] That project, too, had continued to occupy of-

[9]Senate Executive Report 93-15, Sept. 19, 1973, p. 4. For further details see U.S. Senate, Committee on Foreign Relations, 93d Cong., 1st sess., *Nomination of Henry A. Kissinger: Hearings, Parts 1 and 2* (Washington: GPO, 1973).
[10]Cf. Document 21.

ficial Washington, and the new Secretary of State had planned to take advantage of the meetings in New York to discuss its current status with various of his fellow Foreign Ministers from Europe and Japan. While the General Assembly proceeded with the "general debate" that traditionally occupied the first weeks of every session,[11] Secretary Kissinger attempted to bring his conversations on the "Year of Europe" and other current matters into focus at a news conference held in New York on September 26 (**Document 46**).

That the "Year of Europe" plan had run into serious difficulty was frankly admitted by its author. It had been no secret that France and most other members of the European Community had been showing more concern with consolidating their own unity than with humoring the United States by an exercise that could, from a European standpoint, be represented as unnecessary if not positively harmful. This negative attitude had slowed the discussions undertaken in NATO pursuant to the June meeting in Copenhagen,[12] and had exercised an even more negative influence on the posture of the European Community itself. That group, indeed, had recently gone so far as to adopt a procedure that would in effect subvert the link between defense and economic affairs that constituted the distinguishing feature of the American proposal.

This critical decision had been taken at a meeting of the Community's Council of Ministers that had been held in Copenhagen on September 10-11, while Dr. Kissinger's nomination was still under consideration by the Senate Foreign Relations Committee. Instead of a single, all-embracing Atlantic Declaration, these dignitaries had decided, there should be separate declarations issued by the Community and by NATO, with the Community confining itself to the political and economic side while leaving it to NATO to deal with defense angles. A draft Community declaration reflecting these decisions (and promptly leaked to *The New York Times*)[13] had been notable both for its avoidance of the defense question and for its tendency to stress the differences, rather than the identity, between the interests of a uniting Europe and those of the United States.

While complimenting the Europeans on their newfound ability to "speak with one voice," Secretary Kissinger did not conceal from his September 26 news conference the fact that the United States was less than satisfied with their endeavors and would be offering alternative suggestions in the immediate future. The lengthy coun-

---

[11]For subsequent U.N. developments see Chapter 28.
[12]Cf. Document 29.
[13]Text in *New York Times*, Sept. 24, 1973; background in same, Sept. 11 and 20, 1973.

terdraft presented by Assistant Secretary of State Walter J. Stoessel at a working-level meeting with European representatives three days later[14] was laden with new phraseology about "common values and approaches," "faithfulness to existing alliance arrangements," and "a more effective Atlantic community"—language which, in the aggregate, had the effect of reconverting the European draft into an expression of the American rather than the European viewpoint. These differences would still remain unreconciled when the outbreak of war in the Middle East on October 6 initiated a further degeneration of the transatlantic relationship and began to call in question a number of basic premises that had still seemed valid as the new Secretary of State assumed his responsibilities.[15]

(43) Resignation of Secretary of State Rogers and Nomination of Dr. Kissinger: News conference announcement by President Nixon, San Clemente, August 22, 1973.[16]

THE PRESIDENT. Ladies and gentlemen, I have an announcement before going to your questions.

It is with the deep sense of not only official regret, but personal regret, that I announce the resignation of Secretary of State William Rogers, effective September 3. A letter, which will be released to the press after this conference, will indicate my appraisal of his work as Secretary of State.[17]

I will simply say at this time that he wanted to leave at the conclusion of the first 4 years. He agreed to stay on because we had some enormously important problems coming up, including the negotiations which resulted in the end of the war in Vietnam, the Soviet summit, the European Security Conference, as well as in other areas—Latin America and in Asia—where the Secretary of State, as you know, has been quite busy over these past 8 months.

As he returns to private life, we will not only miss him, in terms of his official service, but I shall particularly miss him because of his having been, through the years, a very close personal friend and adviser.

That personal friendship and advice, however, I hope still to have the benefit of, and I know that I will.

As his successor, I shall nominate, and send to the Senate for

---

[14]Same, Nov. 9, 1973.
[15]See further Chapter 27 at notes 1-2.
[16]Text from *Presidential Documents*, vol. 9 (1973), pp. 1016-17.
[17]Cf. note 5.

confirmation, the name of Dr. Henry Kissinger. Dr. Kissinger will become Secretary of State, assume the duties of the office after he is confirmed by the Senate. I trust the Senate will move expeditiously on the confirmation hearings because there are a number of matters of very great importance that are coming up.

There are, for example, some matters that might even involve some foreign travel by Dr. Kissinger that will have to be delayed in the event that the Senate hearings are delayed.

Dr. Kissinger's qualifications for this post, I think, are well known by all of you ladies and gentlemen, as well as those looking to us and listening to us on television and radio.

He will retain the position, after he becomes Secretary of State, of Assistant to the President for National Security Affairs. In other words, he will have somewhat a parallel relationship to the White House which George Shultz has. George Shultz, as you know, is Secretary of the Treasury, but is also an Assistant to the President in the field of economic affairs.

The purpose of this arrangement is to have a closer coordination between the White House and the departments, and in this case, between the White House, the national security affairs, the NSC [National Security Council], and the State Department, which carries a major load in this area.

And also, another purpose is to get the work out in the departments where it belongs, and I believe that this change in this respect, with Dr. Kissinger moving in as Secretary of State and still retaining the position as Assistant to the President for National Security Affairs, will serve the interest not only of coordination but also of the interests of an effective foreign policy.

I will simply say, finally, with regard to Secretary Rogers, that he can look back on what I think, and I suppose it is a self-serving statement but I will say it about him rather than about myself, at the moment one of the most successful eras of foreign policy in any administration in history—an era in which we ended a war, the longest war in America's history; an era, in addition, in which we began to build a structure of peace, particularly involving the two great powers, the People's Republic of China and the Soviet Union, where before there had been nothing but ugly and, at some times, very, very difficult confrontation.

We still have a long way to go. There are trouble spots in the area of the Mideast, others—Southeast Asia, which we could go into in detail.

But as Secretary Rogers looks back on his years—4½ years of service as Secretary of State—he can be very proud that he was one of the major architects of what I think was a very successful foreign policy.

*(44)   Views of the Secretary-designate: News conference statement
by Dr. Kissinger, San Clemente, August 23, 1973.*[18]

DR. KISSINGER. First, I wanted to say that the President has
done me great honor to nominate me for a position that was held
by such great Americans as Secretary [Henry L.] Stimson, George
Marshall, Dean Acheson, John Foster Dulles—all of whom were
united in one basic approach: that the foreign policy of the United
States is not a partisan matter, it concerns the whole Nation, that
the future of our country transcends any particular administration.

That is the spirit in which, if the Senate confirms me, I will attempt to conduct the office of Secretary of State.

I would also like to say a few words about the outgoing Secretary
of State, William Rogers. Many of you, for 4½ years, have commented about the difficult relationship between the White House
Staff and the Secretary of State. And it is, of course, true—you
wouldn't believe me if I said anything else—that there is an institutional problem when there is a strong White House operation
and a strong Secretary of State, which is one reason why we have
combined these positions now.

I would like to say on this occasion that these difficulties which
are inherent in the arrangement were at an absolute minimum. The
Secretary of State has conducted his affairs with enormous dignity,
grace, wisdom, and above all, humanity.

I had a long talk with him on the telephone yesterday, and I look
forward to his continued advice and participation in a policy in
which he played such a large role, in which he was perhaps more instrumental in shaping than he often received credit.

Now, let me say a few things about what is ahead. Any administration wants to leave the world better than it found it, and
the most important challenge before our country in the field of
foreign policy is to bring about a stable peace.

In the first term of the President, many important and some
revolutionary changes were made. These required, to considerable
extent, secret diplomacy, and they were conducted on a rather
restricted basis. But now, we are in a different phase. The foundations that have been laid must now lead to the building of a more
permanent structure. What has been started is still very tender.

If you think back, it is only 3 years that we had simultaneous
crises in the Caribbean, in the Middle East, and on Berlin. It is only
2 years that we first opened relations with the People's Republic
of China. And in the same period, relations with our traditional
friends have undergone enormous transformation.

[18]Text from *Presidential Documents*, vol. 9 (1973), pp. 1026-7.

So, what we are going to try to do is to solidify what has been started, to put more emphasis on our relationship with Europe and with Japan, and to conclude during the term of the President the building of a structure that we can pass on to succeeding administrations so that the world will be a safer place when they take over.

Now, this requires that there will be a greater institutionalization of foreign policy than has been the case up to now. One of the challenges in going to the State Department will be the ability now to work with the great professionals in the Foreign Service who will be here after this Administration has left, and who, hopefully, will carry on the traditions that are valid, that will, by then, have been established.

It is worthwhile remembering that about 70 percent of my staff has been composed of Foreign Service officers to begin with, and, therefore, now that the entire Foreign Service can be brought more closely into the operation, we should get even more momentum behind our foreign policy.

Those who are worried whether the existing bureaucracy will be used should consult the members of my staff, and my advice to them will be to get to know their wives very well before the confirmation because afterwards they may not see as much of them as until now.

The role of the National Security Council's staff will continue to be interdepartmental. There will be a greater exchange between the State Department and the National Security Council staff personnel than has been possible up to now, but the details of this, I would like to defer until after the confirmation.

Another important aspect in the institutionalization of foreign policy will be to bring the Congress into a close partnership in the development, planning, and execution of our foreign policy.

Yesterday, I called every member of the Senate Foreign Relations Committee and key members of the House Foreign Affairs Committee, and I told them all what I am saying to you ladies and gentlemen today.

The foreign policy of this Administration is designed not on a partisan basis, but on a national basis, and it is essential that the Congress fully understand what we are attempting to do. Even in my present position as Assistant to the President, I met regularly with the Senate Foreign Relations Committee, at first in Chairman Fulbright's house, and later, in a committee room in the Senate—at first, on a very informal basis, but later, with very full notes being taken by the committee staff.

I therefore welcome the opportunity of being able to testify regularly, and as frequently as the chairman and the members of the committee consider desirable, about the purposes and policies of the President and the Administration.

There has been some question about whether the dual position of Assistant to the President and Secretary of State may cause me to invoke executive privilege. Let me answer this now: The purpose of combining the two positions is, as the President pointed out yesterday, an attempt to move policymaking from the White House into the Department and, therefore, to make it more accessible to Congressional and public scrutiny.

I would, therefore, expect to testify about all matters that Secretaries of State have traditionally testified. In addition, I would feel it appropriate to testify about those interdepartmental matters with respect to which I spoke informally previously to the Senate Foreign Relations Committee. I would not be able to testify about personal conversations between the President and myself, or about direct advice I gave to the President, but I could not testify with respect to this in any event, and no Cabinet member is ever asked to testify with respect to conversations he has with the President. So, I know the President's intention in combining these two positions is to increase the information available to the Congress.

And the President, whom I have seen only a few minutes ago, has asked me to say that executive privilege will not be invoked except with respect to the range of issues that I have mentioned. The practical consequence of it will be that more information will be available to the Congressional committees than before.

I am certain that I will be able to work out with the chairmen of the appropriate committees and with the leadership of the Senate and the House a division between the testimony that should be in executive session and that which should be public, but this is an inevitable arrangement that will have to be made between Cabinet members and Congressional committees.

The intention of the President and my intention is to establish a new and full partnership with the Congress in developing policies which are in the national interest, and now that the Vietnamese war is behind us and, therefore, the major source of division in the country about foreign policy, we know that we will be able to work out such an arrangement with the members of the Congressional committees, all of whom I know personally and have worked with in the past.

Now a word about the relationship of the department and of our foreign policy to the public. If we are going to achieve the lasting peace which we seek, and if we are going to leave behind a foreign policy tradition that will be carried on on a nonpartisan basis in succeeding administrations, we have an obligation to explain our philosophy, and purposes, and policies to the public, and after my confirmation I intend to invite leaders of various opinion-forming elements in this country to the State Department to advise us on how we can most effectively discharge this responsibility.

We will do our best to conduct foreign policy in as open a manner as is consistent with the goal which we all share, which is to bring about a lasting peace. The overriding goal, as I have said at the beginning, of any administration must be to distinguish the fluctuations of the day-to-day headlines from the more lasting achievement, and any serious person will remember and will keep in mind that what any administration will be remembered for will be the things that last and that are of benefit to our children. And all I can say is that we will make a major effort to leave behind a more peaceful world and a better America, and that is all that I wanted to say.

Now I will take a few questions, but I would like to have you understand that I will have to appear before the Senate Foreign Relations Committee for confirmation.[19] I don't think it would be appropriate to go into detail about questions that the Senators will want to ask me and to create the impression that I want to take a public position before they have an opportunity to formulate their stand. So I hope you will excuse me if I do not go into detail on some of the questions.[20]

(45) "A Just Consensus, a Stable Order, a Durable Peace": Address by Secretary Kissinger at the 28th Regular Session of the United Nations General Assembly, September 24, 1973.[21]

I come before you today—confirmed in office but two days ago—as probably the world's most junior Foreign Minister. That President Nixon should ask me as my first official act to speak here for the United States reaffirms the importance that my country attaches to the values and ideals of the United Nations.

It would be idle to deny that the American people, like many others, have sometimes been disappointed because this organization has not been more successful in translating the hopes for universal peace of its architects into concrete accomplishments.

But despite our disappointments, my country remains committed to the goal of a world community. We will continue to work in this Parliament of Man to make it a reality.

---

[19]Cf. above at note 9.

[20]For the remainder of the news conference see *Presidential Documents, loc. cit.*, pp. 1027-30, or *Bulletin*, vol. 69 (1973), pp. 370-74.

[21]Department of State Press Release 343; text from *Bulletin*, vol. 69 (1973), pp. 469-73.

Two centuries ago, the philosopher Kant predicted that perpetual peace would come eventually—either as the creation of man's moral aspirations or as the consequence of physical necessity. What seemed utopian then looms as tomorrow's reality; soon there will be no alternative. Our only choice is whether the world envisaged in the charter will come about as the result of our vision or of a catastrophe invited by our shortsightedness.

The United States has made its choice. My country seeks true peace; not simply an armistice. We strive for a world in which the rule of law governs and fundamental human rights are the birthright of all. Beyond the bilateral diplomacy, the pragmatic agreements, and dramatic steps of recent years, we envisage a comprehensive, institutionalized peace—a peace which this organization is uniquely situated to foster and to anchor in the hearts of men.

This will be the spirit of American foreign policy.

This attitude will guide our work in this organization.

We start from a bedrock of solid progress. Many of the crises that haunted past General Assemblies have been put behind us. Agreement has been reached on Berlin; there is a cease-fire in the Middle East; the Viet-Nam war has been ended. The rigid confrontation that has dominated international life and weakened this organization for a quarter of a century has been softened.

The United States and the Soviet Union have perceived a commonality of interest in avoiding nuclear holocaust and in establishing a broad web of constructive relationships. Talks on strategic arms limitation have already produced historic accords aimed at slowing the arms race and insuring strategic stability; we have, today, resumed negotiations on this subject. The positive results we hope for will enhance the security of all mankind.

Two decades of estrangement between the United States and the People's Republic of China have given way to constructive dialogue and productive exchanges. President Nixon has met with the leaders of that nation; we have agreed to a historic communique[22] that honestly sets forth both our differences and our common principles; and we have each opened a Liaison Office in the capital of the other.

Many other countries have seized the initiative and contributed—in substance and spirit—to the relaxation of tensions. The nations of Europe and North America are engaged in a conference to further security and cooperation. The two German states have taken their place in this Assembly.[23] India, Pakistan, and

Bangladesh have begun to move toward a welcome reconciliation. North and South Korea are at last engaged in a dialogue which we hope will lead to a new era of peace and security.

Yet these achievements, solid as they are, have only made less precarious the dangers and divisions inherited from the postwar era. We have ended many of the confrontations of the cold war; yet, even in this room, the vocabulary of suspicion persists. Relaxation of tensions is justified by some as merely a tactical interlude before renewed struggle. Others suspect the emergence of a two-power condominium. And as tension between the two original blocs has eased, a third grouping increasingly assumes the characteristics of a bloc of its own—tne alignment of the nonaligned.

So the world is uneasily suspended between old slogans and new realities, between a view of peace as but a pause in an unending struggle and a vision of peace as a promise of global cooperation.

From Détente to Cooperation

In 1946 James Byrnes, the first Secretary of State to address this Assembly, spoke of how the United Nations could help break down habits of thinking in national isolation and move toward universal understanding and tolerance among all peoples.[24]

The United States will never be satisfied with a world of uneasy truces, of offsetting blocs, of accommodations of convenience. We know that power can enforce a resigned passivity, but only a sense of justice can enlist consensus. We strive for a peace whose stability rests not merely on a balance of forces, but on shared aspirations. We are convinced that a structure which ignores humane values will prove cold and empty and unfulfilling to most of mankind.

The United States deeply believes:

—That justice cannot be confined by national frontiers.
—That truth is universal and not the peculiar possession of a single people or group or ideology.
—That compassion and humanity must ennoble all our endeavors.

In this spirit we ask the Assembly to move with us from détente to cooperation, from coexistence to community.

[24]Address of Feb. 28, 1946; excerpts in *Documents, 1945-46*, pp. 21-6.

Moving Toward Greater Stability

Our journey must begin with the world as it is and with the issues now before us. The United States will spare no effort to ease tensions further and to move toward greater stability:

—We shall continue, in the spirit of the Shanghai communique, our search for a new relationship with the People's Republic of China.

—We shall work to promote positive trends elsewhere in Asia. The uncertain peace in Indochina must be strengthened; the world community cannot afford, or permit, a relapse into war in that region.

—We shall continue to pursue vigorously the building of constructive relations with the Soviet Union.

—We shall strive to promote conciliation in Europe. In the negotiations beginning next month we shall seek a reduction of the military forces that have faced each other for so long across that divided continent.[25]

—We shall give new vigor to our policy of partnership in the Western Hemisphere.[26]

—We shall honor our pledge to promote self-determination, economic development, and human dignity across the continent of Africa.

—We shall press on with strategic arms limitation talks. We consider them crucial for security and stability in this period.

—We shall search for solutions to the worldwide problem of conventional weapons, which drain our resources and fuel the fires of local conflict.

In these efforts, the United States will be guided by fundamental principles:

—We have no desire for domination. We will oppose—as we have consistently opposed throughout this century—any nation that chooses this path. We have not been asked to participate in a condominium; we would reject such an appeal if it were made.

—We will never abandon our allies or our friends. The strengthening of our traditional ties is the essential foundation for the development of new relationships with old adversaries.

—We will work for peace through the United Nations as well as through bilateral relationships.

[25]Cf. Document 79.
[26]Cf. Chapter 20.

We recognize our special obligation, as a permanent member of the Security Council, to assist in the search for just solutions in those parts of the world now torn by strife, such as the Middle East. While we cannot substitute for the efforts of those most directly involved, we are prepared to use our influence to generate a spirit of accommodation and to encourage the parties toward practical progress.

The Quality of Life

But progress on the traditional agenda is not enough. The more we succeed in solving political problems, the more other and perhaps deeper challenges emerge. As the world grows more stable, we must confront the question of the ends of détente. As the threat of war recedes, the problem of the quality of life takes on more urgent significance.

We are, in fact, members of a community drawn by modern science, technology, and new forms of communication into a proximity for which we are still politically unprepared. Technology daily outstrips the ability of our institutions to cope with its fruits. Our political imagination must catch up with our scientific vision. This is at the same time the greatest challenge and the greatest opportunity of this organization:

—The pollution of the skies, the seas, and the land is a global problem.

—The increased consumption of cereals and protein has reduced world food reserves to dangerously low levels.

—The demand for energy is outrunning supply, and the need for technological innovation is urgent.

—The growth of the world's economy is inhibited by restrictive trading blocs and an insufficiently flexible international monetary system.

—The exploitation of the resources of the ocean beds, which is essential for the needs of burgeoning populations, requires global cooperation lest it degenerate into global contention.

Challenges of this magnitude cannot be solved by a world fragmented into self-contained nation-states or rigid blocs.

Areas of Common Action

I do not intend today to cover the whole agenda of international cooperation. Rather, I shall speak briefly of some illustrative areas of common action. I pledge the readiness of the United States to solve these problems cooperatively and to submit proposals aimed at their resolution.

1. *A world community requires the curbing of conflict.*

The United Nations, in its 28-year history, has not always been idle in this sphere. In Indonesia, the Indian Subcontinent, the Middle East, the Congo, and in Cyprus, it has shown its ability for effective factfinding, mediation, and peacekeeping missions. This central aspect of the U.N.'s work must be strengthened. On a small planet, so bound together by technology and so interdependent economically, we can no longer afford the constant eruption of conflict and the danger of its spread.

Yet, in recent years we have found ourselves locked in fruitless debates about the inauguration of peacekeeping operations and over the degree of control the Security Council would exercise over peacekeeping machinery—an impasse which insured only that permanent peacekeeping machinery would not come into being. Each peacekeeping unit we have formed to cope with an emergency has been an improvisation growing out of argument and controversy.

We should delay no longer. The time has come to agree on peacekeeping guidelines so that this organization can act swiftly, confidently, and effectively in future crises. To break the deadlock, the United States is prepared to consider how the Security Council can play a more central role in the conduct of peacekeeping operations. If all countries concerned approach this problem with a desire to achieve a cooperative solution, the United Nations can achieve a major step forward during this session.

2. *A world community must have the widest possible membership.*

The exclusion of any qualified state denies representation not only to governments but to peoples. Membership in this body should be a step toward reconciliation, not a source of conflict. The time has come for North and South Korea to be offered their rightful places here, without prejudice to a future evolution toward unification.[27]

In this spirit also, we support the permanent membership of Japan in the Security Council.

3. *A world community must assure that all its people are fed.*

The growing threat to the world's food supply deserves the

[27]Cf. Chapter 28 at note 7.

urgent attention of this Assembly. Since 1969, global consumption of cereals has risen more rapidly than production; stocks are at the lowest levels in years. We now face the prospect that—even with bumper crops—the world may not rebuild its seriously depleted reserves in this decade.

No one country can cope with this problem. The United States therefore proposes:

—That a World Food Conference be organized under United Nations auspices in 1974 to discuss ways to maintain adequate food supplies, and to harness the efforts of all nations to meet the hunger and malnutrition resulting from natural disasters.[28]

—That nations in a position to do so offer technical assistance in the conservation of food. The United States is ready to join with others in providing such assistance.

4. *A world community cannot remain divided between the permanently rich and the permanently poor.*

Let us therefore resolve that this Assembly, this year, initiate a search—drawing on the world's best minds—for new and imaginative solutions to the problems of development. Our search must be candid and realistic, but it must also be free of peremptory demands, antagonistic propositions, ideological confrontation, or propagandistic rhetoric—or we will surely fail.

The United States is prepared to join in this new search, providing freely of the experience gained over two decades. We have learned not to exaggerate our capacity to transform nations—but we have also learned much about what progress is possible.

We will participate without preconditions, with a conciliatory attitude and a cooperative commitment. We ask only that others adopt the same approach.

In this spirit the United States is willing to examine seriously the proposal by the distinguished President of Mexico for a Charter of the Economic Rights and Duties of States.[29] Such a document will make a significant and historic contribution if it reflects the true aspirations of all nations; if it is turned into an indictment of one group of countries by another, it will accomplish nothing. To command general support—and to be implemented—the proposed rights and duties must be defined equitably and take into account the concerns of industrialized as well as of developing countries.

[28]Cf. Chapter 24 at note 7.
[29]Proposed by Mexican President Luis Echeverria Álvarez at the Third Ministerial Session of the U.N. Conference on Trade and Development (UNCTAD III), held in Santiago, Chile on Apr. 13-May 21, 1972.

The United States stands ready to define its responsibilities in a humane and cooperative spirit.

5. *Finally, a world community must harness science and technology for the benefit of all.*

We must begin to match our remarkable technological skills with our equally remarkable technological needs. We must find the means for the cooperative and judicious development of our energy resources. We must responsibly confront the problems of population growth, which are fast pushing humanity toward the limits of what our earth can sustain. We must embark on a new scientific revolution to increase agricultural productivity in all lands. No field of human endeavor is so dependent upon an open world for its advancement; no field is so in need of international cooperation to cope with its potential dangers.

Mr. President,[30] fellow delegates: Are we prepared to accept the imperatives of a global society and infuse our labors with a new vision? Or shall we content ourselves with a temporary pause in the turmoil that has wracked our century? Shall we proceed with one-sided demands and sterile confrontations? Or shall we proceed in a spirit of compromise produced by a sense of common destiny? We must move from hesitant cooperation born of necessity to genuine collective effort based on common purpose.

It is a choice no country can make alone. We can repeat old slogans or strive for new hope. We can fill the record of our proceedings with acrimony, or we can dedicate ourselves to dealing with man's deepest needs. The ideal of a world community may be decried as unrealistic—but great constructions have always been ideals before they can become realities. Let us dedicate ourselves to this noblest of all possible goals and achieve at last what has so long eluded us: true understanding and tolerance among mankind.

(46) Current Diplomatic Business: News conference statement by Secretary Kissinger, New York, September 26, 1973.[31]

(Excerpt)

Ladies and gentlemen: I wanted to give you a brief account of what I have been doing here and then answer your questions, hopefully relating primarily to my activities in New York.

---

[30]Leopoldo Benites (Ecuador).
[31]Department of State Press Release 349, Sept. 27; text from *Bulletin*, vol. 69 (1973), pp. 475-7.

You know my schedule, so there is no point in repeating that. My activities consisted of the speech to the General Assembly, meetings with various Foreign Ministers, and meetings with my staff in preparation for entering the State Department on Thursday [September 27], where I still haven't been.

Now, about my speech to the General Assembly,[32] the intention was to convey the tone, philosophy, and the attitude of the administration in its conduct of foreign policy for the remainder of this term.

We wanted to convey, beyond the specific initiatives that might be proposed, that the task which is before us now is to consolidate what has been achieved, to construct something that can endure, both within our country—because it has popular and governmental support—and above all, something that can endure internationally—because it is seen to be in the common interest.

This attitude and general philosophy, we felt, was more important at this stage than a list of specific proposals—although some were made—because you are familiar with the main outlines of many of our policies.

So for the President's second term, our agenda is to try to create an international consensus to international order that is seen to be just by all or at least the greatest number—something that embodies humane and progressive ideas.

In my conversations with the Foreign Ministers, I obviously had to deal primarily with the current agenda. On my trip this week I saw a great many of our allies. I saw many of the Foreign Ministers from Europe. I saw, of course, the Foreign Minister of Japan. I spent some time with Foreign Minister Gromyko and today with the Permanent Representative of the People's Republic of China. I had a long and fruitful talk with the Foreign Minister of Brazil to underline the great importance we attach to reinvigorating our relationships in that area. And I saw the Foreign Ministers of Thailand and Korea.

Let me say a word about the conversations with our European friends and also the relation of Japan to that process.

There has been a great deal of speculation tied to a possible trip of the President to Europe. We still, of course, plan this trip, but its exact date will have to be determined by the pace of our preparation.

Much of the speculation has been in terms of an adversary relationship between us and the Europeans and great difficulty in coming to an agreement. I would like to correct this impression. What we are confronting in the dialogue with the Europeans is the

[32]Document 45.

merging of several processes. There is the process of European integration. There is the process of the debate on security within
NATO. And there is the redefinition of the Atlantic relationship,
which covers all these areas.

As you know, on behalf of the President, I proposed a new
Atlantic Declaration of Principles in a speech I gave in April.[33]

There was some uncertainty in Europe on how and in what
forum to respond; several months were spent in internal discussions
within Europe—whether the proper forum would be NATO, a
series of bilateral negotiations with the Europeans, or a series of
talks between the United States and the Common Market.

The result has been that after some months of going all these
routes European opinion crystallized. It was decided that those
economic matters—and political considerations relevant to
economic matters—relevant to Europe as an entity should be
discussed by the Nine, as a unit, with the United States. It was also
decided that security issues—and those political issues relevant to
security matters—should be discussed in the NATO Council. And
then of course bilateral channels have remained open throughout
this process.

With respect to the declaration that the European Nine have
developed and that was presented to me yesterday on behalf of the
Nine by Foreign Minister [Knud B.] Andersen of Denmark,[34] let me
say that the United States recognizes that this first attempt by
Europe to speak with one voice on a political matter of transatlantic relationships is an event of the greatest significance.

The United States in the postwar period has constantly supported
the emergence of a European identity, and we therefore welcome
the fact that Europe has now organized itself well enough so that it
can speak to us with one voice. It may be that in historical
retrospect this meeting of the European Nine in Copenhagen will be
seen as one of the decisive events of the postwar period.

At the same time, the United States of course reserves the right to
its own opinion with respect to the outcome of these deliberations.
They were not presented to the United States on a take-it-or-leave-it
basis. They were presented to us in a spirit of partnership as the
opening of a dialogue. Therefore, this Saturday [September 29] the
Political Directors of the Nine and Assistant Secretary Stoessel are
going to meet for a discussion in which we will blend our ideas—or
attempt to blend our ideas—with those of Europe in this
declaration of economic and political principles.[35]

Secondly, as you know, there are discussions taking place right

---

[33]Document 21.
[34]Cf. above at note 13.
[35]Cf. above at note 14.

now in NATO dealing with the definition of future allied relationships. They concern security and the political aspects of security. There is general agreement that these discussions will be energetically pursued within the context of the NATO Council. We expect to make a significant contribution to this. And so will other countries.

What I want to underline here is that we are not engaged in an adversary procedure. We are engaged in a process in which we intend to give traditional friendship new vitality.

The trip of the President is not an end in itself. The trip of the President will certainly take place in the near future,[36] but our concern is to produce documents that will have some historic significance. We believe that we are now well on the way toward accomplishing what we set out to do earlier this year. The discussions have been useful, and they will proceed in a constructive spirit.

It was of course inevitable in the conversations with Japan that its relationship to these various efforts would be a subject of conversation.

Since the Japanese Foreign Minister and Prime Minister[37] are going to be visiting Europe in the next few weeks, it would not be appropriate for me to comment, except to say that in my speech of April 23 we outlined the American point of view. We believe that at some stage of this process, in some manner, it is important for Japan to participate.

The manner and the kind of declaration remains to be discussed. I think it will continue to be discussed between the Japanese and ourselves and between the Japanese and the Europeans on the trip of senior Japanese officials through Europe.

I will make no comment about the conversations we had with the Representative of the People's Republic of China and the Foreign Minister of the Soviet Union.[38] As you know, Foreign Minister Gromyko will meet the President on Friday in Washington, and after that he and I will have a lunch. Therefore, we are still in the middle of our discussions, which cover the entire agenda of U.S.-Soviet relationships.

While I was here, I also met with the Representatives of African nations and with the Representatives of Arab states here at the United Nations. These meetings were not intended as pronouncements of new policy, but as expressions of our profound concern. We do not want to pretend to answers that have not yet been

---

[36]Cf. Chapter 27 at note 16.
[37]Respectively Masayoshi Ohira and Kakuei Tanaka.
[38]Respectively Huang Hua and Andrei A. Gromyko.

found. But we can pledge in both areas that we will make an effort at understanding and an attempt to find just solutions.

I think now it would be best if I took your questions.[39]

---

[39]For the remainder of the news conference see *Bulletin, loc. cit.*, pp. 477-81.

18. SOUTHEAST ASIAN ADJUSTMENTS

Among the numerous matters that would compete for Secretary Kissinger's attention on his return to Washington was the grievously disappointing state of affairs in Indochina, eight months after the Paris peace agreement and more than three months after its formal reaffirmation at the Paris ceremony of June 13. The herculean diplomatic efforts that had eventually produced the Vietnam peace settlement had wholly failed to harmonize the political ambitions of the Vietnamese parties, and had only temporarily stayed the expression of their hostility on a military level. Although the United States had now denied itself the possibility of further military involvement in Indochina, it still regarded the actions of its adversaries there with profound misgivings. In a note delivered to the North Vietnamese Embassy in Paris on September 10 (**Document 47**), it specifically complained that North Vietnamese forces had built or repaired at least twelve airfields in South Vietnam and, despite an earlier American protest, had continued to introduce SA-2 missiles and antiaircraft units into South Vietnam in contravention of the Paris agreement. In Saigon, it was openly affirmed that such activities spelled "a sinister probability of an offensive in the near future."[1]

In Laos, the situation still appeared distinctly more hopeful. Aided by considerable pressure from American and Soviet representatives, negotiators for the Vientiane government and the Communist-led Pathet Lao or "Patriotic Forces" had belatedly reached agreement on a protocol designed to implement the various clauses of the cease-fire agreement they had concluded February 21. As signed in Vientiane on September 14, this document called for the formation of an elaborately balanced "Provisional Government of National Union," to be headed by Prince Souvanna Phouma, with Prince Souphanouvong as one of his two deputies; a 42-member National Political Consultative Council, made up of

[1]*Keesing's*, pp. 26335-6; for earlier discussion cf. Chapters 2, 11, and 16.

371

Vientiane, "patriotic," and neutralist representatives; a joint police force to ensure the neutralization of Vientiane and Luang Prabang; and a Joint Commission to superintend the implementation of the agreement, particularly the withdrawal of foreign military personnel.[2]

In a congratulatory letter to Souvanna Phouma on the successful completion of these negotiations (**Document 48**), President Nixon assured the veteran Lao statesman of the continued support of the United States, and of its expectation "that others who have participated in this conflict similarly will keep faith with all aspects of the Lao Accords." Although American military power would no longer be available to reinforce this expectation, Laos for the moment appeared well started along "the path to peace and national reconciliation" to which it was generally to adhere until the definitive assertion of Communist control that took place in 1975.

As always, it was Cambodia's situation that appeared the most problematical at the moment, especially now when further American military support of the Khmer Republic forces had been barred by Congress. True, the military pressure on Phnom Penh had eased since midsummer, and the insurgents failed in early September to capture Kompong Cham, Cambodia's third largest city. But though Prince Sihanouk continued to complain about the paucity of ammunition and equipment provided by his North Vietnamese and Chinese allies, his "Royal Government of National Union" was making up for its lack of military success by scoring a whole succession of diplomatic victories. Endorsed by the summit Conference of Nonaligned Countries at Algiers early in September, the Sihanouk regime was for the first time accorded formal diplomatic recognition by the Soviet Union on October 10. Seven days later, the U.N. General Assembly in New York decided, by a vote of 68 to 24 with 29 abstentions, to add to its agenda an item entitled "Restoration of the lawful rights of the Royal Government of National Union of Cambodia in the United Nations"—in other words, a plan for the ouster of the Phnom Penh government and substitution of the Sihanouk group in much the same way that Nationalist China had been ousted to make way for Communist China two years earlier. A vote on this proposal, which was strongly opposed by the United States, was not, however, expected for several weeks.[3]

[2]Summary in *Keesing's*, p. 26191; full texts, translated from the Lao original, in *Australian Foreign Affairs Record* (Canberra), vol. 44 (1973), pp. 676-87, and *Foreign Affairs Reports* (New Delhi), Sept. 1973, pp. 219-35.
[3]See further Chapter 26 at note 3.

Whatever doubts might prevail concerning the long-range prospects in this part of Asia, there was no mistaking the fact that the American power and presence in the area were being rapidly reduced, and that the various mutual defense arrangements erected with American encouragement in earlier years were being correspondingly downgraded. Particularly instructive was the case of Thailand, which had given valued support to the United States throughout the recent conflict and had permitted a substantially increased build-up of American military personnel as U.S. Air Force units had been withdrawn from South Vietnam in the year preceding the cease-fire. By the summer of 1973, however, the emphasis had shifted to a reduction of this U.S. military presence, at that time reckoned at about 44,000 men and 500 aircraft. On August 24 came the announcement that the United States, as a first step, would make immediate arrangements for the withdrawal of 3,550 men and over 100 aircraft.[4] Pressures for an expedited American withdrawal would soon be strengthened following the overthrow on October 14 of the military-dominated government of Field Marshal Thanom Kittikachorn and the installation of a predominantly civilian government of more democratic and neutralist outlook.

Similar tendencies were at work in other parts of Southeast Asia. President Ferdinand E. Marcos of the Philippines, still wielding the virtually dictatorial powers he had assumed in 1972, was giving high priority to a curtailment of U.S. military base rights as well as the establishment of closer relations with Communist governments. Australia and New Zealand, under their new Labor cabinets, continued to debate the wisdom of.participation in the South-East Asia Treaty Organization (SEATO) and other collective defense arrangements inherited from the "cold war" era. SEATO, a relic of the Indochina crisis of 1954 and a prime reflection of the "pactomania" of that period, had for several years been widely regarded as an anachronism. French support had been denied the organization since the mid-1960s, and Pakistan had announced its determination to withdraw from membership following the loss of its eastern province in 1971.

The eighteenth meeting of the SEATO Council, held in New York on September 28 with Deputy Secretary of State Kenneth Rush as the chief U.S. delegate, signaled a further stage in this long-term process. Omitting the customary declaration of anti-Communist solidarity, the representatives of SEATO's six remaining member countries confined themselves to announcing a series of important decisions aimed, they said, at making SEATO's activities "more relevant to the situation in the treaty area today." "In the light of major changes which have occurred in Southeast Asia since the last Council meeting," said the official press release (Document 49) which took the place of a formal communiqué, "the Council agreed to a reduction of SEATO's traditional military activities, with increased emphasis on supporting the national programs of the two regional members, the Philippines and Thailand, in promoting stability and development." To implement this change of emphasis, it was announced, the SEATO military staff would be absorbed into the civilian headquarters organization in Bangkok, a step just short of the "phasing out" of the alliance that was to be announced a scant two years later.[5]

(47) Construction of Airfields in South Vietnam: United States Note delivered to the Embassy of the Democratic Republic of Vietnam (DRV) at Paris September 10, 1973.[6]

The Department of State of the United States of America presents its compliments to the Ministry of Foreign Affairs of the Democratic Republic of Viet-Nam and has the honor to refer to the Agreement on Ending the War and Restoring Peace in Viet-Nam of January 27, 1973.[7]

1. The United States calls the attention of the DRV to the fact that since January 28, when the Paris Agreement on Ending the War and Restoring Peace in Viet-Nam went into effect, the forces of its side have built or repaired at least 12 airfields in South Viet-Nam. It notes that North Vietnamese anti-aircraft units with weapons have been introduced into South Viet-Nam after January 28 in violation of Article 7 of the Paris Agreement and emplaced at these fields.

2. The DRV will recall that the United States on April 20, in its note to the other signatories of the Act of Paris,[8] protested the illegal placing of SA-2 missiles at Khe Sanh airfield in Quang Tri Province. Despite the U.S. protest, the DRV has continued to introduce SA-2 missiles and anti-aircraft units into South Viet-Nam. The U.S. calls upon the DRV side to remove to North Viet-Nam

---

[5]Press statement, Sept. 24, 1975, in *Bulletin*, vol. 73 (1975), p. 575.
[6]Department of State Press Release 325, Sept. 11; text from *Bulletin*, vol. 69 (1973), pp. 423-4.
[7]Document 5.
[8]Document 9.

those missiles and anti-aircraft units which it has illegally introduced into South Viet-Nam since January 28.

3. The United States notes that on June 9 a press spokesman of the DRV side told the press in Saigon that the DRV side has the "right" to develop civil aviation in South Viet-Nam. A spokesman of the DRV side also told the press in Saigon on July 28 that its side would "not permit" the RVN [Republic of Viet-Nam] "exclusive control" of the airspace over South Viet-Nam. The above statements and the DRV side's repair and construction of 12 airfields in South Viet-Nam strongly suggest that the DRV intends to introduce aircraft into the airspace of South Viet-Nam in a way not authorized by the Agreement of January 27 or permitted under international law.

4. The GVN [Government of Viet-Nam] in its September 10, 1973, note to the DRV has clearly indicated that it will not tolerate any unauthorized intrusion by the DRV into the airspace of South Viet-Nam. The United States thus wishes strongly to emphasize the grave risks which the DRV would run by violating the airspace sovereignty of the Republic of Viet-Nam.

(48) Completion of Internal Political Agreement in Laos: United States Government statement, September 14, 1973, and letter from President Nixon to Prime Minister Souvanna Phouma.[9]

The United States welcomes the successful completion of the negotiations on the implementing protocols to carry out the February 21, 1973, Agreement on the Restoration of Peace and Reconciliation in Laos.[10]

We hope the agreement will secure the peace and freedom from aggression for which Prime Minister Souvanna Phouma and Lao people have sacrificed so much in years past.

The United States stands ready to continue cooperation and assistance to the new provisional government which is expected to be formed shortly in Laos.

The United States will, of course, be guided by the provisions of the agreement and its implementing protocols and by the wishes of Prime Minister Souvanna Phouma and the new provisional government. We expect all other parties to do the same and to respect the sovereignty of Laos.

[9]Department of State Press Release 331, Sept. 14; texts from *Bulletin*, vol. 69 (1973), pp. 452-3.
[10]Cf. Chapter 2 at note 9, and note 2 above.

MESSAGE FROM PRESIDENT NIXON
TO PRINCE SOUVANNA PHOUMA

YOUR HIGHNESS: On behalf of the American people, I am pleased to congratulate you on the successful completion of negotiations to carry out the February 21, 1973 Agreement on the Restoration of Peace and Reconciliation in Laos. On this historic occasion, allow me again to assure you that the United States will continue to support your efforts to perfect the neutrality, independence and unity of the Lao Kingdom.

The protocol which has just been signed will, I earnestly hope, secure the peace and freedom from aggression for which you and your people have sacrificed so much in years past. For our part, the actions of the United States Government with respect to Laos will, of course, be guided by the provisions of the agreement and the wishes of the new provisional government under your leadership. We expect that others who have participated in this conflict similarly will keep faith with all aspects of the Lao Accords and we are resolved that henceforth the sovereignty of your country shall be universally respected.

The path to peace and national reconciliation has, I know, not been easy. I am truly gratified that your steadfast pursuit of these goals has culminated in the agreement just signed, and I am confident that with your persistent and vigilant leadership and the support of all true Lao nationalists, you will surely surmount whatever difficulties may lie ahead. As you set about implementing this new agreement, you can be sure that the United States is as ready to support you in assuring peace and healing the wounds of war as we were in assisting with your self-defense.

Sincerely,

RICHARD NIXON.

(49) The South-East Asia Treaty Organization (SEATO): Press Statement issued at the conclusion of the 18th annual meeting of the SEATO Council, New York, September 28, 1973.[11]

Council members of the Southeast Asia Treaty Organization from Australia, New Zealand, the Philippines, Thailand, the United Kingdom and the United States held their 18th annual meeting in New York today.

At the conclusion of the meeting, SEATO Secretary General

---

[11]Text from *Bulletin*, vol. 69 (1973), p. 512.

H. E. Sunthorn Hongladarom announced that the Council upheld the objectives of the Manila Pact[12] and its basic purpose of peace in Southeast Asia. They discussed and agreed on measures to ensure that SEATO's future activities are relevant to the situation in the treaty area brought about by recent international development, notably the movement towards a peaceful and viable settlement of the Indochina conflict.

In the light of major changes which have occurred in Southeast Asia since the last Council meeting,[13] the Council agreed to a reduction of SEATO's traditional military activities, with increased emphasis on supporting the national programs of the two regional members, the Philippines and Thailand, in promoting stability and development.

The Council also agreed with the Secretary General's proposal calling for a complete integration of the military into the civilian staff at SEATO Headquarters in Bangkok which would facilitate the organization's increased focus on cooperating in the support of the internal stability and development measures of the regional members.

Council members believed that these changes would result in SEATO's activities being more relevant to the situation in the treaty area today, noting that the Manila Pact calls for cooperation among member nations to promote peace, economic progress and social well-being.

[12]Southeast Asia Collective Defense Treaty, signed at Manila Sept. 8, 1954 and entered into force Feb. 19, 1955 (TIAS 3170; 6 UST 81); text in *Documents, 1954*, pp. 319-23.
[13]Held in Canberra June 27-28, 1972; *AFR, 1972*, pp. 340-50.

19. MEETINGS ON TRADE AND MONEY

Not all the important foreign policy business of these weeks was handled by the Department of State. Secretary Kissinger's debut occurred at a crucial stage of the multilateral discussions on trade and monetary affairs that had been initiated pursuant to the Smithsonian Agreement of December 1971, and were conducted mainly by other branches of the Federal establishment.[1] Even while Dr. Kissinger was awaiting the Senate's verdict on his Cabinet nomination, there had taken place in Tokyo on September 12-14 a ministerial-level meeting of the Contracting Parties to the General Agreement on Tariffs and Trade (GATT), especially convened to launch the new round of multilateral trade negotiations that would become known as the "Nixon" or "Tokyo" Round. Ten days later, while the newly inducted Secretary of State conferred with Foreign Ministers and others in New York, the world's financial luminaries were reassembled in Nairobi for the annual meetings of the Boards of Governors of the International Bank for Reconstruction and Development (IBRD) and the International Monetary Fund (IMF), held in the Kenyan capital on September 24-28.

There had been no lack of publicity concerning the United States' objectives in the Tokyo negotiations, in which it was represented by a twenty-member delegation headed by Secretary of the Treasury Shultz and by Ambassador William D. Eberle, the President's Special Representative for Trade Negotiations and the regular U.S. spokesman in the 82-member GATT organization. With its decades-old commitment to the principles of trade expansion and liberalization, the United States had eagerly sought an opportunity to bargain with other trading nations for the removal of various disabilities affecting its own commerce—among them, the prevalence of various types of "nontariff" barriers and the pursuit by the European Economic Community of policies in the agricultural and other fields which were felt to place the interests of U.S. exporters at an unfair disadvantage.

[1]For earlier discussion see Chapter 4.

In a statement geared to the opening of the Tokyo meeting,[2] President Nixon on September 8 had summarized American aims as: (1) continuance of the 40-year-old movement toward freer trade; (2) resolution of trade problems that had caused friction between the United States and its partners; (3) reform of guidelines and practices that reduced trading opportunities for the United States and some other producers, and favored some at the expense of others; and (4) finding ways to improve trading relationships with the less developed countries and with countries with differing economic and social systems. These, of course, were essentially the same aims that had been set forth in President Nixon's trade message of April 10. Although the Trade Reform Act proposed at that time had since run into difficulties and had not yet cleared the House Ways and Means Committee,[3] the absence of fresh legislative authority was not expected to hamper the U.S. delegation at the Tokyo meeting, which would be mainly concerned with defining principles and establishing guidelines for the detailed negotiations to follow.

From the standpoint of the United States, it would have been preferable that the negotiations on trade and monetary affairs foreseen in the Smithsonian Agreement should go forward within some common institutional framework that would ensure their treatment in a coordinated manner. Although its partners had rejected this technique and insisted that overall responsibility be divided between GATT and the IMF, American spokesmen continued to emphasize the essential interdependence of trade and monetary matters. "Action in one field can, but should not be allowed to, frustrate the solutions reached in other fields," said Secretary Shultz in his major presentation at Tokyo (**Document 50a**). "There is thus a need for simultaneous improvement in all elements of the international system."

Few if any governments would have disputed this assertion as a theoretical principle; yet quite a number of them differed with American views about its practical application. Where the United States looked to wider trading opportunities as a means of strengthening its overall international financial position, France and its EEC partners had tended to approach the question from an opposite angle and to maintain that trade concessions should be granted only after the United States had brought its finances into equilibrium. There was also a serious difference about the acceptability of floating exchange rates, which, as already noted, had become widely prevalent within the past few months and were

---

[2]*Presidential Documents*, vol. 9 (1973), p. 1068, and *Bulletin*, vol. 69 (1973), p. 446.
[3]Cf. below at note 7.

being much more tolerantly viewed in Washington than in Paris. Recent monetary developments were proving highly favorable to the improvement of the U.S. trade balance, and the American Government had remained unmoved by M. Giscard d'Estaing's insistence on the urgency of returning to "stable currency values."

These and similar differences had precluded any full agreement in advance of the Tokyo meeting, and there was further high-level wrangling before the various controversies could be plastered over with suitably ambiguous phraseology. The end result of this semantic effort was an 11-point "Declaration of Tokyo" (**Document 50b**), made public at the conclusion of the meeting on September 14, which cautiously reviewed the areas of agreement and disagreement and laid down basic procedures for the months ahead. As had been anticipated, responsibility for elaborating detailed negotiating plans and supervising the actual negotiations was entrusted to a special Trade Negotiations Committee, open to participating governments "including the European Communities," which was to begin work not later than November 1 with the intention that the negotiations should be completed in 1975.

Many of those who had participated in the Tokyo meeting turned up again in Nairobi ten days later for the annual meeting of the 123-nation World Bank and affiliated institutions and the 126-nation International Monetary Fund (IMF). These meetings, at which Secretary Shultz served as the principal American representative, had been expected to form a kind of pendant to the Tokyo session and to give the negotiations on monetary reform the same kind of impetus the trade negotiations had received at Tokyo. Throughout most of the past year, the complexities of international monetary reform had been under examination by an *ad hoc* group of IMF member countries, the so-called "Committee on Reform of the International Monetary System and Related Issues" or "Committee of Twenty," which had met under the chairmanship of Finance Minister Ali Wardhana of Indonesia and had been assisted by a committee of deputies whose chairman was C. Jeremy Morse of the United Kingdom. A report on the activities of these groups, together with a "First Outline of Reform" that reflected both the agreements and the disagreements prevailing at the current stage, was released in Nairobi as the Governors began their deliberations on September 24.

A salient feature of the Committee's report (**Document 50a**) and the accompanying outline was an authoritative affirmation of the need for "a reformed world monetary order, based on cooperation and consultation within the framework of a strengthened International Monetary Fund, that will encourage the growth of world trade and employment, promote economic development, and help to avoid both inflation and deflation." In what appeared to be a careful synthesis of conflicting French and American viewpoints, the outline further stated that such a reform should include among its main features "an effective and symmetrical adjustment process, including better functioning of the exchange rate mechanism, with the exchange rate regime based on stable but adjustable par values and [with] floating rates recognized as providing a useful technique in particular situations." Other points on which general agreement was said to exist included the acceptance of the Special Drawing Right (SDR) as the principal reserve asset of the future monetary system, with a reduction in the role of gold and reserve currencies. Issues on which agreement had obviously still to be sought included the working of the adjustment process, the exchange rate mechanism, the treatment of disequilibrating capital flows, valuation of the SDR, consolidation and management of currency reserves, and measures in favor of developing countries.

In making public its results to date, the Committee of Twenty also announced that it intended to persevere and "settle the issues of reform" by July 31, 1974, in time for the Board of Governors meeting in September of that year. Among the many who commended this intention—which turned out, for unforeseeable reasons, to be far too optimistic—were the Fund's new Managing Director, H. Johannes Witteveen of the Netherlands, and Secretary of the Treasury Shultz, who offered an authoritative exposition of U.S. views on monetary reform in his major address to the Governors on September 25 (**Document 51b**).

Acknowledging that the developing countries, too, had a growing stake in the world economy, the U.S. spokesman also took note of an earlier address by World Bank President Robert S. McNamara, in which the former U.S. Secretary of Defense had revealed that financial commitments by the IBRD and affiliated agencies had doubled over the past five years and were expected to increase still further in the future, from $13.4 billion in 1969-73 to $22 billion in 1974-78. Expressing qualified support for this ambitious program, Secretary Shultz revealed that the American administration would seek congressional backing for a replenishment of the resources of the Bank's "soft loan" affiliate, the International Development Association (IDA). This was an important aspect of the overall problem of world development, which was currently being examined in somewhat greater detail by other U.S. authorities.[4]

In concluding his address, Mr. Shultz called special attention to

---

[4]Cf. Documents 70-71, and see further Chapter 24 at note 3.

the ravages of the "storm of worldwide inflation" which, he asserted, was not only threatening to "break down the processes of orderly development" but was "simply incompatible with the stability of any international monetary and trading system." Among the salient causes of the most recent inflationary surge, the Secretary of the Treasury noted, was the pressure on prices in the two key areas of agriculture and energy. But neither the U.S. spokesman nor any of his colleagues of Nairobi could yet foresee the further escalation of petroleum prices that would take place over the next three months, precipitating a global economic crisis in which the interests of both industrial and developing countries would be severely impaired and any comprehensive monetary reform would have to be more or less indefinitely postponed.

(50) The General Agreement on Tariffs and Trade (GATT): Meeting of the Contracting Parties at Ministerial Level, Tokyo, September 12-14, 1973.

(a) Presentation of United States Views: Statement by Secretary of the Treasury Shultz to the Contracting Parties, September 12, 1973.[5]

This is a historic meeting, and I am honored to participate in it. We join here in the first formal step toward a major expansion and improvement of global trading relationships. While these negotiations build upon what has been achieved in the past, in the Kennedy Round and earlier, they are also a bold step beyond our past. Our present undertaking is broader in scope, more ambitious in objective, and guided by a clearer view of economic and political realities.

I was told before I came that Tokyo would be the occasion for many speeches on the benefits of open international trade. I expect that will be true. And I consider it entirely appropriate that it should be true. As we embark upon a course of negotiations to last for many months and involving details of endless complexity, we should remind ourselves of the principles that should underlie our efforts. However obvious these principles may seem to us, the process of putting them into practice has always been difficult and is far from complete.

The basic principle that brings us here is simple and needs no great elaboration. When there is voluntary exchange, both par-

5Department of Treasury Press Release; text from *Bulletin,* vol. 69 (1973), pp. 445-50.

ties—the buyer and the seller—gain. If they did not, one party or the other would refuse to exchange. This principle is as valid when the parties are in different countries as when they are in the same country. Obstacles that governments place in the way of trade, internally or externally, prevent people from doing business that would be beneficial to all participants.

What is involved is more than one country trading what it produces most efficiently today for what another country produces most efficiently today. Open trade forces and stimulates all of us to become more efficient. The wind of foreign competition drives businesses in all countries to more innovation, greater research and development efforts, and better adaptation to the wants of consumers.

Our generation has more cause to recognize the force of these ideas than any before us. We have been living through the greatest and most widely shared economic advance in world history and the greatest expansion of international trade. This combination of developments is of course no coincidence.

The growth of world output has contributed to the rise of trade, but the rise of trade has also contributed to the growth of world output. Greater access to markets has promoted specialization in production and thereby the better use of each country's resources. Competitive pressure from foreign firms has stimulated the growth of technology and business acumen.

As a result of greater openness in the world economy, economic opportunities have been substantially broadened for the citizens of all nations and the standard of living has improved throughout the world. Freer trade has led to higher real wages for working men and women and a wide choice of goods to consumers.

One recent development in economic policy holds a useful lesson for all of us. Governments in many parts of the world, such as Australia, Japan, Canada, some European countries, and the United States, have been led by compelling domestic reasons to reduce unilaterally their tariffs or quotas, without asking for reciprocal concessions from others. Although the circumstances in each case may have differed, this is a reminder that we should not think of every reduction of our own restrictions as a concession made for the benefit of others and worthwhile only if there is a greater or at least equal concession by others. The general principles that guide our work suggest that we gain from reduction of our own barriers as well as from reduction of the barriers of others.

Of course, there are qualifications to the basic ideas of trade liberalization. The participants in this conference, who live in the governmental and political process, are especially aware of these qualifications. Substantial reduction of trade barriers may cause local and temporary difficulties that cannot be ignored, however great the longer run and more general benefits may be. Transitional protection may sometimes permit the achievement of efficiencies that would not be possible without it. Other reservations can be thought of.

These qualifications constitute the case for gradualism, selectivity, and mutuality. No doubt, much of the time in the negotiations now beginning will be devoted to these qualifications. But let us, as we say in the United States, keep our eye on the ball—the liberalization and expansion of trade—and seek to deal with the problems in ways most consistent with that overall objective.

I see a number of important challenges for these negotiations. In listing them, I do not mean to imply they encompass the full range of issues that we expect these negotiations to cover nor that they will necessarily appear as specific items on the agenda for the negotiations.

Guidelines and Procedures

The central challenge for these negotiations is, as I see it, to develop guidelines and procedures that will permit the elimination of barriers to trade while preserving the ability of governments to carry out their domestic responsibilities. Many of the important barriers that still hamper international trade result from the efforts of individual governments to achieve a variety of domestic economic, social, and political objectives. We must develop the means whereby these barriers can be eliminated or minimized. Because national needs and policy preferences frequently differ, we need to develop rules that will give each government considerable leeway in forming and pursuing its own policies. At the same time, we need to encourage countries to devise policy measures that minimize disruption of the economic interests of other nations.

In an interdependent world, the policies pursued by any one government in carrying out its domestic responsibilities are bound to conflict at one time or another with the policies pursued by other governments. We therefore will have to focus on the procedures and arrangements that are designed to minimize these conflicts and effectively to resolve disputes that may arise. Our common institutions, such as the GATT, have performed this role well. These institutions are aging, however, and while they may be structurally sound, it is important that we look closely at our recent experiences in dealing with trade problems to see where the rules and procedures can be updated and improved.

Safeguards Against Disruptive Imports

Our recent experience would indicate that we need particularly to look at the rules and procedures that deal with problems of import disruption. Every country represented here has at one time or another found it necessary to limit imports temporarily in order to permit domestic industry enough time to adjust. Frequently the current rules and procedures covering such actions have proved unsuitable, and governments had to work out informal arrangements. While such arrangements have proved expedient, they have not been able to cope with all problems and have been accompanied by an unnecessary degree of international friction. It is time that we face this issue squarely and together design a mutually acceptable safeguard system.

Agricultural Commodities

Another area where common action would be desirable is the area of agriculture. The current shortage in agricultural supplies and the danger that it will be repeated in the future gives great urgency to the need to find a more rational pattern of production and trade in agricultural commodities. If we take advantage of this occasion to expand opportunities for world trade in this area, we will be able to make available more food at cheaper prices for everyone. A number of thoughts have been expressed on how this might be accomplished. We are willing to examine any serious proposal.

In the past year, we have seen how international trade in agricultural commodities can help to avoid what would otherwise have been critical food shortages. The decline in world grain production was alleviated for many countries by the ability to import, especially from the United States. Despite poor growing weather and poor harvests in our own country, we have supplied greatly enlarged quantities of goods and feeds to countries in every part of the world, partly at the expense of a substantial reduction in our own stocks.

Our exports of wheat in fiscal year 1973 reached 32 million metric tons, almost double the amount shipped in FY 1972, and equivalent to three-fourths of U.S. production. Exports of feed grains jumped sharply from 21 million tons to 35 million tons. And soybean exports rose to 14 million tons, an increase over the previous year of 2 million tons. More than half of our soybean crop went into export. Indeed, all of the increase in our soybean crop was exported last season.

Although our stock position has been sharply reduced, we anticipate that an excellent feed grain and record soybean crop this season will permit us to meet foreign demand for these commodities in FY 1974 with exports at levels higher than the record levels of last year and that our wheat exports will be close to last season's very high level. To meet anticipated world needs this year, we have put millions of acres back into production, and for 1974 all our reserve acreage has been removed from set-aside restrictions. We have proved that in the pinch, the United States is, indeed, a dependable supplier—and that its market-oriented system can be relied upon.

Regional Integration and the MFN Principle

Now let me turn to a development that has been a source of increasing concern to the United States. Over the past few years we have seen a tendency to move away from the notion of a single world trading system in which all nations are treated equally. The most-favored-nation principle has been the cornerstone of our global system. Now we are seeing that principle increasingly disregarded. At a time when the circle of nations participating in the world trading system is increasing, we need to rededicate ourselves to the ideals of a single non-discriminatory trading order.

I should say in this respect that we continue to support the many efforts to achieve political and economic integration. This makes sense where neighboring countries, sharing common traditions, find their economic affairs increasingly linked. We feel compelled to insist, however, that such efforts not undermine the global system that we have built together and from which we have derived great benefit. It is thus important that countries in regional groupings organize themselves in such a way that they can effectively discharge as a unit the responsibilities to which they have committed themselves individually as nations.

Support for Less Developed Countries

We support efforts to give the less developed countries special access to foreign markets. We believe that such arrangements will benefit the industrial nations as well as the developing nations. We also recognize that it would not be appropriate or desirable for us to insist that these countries assume the same responsibilities as we expect from those countries that have achieved a relatively high degree of economic development. At the same time, however, we do expect commitments appropriate to a nation's stage of development and to a sharing of the responsibility for the effective working of the global system. No international undertaking can succeed if those who derive a benefit from it do not contribute to it. And the system as a whole cannot work unless all nations contribute to its effective functioning.

Monetary and Trade Interrelationships

Lastly, let me say a word about the relationship between our efforts here and those related to the reform of the world monetary system. We recognize the interrelationship between monetary affairs and trade matters. A primary goal of an international monetary system, on the one hand, is to facilitate trade; that objective is seriously jeopardized when monetary relations become unstable. On the other hand, the logic is equally strong that the adjustment process in the monetary system is less effective and less responsive when trade is restricted by direct measures and can respond only slowly, and in a partial and distorted way, to the forces of the monetary adjustment process. In short, actions in one field can, but should not be allowed to, frustrate the solutions reached in other fields. There is thus a need for simultaneous improvement in all elements of the international economic system.

Although concrete progress in one area of negotiation should not be held hostage to specific negotiations in another, overall success in one area will ultimately be dependent on success in another. Where specific overlaps do occur, work in one area ought to supplement rather than frustrate work in other areas.

Negotiating Mandate of the United States

My government believes it is important to take advantage of the opportunity presented by these negotiations and is anxious to participate vigorously. In implementing negotiated changes and in strengthening our commitment to the basic objectives, of course we will need the support, advice, and concurrence of our Congress. President Nixon submitted his Trade Reform Act to the Congress in April of this year.[6] That bill has received thoughtful and highly constructive consideration in the Ways and Means Committee of the House of Representatives and will likely remain under con-

---

[6]Cf. Document 14.

sideration in the Congress for a few more months. The ranking
Democratic and Republican members of that committee issued a
statement last week expressing their "hope and belief that we will
complete work on the bill by October 1."[7] They also said:

> We believe that the committee will report a bill that will
> provide sufficient scope for comprehensive negotiations aimed
> at removing trade barriers and substantially expanding world
> trade. It is our hope and purpose that the Congress will act on
> this legislation in ample time to facilitate these negotiations.

The fact that our trade bill is still under congressional review
does not impede our ability to participate actively and fully at this
stage. The negotiations which begin at this conference will, at the
outset, concentrate on preparing the way for the detailed bargaining process to come. We remain committed to the start of substantive work on these negotiations in late October of this year and
to the pursuit of that work on an intensive and continuous basis
without any interim delay.

I must call to your attention the fact that the attitude of the
Congress toward these negotiations—and therefore the mandate
they will be willing to give our negotiators—will be influenced by
the manner in which we are able to settle in coming months some
outstanding issues with our trading partners. We have already
reached satisfactory agreements recently with some of our major
trading partners to eliminate longstanding trade restrictions inconsistent with the GATT. This has been a very positive development and clearly demonstrates to domestic observers that the
GATT does work. There are, nonetheless, some other issues pending at this time. We view the settlement of these issues as an indication of the confidence we can have in the ability of the international community to reach an agreement on a more open and
improved world trading order, and we know that it is essential to
demonstrate the basis for this confidence to the Congress.

U.S. Approach to the Negotiations

In a few words, the U.S. approach to these negotiations will be
based on the following ideas:

1. We desire to expand the opportunities for international
trade and are willing to participate fully in the common effort to

[7]Cf. Chapter 21 at note 8.

eliminate or reduce barriers to all trade, agricultural or industrial.

2. We seek an agreement that will be beneficial to all the participants and recognized as such by them. This will require that the agreement be balanced from the standpoint of each participant. However, we believe that to insist on a balance in every individual component of every agreement is unnecessary and would undesirably limit what can be achieved.

3. We believe that there should be a substantial expansion of duty-free trade as well as a substantial reduction in the average tariff on the remaining dutiable items.

4. We consider it one of the main objectives of these negotiations to remove as many nontariff barriers as possible and to reduce as far as possible those that cannot be removed.

5. Reduction of barriers to agricultural trade is a major goal, and negotiations to that end should move forward together with negotiations on industrial products. We should agree that where we find domestic actions necessary to assist our own farmers, those actions should not be of a kind that injure farmers in other countries.

6. We believe that the maximum liberalization of trade will be achieved if we can agree on a multilateral safeguard system that will allow governments to take appropriate actions when a rapid rise of imports threatens to disrupt domestic production in a particular industry but at the same time will assure that such measures will not be any broader or continued any longer than necessary for the domestic adjustment process.

7. We have an open mind about the specific techniques or arrangements to be employed in achieving the common goals of the negotiations.

8. We are eager to see the negotiations begin promptly and proceed rapidly and pledge our maximum cooperation to that goal.

We look to the Trade Negotiations Committee (TNC) to play an important role in guiding these negotiations toward their desired ends. We hope that the TNC will begin its work as soon as possible, setting up procedures for subgroups, and moving them promptly toward continuous, effective work on the substance of the negotiations. We hope that the participating governments can focus on trade negotiating plans, undertake the basic analytical work which needs to be done at the earliest possible date, and begin this process in the TNC no later than November 1. Once we have begun, we should work in earnest, continuously, so that the target of finishing in 1975 can be met.

In our view, the declaration negotiated by the preparatory committee in July represents a sound basis for beginning these negotiations and provides useful political guidance for our negotiators to follow. While we recognize that there are some disagreements with the declaration based on specific points of substance or emphasis, the declaration does provide a framework for achieving ends desirable to us all. To translate that declaration into change in our trade relations is the task which will be before us throughout these negotiations.

The progress we all want in these negotiations can only be accomplished by a joint effort in which all of us make appropriate contributions and receive appropriate benefits. Let this Declaration of Tokyo serve as a starting point and a point of inspiration. Let the vision which has in the past inspired nations to achieve great goals guide us in a common effort to construct a durable order that will contribute to international harmony and prosperity for us and for future generations.

(b) Guidelines for Multilateral Trade Negotiations: The "Declaration of Tokyo," approved by the Contracting Parties September 14, 1973.[8]

1. The Ministers, having considered the report of the Preparatory Committee for the Trade Negotiations and having noted that a number of governments have decided to enter into comprehensive multilateral trade negotiations in the framework of GATT and that other governments have indicated their intention to make a decision as soon as possible, declare the negotiations officially open. Those governments which have decided to negotiate have notified the Director-General of GATT to this effect, and the Ministers agree that it will be open to any other government, through a notification to the Director-General, to participate in the negotiations. The Ministers hope that the negotiations will involve the active participation of as many countries as possible. They expect the negotiations to be engaged effectively as rapidly as possible, and that, to that end, the governments concerned will have such authority as may be required.

2. The negotiations shall aim to:

—achieve the expansion and ever-greater liberalization of world trade and improvement in the standard of living and welfare of the people of the world, objectives which can be achieved, *inter alia*, through the progressive dismantling of ob-

---

[8]Text from *Bulletin*, vol. 69 (1973), pp. 450-52.

stacles to trade and the improvement of the international framework for the conduct of world trade.

—secure additional benefits for the international trade of developing countries so as to achieve a substantial increase in their foreign exchange earnings, the diversification of their exports, the acceleration of the rate of growth of their trade, taking into account their development needs, an improvement in the possibilities for these countries to participate in the expansion of world trade and a better balance as between developed and developing countries in the sharing of the advantages resulting from this expansion, through, in the largest possible measure, a substantial improvement in the conditions of access for the products of interest to the developing countries and, wherever appropriate, measures designed to attain stable, equitable and remunerative prices for primary products.

To this end, co-ordinated efforts shall be made to solve in an equitable way the trade problems of all participating countries, taking into account the specific trade problems of the developing countries.

3. To this end, the negotiations should aim, *inter alia*, to:

(a) conduct negotiations on tariffs by employment of appropriate formulae of as general application as possible;

(b) reduce or eliminate non-tariff measures or, where this is not appropriate, to reduce or eliminate their trade restricting or distorting effects, and to bring such measures under more effective international discipline;

(c) include an examination of the possibilities for the co-ordinated reduction or elimination of all barriers to trade in selected sectors as a complementary technique;

(d) include an examination of the adequacy of the multilateral safeguard system, considering particularly the modalities of application of Article XIX,[9] with a view to furthering trade liberalization and preserving its results;

(e) include, as regards agriculture, an approach to negotiations which, while in line with the general objectives of the negotiations, should take account of the special characteristics and problems in this sector;

(f) treat tropical products as a special and priority sector.

4. The negotiations shall cover tariffs, non-tariff barriers and

---

[9]Of the General Agreement on Tariffs and Trade, concluded at Geneva Oct. 30, 1947 and entered into force Jan. 1, 1948 (TIAS 1700).

other measures which impede or distort international trade in both industrial and agricultural products, including tropical products and raw materials, whether in primary form or at any stage of processing including in particular products of export interest to developing countries and measures affecting their exports.

5. The negotiations shall be conducted on the basis of the principles of mutual advantage, mutual commitment and overall reciprocity, while observing the most-favored-nation clause, and consistently with the provisions of the General Agreement relating to such negotiations. Participants shall jointly endeavour in the negotiations to achieve, by appropriate methods, an overall balance of advantage at the highest possible level. The developed countries do not expect reciprocity for commitments made by them in the negotiations to reduce or remove tariff and other barriers to the trade of developing countries, i.e., the developed countries do not expect the developing countries, in the course of the trade negotiations, to make contributions which are inconsistent with their individual development, financial and trade needs. The Ministers recognize the need for special measures to be taken in the negotiations to assist the developing countries in their efforts to increase their export earnings and promote their economic development and, where appropriate, for priority attention to be given to products or areas of interest to developing countries. They also recognize the importance of maintaining and improving the Generalized System of Preferences. They further recognize the importance of the application of differential measures to developing countries in ways which will provide special and more favourable treatment for them in areas of the negotiation where this is feasible and appropriate.

6. The Ministers recognize that the particular situation and problems of the least developed among the developing countries shall be given special attention, and stress the need to ensure that these countries receive special treatment in the context of any general or specific measures taken in favour of the developing countries during the negotiations.

7. The policy of liberalizing world trade cannot be carried out successfully in the absence of parallel efforts to set up a monetary system which shields the world economy from the shocks and imbalances which have previously occurred. The Ministers will not lose sight of the fact that the efforts which are to be made in the trade field imply continuing efforts to maintain orderly conditions and to establish a durable and equitable monetary system.

The Ministers recognize equally that the new phase in the liberalization of trade which it is their intention to undertake should facilitate the orderly functioning of the monetary system.

The Ministers recognize that they should bear these considerations in mind both at the opening of and throughout the negotiations. Efforts in these two fields will thus be able to contribute effectively to an improvement of international economic relations, taking into account the special characteristics of the economies of the developing countries and their problems.

8. The negotiations shall be considered as one undertaking, the various elements of which shall move forward together.

9. Support is reaffirmed for the principles, rules and disciplines provided for under the General Agreement.[10] Consideration shall be given to improvements in the international framework for the conduct of world trade which might be desirable in the light of progress in the negotiations and, in this endeavour, care shall be taken to ensure that any measures introduced as a result are consistent with the overall objectives and principles of the trade negotiations and particularly of trade liberalization.

10. A Trade Negotiations Committee is established, with authority, taking into account the present Declaration, *inter alia*:

(a) to elaborate and put into effect detailed trade negotiating plans and to establish appropriate negotiating procedures, including special procedures for the negotiations between developed and developing countries;

(b) to supervise the progress of the negotiations.

The Trade Negotiations Committee shall be open to participating governments.[11] The Trade Negotiations Committee shall hold its opening meeting not later than 1 November 1973.

11. The Ministers intend that the trade negotiations be concluded in 1975.

(51) The International Bank for Reconstruction and Development (IBRD) and the International Monetary Fund (IMF): Annual Meeting of the Boards of Governors, Nairobi, September 24-28, 1973.

(a) An Outline for Monetary Reform: Report to the Board of Governors of the International Monetary Fund by Ali Wardhana, Chairman of the Committee on Reform of the International Monetary System and Related Issues, September 24, 1973.[12]

[10]This does not necessarily represent the views of representatives of countries not now parties to the General Agreement. [Footnote in original.]

[11]Including the European Communities.[Footnote in original.]

[12]Text from *IMF Survey*, vol. 2 (1973), p. 305.

On July 26, 1972, the Board of Governors adopted Resolution 27-10 which established the Committee and instructed it to advise and report to the Board of Governors with respect to all aspects of reform of the international monetary system. During the past year the Committee has met four times, most recently on September 23, 1973, and has been assisted by the Deputies who have worked intensively on the various aspects of reform. I attach a First Outline of Reform[13] which has been prepared by the Chairman and Vice-Chairmen of the Deputies and which, in my view, reflects the stage reached in the Committee's discussions. This Outline covers the main aspects of monetary reform. It does not distinguish between those matters which would have to be dealt with by amendment of the Articles of Agreement of the Fund[14] and those which might be incorporated in a code of conduct outside the Articles. It does not cover questions concerning the quota structure and possible changes in the General Account, which fall to be considered at a later stage; and it makes only a few references to questions of the structure of the Fund, on which discussion is not far advanced.

As is apparent from the Outline, much has been achieved but much remains to be done.

The general shape of the reformed system has been defined and significant progress has been made on some important issues. Arrangements for adjustment and convertibility are to be effective in avoiding the protracted imbalances which led to the breakdown of the Bretton Woods system: symmetrical in relation to all member countries, large or small, developed or developing, in surplus or in deficit; and consistent with each other and with the volume of global liquidity. The SDR is to become the principal reserve asset of the reformed system, with the role of gold and of reserve currencies being reduced. Economic development and the flow of real resources from developed to developing countries are to be promoted.[15]

On the other hand, important issues have not yet been resolved; and further consideration and study must be given to many matters, including the operational provisions of the reformed system.

[13]Text in same, pp. 305-8.

[14]Opened for signature at Washington and entered into force Dec. 27, 1945 (TIAS 1501).

[15]The relevant paragraph of the First Outline of Reform reads as follows:

"1.   It is generally agreed that there is need for a reformed world monetary order, based on cooperation and consultation within the framework of a strengthened International Monetary Fund, that will encourage the growth of world trade and employment, promote economic development, and help to avoid both inflation and deflation. The main features of the international monetary reform should include:

(a) an effective and symmetrical adjustment process, including better functioning of the exchange rate mechanism, with the exchange rate regime based on stable but

This position reflects the complex and difficult nature of international monetary reform which involves changes in the patterns of countries' behavior that have persisted for many years. Moreover, agreement on particular issues reached during the process of discussion must be dependent on final agreement of the whole range of issues of reform; and agreement of principle in particular areas must be dependent on satisfactory settlement of the operational provisions in those areas.

The Committee intends to continue its efforts to arrive as soon as possible at final recommendations for a reform of the international monetary system. In view of the urgency of completing this task, the Committee intends to settle the issues of reform by July 31, 1974, in good time for the Annual Meeting which is to be held in Washington in September 1974.[16] To this end the Committee plans to meet in January and to hold a further meeting in the spring. The Committee has also given instructions to the Deputies to work further on the various aspects of monetary reform, giving attention to the related issues. In particular the Deputies have been asked, in cooperation with the Executive Board of the Fund, to continue their work on future arrangements for adjustment and convertibility, including the details of a reserve indicator structure and of a possible multicurrency intervention system, and to study and advise the Committee further on unresolved issues in the fields of primary reserve assets, consolidation and management of currency reserves, and the link and credit facilities in favor of developing countries, as well as the more general question of how to promote the flow of real resources from developed to developing countries.

(b) Views of the United States: Statement to the Boards of Governors by Secretary of the Treasury Shultz, September 25, 1973.[17]

adjustable par values and floating rates recognized as providing a useful technique in particular situations;

(b) cooperation in dealing with disequilibrating capital flows;

(c) the introduction of an appropriate degree and form of convertibility for the settlement of imbalances, with symmetrical obligations on all countries;

(d) better international management of global liquidity, with the SDR becoming the principal reserve asset and the role of gold and of reserve currencies being reduced;

(e) consistency between arrangements for adjustment, convertibility, and global liquidity;

(f) the promotion of the flow of real resources to developing countries."

[16]The Committee of Twenty completed its work June 13, 1974, its efforts being continued thereafter by an Interim Committee of the IMF Board of Governors. For details see *IMF Survey*, vol. 3 (1974), pp. 177-208.

[17]Department of the Treasury Press Release, Sept. 25; text from *Bulletin*, vol. 69 (1973), pp. 544-50. Secretary Shultz held the position of U.S. Governor of the Fund and Bank.

Nairobi has been a happy choice for this annual meeting. For many of us, the prospect of visiting Kenya and seeing some of its natural splendor provided a special sense of anticipation. Upon arrival, we found these striking and efficient facilities in the setting of a city that epitomizes the rapid progress that independent, self-reliant, and energetic people can make when they have the tools with which to work. I particularly appreciate President [Jomo] Kenyatta's warm words of welcome and his challenge to us all.

Less than two weeks ago in Tokyo, most of the nations here represented pledged themselves to a thorough review of our trading practices and rules. This week we can provide the necessary impetus to complete our work in reshaping our international monetary arrangements. Here in Nairobi—on a continent where vast potential often contrasts starkly with human poverty—we also come face to face with the challenge of economic development.

Trade, money, development—each of these is a large task. Any one of them, it might be said, would be enough for us to deal with alone. Yet, in a larger sense, we are fortunate that the pressure of events forces us to deal with them together. They are related, not by any artificial or self-imposed negotiating calendar, but by reality. It is right to keep in mind that delay in one area could undermine progress in another. It is equally right—and a better omen—that success in one area will support and encourage good results in the others.

These fundamental interrelationships were plainly recognized in the mandate given the Committee of Twenty on monetary reform a year ago.[18] They were recognized in the Tokyo Declaration on trade adopted by GATT earlier this month.[19] Let us keep them in mind in all our work in Nairobi and beyond and emphasize the mutually reinforcing benefits of success in each field.

Monetary Reform

Our monetary discussions are now well advanced, owing in no small part to the patient and effective efforts of Mr. Wardhana and Mr. Morse. We take satisfaction in the extent to which a basic convergence of views on the broad framework of a new system has emerged.

—We all seek a substantial strengthening of the processes of international adjustment through a blending of objective criteria and international judgment, with the recognition of the need for

[18]*AFR, 1972*, pp. 528-9.
[19]Document 50b.

symmetrical and evenhanded pressures on both surplus and deficit countries.

—There is full acceptance of the idea that the center of gravity of the exchange rate system will be a regime of "stable but adjustable par values," with adequately wide margins and with floating "in particular situations."

—We anticipate a general system of convertibility to support the regime of par values, with a modified SDR as the central reserve asset and deemphasis of the roles of gold and reserve currencies.

—There is a common will to explore the complex technical requirements for multi-currency intervention and to find mutually satisfactory terms for consolidating or funding outstanding balances of reserve currencies.

At the same time, my sense of satisfaction is tempered. Issues of critical importance—carefully outlined in the report submitted to us by Mr. Wardhana—remain unresolved. No doubt we could each expound at length views on particular aspects of these issues. However, I believe those issues will be resolved as national governments are able to appraise more thoroughly the operational aspects of different approaches toward adjustment pressures, toward convertibility, and toward the definition and valuation of reserve assets. Moreover, we need to consider answers to each of those questions in the full context of answers to the others.

In constructing a world monetary system we cannot act, as I see it, like merchants in a bazaar bargaining for selfish advantage. Nor should we be concerned out of pride or politics with patching together and compromising components from every national position. All our success depends upon achieving a coherent, workable whole that fairly serves the common interests.

With good will and intensive technical work, the ground can be fully prepared for a comprehensive agreement as soon as next spring. That agreement will then need to be translated into an extensive and detailed rewriting of the IMF Articles of Agreement. Is it wrong to aim to approve those new articles, for submissions to our legislatures, at our next annual meeting?

The Transitional Period

We are all conscious of the stresses in exchange markets arising from time to time during this transitional period. Yet, in broad terms, the substantial exchange rate changes of the past two years—although in some instances clearly exaggerated by speculation and uncertainty—have provided powerful and needed impetus toward correcting persistent structural imbalances.

In the case of the United States, the alarming erosion in our trade position has by now been decisively reversed. In contrast to a deficit of more than $6½ billion in 1972, we should be close to balance in 1973. While an extraordinary surge in agricultural exports has greatly speeded the turnaround, our trade position in manufactured goods has also been improving, even in the face of high domestic demand.

We are also beginning to see welcome evidence that both American and foreign firms are reappraising their investment programs, with more emphasis on U.S. production. Thus, shifts in capital flows should reinforce the favorable effects on our payments of the swing in our trade position. In these circumstances, surpluses in both our trade and basic payments position now appear in sight for next year. Such surpluses for a period seem to me indispensable for full restoration of confidence, for encouraging a reflow of dollars to the United States, and for implementing any lasting monetary reform.

Our contacts with traders, investors, and businessmen suggest they have acclimated themselves reasonably well to the present monetary environment, despite more instability in exchange markets from day to day than they or we like to see. Propelled by boom conditions, world trade is, if anything, expanding even faster than in most earlier years.

It would be a fundamental error, however, to mistake present arrangements for monetary reform. Habits of cooperation and the exercise of good sense have carried us over the rough spots. But what is lacking—and what I believe to be the essence of any lasting monetary system—is a deep sense of commitment to an agreed code of international conduct to help guide us when the actions of one nation impinge on those of another.

Issues Left Open

In one way or another, most of the issues left open in Chairman Wardhana's report deal with delicate and sensitive questions arising out of the inherent tensions between the responsibilities of national governments to meet their domestic priorities and our common commitment to a mutually beneficial international order. We firmly believe these tensions can be constructively resolved, for in the end a well-functioning international system should contribute to the growth and stability of the individual countries operating within that system.

The challenge is to translate that concept into operating reality. To do so will require a commitment to some basic rules established in advance and seen as equitable to all. We must provide for necessary international review and surveillance. Not least, we must permit necessary scope for national decisionmaking.

In seeking an appropriate balance among these components of a new system, we have emphasized the role that quantitative indicators—and in particular reserve indicators—could play in helping discipline the adjustment process in an evenhanded, effective, and politically acceptable manner. I therefore welcome the prospect that in the months immediately ahead a common effort will be made to appraise and test the operational feasibility of that approach, alongside related questions of the operation of the convertibility provisions in the new system.

At the same time, I believe it is common ground among us that effective processes of international consultation and decisionmaking are critical to the operation of the new system. I have been encouraged by the widespread recognition of the need to equip the IMF to play its full role at the center of the system. The logic is strong that, for the Fund to act effectively, member governments should have available a forum of workable size within the organization at which responsible national officials can speak and negotiate with both flexibility and authority. Conversely, we should be sure that the deliberations and concerns of the international community are fully and directly reflected in the internal councils of member governments.

These objectives could be fostered by keeping in being a streamlined Committee of Twenty able to review periodically or in emergencies larger issues with a significant impact on the monetary situation as a whole. Plainly, there will also be a need to retain a body along the lines of the present and highly competent Executive Board, with resident members and the knowledge and insight that come only with intimate day-to-day contact with operations and emerging problems.

In the effort to resolve finally these difficult substantive and organizational questions, I particularly look forward to the participation and fresh insights of our new Managing Director, Mr. Witteveen. He brings to us rich and varied experience as a professional economist and a practicing politician—precisely the disciplines that must be blended in all our work.

Interests of Developing Countries

The day has long passed—and rightly so—when discussions of trade and monetary issues could take place primarily in a relatively closed circle of industrialized countries. We must consider with great care what special arrangements within the trading and monetary systems may be appropriate to help meet development needs more effectively.

In presenting broad trade legislation to our Congress, we incorporated the concept of assisting development by means of generalized preferences, to be granted on a nonreciprocal basis.[20] This approach, undertaken in concert with comparable efforts by other industrialized countries, is consistent with the broad thrust of our mutual effort to reduce barriers to trade and to encourage economic development. We look forward to early passage of this legislation.

We support the idea of freeing flows of capital to developing countries and exempting where possible those countries from controls imposed for balance of payments purposes.

Closer examination should be given to methods of providing credit through our international institutions better tailored to the needs of developing countries experiencing extended periods of difficulty.

Our judgment concerning the value of another proposal has, as is well known, been different. We feel the so-called SDR-aid link would in practice serve well neither monetary stability nor economic development. Experience strongly demonstrates the wisdom of keeping separate the function of money creation—which is what the SDR is all about—and the essentially political decision of resource transfer and redistribution.

As we deal with these specific issues, let us never lose sight of the much larger stake that developing countries—as all of us—have in a well-functioning, stable monetary system and an open trading order. Mr. McNamara has already pointed to the cost to poorer countries of burdens on their exports in the markets of industrialized nations.[21] Long delays and sharp exchange rate adjustments among their more affluent trading partners, responding to imbalances that were permitted to build up over a period of years, have complicated the financial management of developing countries.

At the same time, a number of countries still classified as developing are reaching a stage of industrialization where they can, in the mutual interest, accept their fair share of the responsibilities for a world order. Controls, subsidies, and other impediments to open trade that might have been justified in an earlier stage of development need to be reviewed and eliminated. The disciplines of balance of payments adjustment—whether to correct deficits or

[20]Cf. Chapter 4 at note 10.
[21]President McNamara's address of Sept. 24, 1973 is summarized in *IMF Survey*, vol. 2 (1973), pp. 314-16.

surpluses—need to be observed, and this can be done without sacrificing developmental objectives. Indeed, I believe there are long term dangers to the kind of open, one-world economy we would like to see in casually proliferating arrangements that would divide the world sharply into distinct groupings of "have" and "have-not" nations.

In the short run, the prosperity of developing countries is tied to the prosperity of the industrialized world. In the past two years, relatively high prices for agricultural products and raw materials have directly benefited many. When the labor forces of industrialized economies are fully employed, resistance to imports of labor-intensive products declines, to the benefit of producer and consumer alike.

While uneven country by country, the overall results are apparent in the recent growth of production and monetary reserves of the developing world. Excluding the main oil producers, developing countries had a surplus of over $4½ billion in 1972, and their surpluses appear to have been well maintained this year.

Long-Term Development and Official Assistance

A cyclical surge is of course no substitute for sustained development over a long period of years. In the end, development will succeed or fail as the result of the efforts of the millions of people in the developing countries themselves, working under the direction and leadership of their own governments. Compared to the human and material resources of even the poorest country, the effects of external assistance are bound to be modest. Indeed, all the official assistance of all the donor countries of the Western World amounts to less than 2 percent of the GNP of developing countries.

Effectively used, however, the margin of resources from abroad can be a catalyst—in some instances an essential catalyst—to the development process. I speak of this potential as seen from the particular vantage point of a country whose people and government have had experience in the provision of assistance in amounts, and over a period of time, without parallel in history. Even today, when others have moved to help pick up the burden, the United States provides almost 40 percent of official development assistance from the OECD countries, and it is by far the largest source of private capital as well.

This commitment has been a natural one, for we are a large and relatively rich country, unusually blessed with resources, political stability, and a productive population. We accept today, as we have in the past, the simple premise that no nation—whether the motives are properly considered those of common humanity or enlightened self-interest—can be oblivious to the conditions in which other men and women are living.

Out of this long experience, we have reached certain conclusions and raised certain questions that I want to convey to you today. The questions are no doubt sharpened by the searching look at priorities evoked by long years of an agonizing war and by the evident strains on our external position. Like every other country represented in this room, we face hard decisions about economic and social priorities in many areas.

The strongest of our convictions is that aid stimulates development only where there exists the will and competence to utilize it effectively. This implies a responsibility upon the donor as well as the recipient to identify, develop, and carry through projects of strategic developmental importance. The World Bank Group and its regional financing institutions rightly pride themselves as leaders in efficient project planning and execution and in assessment of those projects as part of a larger development effort. This is not a matter of dramatic new initiatives, but hard persistent effort. We are particularly gratified that the World Bank Group is moving to reinforce its effectiveness by further strengthening postaudit performance evaluation independent of those responsible for project execution.

Second, there is a growing need to place more emphasis on what might be called "people-oriented" projects rather than large-scale civil engineering. We have redirected the emphasis in our own bilateral assistance in support of imaginative new programs in education, agriculture, and population planning. We warmly support the initiatives the World Bank has taken in these same areas. The fresh emphasis that Mr. McNamara placed on rural development in his remarks to us yesterday seems to us entirely appropriate.

Third, and most broadly, a genuine commitment on the part of recipient countries to the idea of development in their own policies is a key ingredient. Experience shows time and again that "growth-oriented" countries rapidly become less dependent on official assistance once internal conditions are right.

There is one aspect of "growth orientation"—the part played by private investment—that I wish to emphasize, sensitive though it may be. In sheer quantitative terms, the potential is clear enough: Net flows of medium- and long-term private capital to developing countries are now as large as official assistance. Moreover, the private investor can bring benefits in skills and experience that simply have no counterpart in governmental aid.

Every sovereign nation has, of course, the right to regulate terms and conditions under which private investment is admitted or to reject it entirely. However, when such capital is rejected, we find it difficult to understand that official donors should be asked to fill the gap. Moreover, we do not find it reasonable that a nation taking confiscatory steps toward investment that it has already accepted from abroad should anticipate official assistance, bilateral or multilateral.

Mr. McNamara has outlined an ambitious program for the next five years. We are in a large measure of agreement with the objectives of that program, and we give them our support. We also appreciate that a consensus has been reached that the traditional share of the United States in IDA [International Development Association] financing should be dropped from 40 percent to one-third, and the shares of Japan, Germany, and others increased, to more accurately reflect the present distribution of economic strength.

On this basis, the U.S. administration will consult with, and strongly recommend to, the Congress our participation in a total fourth replenishment for IDA of $4½ billion.[22] In doing so, I must emphasize that many questions about this program, including those I have discussed with you, are on the minds of the Members of Congress. The large and distinguished delegation from the Congress that has accompanied me to Nairobi and visited a variety of World Bank projects in Africa is evidence that they are interested in finding constructive answers to these questions.

I cannot say with any certainty how long our consultative and legislative process will take or certify its outcome. We do fully recognize that necessary legislative procedures differ among countries and that timetables are pressing. We will therefore remain in close touch with the management and the Executive Board of the Bank during this process.

Worldwide Surge of Inflation

Before concluding, I must underscore the threat to all our constructive labor from the storm of worldwide inflation.

Unfortunately, inflation is no new phenomenon. What is new is that it is now infecting more countries, in a greater degree, than at any time in memory. Speculation in commodities is fed by fear about currencies. Inflation is becoming imbedded in the expectations of too many people. Long maintained, this will break down the processes of orderly development. It is simply in-

[22]Cf. Document 71.

compatible with the stability of any international monetary and trading system.

I am familiar with analyses that trace world inflation to defects in the international monetary system. The Bretton Woods system has itself been criticized as an engine of inflation, and floating rates praised as permitting the restoration of internal monetary discipline. Equally forcibly, we are urged—especially by those who have seen their own exchange rates depreciate and their import bill rise—that floating rates are themselves an inflationary force.

Whatever the technical merits of these analyses in particular circumstances, I submit they place the responsibility for inflation and its correction in the wrong place. Let us not neglect the causes and cures that lie closer to our national actions and powers.

Two factors, mainly unforeseen a year ago, have been at work in the recent surge of inflation. The first is that strong expansionary forces have coincided among virtually all industrialized and developing countries. As a result, increases in cyclical demand have put pressures on supply, exposed unforeseen shortages of capacity, and driven up prices of raw materials. Second, the pressures on prices in two key areas—agriculture and energy—have been greatly aggravated by crop failures and weather and by shifts in production patterns and marketing policies.

In the United States, we have long been accustomed to relatively low prices of basic agricultural commodities. For many years, without adequate markets abroad, we kept a sizable margin of farm resources idle. But in the past crop year, the volume of our wheat exports nearly doubled, feed grain exports rose by two-thirds, and soybeans by one-sixth. And now, with our markets fully open to the surge in world demand, looked to as a residual supplier when other countries are short, and without the price protection afforded those whose exchange rates have appreciated, we have felt the full brunt of the rise in world agricultural prices.

At the same time, our needs for energy imports are rising rapidly. Obviously these commodity flows in both directions have responded to pressing needs. But the price impact is measured by the fact that, taken together, prices of food and energy account for 82 percent of the rise in our wholesale price index and 66 percent of the rise in our consumer price index in the past year.

We believe a market-oriented system will respond flexibly and effectively to changing needs. We are making great efforts to deal with the high price of food by bringing idle acreage back into production. Normal market processes are at work. The prices of soybeans are 50 percent below their speculative peak, feed grains have fallen back by a quarter, and wheat prices—where the worldwide supply situation is most tenuous—have at least stopped rising.

We cannot speed the natural cycle of planting and harvesting and of animal growth. We face for a considerable period ahead a tight situation in agricultural markets. But we have every intention of keeping our markets open, for we are and intend to be a dependable supplier.

Meanwhile, this experience will ultimately redound to our common advantage if we attack with fresh urgency the problem of finding more effective patterns of production and trade to serve our mutual interests in more food at cheaper prices.

Let us work in similar spirit to deal with the problem of developing and distributing energy resources.

We, for our side, have now embarked upon a massive effort to develop the bountiful energy sources within our own country now made economic by higher prices. We look to others to help maintain the flow of energy so long as their own legitimate needs and aspirations are fairly recognized.

A vigorous attack on the special problems of food and energy is not a cure-all for inflation. A number of countries, as ourselves, have resorted to, and even intensified, direct price and wage controls. But we remain convinced that our success will hinge mainly on the firm and persistent application of the traditional tools of fiscal and monetary restraint. I need not belabor, to an audience of Finance Ministers and central bankers, that expenditure and monetary restraints are never popular. Nevertheless, I believe, in the face of the evident need, these policies are broadly accepted by the American people. We mean to see it through. We hope and expect our efforts will be mutually reinforcing with those of others.

20. "NEW ERA" IN THE AMERICAS?

The announcement of a "new era" in the United States' relations with its Latin American neighbors is a virtually automatic consequence of any change in U.S. foreign policy leadership. Almost any new President can be trusted to proclaim his special solicitude for the republics to the south, and to imply that the neglect and ill-judged interference imputed to his predecessors will now at long last be succeeded by a relationship of mutual understanding, confidence, and respect. A similar demonstration is customary at the Secretary of State's level. Secretary Rogers, for example, had given an unusual amount of attention to Latin America, and had made a sixteen-day trip to South America and Jamaica as recently as May 1973.[1] Yet Mr. Rogers' successor had not been long in office before his aides were announcing still another "new era" in U.S.-Latin American relations,[2] this one initiated by a lunchtime invitation to the Latin American Foreign Ministers to join a "dialogue" on the issues of the hemisphere relationship.

That there was need for a thorough reappraisal of U.S. policies and programs in the Western Hemisphere would have been questioned by no one who had observed the course of U.S.-Latin American relations in the months just past. Apart from the chronic Latin American discontent with virtually every aspect of the existing economic relationship, there had been frictions of unusual intensity between the United States and such countries as Cuba, Chile, Ecuador, Peru, and Panama—whose keen dissatisfaction with what was regarded as U.S. "foot-dragging" on the Panama Canal issue had been dramatized at the Security Council meetings in March. In addition, the OAS General Assembly at its April session had noted that there was "general dissatisfaction with the functioning and results of the inter-American system," and had

[1]Cf. Chapter 5 at note 12.
[2]Cf. Deputy Secretary Kenneth Rush, "A New Era in U.S.-Latin American Relations" (address of Dec. 5, 1973), in *Bulletin*, vol. 69 (1973), pp. 765-9.

set up a special committee to propose measures for its restructuring.[3] This new committee, known as CEESI from its initials in Spanish, had since held an inaugural meeting in Lima on June 20-July 14 and decided to recommend a thorough rewriting of the OAS Charter as well as a complete reform of inter-American relations.[4]

Internal conditions in some important Latin American countries were also caught up in a process of evolution that was not always to the advantage of the United States. Of the "big three" nations of South America, only Brazil appeared to be set on a clearly predictable course as General Ernesto Geisel, the presidential candidate approved by the dominant military forces, prepared to succeed the incumbent General Emilio Garrastazú Médici early in 1974. Argentina's new civilian President, Dr. Cámpora, inaugurated as recently as May 25 at the close of a lengthy period of military rule, had resigned just seven weeks later, to be succeeded October 12 by the septuagenerian ex-President Perón following a special election on September 23 in which his wife, Señora Isabel Martínez de Perón, was elected to the vice-presidency. (Perón was to govern for less than nine months, dying July 1, 1974, while his wife was removed from office by another military coup on March 24, 1976.)

More startling, and decidedly more problematical from the standpoint of U.S. interests, was the military *coup d'état* that took place in Chile on September 11, 1973, occasioning the downfall of the Allende government, the death—assertedly by suicide—of President Allende himself, and the setting up of a harshly repressive military dictatorship headed by General Augusto Pinochet Ugarte, the recently appointed Commander-in-Chief of the Army. Essentially the culmination of a rapidly worsening domestic economic crisis that had been accentuated by a prolonged strike of transport vehicle owners, the coup was promptly ascribed by Allende sympathizers to alleged undercover machinations by the Central Intelligence Agency and other U.S. institutions and interests. Such rumors, persisting in the face of emphatic disclaimers from Washington, could be seen as a natural consequence of the Nixon administration's well-known antipathy toward the Allende regime, its steadily proliferating record of clandestine action in other contexts, and its apparent tolerance of the anti-Allende maneuvers by private U.S. interests that had been brought out at congressional hearings earlier in the year.[5]

In spite of a widespread predisposition to believe the worst,

---

[3]OAS document AG/doc.396/73 rev. 2, in *Bulletin*, vol. 68 (1973), pp. 684-5; cf. Chapter 5 at note 11.

[4]*Keesing's*, p. 26252.

[5]Cf. Chapter 5 at note 6.

responsible U.S. officials continued to insist, as they had done in the past, that the United States had been innocent of any attempt to prevent Allende's election, his assumption of office, or the continued exercise of his responsibilities. Former CIA Director Helms, at a hearing in February 1973 preceding his confirmation as Ambassador to Iran, had specifically denied that the CIA had attempted to overthrow the Chilean Government or passed money to Allende's opponents;[6] in addition, he had responded in the negative to a question asked him at another congressional hearing as to whether the CIA had attempted in any way to influence the vote of the Chilean Congress that had confirmed Allende's election on October 24, 1970.[7]

So far as the 1973 coup was concerned, Dr. Kissinger, whose chairmanship of the so-called "40 Committee" had given him a decisive role in the direction of CIA clandestine operations, replied in the following terms to a question put to him at his confirmation hearings on September 17: "The CIA had nothing to do with the coup, to the best of my knowledge and belief, and I only put in that qualification in case some madman appears down there who without instructions, talked to somebody. I have absolutely no reason to suppose it. [Deleted]." Elaborating on his statement, the Secretary of State-designate recalled that he had himself instructed U.S. Ambassador Nathaniel Davis in Santiago to be sure no Embassy personnel had anything to do with reputed plotters.[8] Similar assurances of U.S. noninvolvement were furnished to the interested congressional committees by Dr. Kissinger, CIA Director Colby, Ambassador Davis, and the new Assistant Secretary of State for Inter-American Affairs, Jack B. Kubisch (**Document 52**).

But even assuming that such disclaimers were literally true, the very fact that questions so damaging to the United States continued to be asked was proof that the country had suffered another setback not only in its Latin American relations but in its worldwide reputation. Subsequent disclosures, moreover, would make clear that though apparently not involved in the 1973 coup, the U.S. Government had been far more deeply immersed in anti-Allende activities than it had been willing to admit. In a first updating of the

[6]Statement of Feb. 7, 1973, in U.S. Senate, Committee on Foreign Relations, 93rd Cong., 1st sess., *Nomination of Richard Helms to be Ambassador to Iran and CIA International and Domestic Affairs: Hearings, Feb. 5 and 7 and May 21, 1973* (Washington: GPO, 1973), p. 47.

[7]Statement of Mar. 6, 1973, quoted in U.S. Senate, Committee on Foreign Relations, 94th Cong., 1st sess., *CIA Foreign and Domestic Activities: Hearing, Jan. 22, 1975* (Washington: GPO, 1975), p. 13.

[8]U.S. Senate, Committee on Foreign Relations, 93d Cong., 1st sess., *Nomination of Henry A. Kissinger: Hearings, Part 2* (Washington: GPO, 1973), p. 303.

public record, it was revealed in 1974 that Dr. Kissinger's "40 Committee" had authorized expenditures of over $8 million during 1969-73 for clandestine activities in Chile, for purposes that were described by press reports as "political destabilization";[9] by President Ford, as "to help and assist the preservation of opposition newspapers and electronic media and to preserve opposition political parties";[10] and by CIA Director Colby as to encourage "the continued existence of democratic forces looking toward future elections."

More sinister disclosures were to follow in 1975, when it was established that U.S. authorities, acting under what they conceived to be a direct order from President Nixon, had attempted to foment a military coup in Chile in the fall of 1970 as part of an all-out effort to prevent Allende from coming to power following his election, with 36.22 percent of the popular vote, on September 4, 1970. Developed and carried on under the auspices of Dr. Kissinger's White House office, and without the knowledge of the Secretaries of State and Defense, the plan apparently was shelved some days before the fatal shooting of the then Commander-in-Chief of the Chilean Armed Forces, General René Schneider, and the confirmation of Allende's election by the Chilean Congress on October 24, 1970.[12]

Although the congressional investigators who brought these facts to light discovered no evidence of CIA or Embassy involvement in the successful anti-Allende coup of 1973, some though by no means all of those involved expressed a conviction that "the seeds that were laid in that effort in 1970 had their impact in 1973."[13] Mr. Nixon himself, in a sworn deposition made public in March 1976, disclaimed any recollection of specific plans for a military coup in 1970. Such clandestine actions as were taken during that year with a view to preventing Allende's election, the former President indicated, were terminated with his approval later in 1970 and in his opinion "were not a factor in bringing about the 1973 coup."[14]

However controversial its origins, responsible U.S. authorities

[9]Seymour M. Hersh, in New York Times, Sept. 8, 1974.

[10]News conference, Sept. 16, 1974, in Presidential Documents, vol. 10 (1974), p. 1159.

[11]Letter to the editor, in New York Times, Sept. 18, 1974.

[12]U.S. Senate, Select Committee to Study Governmental Operations with Respect to Intelligence Activities, 94th Cong., 1st sess., Alleged Assassination Plots Involving Foreign Leaders: An Interim Report (S. Rept. 94-465, Nov. 20, 1975; Washington: GPO, 1975), pp. 225-54; same, Covert Action in Chile, 1963-1973 (staff report, Dec. 18, 1975; Washington: GPO, 1975).

[13]Alleged Assassination Plots Involving Foreign Leaders, cited, p. 254.

[14]New York Times, Mar. 12, 1976.

on the whole appeared well satisfied at the emergence of a Chilean government that was vigorously anti-Communist, was clearly intent on reversing Allende's leftist policies, and, despite some undeniably repressive measures directed against supporters of the former regime, had yet to reveal its full indifference to human rights and democratic values. The tragedy in Santiago must nevertheless have strengthened Dr. Kissinger's belief in the advisability of a new departure in this sensitive area of U.S. foreign relations, which was already under examination in connection with the preparaion of a National Security Study Memorandum on over-all Latin American policy.[15] The scene of the novel gesture that marked the new Secretary's fourteenth day in office was a luncheon held October 5 at the Center for Inter-American Relations in New York in honor of Latin American and Caribbean Foreign Ministers and other representatives attending the current General Assembly session.

The genesis and immediate results of this occasion were described by Secretary Kissinger some months later in the following language:[16]

Last year some of my friends, the Foreign Ministers from Latin America, suggested that there had been too many proclamations and too few policies, that the peoples of the Western Hemisphere needed a new approach to their relationship. Picking up this idea, very insistently urged upon me by the distinguished Foreign Minister from Mexico [Emilio O. Rabasa], I invited the Foreign Ministers from Latin America who were at the General Assembly in New York to lunch. I proposed to them a new dialogue among equals. This led the distinguished Foreign Minister of Colombia [Alfredo Vázquez Carrizosa] to call a meeting in Bogotá [in November 1973] which outlined an agenda for common action. And this in turn led to a meeting in Mexico at the Foreign Ministry, located in Tlatelolco—a part of Mexico City—[in February 1974] in which the nations assembled here and two others that are not part of the OAS dedicated themselves to a new dialogue among equals.

Significantly, the Secretary of State in his proposal looking toward "a new dialogue with our friends in the Americas" (Document 53) specified neither the subject matter nor the form the discussion should take. The essential point, he emphasized, was that what was needed was not "a policy designed in Washington for Latin America," but "a policy designed by all of Latin America

[15]Same, Oct. 6, 1973.
[16]Address to the Fourth Regular Session of the OAS General Assembly, Atlanta, Apr. 19, 1974, in *Bulletin*, vol. 70 (1974), p. 509.

for the Americas." The choice of topics for discussion was accordingly left to a subsequent "Conference of Foreign Ministers of Latin America for Continental Cooperation," which took place in Bogotá on November 14-16 and drew up a list of agenda subjects ranging from "Cooperation for Development," "Coercive Measures of an Economic Nature," and "Restructuring of the Inter-American System" to "Solution of the Panama Canal Question," "Structure of International Trade and the Monetary System," "Transnational Enterprises," "Transfer of Technology," and "General Panorama of the Relations between Latin America and the United States of America."[17] These topics, in turn, were earmarked for discussion—together with any topics proposed by the United States—at a conference that would be held in Mexico early in the new year 1974.

There was no need to await this "Conference of Tlatelolco"[18] to perceive that the Latin Americans were desirous of discussing practically everything that separated them from the United States—and, in not a few cases, from one another. Even the vexatious Cuban issue could reasonably be brought up under such headings as the "Restructuring of the Inter-American System," a topic already under discussion in the CEESI as well.[19] How long the new interest professed by the United States would remain alive, and how genuinely Washington was disposed to defer to the views of its Latin American partners, would naturally become apparent only as the dialogue got under way.

At least one favorable augury was seen in the designation of Ambassador at Large Ellsworth Bunker, whose reputation as a conciliator had antedated his recent service in Vietnam, to visit Panama for talks with Foreign Minister Juan Antonio Tack "on a new approach toward reaching agreement on a modernized Panama Canal Treaty."[20] A genuinely fresh approach to this tangled issue, which had increasingly assumed symbolic as well as practical significance for the Americas, might in itself go far to justify the reference to a "new era" encompassing a wider area of U.S.-Latin American relationships.

(52)   The Coup in Chile: Statement by Jack B. Kubisch, Assistant Secretary of State for Inter-American Affairs, before the Subcommittee on Inter-American Affairs of the Committee on Foreign Affairs, House of Representatives, September 20, 1973.[21]

[17]The list is repeated in the preamble to the Declaration of Tlatelolco, Feb. 24, 1974, in *Bulletin*, vol. 70 (1974), p. 262.
[18]Held Feb. 18-23, 1974; documentation in *Bulletin*, vol. 70 (1974), pp. 257-64.
[19]*Keesing's*, p. 26252.
[20]Department of State Press Release 424, Nov. 23, in *Bulletin*, vol. 69 (1973), p. 711.
[21]Text from *Bulletin*, vol. 69 (1973), pp. 464-6.

I am very happy to appear before this committee today and discuss recent events in Chile and U.S. policy. Although this is my first formal appearance before the committee since becoming Assistant Secretary of State for Inter-American Affairs several months ago, I have maintained contact with the chairman[22] and have had opportunities to meet informally from time to time with other members of the committee.

I appreciate this opportunity to make a few opening remarks and will of course be glad to try and answer as many questions as you may care to ask. I will also be most interested in any views you care to express and can assure you they will be carefully considered.

There may be some matters you will wish to cover that should not be taken up at this time in a public session because of the still-evolving situation in Chile. However, I want you to know that I am prepared to discuss as fully and as candidly as I can all pertinent issues and if it appears that some of these would be inappropriate for public session I would be more than willing to continue this hearing in executive session. Subsequently, of course, we could release publicly all of the testimony that did not need to be classified.

If you wish, Mr. Chairman, I am prepared to give you a brief summary of the current situation in Chile as we understand it, although I assume that most of the members present have a good idea of the general conditions in the country now and events leading up to the coup.

However, perhaps I should take this opportunity at the outset to comment on false charges from some quarters that the U.S. Government had advance knowledge of or participated in some way in the overthrow and death of President Allende.

Gentlemen, I wish to state as flatly and as categorically as I possibly can that we did not have advance knowledge of the coup that took place on September 11. In the light of what I consider to be some rather imprecise reporting on the matter, I want to distinguish between our receiving reports about the *possibility* of a coup in Chile and our having advance *knowledge* that a coup would take place.

The facts are that we had received many reports over a long period of time about the possibility of a coup in Chile. Such reports and speculations were rife in Chile itself. Indeed, President Allende himself had commented publicly about them, and there was even a report in a Santiago daily newspaper on September 11 that a coup by the Chilean armed forces was scheduled for that very day.

[22]Representative Thomas E. Morgan, Democrat of Pennsylvania, was Chairman of the Foreign Affairs Committee, and Representative Dante B. Fascell, Democrat of Florida, was Chairman of the Subcommittee on Inter-American Affairs.

All of the earlier reports that had speculated about or predicted coup attempts turned out to be false except the last one, which was received in our offices Tuesday morning, September 11, after the coup had already begun.

However, there was no contact whatsoever by the organizers and leaders of the coup directly with us, and we did not have definite knowledge of it in advance.

In a similar vein, either explicitly or implicitly, the U.S. Government has been charged with involvement or complicity in the coup. This is absolutely false. As official spokesmen of the U.S. Government have stated repeatedly, we were not involved in the coup in any way.

I would at this point like to comment also on the subject of U.S.-Chile economic relations during the past several years.

In my opinion, the position of the U.S. Government was quite correct and fully understandable. The United States had no desire to provoke a confrontation with the Allende government. On the contrary, strong efforts were repeatedly made to seek ways to resolve our differences, although there were expropriations without compensation by the Chilean Government of over $700 million of American private investment during this period. In addition, Chile defaulted on over $100 million in debt to the U.S. Government in the same period.

The facts are that there were no embargoes or restrictions placed on trade with Chile. U.S. firms continued to be major suppliers of food, parts, and equipment for the Chilean economy. Bilaterally, we continued a variety of programs, such as AID people-to-people activities, Food for Peace assistance, the Peace Corps, and scientific and cultural exchanges. We continued to disburse normally on the remaining AID loans after Dr. Allende ascended to office. While there were no new bilateral development loans, it should be noted that we had cut back sharply on AID development lending in Latin America, including Chile, even before the Allende government took office. In any case, the Chilean Government did not request any new development loans.

In the international field, multilateral banks continued to disburse existing loans to Chile totaling $83 million from August 1971 to August 1973, this sum representing an increase in annual disbursements as compared with the three years prior to Dr. Allende's coming to power.

However, the economic policies themselves that were pursued by the Allende government resulted in the steadily deteriorating economic situation. The unwillingness of the government to modify its policies made it inevitable that international lending agencies would curtail their programs for Chile, and in any case, the United States could not have voted favorably for some of this assistance because of legal restrictions.

The Paris Club, consisting of various creditor nations, concluded there was little that could be done for Chile unless the government adopted policies they could support. I repeat, however, that it was not the United States, but the institutions themselves, which made their decisions.

In sum it is untrue to say that the U.S. Government was responsible—either directly or indirectly—for the overthrow of the Allende regime.

Much concern has naturally been shown for the human tragedy that has resulted from recent events in Chile. The American people and their government have traditionally demonstrated such concern for the suffering of others throughout the world. The United States has given active support in numerous ways to alleviating suffering and furthering the respect of human rights. With regard to Chile, we have already expressed regret at the loss of human lives and at the death of President Allende.

We have also been concerned with reports of violations of human rights in Chile. However, to my knowledge, many of these reports are unsubstantiated and not necessarily indicative of the policies to be followed by the new Government of Chile once the situation there has fully stabilized.

Moreover, I understand that the Chilean authorities have already given the U.N. Human Rights Commission assurances with regard to the refugees in that country.

Mr. Chairman, members of the committee, in closing I would like to emphasize once again that the situation in Chile is an evolving one. As the new government begins to set out its economic, social, and other policies, we will endeavor to formulate our own policies to respond to the realities of the new situation.

We were not responsible for the difficulties in which Chile found itself, and it is not for us to judge what would have been best or will now be best for the Chilean people.

That is for Chileans themselves to decide, and we respect their right to do this. If in the tasks that face them now, we can be of help, and if our help is wanted by Chile, I am sure we will do our best to provide it in the spirit of understanding and friendship that the American people have long felt for the people of Chile.

(53) "A Western Hemisphere Relationship of Cooperation": Toast by Secretary Kissinger at a luncheon honoring Latin American delegations to the General Assembly, New York, October 5, 1973.[23]

[23]Text from *Bulletin*, vol. 69 (1973), pp. 542-3.

President Benites,[24] Excellencies, ladies and gentlemen: There is a story of an Englishman who visited Sweden, and when he was going through passport control, he was confronted with two lines. One was marked for Swedes; the other one was marked for foreigners. After a while an official came by and found him sitting between these two lines. And the official said, "Sir, will you please go into one line or the other?" And he said, "That's just my problem. I am not a Swede, and I am obviously not a foreigner." [Laughter.]

I think that story is symbolic of our meeting today. We obviously do not belong all to one country, but we obviously are also not foreigners in this room.

I am grateful that you came and for this opportunity to tell you that we are serious about starting a new dialogue with our friends in the Americas.

As we look back at the history of the relationships of the United States to its neighbors to the south, it has been characterized by alternating periods of what some of you have considered intervention with periods of neglect.

We are proposing to you a friendship based on equality and on respect for mutual dignity.

And such a relationship is needed for all of us, and I believe it is needed also for the rest of the world.

In the United States in the last decade, we have experienced many dramatic changes. Throughout most of our history we could overpower most of our foreign policy problems, and we could also substitute resources for thought. Today, without understanding, we can do very little.

Throughout much of our history, indeed throughout much of this administration, we used to believe with respect to agriculture, for example, that our primary problem was how to get rid of seemingly inexhaustible surpluses. We have now learned that we share the world's problem: how to allocate scarce food resources in relation to world needs.

When I came to Washington, the discussions with respect to energy concerned means of restricting production and allocating it among various allies. Today the problem is to find energy sources around the world that can meet world needs.

So we in this country are going through a revolution of sorts, and the whole world is undergoing a revolution in its patterns. And the basic problem we face is whether we will choose the road of nationalism or the road of cooperation, whether we will approach

[24]Leopoldo Benites (Ecuador), President of the 28th session of the U.N. General Assembly.

it from the perspective of each party trying to get the maximum benefit for itself, or whether we can take a common view based on our common needs. And this is why our relations in this hemisphere are so crucial for all of us in this room and for all the rest of the world as well. We in this room, with all the ups and downs in our relationships, share a common history and similar values and many similar experiences. The value of human dignity is nowhere better understood than in the countries of our friends to the south of us.

.So if the technically advanced nations can ever cooperate with the developing nations, if people with similar aspirations can ever achieve common goals, then it must start here in the Western Hemisphere.

We in the United States will approach this dialogue with an open mind. We do not believe that any institution or any treaty arrangement is beyond examination. We want to see whether free peoples, emphasizing and respecting their diversity but united by similar aspirations and values, can achieve great goals on the basis of equality.

So we are starting an urgent examination of our Western Hemisphere policy within our government. But such a policy makes no sense if it is a U.S. prescription handed over to Latin Americans for your acceptance or rejection. It shouldn't be a policy designed in Washington for Latin America. It should be a policy designed by all of Latin America for the Americas.

And so as we examine our own policy, we must also ask for your help. We know that there isn't one Latin America, but many different countries. We know also that there are certain subregional groupings. But it isn't for us to say with whom to conduct the dialogue. That has to come from our guests here in this room.

And so as we form our policy, I would like to invite your suggestions, whatever form you think appropriate, as groups or subgroups or individual nations.

And when our final policy emerges, we will all have a sense that we all had a share in its making, and we will all have a stake in maintaining it.

So, President Benites and Excellencies, I would like to propose a toast to what can be an adventure of free peoples working together to establish a new relationship that can be an example to many other nations. I would like to propose a toast to Western Hemisphere relationships, to our distinguished guest of honor, President Benites.

21. CONGRESS, TRADE REFORM, AND DÉTENTE

An effective foreign policy must always rest upon an effective working relationship between the administration and the Congress, whose responsibilities in some important areas of foreign affairs are not less fundamental than those of the executive branch. When Secretary-designate Kissinger talked of his intention "to bring the Congress into a close partnership in the development, planning, and execution of our foreign policy,"[1] he spoke in full awareness that Congress had for several years been viewing the administration's foreign policy initiatives with an increasingly dubious eye and had been making resolute efforts to recapture for itself a position of greater authority in the international field.

One of the important landmarks in this campaign had been the recent success of the two houses, after years of struggle aimed at forcing an end to the war in Indochina, in banning the use of U.S. military forces in combat operations in that theater after August 15, 1973.[2] Another, potentially much broader assertion of congressional authority was embodied in the proposed War Powers Act of 1973, which undertook to redefine the respective roles of Congress and the President in regard to the use of the armed forces in hostilities abroad. Passed in different forms by both houses of Congress during the summer of 1973, this legislation had been under study by a House-Senate conference committee at the time of Secretary Kissinger's nomination.[3]

While bent upon increasing its own authority at the expense of the executive, the 93rd Congress elected in November 1972 had paid less heed to the administration's recommendations in foreign policy areas where legislative responsibility was already acknowledged. Nine months after Congress had assembled in January, and two months after the beginning of the new fiscal year on

[1]Document 44.
[2]Document 41.
[3]See further Chapter 23.

July 1, there still had been no final action with respect to President Nixon's major proposals in the fields of trade reform, energy, defense, foreign aid, or foreign policy management. Even the President's nominations to major diplomatic posts had encountered unusual delays and frustrations, in part at least because the prevalent revulsion against recent Indochina policy had tended to take itself out on some of the individuals concerned.

Particularly noticed in this connection had been the persistent failure of the Senate Foreign Relations Committee to act on the nomination of Ambassador G. McMurtrie Godley, U.S. Ambassador to Laos since 1969, who had been named on March 16, 1973 to succeed Marshall Green as Assistant Secretary of State for East Asian and Pacific Affairs. In effect, President Nixon complained on July 12, by refusing to act on the nomination the Foreign Relations Committee was penalizing Ambassador Godley "for faithfully carrying out the policies of his Government"—a practice that amounted, in Mr. Nixon's view, to subjecting Foreign Service officers to "retribution for diligent execution of their instructions."[4] (In the face of continued committee inaction, Ambassador Godley's nomination was withdrawn on November 5. He was later nominated and confirmed as Ambassador to Lebanon.)

Appealing for "swift and decisive action" on a range of unfinished legislative business, the President on September 10 addressed to Congress a somewhat reproachful message whose foreign affairs sections (**Document 54**) amounted to a critical report on the status of pending legislation in the fields of trade reform, energy policy, defense, and foreign aid. Though action on most of these fronts continued to lag in the weeks that followed the presidential reproof, the persistence of major disagreements on global policy in the post-Vietnam period was even better exemplified by a series of Senate votes on the military procurement authorization bill for the ongoing fiscal year 1974.

Undeterred by the impending commencement of East-West negotiations on mutual and balanced force reductions (MBFR) in Central Europe,[5] the Senate was again exhibiting a marked responsiveness to proposals by its Majority Leader, Senator Mansfield, that called for major cutbacks in overseas manpower in Europe and elsewhere. On September 26, a Mansfield initiative envisaging a 40 percent reduction—from 471,000 to 282,600—over the next three years in the number of U.S. ground and air personnel maintained abroad was actually approved by a Senate vote of 49 to 46. Under administration pressure, this particular amendment was repudiated

[4]*Presidential Documents*, vol. 9 (1973), p. 898.
[5]Cf. Document 34a.

later on the same day by a second vote of 51 to 44; but next day, September 27, the Senate did adopt by 48 to 36 a substitute amendment that called for a reduction of 110,000 in U.S. overseas forces as early as the end of 1975.[6] Also on September 27, administration forces in the Senate defeated by only 49 votes to 47 an amendment that would have imposed a two-year slowdown on the development of the Trident missile-launching submarine, the intended backbone of the U.S. strategic forces for the 1980s.[7]

A critical challenge to administration policy in another area of foreign relations had meanwhile developed within the House Ways and Means Committee, which had by now devoted almost six months to hearings and deliberations on the trade reform legislation President Nixon had recommended in his message of April 10.[8] As it prepared to draft its report to the House, the Ways and Means Committee had found itself in agreement with the main lines of the administration's moderate free trade philosophy. It had been less impressed by the protectionist appeals of organized labor, whose misgivings about foreign competition and about the job-exporting proclivities of multilateral corporations had led to an advocacy of strict limits both on imports and on the expatriation of capital and technology. But while the Ways and Means Committee approved the central thrust of the administration's international trade policy, it emphatically did *not* share administration views regarding the expediency of granting nondiscriminatory or most-favored-nation tariff treatment to the Soviet Union and other Communist countries.

To underline its disapproval of the Soviet Union's policy of hindering emigration by some of its own citizens, the committee actually went a considerable part of the way toward adoption of the so-called Jackson-Vanik amendment, which, it will be recalled, barred certain types of economic concessions to Communist countries that limited the freedom to emigrate. Under the terms of the

---

[6]This provision, in turn, was eventually superseded by the so-called Jackson-Nunn amendment, named for Democratic Senators Jackson of Washington and Sam Nunn of Georgia, which called for a reduction of U.S. troops in Europe proportionate to any failure by the United States' allies in Europe to offset the U.S. balance-of-payments deficit for fiscal year 1974 resulting from the deployment of U.S. forces in NATO Europe. This amendment became Sec. 812(d) of the Department of Defense Appropriation Authorization Act, 1974 (Public Law 93-155, Nov. 16, 1973). In the last of a series of required reports to Congress, President Ford disclosed on May 27, 1975 "that our Allies have fully offset the U.S. fiscal year 1974 deficit and that the troop reduction provision will not have to be implemented." (*Presidential Documents*, vol. 11 [1975], p. 561.)

[7]*New York Times*, Sept. 27 and 28, 1973.

[8]Document 14.

original Jackson-Vanik amendment, restrictions on freedom of emigration would result in a twofold penalty, involving (1) a ban on U.S. credits and credit and investment guarantees, and (2) a ban on nondiscriminatory tariff treatment of the country's imports to the United States. The first of these prohibitions was, in fact, rejected by the Ways and Means Committee, though only by a tie vote of 12 to 12. The second was accepted, in the form of a committee recommendation opposing the extension of nondiscriminatory treatment to those nonmarket economy (i.e., Communist) countries—other than Poland and Yugoslavia—that denied their citizens the right or opportunity to emigrate, imposed more than a nominal tax on emigration or on the necessary documents, or imposed more than nominal taxes, fines, or other charges on any citizen as a consequence of his desire to emigrate to the country of his choice. Subjecting nondiscriminatory tariff treatment to these conditions, the committee maintained in its report, not only would "place humanitarian concerns and closer economic ties . . . in their proper perspective" but, hopefully, would "provide an incentive to the Soviet Union and other Communist countries to permit freedom of emigration."[9]

President Nixon, however, persisted in his previously expressed opinion[10] that the denial of most-favored-nation treatment would not be "a proper or even an effective way" of dealing with the problem of restrictions on Soviet emigration. In most respects, the President conceded in a statement made public October 4 (**Document 55**), the committee's bill was "a highly responsible piece of legislation"; but Mr. Nixon found it "clearly inadequate" in its failure "to provide the tools we need to expand healthy commercial relationships with the Soviet Union and other Communist countries." "This administration," the President continued, "is committed to seeking most-favored-nation treatment for the Soviet Union. Indeed, the United States has made a formal commitment to the Soviet Union to seek the necessary legislative approval for such treatment in the firm belief that it is in the best interests of both our countries. Therefore, once again I strongly urge the Congress to restore the authority to grant nondiscriminatory tariff treatment to all countries."

Dr. Kissinger offered much the same plea in his second major pronouncement as Secretary of State, an October 8 address in Washington before the Third "Pacem in Terris" Conference sponsored by the Center for the Study of Democratic Institutions. As in his earlier appearance at the United Nations, the Secretary's Pacem

[9]House Report 93-571, Oct. 10, 1973, pp. 3 and 80.
[10]Document 14.

in Terris address exuded an air of philosophic statesmanship appropriate to the status of one who not only embodied all the majesty of American foreign policy but would, in addition, shortly be honored by the award of a Nobel Peace Prize, to be shared with North Vietnam's Le Duc Tho in recognition of their joint peacemaking efforts. (While Secretary Kissinger would use his share of the prize money to establish a scholarship fund for children of U.S. servicemen killed in Indochina, Le Duc Tho was to refuse any part of the prize on the ground that "real peace" had not yet been established.)[11]

"Peace on earth," the acknowledged theme of the Pacem in Terris deliberations, had once again been violently ruptured, 60 hours before the Kissinger speech, by the outbreak of still another round of full-scale warfare in the Middle East. The commencement on Saturday morning, October 6, of the fourth and in many ways the most serious of the recurring military encounters between Arab states and Israel would in due course open new doors to the diplomatic talents of the Secretary of State, but would also subject the "structure of peace" in course of erection by the Nixon administration to the severest test it had yet experienced.[12]

Secretary Kissinger seemed well aware of these hazards as he rose to address the Pacem in Terris Conference on the evening of October 8 (**Document 56**). "Détente cannot survive irresponsibility in any area, including the Middle East," he interpolated, in what was plainly intended as a serious warning to Moscow to avoid the risk of pursuing unilateral advantage in so dangerously explosive a situation. On the whole, however, Dr. Kissinger at this early stage of the developing Mideast crisis still appeared more concerned with countering that other threat to détente that he discerned in the apparent congressional determination to try to force a change in Soviet policy on the emigration issue.

"How hard can we press without provoking the Soviet leadership into returning to practices in its foreign policy that increase international tensions?" the Secretary of State inquired, in obvious reference to the Jackson-Vanik school of thought. "Are we ready to face the crises and increased defense budgets that a return to cold war conditions would spawn? And will this encourage full emigration or enhance the well-being or nourish the hope for liberty of the peoples of Eastern Europe and the Soviet Union? Is it détente that has prompted repression—or is it détente that has generated the ferment and the demand for openness which we are now witnessing?"

[11]For details cf. *Bulletin*, vol. 69 (1973), p. 560, and *Keesing's*, p. 26216.
[12]For details cf. Chapter 22.

Inevitably, the emphasis on this immediate, partly tactical issue diluted to some extent the impact of the Secretary's more philosophic reflections. Nor did his warnings seem to influence the members of the House Ways and Means Committee, whose formal report on the trade bill, including the recommendations on most-favored-nation treatment, was issued only two days later.[13] Presumably, moreover, the Secretary's admonitions had no greater effect upon the thinking of the Soviet leaders, who had undoubtedly followed the trade bill's progress with close attention and could form their own estimate of the likelihood that the administration's commitment would be fulfilled. Whether or not the men in the Kremlin were already having second thoughts about the usefulness of a détente that might be obtainable only at the cost of a change in Soviet domestic policy, Soviet actions in the weeks immediately ahead were to create a situation so grave that President Nixon, at least, could characterize it as "the most difficult crisis we have had since the Cuban confrontation of 1962."[14]

(54) National Legislative Goals: Message of President Nixon to the Congress, September 10, 1973.[15]

(Excerpts)

To the Congress of the United States:

As the Congress reconvenes for the closing months of the 1973 legislative season, it returns to a critical challenge.

Our country faces many pressing problems which must be solved with dispatch.

Americans want and deserve decisive action to fight rising prices. And they want every possible step taken now—not a year from now or in the next session of the Congress.

Americans want and deserve decisive action this year to ensure that we will have enough heat for our homes, enough power for our factories, and enough fuel for our transportation.

They want and deserve decisive action this year to combat crime and drug abuse. The national rate of serious crime is now heading down for the first time in 17 years, and they want that downward spiral to continue

There is also an immediate need to improve the quality of our schools, reform Federal programs for our cities and towns, provide

---

[13]For the subsequent history of the trade bill see Chapter 30 at note 8.
[14]Cf. Chapter 22 at note 13.
[15]Text from *Presidential Documents*, vol. 9 (1973), pp. 1074-99.

better job training, revamp our housing programs, institute lasting reforms in campaign practices, and strengthen our position in world markets.

Of transcending importance is America's continuing commitment to building a lasting structure of world peace. Our people are now at peace for the first time in more than a decade, and they expect their leaders to do all that is necessary to maintain the peace, including those actions which preserve the Nation's strong defense posture.

At the same time, it is apparent as the fall legislative season begins that many Members of the Congress wish to play a larger role in governing the Nation. They want to increase the respect and authority which the American people feel for that great institution.

Personally, I welcome a Congressional renaissance. Although I believe in a strong Presidency—and I will continue to oppose all efforts to strip the Presidency of the powers it must have to be effective—I also believe in a strong Congress.

In campaigning for the Presidency in 1968, I called for "national leadership that recognizes the need in this country for a balance of power. We must maintain," I said, "a balance of power between the legislative and the judicial and the executive branches of Government."

I still believe in that division of responsibility. There can be no monopoly of wisdom on either end of Pennsylvania Avenue—and there should be no monopoly of power.

The challenge is thus clear. The problems of the Nation are pressing, and our elected leaders must rise to the occasion. These next four months will be a time of great testing. If the Congress is to play its proper role in guiding the affairs of the Nation, now is the time for it to take swift and decisive action.

In sending this message to the Congress today, I want to refocus attention on more than 50 legislative measures which I proposed earlier this year. These proposals, along with my regular authorization requests, are now of the highest priority if we are to meet our responsibilities.

* * *

TRADE REFORM ACT

One of the most important of all the bills now before the Congress is my proposed Trade Reform Act of 1973.[16] It is important that final action on this measure be taken in the next four months.

[16]Cf. Document 14.

This legislation represents the most significant reform of our approach to world trade in more than a decade. But it builds on a strong tradition, steadily maintained since the days of Franklin Roosevelt, of giving the executive branch the authority it needs to represent the Nation effectively in trade negotiations with other countries.

The weeks and months ahead are a particularly important time in international economic history. This month sees the formal opening of a new and highly important round of trade negotiations in Tokyo and the annual meeting of the International Monetary Fund and World Bank in Nairobi.[17] The Nairobi meeting is highly important to international monetary reform negotiations. Decisions which grow out of both of these meetings will shape the world's economy for many years to come. The United States can be a much more effective participant in such discussions if the Congress provides the tools contained in my proposed trade reform legislation.

The United States continues to seek a more open trading world. We believe that artificial barriers against trade among nations are often barriers against prosperity within nations. But while the trading system should be more open, it should also be more fair. The trading game must be made equitable for all countries—giving our workers, farmers and businessmen the opportunity to sell to other countries goods which they produce most competitively and, as consumers, to buy goods which their counterparts in other countries produce most competitively. In bargaining for a more open and more equitable trading system, our negotiators must be equipped with authorities comparable to those of their counterparts from other nations.

My trade reform legislation would provide a number of such authorities and thus would strengthen our bargaining position. I emphasize again that the Congress should set up whatever mechanism it deems best for closer consultation and cooperation with the executive branch to ensure that its views are properly represented as trade negotiations go forward.

At the same time, I have also requested actions to ensure that the benefits of expanding international trade are fairly distributed among our own people and that no segment of our economy is asked to bear an unfair burden. My proposals would give us greater flexibility in providing appropriate relief from imports which cause severe domestic problems and would also liberalize our programs of adjustment assistance and other forms of compensation to help workers who are displaced because of rising imports. They would

[17]Cf. Chapter 19.

also equip us to deal more adequately with the unfair trading practices of other countries, and through expanded trade, to "sop up" some of the excess dollar credits now held abroad which can play havoc with domestic markets.

Other authorities contained in the bill would give us greater flexibility to use trade policy in fighting inflation, correcting our balance of payments, expanding our exports, and advancing our foreign policy goals. One provision of this bill, authorizing the President to extend Most Favored Nation treatment to those countries which lack that status, would be particularly helpful in carrying out our foreign policy and I continue to give it my strong support.

Altogether, the proposed Trade Reform Act of 1973 represents a critical building block as we seek to construct a durable structure of peace in the world and a vibrant and stable economy at home. In the difficult negotiations which lie ahead, this legislation would enable us to assure more jobs for American workers, better markets for American producers, wider opportunities for American investors and lower prices for American consumers.

* * *

MEETING THE ENERGY CHALLENGE

I have previously stated, and wish to restate in the most emphatic terms, that the gap between America's projected short-term energy needs and our available domestic energy supplies is widening at a rate which demands our immediate attention.[18]

I am taking all appropriate measures within my authority to deal with this problem, seeking to increase our supplies and moderate our demands. Looking to the future, I have announced plans for a large scale increase in our research and development effort, and I have asked my top energy advisor, Governor John Love, to meet with State officials to seek temporary modifications of air quality standards. Such modifications would help to minimize fuel shortages this winter. In addition, I will soon be meeting with members of the Atomic Energy Commission to determine whether we can bring nuclear power plants on line more quickly. But the energy problem requires more than Presidential action; it also requires action by the Congress.

It is absolutely essential that the Congress not wait for the stimulation of energy shortage to provide the legislation necessary

---

[18]Cf. Chapter 10 at note 6.

to meet our needs. Already we have seen some regional inconveniences this summer with respect to gasoline and this winter we may experience a similar problem with regard to heating fuels.

Over the long term, the prospects for adequate energy for the United States are excellent. We have the resources and the technology to meet our growing needs. But to meet those long-term needs and to avoid severe problems over the short term, we must launch a concentrated effort which mobilizes the Government, American industry and the American people.

I have recently called for passage of seven major energy bills now before the Congress.[19] Not all of those can be acted upon with equal speed, but four of these bills are of the highest urgency and must be acted upon before the end of this year. These four would provide for the construction of the Alaskan pipeline, construction of deepwater ports, deregulation of natural gas and establishment of new standards for surface mining. All four of these bills are addressed to both our short-term and long-term needs.

* * *

KEEPING THE PEACE

For the first time in more than a decade, America is at peace. Now we must learn how to keep that peace—a task that is at least as demanding and in many ways even more subtle than the struggle to end a war.

There is always a temptation after war to enter into a period of withdrawal and isolation. But surely we have learned from past lessons of precipitate disarmament that this temptation must be resisted. And surely we have also learned that our progress in securing peace is due in large measure to our continued military strength and to the steadfast, responsible role we have played in the affairs of our world.

DEFENSE SPENDING

In recent years, it has been fashionable to suggest that whatever we want in the way of extra programs at home could be painlessly financed by lopping 5 or 10 or 20 billion dollars off the defense budget. This approach is worse than foolhardy; it is suicidal. We could have the finest array of domestic programs in the world, and

[19]Statement of Sept. 8, in *Presidential Documents*, vol. 9 (1973), pp. 1066-8.

they would mean nothing if we lost our freedom or if, because of our weakness, we were plunged into the abyss of nuclear war.

The world's hope for peace depends on America's strength—it depends absolutely on our never falling into the position of being the world's second strongest nation in the world.

For years now we have been engaged in a long, painstaking process of negotiating mutual limits on strategic nuclear arms. Historic agreements have already been reached and others are in prospect. Talks are also going forward this year aimed at a mutual and balanced reduction of forces in Europe. But the point of all these negotiations is this: if peace is to be preserved the limitations and the reductions must be mutual. What one side is willing to give up for free, the other side will not bargain for.

If America's peace and America's freedom are worth preserving, then they are worth the cost of whatever level of military strength it takes to preserve them. We must not yield to the folly of breaching that level and so undermining our hopes and the world's hopes for a peaceful future.

Although my military budget—measured in constant dollars— is down by almost one-third since 1968, the Congress is now threatening further defense cuts which would be the largest since 1949. To take such unilateral action—without exacting similar concessions from our adversaries—could undermine the chances for further mutual arms limitations or reductions. I will therefore actively oppose these cuts.

The arms limitations agreement signed with the Soviet Union last year[20] has at last halted the rapid growth in the numbers of strategic weapons. Despite this concrete achievement, much needs to be done to ensure continued stability and to support our negotiation of a permanent strategic arms agreement. A vigorous research and development program is essential to provide vital insurance that no adversary will ever gain a decisive advantage through technological breakthrough and that massive deployment expenditures will therefore not become necessary. Yet the Congress is in the process of slashing research and development funding below minimum prudent levels, including elimination of our cruise missile and air defense programs. The Trident and B-1 programs, which are critical to maintaining a reliable deterrent into the next decade, are also facing proposals to cut them to the bone.

On top of this, the Senate has approved a staggering and unacceptable cut of 156,000 men in our military manpower. Such action would force us to reduce the number of ships in our Navy while the

---

[20] *AFR, 1972*, pp. 97-101; cf. Chapter 12 at note 9.

Soviet Union continues an unprecedented naval buildup and to reduce the size of our Army and Air Force while the Soviet Union and the Chinese continue to maintain far larger forces.

In addition to these cuts, there is also a major Senate proposal requiring substantial unilateral troop withdrawals from Europe, a mistake that could begin a serious unraveling of the NATO alliance. Negotiations for mutual and balanced force reductions begin on October 30. On the very eve of negotiations, the troop cuts in Europe and the reduction in military manpower would destroy our chances of reaching an agreement with the Warsaw Pact countries to reduce troop levels in Europe on a mutual basis. If the Congress were to succeed in making these proposed cuts, the United States would be making far-reaching concessions even before the talks begin.

Cuts in other defense programs are equally unacceptable. It is illogical to cut America's capabilities at the very time the Soviet Union increases hers. And it would be difficult to stabilize delicate situations in the Middle East and Asia if the Congress removes the influential tools which have made stability possible.

FOREIGN ASSISTANCE ACT

Another matter of prime concern to me is our commitment to a sound program of bilateral and multilateral foreign aid. Last spring I sent to the Congress reasonable requests for our economic and military assistance programs.[21] These programs represent a central element in America's ability to work with her allies to maintain peace and stability in the world. Unfortunately, the Congress has not treated these requests favorably.

The House has already cut about 25 percent from the military aid program and the Senate has cut it by one-half. Not only have extraordinary cuts been made in the funding, but restrictive amendments have been added in committee and others may be suggested on the floor. I cannot stand by while these crucial programs are gutted in haste and reaction.

Current foreign aid programs are being funded through a continuing resolution which ends on September 30.[22] This approach is unsatisfactory, especially in light of demands resulting from North Vietnamese truce violations in Cambodia. Yet the Congress continues not only to provide smaller dollar amounts but also to make unreasonable requests for access to sensitive information and im-

---

[21]Document 24.
[22]Public Law 93-52, July 1, 1973 (excerpt in Document 41b).

pose counterproductive conditions on specific programs. Such demands are unacceptable; they would badly compromise our ability to maintain security around the world.

I intend to make every effort to increase the funding for fiscal year 1974 security assistance requirements. I shall also strongly resist efforts by the Congress to impose unreasonable demands upon necessary foreign policy prerogatives of the executive branch. A spirit of bipartisan cooperation provided the steel which saw America through the Cold War and then through Vietnam. We must not jeopardize the great potential for peaceful progress in the post Vietnam era by losing that strong bipartisan spirit.

To build a truly durable structure of peace, our progress in re-forming the world's trade and monetary systems must be ac-companied by efforts to help the poorer countries share more equitably in the world's growing prosperity. To this end, I ask the Congress to support our fair share of contributions to the multilateral development banks—both the proposed contributions now pending in the Congress and other proposals about which I am currently consulting with the Congress and which will be formally submitted in the near future.[23] Our bilateral assistance programs are also an essential part of our effort to stimulate world develop-ment and I urge the Congress to give them full support.

All these efforts represent short-range investments in peace and progress which are of enormous long-range importance. To try to save a few dollars on these programs today could cost us far more tomorrow.

CONCLUSION

With the Congress, the Administration and the people working together during the coming weeks, we can achieve many of the goals described in this message. And we will work together most ef-fectively if we remember that our ultimate responsibility is not to one political party, nor to one philosophical position, nor even to one branch of the Government. Our ultimate responsibility is to the people—and our deliberations must always be guided by their best interests.

Inevitably, we will have different opinions about what those in-terests demand. But if we proceed in a spirit of constructive part-nership, our varying perspectives can be a source of greater creativ-ity rather than a cause of deadlock.

We already know that the year 1973 will be recalled in history

[23]Cf. Document 71.

books as the year in which we ended the longest war in American history. Let us conduct ourselves in the next four months so that 1973 will also be remembered as the time in which we began to turn the blessings of peace into a better life for all.

RICHARD NIXON

The White House,
  September 10, 1973.

(55) *Status of Trade Reform Legislation: Statement by President Nixon, October 4, 1973.*[24]

Over the past several months, the House Ways and Means Committee has held exhaustive hearings and made a number of changes in the Trade Reform Act which I proposed last April. Its work was completed yesterday, and the trade bill will soon be considered by the House of Representatives.

Many of the committee's changes were made over the strong objections of the Administration. Many others were accepted as significant improvements. In assessing the impact of the committee's changes, I have tried to determine how they would affect the purposes for which this legislation was originally designed.

In most respects, the bill submitted to the House by the Ways and Means Committee is a highly responsible piece of legislation.

—It would permit the United States to enter major trade negotiations with the authorities needed to achieve broad gains in trade liberalization with a strong and proper emphasis both on equity and reciprocity.
—It would significantly ease access to escape clause relief and adjustment assistance for American workers and firms suffering injury or threat of injury from growing import competition.
—It would broaden the range of actions the United States can take in responding to unfair international trade practices.
—It would introduce several new authorities which can be used to manage domestic and international economic policies more effectively.
—It would allow the United States to fulfill its international pledge to establish a plan of generalized tariff preferences for the less developed countries of the world.

[24]Text from *Presidential Documents*, vol. 9 (1973), pp. 1224-5; for related documentation see above at notes 8-9.

In short, the Trade Reform Act as reported to the House holds out the promise of more and better jobs for American workers, of more products at lower prices for the American consumer, of expanding exports for the United States and other nations and, most importantly, of reduced international tensions and a strengthened structure of peace.

In one important area, however, the committee bill is clearly inadequate. I am deeply concerned about the bill's failure to provide the tools we need to expand healthy commercial relationships with the Soviet Union and other communist countries. This Administration is committed to seeking most-favored-nation treatment for the Soviet Union. Indeed, the United States has made a formal commitment to the Soviet Union to seek the necessary legislative approval for such treatment in the firm belief that this is in the best interests of both our countries. Therefore, once again, I strongly urge the Congress to restore the authority to grant non-discriminatory tariff treatment to all countries.

(56) *"Moral Purpose and Policy Choices": Address by Secretary of State Kissinger before the Third Pacem in Terris Conference, sponsored by the Center for the Study of Democratic Institutions, Washington, October 8, 1973.*[25]

This is an important anniversary. A year ago today, on October 8, came the breakthrough in the Paris negotiations[26] which led soon afterward to the end of American military involvement in Viet-Nam. It is strangely difficult now to recapture the emotion of that moment of hope and uncertainty when suddenly years of suffering and division were giving way to new possibilities for reconciliation.

We meet, too, at a time when renewed conflict in the Middle East reminds us that international stability is always precarious and never to be taken for granted. Pacem in Terris remains regrettably elusive. However well we contain this crisis, as we have contained others, we must still ask ourselves what we seek beyond the management of conflict.

The need for a dialogue about national purposes has never been more urgent, and no assembly is better suited for such a discussion than those gathered here tonight.

Dramatic changes in recent years have transformed America's position and role in the world:

[25]Department of State Press Release 362; text from *Bulletin*, vol. 69 (1973), pp. 525-31.
[26]Cf. *AFR, 1972*, p. 273.

—For most of the postwar period America enjoyed pre-dominance in physical resources and political power. Now, like most other nations in history, we find that our most difficult task is how to apply limited means to the accomplishment of carefully defined ends. We can no longer overwhelm our problems; we must master them with imagination, understanding, and patience.

—For a generation our preoccupation was to prevent the cold war from degenerating into a hot war. Today, when the danger of global conflict has diminished, we face the more profound problem of defining what we mean by peace and determining the ultimate purpose of improved international relations.

—For two decades the solidarity of our alliances seemed as constant as the threats to our security. Now our allies have regained strength and self-confidence, and relations with adversaries have improved. All this has given rise to uncertainties over the sharing of burdens with friends and the impact of reduced tensions on the cohesion of alliances.

—Thus, even as we have mastered the art of containing crises, our concern with the nature of a more permanent international order has grown. Questions once obscured by more insistent needs now demand our attention: What is true national interest? To what end stability? What is the relationship of peace to justice?

It is characteristic of periods of upheaval that to those who live through them they appear as a series of haphazard events. Symptoms obscure basic issues and historical trends. The urgent tends to dominate the important. Too often goals are presented as abstract utopias, safe havens from pressing events.

But a debate, to be fruitful, must define what can reasonably be asked of foreign policy and at what pace progress can be achieved. Otherwise it turns into competing catalogues of the desirable rather than informed comparisons of the possible. Dialogue degenerates into tactical skirmishing.

The current public discussion reflects some interesting and significant shifts in perspective:

—A foreign policy once considered excessively moralistic is now looked upon by some as excessively pragmatic.

—The government was criticized in 1969 for holding back East-West trade with certain countries until there was progress in their foreign policies. Now we are criticized for not holding back East-West trade until there are changes in those same countries' domestic policies.

—The administration's foreign policy, once decried as too cold war oriented, is now attacked as too insensitive to the profound moral antagonism between communism and freedom.

One consequence of this intellectual shift is a gap between conception and performance on some major issues of policy:

—The desirability of peace and détente is affirmed, but both the inducements to progress and the penalties to confrontation are restricted by legislation.
—Expressions of concern for human values in other countries are coupled with failure to support the very programs designed to help developing areas improve their economic and social conditions.
—The declared objective of maintaining a responsible American international role clashes with nationalistic pressures in trade and monetary negotiations and with calls for unilateral withdrawal from alliance obligations.

It is clear that we face genuine moral dilemmas and important policy choices. But it is also clear that we need to define the framework of our dialogue more perceptively and understandingly.

The Competing Elements of Foreign Policy

Foreign policy must begin with the understanding that it involves relationships between sovereign countries. Sovereignty has been defined as a will uncontrolled by others; that is what gives foreign policy its contingent and ever-incomplete character.

For disagreements among sovereign states can be settled only by negotiation or by power, by compromise or by imposition. Which of these methods prevails depends on the values, the strengths, and the domestic systems of the countries involved. A nation's values define what is just; its strength determines what is possible; its domestic structure decides what policies can in fact be implemented and sustained.

Thus foreign policy involves two partially conflicting endeavors: defining the interests, purposes, and values of a society and relating them to the interests, purposes, and values of others.

The policymaker therefore must strike a balance between what is desirable and what is possible. Progress will always be measured in partial steps and in the relative satisfaction of alternative goals. Tension is unavoidable between values, which are invariably cast in maximum terms, and efforts to promote them, which of necessity involve compromise. Foreign policy is explained domestically in terms of justice. But what is defined as justice at home becomes the subject of negotiation abroad. It is thus no accident that many nations, including our own, view the international arena as a forum in which virtue is thwarted by the clever practice of foreigners.

In a community of sovereign states, the quest for peace involves a paradox: The attempt to impose absolute justice by one side will be seen as absolute injustice by all others; the quest for total security for some turns into total insecurity for the remainder. Stability depends on the relative satisfaction and therefore also the relative dissatisfaction of the various states. The pursuit of peace must therefore begin with the pragmatic concept of coexistence—especially in a period of ideological conflict.

We must, of course, avoid becoming obsessed with stability. An excessively pragmatic policy will be empty of vision and humanity. It will lack not only direction but also roots and heart. General de Gaulle wrote in his memoirs that "France cannot be France without greatness." By the same token, America cannot be true to itself without moral purpose. This country has always had a sense of mission. Americans have always held the view that America stood for something above and beyond its material achievements. A purely pragmatic policy provides no criteria for other nations to assess our performance and no standards to which the American people can rally.

But when policy becomes excessively moralistic it may turn quixotic or dangerous. A presumed monopoly on truth obstructs negotiation and accommodation. Good results may be given up in the quest for ever-elusive ideal solutions. Policy may fall prey to ineffectual posturing or adventuristic crusades.

The prerequisite for a fruitful national debate is that the policymakers and critics appreciate each other's perspectives and respect each other's purposes. The policymaker must understand that the critic is obliged to stress imperfections in order to challenge assumptions and to goad actions. But equally the critic should acknowledge the complexity and inherent ambiguity of the policymaker's choices. The policymaker must be concerned with the best that can be achieved, not just the best that can be imagined. He has to act in a fog of incomplete knowledge without the information that will be available later to the analyst. He knows—or should know—that he is responsible for the consequences of disaster as well as for the benefits of success. He may have to qualify some goals, not because they would be undesirable if reached but because the risks of failure outweigh potential gains. He must often settle for the gradual, much as he might prefer the immediate. He must compromise with others, and this means to some extent compromising with himself.

The outsider demonstrates his morality by the precision of his perceptions and the loftiness of his ideals. The policymaker expresses his morality by implementing a sequence of imperfections and partial solutions in pursuit of *his* ideals.

There must be understanding, as well, of the crucial importance of timing. Opportunities cannot be hoarded; once past, they are usually irretrievable. New relationships in a fluid transitional period—such as today—are delicate and vulnerable; they must be nurtured if they are to thrive. We cannot pull up young shoots periodically to see whether the roots are still there or whether there is some marginally better location for them.

We are now at such a time of tenuous beginnings. Western Europe and Japan have joined us in an effort to reinvigorate our relationships. The Soviet Union has begun to practice foreign policy, at least partially, as a relationship between states rather than as international civil war. The People's Republic of China has emerged from two decades of isolation. The developing countries are impatient for economic and social change. A new dimension of unprecedented challenges—in food, oceans, energy, environment—demands global cooperation.

We are at one of those rare moments where through a combination of fortuitous circumstances and design man seems in a position to shape his future. What we need is the confidence to discuss issues without bitter strife, the wisdom to define together the nature of our world, as well as the vision to chart together a more just future.

Détente With the Soviet Union

Nothing demonstrates this need more urgently than our relationship with the Soviet Union.

This administration has never had any illusions about the Soviet system. We have always insisted that progress in technical fields, such as trade, had to follow—and reflect—progress toward more stable international relations. We have maintained a strong military balance and a flexible defense posture as a buttress to stability. We have insisted that disarmament had to be mutual. We have judged movement in our relations with the Soviet Union not by atmospherics but by how well concrete problems are resolved and by whether there is responsible international conduct.

Coexistence, to us, continues to have a very precise meaning:

—We will oppose the attempt by any country to achieve a position of predominance either globally or regionally.

—We will resist any attempt to exploit a policy of détente to weaken our alliances.

—We will react if relaxation of tensions is used as a cover to exacerbate conflicts in international trouble spots.

The Soviet Union cannot disregard these principles in any area of the world without imperiling its entire relationship with the United States.

On this basis we have succeeded in transforming U.S.-Soviet relations in many important ways. Our two countries have concluded a historic accord to limit strategic arms. We have substantially reduced the risk of direct U.S.-Soviet confrontation in crisis areas. The problem of Berlin has been resolved by negotiation. We and our allies have engaged the Soviet Union in negotiations on major issues of European security, including a reduction of military forces in central Europe. We have reached a series of bilateral agreements on cooperation—health, environment, space, science and technology, as well as trade. These accords are designed to create a vested interest in cooperation and restraint.

Until recently the goals of détente were not an issue. The necessity of shifting from confrontation toward negotiation seemed so overwhelming that goals beyond the settlement of international disputes were never raised. But now progress has been made—and already taken for granted. We are engaged in an intense debate on whether we should make changes in Soviet society a precondition for further progress or indeed for following through on commitments already made. The cutting edge of this problem is the congressional effort to condition most-favored-nation (MFN) trade status for other countries on changes in their domestic systems.

This is a genuine moral dilemma. There are genuine moral concerns on both sides of the argument. So let us not address this as a debate between those who are morally sensitive and those who are not, between those who care for justice and those who are oblivious to humane values. The attitude of the American people and government has been made emphatically clear on countless occasions in ways that have produced effective results. The exit tax on emigration is not being collected, and we have received assurances that it will not be reapplied; hardship cases submitted to the Soviet Government are being given specific attention; the rate of Jewish emigration has been in the tens of thousands, where it was once a trickle. We will continue our vigorous efforts on these matters.

But the real debate goes far beyond this: Should we now tie demands which were never raised during negotiations to agreements that have already been concluded? Should we require as a formal condition internal changes that we heretofore sought to foster in an evolutionary manner?

Let us remember what the MFN question specifically involves. The very term "most favored nation" is misleading in its implication of preferential treatment. What we are talking about is whether to allow *normal* economic relations to develop—of the kind we now have with over 100 other countries and which the Soviet Union enjoyed until 1951. The issue is whether to abolish discriminatory trade restrictions that were imposed at the height of the cold war. Indeed, at that time the Soviet Government discouraged commerce because it feared the domestic impact of normal trading relations with the West on its society.

The demand that Moscow modify its domestic policy as a precondition for MFN or détente was never made while we were negotiating; now it is inserted after both sides have carefully shaped an overall mosaic. Thus it raises questions about our entire bilateral relationship.

Finally, the issue affects not only our relationship with the Soviet Union but also with many other countries whose internal structures we find incompatible with our own. Conditions imposed on one country could inhibit expanding relations with others, such as the People's Republic of China.

We shall never condone the suppression of fundamental liberties. We shall urge humane principles and use our influence to promote justice. But the issue comes down to the limits of such efforts. How hard can we press without provoking the Soviet leadership into returning to practices in its foreign policy that increase international tensions? Are we ready to face the crises and increased defense budgets that a return to cold war conditions would spawn? And will this encourage full emigration or enhance the well-being or nourish the hope for liberty of the peoples of Eastern Europe and the Soviet Union? Is it détente that has prompted repression—or is it détente that has generated the ferment and the demand for openness which we are now witnessing?

For half a century we have objected to Communist efforts to alter the domestic structures of other countries. For a generation of cold war we sought to ease the risks produced by competing ideologies. Are we now to come full circle and insist on domestic compatibility as a condition of progress?

These questions have no easy answers. The government may underestimate the margin of concessions available to us. But a fair debate must admit that they are genuine questions, the answers to which could affect the fate of all of us.

Our policy with respect to détente is clear: We shall resist aggressive foreign policies. Détente cannot survive irresponsibility in any area, including the Middle East. As for the internal policies of closed systems, the United States will never forget that the antagonism between freedom and its enemies is part of the reality of the modern age. We are not neutral in that struggle. As long as we remain powerful, we will use our influence to promote freedom, as we always have. But in the nuclear age we are obliged to recognize that the issue of war and peace also involves human lives and that the attainment of peace is a profound moral concern.

The World as It Is and the World We Seek

Addressing the United Nations General Assembly two weeks ago,[27] I described our goal as a world where power blocs and balances are no longer relevant; where justice, not stability, can be our overriding preoccupation; where countries consider cooperation in the world interest to be in their national interest.

But we cannot move toward the world of the future without first maintaining peace in the world as it is. These very days we are vividly reminded that this requires vigilance and a continuing commitment.

So our journey must start from where we are now. This is a time of lessened tension, of greater equilibrium, of diffused power. But if the world is better than our earlier fears, it still falls far short of our hopes. To deal with the present does not mean that we are content with it.

The most striking feature of the contemporary period, the feature that gives complexity as well as hope, is the radical transformation in the nature of power. Throughout history power has generally been homogeneous. Military, economic, and political potential were closely related. To be powerful, a nation had to be strong in all categories. Today the vocabulary of strength is more complex. Military muscle does not guarantee political influence. Economic giants can be militarily weak, and military strength may not be able to obscure economic weakness. Countries can exert political influence even when they have neither military nor economic strength.

It is wrong to speak of only one balance of power, for there are several, which have to be related to each other. In the military sphere, there are two superpowers. In economic terms, there are at least five major groupings. Politically, many more centers of in-

[27]Document 45.

fluence have emerged; some 80 new nations have come into being since the end of World War II, and regional groups are assuming ever-increasing importance.

Above all, whatever the measure of power, its political utility has changed. Throughout history increases in military power, however slight, could be turned into specific political advantage. With the overwhelming arsenals of the nuclear age, however, the pursuit of marginal advantage is both pointless and potentially suicidal. Once sufficiency is reached, additional increments of power do not translate into usable political strength, and attempts to achieve tactical gains can lead to cataclysm.

This environment both puts a premium on stability and makes it difficult to maintain. Today's striving for equilibrium should not be compared to the balance of power of previous periods. The very notion of "operating" a classical balance of power disintegrates when the change required to upset the balance is so large that it cannot be achieved by limited means.

More specifically, there is no parallel with the 19th century. Then the principal countries shared essentially similar concepts of legitimacy and accepted the basic structure of the existing international order. Small adjustments in strength were significant. The "balance" operated in a relatively confined geographic area. None of these factors obtain today.

Nor when we talk of equilibrium do we mean a simplistic mechanical model devoid of purpose. The constantly shifting alliances that maintained equilibrium in previous centuries are neither appropriate nor possible in our time. In an age of ideological schism the distinction between friends and adversaries is an objective reality. We share ideals as well as interests with our friends, and we know that the strength of our friendships is crucial to the lowering of tensions with our opponents.

When we refer to five or six or seven major centers of power, the point being made is not that others are excluded but that a few short years ago everyone agreed that there were only two. The diminishing tensions and the emergence of new centers of power have meant greater freedom of action and greater importance for all other nations.

In this setting, our immediate aim has been to build a stable network of relationships that offers hope of sparing mankind the scourges of war. An interdependent world community cannot tolerate either big-power confrontations or recurrent regional crises.

But peace must be more than the absence of conflict. We perceive stability as the bridge to the realization of human aspirations, not an end in itself. We have learned much about containing crises, but we have not removed their roots. We have begun to accommodate our differences, but we have not affirmed our commonality. We may have improved the mastery of equilibrium, but we have not yet attained justice.

In the encyclical for which this conference is named, Pope John [XXIII] sketched a greater vision. He foresaw "that no political community is able to pursue its own interests and develop itself in isolation" for "there is a growing awareness of all human beings that they are members of a world community."

The opportunities of mankind now transcend nationalism and can only be dealt with by nations acting in concert:

—For the first time in generations mankind is in a position to shape a new and peaceful international order. But do we have the imagination and determination to carry forward this still-fragile task of creation?

—For the first time in history we may have the technical knowledge to satisfy man's basic needs. The imperatives of the modern world respect no national borders and must inevitably open all societies to the world around them. But do we have the political will to join together to accomplish this great end?

If this vision is to be realized, America's active involvement is inescapable. History will judge us by our deeds, not by our good intentions.

But it cannot be the work of any one country. And it cannot be the undertaking of any one administration or one branch of government or one party. To build truly is to chart a course that will be carried on by future leaders because it has the enduring support of the American people.

So let us search for a fresh consensus. Let us restore a spirit of understanding between the legislative and the executive, between the government and the press, between the people and their public servants. Let us learn once again to debate our methods and not our motives, to focus on our destiny and not on our divisions. Let us all contribute our different views and perspectives, but let us once again see ourselves as engaged in a common enterprise. If we are to shape a world community we must first restore community at home.

With Americans working together, America can work with others toward man's eternal goal of a Pacem in Terris—peace abroad, peace at home, and peace within ourselves.

22. THE GUNS OF OCTOBER

Whether the October crisis in U.S.-Soviet relations was as grave as President Nixon later asserted[1] cannot be judged with certainty at a time when essential parts of the record are still unavailable for examination. It is a natural assumption, borne out to some extent by contemporary testimony, that the President was indulging in a measure of rhetorical exaggeration only too comprehensible in the light of his increasing personal difficulties. There cannot, however, be any doubt that the explosive mixture of domestic and foreign anxieties that plagued the United States at the time of the October War between Israel and its Arab neighbors added up to a traumatic experience as severe as it was many-sided. To the remorseless unfolding of the Watergate investigation and related scandals were added, first, the stresses and strains attendant on the violent renewal of the Arab-Israeli conflict; second, the sudden, sickening possibility of another nuclear confrontation with the Soviet Union; and third, the novel, almost unbelievable threat of a large-scale petroleum shortage that could require far-reaching and possibly permanent changes in American life styles.

Events succeeded one another during these days with ever more shattering effect. There had been a few premonitory signals in the preceding weeks—an attempt by Arab terrorists to shoot down an Israeli airliner at Rome's Fiumicino airport; the seizure and abduction of hostages from the Saudi Arabian Embassy in Paris; the seizure of more hostages on a Moscow-Vienna express train, in a partially successful attempt to force the closure of Austrian transit facilities for Israel-bound Soviet Jews.[2] But neither this activity nor the continuing, ominous flow of Soviet arms to Egypt and Syria had prepared Americans (or Israelis) for the outbreak of actual, large-scale warfare in the Middle East. Arab military capabilities, even when buttressed by Soviet equipment, had been less highly

[1] Cf. Chapter 21 at note 14.
[2] *Keesing's*, pp. 26121 and 26159-61.

regarded in Washington than they perhaps deserved. As late as September 30, six days before hostilities began, the Central Intelligence Agency is said to have advised Secretary Kissinger that "the whole thrust of President Sadat's activities since last spring has been in the direction of bringing moral, political, and economic force to bear on Israel in tacit acknowledgement of Arab unreadiness to make war."[3]

American authorities, therefore, were no less rudely surprised than their Israeli friends by the audacious attack launched by Egyptian and Syrian regular forces on the morning of October 6, the Jewish Yom Kippur, against Israeli military positions at the Suez Canal and in the Golan Heights. (The Jordanian and Lebanese fronts were not involved, although Jordan, Iraq, and Saudi Arabia all sent military contingents to Syria's aid.) Taken unawares by the violence of the Arab attacks, the Israelis suffered extremely heavy losses and did not begin to retrieve their position until after a period of Arab success so striking as virtually to erase the sense of military inferiority that had so long weighed upon the pride of the Arab peoples.

Despite the violence of the fighting, however, this fourth in the series of Arab-Israeli wars did not at first appear to harbor as vital a threat to the world's peace as had the earlier conflicts of 1956 and 1967. It was obvious, of course, that the Soviets must have been deeply involved in the military build-up that had preceded the Egyptian-Syrian attack; and Secretary Kissinger was quick to warn in his Pacem in Terris address[4] that "Détente cannot survive irresponsibility in any area, including the Middle East." But since the American and Soviet governments had repeatedly affirmed their determination to avoid serious conflict with one another—renewing their pledge as recently as Brezhnev's June visit to the United States[5]—it seemed reasonable to suppose that they would give great weight to the preservation of their mutual understanding, even if they differed to some extent about the details of the current conflict. In the circumstances, as Secretary Kissinger later explained (**Document 62**), the obvious American objectives were, first, to get the fighting stopped, and then to try to get rid of the underlying conditions that had caused it.

The initial encounter of the interested parties in the U.N. Security Council, which convened at U.S. request on October 8, did not appear to invalidate such an approach. Speaking for the United States, Ambassador Scali took an easily predictable line in

[3]Excerpt from the report of the House Select Committee on Intelligence, in *The Village Voice*, Feb. 16, 1976, p. 78.
[4]Document 56.
[5]Document 32b.

suggesting that the combatants stop fighting and withdraw to the positions they had occupied before the outbreak of hostilities (**Document 57**). No one was specially surprised, however, that Soviet delegate Yakov A. Malik should think fit to subordinate a cease-fire to the evacuation by Israel of all the Arab territories it had been occupying since the previous war in June 1967. It would, perhaps, have been too much to expect that the Russians should press for an immediate cease-fire at a moment when their clients all too obviously held the upper hand.[6]

The situation began to take on a different aspect as Israel's military fortunes improved. By mid-October, Israeli forces once again had seized the initiative, had regained control of the Golan Heights, and were well along the road to Damascus. On the Suez front, where a major tank battle was developing between Israeli and Egyptian forces east of the waterway, an Israeli task force led by Major General Ariel Sharon crossed the Canal from east to west on October 16, wiping out a number of antiaircraft missile sites and establishing an important bridgehead on the Egyptian-held west bank that extended to within some 70 miles of Cairo.

There were also growing indications during this period that the Soviets, in spite of Secretary Kissinger's admonitions, were not limiting themselves to political support of Israel's foes but were in addition sending large amounts of military equipment to Egypt and Syria, mainly by military airlift routed across Hungary and Yugoslavia. Dismayed by what was soon being described in Washington as a "massive" Soviet resupply effort, the United States lost several days in bureaucratic confusion and recrimination but, by October 13, had initiated its own, "appreciable" airlift of military supplies to Israel, relying mainly on C-5 transport aircraft which traveled via the Portuguese Azores in view of the unwillingness of most other allied countries to provide the necessary facilities. Leaving no doubt of U.S. support for Israel, President Nixon in a special message to Congress on October 19 (**Document 58**) called attention to the heavy Israeli losses in the current fighting and proposed the allocation of no less than $2.2 billion in security assistance to that country as a contribution to what he called "maintaining a balance of military capabilities and achieving stability in the area."[7]

[6] Detailed accounts of the Security Council discussions during the October War will be found in *UN Monthly Chronicle*, vol. 10 (Nov. 1973), pp. 3-66, and *U.S. Participation, 1973*, pp. 6-9. For a general account of American diplomacy in the war see especially Kalb, *Kissinger*, pp. 450-99. Additional details are furnished by Matti Golan, *The Secret Conversations of Henry Kissinger: Step-by-Step Diplomacy in the Middle East* (New York: Quadrangle/The New York Times Book Co., 1976), which was published too late for use in preparing the present text.

[7] Also requested was a more modest $200 million for Cambodia (cf. Chapter 26).

Two other factors accentuated the sense of gathering crisis. One was a competitive build-up of Soviet and American naval strength in the Mediterranean; the other, a decision by the Arab oil-producing countries to make a collective display of solidarity with Egypt and Syria and try to exert pressure on the United States and other friends of Israel. At meetings held in Kuwait on October 16-17, the Persian Gulf oil states (including Iran) announced a steep increase in posted prices, mainly for economic reasons; in addition, Arab oil states decided to reduce production by 10 percent immediately and at least 5 percent a month thereafter, pending an Israeli withdrawal from the occupied territories and restoration of what were termed the "legitimate rights" of the Palestinians. Even more eloquent was the action of most Arab countries in suspending *all* petroleum exports to the United States and the Netherlands because of their alleged partiality to Israel.[8]

Proceeding in counterpoint with these overseas developments were sensational domestic occurrences that spelled a new and drastic impairment in the position of the Nixon administration. The war in the Middle East was only five days old when Vice-President Agnew resigned his office in order to plead "no contest" to a charge of income tax evasion, in this way avoiding prosecution on a variety of charges centering in the improper acceptance of substantial cash payments before and during his tenure of the vice-presidency. President Nixon, whose own position by now looked rather less secure than formerly, lost little time in designating Republican Representative Gerald R. Ford of Michigan, the House Minority Leader, to fill the vacant vice-presidential seat. The need for confirmation by both houses of Congress would, however, delay the actual swearing in of a new Vice-President until December 6.

The Watergate situation, meanwhile, had also been advancing toward another of its periodic climaxes in the political and constitutional struggle that culminated in the celebrated "Saturday night massacre" of October 20. The events of that day formed a natural counterpart to those of Monday, April 30, when the President had announced the departure of Messrs. Haldeman, Ehrlichman, Kleindienst, and Dean and designated Elliot Richardson as Attorney-General with authority to name a special prosecutor for Watergate matters.[9] It was the diligent pursuit of his investigative responsibilities by Special Prosecutor Archibald Cox—specifically, his insistence on obtaining access to certain White House tapes, and his refusal either to accept a compromise

[8]For further details see Chapter 24 at note 10.
[9]Cf. Chapter 9 at note 4.

arrangement or to resign—that led on October 20 to the announcement of his abrupt dismissal at the President's order, and of the resignation of Attorney-General Richardson and Deputy Attorney-General William D. Ruckelshaus, neither of whom had been willing to carry out the dismissal order.[10] This startling exercise of presidential authority produced the opposite of its intended effect, unloosing a storm of criticism and acting as a powerful spur to impeachment talk. Undoubtedly it suggested to some observers that the harassed President was overindulging his penchant for abrupt and vigorous action and might at some point be tempted to make a similar demonstration on the international scene.

Secretary Kissinger was not in Washington on that fateful Saturday night, having gone to Moscow earlier in the day in response to an invitation from General Secretary Brezhnev to fly to the Soviet capital for urgent consultations on the Middle East. As the military situation developed increasingly in Israel's favor, Moscow's earlier indifference with regard to a cease-fire had given way to ill-concealed alarm. The need to find a basis for an early cessation of hostilities had already been discussed with President Sadat by Premier A.N. Kosygin at meetings held in Cairo on October 16-19. The Brezhnev-Kissinger consultations over the October 20-21 weekend now resulted in an agreement that the two powers should jointly approach the Security Council with a cease-fire plan, and that they should also concert their efforts with a view to promoting a negotiated settlement of the whole issue. By Monday evening, October 22, as the Secretary of State flew homeward after brief stopovers in Israel and England, Security Council action pursuant to the Moscow conversations had already brought about a partial cease-fire and established somewhat modified ground rules for the future handling of the Middle East conflict.

The draft resolution proposed by Ambassador Scali on the evening of October 21 (**Document 59a**) and formally adopted as Security Council Resolution 338 at 12:50 A.M., New York time (0450 hours Greenwich Mean Time) on October 22, was to become almost as famous as the basic Resolution 242 of November 22, 1967. Besides calling for a cease-fire in place within twelve hours and an immediate start on the implementation of Resolution 242, this new resolution (**Document 59b**) embodied a most significant novelty: a decision, that is, "that, immediately and concurrently with the cease-fire, negotiations start between the parties concerned under appropriate auspices aimed at establishing a just and durable peace in the Middle East."

---

[10]For the White House announcement see *Presidential Documents*, vol. 9 (1973), p. 1271.

This paragraph, which was to become the point of departure for the later Geneva Conference on the Middle East, was distinctly a new departure in a situation in which direct negotiations between the parties had never yet been possible. It gained additional authority, moreover, from the implied promise of the American and Soviet governments to make their joint good offices available to facilitate the negotiating process. The idea of a later peace conference appears to have been a part of the Brezhnev-Kissinger understandings from the very beginning, although it was to receive comparatively little notice at a time when world attention was still concentrated on battlefield developments.

Fourteen of the Security Council's fifteen members voted to approve the U.S.-Soviet resolution, though China refused to participate as a protest against alleged dictation by the "superpowers." Acceptance of the cease-fire order was made known by Israel, Egypt, and Jordan, and fighting was halted on the Suez front on the expiration of the Council's twelve-hour deadline at 1650 hours G.M.T. (12:50 P.M., New York time) on Monday, October 22. Syria, however, did not accept, and military operations in the north continued. To the dismay of both Egyptians and Russians, moreover, heavy fighting soon resumed also in the south, where General Sharon's forces, ostensibly responding to Egyptian attacks, were endeavoring to improve their position west of the Canal and to complete their encirclement of the Egyptian Third Army based on Suez City. At Egypt's urgent request, the Security Council was accordingly summoned to convene once more on Tuesday evening, October 23.

Still operating within the terms of the Brezhnev-Kissinger understandings, the United States and the U.S.S.R. joined forces at the October 23 meeting in submitting for the Council's consideration a new cease-fire draft going well beyond the terms of the previous resolution. In this more peremptory text (Document 60a), forces of the two sides were told not merely to stop fighting but to return to the positions they had occupied at the moment the cease-fire became effective. In addition, the Secretary-General was now requested to assign personnel of the U.N. Truce Supervision Organization (UNTSO), previously deployed along the 1967 cease-fire line at the Suez Canal, to supervise observance of the new cease-fire. This resolution, No. 339 in the series, was likewise adopted by 14 votes to 0, with China not participating. Ambassador Scali, while stressing American support for prompt application of the cease-fire, cautioned in a statement following the vote (Document 60b) that there was bound to be great difficulty "in establishing actual cease-fire lines and in fixing the positions of forces which have been maneuvering in the desert."

The immediate sequel to this resolution was a cessation of fighting in the north, where Syria, having perceived the impossibility of fighting on alone, now accepted not only the cease-fire order but also the basic Security Council Resolution 242 of 1967, whose terms it had previously rejected. But no such favorable evolution occurred on the southern front, where the isolation of Egypt's Third Army was now complete and Israeli forces showed no sign of drawing back to previous positions as the Security Council had ordered.

Increasingly concerned at the difficult plight of the Egyptian armies, President Sadat on the morning of Wednesday, October 24, put forward the somewhat unusual proposal that the United States and the Soviet Union, in their capacity as "guarantors," should themselves send units of their armed forces to supervise the implementation of the cease-fire. But while apparently acceptable to the Russians, such a proposal was very far from being acceptable to the American side. "In the view of the United States," Ambassador Scali warned the Security Council that Wednesday evening **(Document 61)**, "this is not a time in which involvement by the great powers through the dispatch of their armed forces could be helpful in creating conditions of peace. Our objective in the Middle East has not been to produce a military confrontation but rather to encourage restraint and caution on both sides."

Little as the United States might like Sadat's idea, however, there was one possible alternative that would be still more objectionable. Even less desirable than a parallel introduction of American and Soviet forces into the Middle East, as Secretary Kissinger explained at a news conference next day **(Document 62)**, would be the *unilateral* introduction "by any great power, especially by any nuclear power, of military forces into the Middle East in whatever guise those forces should be introduced." And it was precisely this supremely distasteful possibility that increasingly suggested itself to American authorities in the hours that followed Sadat's proposal. Their observation of Soviet military moves seemed to raise a definite possibility that Moscow was preparing for unilateral intervention in the Middle East; and this impression appeared to be confirmed by a message from Brezhnev that stated, in effect, that if the United States would not cooperate, the Soviet Union would proceed independently.

Senator Jackson, although he did not himself see the Brezhnev message, immediately advised the world that its tone was "brutal, rough"; and President Nixon later agreed that "it was very firm, and . . . left very little to the imagination as to what he intended."[11] The key passage, unpublicized at the time but sub-

[11]News conference, Oct. 26, in same, p. 1292.

sequently printed in *The New York Times* of April 10, 1974, read:
"I will say it straight, that if you find it impossible to act with us in
this matter, we should be faced with the necessity urgently to consider the question of taking appropriate steps unilaterally. Israel
cannot be permitted to get away with the violations [of the
cease-fire]."

In a personal review of these events some 48 hours later,
President Nixon stated also that Brezhnev might have found his
own communications "rather rough." The American response,
said the President, "was also very firm and left little to the
imagination of how we would react." The nature of the response
apparently was worked out during the night of October 24-25 at a
somewhat unconventional meeting of some members of the
National Security Council, at which Secretary Kissinger presided
while the President remained upstairs in his private White House
quarters.

As was often the case, American policy in this emergency un-
folded simultaneously in several directions. Israel was severely admonished to abide by the cease-fire. Moscow was advised in
diplomatic language that the United States opposed joint intervention in the Middle East and would not stand for unilateral
Soviet action, but would have no objection to the assignment of a
United Nations force to the area on the understanding that it must
not include contingents from any of the major world powers. At
the same time, a more sensational message that revealed the depth
of U.S. opposition to any unilateral Soviet moves was conveyed by
"certain precautionary measures" of a military character involving
nothing less than the alerting of American military forces,
both nuclear and non-nuclear, throughout the world. These
measures, the most far-reaching American military moves since the
Jordanian crisis of 1970, were of a nature to be picked up immediately by Soviet intelligence, just as U.S. intelligence had
previously been made aware of the more limited Soviet actions.

The alert of American military forces, according to Secretary
Kissinger's statements at a midday news conference next day
(Thursday, October 25), had been ordered at 3 o'clock that morning after the President had concurred in the unanimous recommendation of his senior advisers (**Document 62**). Other accounts
would indicate that the basic decisions had perhaps been reached
some hours earlier, possibly without full consultation within the
government.[12] Dr. Kissinger, who had not expected the alert to

[12]In addition to Kalb, *Kissinger*, pp. 489-99, the events of Oct. 24-25 are discussed in
some detail in Ray S. Cline, "Policy Without Intelligence," *Foreign Policy*, No. 17
(Winter 1974-75), pp. 121-35. The Kissinger remarks quoted in this and the follow-

become public knowledge, appeared concerned that the seriousness of the situation should not be exaggerated. "We do not consider ourselves in a confrontation with the Soviet Union," he emphasized. "We do not believe it is necessary, at this moment to have a confrontation. . . . We are not talking of a missile-crisis-type situation."

With equal certitude, the Secretary of State repudiated any suggestion that the crisis might have been artificially created to distract attention from Watergate. "It is a symptom of what is happening to our country," he lamented, "that it could even be suggested that the United States would alert its forces for domestic reasons." Nor did Dr. Kissinger at all accept the view that the United States had reacted in an exaggerated manner unwarranted by the circumstances. "There has to be a minimum of confidence that the senior officials of the American government are not playing with the lives of the American people," he said.

The Secretary's overall appraisal was not without its reassuring side. "From many points of view," he observed, "the chances for peace in the Middle East are quite promising." The situation would be greatly eased, he suggested, should the Security Council in fact decide to set up an international force for the Middle East *from which the great powers would be excluded*. President Nixon, indeed, said later that a suggestion along these lines had already been conveyed to Brezhnev as part of the diplomatic effort initiated "in the early morning hours" concurrently with the military alert (**Document 64**). Word had also been flashed to New York, where diplomats at the United Nations were even then bestowing the final touches on a draft Security Council resolution amended to reflect the American view.

Briefly introduced by Ambassador Scali (**Document 63a**) and rather coolly accepted by Soviet Representative Malik, this latest Security Council resolution was adopted later on October 25 by the now familiar vote of 14 to 0, with China not participating. In addition to establishing a United Nations Emergency Force (UNEF) "composed of personnel drawn from States Members of the United Nations except the permanent members of the Security Council," Resolution 340 (**Document 63b**) demanded an immediate and complete cease-fire and a return to previous positions; requested an immediate increase in the number of U.N. military observers on both sides; and asked the Secretary-General to report within 24 hours on the steps taken to organize the Emergency Force.

As Secretary Kissinger had hoped, this action ended the most acute phase of the crisis and cleared the way for a gradual cutback

ing paragraph are from the continuation of his Oct. 25 news conference in *Bulletin*, vol. 69 (1973), pp. 588-94.

in the alert status of the U.S. military forces. It was President Nixon himself who announced the de-alerting of the North American Air Defense Command (NORAD) and the Strategic Air Command (SAC) at a televised news conference on Friday evening, October 26.[13] Asserting that recent events had amounted to "the most difficult crisis . . . since the Cuban confrontation of 1962," the President also offered the unexpectedly optimistic judgment that the outlook for permanent peace in the Middle East was now "the best that it has been in 20 years."

The real significance of the events just past, in Mr. Nixon's view, lay in the vindication not only of détente as such, but of his personal relationship with Brezhnev—a relationship which, he asserted, had enabled him to match the Soviet leader's firmness and had made it possible not only to avoid a confrontation, but to move "a great step forward toward real peace in the Mideast." The threatened interruption of Middle East oil shipments, Mr. Nixon observed in passing, had given "enormous urgency" to the settlement of the crisis, and had made it "indispensable at this time that we avoid any further Mideast crisis so that the flow of oil to Europe, to Japan, and to the United States can continue."

Although there was no longer any realistic possibility of avoiding a major international oil crisis, the chances of maintaining a military cease-fire in the Middle East were heightened in the following days by the successful exertions of Secretary-General Waldheim and other U.N. officials. With the consent of the Security Council, contingents supplied by Austria, Finland, and Sweden had already been detached from the U.N. Peacekeeping Force in Cyprus for emergency Middle East duty under General Ensio Siilasvuo of Finland, Chief of Staff of UNTSO and Commander-to-be of the new U.N. Emergency Force (UNEF). Detailed guidelines for the operation of a 7,000-man Emergency Force over a six-month period were drawn up by the Secretary-General (**Document 65a**) and approved on September 27 by still another 14 to 0 vote of the Security Council (**Document 65b**). "Supervising cease-fire lines in an area in the wake of war will not be easy," Ambassador Scali warned in commenting on this action (**Document 65c**). There was no need for him to point out that the situation would remain extremely dangerous as long as the Egyptian Third Army was cut off and Israel, increasingly concerned about the fate of its prisoners in Egyptian and Syrian hands, made no move to withdraw to its October 22 positions as the Security Council had twice demanded.

---

[13]Full text in *Presidential Documents*, vol. 9 (1973), pp. 1287-94; partial texts in *Bulletin*, vol. 69 (1973), pp. 581-4 and in Document 64 below.

Israeli forces were still maintaining their stranglehold on Egypt's Third Army when the Security Council met again on November 1 and 2 to consider what further countries might be asked to supply contingents to the newly constituted UNEF **(Document 66a)**. "The situation remains tense and dangerous," Ambassador Scali observed once more **(Document 66b)**. "The unforeseen can easily happen." Nevertheless, the U.S. Rpresentative added, "For the present we can take satisfaction that this Council has worked tirelessly and constructively to fulfill in this instance one of its highest responsibilities under the Charter—that of peacekeeping. We can only hope that our efforts will make possible a further success—the creation of a just and durable peace in the Middle East."

(57) The Responsibilities of the United Nations: Statement by Ambassador Scali to the Security Council regarding the situation in the Middle East, October 8, 1973. [14]

The United States has requested that the Security Council be convened today in order that it might deal urgently with the current situation in the Middle East.

For the first time in more than three years, armed hostilities have broken out on a massive scale in the Middle East. The cease-fire we have sought to maintain has been broken. The recourse to tragic violence we have sought to avoid is upon us.

Reports based on U.N. sources appear to indicate that the air attacks in the Golan Heights were initiated by Syrian MIG aircraft and that the first firing on the Suez front, which took place at the same time as the Syrian attack, was from west to east. The subsequent development of the fighting has been fully covered in the press.

In the days before fighting broke out, we received reports of intensified military activities in the Middle Eastern area. We watched these developments closely, but until a few hours before military operations started we were unable to conclude that these activities were a prelude to actual fighting. This is a region in which alarms and alerts are fairly frequent. In themselves, military movements would not necessarily indicate that combat was about to begin. When, very shortly before the initial attacks took place, we received indications that this was the fact, we immediately undertook intensive diplomatic efforts in hopes that the outbreak of hostilities might be prevented. We discussed the situation directly with Israel and Egypt. We consulted other permanent members and

[14]USUN Press Release 91, Oct. 8; text from *Bulletin*, vol. 69 (1973), pp. 598-9.

exchanged views with many governments represented on this Council. Others in and outside of the area pursued parallel efforts. We kept in close touch with Secretary General Waldheim, who also lent his great weight and prestige to the efforts. Unfortunately these efforts did not prevent the outbreak, and intense fighting continues.

In so serious a situation we felt that we could not fail to exercise our responsibility, as a permanent member of the Security Council, to request a meeting of the Council in order that it might be seized of the grave situation which had arisen. Not to have done this would have been to fail in our obligations under the charter. We hope that in the days ahead the Council by its deliberations can restore in some measure its historic role of constructive ameliorator in the most critical and explosive area in the world.

Definitive judgments as to constructive action are difficult in view of the fluidity of the situation. My government has itself made no such judgments. Nor have we felt it would be constructive to divert the Council's energies and attention to the question of assessing blame.

Our purpose today is not to sift conflicting reports or to assess responsibility for what has occurred. Our purpose is to help promote a solution for the tense and dangerous situation confronting us.

We recognize that it is difficult to separate proximate from underlying causes. The former may be clear-cut, but the latter are complex, and perceptions of right and wrong inevitably vary. It has been over six years since the present abnormal situation was created in the wake of the 1967 Arab-Israeli war. That war in turn followed 18 years of abnormal armistice. For the failure to move from abnormal armistice and cease-fire to political accommodation and peace, there is more than enough blame to go around. All concerned have missed opportunities to make the transition over the past 25 years.

We have given preliminary thought to the direction in which this Council might move in dealing with this problem so that new opportunities to make practical progress toward peace can be created and the present tragedy can be made a new beginning rather than simply another lost opportunity. As we see it, there are a number of principles which the Council must seek to apply:

—First, in a situation where fighting is raging unchecked, the most appropriate means must be found for bringing the hostilities to an end. Military operations must be halted. The guns must fall silent so that additional human suffering may be avoided and the search for peace may proceed.

—Second, conditions must be restored in the area that would be conducive to a settlement of the longstanding differences in the

Middle East. There must be respect for the rights and positions of all the states in the region. A beginning must be made toward converting the sharp confrontation of violently opposing claims and counterclaims, which for over a quarter of a century has made true stability impossible, to a more reasoned discourse aimed at genuine reconciliation. The least damaging way to bring this about is to have the parties concerned return to the positions before hostilities broke out.

—Third, in all its efforts the Council must be mindful of the need for universal respect for the integrity of those instruments and principles of settlement for the Middle Eastern dispute which have received the adherence of the interested parties and the support of the Council's authority. The foundations so laboriously achieved in the past for negotiations looking toward a Middle Eastern peace must not be destroyed under the stress of a military emergency.

These principles, in the opinion of my government, constitute the framework within which we can act in this Council to reduce the prevailing tension in the Middle East and to prepare for a reinvigoration of the process of peacemaking. We are prepared to discuss these principles, and any others which other members may put forward, as a basis for our further action.

What we seek in this Council is not a war of words, but a broad consensus which will enable the Council to put the full weight of its influence behind the task of restoring peace so that the Middle East can be set on a new course pointing toward a better era in the region.

Let us then renounce the sterile gains of propaganda and turn to serious discussion. The situation is urgent; the need is great; and time presses.

(58) Emergency Security Assistance for Israel and Cambodia: Message from President Nixon to the Congress, October 19, 1973.[15]

To the Congress of the United States:

I am today requesting that the Congress authorize emergency security assistance of $2.2 billion for Israel and $200 million for Cambodia. This request is necessary to permit the United States to follow a responsible course of action in two areas where stability is vital if we are to build a global structure of peace.

For more than a quarter of a century, as strategic interests of the

---

[15]Text from *Presidential Documents*, vol. 9 (1973), p. 1264. For congressional action on aid to Israel see Chapter 29 at note 7.

major powers have converged there, the Middle East has been a flashpoint for potential world conflict. Since war broke out again on October 6, bringing tragedy to the people of Israel and the Arab nations alike, the United States has been actively engaged in efforts to contribute to a settlement. Our actions there have reflected my belief that we must take those steps which are necessary for maintaining a balance of military capabilities and achieving stability in the area. The request I am submitting today would give us the essential flexibility to continue meeting those responsibilities.

To maintain a balance of forces and thus achieve stability, the United States Government is currently providing military material to Israel to replace combat losses. This is necessary to prevent the emergence of a substantial imbalance resulting from a large-scale resupply of Syria and Egypt by the Soviet Union.

The costs of replacing consumables and lost equipment for the Israeli Armed Forces have been extremely high. Combat activity has been intense, and losses on both sides have been large. During the first 12 days of the conflict, the United States has authorized shipments to Israel of material costing $825 million, including transportation.

Major items now being furnished by the United States to the Israeli forces include conventional munitions of many types, air-to-air and air-to-ground missiles, artillery, crew-served and individual weapons, and a standard range of fighter aircraft ordnance. Additionally, the United States is providing replacements for tanks, aircraft, radios, and other military equipment which have been lost in action.

Thus far, Israel has attempted to obtain the necessary equipment through the use of cash and credit purchases. However, the magnitude of the current conflict coupled with the scale of Soviet supply activities has created needs which exceed Israel's capacity to continue with cash and credit purchases. The alternative to cash and credit sales of United States military materials is for us to provide Israel with grant military assistance as well.

The United States is making every effort to bring this conflict to a very swift and honorable conclusion, measured in days not weeks. But prudent planning also requires us to prepare for a longer struggle. I am therefore requesting that the Congress approve emergency assistance to Israel in the amount of $2.2 billion. If the conflict moderates, or as we fervently hope, is brought to an end very quickly, funds not absolutely required would of course not be expended.

I am also requesting $200 million emergency assistance for Cambodia. As in the case of Israel, additional funds are urgently needed for ammunition and consumable military supplies. The increased requirement results from the larger scale of hostilities and the higher levels of ordnance required by the Cambodian Army and Air Force to defend themselves without American air support.

The end of United States bombing on August 15[16] was followed by increased communist activity in Cambodia. In the ensuing fight, the Cambodian forces acquitted themselves well. They successfully defended the capital of Phnom Penh and the provincial center of Kampong Cham, as well as the principal supply routes. Although this more intense level of fighting has tapered off somewhat during the current rainy season, it is virtually certain to resume when the dry season begins about the end of the year.

During the period of heaviest fighting in August and September, ammunition costs for the Cambodian forces were running almost $1 million per day. We anticipate similar average costs for the remainder of this fiscal year. These ammunition requirements, plus minimum equipment replacement, will result in a total funding requirement of $380 million for the current fiscal year, rather than the $180 million previously requested. To fail to provide the $200 million for additional ammunition would deny the Cambodian Armed Forces the ability to defend themselves and their country.

We remain hopeful that the conflict in Cambodia be resolved by a negotiated settlement. A communist military victory and the installation of a government in Phnom Penh which is controlled by Hanoi would gravely threaten the fragile structure of peace established in the Paris agreements.

I am confident that the Congress and the American people will support this request for emergency assistance for these two beleaguered friends. To do less would not only create a dangerous imbalance in these particular arenas but would also endanger the entire structure of peace in the world.

RICHARD NIXON

The White House,
    October 19, 1973.

(59) First U.N. Cease-fire Resolution, October 22, 1973.

(a) Statement of Ambassador Scali to the Security Council, October 21, 1973.[17]

The United States, together with the U.S.S.R., has called for this meeting of the Security Council with one purpose in mind: to take

---

[16]Document 42b. For further discussion of Cambodia see Chapter 26.
[17]USUN Press Release, Oct. 21; text from *Bulletin*, vol. 69 (1973), pp. 599-600.

joint action and to present a joint proposition to the Council whose aim is to bring an immediate cease-fire-in-place and to begin promptly negotiations between the parties under appropriate auspices looking toward a just and durable peace based on the November 1967 Security Council resolution.[18]

As the members of this Council know, the tragic fighting over the past 17 days has been both furious and costly. We believe that the prolongation of the war is not in the interests of the parties or the peoples in the area and that its continuance carries grave risks for the peace of the world. Because of this, President Nixon agreed that Secretary of State Kissinger should fly to Moscow in response to an invitation of General Secretary Brezhnev. As a result of these discussions the Council has before it the resolution agreed jointly by the United States and the Soviet Governments on which both our governments request immediate action on the part of the Security Council. The resolution has already been circulated to the members of the Council.

Let me make a few brief remarks regarding the three short paragraphs of the resolution,[19] for they all stand clearly on their own words and speak for themselves.

The first paragraph calls for an immediate cease-fire. In our view as well as that of the Soviet Union, this applies not only to the parties directly concerned but also to those who have joined in the fighting by sending units. This paragraph calls for the stopping of fighting in the positions presently occupied by the two sides. We believe that 12 hours should allow ample time to achieve the practical implementation of this paragraph.

The second paragraph calls for the implementation of the Security Council resolution in all of its parts after the cease-fire. The members of this Council, as well as the parties concerned, are fully familiar with Security Council Resolution 242, and it needs no elaboration here. The paragraph is linked to paragraph 3, which calls for the immediate beginning of negotiations between the parties concerned under appropriate auspices aimed at establishing a just and durable peace in the Middle East. We believe that from the tragic events of the past 17 days there must be a new resolve, a new attempt to remove the fundamental causes that have brought war to the Middle East so frequently and so tragically. Another respite between two wars is just not good enough. And for our part, both the United States and the Soviet Union are ready to make our joint good offices available to the parties as a means to facilitate the negotiating process.

[18]Security Council Resolution 242 (1967), Nov. 22, 1967, in *Documents, 1967*, pp. 169-70.
[19]Document 59b.

Finally, I want to report to the Council that both the Soviet Union and the United States believe that there should be an immediate exchange of prisoners of war.

Mr. President,[20] we believe this is a historic moment for the Council. We believe that this Council, in exercising its primary responsibility in the field of peace and security, can make a major contribution to this end by adopting this resolution promptly.

(b) Security Council Resolution 338 (1973), adopted October 22, 1973.[21]

The Security Council

1. *Calls upon* all parties to the present fighting to cease all firing and terminate all military activity immediately, no later than 12 hours after the moment of the adoption of this decision,[22] in the positions they now occupy;

2. *Calls upon* the parties concerned to start immediately after the cease-fire the implementation of Security Council resolution 242 (1967) in all of its parts;

3. *Decides* that, immediately and concurrently with the cease-fire, negotiations shall start between the parties concerned under appropriate auspices aimed at establishing a just and durable peace in the Middle East.

(60) Second U.N. Cease-fire Resolution, October 23, 1973.

(a) Security Council Resolution 339 (1973), adopted October 23, 1973.[23]

The Security Council,

Referring to its resolution 338 (1973) of 22 October 1973,[24]

1. *Confirms* its decision on an immediate cessation of all kinds of firing and of all military action, and urges that the forces of the two sides be returned to the positions they occupied at the moment the cease-fire became effective;[25]

---

[20]Sir Laurence McIntyre of Australia served as President of the Security Council for Oct. 1973.

[21]Text from Security Council, *Official Records: 28th Year, Resolutions and Decisions 1973*, p. 10; adopted by a vote of 14-0 with China not participating.

[22]12:50 A.M., Eastern Standard Time; 0450 hours Greenwich Mean Time.

[23]Text from Security Council, *Official Records: 28th Year, Resolutions and Decisions 1973*, p. 11; adopted by a vote of 14-0 with China not participating.

[24]Document 59b.

[25]1650 hours G.M.T., Oct. 22, 1973.

2. *Requests* the Secretary-General to take measures for immediate dispatch of United Nations observers to supervise the observance of the cease-fire between the forces of Israel and the Arab Republic of Egypt, using for this purpose the personnel of the United Nations now in the Middle East and first of all the personnel now in Cairo.

(b) Statement of Ambassador Scali to the Security Council, October 23, 1973.[26]

(*Excerpt*)

*   *   *

Mr. President, the United States has joined with the Soviet Union in introducing this draft resolution before the Council because of its concern that the cease-fire ordered by the Council on October 22[27] be made fully effective at the earliest possible moment.

There have been charges from each side of violations allegedly committed by the other. It is obviously impossible at this moment to determine the accuracy of these charges. No third-party evidence from an objective source is available to us.

The resolution before us[28] confirms the Council's decision of October 22 on an immediate cessation of all kinds of firing and of all military action and urges that the forces of the two sides be returned to the positions they occupied at the moment the cease-fire became effective. The resolution also suggests that the Secretary General take measures to dispatch United Nations observers immediately to supervise the observance of the cease-fire, including personnel of the United Nations now in the Middle East and first of all those in Cairo.

We consider the central features of the resolution to be those in which the Council confirms its position for a cease-fire and in which it provides for the stationing of observers between the forces of Israel and the Arab Republic of Egypt. The former provision will put an end to bloodshed; the latter will result in the creation of a clear line of demarcation separating the forces of the two sides.

We have agreed, for reasons of principle, with the provision of the resolution urging the forces to return to the positions they oc-

[26]USUN Press Release 98, Oct. 23; text from *Bulletin*, vol. 69 (1973), pp. 600-601.
[27]Document 59b.
[28]Document 60a.

cupied when the cease-fire became effective. We put forward that principle of return to positions occupied before hostilities broke out in a statement I made in this chamber on October 8.[29] At that time the principles did not receive the support from the Council. Consistent with our argument at that time, we agree today that forces should return to the positions occupied at the time the cease-fire became effective. But we must point out that there will be great difficulty in establishing actual cease-fire lines and in fixing the positions of forces which have been maneuvering in the desert. I hope that this will not become our central preoccupation as we search for a just and durable peace.

It is important that the United Nations resume at once the function of observation of the forces of the parties. Fortunately the United Nations has in the area officers of the United Nations Truce Supervision Organization, who can proceed quickly to the cease-fire area. On the passage of this resolution, we would expect the Secretary General, through the Chief of Staff of the Truce Supervision Organization [General Ensio Siilasvuo], to put observers in place at once and to receive immediately reports from them on events in the areas of contact between the two sides. These reports would of course be transmitted to the Security Council forthwith.

Finally, Mr. President, we must look to the future. Our paramount task is to bring about a cease-fire and to halt the bloodshed. We hope, therefore, that the Security Council can give prompt consideration to the U.S.-Soviet resolution, as it has, so that the fighting may be stopped and negotiations begin, looking toward a just and lasting peace.

(61) Request for Soviet and American Forces: Statement of Ambassador Scali to the Security Council, October 24, 1973.[30]

The Security Council meets tonight, for the third time in four days, on a note of increasing urgency. In spite of two Security Council resolutions adopted without a dissenting vote,[31] calling upon the parties in the strongest terms to cease all fighting and to terminate all military activity, military operations have recurred in the zones of combat. As long as the fighting goes on, even intermittently, the parties incur increasing losses; the forces of hate and fear are strengthened; the difficulty of attaining a lasting peace deepens; and the task of reconciliation becomes more difficult.

[29]Document 57.
[30]USUN Press Release 99, Oct. 24; text from *Bulletin*, vol. 69 (1973), pp. 601-2.
[31]Documents 59b and 60a.

Tonight this Council is convened at the request of the delegation of Egypt. The distinguished Foreign Minister of Egypt [Muhammad Hasan al-Zayyat] has suggested the Security Council invite the Soviet Union and the United States to send forces to the area to supervise the implementation of the cease-fire on the part of Israel and to insure its effectiveness.

At the same time the Council is confronted by claims from the Israeli side that Egyptian forces failed to abide by the cease-fire and are accordingly responsible for the fact that hostilities have recurred.

Let me say again, as I said yesterday,[32] that it remains impossible to determine the accuracy of these contradictory charges. Until the impartial observers of the United Nations Truce Supervision Organization can reach their posts in the areas of contact and can report to the Chief of Staff of the Organization, we will be unable to assess with certainty these conflicting claims.

Accordingly, the United States believes that the Council has before it two urgent tasks. First, it must impress upon the parties with renewed vigor that each of them must comply immediately and fully with the cease-fire resolutions we have adopted. Second, it should urge and encourage the Secretary General and the Chief of Staff of the U.N. Truce Supervision Organization to move as promptly as possible to place additional observers on the spot.

Mr. President, the distinguished Foreign Minister of Egypt has suggested that the United States send armed forces to the area of fighting in order to supervise implementation of the cease-fire. In the view of the United States, this is not a time in which involvement by the great powers through the dispatch of their armed forces could be helpful in creating conditions of peace. Our objective in the Middle East has not been to produce a military confrontation but rather to encourage restraint and caution on both sides.

The United States remains committed to Resolution 338 and Resolution 339 of this Council, in all their parts. We believe that the parties, with the assistance of the United Nations observers, can and will bring the fighting to an end. For our part, I can state that we have been in active and serious consultation with the Government of Israel to impress upon it the urgency of absolute adherence to the Security Council's cease-fire resolutions. We will continue to make these representations as required.

We also agree, as I said yesterday, that the forces of the parties should return to the positions they occupied when the cease-fire became effective. Mr. Malik, I believe, knows that we have exerted

[32]Document 60b.

all of our efforts to put the cease-fire into effect, to translate it from a careful, balanced appeal to a reality which will end the killing. In keeping with the understanding that Secretary Kissinger negotiated with the Soviet leaders in Moscow, in a spirit of friendship, as part of our efforts to improve relations on a broad front with the Soviet Union, we have done our part to carry out this agreement—calmly and without seeking to extract propaganda advantage. But this, Mr. President, cannot be done merely by snapping our fingers. In a highly emotional state of affairs, in time of war, it is not easy. As a matter of principle, the United States believes today, as it made clear in my statement of October 8,[33] that return to positions held before hostilities broke out is the preferred means of opening the way to genuine reconciliation.

We will continue to support this principle. But it can only be applied in the context of agreement as to the geographical and physical facts. Until actual cease-fire lines are demarcated and it becomes clear where the opposing forces were stationed at a given moment in time, there can be no agreed basis for firm truce lines. This emphasizes still further the need for completing the organization and placement of the Truce Supervision force and for insuring that the Council and the parties are fully informed of developments and the military commanders of the two sides instructed in compelling terms to stop the fighting.

(62) Significance of the Military Alert: News conference comments by Secretary Kissinger, October 25, 1973.[34]

(Excerpts)

Secretary Kissinger: Ladies and gentlemen, I thought the most useful introduction to your questions would be a summary of events between October 6 and today so that you can evaluate our actions, the situation in which we find ourselves, and our future course.

The crisis for us started at 6 a.m. on October 6, when I was awakened with the information that another Arab-Israeli war was in progress. I mention this personal detail because it answers the question that the United States intervention prevented Israel from taking preemptive action. The United States made no demarche to either side before October 6, because all the intelligence at our

---

[33]Document 57.
[34]Department of State Press Release 390, Oct. 25; text from *Bulletin*, vol. 69 (1973), pp. 585-8.

disposal and all the intelligence given to us by foreign countries suggested that there was no possibility of the outbreak of a war. We had no reason to give any advice to any of the participants, because we did not believe—nor, may I say, did the Israeli Government—that an attack was imminent.

In the three hours between 6 a.m. and 9 a.m., we made major efforts to prevent the outbreak of the war by acting as an intermediary between the parties, of assuring each of them that the other one was—attempting to obtain the assurance of each side that the other one had no aggressive intention.

Before this process could be completed, however, war had broken out. And it started the process in which we are still engaged.

I do not think any useful purpose is served in reviewing every individual diplomatic move, but I thought it would be useful to indicate some of the basic principles we attempted to follow.

Throughout the crisis the President was convinced that we had two major problems: first, to end hostilities as quickly as possible—but, secondly, to end hostilities in a manner that would enable us to make a major contribution to removing the conditions that have produced four wars between Arabs and Israelis in the last 25 years.

We were aware that there were many interested parties. There were, of course, the participants in the conflict—Egypt and Syria on the Arab side, aided by many other Arab countries; Israel on the other. There was the Soviet Union. There were the other permanent members of the Security Council. And, of course, there was the United States.

It was our view that the United States could be most effective in both the tasks outlined by the President—that is, of ending hostilities, as well as of making a contribution to a permanent peace in the Middle East—if we conducted ourselves so that we could remain in permanent contact with all of these elements in the equation.

Throughout the first week, we attempted to crystallize a consensus in the Security Council which would bring about a cease-fire on terms that the world community could support. We stated our basic principles on October 8.[35] We did not submit them to a formal vote, because we realized that no majority was available and we did not want sides to be chosen prematurely. On October 10 the Soviet Union began an airlift, which began fairly moderately but which by October 12 had achieved fairly substantial levels.

Let me say a word here about our relationship with the Soviet Union throughout this crisis and what we have attempted to

[35]Document 57.

achieve. The United States and the Soviet Union are, of course, ideological and, to some extent, political adversaries. But the United States and the Soviet Union also have a very special responsibility. We possess—each of us—nuclear arsenals capable of annihilating humanity. We—both of us—have a special duty to see to it that confrontations are kept within bounds that do not threaten civilized life. Both of us, sooner or later, will have to come to realize that the issues that divide the world today, and foreseeable issues, do not justify the unparalleled catastrophe that a nuclear war would represent. And therefore, in all our dealings with the Soviet Union, we have attempted to keep in mind and we have attempted to move them to a position in which this overriding interest that humanity shares with us is never lost sight of.

In a speech—Pacem in Terris[36]—I pointed out that there are limits beyond which we cannot go. I stated that we will oppose the attempt by any country to achieve a position of predominance, either globally or regionally; that we would resist any attempt to exploit a policy of détente to weaken our alliances; and that we would react if the relaxations of tensions were used as a cover to exacerbate conflicts in international trouble spots. We have followed these principles in the current situation.

It is easy to start confrontations, but in this age we have to know where we will be at the end and not only what pose to strike at the beginning.

Throughout the first week we attempted to bring about a moderation in the level of outside supplies that were introduced into the area and we attempted to work with the Soviet Union on a cease-fire resolution which would bring an end to the conflict.

This first attempt failed, on Saturday, October 13, for a variety of reasons—including, perhaps, a misassessment of the military situation by some of the participants. We were then faced with the inability to produce a Security Council resolution that would command a consensus, and the substantial introduction of arms by an outside power into the area. At this point, on Saturday, October 13, the President decided that the United States would have to start a resupply effort of its own. And the United States, from that time on, has engaged in maintaining the military balance in the Middle East in order to bring about a negotiated settlement that we had sought.

Concurrently with this, we informed the Soviet Union that our interest in working out an acceptable solution still remained very strong and that as part of this solution we were prepared to discuss a mutual limitation of arms supply into the area.

[36]Document 56.

In the days that followed, the Soviet Union and we discussed various approaches to this question, the basic difficulty being how to reconcile the Arab insistence on an immediate commitment to a return to the 1967 borders with Israeli insistence on secure boundaries and a negotiated outcome.

As you all know, on October 16, Prime Minister Kosygin went to Cairo to work on this problem with the leaders of Egypt. He returned to the Soviet Union on October 19.

We began exploring a new formula for ending the war that evening, though it was still unacceptable to us. And while we were still considering that formula, General Secretary Brezhnev sent an urgent request to President Nixon that I be sent to Moscow to conduct the negotiations in order to speed an end to hostilities that might be difficult to contain were they to continue.

The President agreed to Mr. Brezhnev's request, and as all of you know, I left for Moscow in the early morning of October 20.

We spent two days of very intense negotiations, and we developed a formula which we believe was acceptable to all of the parties and which we continue to believe represented a just solution to this tragic conflict.

The Security Council resolution[37] had, as you all know, three parts. It called for an immediate cease-fire-in-place. It called for the immediate implementation of Security Council Resolution 242, which was adopted in November 1967 and which states certain general principles on the basis of which peace should be achieved in the Middle East. And, thirdly, it called for negotiations between the parties concerned under appropriate auspices to bring about a just and durable peace in the Middle East.

This third point was the first international commitment to negotiations between the parties in the Middle East conflict. The United States and the Soviet Union were prepared to offer their auspices, if this proved to be acceptable to the parties, to bring about and then to speed the process of negotiations. The United States continues to be ready to carry out this understanding. This, then, was the situation when I returned from Moscow and Tel Aviv on Monday evening [October 22].

Since then, events have taken the following turn. On the first day—that is, Tuesday—of the implementation of the cease-fire, there was a breakdown of the cease-fire which led to certain Israeli territorial gains. The United States supported a resolution[38] which called on the participants to observe the cease-fire, to return to the places from which the fighting started, and to invite United Nations

[37]Document 59b.
[38]Document 60a.

observers to observe the implementation of the cease-fire. This seemed to us a fair resolution.

In the last two days, the discussion in the Security Council and the communications that have been associated with it have taken a turn that seemed to us worrisome. We were increasingly confronted with a cascade of charges which were difficult to verify in the absence of United Nations observers and a demand for action that it was not within our power to take. There was a proposal, for example, that joint U.S. and Soviet military forces be introduced into the Middle East to bring about an observance of the cease-fire.

I would like to state on behalf of the President the United States position on this matter very clearly. The United States does not favor and will not approve the sending of a joint Soviet-United States force into the Middle East. The United States believes that what is needed in the Middle East above all is a determination of the facts, a determination where the lines are, and a determination of who is doing the shooting, so that the Security Council can take appropriate action. It is inconceivable that the forces of the great powers should be introduced in the numbers that would be necessary to overpower both of the participants. It is inconceivable that we should transplant the great-power rivalry into the Middle East or, alternatively, that we should impose a military condominium by the United States and the Soviet Union. The United States is even more opposed to the unilateral introduction by any great power, especially by any nuclear power, of military forces into the Middle East in whatever guise those forces should be introduced. And it is the ambiguity of some of the actions and communications and certain readiness measures that were observed that caused the President at a special meeting of the National Security Council last night, at 3 a.m., to order certain precautionary measures to be taken by the United States.

The United States position with respect to peace in the Middle East is as follows: The United States stands for a strict observance of the cease-fire as defined in the United Nations Security Council Resolution 338, adopted on October 22.[39] The United States will support and give all assistance and is willing to supply some personnel to a United Nations observer force whose responsibility it is to report to the Security Council about the violations of the cease-fire and which would have the responsibility, in addition, of aiding the parties in taking care of humanitarian and other concerns that are produced by the fact that on the Egyptian-Israeli front a series of enclaves exist in which demarcation is extremely difficult.

If the Security Council wishes, the United States is prepared to

[39]Document 59b.

agree to an international force, provided it does not include any participants from the permanent members of the Security Council, to be introduced into the area as an additional guarantee of the cease-fire.

The United States is prepared to make a major effort to help speed a political solution which is just to all sides.

The United States recognizes that the conditions that produced the war on October 6 cannot be permitted to continue, and the United States, both bilaterally and unilaterally, is prepared to lend its diplomatic weight to a serious effort in the negotiating process foreseen by paragraph 3 of Security Council Resolution 338.

We are therefore at a rather crucial point.

From many points of view, the chances for peace in the Middle East are quite promising.

Israel has experienced once more the trauma of war and has been given an opportunity for the negotiations it has sought for all of its existence, and it must be ready for the just and durable peace that the Security Council asks for.

The Arab nations have demonstrated their concern and have received international assurances that other countries will take an interest in these negotiations.

The Soviet Union is not threatened in any of its legitimate positions in the Middle East. The principles I mentioned earlier of the special responsibility of the great nuclear powers to strike a balance between their local interests and their global interest and their humane obligations remain.

And, seen in this perspective, none of the issues that are involved in the observance of the cease-fire would warrant unilateral action.

As for the United States, the President has stated repeatedly that this administration has no higher goal than to leave to its successors a world that is safer and more secure than the one we found. It is an obligation that any President, of whatever party, will have to discharge, and it is a responsibility which must be solved—if mankind is to survive—by the great nuclear countries at some point, before it is too late.

But we have always stated that it must be a peace with justice. The terms that have been agreed to in the United Nations provide an opportunity for the peoples of the Middle East to determine their own fate in consultation and negotiation—for the first time in 25 years.

This is an opportunity we are prepared to foster. It is an opportunity which is essential for this ravaged area and which is equally essential for the peace of the world. And it is an opportunity that the great powers have no right to be permitted to miss.

Now I'll be glad to answer questions.[40]

(63) Third U.N. Cease-fire Resolution, October 25, 1973.

(a) Statement of Ambassador Scali to the Security Council, October 25, 1973.[41]

The United States supports the eight-power resolution presented to this Council last night[42] as amended this morning.[43]

We have from the first advocated an immediate cease-fire at the positions occupied when Security Council Resolution 338[44] came into effect at 1650 GMT on October 22.

We agree on the need to increase the number of observers of the United Nations Truce Supervision Organization immediately.

We approve of the establishment of a new United Nations Emergency Force to be composed of personnel from member states except those of the permanent members of the Security Council. We will seek to be helpful in facilitating the transportation of this Force to the area.

We trust that the Secretary General will proceed with the utmost despatch to carry out the functions entrusted to him under the resolution.

Mr. President, we believe that the resolution now before us will, if faithfully implemented by all concerned, result in the prompt and effective establishment of a true cease-fire in the Middle East. Nothing could be more important as a step toward peace. We urge the Security Council to adopt this resolution as a matter of highest priority.

(b) Security Council Resolution 340 (1973), adopted October 25, 1973.[45]

The Security Council,
Recalling its resolutions 338 (1973) of 22 October and 339 (1973) of 23 October 1973.[46]

---

[40]For the remainder of the news conference see *Bulletin, loc. cit.,* pp. 588-94. (Certain passages are quoted above at note 12.)

[41]USUN Press Release 101, Oct. 25; text from *Bulletin,* vol. 69 (1973), pp. 602-3.

[42]U.N. document S/11046, Oct. 24, in Security Council, *Official Records: 28th Year, Supplement for Oct., Nov. and Dec. '973,* p. 88.

[43]U.N. document S/11046/Rev. 1, Oct. 25, identical with Document 63b.

[44]Document 59b.

[45]Text from Security Council, *Official Records: 28th Year, Resolutions and Decisions 1973,* p. 11; adopted by a vote of 14-0 with China not participating.

[46]Documents 59b and 60a.

Noting with regret the reported repeated violations of the cease-fire in non-compliance with resolutions 338 (1973) and 339 (1973),

Noting with concern from the Secretary-General's report[47] that the United Nations military observers have not yet been enabled to place themselves on both sides of the cease-fire line,

1. *Demands* that immediate and complete cease-fire be observed and that the parties return to the positions occupied by them at 1650 hours GMT on 22 October 1973;

2. *Requests* the Secretary-General, as an immediate step, to increase the number of United Nations military observers on both sides;

3. *Decides* to set up immediately, under its authority, a United Nations Emergency Force to be composed of personnel drawn from States Members of the United Nations except the permanent members of the Security Council, and requests the Secretary-General to report within 24 hours on the steps taken to this effect;[48]

4. *Requests* the Secretary-General to report to the Council on an urgent and continuing basis on the state of implementation of the present resolution, as well as resolutions 338 (1973) and 339 (1973);

5. *Requests* all Member States to extend their full co-operation to the United Nations in the implementation of the present resolution, as well as resolutions 338 (1973) and 339 (1973).

(64) Views of President Nixon: News conference statement, October 26, 1973.[49]

THE PRESIDENT. Ladies and gentlemen, before going to your questions, I have a statement with regard to the Mideast which I think will anticipate some of the questions, because this will update the information which is breaking rather fast in that area, as you know, for the past 2 days.

The cease-fire is holding. There have been some violations, but generally speaking it can be said that it is holding at this time. As you know, as a result of the U.N. resolution which was agreed to yesterday by a vote of 14 to 0,[50] a peacekeeping force will go to the Mideast, and this force, however, will not include any forces from the major powers, including, of course, the United States and the Soviet Union.

The question, however, has arisen as to whether observers from

---

[47]U.N. document S/7930/Add. 2219, Oct. 24, in Security Council, *Official Records: Supplement for Oct., Nov. and Dec. 1973*, pp. 52-3.
[48]Cf. Document 65a.
[49]Text from *Presidential Documents*, vol. 9 (1973), pp. 1287-9.
[50]Document 63b.

major powers could go to the Mideast. My up-to-the-minute report on that, and I just talked to Dr. Kissinger 5 minutes before coming down, is this: We will send observers to the Mideast if requested by the Secretary General of the United Nations, and we have reason to expect that we will receive such a request.

With regard to the peacekeeping force, I think it is important for all of you ladies and gentlemen, and particularly for those listening on radio and television, to know why the United States has insisted that major powers not be part of the peacekeeping force, and that major powers not introduce military forces into the Mideast. A very significant and potentially explosive crisis developed on Wednesday of this week [October 24]. We obtained information which led us to believe that the Soviet Union was planning to send a very substantial force into the Mideast, a military force.

When I received that information, I ordered, shortly after midnight on Thursday morning, an alert for all American forces around the world. This was a precautionary alert. The purpose of that was to indicate to the Soviet Union that we could not accept any unilateral move on their part to move military forces into the Mideast. At the same time, in the early morning hours, I also proceeded on the diplomatic front. In a message to Mr. Brezhnev, an urgent message, I indicated to him our reasoning, and I urged that we not proceed along that course, and that, instead, that we join in the United Nations in supporting a resolution which would exclude any major powers from participating in a peacekeeping force.

As a result of that communication, and the return that I received from Mr. Brezhnev—we had several exchanges, I should say—we reached the conclusion that we would jointly support the resolution which was adopted in the United Nations.

We now come, of course, to the critical time in terms of the future of the Mideast. And here, the outlook is far more hopeful than what we have been through this past week. I think I could safely say that the chances for not just a cease-fire—which we presently have and which, of course, we have had in the Mideast for some time—but the outlook for a permanent peace is the best that it has been in 20 years.

The reason for this is that the two major powers, the Soviet Union and the United States, have agreed—this was one of the results of Dr. Kissinger's trip to Moscow—have agreed that we would participate in trying to expedite the talks between the parties involved. That does not mean that the two major powers will impose a settlement. It does mean, however, that we will use our influence with the nations in the area to expedite a settlement.

The reason we feel this is important is that first, from the standpoint of the nations in the Mideast, none of them, Israel, Egypt, Syria, none of them can or should go through the agony of another war.

The losses in this war on both sides have been very, very high. And the tragedy must not occur again. There have been four of these wars, as you ladies and gentlemen know, over the past 20 years. But beyond that, it is vitally important to the peace of the world that this potential trouble-spot, which is really one of the most potentially explosive areas in the world, that it not become an area in which the major powers come together in confrontation.

What the developments of this week should indicate to all of us is that the United States and the Soviet Union, who admittedly have very different objectives in the Mideast, have now agreed that it is not in their interest to have a confrontation there, a confrontation which might lead to a nuclear confrontation and neither of the two major powers wants that.

We have agreed, also, that if we are to avoid that, it is necessary for us to use our influence more than we have in the past, to get the negotiating track moving again, but this time, moving to a conclusion—not simply a temporary truce, but a permanent peace.

I do not mean to suggest that it is going to come quickly because the parties involved are still rather far apart. But I do say that now there are greater incentives within the area to find a peaceful solution, and there are enormous incentives as far as the United States is concerned, and the Soviet Union and other major powers, to find such a solution.

Turning now to the subject of our attempts to get a cease-fire on the home front, that is a bit more difficult.[51]

* * *

(65) Establishment of the U.N. Emergency Force (UNEF), October 27, 1973.

(a) Plans for the Force: Report of Secretary-General Kurt Waldheim to the Security Council, October 27, 1973.[52]

Report of the Secretary-General on the implementation of Security Council resolution 340 (1973)

[*Original: English*]
[*27 October 1973*]

---

[51]For the remainder of the news conference see *Presidential Documents, loc. cit.*, pp. 1289-94; excerpts appear also in *Bulletin*, vol. 69 (1973), pp. 582-4. (Certain passages are quoted above at note 11.)
[52]U.N. document S/11052/Rev.1, Oct. 27, in Security Council, *Official Records: 28th Year, Supplement for Oct., Nov. and Dec. 1973*, pp. 91-2.

1. The present report is submitted in pursuance of Security Council resolution 340 (1973) of 25 October 1973[53] in which the Council, among other things, decided to set up immediately a United Nations Emergency Force under its authority and requested the Secretary-General to report within 24 hours on the steps taken to this effect.

Terms of reference

2. (a) The Force will supervise the implementation of paragraph 1 of resolution 340 (1973), which reads as follows:

"1. *Demands* that immediate and complete cease-fire be observed and that the parties return to the positions occupied by them at 1650 hours GMT on 22 October 1973."

(b) The Force will use its best efforts to prevent a recurrence of the fighting, and co-operate with the International Committee of the Red Cross in its humanitarian endeavours in the area.

(c) In the fulfilment of its tasks, the Force will have the co-operation of the military observers of UNTSO [U.N. Truce Supervision Organization].

General considerations

3. Three essential conditions must be met for the Force to be effective. Firstly, it must at all times have the full confidence and backing of the Security Council. Secondly, it must operate with the full co-operation of the parties concerned. Thirdly, it must be able to function as an integrated and efficient military unit.

4. Having in mind past experience, I would suggest the following guidelines for the proposed Force:

(a) The Force will be under the command of the United Nations, vested in the Secretary-General, under the authority of the Security Council. The command in the field will be exercised by a Force Commander appointed by the Secretary-General with the consent of the Security Council. The Commander will be responsible to the Secretary-General.

The Secretary-General shall keep the Security Council fully informed of developments relating to the functioning of the Force. All matters which may affect the nature or the continued effective functioning of the Force will be referred to the Council for its decision.

(b) The Force must enjoy the freedom of movement and communication and other facilities that are necessary for the performance of its tasks. The Force and its personnel should be granted all relevant privileges and immunities provided for by the Convention on the Privileges and Immunities of the United Nations.[54] The Force should operate at all times separately from the armed forces of the parties concerned. Consequently separate quarters and, wherever desirable and feasible, buffer zones will have to be arranged with the co-operation of the parties. Appropriate agreements on the Status of the Force will have to be concluded with the parties to cover the above requirements.

(c) The Force will be composed of a number of contingents to be provided by selected countries, upon the request of the Secretary-General. The contingents will be selected in consultation with the Security Council and with the parties concerned, bearing in mind the accepted principle of equitable geographic representation.

(d) The Force will be provided with weapons of a defensive character only. It shall not use force except in self-defence. Self-defence would include resistance to attempts by forceful means to prevent it from discharging its duties under the mandate of the Security Council. The Force will proceed on the assumption that the parties to the conflict will take all the necessary steps for compliance with the decisions of the Security Council.

(e) In performing its functions, the Force will act with complete impartiality and will avoid actions which could prejudice the rights, claims or positions of the parties concerned which in no way affect the implementation of paragraph 1 of resolution 340 (1973) and paragraph 1 of resolution 339 (1973).[55]

(f) The supporting personnel of the Force will be provided as a rule by the Secretary-General from among existing United Nations staff. Those personnel will, of course, follow the Staff Rules and Regulations of the United Nations Secretariat.

Proposed plan of action

5. If the Security Council is in agreement with the principles outlined above, I intend to take the following urgent steps:

(a) I propose, with the consent of the Security Council, to appoint the Commander of the Emergency Force as soon as possible. Pending the Commander's arrival in the mission area, with the consent of the Council given at its meeting of 25 October 1973 [*1750th*

---

[54]Done at New York Feb. 13, 1946 and entered into force for the U.S. Apr. 29, 1970 (TIAS 6900; 21 UST 1418).
[55]Respectively Documents 63b and 60a.

meeting], I have appointed the Chief of Staff of UNTSO, Major-General E. Siilasvuo, as interim Commander of the Emergency Force, and have asked him to set up a provisional headquarters staff consisting of personnel from UNTSO.

(*b*) In order that the Force may fulfil the responsibilities entrusted to it, it is considered necessary that it have a total strength in the order of 7,000.

(*c*) The Force would initially be stationed in the area for a period of six months.

(*d*) In my letter of 25 October to the President of the Security Council [*S/11049*], I proposed, as an urgent interim measure and in order that the Emergency Force may reach the area as soon as possible, to arrange for the contingents of Austria, Finland and Sweden now serving with the United Nations Peacekeeping Force in Cyprus (UNFICYP) to proceed immediately to Egypt. I am at present actively engaged in the necessary consultations, bearing in mind the considerations in paragraph 4 (*c*) above, with a view to making requests to a number of other Governments to provide contingents of suitable size for the Force at the earliest possible time. As the Members of the Council are aware, this is a complex matter in which a number of factors have to be taken into account. I shall report further to the Council as soon as possible.

(*e*) In addition to the countries requested to provide contingents for the Force, I propose to request logistic support as necessary from a number of other countries, which may include the permanent members of the Security Council.

Estimated cost and method of financing

6. At the present time there are many unknown factors. The best possible preliminary estimate based upon past experience and practice is approximately $30,000,000 for a Force of 7,000, all ranks, for a period of six months.

7. The cost of the Force shall be considered as expenses of the Organization to be borne by the Members in accordance with Article 17, paragraph 2, of the Charter.

(b) Security Council Resolution 341 (1973), adopted October 27, 1973.[56]

The Security Council

1. *Approves* the report of the Secretary-General on the im-

[56]Text from Security Council, *Official Records: 28th Year, Resolutions and Decisions 1973*, p. 11; adopted by a vote of 14-0 with China not participating.

plementation of Security Council resolution 340 (1973) contained in document S/11052/Rev.1 dated 27 October 1973;[57]

2. *Decides* that the Force shall be established in accordance with the above-mentioned report for an initial period of six months, and that it shall continue in operation thereafter, if required, provided the Security Council so decides.

(c) *Statement of Ambassador Scali to the Council, October 27, 1973.*[58]

The United States welcomes with great satisfaction the action of the Council in approving the Secretary General's report.[59] We have demonstrated that indeed this organ can act effectively to fulfill its responsibilities for the maintenance of international peace and security.

But even as we rejoice in our agreement it is important to recognize the difficult task confronting the Emergency Force. Supervising cease-fire lines in an area in the wake of war will not be easy. The Force from its inception will require the full cooperation of the parties concerned—as the Secretary General's report states. In addition, it must operate as an integrated military unit with efficiency and with special privileges for none.

We consider the language of the report carefully drawn. For instance, the statement "All matters which may affect the nature or the continued effective functioning of the Force will be referred to the Council for its decision" assures an orderly, agreed withdrawal of the Force, but only when the Council so decides. We are also satisfied that the phrase "bearing in mind the accepted principle of equitable geographic distribution" is consistent with article 101 of the charter and assures that all of the obvious and necessary criteria will be given appropriate consideration in the composition of the Force.

Looking to the future, we hope that the Secretary General can move as swiftly as possible to implement the resolution we have just approved. The United States, as I said in my statement of October 25,[60] is prepared to consider requests for assistance to this end.

Finally, Mr. President, I would like to express my personal satisfaction that my government has helped to arrange for a meeting on the ground of Egyptian and Israeli military representatives under U.N. auspices to discuss the practical application of the

[57]Document 65a.
[58]USUN Press Release 104, Oct. 17; text from *Bulletin*, vol. 69 (1973), pp. 603-4.
[59]Documents 65a and 65b.
[60]Document 63a.

cease-fire.[61] This is a significant practical result of the thorough deliberations in this chamber. I regard it as especially noteworthy that arrangements are now being made to provide nonmilitary supplies for the 3d Army area. For us the humanitarian aspect of the U.N. effort is a critically important element in this peacekeeping mission.

Mr. President, may I once again express my delegation's firm support for this constructive action of the Council. The future will record this as a historic moment in the annals of the United Nations if we can maintain the momentum generated here and move on to a peaceful, durable settlement.

(66) Further Action by the Security Council, November 1-2, 1973.

(a) Statement by Security Council President Peter Jankowitsch of Austria, November 2, 1973.[62]

At the 1754th meeting, on 2 November 1973, the President of the Council made the following statement representing the agreement of the members of the Council:

"United Nations Emergency Force (Security Council resolution 340 (1973) of 25 October 1973):[63] implementation—second phase

"1. The members of the Security Council met for informal consultations on the morning of 1 November 1973 and heard a report from the Secretary-General on the progress so far made in the implementation of Security Council resolution 340 (1973).

"2. After a lengthy and detailed exchange of views it was agreed that in regard to the next stage of implementation of resolution 340 (1973):

"(a) The Secretary-General will immediately consult, to begin with, Ghana (from the African regional group), Indonesia and Nepal (from the Asian regional group), Panama and Peru (from the Latin American regional group), Poland (from the Eastern European regional group) and Canada (from the Western European and other States group), the latter two with particular responsibility for logistic support,

---

[61]Cf. Chapter 25.

[62]Text from Security Council, *Official Records: 28th Year, Resolutions and Decisions 1973*, p. 12. Under the principle of rotation, Austria held the presidency of the Security Council for the month of Nov. 1973.

[63]Document 63b.

with a view to dispatching contingents to the Middle East pursuant to Security Council resolution 340 (1973). The Secretary-General will dispatch troops to the area from these countries as soon as the necessary consultations have been completed. The Council members agreed that at least three African countries are expected to send contingents to the Middle East. The present decision of the Council is intended to bring about a better geographical distribution of the United Nations Emergency Force.

"(b) The Secretary-General will regularly report to the Council on the results of his efforts undertaken pursuant to sub-paragraph (a) so that the question of balanced geographical distribution in the force can be reviewed.

"3. The above-mentioned agreement was reached by members of the Council with the exception of the People's Republic of China which dissociates itself from it."

(b) Statement of Ambassador Scali to the Council, November 2, 1973.[64]

My delegation is deeply gratified that the Council has reached agreement on important steps to be taken in implementation of Security Council Resolution 340.

In the lengthy consultations that have led to this result, my delegation has held firmly to the view that our first responsibility has been to create an effective UNEF.

Of course, my government fully believes in a broadly based geographic representation in the peacekeeping force. But I am confident that no member would disagree that it must be consistent with the overriding importance of having an effective force. We must remember that we now enter the phase of practical operations. We are dispatching the forces of several nations into lines which only a few days ago were battlefields. Three armies have fought in harsh conflict in this area. The lines are tenuous and uncertain in many places. The situation remains tense and dangerous. The unforeseen can easily happen. It is critically important that we have an integrated, harmonious, and impartial force which can efficiently carry out its duties. To do less is to betray the trust of those countries which have generously offered their young men for this delicate and dangerous task. We wish them well in their mission. Our plan is perhaps less than perfect. We shall be trying to improve it in the days ahead.

For the present, we can take satisfaction that this Council has worked tirelessly and constructively to fulfill in this instance one of its highest responsibilities under the Charter—that of peacekeeping.

We can only hope that our efforts will make possible a further success—the creation of a just and durable peace in the Middle East.[65]

[65]See further Chapter 25.

23. RESTRICTING PRESIDENTIAL WAR POWERS

The sensational events that centered in the military alert of October 25 did nothing to dampen the resolve of those in Congress who believed the time had come for definite restrictions on the President's authority to order the Armed Forces into combat on his own initiative. Admittedly, the current Arab-Israeli crisis was not the kind of situation to which the various legislative proposals dealing with the "war powers" question had been primarily addressed. Aside from a general interest in improving the constitutional balance between executive and legislature in the conduct of foreign affairs, the principal concern of most members of Congress had been to forestall new military engagements analogous to the one in Vietnam. By the autumn of 1973, however, the growing frequency of swift and sudden presidential actions in various areas of national affairs—the "Saturday night massacre" and the Wednesday night alert, to cite two examples occurring within a single week—appeared to many of the President's critics to increase the urgency of some restraint upon the exercise of his military prerogatives as Commander-in-Chief.

By coincidence, it was only a few hours before the October 25 alert that President Nixon had invoked his veto power in an unsuccessful attempt to prevent the enactment of the first serious war powers legislation to have won the approval of both houses of Congress. Although attempts to draft such a measure had been gathering momentum ever since the incursion of U.S. forces into Cambodia early in 1970, the zeal displayed by a bipartisan group of Senators, led by Republican Senator Jacob K. Javits of New York and supported by a majority of the upper house, had failed thus far to evoke a corresponding echo in the more cautious House of Representatives. In 1972, the Senate had adopted by a 68 to 16 vote a war powers bill which set a 30-day limit on any emergency use of the Armed Forces by the President in the absence of a declaration of war or specific authorization by the Congress. The House, however, had declined to go beyond an earlier resolution, drafted by Democratic Representative Clement J. Zablocki of Wisconsin, which merely called on the President to consult with Congress and submit a written report in the event of any significant military action undertaken without prior congressional authorization.[1]

By 1973, however, congressional attitudes were evolving rapidly under the influence of such developments as the gradual disintegration of the Vietnam peace settlement, the continued fighting in Cambodia, and the revelation of the secret bombing carried out in that country earlier in the war. In June, as previously noted, the Congress managed to impose an August 15 deadline for the cessation of all U.S. combat activities in Indochina.[2] In July, both houses enacted different versions of a general war powers bill (House Joint Resolution 542) that for the first time incorporated real restraints on the presidential war-making power. The House version, approved on July 18 by a vote of 244 to 170, imposed a still rather generous 120-day time limit on the commitment of U.S. troops to combat abroad in the absence of prior approval by the Congress. The Senate, in contrast, reaffirmed on July 20 its preference for a more stringent 30-day limit, approving the restriction by a vote of 70 to 18 that was more than enough to override a presidential veto.

The task of reconciling these divergent positions was undertaken by a Senate-House conference committee, which eventually agreed to a compromise 60-day limit on the use of troops in hostilities or near-hostilities in the absence of a declaration of war or other specific authorization from the Congress. Reported to the two houses on October 4—two days before the outbreak of war in the Middle East—the conference version of the War Powers Resolution (**Document 67**) also allowed for a subsequent 30-day extension, on written notification to the Congress of "unavoidable military necessity" respecting the safety of U.S. Armed Forces. On the other hand, it also left open the possibility of earlier termination by the Congress itself through passage of a concurrent resolution, which would require no presidential signature. The conference report setting forth this compromise was accepted by a Senate vote of 75 to 20 on October 10—the day of Vice-President Agnew's resignation—and by a House vote of 238 to 123 on October 12.[3]

Administration spokesmen had never concealed their disapproval of such legislative experiments. An earlier version of the Senate bill had been described by Secretary Rogers as "un-

---

[1]For background cf. *AFR, 1971*, pp. 17-41; same, *1972*, pp. 16-21.
[2]Cf. Document 41.
[3]Details in *Senate Foreign Relations Committee History, 1973-4*, pp. 114-17.

constitutional and unwise"; and a State Department spokesman used similar language in characterizing the bills before the Congress in 1973.[4] Thus no one was surprised when President Nixon, emerging briefly from his preoccupation with Watergate and the Middle East, returned the War Powers Resolution to the House of Representatives on October 24 with an energetic veto message (**Document 68**) in which he asserted that the proposed restrictions on presidential authority were "both unconstitutional and dangerous to the best interests of our Nation." Not only would the proposed legislation "attempt to take away, by a mere legislative act, authorities which the President has properly exercised under the Constitution for almost 200 years," Mr. Nixon argued. It "would seriously undermine this Nation's ability to act decisively and convincingly in times of international crisis," thus perhaps diminishing the confidence of allies and the respect of adversaries as well as injecting a "permanent and substantial element of unpredictability . . . into the world's assessment of American behavior."

In what might have been a reference to his administration's efforts in the current Middle East crisis, Mr. Nixon further asserted that the proposed measure would "strike from the President's hand a wide range of important peace-keeping tools by eliminating his ability to exercise quiet diplomacy backed by subtle shifts in our military deployments." A better approach to executive-legislative cooperation in foreign affairs, he suggested in closing, could be initiated with a "careful and dispassionate study" by a qualified commission.

The Middle East crisis, which reached its climax within hours of the presidential message, had partially subsided by the time Congress was ready to address itself to the situation created by the presidential veto. But though the immediate fear of conflict had abated, the crisis had left new grounds for uneasiness about the state of the national foreign relations—deep fissures in the Atlantic alliance, an interruption of Middle East oil shipments, and a dawning realization that the United States, in President Nixon's words, was "heading toward the most acute shortages of energy since World War II."[5] Mr. Nixon's personal position had also suffered fresh damage, in no way lessened by the displays of personal petulance that marked his October 26 news conference.[6] A decision to yield disputed tapes and documents to Judge Sirica, and to appoint a new special prosecutor, Leon Jaworski, to succeed the

---

[4]The administration position is set forth at length in *AFR, 1971*, pp. 35-41, and in *Bulletin*, vol. 69 (1973), pp. 434-9.

[5]Document 73.

[6]Cf. Chapter 22 at note 13.

dismissed Archibald Cox, had failed to forestall the commencement of impeachment proceedings in the House of Representatives or to discourage demands for the President's resignation by, among others, *Time* magazine and *The New York Times*.

The dwindling of Mr. Nixon's personal ascendancy could be measured by the majorities with which both House and Senate moved to override his veto of the War Powers Resolution on November 7, the anniversary of his triumphant reelection in 1972. In the House, the vote was 284 to 135; in the Senate, it was 75 to 18. The President was "extremely disappointed," said a White House statement **(Document 70)** issued after the House vote and in obvious expectation of the parallel Senate action that would bring the resolution into force. "He feels the action seriously undermines the nation's ability to act decisively and convincingly in times of international crisis. The confidence of our allies in our ability to assist them will be diminished. . . . Our potential adversaries may be encouraged to engage in future acts of international mischief because of this blow to our deterrent posture."

Not all the critics of the War Powers Resolution were troubled by these particular objections. There were also those who contended that in imposing a 60-day limit on the President's untrammeled use of the Armed Forces, Congress had inadvertently provided him with a "blank check" for the duration of that 60-day period. (A rather similar objection would presently be raised concerning the fresh grant of authority that would necessarily accompany the pending $2.2 billion in security assistance for Israel. Since less than half of that amount would be needed to make up Israel's recent losses, the balance would constitute a fund available for use at the President's own discretion.)

Some Senators also perceived a need to try to shield the national foreign relations against the harmful impact of Watergate and related home front developments. On November 9, the Senate adopted by voice vote Senate Resolution 200, introduced by Senator Humphrey and 29 cosponsors, in which was expressed the sense of the Senate that other nations should not consider domestic events to be adversely affecting the American resolve to uphold vital U.S. national interests, nor be tempted to seize upon such events as an opportunity to undermine the security of the United States. Such a reminder might prove decidedly relevant in the still perilous situation through which American diplomacy was trying to grope its way.

(67) The War Powers Resolution: House Joint Resolution 542,

93rd Congress, passed by the Senate October 10 and by the House of Representatives October 12, 1973.[7]

JOINT RESOLUTION

Concerning the war powers of Congress and the President

Resolved by the Senate and House of Representatives of the United States of America in Congress assembled,

SHORT TITLE

SECTION 1. This joint resolution may be cited as the "War Powers Resolution".

PURPOSE AND POLICY

SEC. 2. (a) It is the purpose of this joint resolution to fulfill the intent of the framers of the Constitution of the United States and insure that the collective judgment of both the Congress and the President will apply to the introduction of United States Armed Forces into hostilities, or into situations where imminent involvement in hostilities is clearly indicated by the circumstances, and to the continued use of such forces in hostilities or in such situations.

(b) Under article I, section 8, of the Constitution, it is specifically provided that the Congress shall have the power to make all laws necessary and proper for carrying into execution, not only its own powers but also all other powers vested by the Constitution in the Government of the United States, or in any department or officer thereof.

(c) The constitutional powers of the President as Commander-in-Chief to introduce United States Armed Forces into hostilities, or into situations where imminent involvement in hostilities is clearly indicated by the circumstances, are exercised only pursuant to (1) a declaration of war, (2) specific statutory authorization, or (3) a national emergency created by attack upon the United States, its territories or possessions, or its armed forces.

---

[7]Originally voted 75-20 by the Senate and 238-123 by the House, the resolution was vetoed by the President on Oct. 24 (Document 68) but repassed by both houses on Nov. 7, 1973, becoming law as Public Law 93-148 (87 Stat. 555).

CONSULTATION

SEC. 3. The President in every possible instance shall consult with Congress before introducing United States Armed Forces into hostilities or into situations where imminent involvement in hostilities is clearly indicated by the circumstances, and after every such introduction shall consult regularly with the Congress until United States Armed Forces are no longer engaged in hostilities or have been removed from such situations.

REPORTING

SEC. 4. (a) In the absence of a declaration of war, in any case in which United States Armed Forces are introduced—

(1) into hostilities or into situations where imminent involvement in hostilities is clearly indicated by the circumstances;

(2) into the territory, airspace or waters of a foreign nation, while equipped for combat, except for deployments which relate solely to supply, replacement, repair, or training of such forces; or

(3) in numbers which substantially enlarge United States Armed Forces equipped for combat already located in a foreign nation;

the President shall submit within 48 hours to the Speaker of the House of Representatives and to the President pro tempore of the Senate a report, in writing, setting forth—

(A) the circumstances necessitating the introduction of United States Armed Forces;

(B) the constitutional and legislative authority under which such introduction took place; and

(C) the estimated scope and duration of the hostilities or involvement.

(b) The President shall provide such other information as the Congress may request in the fulfillment of its constitutional responsibilities with respect to committing the Nation to war and to the use of United States Armed Forces abroad.

(c) Whenever United States Armed Forces are introduced into hostilities or into any situation described in subsection (a) of this section, the President shall, so long as such armed forces continue to be engaged in such hostilities or situation, report to the Congress periodically on the status of such hostilities or situation as well as on the scope and duration of such hostilities or situation, but in no event shall he report to the Congress less often than once every six months.

CONGRESSIONAL ACTION

SEC. 5. (a) Each report submitted pursuant to section 4(a) (1) shall be transmitted to the Speaker of the House of Representatives and to the President pro tempore of the Senate on the same calendar day. Each report so transmitted shall be referred to the Committee on Foreign Affairs of the House of Representatives and to the Committee on Foreign Relations of the Senate for appropriate action. If, when the report is transmitted, the Congress has adjourned sine die or has adjourned for any period in excess of three calendar days, the Speaker of the House of Representatives and the President pro tempore of the Senate, if they deem it advisable (or if petitioned by at least 30 percent of the membership of their respective Houses) shall jointly request the President to convene Congress in order that it may consider the report and take appropriate action pursuant to this section.

(b) Within sixty calendar days after a report is submitted or is required to be submitted pursuant to section 4(a)(1), whichever is earlier, the President shall terminate any use of United States Armed Forces with respect to which such report was submitted (or required to be submitted), unless the Congress (1) has declared war or has enacted a specific authorization for such use of United States Armed Forces, (2) has extended by law such sixty-day period, or (3) is physically unable to meet as a result of an armed attack upon the United States. Such sixty-day period shall be extended for not more than an additional thirty days if the President determines and certifies to the Congress in writing that unavoidable military necessity respecting the safety of United States Armed Forces requires the continued use of such armed forces in the course of bringing about a prompt removal of such forces.

(c) Notwithstanding subsection (b), at any time that United States Armed Forces are engaged in hostilities outside the territory of the United States, its possessions and territories without a declaration of war or specific statutory authorization, such forces shall be removed by the President if the Congress so directs by concurrent resolution.

CONGRESSIONAL PRIORITY PROCEDURES
FOR JOINT RESOLUTION OR BILL

SEC. 6. (a) Any joint resolution or bill introduced pursuant to section 5(b) at least thirty calendar days before the expiration of the sixty-day period specified in such section shall be referred to the Committee on Foreign Affairs of the House of Representatives or the Committee on Foreign Relations of the Senate, as the case may be, and such committee shall report [on] such joint resolution or bill, together with its recommendations, not later than twenty-four calendar days before the expiration of the sixty-day period specified in such section, unless such House shall otherwise determine by the yeas and nays.

(b) Any joint resolution or bill so reported shall become the pending business of the House in question (in the case of the Senate the time for debate shall be equally divided between the proponents and the opponents), and shall be voted on within three calendar days thereafter, unless such House shall otherwise determine by yeas and nays.

(c) Such a joint resolution or bill passed by one House shall be referred to the committee of the other House named in subsection (a) and shall be reported out not later than fourteen calendar days before the expiration of the sixty-day period specified in section 5(b). The joint resolution or bill so reported shall become the pending business of the House in question and shall be voted on within three calendar days after it has been reported, unless such House shall otherwise determine by yeas and nays.

(d) In the case of any disagreement between the two Houses of Congress with respect to a joint resolution or bill passed by both Houses, conferees shall be promptly appointed and the committee of conference shall make and file a report with respect to such resolution or bill not later than four calendar days before the expiration of the sixty-day period specified in section 5(b). In the event the conferees are unable to agree within 48 hours, they shall report back to their respective Houses in disagreement. Notwithstanding any rule in either House concerning the printing of conference reports in the Record or concerning any delay in the consideration of such reports, such report shall be acted on by both Houses not later than the expiration of such sixty-day period.

CONGRESSIONAL PRIORITY PROCEDURES FOR CONCURRENT RESOLUTION

SEC. 7. (a) Any concurrent resolution introduced pursuant to section 5(c) shall be referred to the Committee on Foreign Affairs of the House of Representatives or the Committee on Foreign Relations of the Senate, as the case may be, and one such concurrent resolution shall be reported out by such committee together with its recommendations within fifteen calendar days, unless such House shall otherwise determine by the yeas and nays.

(b) Any concurrent resolution so reported shall become the pending business of the House in question (in the case of the Senate the time for debate shall be equally divided between the proponents and the opponents) and shall be voted on within three calendar days thereafter, unless such House shall otherwise determine by yeas and nays.

(c) Such a concurrent resolution passed by one House shall be referred to the committee of the other House named in subsection (a) and shall be reported out by such committee together with its recommendations within fifteen calendar days and shall thereupon become the pending business of such House and shall be voted upon within three calendar days, unless such House shall otherwise determine by yeas and nays.

(d) In the case of any disagreement between the two Houses of Congress with respect to a concurrent resolution passed by both Houses, conferees shall be promptly appointed and the committee of conference shall make and file a report with respect to such concurrent resolution within six calendar days after the legislation is referred to the committee of conference. Notwithstanding any rule in either House concerning the printing of conference reports in the Record or concerning any delay in the consideration of such reports, such report shall be acted on by both Houses not later than six calendar days after the conference report is filed. In the event the conferees are unable to agree within 48 hours, they shall report back to their respective Houses in disagreement.

INTERPRETATION OF JOINT RESOLUTION

SEC. 8. (a) Authority to introduce United States Armed Forces into hostilities or into situations wherein involvement in hostilities is clearly indicated by the circumstances shall not be inferred—

(1) from any provision of law (whether or not in effect before the date of the enactment of this joint resolution), including any provision contained in any appropriation Act, unless such provision specifically authorizes the introduction of United States Armed Forces into hostilities or into such situations and states that it is intended to constitute specific statutory authorization within the meaning of this joint resolution; or

(2) from any treaty heretofore or hereafter ratified unless such treaty is implemented by legislation specifically authorizing the introduction of United States Armed Forces into hostilities or into such situations and stating that it is intended to constitute specific statutory authorization within the meaning of this joint resolution.

(b) Nothing in this joint resolution shall be construed to require any further specific statutory authorization to permit members of United States Armed Forces to participate jointly with members of the armed forces of one or more foreign countries in the headquarters operations of high-level military commands which were established prior to the date of enactment of this joint resolution and pursuant to the United Nations Charter or any treaty ratified by the United States prior to such date.

(c) For purposes of this joint resolution, the term "introduction of United States Armed Forces" includes the assignment of members of such armed forces to command, coordinate, participate in the movement of, or accompany the regular or irregular military forces of any foreign country or government when such military forces are engaged, or there exists an imminent threat that such forces will become engaged, in hostilities.

(d) Nothing in this joint resolution—

(1) is intended to alter the constitutional authority of the Congress or of the President, or the provisions of existing treaties; or

(2) shall be construed as granting any authority to the President with respect to the introduction of United States Armed Forces into hostilities or into situations wherein involvement in hostilities is clearly indicated by the circumstances which authority he would not have had in the absence of this joint resolution.

SEPARABILITY CLAUSE

SEC. 9. If any provision of this joint resolution or the application thereof to any person or circumstance is held invalid, the remainder of the joint resolution and the application of such provision to any other person or circumstance shall not be affected thereby.

EFFECTIVE DATE

SEC. 10. This joint resolution shall take effect on the date of its enactment.

(68) Veto of the War Powers Resolution: Message from President Nixon to the House of Representatives, returning House Joint Resolution 542 without his approval, October 24, 1973.[8]

[8]Text from *Presidential Documents*, vol. 9 (1973), pp. 1285-7.

To the House of Representatives:

I hereby return without my approval House Joint Resolution 542—the War Powers Resolution.[9] While I am in accord with the desire of the Congress to assert its proper role in the conduct of our foreign affairs, the restrictions which this resolution would impose upon the authority of the President are both unconstitutional and dangerous to the best interests of our Nation.

The proper roles of the Congress and the Executive in the conduct of foreign affairs have been debated since the founding of our country. Only recently, however, has there been a serious challenge to the wisdom of the Founding Fathers in choosing not to draw a precise and detailed line of demarcation between the foreign policy powers of the two branches.

The Founding Fathers understood the impossibility of foreseeing every contingency that might arise in this complex area. They acknowledged the need for flexibility in responding to changing circumstances. They recognized that foreign policy decisions must be made through close cooperation between the two branches and not through rigidly codified procedures.

These principles remain as valid today as they were when our Constitution was written. Yet House Joint Resolution 542 would violate those principles by defining the President's powers in ways which would strictly limit his constitutional authority.

Clearly Unconstitutional

House Joint Resolution 542 would attempt to take away, by a mere legislative act, authorities which the President has properly exercised under the Constitution for almost 200 years. One of its provisions would automatically cut off certain authorities after sixty days unless the Congress extended them. Another would allow the Congress to eliminate certain authorities merely by the passage of a concurrent resolution—an action which does not normally have the force of law, since it denies the President his constitutional role in approving legislation.

I believe that both these provisions are unconstitutional. The only way in which the constitutional powers of a branch of the Government can be altered is by amending the Constitution—and any attempt to make such alterations by legislation alone is clearly without force.

Undermining Our Foreign Policy

While I firmly believe that a veto of House Joint Resolution 542

[9]Document 67.

is warranted solely on constitutional grounds, I am also deeply disturbed by the practical consequences of this resolution. For it would seriously undermine this Nation's ability to act decisively and convincingly in times of international crisis. As a result, the confidence of our allies in our ability to assist them could be diminished and the respect of our adversaries for our deterrent posture could decline. A permanent and substantial element of unpredictability would be injected into the world's assessment of American behavior, further increasing the likelihood of miscalculation and war.

If this resolution had been in operation, America's effective response to a variety of challenges in recent years would have been vastly complicated or even made impossible. We may well have been unable to respond in the way we did during the Berlin crisis of 1961, the Cuban missile crisis of 1962, the Congo rescue operation in 1964, and the Jordanian crisis of 1970—to mention just a few examples. In addition, our recent actions to bring about a peaceful settlement of the hostilities in the Middle East would have been seriously impaired if this resolution had been in force.

While all the specific consequences of House Joint Resolution 542 cannot yet be predicted, it is clear that it would undercut the ability of the United States to act as an effective influence for peace. For example, the provision automatically cutting off certain authorities after 60 days unless they are extended by the Congress could work to prolong or intensify a crisis. Until the Congress suspended the deadline, there would be at least a chance of United States withdrawal and an adversary would be tempted therefore to postpone serious negotiations until the 60 days were up. Only after the Congress acted would there be a strong incentive for an adversary to negotiate. In addition, the very existence of a deadline could lead to an escalation of hostilities in order to achieve certain objectives before the 60 days expired.

The measure would jeopardize our role as a force for peace in other ways as well. It would, for example, strike from the President's hand a wide range of important peace-keeping tools by eliminating his ability to exercise quiet diplomacy backed by subtle shifts in our military deployments. It would also cast into doubt authorities which Presidents have used to undertake certain humanitarian relief missions in conflict areas, to protect fishing boats from seizure, to deal with ship or aircraft hijackings, and to respond to threats of attack. Not the least of the adverse consequences of this resolution would be the prohibition contained in section 8 against fulfilling our obligations under the NATO treaty as ratified by the Senate. Finally, since the bill is somewhat vague as to when the 60 day rule would apply, it could lead to extreme confusion and dangerous disagreements concerning the prerogatives of the two branches, seriously damaging our ability to respond to international crises.

Failure to Require Positive Congressional Action

I am particularly disturbed by the fact that certain of the President's constitutional powers as Commander in Chief of the Armed Forces would terminate automatically under this resolution 60 days after they were invoked. No overt Congressional action would be required to cut off these powers—they would disappear automatically unless the Congress extended them. In effect, the Congress is here attempting to increase its policy-making role through a provision which requires it to take absolutely no action at all.

In my view, the proper way for the Congress to make known its will on such foreign policy questions is through a positive action, with full debate on the merits of the issue and with each member taking the responsibility of casting a yes or no vote after considering those merits. The authorization and appropriations process represents one of the ways in which such influence can be exercised. I do not, however, believe that the Congress can responsibly contribute its considered, collective judgment on such grave questions without full debate and without a yes or no vote. Yet this is precisely what the joint resolution would allow. It would give every future Congress the ability to handcuff every future President merely by doing nothing and sitting still. In my view, one cannot become a responsible partner unless one is prepared to take responsible action.

Strengthening Cooperation Between the Congress and the Executive Branches

The responsible and effective exercise of the war powers requires the fullest cooperation between the Congress and the Executive and the prudent fulfillment by each branch of its constitutional responsibilities. House Joint Resolution 542 includes certain constructive measures which would foster this process by enhancing the flow of information from the executive branch to the Congress. Section 3, for example, calls for consultations with the Congress before and during the involvement of the United States forces in hostilities abroad. This provision is consistent with the desire of this Administration for regularized consultations with the Congress in an even wider range of circumstances.

I believe that full and cooperative participation in foreign policy matters by both the executive and the legislative branches could be enhanced by a careful and dispassionate study of their constitutional roles. Helpful proposals for such a study have already been made in the Congress. I would welcome the establishment of a non-partisan commission on the constitutional roles of the Congress and the President in the conduct of foreign affairs. This commission could make a thorough review of the principal constitutional issues in Executive-Congressional relations, including the war powers, the international agreement powers, and the question of Executive privilege, and then submit its recommendations to the President and the Congress. The members of such a commission could be drawn from both parties—and could represent many perspectives including those of the Congress, the executive branch, the legal profession, and the academic community.

This Administration is dedicated to strengthening cooperation between the Congress and the President in the conduct of foreign affairs and to preserving the constitutional prerogatives of both branches of our Government. I know that the Congress shares that goal. A commission on the constitutional roles of the Congress and the President would provide a useful opportunity for both branches to work together toward that common objective.

RICHARD NIXON

The White House,
    October 24, 1973.

(69) Enactment of the War Powers Resolution over the President's Veto: White House statement, November 7, 1973.[10]

The President is extremely disappointed with the House vote to override his veto of House Joint Resolution 542.[11]

He feels the action seriously undermines this Nation's ability to act decisively and convincingly in times of international crisis.

The confidence of our allies in our ability to assist them will be diminished by the House's action. Our potential adversaries may be encouraged to engage in future acts of international mischief because of this blow to our deterrent posture.

---

[10]Text from *Presidential Documents*, vol. 9 (1973), p. 1312.
[11]Document 67. The President's veto (Document 68) was overridden by a House vote of 284-135 and a Senate vote of 75-18, whereupon the resolution entered into force as Public Law 93-148 of Nov. 7, 1973.

24. DEVELOPMENT, FOOD, AND ENERGY PROBLEMS (II)

Even without the war in the Middle East, the final third of 1973 would have been an exceptionally difficult period for a world already racked by runaway inflation and committed to a struggle of indefinite duration against the complex problems of under-development, famine, and potential energy shortfalls.[1] Aggravated, in many respects, by the circumstances of the Mideast conflict, these problems were now beginning to combine and interact in such a way as to confront the world with the gravest international economic crisis it had endured since the Great Depression of the 1930s.

A disconcerting feature of this period was a sharply accentuated sense of opposition, even of confrontation, as between industrialized and developing countries—a feeling on both sides that the destinies of the planet, particularly in economic affairs, were beginning to hinge far more directly upon a somewhat antagonistic "North-South" relationship than on the more familiar East-West polarity between Communist and democratic states, "free market" and "centrally planned" economies. This trend received a powerful impulse from developments surrounding the Fourth Conference of Heads of State and Government of Nonaligned Countries, held in Algiers on September 5-9, 1973 with the participation of 76 member states, 9 observer countries, and 3 guest nations. Attended by such world figures as Marshal Tito of Yugoslavia, Indira Gandhi of India, and Fidel Castro of Cuba, the conference provided an ample sounding board for the preachments of Algerian President Houari Boumediene, the leader of the host government, regarding what he perceived as a fundamental clash of interests between "haves" and "have-nots," between the industrialized peoples of the North and the developing peoples of the South.[2] In articulating a clear-cut philosophy of North-South conflict, the Algiers meeting

---

[1]For background see Chapter 10.
[2]*Keesing's*, pp. 26117-21.

helped establish the tone of subsequent international discussions dealing with more specific issues of development, food supplies, and energy resources.

An American philosophy of economic development, imbued with a spirit of cooperation rather than of conflict, had been repeatedly set forth over the years in documents of the type of President Nixon's May 1 message on the foreign aid program.[3] An even broader statement of the American viewpoint, as notable for its comprehensiveness as for its conciliatory tone, was offered by Under Secretary of State Casey in an October 25 address to the Overseas Development Council in Washington (Document 70). "We cannot carry on economic negotiations in an atmosphere of peremptory demands and confrontation," observed the State Department's leading economic spokesman in a comment on what had become the United States' habitual isolation in U.N. economic forums. "This is eminently a field where all gain or all lose. The nations of the world are inextricably tied together, and the intensity with which economic interests are pursued reflects not a basic disparity of interest, but the closeness of our interdependence."

The Casey statement was of special interest because it brought together within a single focus a number of aspects of the development problem that were often treated as separate and even as unrelated issues. Trade, investment, and monetary relationships, the Under Secretary pointed out, were even more important to the less developed countries (LDC's) than the official development assistance provided through national and multilateral channels. Aid in the strict sense, he noted, "contributes only a tenth of the foreign exchange receipts of the LDC's and represents only 2 percent of their GNP," though it admittedly could in favoring circumstances perform "a critical role in providing the impetus for rapid development." But both the developing countries and their friends of the industrial world would be making a grave mistake, Mr. Casey intimated, if they neglected measures to promote the trade of the former group, encourage a continued flow of investment capital, and ensure that developing country interests were appropriately reflected in the pending reform of the international monetary system.

As was frequently the case, the American approach to world development problems in 1973 was noticeably stronger in philosophy than in purposeful action. The system of generalized trade preferences for developing countries, announced by President Nixon in 1969 and belatedly put forward in his April 10 trade message, was by now bogged down in Congress and would not ac-

[3]Document 24.

tually be placed in effect until 1976. The President's recommendations regarding the current foreign aid program were likewise caught in an intricate congressional battle and would not be finally acted upon until December, by which time the already modest allocations for development assistance would also have been subjected to the usual deep congressional cuts.[4]

The United States had also fallen seriously behind in the payment of its promised contributions to multilateral development lending agencies, particularly the International Development Association (IDA) and the Asian Development Bank (ADB). In a special message to Congress on October 31 that stressed the need to "show other nations that the United States will continue to meet its international responsibilities" **(Document 71)**, President Nixon proposed an authorization of $1.5 billion, to be made available in four annual installments, as the U.S. contribution to a $4.5 billion replenishment of IDA resources worked out at the recent World Bank meeting in Nairobi. (Other IDA contributors had agreed that the U.S. share in IDA financing should be reduced to one-third from its previous level of 40 percent.) Also requested in the same message was an additional authorization of $50 million for the "soft loan" fund of the Asian Development Bank, for which Congress had previously authorized $100 million. Both authorizations would be approved, after some vicissitudes, in the course of 1974,[5] although the appropriation and actual payment of the funds in question would as usual proceed at a slower pace.

One aspect of the developing nations' plight that was receiving markedly increased attention during 1973 was the threatened insufficiency of regional and even global food supplies to sustain a population which, in many countries, continued to increase at an alarming rate in spite of growing acceptance of "family planning" methods. Conditions in the Sahelian region of Africa, where drought and famine had focused world attention earlier in the year, had by autumn been considerably ameliorated, thanks in part to vigorous relief efforts by the United States and other countries.[6] But there had been suffering in other areas, too; and Secretary Kissinger, in his September 24 address to the U.N. Assembly, direc-

---

[4]Foreign Assistance Act of 1973 (Public Law 93-189), Dec. 17, 1973; Foreign Assistance and Related Programs Appropriation Act, 1974 (Public Law 93-240), Jan. 2, 1974. For details cf. *Senate Foreign Relations Committee History, 1973-4*, pp. 26-51.

[5]Public Law 93-373, Aug. 14, and 93-537, Dec. 22, 1974. For further details see *Bulletin*, vol. 69 (1973), pp. 731-9, and *Senate Foreign Relations Committee History, 1973-4*, pp. 127-33.

[6]*Bulletin*, vol. 69 (1973), pp. 380-83 and 669-73.

ted special attention to the broader problems that would have to be addressed in planning food policies for the future.

No single country could any longer expect to cope with the growing threat to the world's food supply, the Secretary of State averred (**Document 45**). Common action had become essential. To formulate a comprehensive attack on the problem, Dr. Kissinger had offered his proposal that a U.N.-sponsored World Food Conference be held in 1974, and that technical assistance in food conservation be made available by nations able to provide it. Subsequently endorsed by the Food and Agriculture Organization of the United Nations (FAO) at its Seventeenth Conference in Rome, the conference plan was ratified later in the year by the U.N. Economic and Social Council (ECOSOC) and the General Assembly, which determined that it should be convened in Rome for about two weeks in November 1974.[7]

Some of the problems with which any food conference would have to deal were touched upon in a statement by Maurice J. Williams, Acting Administrator of the Agency for International Development (AID) and the President's Special Relief Coordinator for Major Disasters Abroad. Action on three fronts, Mr. Williams emphasized (**Document 72**), was essential to staving off continued hunger and malnutrition and recurring food crises: (1) adequate food supplies on special terms to meet the immediate needs of the developing world; (2) better cooperative mechanisms to assure adequate world stocks and harness the efforts of all nations in meeting problems of hunger and malnutrition; and (3) expanded research and development aimed at accelerating production increases in the less developed countries. "Events of the last several months have brought home more sharply than ever before one simple central fact," Mr. Williams observed. "All of us in the world live out of the same food basket. . . . We all have good reason to be concerned about the future of this world food basket."

A more immediate concern, particularly for people in the industrial countries in the late autumn of 1973, was the global energy shortage which had been repeatedly foretold by American and other specialists and now acquired a sudden grim reality thanks to the actions of several Mideast oil exporting countries. The elements of this problem—the rapidly increasing worldwide consumption of a scarce resource controlled by a limited number of governments, many of them with strongly marked "third world" views—had been repeatedly pointed out to the Western peoples, without, as

[7]General Assembly Resolution 3180 (XXVIII), Dec. 17, 1973, adopted without vote; details in *U.S. Participation, 1973*, pp. 75-6 and 156-7, and *Bulletin*, vol. 70 (1974), pp. 97-9. The conference took place in Rome Nov. 5-16, 1974.

yet, enlisting much support for practical steps designed to reduce their shared dependence on imported petroleum. Only a month before the Yom Kippur War, President Nixon had renewed his own advocacy of national energy independence in a statement that urged congressional action on various pieces of legislation put forward in the context of his April 18 energy message.[8] Not many weeks thereafter, the penalties of external dependence were being made evident to all by the combined effect of steep price increases and calculated interruptions of supply.

Even before the beginning of the October War, the continuing economic struggle over ownership and control of the international petroleum industry had destroyed such prospects of long-range stability as had appeared to have been established earlier in the decade. Posted prices for crude petroleum, supposedly settled for a five-year period by an agreement signed at Tehran in February 1971, had already been twice increased, ostensibly to indemnify the members of the eleven-nation Organization of Petroleum Exporting Countries (OPEC) for losses due to dollar devaluation. The so-called New York agreement of October 1972, which provided for a steady increase in producer country participation in ownership and management of the oil companies, was also being called in question as Libya and various Middle Eastern countries attempted to quicken the pace through outright nationalization or accelerated participation arrangements.[9]

These tendencies had been given fresh stimulus by the outbreak of the October War, which also brought into play the first large-scale use of the "oil weapon" as a political instrument by countries belonging to the Organization of Arab Petroleum Exporting Countries (OAPEC), a separate group whose membership included not only strongly "anti-imperialist" countries like Libya and Iraq but also Saudi Arabia and other traditional friends of the United States. As noted earlier, these countries on October 17 announced a collective decision to reduce their petroleum output by 10 percent across the board and to make further cuts of 5 percent a month thereafter—at the same time imposing a complete embargo on shipments to the United States and the Netherlands, but assuring "friendly" nations of normal supplies. Also on October 17, the Gulf members of OPEC, among them Iran as well as the neighboring Arab states, definitively abandoned the Tehran pricing agreement by decreeing a further provisional price increase, nominally of 17 percent but actually closer to 70 percent, which

---

[8]Cf. note 19 to Document 54.
[9]Details in *Keesing's*, pp. 26194-6.

would raise the locally posted price of crude oil from around $3 to around $5 per barrel.[10]

While the 30 days' supply of oil already in transit would mitigate the immediate effect of the cutbacks, it was estimated that continuance of the embargo would cost the United States some 25 percent of its oil imports and upward of 10 percent of its total consumption. Japan and Western Europe, with their heavier dependence on Arab oil, would be even harder hit, despite the fact that the United Kingdom, France, and Spain were being listed as "friendly" countries (from the Arab standpoint) in view of their nonsupport of U.S. policy in the October War.[11] Possibly not less ominous than the restriction of supplies, moreover, was the effect of these sudden price increases on the balance of payments of the industrial nations, to say nothing of the non-oil-exporting developing countries and, ultimately, the oil nations themselves.

President Nixon described the situation in unusually somber tones in a radio-television address of November 7—the day his veto of the War Powers Resolution was overridden by both houses of Congress—in which he once again repudiated current speculation as to his own resignation (**Document 73**). Beyond such short-term expedients as 68-degree thermostat settings and 50-mile highway speeds, the President urged commitment to an ambitious "Project Independence" program designed, he said, to emancipate the nation completely from its dependence on foreign energy sources by 1980.

But though the nation signally failed in this instance to heed the admonitions of its embattled chief executive, it was destined to feel the lash of the Arab "oil weapon" for some time to come, despite its vigorous efforts to speed the process of Mideast peacemaking. Most of the Arab oil producers imposed a further 5 percent production cut at the beginning of December—the members of the European Economic Community (except the Netherlands) being exempted in recognition of their relatively pro-Arab political stand. The embargo on exports to the United States was actually continued until March 1974, while that against the Netherlands was not formally lifted until the following July.[12]

Still more disturbing in its implications for the future of the world economy—and, not least, for those among the developing countries that were themselves dependent on imported petroleum—was a pre-Christmas decision by the Gulf states to effect a further increase in posted prices, this time from a current level of

[10]Same, pp. 26224-5.
[11]Details in *Bulletin*, vol. 69 (1973), pp. 696-7 and 770-73.
[12]*Keesing's*, pp. 26224 and 26617-8.

$5.11 to a staggering $11.651. Ostensibly designed to safeguard the exporting countries' interests until a long-term pricing policy could be formulated,[13] this action was possibly the most important among the factors that served to plunge the entire world into a gloom both literal and figurative during the midwinter season of 1973-74. It lent a further measure of timeliness to Dr. Kissinger's suggestion, in a celebrated London address of December 12 **(Document 81)**, that the industrialized nations make haste to develop "an initial action program for collaboration in all areas of the energy problem."

(70) "A Comprehensive Development Policy for the United States": Address by Under Secretary of State Casey before the Overseas Development Council, October 25, 1973.[14]

Government officials who speak in public on development and foreign assistance sometimes feel like the proverbial Christian being thrown into the lion's den. Appearing here today I have more a feeling of being cast into the communion of saints. The Overseas Development Council needs no evangelizing on our relationship with the less developed countries (LDC's). As a matter of fact, given some of the criticisms that you have made about U.S. policy toward the less developed countries, perhaps I should feel like a beleaguered lion being thrown into a den of Christians.

But the very fact that so many audiences today question the involvement of the United States in the development process indicates that something may be amiss. Our governmental role in the economic and social development of the poorer countries of the world was launched about a quarter of a century ago. Most of the tools which we are using today date from a decade ago. Dwindling appropriations for development purposes bespeak the need for a new thrust and a new articulation of our self-interest in development. This organization, along with the House Foreign Affairs Committee, produced a valuable new initiative to serve both our self-interest and humanitarian purposes in the concept of a special export credit fund to bring technology and modern productivity embodied in American equipment to poor countries to further their development programs. I'd like to take this occasion to pay tribute to Senator Humphrey for his gallant fight to resurrect the Export Development Credit Fund after it was voted down on the floor of the House.

---

[13]Same, p. 26355; *New York Times*, Dec. 24, 1973.
[14]Text from *Bulletin*, vol. 69 (1973), pp. 688-94.

For 1974 and beyond, where do we find the real and durable rationale for development assistance which will command public acceptance? I believe it lies in the combination of the humanitarian aspirations which have always moved large numbers of Americans and our self-interest in an international economic system which works better and in which nations and their policies mesh better. I believe that the fuller participation of the poorer countries in the world economic system is as necessary to make that system work right as it is to the social and economic development of the poor countries.

We hear a lot about the three pillars of money, trade, and investment on which the new and better international economic system is to be built. I believe that there must be a fourth pillar to support that structure. I believe that development is that fourth pillar; and I believe that it consists of transfers of resources, technology, and training to the poor countries so that they can both benefit from and contribute to the worldwide flow of money, trade, investment, and technology. I believe that represents a rationale for loans and grants and technical assistance which can carry us through the second 25 years of development.

Seventy-five percent of the foreign exchange earnings of the developing countries come from their exports. Their ability to earn their own way through trade is compatible with their national dignity and economic aspirations. It is also compatible with our economic interests. We want to see the scarce resources which our economy needs produced efficiently and exported to us. We want to be able to buy abroad the products that can be better produced there and to sell abroad the products that we can produce better here.

The United States has a particular role to play. We must keep up the momentum toward increasing liberalization of world trade. This policy has become traditional for us and has today a significant practical dimension. From an economic point of view, as the world's largest trading nation we stand to be large gainers from trade liberalization. LDC's are important to us in this respect, for they are the market for 30 percent—some $15 billion last year—of our annual exports. From a political point of view, as these countries acquire a larger stake in international trade they will be less likely to take political actions that would disrupt international economic and political systems. In this sense, our approach to trade with the LDC's is consistent with our approach to trade with the Soviet Union and other Socialist countries.

This administration has taken a forward position on trade with the developing countries. We have opposed the formation of trading blocs that would artificially restrict trade, and we have pressed for the inclusion of developing countries in multilateral trade negotiations, where we share substantial interests with them—especially in freer trade in agricultural products. Our record in trade with the LDC's is good. The United States alone takes 40 percent of LDC manufactured exports. We can and should take more, but others must also. Europe and Japan must share with us the benefits and the costs of a more open trading system.

As you know, we already have prepared a program that would represent a giant step forward. The administration remains firmly committed to the generalized system of preferences set forth in title V of the Trade Reform Act of 1973.[15] This act provides a framework for the U.S. role in a more open global trading system. Title V, which would authorize the President to grant preferential treatment to the exports of developing countries, is an integral part of this framework.

If this country is serious about helping the developing countries help themselves, we must participate in a generalized system of preferences. The developing countries must be given a chance to increase their export earnings, particularly in the areas of low-technology manufactures where they can achieve a natural competitive advantage. But they can only do this if they have access to markets in the developed countries such as the United States—where, in fact, low-technology manufacturing is increasingly uneconomic and unsatisfactory to both labor and capital. A generalized preference system would have to be well safeguarded, of course; and its duration and availability would be limited in time—until the LDC exporters become competitive in international markets.

The developing countries themselves must also take the actions necessary to rationalize international trade. They must concentrate on areas where they do in fact enjoy a comparative advantage and move away from artificial incentives, unnecessary import substitution, reverse and special preferences, and regional trading arrangements that are not economically sound. And of course we can reasonably expect these countries to dismantle unnecessary import-restriction policies that deprive them of enjoying the comparative advantage possessed by others.

What this means is that the principle of comparative advantage must come out of the textbooks and be reflected in actual policy. As resource supply becomes a greater problem, we must make sure that available resources are used more efficiently. If disruptions in trade patterns lead to short-term domestic difficulties, we must provide the mechanisms for facilitating adjustments. The cost of

[15]Cf. Document 55.

the adjustments—both human and economic—should not be underestimated. But we must keep in mind the ultimate benefit to both the individual U.S. consumer and the U.S. economy as a whole.

Private Investment in Developing Countries

Although investment flows are small compared to export earnings, investment not only provides capital but brings with it a whole series of ancillary benefits in technology, management, and training that neither trade nor governmental aid can normally provide.

Our basic view on private investment in developing countries is that market forces should determine allocation. And we do not want to press our investment in areas where it is not wanted; to do so would only create political problems. We do, however, have legitimate reason to wonder how effectively a country is committed to economic development when it impedes mutually beneficial investment. Certainly we are not prepared to look to governmental assistance to fill gaps that could equally well be filled by private sources. Our technical assistance, development assistance, and export credits can compound benefits when they stimulate investment in LDC's from local or foreign capital and particularly when they generate indigenous capital markets and other sources of local funding.

We must work to make American investment abroad more compatible with the attitudes of the recipient countries. This is a process in which the U.S. Government can play primarily an advisory role, for investors and recipient governments must work out arrangements that meet their own needs. But we should encourage potential investors to consider new investment arrangements. There are formulas, such as equity participation rather than wholly owned subsidiaries or a phased evolution from one to the other, that would permit an investor-host relationship acceptable to all parties. I have confidence in the ingenuity of the U.S. businessman to respond to this challenge.

The International Monetary System

Whether we reach our trade, investment, and development goals will be closely linked to our success in renovating the international monetary system. LDC trade is closely linked to international economic patterns that interact sensitively with monetary matters. The recent monetary crises affected the economic life of many LDC's in clearly measurable terms. The developing countries are aware of this.

In addition, a number of developing countries have very large sums of foreign exchange reserves—derived in the most part from petroleum exports. These funds find only limited absorption at home and thus enter international markets. By 1980, the oil-exporting countries will be accumulating $55 billion a year over their domestic needs. They are entitled to a fair return on their holdings. We and other countries are entitled to expect that these holdings will not be used to the detriment of the world community as a whole.

Our philosophy in approaching the international monetary problem is simple: These relationships should be managed in a way that is orderly and designed to bring benefit to all. This entails strict responsibility on the part of all participants in the system and cooperative efforts to build a sense of confidence—for without confidence the system simply will not work.

I would like to touch on two aspects of U.S. policy on monetary matters that are of particular concern to the less developed countries.

First, we have taken leadership in involving representatives of the less developed countries in monetary decisionmaking. It was on our initiative that LDC representation was brought into the Committee of Twenty. I believe that this was an extremely constructive step—politically in the short run and economically as we look further into the future.

On the other hand, the United States has felt it necessary to take a position with regard to the allocation of special drawing rights (SDR's) that is not popular in the less developed world—and I would guess not popular at this luncheon.

Our position on SDR's rests on the conviction that the monetary system is critical to trade, investment, and development and that it must be orderly and command confidence. SDR's have a crucial role to play in this new system, and they can play it only if there is confidence that their creation will be limited by the need for liquidity in the world trading system. If we create them for other purposes we will impart a bias and a lack of confidence which will be inflating. We have seen that inflation hurts LDC's most of all. SDR's were not intended to be a means of reallocating resources among countries; to give them this role would run the risk of undermining a novel and sensitive mechanism to the detriment of all of those who have a stake in it—including the less developed countries. There is a real need for transferring resources to the poorer countries. I believe that it must be met directly and that if we short-circuit the appropriations process, the public will resent it and legislators will turn away from development assistance.

Official Development Assistance

Official government assistance transfers, either bilateral or through multilateral organizations, receive by far the lion's share of attention in most discussions of development. Yet aid contributes only a tenth of the foreign exchange receipts of the LDC's and represents only 2 percent of their total GNP. It is tempting to minimize the role of aid in light of these figures and thereby rationalize the declining contribution of our own country in the development assistance field.

But aggregate statistics are deceptive. Given the proper environment, aid can perform and has performed a critical role in providing the impetus for rapid development. The success stories of our aid programs—ranging from Germany through Korea—are familiar and gratifying to us all. While there have also been failures, the historical record of our aid programs over 25 years, in both quantitative and qualitative terms, is one of which we can be proud.

Official development assistance has a political and symbolic importance that cannot be captured in statistics. It provides tangible evidence of American concern for a large and important part of the world and is part of the price that we pay to bring the developing countries into the relationships of interdependence that in the long term benefit us. In addition, of course, aid frequently plays an important short-term role in providing support to governments that have interests parallel to our own or as a quid pro quo for direct benefits that we may receive from certain governments.

Aside from these "practical" concerns, the American aid program is a manifestation of the traditional American desire to help others who are in need. Too often, in an age where calculations of national interest are seen as the only acceptable basis for policy, we have played down this humanitarian aspect. Were the United States, with its unparalleled wealth and standard of living, to turn away from development assistance as "not cost effective," this country would make a tragic break with its traditions and values.

Secretary Kissinger said in his speech before this year's U.N. General Assembly:[16] "A world community cannot remain divided

---

[16]Document 45.

between the permanently rich and the permanently poor"—just as our own nation was unable to continue half slave and half free a century ago. A world that is so permanently and unjustly divided is not the kind of world that either the rich or the poor can live in. It is not the kind of world that you and I would want to live in.

But an aid program must deal with realities. A recipient will benefit from aid only if it is willing and able to mobilize its own efforts. Aid can only be effective where there is a mutuality of interest between recipient and donor. There have to be clearly understood ground rules governing aid programs in both the economic and political fields. Aid should not be given to those who do not want it or are not willing to use it effectively—there are too many competing claims on our resources both abroad and at home.

Where aid is wanted and can be effectively used, it must take into account that growth must be spread in some equitable manner among the peoples and nations of the world. This does not mean that the United States should not concentrate its efforts where its interests are greatest. But we cannot be satisfied with aggregate performance statistics that show glowing rates of growth but hide the fact that great numbers of people have seen their lot in life stagnate while others grow prosperous around them. I would hope that we will get away from using statistics that show an annual growth rate of LDC's of 6 percent but neglect to mention that the largest of the less developed countries, India, has barely grown at all on a per capita basis. And we should be suspicious of statistics that show prodigious growth rates for individual countries but are not disaggregated to show whether all social and regional groups in the country have participated in that growth.

It is scarcely necessary to discuss before this group the various modalities of development assistance: the bilateral versus multilateral question; the relative importance of technical, sectoral, and other program types; and the many other issues with which the Overseas Development Council has dealt so penetratingly and intelligently.

There is little of a concrete nature for me to say about aid levels except that we are sending a request for $1½ billion in IDA replenishment up to the Hill[17] and that in 1974 we must start anew to work toward a proper level of continuing development assistance. That's why it's so critical now that we properly relate development and its importance to both the United States and the LDC's to the other elements in an effective worldwide international economic system. We must create better and broader public understanding that the international economic order can run into dif-

[17]Document 71.

ficulties and political order can be jeopardized if the poorer countries are not brought into successful participation in a reformed world economic system and thereby afforded the opportunity to achieve their development aspirations. The United States and the rest of the industrialized world share with the developing countries a mutual interest in a renewed and open world economic system—built on the four pillars of trade, investment, development assistance, and monetary reform—from which all nations can benefit.

Development Policy and U.S. Interests

U.S. policies toward the LDC's must be consonant with our perceived national interests. Foreign policy considerations—long term rather than short term—will include security and strategic factors and our desire to foster a climate of international cooperation conducive to solution of such problems as preservation of the environment, narcotics control, sanctity of contracts, and security of travel. International economic considerations include the implications of our policies on U.S. access to needed raw materials, on expanded export markets, and on the investment climate in LDC's. Domestic economic considerations are equally relevant: balance of payments and budget constraints, the possibility of shortrun employment dislocations, the interests of our consumers, the long-term efficiency of the U.S. economy.

These U.S. interests are clearly interrelated. We recognize that all nations benefit most under an international economic system where scarce resources are used most efficiently. Our purchases of LDC raw materials and manufactured goods contribute to the well-being of U.S. industry and consumers while providing the LDC's with foreign exchange for their development requirements and for purchases of U.S. products. Similarly, when the LDC's can attract private U.S. investment, they open up an invaluable source of capital, technology, and managerial skills to contribute to their further development.

For its part, the United States needs the foreign exchange from expanded exports and from investment earnings to pay for our growing raw material requirements. The expansion of markets for our own exports of those goods and services which we produce best, and our purchase of resources from the lowest cost foreign suppliers, will contribute to higher productivity of the U.S. economy. For the United States, higher incomes, foreign exchange earnings, and gross employment all flow from the most efficient use of resources. This in turn will permit easier absorption of relatively less efficient domestic industry and labor which are temporarily displaced in the course of this evolution of the world economy. Thus, U.S. interests are more than ever directly affected by the degree to which other countries develop and become successful participants in a market-oriented world economy.

At the same time, development can be accelerated in the LDC's by focusing financial and technical assistance more sharply on increasing their participation in and commitment to an open market-oriented world economy. Increased trade enables the LDC's to increase their export earnings, which are their largest source of development funds. Export growth generates foreign investment in export industries and in sales, service, and financial industries which are attracted by increased foreign exchange earnings. The increased LDC dependence upon world markets helps to protect our investment from arbitrary actions by LDC governments.

In addition, a trade policy emphasizing comparative advantage encourages the LDC's to forgo wasteful import-substitution industries which deprive us of important markets. Finally, as the LDC's build manufacturing, agricultural, and raw material processing industries that depend upon developed country markets, they have less need for artificially high mineral and petroleum prices and are less well situated to withhold production. Our specialized technical assistance can foster market-oriented growth and help the private sector, which is crucial to the development of LDC export industries.

In this world of growing economic interdependence, the U.S. self-interest requires that we play a significant role and provide our "fair share" in support of the development process. To do otherwise would jeopardize our political and economic relations with both developing and developed countries. We could find it more difficult in the future to wield sufficient influence on matters of importance to us.

The way in which we play this role, however, must reflect the realities of recent important developments in the world economic system. Sustained high levels of growth in other industrialized countries enable these countries to assume a larger share of the development assistance burden; balance of payments, inflation, and budgetary problems in the U.S. require solution; the international monetary system is in need of reform; growing differences among LDC's require different packages of development tools. As the health of the U.S. economy improves, the United States should move forward and again provide leadership in formulating for the 1970's and 1980's development policies which recognize that we and other industrialized countries are linked to developing countries by mutual interests of trade and investment.

What is required are flexible and realistic development policies which, with continued attention to basic human problems, interrelate trade, investment, technological developments, and foreign assistance.

To realize the goals of development, the world must, as Secretary Kissinger said in his address to the General Assembly, draw upon the world's best minds for new and imaginative solutions to the problems of development. Concrete contributions are needed in such fields as food production, sectoral development, indigenous economic institutions like capital markets and distribution and servicing systems, and the myriad problems attendant upon development—the critical issue of our time and the years to come. We can spend no less effort on development than we have on dealing with monetary reform, trade, and investment problems. Each element must be equally strong; each must contribute to the other.

I would like to conclude my remarks with some observations that are primarily political in tone but reflect considerations that are integral to any development effort.

We should not hesitate to stand up for our principles in international forums—alone if necessary. But I am disturbed by the U.S. isolation in such groups as the U.N. Economic and Social Council and UNCTAD [U.N. Conference on Trade and Development], where the majority of members are less developed. We need to find ways of relating better to the dissatisfied and restive majority of humanity—ways that are acceptable to them and can form the basis for fruitful cooperation. The issues are no more intractable than those that we face in our economic dealings with the developed countries.

We cannot carry on economic negotiations in an atmosphere of peremptory demands and confrontation. This is eminently a field where all gain or all lose. The nations of the world are inextricably tied together, and the intensity with which economic interests are pursued reflects not a basic disparity of interest, but the closeness of our interdependence.

By building on this interdependence with a comprehensive policy such as I have outlined this afternoon, we and our neighbors on this planet can have a realistic expectation of success in meeting the challenge of development.

(71) Funds for the International Development Association and the Asian Development Bank: Message from President Nixon to the Congress, October 31, 1973.[18]

[18]Text from *Presidential Documents*, vol. 9 (1973), pp. 1299-1301.

To the Congress of the United States:

As their role in conveying financial assistance to developing countries has steadily enlarged in recent years, multilateral lending institutions have become vital to our hopes for constructing a new international economic order.

One of the most important of these institutions is the International Development Association, a subsidiary of the World Bank that provides long-term loans at low interest rates to the world's poorest nations. During the 13 years of its operation, IDA has provided over $6.1 billion of development credits to nearly 70 of the least developed countries of the world. Two dozen countries have contributed funds for this effort.

By next June, however, the International Development Association will be out of funds unless it is replenished. As a result of an understanding reached in recent international negotiations, I am today proposing to the Congress that the United States join with other major industrialized nations in pledging significant new funds to this organization. Specifically, I am requesting that the Congress authorize for future appropriation the sum of $1.5 billion for the fourth replenishment of IDA. Initial payments would be made in fiscal year 1976 and the full amount would be paid out over a period of years.

I am also requesting that the Congress authorize an additional $50 million for the Special Funds of the Asian Development Bank. The bank is one of the major regional banks in the world that complements the work of the International Development Association and the World Bank.

Legislation for both of these authorities is being submitted to the Congress today by the Secretary of the Treasury.

Strengthening the International Economic System

Just over a year ago, in September 1972 at the annual meeting in Washington of the International Monetary Fund and the World Bank, I stressed the urgent need to build a secure structure of peace, not only in the political realm but in the economic realm as well.[19] I stated then that the time had come for action across the entire front of international economic problems, and I emphasized that recurring monetary crises, incorrect alignments, distorted trading arrangements, and great disparities in development not only injured our economies, but also created political tensions that subvert the cause of peace. I urged that all nations come together to deal promptly with these fundamental problems.

AFR, 1972, pp. 529-34.

I am happy to be able to report that since that 1972 meeting, we have made encouraging progress toward updating and revising the basic rules for the conduct of international financial and trade affairs that have guided us since the end of World War II. Monetary reform negotiations, begun last year, are now well advanced toward forging a new and stronger international monetary system. A date of July 31, 1974, has been set as a realistic deadline for completing a basic agreement among nations on the new system.[20]

Concurrently, we are taking the fundamental steps at home and abroad that will lead to needed improvement in the international trading system. On September 14, while meeting in Tokyo, the world's major trading nations launched new multilateral trade negotiations which could lead to a significant reduction of world trade barriers and reform of our rules for trade.[21] The Congress is now considering trade reform legislation that is essential to allow the United States to participate effectively in these negotiations.

Essential Role of Development Assistance

While there is great promise in both the trade and monetary negotiations, it is important that strong efforts also be made in the international effort to support economic development—particularly in providing reasonable amounts of new funds for international lending institutions.

A stable and flexible monetary system, a fairer and more efficient system of trade and investment, and a solid structure of cooperation in economic development are the essential components of international economic relations. We must act in each of these interdependent areas. If we fail or fall behind in one, we weaken the entire effort. We need an economic system that is balanced and responsive in all its parts, along with international institutions that reinforce the principles and rules we negotiate.

We cannot expect other nations—developed or developing—to respond fully to our call for stronger and more efficient trading and monetary systems, if at the same time we are not willing to assume our share of the efforts to ensure that the interests of the poorer nations are taken into account. Our position as a leader in promoting a more reasonable world order and our credibility as a negotiator would be seriously weakened if we do not take decisive and responsible action to assist those nations to achieve their aspirations toward economic development.

There are some two dozen non-communist countries which provide assistance to developing countries. About 20 percent of the

[20]Document 51a.
[21]Document 50b.

total aid flow from these countries is now channeled through multilateral lending institutions such as the World Bank group—which includes IDA—and the regional development banks.

These multilateral lending institutions play an important role in American foreign policy. By encouraging developing countries to participate in a joint effort to raise their living standards, they help to make those countries more self reliant. They provide a pool of unmatched technical expertise. And they provide a useful vehicle for encouraging other industrialized countries to take a larger responsibility for the future of the developing world, which in turn enables us to reduce our direct assistance.

The American economy also benefits from our support of international development. Developing countries today provide one-third of our raw material imports, and we will increasingly rely upon them in the future for essential materials. These developing countries are also good customers, buying more from us than we do from them.

New Proposals for Multilateral Assistance

Because multilateral lending institutions make such a substantial contribution to world peace, it must be a matter of concern for the United States that the International Development Association will be out of funds by June 30, 1974, if its resources are not replenished.

The developing world now looks to the replenishment of IDA's resources as a key test of the willingness of industrialized, developed nations to cooperate in assuring the fuller participation of developing countries in the international economy. At the Nairobi meeting of the World Bank last month, it was agreed by 25 donor countries to submit for approval of their legislatures a proposal to authorize $4.5 billion of new resources to IDA. Under this proposal, the share of the United States in the replenishment would drop from 40 percent to 33 percent. This represents a significant accomplishment in distributing responsibility for development more equitably. Other countries would put up $3 billion, twice the proposed United States contribution of $1.5 billion. Furthermore, to reduce annual appropriations requirements, our payments can be made in installments at the rate of $375 million a year for four years, beginning in fiscal year 1976.

We have also been negotiating with other participating nations to increase funds for the long-term, low-interest operation of the Asian Development Bank. As a result of these negotiations, I am requesting the Congress to authorize $50 million of additional contributions to the ADB by the United States—beyond a $100 million contribution already approved. These new funds would be associated with additional contributions of about $350 million from other nations.

Meeting our Responsibilities

In addition to these proposals for pledging future funds, I would point out that the Congress also has before it appropriations requests for fiscal year 1974—a year that is already one-third completed—for bilateral and multilateral assistance to support our role in international cooperation.[22] It is my profound conviction that it is in our own best interest that the Congress move quickly to enact these pending appropriations requests. We are now behind schedule in providing our contributions to the International Development Association, the Inter-American Development Bank and the Asian Development Bank, so that we are not keeping our part of the bargain. We must show other nations that the United States will continue to meet its international responsibilities.

All nations which enjoy advanced stages of industrial development have a grave responsibility to assist those countries whose major development lies ahead. By providing support for international economic assistance on an equitable basis, we are helping others to help themselves and at the same time building effective institutions for international cooperation in the critical years ahead. I urge the Congress to act promptly on these proposals.[23]

RICHARD NIXON

The White House,
    October 31, 1973.

(72) *"A Comprehensive Approach to Worldwide Problems of Food Shortages and Malnutrition": Statement by Maurice J. Williams, Acting Administrator of the Agency for International Development (AID) and the President's Special Relief Coordinator for Major Disasters Abroad, October 5, 1973.*[24]

Events of the last several months have brought home more sharply than ever before one simple central fact. All of us in the

[22]Cf. above at note 4.
[23]Cf. above at note 5.
[24]AID Press Release 73-73, Oct. 5; text from *Bulletin*, vol. 69 (1973), pp. 573-6. The statement was submitted to the Subcommittees on African and South Asian Affairs of the Senate Committee on Foreign Relations.

world live out of the same food basket. A major drought in Asia affects supplies throughout the world. Rising prices make it difficult for poor countries to import essential food. All countries must work to meet the hunger and malnutrition resulting from natural disasters. A bad harvest of Peruvian anchovies can tip the balance between a healthy export market for U.S. soybeans and a necessity to disappoint our best overseas customers for our farm products. We all have good reason to be concerned about the future of this world food basket.

World cereal and protein consumption has been running slightly ahead of food production in recent years. Our food reserve margins now are close—too close for comfort or complacency.

In this period of reduced food supply and rapidly rising demand, the United States has held open the door of its granary. Commercial exports of grains are at record level, and Public Law 480[25] programs are continuing, although on a drastically reduced scale.

In a situation of short supply and high prices, the less developed countries (LDC's) who must import grain for essential needs are at a particular disadvantage. In some cases, because of natural disaster or economic difficulties of long standing, they are dependent on donations or concessional sales from the United States and other food-exporting nations. For others, even though able to purchase grains commercially, the present high prices constitute a significant drain on foreign exchange and budget resources. For them grain supplies for their people at basic sustenance levels are a political and economic necessity.

U.S. Food Assistance

The current Food for Peace legislation requires that commodities shipped under the concessional sales and donation programs be in excess of the amounts required for domestic consumption, adequate carryover of stocks, and anticipated sales for dollars, as determined by the Secretary of Agriculture. For these reasons, the amount of commodities made available for Food for Peace in fiscal year 1974 is likely to be only half of the amount shipped in FY 1973. We have had to drastically curtail P.L. 480 programs in many other developing countries.

Even with a cut of this magnitude, the importance of continuing humanitarian food programs is fully recognized. The United States continues to be the principal contributor to the World Food

[25]Agricultural Trade Development and Assistance Act of 1954 (Public Law 83-480, July 10, 1954).

Program, sponsored jointly by the Food and Agriculture Organization (FAO) and the United Nations. The U.S. pledge for the 1973-74 biennium is $136 million—in commodities and freight, cash contribution, and shipping costs. The commodity portion is charged to title II of P.L. 480. We expect to fulfill the present pledge.

The United States is also signatory to the Food Aid Convention of 1971.[26] By that convention it is committed to donate or sell concessionally a minimum of 1,890,000 metric tons of wheat and coarse grains in fiscal years 1972, 1973, and 1974. We have met and will continue meeting that commitment.

Donations of food to U.S. voluntary agencies for their overseas distribution programs to the needy are also continuing. While some reductions in the volume of food donations must be made, the voluntary agencies are cooperating in focusing the use of available supplies to help the most nutritionally vulnerable groups—in maternal/child health programs, preschool and primary school feeding. And to upgrade the nutritional quality of the food, we are continuing to put strong emphasis on the use of high-protein blended and fortified foods, such as corn-soya blend, wheat-soya blend, and soy-fortified flour and bulgur.

Food for Peace commodities will continue to be made available for drought relief in the Sahelian zone of Africa. The United States has been by far the largest single donor of food to the Sahel—about 40 percent of the amount pledged so far. Under the leadership of the FAO, a survey of food needs for the months ahead is nearing completion. The United States will continue to participate in the international effort to help the drought victims.[27]

In the case of Pakistan, the President recently announced that 100,000 tons of wheat would be made available as part of our assistance following the disastrous floods. We cannot, however, meet all of Pakistan's needs for grain on concessional terms. In response to U.N. requests, the United States has contributed about half of all the grain which will be supplied to Bangladesh during this calendar year. We are also meeting the minimum essential food requirements of south Indochina.

The situation we face this year points up the great importance of the Food for Peace program in our relations with developing countries. Food for Peace enables the United States to carry out its longstanding tradition of humanitarian assistance to the needy, to provide help in time of disaster, and to boost the efforts of less developed countries to help themselves. I fervently hope that

[26]TIAS 7144 (22 UST 820); cf. *AFR, 1971*, pp. 612-14.
[27]Cf. above at note 6.

Secretary [of Agriculture Earl L.] Butz' drive to maximize U.S. farm production next year is so successful that Food for Peace can be fully restored. It is of utmost importance that the continuing need for food aid be fully a part of our agricultural policy.

Joint International Action Required

The current situation also points up the need for a coordinated approach with other donors and major food producers. In 1972 the United States provided 75 percent of all bilateral and multilateral food aid. The world food problem requires a joint review with other donors, both major cereal and noncereal producers, to analyze (a) world food demands, (b) the overall supply situation, and (c) the need and provision of concessional food aid and other means to address the food problem, including more assistance to agricultural production.

As a first step in achieving joint action, the Secretary of State has proposed that the United Nations call a World Food Conference in 1974 to consider ways to maintain adequate food supplies and harness the efforts of all nations to meet hunger.[28]

The less developed nations have made rapid progress in agricultural production, but more needs to be done in relation to their needs. Since 1955 agricultural production in the LDC's has increased some 62 percent. This is in fact a more rapid rate of growth than the developed countries, which increased production 51 percent, achieved during the same period. However, per capita agricultural output in the LDC's only increased 3 percent during the same period. Hence, food production in these countries is just holding its own against population growth. These countries remain, therefore, close to the edge of malnutrition and hunger—dependent increasingly on imports and on the world's stocks when an emergency arises.

In the years ahead appropriately directed economic and technical assistance for agriculture in the developing countries will be the difference between adequate food and nutrition or mass starvation in many areas. U.S. economic assistance is primarily directed to agricultural and family planning problems.

Research To Increase Crop Yields

With very little new land to develop, food production increases

[28]Document 45.

must come from higher yields of land already in farming. This requires new farming technologies, new farming methods, new institutional capabilities, and usually new governmental policy approaches.

We all know of the new wheat, rice, and corn varieties that scientists have developed in the last several years. Led largely by American scientists and supported by work in our universities and Department of Agriculture, an International Research Center in Mexico has made basic genetic improvements in the spring wheats of the type grown widely in the tropics. These varieties have been adapted to local conditions by additional work done locally in several Asian countries, often with American scientific help and in research institutions we helped to build. The same thing has been done with rice through an International Research Center located in the Philippines. Other international centers are working on other crops and livestock. American universities are collaborating with these centers and are themselves taking the lead on similar efforts with sorghum, winter wheat, soybeans, and livestock, as well as basic research on soil and water management. The United States contributes to all phases of these research efforts through the foreign aid program.

Of the 12 less developed Asian countries for which comparable data are available, the six which led the way in the shift to new varieties increased total rice production almost 40 percent in the last six years. The six which made the least such changes increased total rice production only about 11 percent—nearly a 4 to 1 difference.

For wheat the difference was even more dramatic. The top four countries in the rate of adoption of new wheat varieties more than doubled total wheat production in six years. This is an astounding accomplishment. The remaining 10 countries, which made only minor shifts toward the new technologies, increased their total production only some 12 percent. In other words, countries which shifted heavily to new varieties and the necessary related technological improvements increased their total wheat production some nine times as much as did those which did not make these changes.

Benefits of Collaborative Research

Important total production increases have been limited essentially to those crops on which substantial scientific research and development have taken place on an organized worldwide basis and to those countries where the results of this research have been vigorously incorporated into public and private action.

This progress is due in large part to the fact that we, other donor countries, and the developing countries have really begun to learn how to work together under close collaborative research and development arrangements to tackle the central problems of food production, nutrition, and human reproduction. We have learned that unorganized bits and pieces of effort carried out in many places seldom carry us far. But the same effort, when put to work in a systematic mutually supporting way, gets results. The arrangements are supported by the self-interest of the participating countries, who are learning that this is the only way to solve their own problems. The United States finances only a small fraction of the cost, but it provides the impetus and often the central scientific skill essential to the success of the entire enterprise.

As with the other participants, we are direct beneficiaries of these organized research and development efforts. Often the feedback of this research to American agriculture far exceeds its cost. Plant and animal disease resistance factors discovered overseas are priceless to us when the disease breaks out here. High-protein cereals developed through these efforts can contribute importantly to the diets of our poorest people and should bring down the cost of animal feed rations—a great need at the present time, as we all know.

Immediately before us is the task of broadening the base of agricultural production increases, both in the number of crops and of countries making rapid production increases. Fortunately, the background work for much of this is well underway. You may have read in last weekend's press of a plant-breeding "breakthrough" by Purdue University in radically increasing, by at least 300 percent, the human nutritional value of sorghum. We are at almost this same point of accomplishment in improving nutritional values of wheat, through a research project led by the University of Nebraska, collaborating with the U.S. Department of Agriculture, the International Research Center in Mexico, and some 35 or more LDC's.

The Canadians are taking the lead, under similar collaborative arrangements, in work on the root crop "manioc"—often called cassava or a half-dozen other names—a crop grown largely, also, by very poor people on over-poor lands.

All this means, to me, that we are on the right track and that there is much reason for optimism regarding the medium and long term, if we persevere in our economic assistance efforts.

The availability of a scientific and technological base for rapid agricultural production increases by no means assures that individual farmers, or countries, will have the institutions and resources to translate these technical possibilities into production performance.

New technological potentialities do not take root unless certain requisite institutional capabilities exist in the country, unless adequate numbers of skilled ·personnel are available to guide the process and a competent citizenry exists to put it to work on the farms and throughout the distributional system, and unless the capital is available so the farmer can buy fertilizer and other essential production inputs.

The congressional initiatives to focus the bilateral economic aid program more directly on the problems of food production, rural development, and population are an important step in the right direction, but the resources must be adequate to the task before us. We need the economic assistance tools if research is to continue and the needed production increases in the poor countries are to be realized.

Additionally, the extraordinary disasters of the Sahel and Pakistan have put large demands on economic assistance resources which had not been foreseen.

In closing I want to emphasize the importance of moving on all these fronts:

—We need adequate concessional food supplies to meet the immediate needs of the developing world which press against basic subsistence levels;

—We need better mechanisms for international cooperation to assure adequate world stocks and to harness the efforts of all nations to meet the problems of hunger and malnutrition; and

—We need to expand our research and development efforts in agriculture and related areas to accelerate production increases in the less developed countries.

Only with a comprehensive approach to these problems can we stave off continuing hunger and malnutrition and recurring food crises in the world.

(73) "The Energy Emergency": Radio-television address by President Nixon, November 7, 1973.[29]

Good evening.

I want to talk to you tonight about a serious national problem, a problem we must all face together in the months and years ahead.

As America has grown and prospered in recent years, our ener-

---

[29]Text from *Presidential Documents*, vol. 9 (1973), pp. 1312-18. For the President's formal message to Congress of Nov. 8, see same, pp. 1319-22.

gy demands have begun to exceed available supplies. In recent months, we have taken many actions to increase supplies and to reduce consumption. But even with our best efforts, we knew that a period of temporary shortages was inevitable.

Unfortunately, our expectations for this winter have now been sharply altered by the recent conflict in the Middle East. Because of that war, most of the Middle Eastern oil producers have reduced overall production and cut off their shipments of oil to the United States. By the end of this month, more than 2 million barrels a day of oil we expected to import into the United States will no longer be available.

We must, therefore, face up to a very stark fact: We are heading toward the most acute shortages of energy since World War II. Our supply of petroleum this winter will be at least 10 percent short of our anticipated demands, and it could fall short by as much as 17 percent.

Now, even before war broke out in the Middle East, these prospective shortages were the subject of intensive discussions among members of my Administration, leaders of the Congress, Governors, mayors, and other groups. From these discussions has emerged a broad agreement that we, as a Nation, must now set upon a new course.

In the short run, this course means that we must use less energy—that means less heat, less electricity, less gasoline. In the long run, it means that we must develop new sources of energy which will give us the capacity to meet our needs without relying on any foreign nation.

The immediate shortage will affect the lives of each and every one of us. In our factories, our cars, our homes, our offices, we will have to use less fuel than we are accustomed to using. Some school and factory schedules may be realigned, and some jet airplane flights will be canceled.

This does not mean that we are going to run out of gasoline or that air travel will stop or that we will freeze in our homes or offices anyplace in America. The fuel crisis need not mean genuine suffering for any American. But it will require some sacrifice by all Americans.

We must be sure that our most vital needs are met first—and that our least important activities are the first to be cut back. And we must be sure that while the fat from our economy is being trimmed, the muscle is not seriously damaged.

To help us carry out that responsibility, I am tonight announcing the following steps:

First, I am directing that industries and utilities which use coal—which is our most abundant resource—be prevented from converting from coal to oil. Efforts will also be made to convert powerplants from the use of oil to the use of coal.

Second, we are allocating reduced quantities of fuel for aircraft. Now, this is going to lead to a cutback of more than 10 percent of the number of flights and some rescheduling of arrival and departure times.

Third, there will be reductions of approximately 15 percent in the supply of heating oil for homes and offices and other establishments. To be sure that there is enough oil to go around for the entire winter, all over the country, it will be essential for all of us to live and work in lower temperatures. We must ask everyone to lower the thermostat in your home by at least 6 degrees, so that we can achieve a national daytime average of 68 degrees. Incidentally, my doctor tells me that in a temperature of 66 to 68 degrees, you are really more healthy than when it is 75 to 78, if that is any comfort. In offices, factories, and commercial establishments, we must ask that you achieve the equivalent of a 10-degree reduction by either lowering the thermostat or curtailing working hours.

Fourth, I am ordering additional reductions in the consumption of energy by the Federal Government. We have already taken steps to reduce the Government's consumption by 7 percent. The cuts must now go deeper and must be made by every agency and every department in the Government. I am directing that the daytime temperatures in Federal offices be reduced immediately to a level of between 65 and 68 degrees, and that means in this room, too, as well as in every other room in the White House. In addition, I am ordering that all vehicles owned by the Federal Government—and there are over a half-million of them—travel no faster than 50 miles per hour except in emergencies. This is a step which I have also asked Governors, mayors, and local officials to take immediately with regard to vehicles under their authority.

Fifth, I am asking the Atomic Energy Commission to speed up the licensing and construction of nuclear plants. We must seek to reduce the time required to bring nuclear plants on line—nuclear plants that can produce power—to bring them on line from 10 years to 6 years, reduce that time lag.

Sixth, I am asking that Governors and mayors reinforce these actions by taking appropriate steps at the State and local level. We have already learned, for example, from the State of Oregon, that considerable amounts of energy can be saved simply by curbing unnecessary lighting and slightly altering the school year. I am recommending that other communities follow this example and also seek ways to stagger working hours, to encourage greater use of mass transit and car pooling.

How many times have you gone along the highway or the freeway, wherever the case may be, and see hundreds and hundreds of cars with only one individual in that car. This we must all cooperate to change.

Consistent with safety and economic considerations, I am also asking Governors to take steps to reduce highway speed limits to 50 miles per hour. This action alone, if it is adopted on a nationwide basis, could save over 200,000 barrels of oil a day—just reducing the speed limit to 50 miles per hour.

Now, all of these actions will result in substantial savings of energy. More than that, most of these are actions that we can take right now—without further delay.

The key to their success lies, however, not just here in Washington, but in every home, in every community across this country. If each of us joins in this effort, joins with the spirit and the determination that have always graced the American character, then half the battle will already be won.

But we should recognize that even these steps, as essential as they are, may not be enough. We must be prepared to take additional steps, and for that purpose, additional authorities must be provided by the Congress.

I have therefore directed my chief adviser for energy policy, Governor [John A.] Love, and other Administration officials, to work closely with the Congress in developing an emergency energy act.

I met with the leaders of the Congress this morning, and I asked that they act on this legislation on a priority, urgent basis. It is imperative that this legislation be on my desk for signature before the Congress recesses this December.

Because of the hard work that has already been done on this bill by Senators Jackson and Fannin[30] and others, I am confident that we can meet that goal and that I will have the bill on this desk and will be able to sign it.[31]

This proposed legislation would enable the executive branch to meet the energy emergency in several important ways:

First, it would authorize an immediate return to Daylight Saving Time on a year-round basis.

Second, it would provide the necessary authority to relax environmental regulations on a temporary, case-by-case basis, thus permitting an appropriate balancing of our environmental interests, which all of us share, with our energy requirements, which, of course, are indispensable.

Third, it would grant authority to impose special energy con-

---

[30]Paul J. Fannin, Democrat of Arizona.

[31]The Emergency Petroleum Allocation Act of 1973, embodying a part of the President's recommendations, was signed Nov. 27, 1973 as Public Law 93-159.

servation measures, such as restrictions on the working hours for shopping centers and other commercial establishments.

And fourth, it would approve and fund increased exploration, development, and production from our Naval Petroleum Reserves. Now, these reserves are rich sources of oil. From one of them alone—Elk Hills in California—we could produce more than 160,000 barrels of oil a day within 2 months.

Fifth, it would provide the Federal Government with authority to reduce highway speed limits throughout the Nation.

And finally, it would expand the power of the Government's regulatory agencies to adjust the schedules of planes, ships, and other carriers.

If shortages persist despite all of these actions and despite inevitable increases in the price of energy products, it may then become necessary—may become necessary—to take even stronger measures.

It is only prudent that we be ready to cut the consumption of oil products, such as gasoline, by rationing, or by a fair system of taxation, and consequently, I have directed that contingency plans, if this becomes necessary, be prepared for that purpose.

Now, some of you may wonder whether we are turning back the clock to another age. Gas rationing, oil shortages, reduced speed limits—they all sound like a way of life we left behind with Glenn Miller and the war of the forties. Well, in fact, part of our current problem also stems from war—the war in the Middle East. But our deeper energy problems come not from war, but from peace and from abundance. We are running out of energy today because our economy has grown enormously and because in prosperity what were once considered luxuries are now considered necessities.

How many of you can remember when it was very unusual to have a home air-conditioned? And yet, this is very common in almost all parts of the Nation.

As a result, the average American will consume as much energy in the next 7 days as most other people in the world will consume in an entire year. We have only 6 percent of the world's people in America, but we consume over 30 percent of all the energy in the world.

Now, our growing demands have bumped up against the limits of available supply, and until we provide new sources of energy for tomorrow, we must be prepared to tighten our belts today.

Let me turn now to our long-range plans.

While a resolution of the immediate crisis is our highest priority, we must also act now to prevent a recurrence of such a crisis in the future. This is a matter of bipartisan concern. It is going to require a bipartisan response.

Two years ago, in the first energy message any President has ever sent to the Congress, I called attention to our urgent energy problem.[32] Last April, this year, I reaffirmed to the Congress the magnitude of that problem, and I called for action on seven major legislative initiatives.[33] Again in June, I called for action. I have done so frequently since then.

But thus far, not one major energy bill that I have asked for has been enacted. I realize that the Congress has been distracted in this period by other matters. But the time has now come for the Congress to get on with this urgent business—providing the legislation that will meet not only the current crisis but also the long-range challenge that we face.

Our failure to act now on our long-term energy problems could seriously endanger the capacity of our farms and of our factories to employ Ameicans at record-breaking rates—nearly 86 million people are now at work in this country—and to provide the highest standard of living we, or any other nation, has ever known in history.

It could reduce the capacity of our farmers to provide the food we need. It could jeopardize our entire transportation system. It could seriously weaken the ability of America to continue to give the leadership which only we can provide to keep the peace that we have won at such great cost, for thousands of our finest young Americans.

That is why it is time to act now on vital energy legislation that will affect our daily lives, not just this year, but for years to come.

We must have the legislation now which will authorize construction of the Alaska pipeline—legislation which is not burdened with irrelevant and unnecessary provisions.

We must have legislative authority to encourage production of our vast quantities of natural gas, one of the cleanest and best sources of energy.

We must have the legal ability to set reasonable standards for the surface mining of coal.

And we must have the organizational structures to meet and administer our energy programs.

And therefore, tonight, as I did this morning in meeting with the Congressional leaders, I again urge the Congress to give its attention to the initiatives I recommended 6 months ago to meet these needs that I have described.

Finally, I have stressed repeatedly the necessity of increasing our energy research and development efforts. Last June, I announced a 5-year, $10 billion program to develop better ways of using energy

---

[32]*Public Papers, 1971*, pp. 703-14.
[33]Cf. Chapter 10 at note 6, and note 19 to Document 54.

and to explore and develop new energy sources. Last month I announced plans for an immediate acceleration of that program.

We can take heart from the fact that we in the United States have half the world's known coal reserves. We have huge, untapped sources of natural gas. We have the most advanced nuclear technology known to man. We have oil in our continental shelves. We have oil shale out in the Western part of the United States, and we have some of the finest technical and scientific minds in the world. In short, we have all the resources we need to meet the great challenge before us. Now we must demonstrate the will to meet that challenge.

In World War II, America was faced with the necessity of rapidly developing an atomic capability. The circumstances were grave. Responding to that challenge, this Nation brought together its finest scientific skills and its finest administrative skills in what was known as the Manhattan Project. With all the needed resources at its command, with the highest priority assigned to its efforts, the Manhattan Project gave us the atomic capacity that helped to end the war in the Pacific and to bring peace to the world.

Twenty years later, responding to a different challenge, we focused our scientific and technological genius on the frontiers of space. We pledged to put a man on the moon before 1970, and on July 20, 1969, Neil Armstrong made that historic "giant leap for mankind" when he stepped on the moon.

The lessons of the Apollo project and of the earlier Manhattan Project are the same lessons that are taught by the whole of American history: Whenever the American people are faced with a clear goal and they are challenged to meet it, we can do extraordinary things.

Today the challenge is to regain the strength that we had earlier in this century, the strength of self-sufficiency. Our ability to meet our own energy needs is directly limited to our continued ability to act decisively and independently at home and abroad in the service of peace, not only for America, but for all nations in the world.

I have ordered funding of this effort to achieve self-sufficiency far in excess of the funds that were expended on the Manhattan Project. But money is only one of the ingredients essential to the success of such a project. We must also have a unified commitment to that goal. We must have unified direction of the effort to accomplish it.

Because of the urgent need for an organization that would provide focused leadership for this effort, I am asking the Congress to consider my proposal for an Energy Research and Development Administration separate from any other organizational initiatives, and to enact this legislation in the present session of the Congress.

Let us unite in committing the resources of this Nation to a major new endeavor, an endeavor that in this Bicentennial Era we can appropriately call "Project Independence."

Let us set as our national goal, in the spirit of Apollo, with the determination of the Manhattan Project, that by the end of this decade we will have developed the potential to meet our own energy needs without depending on any foreign energy sources.

Let us pledge that by 1980, under Project Independence, we shall be able to meet America's energy needs from America's own energy resources.

In speaking to you tonight in terms as direct as these, my concern has been to lay before you the full facts of the Nation's energy shortage. It is important that each of us understands what the situation is and how the efforts we together can take to help to meet it are essential to our total effort.

No people in the world perform more nobly than the American people when called upon to unite in the service of their country. I am supremely confident that while the days and weeks ahead may be a time of some hardship for many of us, they will also be a time of renewed commitment and concentration to the national interest.

We have an energy crisis, but there is no crisis of the American spirit. Let us go forward, then, doing what needs to be done, proud of what we have accomplished together in the past, and confident of what we can accomplish together in the future.

Let us find in this time of national necessity a renewed awareness of our capacities as a people, a deeper sense of our responsibilities as a Nation, and an increased understanding that the measure and the meaning of America has always been determined by the devotion which each of us brings to our duty as citizens of America.

I should like to close with a personal note.

It was just one year ago that I was reelected as President of the United States of America. During this past year we have made great progress in achieving the goals that I set forth in my reelection campaign.

We have ended the longest war in America's history. All of our prisoners of war have been returned home. And for the first time in 25 years, no young Americans are being drafted into the Armed Services. We have made progress toward our goal of a real prosperity, a prosperity without war. The rate of unemployment is down to 4½ percent, which is the lowest unemployment in peacetime that we have had in 16 years, and we are finally beginning to make progress in our fight against the rise in the cost of living.

These are substantial achievements in this year 1973. But I would be less than candid if I were not to admit that this has not been an easy year in some other respects, as all of you are quite aware.

As a result of the deplorable Watergate matter, great numbers of Americans have had doubts raised as to the integrity of the President of the United States. I have even noted that some publications have called on me to resign the Office of President of the United States.

Tonight I would like to give my answer to those who have suggested that I resign.

I have no intention whatever of walking away from the job I was elected to do. As long as I am physically able, I am going to continue to work 16 to 18 hours a day for the cause of a real peace abroad, and for the cause of prosperity without inflation and without war at home. And in the months ahead, I shall do everything that I can to see that any doubts as to the integrity of the man who occupies the highest office in this land—to remove those doubts where they exist.

And I am confident that in those months ahead, the American people will come to realize that I have not violated the trust that they placed in me when they elected me as President of the United States in the past, and I pledge to you tonight that I shall always do everything that I can to be worthy of that trust in the future.

Thank you and good night.

25. STARTING THE DIPLOMATIC SHUTTLE

An official who had traveled so extensively in his capacity as a Presidential Assistant would hardly have adopted a sedentary view of his responsibilities as Secretary of State. Dr. Kissinger had been less than a fortnight in his new post when President Nixon revealed that the new Secretary would be going to Peking in late October as part of the continuing U.S.-Chinese dialogue, and that he would also be stopping over in Japan—a country, Mr. Nixon emphasized, to whose position in "the club" of "free world" nations the United States continued to attach vital importance.[1] Subsequently postponed for approximately a fortnight because of the war in the Middle East, the Secretary's Far Eastern trip eventually developed in somewhat altered form as a kind of appendage to Dr. Kissinger's more sensational foray into the Middle Eastern theater.

The Secretary of State and the President had not lacked justification for their assertions in the wake of the October 25 alert that the Middle East situation contained hopeful as well as dangerous elements. Aside from the supremely reassuring fact that a threatened clash involving the major powers had been avoided, there were signs that some of the Arab countries, having managed to put on a creditable military performance in relation to Israel, might possibly be prepared to moderate to some extent their political intransigence toward that country and also toward the United States, its principal international sponsor. One encouraging sign was the prompt acceptance by President Sadat of Egypt of Dr. Kissinger's offer to stop over in Cairo to discuss the current situation on his way to the Far East.

There would be no lack of topics for joint examination on such a visit. Even with the fighting stopped, there remained an obvious need for diplomatic initiatives aimed at resolving the tense and difficult situation at the Suez Canal, relieving the plight of the beleaguered Egyptian Third Army, and encouraging the Israelis to

---

[1]News conference, Oct. 3, in *Bulletin*, vol. 69 (1973), pp. 501-3.

begin their pullback to the October 22 cease-fire line as demanded
by the Security Council. Thanks to the unexpected measure of confidence accorded the new Secretary of State by both Arabs and
Israelis, Dr. Kissinger soon would find himself performing an
honest broker's role of a sort no other American had been able to
play since the U.N. mediation mission of Dr. Ralph Bunche in
1948-49.

A start on the ticklish task of disengaging the hostile armies at
Suez was facilitated by the presence in Washington during the postwar days of Israel's Premier Golda Meir and of Ismail Fahmy, a
Sadat emissary who was soon to be named Egyptian Foreign
Minister. Repeated contact with the two envoys, in what amounted to a preview of the famous Kissinger "shuttle diplomacy,"
proved helpful in identifying the principal points with which any
agreement would have to deal,[2] among them the opening of a supply route to Suez city, an exchange of prisoners, and some pullback
of Israeli military forces. The filling in of the details, it was
recognized, would have to await further discussion nearer the scene
of action.

Secretary Kissinger's first official visit to the Middle East[3] got
under way on November 5-6 with brief stopovers in Morocco and
Tunisia for consultations with those countries' heads of state, both
of whom were traditionally well disposed toward the United States.
On Wednesday, November 7, there took place a first, remarkably
cordial meeting with President Sadat in Cairo, marked not only by
progress toward resolving the Suez difficulty but also by an
agreement in principle on the early resumption of diplomatic
relations between Egypt and the United States. On Thursday,
November 8, the Secretary of State proceeded via Amman to
Riyadh, Saudi Arabia, where he obtained King Faisal's promise to
intercede with Syria in the interests of peacemaking but failed to
convince this hitherto friendly monarch that the time had come to
relax the oil embargo.[4] Assistant Secretary Sisco, meanwhile, had
flown to Jerusalem and was working with the Israelis to pin down
details of the Suez disengagement plan as it had emerged from the
Cairo conversations.

The results of this complicated endeavor were embodied in the
message that Secretary Kissinger dispatched to U.N. Secretary-
General Waldheim early on Friday, November 9, as the Secretary

[2]For details see Kalb, *Kissinger*, pp. 500-505, and cf. note 6 to Chapter 22.
[3]Narrative in same, pp. 505-18; documentation in *Bulletin*, vol. 69 (1973), pp. 712-17.
[4]Edward R. F. Sheehan, "Step by Step in the Middle East," *Foreign Policy*, No. 22 (Spring 1976), pp. 18-22.

of State continued his journey to Peking via Tehran and Islamabad. This communication (**Document 74**), transmitted through American diplomatic channels, contained the terms of a crucial accord between Egyptians and Israelis with regard to the procedure for implementing the cease-fire and withdrawal provisions of the recent Security Council resolutions. In addition to arrangements for provisioning the town of Suez and exchanging prisoners of war, the document confirmed the agreement of the two sides that discussions between them should begin immediately "to settle the question of the return to the October 22 positions in the framework of agreement on the disengagement and separation of forces under the auspices of the UN." To sign this bilateral agreement and provide for its implementation, Dr. Kissinger advised, the Egyptians and Israelis had also agreed that a meeting would be held the following day—or at another mutually convenient time—under the auspices of the U.N. Commander at Kilometer 109 on the Suez-Cairo road, an Israeli checkpoint which had previously served as a meeting place of Egyptian and Israeli military representatives.

In a slight departure from the advance program, the actual signature of the agreement took place two days later, on Sunday, November 11, and at Kilometer marker 101 (rather than 109) on the same highway. General Siilasvuo, as Commander-designate of the new U.N. Emergency Force, presided, Egypt being represented by Major General Mohammed el-Gamasy and Israel by Major General Aharon Yaariv. Once the agreement was signed, the three generals plunged immediately into a first discussion of "the modalities of its implementation."[5]

That this bilateral agreement represented no more than an opening step in the peacemaking process was strongly emphasized by Secretary Kissinger in response to questions from newsmen accompanying him on the Peking trip. "We have had from the beginning two objectives," the Secretary of State explained. "One is to stabilize the cease-fire, and then once the cease-fire was stabilized, we move from there to a peace conference." Having signed the cease-fire stabilization agreement, Dr. Kissinger continued, it still remained for Israel and Egypt "to negotiate some of the implementation of modalities of this. When that is completed, which we hope will be soon, we will move into setting up the peace conference. Our expectations is that this should not be more than a matter of weeks."[6]

---

[5]U.N. document S/11056/Add.3, Nov. 11, in Security Council, *Official Records: Supplement for Oct., Nov. and Dec. 1973*, pp. 97-8.

[6]Peking interview, Nov. 12, in *Bulletin*, vol. 69 (1973), pp. 714-15.

In the meantime, the Secretary had already immersed himself in an assessment of the development of the Sino-American relationship since his previous visit in February.[7] The August Congress of the Chinese Communist Party had wrought few visible changes in the top leadership of the People's Republic, and it was not yet realized that Premier Chou En-lai, the principal architect of the *rapprochement* with the United States, was stricken with cancer and would in the next couple of years increasingly delegate administrative responsibilities to Teng Hsiao-ping, a rehabilitated victim of the "Cultural Revolution." It was, however, entirely evident by November 1973 that Chairman Mao and his associates were puzzled and concerned about the implications of Watergate; and Secretary Kissinger appears to have made a special effort to assure his hosts that U.S. friendship for China was too firmly rooted to be affected by any vicissitudes of domestic American politics.[8]

The concrete results of the Peking visit were not intended to be dramatic. There was drama enough in current figures on the expansion of U.S.-Chinese trade, which would depict an increase from $4.9 million in 1971 to $803.6 million in 1973. "On the trip," Secretary Kissinger later summarized, "we brought about an expansion of the functions of the Liaison Offices, a continuation of the exchange programs, an expansion of trade, and a substantial expansion of the consultative processes. This was the maximum that we had set ourselves as a goal."[9] Aside from the recitation of a mutual commitment to continued normalization efforts and strengthened bilateral ties, the formal communiqué made public in Peking and Washington (**Document 75**) was mainly notable for its repetition of earlier language setting forth the two governments' views on the Taiwan issue and rejecting "hegemony" in the Asia-Pacific region, a harmless-sounding formula that was equated by the Chinese with opposition to Soviet influence.

Following brief stopovers in Japan and Korea—where, he reported, "we strengthened the friendships that have lasted now for most of the postwar period"[10]—Secretary Kissinger returned to Washington on November 16 amid quickening hopes for a commencement of genuine peace negotiations on the Middle East. The most pressing local issues had by this time been resolved at the Kilometer 101 talks, with U.N. checkpoints replacing Israeli checkpoints and an exchange of prisoners—some 8,300 Egyptians against 241 Israelis—already under way. Although there had been

---

[7]Cf. Chapter 8.
[8]Kalb, *Kissinger*, pp. 436-8.
[9]News conference, Nov. 21, in *Bulletin*, vol. 69 (1973), pp. 702-3.
[10]Homecoming remarks, Nov. 16, in same, p. 717.

no progress on the Syrian front—and, perhaps, even more important, no progress on the vital question of a general Israeli-Egyptian disengagement and return to the October 22 cease-fire lines—fears of a new clash between Egyptians and Israelis had been progressively reduced with the expansion of the new U.N. Emergency Force to a strength (as of November 23) of 2,566 men from nine countries.[11]

All in all, the Secretary of State indicated at a November 21 news conference,[12] there had been sufficient progress in the Egyptian-Israeli talks "so that we can look forward with some confidence to the beginning of peace negotiations." Security Council Resolution 338,[13] Dr. Kissinger recalled, had contemplated an immediate commencement of negotiations "under appropriate auspices"; and the Secretary of State again affirmed that in the American view such auspices could best be furnished by the United States and the Soviet Union. In addition, he conceded, it would be desirable that the proposed negotiations "should be generally blessed by the United Nations," and should assume a form that would permit participation by the Secretary-General in a symbolic role. Citing "rather substantial understandings with all of the parties" which indicated that the negotiating process might begin in the course of December, the Secretary suggested that agreement would soon be reached on both the site of the conference and the identity of the participants.

Given these rather encouraging prospects, Secretary Kissinger was plainly unconvinced of the relevance of "the various oil pressures" that had been invoked against the United States during hostilities, and were still being applied with full rigor despite its constructive diplomatic efforts. American policy, Dr. Kissinger stressed, had been and would continue to be determined "not by the pressures that this or that nation may attempt to generate, but by the American conception of the national interest and of the interest of general peace." Responding to a question about unspecified "countermeasures" the United States might take if pressures continued, the Secretary again stressed his hope that the embargo would be lifted "when it becomes apparent that we are attempting to bring about a just peace." "However," he added, "it is clear that if pressures continue unreasonably and indefinitely, then the United States will have to consider what countermeasures it may have to take. We would do this with enormous reluctance, and we are still hopeful that matters will not reach this point."

[11]U.N. document S/11056/Add.6, Nov. 24, *loc. cit.*, p. 100.
[12]Partial text in Document 76; full text in *Bulletin*, vol. 69 (1973), pp. 701-10.
[13]Document 59b.

The Arab nations, however, were plainly disinclined to hearken to American advice in this matter. Meeting in Algiers on November 26-28, the leaders of fifteen Arab countries and the Palestine Liberation Organization decided (in the absence of Iraq and Libya) that the embargo should *not* be lifted, but that the use of the oil weapon should continue until the Arabs' supreme political aims had been achieved—i.e., "until the withdrawal from occupied Arab lands is realized and the rights of the Palestinian people are assured."[14] Grievously as it had suffered in the recent war, there was no prospect whatever that Israel would meet such terms as they were understood by the Arab governments. Much had nevertheless been accomplished in defusing the immediate situation, and Secretary Kissinger, anxious to prevent a loss of momentum, was already contemplating a second visit to the area in advance of the proposed peace conference. In the meantime, the United States faced other problems of a critical nature both in Southeast Asia and in Europe.

(74) Egyptian-Israeli Disengagement Agreement: Letter from Secretary Kissinger to Secretary-General Waldheim, November 9, 1973.[15]

NOVEMBER 9, 1973.

DEAR MR. SECRETARY GENERAL: I have the honor to inform you that the governments of Egypt and Israel are prepared to accept the following agreement which implements Article I of the United Nations Security Council Resolution 338 and Article I of United Nations Security Council Resolution 339.[16]

The text of this agreement is as follows:

A. Egypt and Israel agree to observe scrupulously the ceasefire called for by the UN Security Council.

B. Both sides agree that discussions between them will begin immediately to settle the question of the return to the October 22 positions in the framework of agreement on the disengagement and separation of forces under the auspices of the UN.

C. The town of Suez will receive daily supplies of food, water and medicine. All wounded civilians in the town of Suez will be evacuated.

---

[14]*Keesing's*, p. 26245. For further developments see Chapter 29.
[15]White House Press Release, Nov. 9, text from *Bulletin*, vol. 69 (1973), p. 711. A slightly different text, incorporated in a letter from Ambassador Scali to Secretary-General Waldheim, appears in U.N. document S/11091, Nov. 9, *loc. cit.*, p. 217.
[16]Respectively Documents 59b and 60a.

D. There shall be no impediment to the movement of non-military supplies to the East Bank.

E. The Israeli checkpoints on the Cairo-Suez road will be replaced by UN checkpoints. At the Suez end of the road Israeli officers can participate with the UN to supervise the non-military nature of the cargo at the bank of the Canal.

F. As soon as the UN checkpoints are established on the Cairo-Suez road, there will be an exchange of all prisoners of war, including wounded.

It has also been agreed by the two parties that they will hold a meeting under the auspices of the United Nations Commander at the usual place (kilometer 109 on the Suez-Cairo road) to sign this agreement and to provide for its implementation. I would be most grateful if you would take the appropriate steps to insure that a meeting is held on Saturday, November 10, 1973, or at such other time as may be mutually convenient of representatives of the parties to take the appropriate steps.

We intend to announce publicly the agreement at noon New York time on Friday, November 9, 1973.

Best regards,

HENRY A. KISSINGER.

(75) Visit to the People's Republic of China, November 10-14, 1973: Joint Communiqué issued in Washington and Peking, November 14, 1973.[17]

Dr. Henry A. Kissinger, U.S. Secretary of State and Assistant to the President for National Security Affairs, visited the People's Republic of China from November 10 to November 14, 1973. He was accompanied by Robert Ingersoll, Robert McCloskey, Arthur Hummel, Winston Lord, Oscar Armstrong, Jonathan Howe, and Richard Solomon.

Chairman Mao Tse-tung received Secretary Kissinger. They held a wide-ranging and far-sighted conversation in a friendly atmosphere. Secretary Kissinger conveyed greetings from President Nixon, and Chairman Mao Tse-tung sent his greetings to the President.

Secretary Kissinger and members of his party held frank and serious talks with Premier Chou En-lai, Foreign Minister Chi Peng-fei, Vice Foreign Minister Chiao Kuan-hua, Assistant Foreign Minister Wang Hai-jung, Director Lin Ping, Director Peng Hua, Tsien Ta-yung, Ting Yuan-hung and others.

[17]Text from *Presidential Documents*, vol. 9 (1973), p. 1332.

Officials of the two sides conducted counterpart talks on bilateral issues of mutual concern and made good progress.

The two sides reviewed international developments since Dr. Kissinger's visit to the People's Republic of China in February, 1973.[18] They noted that international relationships are in a period of intense change. They reaffirmed that they are committed to the principles established in the Shanghai Communiqué[19] and that disputes between states should be settled without resorting to the use or threat of force, on the basis of the principles of respect for the sovereignty and territorial integrity of all states, non-aggression against other states, non-interference in the internal affairs of other states, equality and mutual benefit, and peaceful coexistence. In particular, they reiterated that neither should seek hegemony in the Asia-Pacific region or any other part of the world and that each is opposed to efforts by any other country or group of countries to establish such hegemony.

The two sides agreed that in present circumstances it is of particular importance to maintain frequent contact at authoritative levels in order to exchange views and, while not negotiating on behalf of third parties, to engage in concrete consultations on issues of mutual concern.

Both sides reviewed progress made during 1973 in their bilateral relations. The U.S. side reaffirmed: The United States acknowledges that all Chinese on either side of the Taiwan Strait maintain there is but one China and that Taiwan is a part of China; the United States Government does not challenge that position. The Chinese side reiterated that the normalization of relations between China and the United States can be realized only on the basis of confirming the principle of one China.

Both sides noted with satisfaction that the liaison offices in Peking and Washington are functioning smoothly. Both sides agreed that the scope of the functions of the liaison offices should continue to be expanded.

Exchanges have deepened understanding and friendship between the two peoples. The two sides studied the question of enlarging the exchanges between the two countries and agreed upon a number of new exchanges for the coming year.

Trade between the two countries has developed rapidly during the past year. The two sides held that it is in the interest of both countries to take measures to create conditions for further development of trade on the basis of equality and mutual benefit.

The two sides stated that they would continue their efforts to

[18]Document 11.
[19]*AFR, 1972*, pp. 307-11.

promote the normalization of relations between China and the United States on the basis of the Shanghai Communiqué.

Secretary Kissinger and his party expressed their gratitude for the warm hospitality extended to them by the Government of the People's Republic of China.

(76) "Where We Stand": News conference statement by Secretary Kissinger, November 21, 1973.[20]

Secretary Kissinger: Ladies and gentlemen, I will just make a very few brief observations about where we stand in the Middle East, where we expect to go, then say a word about our attitude toward the various oil pressures.

First, with respect to the situation in the Middle East. As I have pointed out before, our objective was to solidify the cease-fire so that we could move forward, together with the other interested parties, toward peace negotiations.

Now, in the complex situation that exists on the Egyptian-Israeli front, sufficient progress has been made on the cease-fire, in the cease-fire negotiations, so that we can look forward with some confidence to the beginning of peace negotiations.

Our effort will be to create the appropriate auspices called for in Security Council Resolution 338[21] and under the auspices of the United Nations, to begin a negotiating process—hopefully, during the month of December—that we believe and that we expect and hope will lead toward the just and lasting peace that all parties have pledged themselves to attempt to negotiate.

The United States has committed itself, in Security Council Resolution 338, to support the implementation of Security Council Resolution 242[22] in all of its parts.

We will make a major effort to narrow the differences between the parties, to help the parties move toward the peace that all the peoples in the area need and that the peace of the world requires.

Now, this will be our policy in the Middle East.

We stated this policy to the Arab Foreign Ministers at the United Nations prior to the outbreak of the Arab-Israeli war. And I lay stress on this because the United States policy is determined not by the pressures that this or that nation may attempt to generate, but

---

[20]Department of State Press Release 423, Nov. 21; text from *Bulletin*, vol. 69 (1973), pp. 701-2.

[21]Document 59b.

[22]*Documents, 1967*, pp. 169-70.

by the American conception of the national interest and of the interest of general peace.

Now, the United States has full understanding for actions that may have been taken when the war was going on, by which the parties and their friends attempted to demonstrate how seriously they took the situation.

But as the United States has committed itself to a peaceful process, as the United States has pledged that it would make major efforts to bring about the implementation of Security Council Resolution 242, those countries who are engaging in economic pressures against the United States should consider whether it is appropriate to engage in such steps while peace negotiations are being prepared and, even more, while negotiations are being conducted.

I would like to state for the United States Government that our course will not be influenced by such pressures, that we have stated our policy, that we have expressed our commitments, and that we will adhere to those and will not be pushed beyond this point by any pressures.

Now, this is all I will say on the Middle East. But of course I will be delighted to answer your questions.

There is one matter that I wanted to raise with you ladies and gentlemen, growing out of my last press conference, in which I promised, within a week, to supply the material or the evidence on which our decision to go on alert was based.[23] It was a statement that, quite frankly, I regretted having made in terms of the short deadline immediately afterward. The reason is that as we are now moving toward peace negotiations, which we expect to conduct with the cooperation of the Soviet Union, I do not believe any useful purpose would be served if the United States recited confidential communications that had taken place and tried to recreate an episode of confrontation that, hopefully, has been transcended.

As time goes on and as the spirit of cooperation which we are attempting to foster in the Middle East takes hold, as things can be seen in fuller perspective, we still expect to fulfill what I have stated.

I am also glad to note that whatever the formal cooperation of the government, reportorial enterprise and the reluctance of associates to admit anything less than full knowledge of participation in events have both combined to produce journalistic ef-

---

[23]*Bulletin*, vol. 69 (1973), pp. 589 and 593.

forts that have given a fuller picture of events than those that were available on the morning of my last press conference.

So with these two observations, I will turn to your questions.[24]

---

[24]For the remainder of the news conference see *Bulletin, loc. cit.*, pp. 702-10. (Quotations appear above at note 13.)

26. NO PEACE FOR INDOCHINA

In the course of his November 21 news conference, Secretary Kissinger was asked in what way the American-Chinese "normalization process" he had been promoting in Peking might affect U.S. relations in Southeast Asia, particularly Cambodia. ". . . It has always been understood," the Secretary of State replied, "that progress toward normalization would be aided by a general condition of stability and tranquillity in Asia and that both sides had an obligation to do their utmost to bring this about. So we are hopeful that the situation in Southeast Asia will not be exacerbated by the actions of any outside country."[1] While there seemed at the moment to be no special reason to suspect the Chinese, at any rate, of deliberately muddying the waters in Southeast Asia, Dr. Kissinger's comment bore witness to a realization that conditions in that area had continued to deteriorate even while the United States had been so preoccupied with developments in the Middle East.

Since August 15, a resumption of American military activity in Indochina had been definitively barred by Act of Congress; and the Communist forces and movements operating in the different Indochinese countries had appeared to see less reason than ever to abide by the fragile restraints set up by the Paris peace agreement and related understandings. It was true that North Vietnam had not yet mounted the large-scale offensive in the south that had been so often predicted; yet the scale of localized conflict within South Vietnam was undeniably increasing from week to week as both Hanoi and Saigon prepared themselves for what both parties seemed to regard as an inevitable showdown.

Renewed North Vietnamese charges about the United States' alleged furnishing of illegal military assistance to South Vietnam were sharply contradicted in a new American note delivered to the North Vietnamese Embassy in Paris on October 26 (**Document 77**). In point of fact, the United States asserted in rejecting Hanoi's

---

[1]*Bulletin*, vol. 69 (1973), p. 702. For background cf. Chapter 16.

allegations, the North Vietnamese themselves were chronic of-fenders, whose record of habitual armistice violations ranged from illegal introduction of "vast quantities of war material" and "large numbers of North Vietnamese troops" into South Vietnam to a persistent refusal to permit the establishment and functioning of the agreed control organs. "The Democratic Republic of Viet-Nam will recognize that it has a grave responsibility in this matter and that on the course it elects to follow the prospects for lasting peace in Viet-Nam will depend," the note concluded.

North Vietnamese interference in Cambodia was less easily documented. Indeed, exiled Prince Sihanouk continued to insist that Hanoi had virtually ceased its aid to the insurgent Khmer Rouge forces, presumably in what to him appeared as ill-advised deference to American wishes.[2] Yet among all the countries of In-dochina and Southeast Asia, it was precisely in Cambodia that elements friendly to the United States had been placed in greatest difficulty as the Khmer Republic government struggled for survival under the enfeebled guidance of President Lon Nol.

President Nixon had taken notice of the difficult plight of the Cambodian military forces in his October 19 message asking for $2.2 billion in emergency security assistance for Israel (**Document 58**). The heavy fighting that had followed the termination of U.S. bombing in Cambodia on August 15 had abated somewhat during the subsequent rainy season, the President noted; but it would almost certainly resume by the end of the year, at which time the loyalist forces would face a critical shortage of ammunition unless an additional allotment of $200 million in American funds could be made available before the end of the fiscal year on June 30, 1974. "We remain hopeful that the conflict in Cambodia be resolved by a negotiated settlement," Mr. Nixon added. "A Communist military victory and the installation of a government in Phnom Penh which is controlled by Hanoi would gravely threaten the fragile structure of peace established in the Paris agreements."

In addition to a Communist insurgency extending over what had become virtually a nationwide battlefield, the Lon Nol government was menaced by a phalanx of nonaligned and Communist nations drawn up upon that global diplomatic battlefield, the United Nations General Assembly. The question of disaccrediting the Phnom Penh government and substituting Prince Sihanouk's "Royal Government of National Union" as the proper representa-tive of Cambodia in the United Nations had been placed on the Assembly's agenda in October, as already noted, and was taken up in an acrimonious two-day debate on December 4-5. In a

[2]*Keesing's*, p. 26187.

passionate defense of the Khmer Republic **(Document 78)**, Ambassador W. Tapley Bennett, Jr., of the United States denounced its enemies' campaign as "gross . . . blatant" interference in the internal affairs of a U.N. member state. Many other U.N. members, among them all of the non-Communist states of Southeast Asia, took a similar view, and the Assembly eventually decided, by a procedural vote of 53 to 50 with 22 abstentions, to postpone further consideration of the matter until 1974.[3]

The Nixon administration was less successful in winning the support of Congress for the President's plan to give Cambodia an extra $200 millions' worth of ammunition. Having already decided that the war in Indochina was over so far as the United States was concerned, American legislators were unenthusiastic about a project which, in the view of most of them, would only serve to prolong hostilities without regard to the merits of the rival governments. In passing the annual foreign aid appropriation bill a few days before Christmas,[4] Congress did include $150 million (rather than $200 million) in emergency aid for Cambodia, along with $2.2 billion for Israel. But this appropriation was made contingent on the enactment of separate authorizing legislation; and the separate authorization bill enacted the same day[5] provided full funding for Israel but nothing for Cambodia.

In justification of this omission, it was noted that the President still possessed authority to help Cambodia by drawing down items from U.S. defense stocks.[6] Any vestigial possibilities of aiding the crumbling Lon Nol regime would surely be eagerly canvased in Washington as the military ring around Phnom Penh again began to tighten in the closing days of 1973.

(77) Admonition to North Vietnam: United States note delivered to the Embassy of the Democratic Republic of Vietnam at Paris, October 26, 1973.[7]

The Department of State of the United States of America presents its compliments to the Ministry of Foreign Affairs of the Democratic Republic of Viet-Nam and has the honor to refer to the

[3]Details in *UN Monthly Chronicle*, vol. 11 (Jan. 1974), pp. 40-41, and *U.S. Participation, 1973*, pp. 61-4.

[4]Foreign Assistance and Related Programs Appropriation Act, 1974 (Public Law 93-240), Jan. 2, 1974.

[5]Emergency Security Assistance Act of 1973 (Public Law 93-199), Dec. 26, 1973.

[6]*Senate Foreign Relations Committee History, 1973-4*, p. 51.

[7]Department of State Press Release 394, Oct. 30; text from *Bulletin*, vol. 69 (1973), pp. 626-7.

Agreement on Ending the War and Restoring Peace in Viet-Nam of January 27, 1973.[8]

The United States refers to recent statements by the Democratic Republic of Viet-Nam that the United States is illegally providing military assistance to the Republic of Viet-Nam and states that these charges are without any foundation and intended to mask the Democratic Republic of Viet-Nam's own continuing violations of the Paris Agreement. The United States draws the Democratic Republic of Viet-Nam's attention to the fact that, as set forth in the United States note of April 20, 1973,[9] to the signatories of the March 2, 1973, Act of the International Conference on Viet-Nam and in the United States note to the Democratic Republic of Viet-Nam dated September 10, 1973,[10] the Democratic Republic of Viet-Nam side has shipped vast quantities of war material into South Viet-Nam since January 28 in violation of Article 7 of the Paris Agreement.

The United States notes that also in contravention of Article 7 of the Paris Agreement the Democratic Republic of Viet-Nam side has dispatched large numbers of North Vietnamese troops into South Viet-Nam since January 28, 1973. Some of these troops entered South Viet-Nam by crossing the Demilitarized Zone in violation of Article 15(b) of the Agreement, while others entered through Laos and Cambodia, violating Article 20(a).

The United States further notes that the Democratic Republic of Viet-Nam has failed to honor its commitment in the Joint Communique of June 13[11] to designate three additional points of entry and to discuss in the Two-Party Joint Military Commission modalities for the supervision of the replacement of armaments, munitions, and war material permitted under Article 17 of the Paris Agreement.

In addition, because of the Democratic Republic of Viet-Nam side's failure to cooperate with the International Commission of Control and Supervision (ICCS) and to provide it assistance and protection as required by Article 10 of the ICCS Protocol, the ICCS has been unable to station and maintain teams at certain locations where Article 4(d) of the ICCS Protocol requires that such teams be stationed: Gio Linh, Lao Bao, Duc Co and Xa Mat. In consequence of these failures by the Democratic Republic of Viet-Nam to honor its commitments under the Paris Agreement and its Protocols, the machinery provided for in the Agreement to

[8]Document 5.
[9]Document 9.
[10]Document 47.
[11]Document 30a.

supervise replacement of war materials by the two South Vietnamese parties has never been established. Responsibility for the lack of supervision of, and control over, import of war materials into South Viet-Nam lies entirely with the Democratic Republic of Viet-Nam.

The United States urges the Democratic Republic of Viet-Nam side to remedy this dangerous situation by ceasing all violations of Article 7 of the Paris Agreement; by at once formally designating three additional points of entry; by at once beginning discussions in the Two-Party Joint Military Commission regarding the modalities for the supervision of the replacement of war materials permitted under Article 7; and by immediately inviting the ICCS to send its teams to Gio Linh, Lao Bao, Duc Co, and Xa Mat, providing them with suitable quarters and other amenities. Only in this way can Article 7 of the Paris Agreement be implemented and violations by either side be prevented.

The Democratic Republic of Viet-Nam will recognize that it has a grave responsibility in this matter and that on the course it elects to follow the prospects for lasting peace in Viet-Nam will depend.

(78) *The Crisis of the Khmer Republic: Statement by Ambassador W. Tapley Bennett, Jr., United States Deputy Permanent Representative, to the United Nations General Assembly, December 5, 1973.*[12]

(Excerpts)

Last week this Assembly discussed means of strengthening the United Nations. During that debate the United States called attention to the growing tendency of some of our members to propose simplistic one-sided resolutions on the most complex and difficult of issues, resolutions often totally unacceptable to the parties concerned. My delegation pointed out then that in divorcing itself from reality in this manner, the General Assembly was weakening its ability to have impact on the real problems we face in many parts of the world.

Regrettably, the resolution we are considering today[13] is par-

[12]USUN Press Release 126, Corr.1; text from *Bulletin*, vol. 70 (1974), pp. 100-103.
[13]U.N. document A/L.714, a 33-nation draft resolution which would restore the "lawful rights" of the Royal Cambodian Government of National Union in the United Nations, recognize its representatives as the sole lawful representatives of Cambodia, and "expel the representatives of the Lon Nol group from the seat they illegally occupy in the United Nations and in all the organizations related to it."

ticularly notable both for its one-sidedness and for its failure to take account of the real situation as it presently exists in Cambodia and in East Asia. One can only wonder at the curious twists of logic which have produced a resolution through which some members of the nonaligned movement appear to support great-power hegemony in Asia, through which self-proclaimed revolutionary governments appear to support the divine right of a royal pretender, and through which some of those among us who are the most vociferous in denouncing outside interference in the affairs of sovereign states now propose that this Assembly instruct the Khmer people on who is to represent them.

Certainly the complexities of the issue before us are worthy of a more balanced, considered approach than that taken by this resolution. One must wonder whether its sponsors have thought through seriously the consequences of what they propose. Have they asked themselves, for example, why it is that only one East Asian member government supports seating Prince Sihanouk's "government"?

Many delegations here have been quick to voice their concern over any appearance of great-power domination and their resentment whenever they believe they sense the possibility of a great-power dictate. Have they, I wonder, thought about the implications of this resolution for Asia? Have they asked the views of their many East Asian colleagues? Have they considered that they would be siding with the great power of the area against the smaller ones?

Yesterday the distinguished Representative of Thailand referred to the views of seven Asian and Pacific states—Indonesia, Japan, Malaysia, New Zealand, the Philippines, Singapore, and Thailand. These states have formulated their position on the issue before us and have circulated it among the U.N. membership in document A/9254.[14] I believe that all of us have an obligation to examine these views carefully. Many members here have, in other circumstances, insisted on the importance of giving primacy to states of a region or their regional grouping in seeking solutions to problems of their respective area. In this case, it seems to me, we are fortunate to have a regional consensus before us, and we should certainly give it the greatest weight in our considerations.

The argumentation made in support of the "Royal Government

[14]The authors of U.N. document A/9254 "had asked that the Khmer people themselves be allowed to solve their own problems peacefully and free from outside interference in whatever form, that the political settlement be reached by the indigenous parties concerned, and that the United Nations not take any action which might prejudge the decision of the Khmer people and prolong their tragic suffering" (*U.S. Participation, 1973*, pp. 61-2).

of National Union of Cambodia" seems to rest largely on the principle that since Prince Sihanouk is at its head, it must be the true government of Cambodia. But with all due respect to Prince Sihanouk's once intimate, often constructive role in earlier Cambodian developments, I submit that we can find some more objective and reliable criteria for deciding who governs Cambodia. Better yet, can we not allow the Cambodian people the privilege of making this determination themselves? The Cambodian people have not, so far as I know, granted Prince Sihanouk any irrevocable right to rule over them. Neither, I submit, should we.

Among the sponsors of the resolution before us are some of the most vocal supporters of the principle of noninterference in the internal affairs of sovereign states. Have they fully considered the basic conflict between this principle and support for a resolution by which foreigners would tell the Khmer people who is to represent them in this world organization?

It is hard to conceive of a more gross or more blatant interference in the internal affairs of a member state. If this were to become a precedent, who is to say what member state in this Assembly might not be the next victim of such a procedure?

All of us who have been reading the international press —reputable journals such as *Le Monde* of Paris and the Guardian of Britain, which enjoy a large audience here in the United Nations—are aware that Prince Sihanouk himself admits that he is not in control of his "government" and that his "government" is not in control of Cambodia. Prince Sihanouk does not head a government-in-exile; he is a non-government-in-exile. Have the supporters of the resolution before us given thought to the precedent they are setting in seeking to have the United Nations decide the issue of Cambodian representation not on the basis of who actually governs Cambodia, but rather who they would like to have govern Cambodia?

But let us leave the never-never land of the "Royal Government of National Union of Cambodia" and resolution A/L.714. Let us turn our attention to the real world, to what has happened in Cambodia, what is happening, and what my delegation believes most of us hope will happen.

In March of 1970, Prince Norodom Sihanouk was removed as the Chief of State of Cambodia by a unanimous vote of the Cambodian Parliament under the terms of the constitution then in effect, the constitution that Prince Sihanouk himself had proclaimed. The complaint against the Prince which led to his removal was his open and since publicly admitted complicity with North Vietnamese forces in the prosecution of their war against the Republic of Viet-Nam. His activity included his giving permission for large-scale use of Cambodian territory by South Vietnamese Communists and the North Vietnamese Army over a period of years. This occupation began to supplant the indigenous Cambodian inhabitants and, in a de facto manner, to annex the areas occupied. Here is the real intervention by a foreign force. This is the intervention that began the tragedy of Cambodia.

The removal of Prince Sihanouk was not a palace coup. It resulted from popular disaffection and general discontent with the then existing situation. The initial demonstrations began in the provinces, protesting North Vietnamese occupation of their territory, and quickly spread to the capital, culminating in the Parliament's unanimous decision to remove Prince Sihanouk from the office.

I might note that Prince Sihanouk's removal from office was not accompanied by any change of government. The government in existence at the time had been chosen by the Prince in August of the preceding year, and the Parliament had been elected in 1966 from his own political organization. This government remained in office, reiterated its adherence to all treaties and agreements, and made no substantive changes in its own composition.

No sooner had the Cambodian Government made the single change of removing Sihanouk and begun negotiations with Vietnamese Communist representatives for the withdrawal of their troops from Cambodia, than those troops began to attack police and army posts in and near their areas of occupation, to widen their zones of control, and to protect their base areas. How many here protested that interference by foreign forces in the internal affairs of a member state?

Following his removal from office, Sihanouk turned to an insurgent group which he had previously tried, with considerable success, to suppress, the Khmer Rouge, and to the Vietnamese occupation forces in an effort to regain his personal power. He himself has chosen to live in Peking. The principal bases of his mandate to rule Cambodia—North Vietnamese troops, Chinese diplomacy, and an externally supported insurgency—do not enhance the legitimacy of his claim.

The situation at present is that the Government of Cambodia is fighting alone, without the assistance of foreign troops or foreign advisers, against a local insurgency led, equipped, and substantially assisted by the forces of a foreign country, North Viet-Nam.

The Government of the Khmer Republic has never ceased to maintain its clear control of the machinery of government, the support of a great majority of the population, and administration of the crucial urban areas and territories in which the greatest portion of the economic, social, and political life of the Khmer people takes place. It thus commands the resources and enjoys the support of the people of the state and consequently is in a position to carry out the obligations of Cambodia under the U.N. Charter.

* * *

It is true that North Vietnamese and insurgent forces have disrupted government control, in the military sense, of some parts of the territory of Cambodia. Claims by the insurgents and their foreign supporters that they control 90 percent of the territory and 80 percent of the population are patently false. The deep water port of Kompong Som [Sihanoukville] and 16 of the 20 Provincial capitals are controlled by the Government of the Khmer Republic. The four Provincial capitals excepted, all in the northeast of the country, were abandoned to the North Vietnamese Army in June of 1970. The bulk of the Khmer population lives along the lines of communications and rivers. These are generally controlled by forces loyal to the government in Phnom Penh. We estimate that more than 70 percent of the population is administered by the Government of the Khmer Republic.

The territory in which the North Vietnamese and the Khmer Rouge hold sway is primarily rural in character. The areas of central importance to the main functions of government and the social patterns of Cambodian life, as well as the major markets and other ports, are clearly under full government control. Neutral foreign observers are free to visit the areas under Phnom Penh control and do so as a matter of course. It should also be noted that even in those areas under the military control of North Vietnamese and insurgent forces, a large part of the population retains its allegiance to the Government of the Khmer Republic. The thousands of refugees who flee the fighting in contested zones go only to territories in which the government has clear control.

In any case, the fact that government control of certain parts of the territory of Cambodia has been interrupted by North Vietnamese and insurgent forces has no necessary relationship to the question of the degree of effective authority exercised by the self-styled Sihanouk "government." That entity, which has long had its base in a foreign capital far distant from the territory of Cambodia, has not even demonstrated its control over the insurgent forces operating in Cambodia. Nor is there any indication that that entity controls any sort of administrative machinery which might exercise governmental authority in territory under the military control of insurgent and North Vietnamese forces.

The fighting in Cambodia goes on, and as long as the North Vietnamese are willing to continue, there is no end in sight. Should we, in view of this long, costly, and still-unresolved conflict, conclude that the Khmer people were wrong to resent and resist foreign aggression? Should we declare that they were naive to believe their country could avoid the domination of its powerful neighbors to the north? Should we now explain to them that they must accept a regime based in Peking, that they must allow North Viet-Nam to occupy and control much of their territory, and that they must never again seek to change their policies, nor their Chief of State, without first securing the approval of China, North Viet-Nam, and this Assembly? We cannot believe that states valuing their own sovereignty and represented in this Assembly would display such arrogance in trying to dictate to the people of a member state of the United Nations.

As for the Khmer people, they chose not to accept the dictates of a cynical *realpolitik* which took no account of their national pride, their dignity, and their freedom. In removing Prince Sihanouk from office, the Government of Cambodia sought to preserve its neutrality, its independence, and its sovereignty, national rights which it felt Prince Sihanouk had ceased to defend. Are we to tell the Khmer people that these principles are only words, that they do not apply to small, weak states with strong aggressive neighbors? Has this organization so forgotten the ideals of its founders? Have we so departed from the principles of our charter?

Clearly there is much disagreement among us as to how the present situation in Cambodia came about or as to how it should be resolved. But the United States would hope that we could all agree that a negotiated settlement is preferable to a military solution. Let us all read the public statements and study the private actions of the Government of the Khmer Republic, and on the other hand those of Prince Sihanouk, to determine which of the two is truly seeking peace, which of the two has offered to negotiate, and which of the two has accepted the need for conciliation. It is the Government of the Khmer Republic that has repeatedly stated its willingness to negotiate a political settlement. It is Prince Sihanouk and the Khmer Rouge who seek to prolong the violence and the bloodshed. Let us not therefore seek to discredit those who are seeking a peaceful settlement. Let us not take any action which can only complicate the situation and further block the path to peace.

27. ATLANTIC DIALOGUE, PART TWO

Though some Americans undoubtedly viewed with equanimity the crumbling of their government's hopes in Indochina, few could display an equal indifference with regard to the disarray prevailing in the Atlantic Community in these closing months of 1973. The "Year of Europe," instead of moving majestically forward to a solemn reaffirmation of Atlantic solidarity, had disclosed a depth of division and recrimination unseen since the difficult 1950s. Disharmonies already existing between the United States and its European allies had been immeasurably aggravated by the events of the October War. Less committed than the United States to the cause of Israel, and far more vulnerable to any interruption of their oil supplies, the NATO countries (other than Portugal) had mortified the White House and the State Department by refusing to assist in the emergency airlift of military equipment to Israel. Europeans, uneasy over the alignment of Soviet and American diplomacy at the time of the cease-fire resolutions, had subsequently become enraged by Washington's failure to consult them before alerting its military forces on the morning of October 25.

More was behind these European criticisms than a lack of information about American aims and intentions. In many instances, as Secretary Kissinger acknowledged at his November 21 news conference, the Europeans' complaints arose from what was fundamentally "a different perception of their role." That the Middle East crisis was viewed quite differently in Europe and in the United States had been sufficiently evidenced by an October 31 statement by President Pompidou in which the French leader had bewailed the exclusion of "Europe" from the cease-fire negotiations and proposed a European meeting "at the summit" as the only fitting riposte to what he called the "tête-à-tête of the two superpowers."[1] Said Secretary Kissinger, "One cannot avoid the perhaps melancholy conclusions that some of our European allies saw their in-

[1] *Keesing's*, p. 26349.

551

terests [as] so different from those of the United States that they
were prepared to break ranks with the United States on a matter of
very grave international consequence and that we happen to believe
was of very profound consequence to them as well."[2]

This was hardly the most auspicious moment for the commencement of the nineteen-nation Conference on Mutual Reduction of Forces and Armaments and Associated Measures in Central
Europe, which, nevertheless, was duly opened in Vienna on October 30 in accordance with the decisions reached at the preliminary
MBFR consultations four months earlier.[3] Here was another
question on which there remained sharp differences of opinion between the United States and many of its European partners.
Representatives of the interested NATO members—always excluding France—had been engaged for months in trying to devise a
negotiating formula that might possibly interest the Warsaw Pact
governments, yet would also give due weight to the Europeans'
determination "to limit the risks which they believe will accompany
any U.S. withdrawals and to protect themselves from domestic
political pressure in their own countries."[4]

All of the interested Western countries could at least agree on the
central objective of the negotiations and the basic strategy to be
pursued. As phrased in a later report of the U.S. Arms Control and
Disarmament Agency (ACDA), "The purpose is to achieve a more
stable military balance at lower levels of forces in Central Europe
while maintaining undiminished security for all parties. A reduction agreement must, therefore, take into account major disparities
favoring the Warsaw Pact in geography, manpower and character
of opposing forces."[5] A new balance, in other words, should be
sought primarily by trimming the special advantages enjoyed by the
Warsaw Pact in regard to such factors as ground personnel, heavy
armor, and the proximity of a major ally. The best approach, said
Ambassador Stanley H. Resor in his opening statement to the conference as chairman of the U.S. delegation (Document 79), would
be to seek a common ceiling for the ground forces of the two sides,
focusing in the initial phase on a reduction of American and Soviet
ground forces.

[2]*Bulletin*, vol. 69 (1973), p. 710.
[3]Document 34a.
[4]U.S. Senate, Committee on Foreign Relations, 93d Cong., 1st sess., *U.S. Security
Issues in Europe: Burden Sharing and Offset, MBFR and Nuclear Weapons, September 1973: A Staff Report prepared for the use of the Subcommittee on U.S.
Security Agreements and Commitments Abroad, Dec. 2, 1973* (Committee print;
Washington: GPO, 1973), p. 11.
[5]13th Annual Report of the United States Arms Control and Disarmament Agency,
Feb. 20, 1974, in *Documents on Disarmament, 1973*, p. 919.

But why should Moscow oblige the West by cutting back the very elements in which it could most easily maintain superiority? The Western representatives were undoubtedly aware that their prescription conflicted radically with the Soviet approach, made public by General Secretary Brezhnev in addressing a "World Congress of Peace Forces" in the Soviet capital on October 26. Like the West, the U.S.S.R. intended to use the negotiations to attack those elements of military power in which the advantage currently lay with the other side. "Our stand is clear and understandable," Brezhnev declared. "We believe that agreement must be reached on a reduction . . . of both foreign [mainly Soviet and American] and national land and air forces of the states party to the talks. . . . Moreover, it obviously must be recognized that the reduction should also apply to units equipped with nuclear weapons." Although Brezhnev also stated that the Soviet Union favored a "specific agreement . . . in the immediate future" and would be "prepared to take practical steps in this direction as early as 1975,"[6] the end of that year would find the two sides still far short of agreement and still impaled upon the fundamental differences between the NATO and Soviet positions.

The opening of the Vienna conference, with its emphasis on the persistent differences between East and West, offered at most a momentary distraction from the continuing difficulties among the Western countries themselves. If anything, these difficulties seemed still to be increasing as the significance of recent Middle Eastern events sank in, petroleum stocks dwindled, and individual European countries intensified their efforts to protect their national oil supplies. A new source of recrimination was opened up when ministers of the European Community member states, meeting in Brussels on November 5-6, agreed to issue a statement on the Middle East[7] that closely echoed Arab doctrine with regard to Israeli withdrawal from occupied territories and "the legitimate rights of the Palestinians"—matters which, in the American view, could be worked out only as part of the eventual peace settlement. (An even stronger statement in support of the Arab stand was issued by the Japanese Government on November 22,[8] a few days after Secretary Kissinger's visit to Tokyo.)

These divisive trends could hardly fail to affect the course of the December ministerial meeting of the North Atlantic Council, which was to be followed within a day or two by the summit meeting of

---

[6]*Soviet News*, No. 5711 (1973), p. 452. For the Soviet position at the Vienna conference cf. same, No. 5713 (1973), p. 476.

[7]*Keesing's*, p. 26227.

[8]Same, p. 26323.

European Community members proposed by President Pompidou. Each of these meetings would presumably have to take some further notice of the months-old American plan for one or more symbolic declarations on Atlantic relations, a scheme that dated from Dr. Kissinger's "Year of Europe" speech of April 23[9] and had not been wholly lost to view in the turmoil of recent months. Discussion of a possible declaration by the North Atlantic allies had, in fact, continued throughout the autumn under the aegis of the permanent NATO Council, where the submission in mid-November of an unexpectedly conciliatory French draft[10] had given the impression that even President Pompidou's government was reluctant to alienate the United States beyond a certain point.

An agreement to pursue "this important work . . . to a successful conclusion" was among the highlights of NATO's ministerial session, which took place in Brussels on December 10-11 and was chronicled in the usual formal communiqué **(Document 80)**. In reaffirming the fundamental role of the alliance, the participating ministers also promised with their habitual blandness to "continue to maintain the fullest possible exchange of views and information, and close consultation and cooperation, in a spirit of mutual trust, on all problems of mutual concern." Going on to reiterate familiar views on European security, MBFR, and SALT, the ministers also showed awareness of the link established by Congress between the U.S. balance of payments and the continued maintenance of American troops in Europe.[11] Acknowledging the need for "a common effort . . . to achieve a solution to the financial problems which the United States consequently faces," they endorsed the judgment of the NATO Defense Ministers[12] that there was need to foster a "common solution" to these problems through specific multilateral or bilateral arrangements.

The euphemistic tone so characteristic of NATO's formal communiqués did less than justice to the vigorous exchanges that were said to have taken place around the Council table, particularly between Secretary Kissinger and Foreign Minister Jobert of France. But any feelings that might have been ruffled at the NATO meeting were largely assuaged in the course of an informal session, later on December 11, at which the Secretary of State was invited to join an exchange of views with the Foreign Ministers of the European Community member states. This first encounter of its kind, which had been assiduously sought by the United States, was generally

<hr>

[9]Document 21; see also Chapter 17 at notes 10-14.

[10]*New York Times*, Nov. 19, 1973; for background see same, Oct. 11 and Nov. 9, 1973.

[11]Cf. note 6 to Chapter 21.

[12]Defense Planning Committee communiqué, Dec. 7, in *Keesing's*, pp. 26283-4.

felt to have provided a most valuable means of clearing up misunderstandings and reducing friction.[13]

Secretary Kissinger's more formal appraisal of the state of the Western world was reserved for a dinner sponsored by the Pilgrims of Great Britain and held in London on the following day, December 12. The somber language which the Secretary of State employed on this occasion contrasted with the somewhat more optimistic tone of his "Year of Europe" speech. "There exists," he now declared (**Document 81**), ". . . a real danger of a gradual erosion of the Atlantic community which for 25 years has insured peace to its nations and brought prosperity to its peoples. . . . A comprehensive reexamination of all aspects of our relationship, economic, political, and military, is imperative." The central threat to the Atlantic community, Secretary Kissinger quite obviously felt, lay in the current efforts of Europeans to define a "European identity" that was, in his view, too frequently conceived in terms of opposition to American (or "Atlantic") purposes. "Europe's unity must not be at the expense of Atlantic community, or both sides of the Atlantic will suffer," the American visitor warned.

So far as the concrete requirements of the situation were concerned, the Secretary of State referred particularly to the need for better consultation, the importance of completing the pending Atlantic declarations, and the necessity of transforming these declarations into "practical and perceptible progress" so that "our policies begin to reinforce rather than work against our common objectives." Recalling the intimate historical association between the United States and Britain, Dr. Kissinger now seemed to contemplate a similar relationship with Europe as a whole: "We are prepared to offer a unifying Europe a 'special relationship', for we believe that the unity of the Western world is essential for the well-being of all its parts."

As an immediate step, and one directed to what had obviously become an imminent threat to the life of the industrialized nations, Dr. Kissinger called for purposeful action by "the nations of Europe, North America, and Japan" to meet the current energy crisis. None of his British listeners had need to be reminded of the seriousness of the situation created by the Arab oil cutbacks, particularly for the United Kingdom, where labor disputes had combined with dwindling imports to cause a severe depletion of fuel stocks. Already living under a month-old state of emergency, the British people were to be advised within hours of the Kissinger speech that the supply of electricity to most industrial and com-

[13]*New York Times*, Dec. 12, 1973; cf. also Kissinger news conference, Dec. 11, in *Bulletin*, vol. 69 (1973), pp. 783-5.

mercial sites would be limited to three days a week until further notice. (These restrictions would remain in force until their removal by a new Labour government on March 7, 1974.)

Dr. Kissinger's specific recommendation on the energy crisis involved the establishment of "an Energy Action Group of senior and prestigious individuals with a mandate to develop within three months an initial action program for collaboration in all areas of the energy problem." The ultimate result of his proposal would be the establishment on November 15, 1974, of a sixteen-nation International Energy Agency within the framework of the Organization for Economic Cooperation and Development.[14]

The views expressed by the American Secretary of State with regard to more abstruse topics, like European identity and Atlantic solidarity, appeared to arouse no great enthusiasm, and were to be largely ignored by the heads of government of the nine-member Community when they assembled for their two-day summit meeting in Copenhagen on December 14-15. Among the very first actions of the European leaders was the issuance of a pre-packaged "Declaration on the European Identity" that stressed the resolute "construction of a united Europe" but took only minimal notice of Europe's relations with the United States. A final communiqué, keyed to the theme that Europe should "speak with one voice in important world affairs," gave slightly more weight to the pending transatlantic declaration, which, the nine Community states affirmed, would form "the basis for their friendly and cooperative relations with the United States."[15]

All in all, this piecemeal renewal of the Atlantic dialogue served to restore at least an appearance of normality to the Atlantic relationship; but Dr. Kissinger's hopes for the completion of a pair of declarations "equal to the occasion" were to be very imperfectly realized in the following months. A "Declaration on Atlantic Relations," adopted by the North Atlantic Council at its spring ministerial meeting in Ottawa on June 18-19, 1974, was signed by President Nixon and other heads of government at a special meeting of the North Atlantic Council in Brussels on June 26, 1974.[16] But no joint declaration was issued by the United States and the European Community, the members of the latter group having decided in the course of 1974 to bury the idea of a formal declaration and settle for a policy of improved consultation with the United States. The proposed joint declaration between the United States and Japan eventually took the form of a statement of

[14]*Keesing's*, p. 26845.
[15]Same, pp. 26350-52.
[16]*Presidential Documents*, vol. 10 (1974), pp. 729-30.

principles in the communiqué that was issued by Prime Minister Tanaka and President Ford at Tokyo on November 20, 1974.[17]

(79) Conference on Mutual Reduction of Forces and Armaments and Associated Measures in Central Europe, opened in Vienna October 30, 1973.

(a) Statement to the Conference by Ambassador Stanley H. Resor, Chairman of the United States Delegation, October 31, 1973.[18]

My government warmly welcomes the beginning of these negotiations on the mutual reduction of forces and armaments and associated measures in Central Europe.

A great challenge lies before us. Central Europe is the focus of one of the greatest concentrations of military power in peacetime history. For more than two decades, the armed forces of East and West have confronted each other there. This confrontation has given rise to abiding apprehension and concern. And it represents a formidable burden on us all.

The time has come to change this situation. Successive changes in East-West relations have made it possible to seek to reduce the scale and intensity of the confrontation.

This is surely one of the central tasks of our time. It is also a delicate one. The present security situation in Europe is unsatisfactory in many ways, but we would not wish it to worsen through unwise measures. Therefore we must carry out our task in such a way as to strengthen peace and stability in Europe, not weaken them. The structure of security in Europe is a delicate one; and in the interests of all we will have to proceed cautiously and step by step, realizing that all parties will wish to be assured of their security at each stage.

We do not expect this task to be easy. These negotiations represent a radical new departure in international diplomacy. There has been nothing quite like them before. Both in the subject matter they will address and in their pattern of participation, they break new ground. But their importance justifies an extraordinary effort on the part of us all.

My government's approach to these negotiations is a practical one. We are interested in concrete results. At the same time, we are not setting any artificial deadlines for ourselves. We consider that

[17]Cf. note 40 to Chapter 14.
[18]ACDA Press Release 73-9, Oct. 31; text from *Bulletin*, vol. 69 (1973), pp. 657-61.

the negotiations should move ahead at a steady, even tempo, keeping pace with the development of the subject matter, without an artificial preordained pattern of breaks.

Further, we will strive for a businesslike atmosphere. We are here to perform a specific task. We are interested in seeking mutually acceptable solutions to the problems we will have to address together. We are not interested in polemical debates. Many aspects of the subject matter are controversial, and viewpoints will diverge. We believe that it would be helpful in this context if all participants made it a conscious rule to discuss the subject matter and present their points of view in terms of concrete, objective facts, and not in terms of the presumed intentions of other participants.

The enterprise on which we are now embarking provides us with an opportunity of historic importance to move from confrontation to negotiation on a problem area of key importance for all of us. The military confrontation in Central Europe is the product of history. It is a result of past tensions, and at the same time a cause of tension.

In keeping with the businesslike and objective spirit which I have suggested should govern the tone of our discussions, we do not wish to engage in debates over how or why the present situation arose. We should move directly to the task of seeking to change that situation in ways that will benefit all of us. Thus we hope to reduce the risks for all arising from miscalculation, misunderstanding, or misinterpretation of actions of either side.

Our main task will be to achieve a more stable military balance at lower levels of forces with undiminished security—undiminished security for all participants in these talks. If we can achieve this goal—and my government believes we can—then an MBFR agreement or agreements will be a highly important contribution to strengthening peace, security, and mutual confidence in Europe and to improved, more fruitful relations among us all. Such a result would be welcomed by all our peoples. With this prospect before us, my government considers that these negotiations will test the willingness of all participants to address and to resolve the hard, concrete military security issues in Central Europe.

Our negotiations were preceded earlier this year in Vienna by preparatory talks.[19] In those talks, the following principles were agreed as guidance for the negotiations:

—Mutual reduction of forces and armaments and associated measures in Central Europe would be considered.
—The general objective of the negotiations will be to con-

[19]Cf. Document 34a.

tribute to a more stable relationship in Europe and to the strengthening of peace and security.

—In the negotiations, an understanding should be reached to conduct them in such a way as to insure the most effective and thorough approach to the consideration of the subject matter, with due regard to its complexity.

—Specific arrangements will have to be carefully worked out in scope and timing in such a way that they will in all respects and at every point conform to the principle of undiminished security for each party.

—Any topic relevant to the subject matter may be introduced for negotiation.

We believe these agreed guidelines form a sound basis for our work. The proposals we will make during the course of these negotiations, and our approach to the negotiations themselves, will be consistent with these guidelines.

In the preparatory talks, we also agreed on procedures for these negotiations. We feel that no further general discussion of procedural matters is needed at this time. Our task is now to address questions of substance relating to the subject matter. We believe that day-to-day procedural business, such as the scheduling of meetings, can be handled in appropriate ways.

The preparatory talks recorded agreement on a further point; namely, the region on which the negotiations will focus. That region was defined in the June 28 communique as Central Europe.

General U.S. Approach in Negotiations

Based on the points of agreement between us which I have just enumerated, I should like now to outline for you the general approach of my government to the substance of these negotiations.

In our view, the subject matter of these negotiations is the size, character, and activities of armed forces in Central Europe.

We aim to reduce the size of those forces in such a way as to lead to a more stable military balance at lower levels of forces while maintaining undiminished security for each party.

We aim at affecting the character of these military forces by reducing those aspects or characteristics of the forces which are of particular concern to us because of their intrinsic capabilities. Agreements on topics of this kind would contribute to the creation of a more stable military balance.

Finally, we aim at dealing in these negotiations with the activities of these military forces in a manner which will minimize the risk of miscalculation, surprise, or their use in a destabilizing manner. Agreements on measures to accomplish this would also enhance stability and mutual confidence.

We have agreed that the outcome of these negotiations must be one which preserves undiminished security for each party. No participant or group of participants should gain unilateral advantage from an agreement. It is the considered view of my government that the aims I have outlined above with respect to the size, character, and activities of military forces in Central Europe can and should be realized in a manner that preserves undiminished security for my country and all its allies when appropriate account is taken of significant objective disparities affecting the current situation in Central Europe. The disparities which we view as operating to our disadvantage in Central Europe are: disparities in manpower, in the character of forces, and in geography.

Let me elaborate on these. In manpower, the countries of the Warsaw Pact have more ground personnel on active duty in Central Europe than does NATO. We consider that to narrow and finally eliminate this disparity in manpower through mutual reductions would improve stability in Central Europe.

With respect to character of forces, the Warsaw Pact forces maintain a concentration of heavy armor in Central Europe. I have said that we shall seek to avoid debates over each other's intentions or motives. Therefore I am not remarking on the possible intentions of anyone when I say that it is an objective fact that a marked imbalance in tanks exists in Central Europe.

We consider that stability is enhanced when all participants in these talks are able to see each other's purpose as a defensive one and when they perceive each other's forces to be configured in a way consistent with defensive purposes. A substantial reduction in the armored capability of the U.S.S.R. in Central Europe would, in our view, be consistent with defensive purposes and would constitute a major contribution to enhanced stability in Europe.

The third major disparity to which I have referred —geography—is also basic to the situation in Central Europe. The United States and the U.S.S.R., which station significant forces in Central Europe, are located at vastly unequal distances from the area. The territory of the Soviet Union directly and immediately adjoins Central Europe. Soviet forces, located in Soviet territory, have ready access over the Polish plain to the very heart of the area. The United States, on the other hand, is located at a great distance from Central Europe and is separated from the area by the Atlantic Ocean. Thus, access to Central Europe is far more difficult for U.S. forces.

The geographic disparity has this consequence for mutual reductions: Any Soviet forces withdrawn from Central Europe into the territory of the Soviet Union could return quickly and easily; U.S. forces withdrawn to the United States would be an ocean away. This point applies equally to reinforcement capability. A reduction agreement would have to deal with this inherent inequity in a manner that did not result in any diminution of our security. There are also other geographic disparities of considerable importance.

Size and Activities of Forces

Implicit in all that I have said on the need to deal with these major disparities is the concept that these negotiations must achieve equitable results, arrived at in an equitable manner. In keeping with this concept and with the actual nature of the problem at hand, we consider that an ultimate goal of these negotiations should be approximate parity in the form of a common ceiling for the ground forces of each side in Central Europe. Our approach to these negotiations, as I have already said, is a realistic one. In view of the complexities of the subject matter, we believe that our initial goal would have to be a more modest one than the achievement, in one step, of a common ceiling for ground forces in Central Europe.

Thus we consider that our negotiations should proceed in more than one phase. The first phase should focus on U.S. and Soviet ground forces. Their reduction in a manner consistent with the principle of undiminished security would be a particularly valuable contribution to stability in Europe. Moreover, it would be logical if the two largest powers with forces in the area should take the first step.

It is our view that reduction of forces in Central Europe will not of itself be sufficient to result in greater stability. Other measures will also be needed. These should include stabilizing measures, verification measures, and noncircumvention provisions.

For example, not only the size and character, but also the activities of armed forces affect the stability of the military situation in Europe. Therefore we consider that measures affecting certain military activities are necessary. As participants will be aware, this is what we had in mind when we introduced the term "associated measures" into the communique of last June. Activities of the forces in the area, if their purpose is ambiguous or if they are carried out on such a scale or in such a manner as to be perceived by other participants as a potential threat, could be destabilizing. Agreed measures relating to force activities and arrangements designed to reduce the possibility of miscalculation—that is, what may be termed stabilizing measures—would be a significant contribution to stability in the area and could enhance mutual confidence. We shall have a number of such measures to propose.

Verification and Noncircumvention Measures

It is also our view that appropriate provisions concerning verification of a reduction agreement will need to be agreed. Each participant or group of participants will wish to have adequate assurance that the terms of a reduction agreement are being faithfully carried out. That will clearly be in the interests of all. It will be necessary, therefore, to deal with this matter in the context of agreement on the substance of reductions.

We consider that each participant will also wish to have appropriate assurances that each party to possible agreements will refrain from any action which would circumvent or undermine an agreement. We will need to take this matter up in detail at a later stage in our negotiations, when the outlines of a possible reduction agreement may have begun to emerge.

We believe, in sum, that appropriate provisions and assurances regarding the activities of forces in Central Europe, regarding verification of the observance of a reduction agreement, and regarding measures to assure that a reduction agreement will not be circumvented will be necessary to preserve undiminished security for each party. In accordance with this same principle of undiminished security for each party, we will also wish to insure that agreed measures in Central Europe not result in reduced stability or security outside the area.

Finally, as a last major point, I wish to remind you of the statement made at the May 14 plenary of the preparatory talks by Ambassador [Bryan] Quarles Van Ufford [of the Netherlands] on behalf of my government and the other governments represented by my colleagues. That statement[20] said that:

> The representatives of Belgium, Canada, the Federal Republic of Germany, Luxembourg, the Netherlands, the United Kingdom, and the United States of America wish to point out that the arrangements for the participation of Hungary in these consultations are without prejudice to the nature of Hungary's participation in future negotiations, decisions, or agreed measures or to the security of any party, and that, in particular, the question of how and to what extent Hungary will be included

[20]*Documents on Disarmament, 1973*, p. 254.

in future decisions, agreements, or measures must be examined and decided during the pending negotiations.

This represents our continued intention.

I have outlined for you the overall American approach to the subject matter of these negotiations. As will have been evident from statements made earlier, this approach is shared by our allies. Our general method of exposition over the next weeks and months will be to proceed from the general to the specific. This initial exposition of our approach to the subject matter has dealt with general concepts. We will return to these concepts in our ensuing discussions in the next days. We hope to elaborate on them and examine their practical implications with you in increasing detail.

I wish to stress in closing that my government attaches great weight to these negotiations. We believe that the goal we seek—a more stable military balance in Central Europe at lower levels of forces with undiminished security for each party—is of immense potential importance to us all. Success in achieving this goal would surely be regarded by all our peoples as a great and valuable contribution to a lasting peace in Europe and in the world. In view of the importance of this goal, it is up to all of us here to exert every effort to achieve it. We, for our part, are ready to move ahead.

On behalf of my government, I would like to thank the Austrian authorities for agreeing to host our conference in Vienna and for making available facilities to help us in our work. There could be no better site for this important conference.

(80) Ministerial Session of the North Atlantic Council, Brussels, December 10-11, 1973.

(a) Final Communiqué.[21]

1. The North Atlantic Council met in Ministerial session in Brussels on 10th and 11th December, 1973.

2. Ministers considered international developments since their previous meeting in June.[22] They drew encouragement from the continuing development of both bilateral and multilateral East-West contacts over a wide field. They recognized, however, that international peace remains fragile and stressed once again the im-

---

[21]Department of State Press Release 453, Dec. 12; text from *Bulletin*, vol. 69 (1973), pp. 785-6.
[22]Document 29.

portance for the Alliance of maintaining to the full its defensive and deterrent military capacity.

3. Ministers recalled their decision in June to examine the relationship between the countries of the Alliance in the light of the profound changes which were taking place in every field of international activity. They noted that examination of these changes had led to substantial progress towards agreement on a joint declaration on Atlantic relations. They agreed that this important work should be pursued to a successful conclusion. Such a declaration, reflecting a perspective commensurate with the challenges of the future, would serve to guide the Alliance in its vital tasks of maintaining peace, improving East-West relations and promoting greater security and well-being.

4. Ministers reaffirmed that the solidarity of the Alliance, and thereby its success in maintaining effective deterrence and reliable defense were the foundations of continuing progress towards detente. In this perspective, they will continue to maintain the fullest possible exchange of views and information, and close consultation and cooperation, in a spirit of mutual trust, on all problems of common concern. They instructed the Council in permanent session to consider the most appropriate means of ensuring the full effectiveness of this consultation.

5. Ministers reviewed events in the Middle East. They welcomed the establishment of a UN Emergency Force and noted with satisfaction progress towards the holding of a peace conference. They reaffirmed the support of all their Governments for the relevant resolutions of the UN Security Council and they expressed their over-riding concern to see a just and lasting settlement in the Middle East. Ministers further took note of the report by the Council in permanent session on the situation in the Mediterranean prepared on their instructions given at their previous meeting. Ministers invited the Council in permanent session to continue to keep the situation under review and to report further.

6. Ministers reviewed developments in the Conference on Security and Cooperation in Europe. They noted that, following the Ministerial Meeting in Helsinki[23] at which the agenda for the Conference had been approved, the methodical work which had taken place thus far in Geneva had been successful in bringing about the thorough examination of specific issues which, in their view, was essential if the Conference was to lead in due course to satisfactory results. They reaffirmed the determination of their Governments to continue to pursue the negotiations constructively,

[23]Document 35.

having regard to the importance of all of the subjects under discussion, in particular in the field of human contacts.

7. Ministers noted that the Federal Republic of Germany and the German Democratic Republic were admitted simultaneously as members of the United Nations in September 1973.[24] They reaffirmed their view that satisfactory development of the relations between the two German states, taking into account the special situation in Germany, can make a significant contribution to the further relaxation of tensions in Europe.

8. As regards Berlin, Ministers paid particular attention to the experience so far gained in the application of the Quadripartite Agreement of 3rd September, 1971.[25] They reaffirmed their conviction that the strict observance and full application of this agreement make possible a satisfactory solution of practical questions in the interest of the people of Berlin and constitute a condition for lasting detente and stability in Europe.

9. Ministers representing countries which participate in NATO's integrated defense program welcomed the opening, on 30th October, of the negotiations on Mutual and Balanced Force Reductions [MBFR][26] which they had proposed. They considered a report by Allied negotiators in Vienna, and noted that the talks were proceeding in a businesslike way. They instructed the Council in permanent session to continue its work on the negotiations.

10. These Ministers recalled that, as agreed on 28th June at the preparatory consultations in Vienna,[27] the general objective of the negotiations would be to contribute to a more stable relationship and to the strengthening of peace and security in Europe. To this end the Allied negotiators in Vienna have proposed the establishment of approximate parity between the two sides, in the form of a common ceiling for overall ground force manpower on each side in the area in which reductions would take place, having regard to combat capability. They have also proposed a first phase agreement providing for reductions of Soviet and US ground forces in the area. These Ministers reaffirmed their resolve, on the basis of the agreed Allied approach to Mutual and Balanced Force Reductions including associated measures, to strive for an outcome which was both balanced and equitable, and which would ensure undiminished security for all parties.

11. These Ministers reaffirmed the need to maintain and improve Allied Forces in Europe, and expressed their conviction that reduc-

[24]Cf. Chapter 28 at note 4.
[25]*AFR, 1971*, pp. 166-70.
[26]Document 79.
[27]Document 34a.

tions should take place only in the context of MBFR. They also recognized that the maintenance of United States Forces in Europe at their present level calls for a common effort on the part of the Allies to achieve a solution to the financial problems which the United States consequently faces. To this end, these Ministers reaffirmed the decisions taken by the Defense Ministers and expressed their support for the statements contained in paras. 9-12 of the communique of the Defense Planning Committee issued on 7th December, 1973.[28]

12. Ministers expressed appreciation for the continuing efforts undertaken by the United States in SALT II [Strategic Arms Limitation Talks] towards a permanent agreement limiting strategic offensive arms. They took note of the Declaration on the Basic Principles of Negotiations on the Further Limitation of Strategic Offensive Arms signed on 21st June, 1973,[29] including, in particular, the recognition of each side's equal security interest.

13. In noting the progress reported by the Chairman of the Committee on the Challenges of Modern Society (CCMS), Ministers welcomed the start on cooperation in the development of supplemental energy sources through the use of solar and geothermal energy, and in the disposal of hazardous wastes and toxic industrial effluents. Ministers took note of the CCMS International Road Safety Resolution, and the CCMS guidelines on National Planning for Regional Development. Ministers expressed satisfaction at the practical work of the CCMS in such other fields as air and water pollution, health care and urban transportation.

14. The Ministers directed the Council in permanent session to consider and decide on the date and place of the next session of the Ministerial Meeting of the North Atlantic Council, taking into account that 1974 will mark the 25th anniversary of the signing of the treaty.[30]

(81) *"The United States and a Unifying Europe—The Necessity for Partnership": Address by Secretary of State Kissinger before the Pilgrims of Great Britain, London, December 12, 1973.*[31]

I am grateful for the opportunity to speak to you this evening because, like most Americans, I am seized by a mixture of pride

[28]Cf. note 12 above.
[29]Document 31b.
[30]The Council met in ministerial session in Ottawa on June 18-19, 1974; cf. above at note 16.
[31]Department of State Press Release 452; text from *Bulletin*, vol. 69 (1973), pp. 777-82.

and terror when invited to appear before a British audience. In my particular case, and without any reflection on this distinguished assemblage, it is probably more terror than pride; for there is no blinking the fact—it is there for all to hear—that my forebears missed the Mayflower by some 300 years.

Our two peoples have been more closely associated than any other two nations in modern history—in culture and economics, in peace and in war. We have sometimes disagreed. But the dominant theme of our relationship in this century has been intimate alliance and mighty creations.

In 1950, while the Atlantic alliance was considering a continuing political body, my great predecessor Dean Acheson spoke to this society.[32] Describing the travails of creation, Acheson noted that a "strange and confusing dissonance has crowded the trans-Atlantic frequencies." But he added that this "dissonance flows from the very awareness that difficult decisions must be made and is a part of the process of making them."

Again today America and Western Europe find themselves at a moment of great promise and evident difficulty, of renewed efforts to unite and old problems which divide. It is a time of both hope and concern for all of us who value the partnership we have built together. Today, as in 1950, we and Europe face the necessity, the opportunity, and the dilemma of fundamental choice.

The Year of Europe

Because we have a historical and intimate relationship, I want to speak tonight frankly of what has been called the "Year of Europe"—of the difficulties of 1973 and the possibilities of 1974 and beyond.

Last April the President asked me to propose that Europe and the United States strive together to reinvigorate our partnership.[33] He did so because it was obvious that the assumptions on which the alliance was founded have been outstripped by events:

—Europe's economic strength, political cohesion, and new confidence—the monumental achievements of Western unity—have radically altered a relationship that was originally shaped in an era of European weakness and American predominance.

—American nuclear monopoly has given way to nuclear parity, raising wholly new problems of defense and deterrence—

[32]Speech of May 10, 1950 in *Bulletin*, vol. 22 (1950), pp. 789-91.
[33]Document 21.

problems which demand a broad reexamination of the requirements of our security and the relative contribution to it of
the United States and its allies.

—The lessening of confrontation between East and West has
offered new hope for a relaxation of tensions and new opportunities for creative diplomacy.

—It has become starkly apparent that the great industrialized
democracies of Japan, Europe, and North America could pursue divergent paths only at the cost of their prosperity and their
partnership.

These historic changes were occurring in a profoundly changed
psychological climate in the West. The next generation of leaders in
Europe, Canada, and America will have neither the personal
memory nor the emotional commitment to the Atlantic alliance of
its founders. Even today, a majority on both sides of the Atlantic
did not experience the threat that produced the alliance's creation
or the sense of achievement associated with its growth. Even today,
in the United States over 40 Senators consistently vote to make
massive unilateral reductions of American forces in Europe. Even
today, some Europeans have come to believe that their identity
should be measured by its distance from the United States. On both
sides of the Atlantic we are faced with the anomalous—and
dangerous—situation in which the public mind identifies foreign
policy success increasingly with relations with adversaries while
relations with allies seem to be characterized by bickering and drift.
There exists, then, a real danger of a gradual erosion of the
Atlantic community which for 25 years has insured peace to its
nations and brought prosperity to its peoples. A major effort to
renew Atlantic relations and to anchor our friendship in a fresh act
of creation seemed essential. We hoped that the drama of the great
democracies engaging themselves once again in defining a common
future would infuse our Atlantic partnership with new emotional
and intellectual excitement. This was the origin of the initiative
which came to be called the "Year of Europe."
Let me lay to rest certain misconceptions about American intentions:

—The President's initiative was launched after careful
preparation. In all of our conversations with many European
leaders during the winter and spring of 1972-73 there was
agreement that Atlantic relations required urgent attention to
arrest the potential for growing suspicion and alienation between Europe and America.
—We do not accept the proposition that the strengthening of

Atlantic unity and the defining of a European personality are incompatible. The two processes have reinforced each other from the outset and can continue to do so now. The United States has repeatedly and explicitly welcomed the European decision to create an independent identity in all dimensions, political and economic. Indeed, we have long—and more consistently than many Europeans—supported the goal of political cohesion.

—We have no intention of restricting Europe's international role to regional matters. From our perspective, European unification should enable Europe to take on broader responsibilities for global peace that ultimately can only contribute to the common interest. The American initiative was meant to mark Europe's new preeminence on the world scene as well as within the North Atlantic community.

A comprehensive reexamination of all aspects of our relationship, economic, political, and military, is imperative. It is a fact that our troops are in Europe as a vital component of mutual defense. It is also a fact—indeed, a truism—that political, military, and economic factors are each part of our relationship. In our view, the affirmation of the pervasive nature of our interdependence is not a device for blackmail. On the contrary, it is the justification for conciliatory solutions. For the specialized concerns of experts and technicians have a life of their own and a narrow national or sectarian bias. The purpose of our initiative was to override these divisive attitudes by committing the highest authority in each country to the principle that our common and paramount interest is in broadly conceived cooperation.

The European Identity

Since last April Europe has made great strides toward unity—particularly in political coordination. The United States strongly supports that process. But as an old friend we are also sensitive to what this process does to traditional ties that, in our view, remain essential to the common interest.

Europe's unity must not be at the expense of Atlantic community, or both sides of the Atlantic will suffer. It is not that we are impatient with the cumbersome machinery of the emerging Europe. It is rather the tendency to highlight division rather than unity with us which concerns us.

I would be less than frank were I to conceal our uneasiness about some of the recent practices of the European Community in the political field. To present the decisions of a unifying Europe to us as faits accomplis not subject to effective discussion is alien to the tradition of U.S.-European relations.

This may seem a strange complaint from a country repeatedly accused of acting itself without adequately consulting with its allies. There is no doubt that the United States has sometimes not consulted enough or adequately—especially in rapidly moving situations. But this is not a preference; it is a deviation from official policy and established practice—usually under pressure of necessity. The attitude of the unifying Europe, by contrast, seems to attempt to elevate refusal to consult into a principle defining European identity. To judge from recent experience, consultation with us before a decision is precluded, and consultation after the fact has been drained of content. For then Europe appoints a spokesman who is empowered to inform us of the decisions taken but who has no authority to negotiate.

We do not object to a single spokesman, but we do believe that as an old ally the United States should be given an opportunity to express its concerns before final decisions affecting its interests are taken. And bilateral channels of discussion and negotiation should not be permitted to atrophy—at least until European political unity is fully realized. To replace the natural dialogue with extremely formalistic procedures would be to shatter abruptly close and intangible ties of trust and communication that took decades to develop and that have served our common purposes well.

The United States recognizes the problems of a transitional period as Europe moves toward unity. We understand the difficulty of the first hesitant steps of political coordination. But we cannot be indifferent to the tendency to justify European identity as facilitating separateness from the United States; European unity, in our view, is not contradictory to Atlantic unity.

For our part, we will spare no effort to strengthen cooperative relationships with a unifying Europe, to affirm the community of our ideals, and to revitalize the Atlantic relationship. That was the purpose of our initiative last April. It remains the central goal of our foreign policy.

The Common Challenge

The leaders of the European Community meet this week. They will consider the nature of European identity; no doubt they will adopt common policies and positions.[34] In the light of this important meeting, let me outline the position of the United States:

---

[34]Cf. above at note 15.

—Détente is an imperative. In a world shadowed by the danger of nuclear holocaust, there is no rational alternative to the pursuit of relaxation of tensions. But we must take care that the pursuit of détente not undermine the friendships which made détente possible.

—Common defense is a necessity. We must be prepared to adjust to changing conditions and share burdens equally. We need a definition of security that our peoples can support and that our adversaries will respect in a period of lessened tensions.

—European unity is a reality. The United States welcomes and supports it in all its dimensions, political as well as economic. We believe it must be made irreversible and that it must strengthen transatlantic ties.

—Economic interdependence is a fact. We must resolve the paradox of growing mutual dependence and burgeoning national and regional identities.

We are determined to continue constructive dialogue with Western Europe. We have offered no final answers: we welcome Europe's wisdom. We believe that this opportunity will not come soon again.

So let us rededicate ourselves to finishing the task of renewing the Atlantic community.

First, let us complete the work before us; let us agree on a set of declarations equal to the occasion so that they may serve as an agenda for our governments and as an example and inspiration for our peoples.

Second, let us then transform these declarations into practical and perceptible progress. We will restore mutual confidence if our policies begin to reinforce rather than work against our common objectives. And let us move quickly to improve the process of consultation in both directions. The U.S. Government made concrete suggestions in this regard at the recent meeting of the Foreign Ministers in the North Atlantic Council.[35]

But let us also remember that even the best consultative machinery cannot substitute for common vision and shared goals; it cannot replace the whole network of intangible connections that have been the real sinews of the transatlantic and especially the Anglo-American relationship. We must take care lest in defining European unity in too legalistic a manner we lose what has made our alliance unique: that in the deepest sense Europe and America do not think of each other as foreign entities conducting traditional diplomacy, but as members of a larger community engaged,

[35]Document 80.

sometimes painfully but ultimately always cooperatively, in a common enterprise. The meeting to which the Foreign Ministers of the Community were courteous enough to invite me[36] marks a significant step forward in restoring the intangibles of the transatlantic dialogue.

Let us put false suspicions behind us. The President did not fight so hard in Congress for our troops in Europe, for strong defenses, for a conciliatory trade bill, for support for allies around the world; he did not strive so continually to consult on SALT and develop common positions on MBFR; he did not stand up so firmly to challenges in crises around the world—suddenly to sacrifice Western Europe's security on the altar of condominium. Our destiny, as well as the full strength of our military power, is inextricably linked with yours.

As we look into the future we can perceive challenges compared to which our recent disputes are trivial. A new international system is replacing the structure of the immediate postwar years. The external policies of China and the Soviet Union are in periods of transition. Western Europe is unifying. New nations seek identity and an appropriate role. Even now, economic relationships are changing more rapidly than the structures which nurtured them. We— Europe, Canada, and America—have only two choices: creativity together or irrelevance apart.

The Middle East and Energy

The Middle East crisis illustrates the importance of distinguishing the long-range from the ephemeral. The differences of recent months resulted not so much from lack of consultation as from a different perception of three key issues: Was the war primarily a local conflict, or did it have wider significance? Has the energy crisis been caused primarily by the war, or does it have deeper causes? Can our common energy crisis be solved by anything but collective action?

As for the nature of the Middle East conflict, it is fair to state—as many Europeans including your Foreign Secretary [Sir Alec Douglas-Home] have—that the United States did not do all that it might have done before the war to promote a permanent settlement in the Middle East. Once the war began, the United States demonstrated great restraint until the Soviet effort reached the point of massive intervention. Once that happened, it became a question of whether the West would retain any influence to help

[36]Cf. above at note 13.

shape the political future of an area upon which Europe is even more vitally dependent than the United States. We involved ourselves in a resupply effort not to take sides in the conflict but to protect the possibility of pursuing after the war the objective of a just, permanent settlement which some of our allies have urged on us ever since 1967.

At the same time, we must bear in mind the deeper causes of the energy crisis: It is not simply a product of the Arab-Israeli war; it is the inevitable consequence of the explosive growth of worldwide demand outrunning the incentives for supply. The Middle East war made a chronic crisis acute, but a crisis was coming in any event. Even when prewar production levels are resumed, the problem of matching the level of oil that the world produces to the level which it consumes will remain.

The only long-term solution is a massive effort to provide producers an incentive to increase their supply, to encourage consumers to use existing supplies more rationally, and to develop alternate energy sources.

This is a challenge which the United States could solve alone with great difficulty and that Europe cannot solve in isolation at all. We strongly prefer, and Europe requires, a common enterprise.

To this end, the United States proposes that the nations of Europe, North America, and Japan establish an Energy Action Group of senior and prestigious individuals with a mandate to develop within three months an initial action program for collaboration in all areas of the energy problem. We would leave it to the members of the Nine whether they prefer to participate as the European Community.

The Group would have as its goal the assurance of required energy supplies at reasonable cost. It would define broad principles of cooperation, and it would initiate action in specific areas:

—To conserve energy through more rational utilization of existing supplies;
—To encourage the discovery and development of new sources of energy;
—To give producers an incentive to increase supply; and
—To coordinate an international program of research to develop new technologies that use energy more efficiently and provide alternatives to petroleum. The United States would be willing to contribute our particular skills in such areas as the development of the deep seabed.

The Energy Action Group should not be an exclusive organization of consumers. The producing nations should be invited to join it from the very beginning with respect to any matters of common interest. The problem of finding adequate opportunity for development, and the investment of the proceeds from the sale of energy sources, would appear to be a particularly important area for consumer-producer cooperation.

As an example of a task for the Energy Action Group, I would cite the field of enriching uranium for use in nuclear power reactors. We know that our need for this raw material will be great in the 1980's. We know that electric utilities will wish to assure their supply at the least possible cost. We know that European countries and Japan will wish to have their own facilities to produce at least part of their needs for enriched uranium. Such plants require huge capital investment. What could be more sensible than that we plan together to assure that scarce resources are not wasted by needless duplication?

The United States is prepared to make a very major financial and intellectual contribution to the objective of solving the energy problem on a common basis. There is no technological problem that the great democracies do not have the capacity to solve together—if they can muster the will and the imagination. The energy crisis of 1973 can become the economic equivalent of the sputnik challenge of 1957. The outcome can be the same. Only this time, the giant step for mankind will be one that America and its closest partners take together for the benefit of all mankind.

We have every reason of duty and self-interest to preserve the most successful partnership in history. The United States is committed to making the Atlantic community a vital positive force for the future as it was for the past. What has recently been taken for granted must now be renewed. This is not an American challenge to Europe; it is history's challenge to us all.

The United Kingdom, we believe, is in a unique position. We welcome your membership in the European Community—though the loosening of some of our old ties has been painful at times. But you can make another historic contribution in helping develop between the United States and a unifying Europe the same special confidence and intimacy that benefited our two nations for decades. We are prepared to offer a unifying Europe a "special relationship," for we believe that the unity of the Western world is essential for the well-being of all its parts.

In his memoirs Secretary Acheson described the events of his visit to London in the spring of 1950.[37] He described the need of his

[37]Dean Acheson, *Present at the Creation: My Years in the State Department* (New York: W.W. Norton, 1969), p. 399.

time for an "act of will, a decision to do something" at a crucial juncture.

We require another act of will—a determination to surmount tactical squabbles and legalistic preoccupations and to become the master of our destinies. We in this room are heirs to a rich heritage of trust and friendship. If we are true to ourselves, we have it in our power to extend it to a united Europe and to pass it on, further enriched and ennobled, to succeeding generations.

28. BREATHING SPELL AT THE UNITED NATIONS

The annual session of the U.N. General Assembly invariably marks an important phase in the cyclical movement of American foreign policy. When Secretary Kissinger addressed the Assembly on September 24, immediately following his assumption of office and shortly after the start of the Assembly's 28th Regular Session,[1] there appeared to be every reason to suppose that most of the principal currents of international life would again be flowing into and through New York in the coming weeks. It seemed a foregone conclusion, moreover, that this Assembly session would derive its special character from the interaction of what already ranked as two of the dominant trends of the 1970s: the growing need for international cooperation in dealing with a host of issues born of rapid, global technological evolution; and the growing rift between the "have" and "have-not" nations that had been increasingly brought to world attention over the past few years and had been most conspicuously placed on view at the Algiers conference of nonaligned nations a few days before the Assembly met.[2]

As matters turned out, however, the 1973 General Assembly was denied its customary share of the limelight by the cataclysmic events associated with the outbreak of war in the Middle East, the threatened Soviet-American confrontation of October 24-25, the imposition of the Arab oil embargo, and the sharp increases in petroleum prices that bore so heavily on developing as well as developed countries. With such events in progress, the Assembly seemed at times to have been reduced to little more than a side show, a backwater far removed from the mainstream of world affairs. Admittedly, the trend was not entirely unwelcome from the standpoint of the United States, which was being bitterly attacked from various directions in the world outside but experienced at least some temporary alleviation of the unenviable position it had

---

[1]Document 45.
[2]Cf. Chapter 24 at note 2.

come to occupy within the Assembly itself. In spite of numerous instances in which the U.S. delegation felt quite unable to swim with the tide of majority sentiment, the United States experienced no such humiliating defeats as had fallen to its lot in 1971 with the expulsion of the Republic of China, or in 1972 with the rejection of its carefully wrought proposals for international action against terrorism.[3]

There was, for instance, no longer any implied affront to the United States in the simultaneous admission to U.N. membership on September 18, the opening day of the session, of the German Democratic Republic and the Federal Republic of Germany, together with the newly independent Commonwealth of the Bahamas.[4] These actions, which increased the roster of U.N. members from 132 to 135, had the welcome effect of clearing the way for the realization of an important U.S. fiscal objective, the reduction of the annual U.S. assessment in support of the regular U.N. budget from 31.52 percent to a maximum of 25 percent.[5] As previously recounted, the United States was able to stave off a threatened change in the representation of Cambodia (the Khmer Republic);[6] and it also helped postpone a major clash regarding Korea by accepting a consensus statement that took note of the dialogue initiated between the two Korean governments, expressed hope for its success, and sanctioned the dissolution of the 23-year-old U.N. Commission on the Unification and Rehabilitation of Korea (UNCURK).[7] None of these actions would affect the status of the local U.N. military command, which still served as umbrella for approximately 38,000 U.S. troops remaining in South Korea.

A copious debate on disarmament questions found the United States quite often in alignment with majority sentiment, although the American delegation abstained as usual on various proposals

---

[3]*AFR, 1971*, pp. 500-515; same, *1972*, pp. 486-515. For more detailed background see especially *Nixon Report, 1973*, pp. 210-29, and *Rogers Report, 1972*, pp. 101-85. Official texts of resolutions and decisions of the 28th General Assembly will be found in General Assembly, *Official Records: 28th Session, Supplement No. 30* (A/9030); details of the debates on particular agenda items will be found in *UN Monthly Chronicle*, vol. 10 (Oct.-Dec. 1973) and vol. 11 (Jan. 1974), and in *U.S. Participation, 1973*.

[4]Resolutions 3050 and 3051 (XXVIII), Sept. 18, adopted respectively without vote and by acclamation.

[5]Resolution 3072 (XXVIII), Nov. 9, adopted by a vote of 90 (U.S.)-1-1. By Resolution 3131 (XXVIII), Dec. 11, adopted by a vote of 108 (U.S.)-3-1, the U.S. agreed to contribute 28.894 percent of the initial expenses of the new U.N. Emergency Force in the Middle East.

[6]Cf. Chapter 26 at note 3.

[7]Text in *Official Records, Supplement 30*, cited, p. 24; details in *U.S. Participation, 1973*, pp. 22-5.

that it considered laudable in intent but impractical or dangerous in their probable effect. Since disagreement over the verification problem continued to impede the longstanding quest for treaties limiting chemical weapons and barring underground nuclear weapon tests, the most positive action open to the Assembly at its 1973 session was the establishment of a 40-nation *ad hoc* committee to examine governmental views on the holding of a world disarmament conference, as previously proposed by the Soviet Union.[8] Although the United States continued to oppose the actual convening of such a conference, it did not object to a preliminary study on terms acceptable to the other four nuclear powers.

As always, it was on issues of special interest to "third world" and "anticolonial" countries that the United States most frequently found itself in a minority position, thanks mainly to the insistence of such countries on enunciating an activist point of view with which the American delegation could not or would not associate itself. Typical of the many such instances that stud the Assembly's records were strongly worded resolutions denouncing Israeli practices in occupied territories, insisting on the "rights" of Palestinians, castigating the activities of foreign economic and other interests in dependent territories, and urging moral and material assistance to African liberation movements.[9]

In one widely noted instance, the United States itself was singled out for Assembly censure in consequence of its failure, unavoidable under the "Byrd amendment" of 1971, to observe the Security Council ban on the import of chrome ore and other strategic materials from Southern Rhodesia.[10] Congressional opponents of the Byrd provision, led by Senator Humphrey, had mounted a new repeal effort early in the 1973 congressional session, and their efforts had in due course been endorsed not only by Ambassador Scali and Assistant Secretary Newsom but also by Secretary Kissinger, who had avowed in writing a conviction that "the Byrd provision is not essential to our national security, brings us no real economic advantage, and is detrimental to the conduct of foreign relations."[11] In spite of such endorsements, however, the repeal

[8]Resolution 3183 (XXVIII), Dec. 18, adopted unanimously. Details of the U.S. position on disarmament items will be found in *Documents on Disarmament, 1973, passim.*
[9]Respectively Resolutions 3092 B (XXVIII), Dec. 7, adopted by 90-7 (U.S.)-27; 3089 D (XXVIII), Dec. 7, adopted by 87-6 (U.S.)-33; 3117 (XXVIII), Dec. 12, adopted by 103-3 (U.S.)-23; and 3118 (XXVIII), Dec. 12, adopted by 108-4 (U.S.)-17.
[10]Cf. Chapter 6 at note 5.
[11]Scali and Newsom in *Bulletin*, vol. 69 (1973), pp. 434-9; Kissinger letter to Rep. Charles C. Diggs, Jr., Oct. 3, in *Congressional Record* (Daily Edition), Dec. 11, 1973, p. S 22498.

measure encountered heavy opposition when it reached the Senate floor on November 20. A first attempt to cut off debate by invoking cloture failed on December 11 by a vote of 59 to 35, and a second attempt on December 13 was likewise unsuccessful. Not until December 18 was cloture successfully invoked by a vote of 63 to 26, after which the Senate passed the bill itself by a vote of 54 to 37. Any consideration by the House of Representatives, however, would obviously have to await the next session of Congress in 1974.[12]

In the meantime, the U.N. Assembly had adopted on December 12 a pair of resolutions voicing grave impatience with the United Kingdom, as legal sovereign in Rhodesia, and with the United States and other, unnamed violators of the sanctions program. As was normal, the United States (together with Portugal, South Africa, and Great Britain) opposed the first of these two resolutions "because of its unrealistic, violent demands on the United Kingdom."[13] The U.S. delegation had even more cogent reasons for opposing the second resolution, which was sponsored by 50 African, Asian, Latin American, and Eastern European states and included a special paragraph condemning U.S. chrome and nickel imports from Southern Rhodesia and admonishing the United States to live up to its obligations under the U.N. Charter.[14] Adopted by a vote of 101 to 5 with 22 abstentions, this resolution (Document 82) incurred the opposition of France, Portugal, South Africa, and the United Kingdom as well as the United States— which took the position that "it could not accept language that condemned actions it had taken in compliance with its own laws and that focused attention on the United States while largely ignoring the violations of others."[15]

On other Southern African matters, the United States as usual turned in a mixed voting record reflecting both its abhorrence of racial discrimination and oppression and its misgivings about the impetuosity of the African liberation movements and their supporters. Among other actions exhibiting this characteristic mixture of motives, the United States opposed a resolution hailing the newly proclaimed "sovereign State of the Republic of Guinea-Bissau" (Portuguese Guinea), and abstained on (but did not oppose) a lengthy call to action against South Africa's illegal occupa-

---

[12]Details in *Senate Foreign Relations Committee History, 1973-4*, pp. 169-72. The House did not consider the bill in 1974, but rejected a similar bill on Sept. 25, 1975.
[13]Resolution 3115 (XXVIII), Dec. 12, adopted by 108-4 (U.S.)-15; *U.S. Participation, 1973*, p. 214.
[14]Resolution 3116 (XXVIII), Dec. 12, adopted by 101-5 (U.S.)-22.
[15]*U.S. Participation, 1973*, p. 214.

tion of Namibia.[16] In a concurrent discussion of Namibia in the Security Council, the United States supported that body's action in calling a halt to the Secretary-General's efforts to negotiate a solution with South Africa[17]—at the same time, however, voicing a hope that further discussions with the Pretoria government might yet encourage desirable modifications of South African policy.[18]

Perhaps the most acceptable American initiative of the session was Secretary Kissinger's proposal relating to a World Food Conference, which, as already noted, was given strong endorsement by the Food and Agriculture Organization, the Economic and Social Council, and the General Assembly itself.[19] Among other matters of special interest to the United States, there was ground for renewed disappointment in the Assembly's failure to address itself more resolutely to the problems of international terrorism that had been brought to its attention by Secretary Rogers the year before.[20] This negative performance was only partially redeemed, in American eyes, by the adoption of a Convention on the Prevention and Punishment of Crimes Against Internationally Protected Persons, Including Diplomatic Agents (**Document 83a**),[21] which dealt with only a small segment of the terrorist problem but was warmly praised by the U.S. spokesman in the Assembly (**Document 83b**). Although the United States was first to sign the convention in a brief ceremony at U.N. Headquarters on December 28,[22] official enthusiasm seems to have cooled thereafter. Transmitted to the Senate by President Ford on November 13, 1974, the convention was approved by that body on October 28, 1975 but was still awaiting formal ratification more than two years after its initial adoption.

No subject on the Assembly's 1973 agenda was more important to the United States and other maritime nations than the completion of arrangements for the Third U.N. Conference on the Law of the Sea, a meeting that had been in preparation for a number of years and would, it was hoped, resolve a multitude of pending questions relating to such matters as the breadth of the territorial

---

[16]Resolutions 3061 (XXVIII), Nov. 2, adopted by 93-7 (U.S.)-30, and 3111 (XXVIII), Dec. 12, adopted by 107-2-17 (U.S.).

[17]Security Council Resolution 342 (1973), Dec. 11, adopted unanimously.

[18]Statement by Ambassador Bennett, Dec. 11, 1973, in *Bulletin*, vol. 70 (1974), pp. 104-5.

[19]Cf. Chapter 24 at note 7.

[20]For background cf. *AFR, 1972*, pp. 490-516. On recommendation of its Sixth (Legal) Committee, the Assembly decided on Dec. 12, 1973 to defer consideration of terrorism to its 29th Session in 1974.

[21]Resolution 3166 (XXVIII), Dec. 14, adopted without objection.

[22]*UN Monthly Chronicle*, vol. 11 (Jan. 1974), p. 91; *Bulletin*, vol. 70 (1974), p. 90.

sea, the exploitation of the continental shelf, the regulation of
fisheries, the regime of the deep seabed, and the protection of the
marine environment.[23] Originally scheduled to take place in 1973,
the conference had already been once postponed because of the
complexity and difficulty of the issues involved. Under a final
timetable approved by the General Assembly on November 16,
1973 (**Document 84**), it was decided that the first session of the conference, dealing only with organizational and procedural matters,
would be convened in New York on December 3-14, 1973; the
second session, dealing with the substantive work of the conference, would be held in Caracas from June 20 to August 29, 1974;
and any subsequent session or sessions that might prove necessary
would be convened not later than 1975, taking due note of
Austria's offer to provide a site in Vienna in that year.[24] Sup-
plementing this resolution, the Assembly in a so-called "gentleman's agreement" admonished the conference to "make every
effort to reach agreement on substantive matters by way of consensus" and not to resort to voting until all efforts at consensus had
been exhausted.[25]

Partly because of complications relating to this gentleman's
agreement, no definitive rules of procedure could be adopted when
the opening session of the Law of the Sea Conference was held in
New York on December 3-15. The main achievements of the
session were the adoption of an agenda, the establishment of a
committee structure, and the election of officers. H.S.
Amerasinghe of Sri Lanka, who had previously served as Chairman
of the U.N.'s 91-member Committee on the Peaceful Uses of the
Seabed and the Ocean Floor Beyond the Limits of National
Jurisdiction, was chosen President of the conference by acclamation. The United States, after protracted disagreements over
the allocation of committee seats, eventually secured election to
both the 48-member General Committee and the 23-member
Drafting Committee, thus assuring itself a strong position for the
real work of the conference that would begin in Caracas in June
1974.[26]

An agenda item on "The situation in the Middle East" was still
awaiting consideration by the General Assembly when the time for
that body's adjournment arrived on December 18, 1973. Extensive
consultations by the Assembly's President, Leopoldo Benites of
Ecuador, had disclosed a prevalent reluctance to take up the Mid-

[23]For background see *AFR, 1971*, pp. 533-6 and 543-8; same, *1972*, pp. 477-85.
[24]Resolution 3067 (XXVIII), Nov. 16, adopted without objection.
[25]Text in *Official Records, Supplement 30*, cited, p. 24; details in *U.S. Participation, 1973*, pp. 56-7.
[26]*UN Monthly Chronicle*, vol. 11 (Jan. 1974), pp. 84-5; *U.S. Participation, 1973*,
pp. 57-9.

dle Eastern question at a time when a special diplomatic conference on the subject was about to convene in Geneva under the auspices of the United States and the Soviet Union. But since there was also a feeling that an Assembly discussion of the Middle East might be desirable at a later date, it was agreed that the 28th Session should be suspended, rather than adjourned, so that it could later be reconvened if circumstances warranted.[27] (In point of fact, the session was reconvened only for purposes of its final dissolution on September 16, 1974.) As one of its final actions before dispersing for the year-end holidays, the Assembly acted on a proposal by the Algiers conference in scheduling a special session on development problems, to be held immediately preceding its 30th Regular Session in September 1975.[28]

(82) *Criticism of United States Policy toward Southern Rhodesia: General Assembly Resolution 3116 (XXVIII), December 12, 1973.*[29]

Question of Southern Rhodesia

The General Assembly,
Having examined the critical and deteriorating situation in Southern Rhodesia (Zimbabwe), which the Security Council, in its resolution 277 (1970) of 18 March 1970,[30] reaffirmed as constituting a threat to international peace and security,

Deeply disturbed that measures taken so far have failed to bring the rebellion in Southern Rhodesia (Zimbabwe) to an end, owing primarily to the continued and increasing collaboration which certain States, in particular Portugal and South Africa, in violation of Article 25 of the Charter of the United Nations[31] and of the relevant decisions of the United Nations, maintain with the illegal

---

[27] *UN Monthly Chronicle,* vol. 11 (Jan. 1974), p. 22.

[28] Resolution 3172 (XXVIII), Dec. 17, adopted by 123 (U.S.)-0-0. The Seventh Special Session of the Assembly, convened pursuant to this resolution and held in New York Sept. 1-16, 1975, was preceded by a Sixth Special Session, on raw materials and development, which was held in New York Apr. 9-May 2, 1974.

[29] Text from General Assembly, *Oﬃcial Records: 28th Session, Supplement No. 30* (A/9030), pp. 99-100; adopted by a vote of 101-5 (U.S.)-22. For background cf. above at notes 10-15.

[30] *Documents, 1970,* pp. 247-51.

[31] "The Members of the United Nations agree to accept and carry out the decisions of the Security Council in accordance with the present Charter."

régime, thereby seriously impeding the effective application of sanctions against the illegal régime,

Gravely concerned that the Government of the United States of America continues to permit the importation of chrome and nickel into the United States from Southern Rhodesia, in violation of the relevant provisions of Security Council resolutions 253 (1968) of 29 May 1968, 277 (1970) of 18 March 1970, 288 (1970) of 17 November 1970, 314 (1972) of 28 February 1972,[32] 318 (1972) of 28 July 1972 and 320 (1972) of 29 September 1972,[33] and in disregard of General Assembly resolutions 2765 (XXVI) of 16 November 1971[34] and 2946 (XXVII) of 7 December 1972,[35]

Taking into consideration the programme of action adopted by the International Conference of Experts for the Support of Victims of Colonialism and *Apartheid* in Southern Africa, held at Oslo from 9 to 14 April 1973,

Deeply disturbed at recent reports of widespread violations of United Nations sanctions, including the regular operation of Southern Rhodesian aircraft for exporting Southern Rhodesian cargo to Europe and the participation of Southern Rhodesian teams at various sporting events, as well as the continued functioning of information and airline offices of the illegal régime outside Southern Rhodesia,

Bearing in mind the views expressed by the representatives of the Zimbabwe African People's Union and the Zimbabwe African National Union and by the petitioners,

Reaffirming its conviction that the sanctions will not put an end to the illegal racist minority régime unless they are comprehensive, mandatory, effectively supervised, enforced and complied with, particularly by Portugal and South Africa,

1. *Condemns* the failure of the Government of the United Kingdom of Great Britain and Northern Ireland to take effective measures in accordance with the relevant decisions of the United Nations to put an end to the illegal racist minority régime in Southern Rhodesia (Zimbabwe), and calls upon that Government to take forthwith all effective measures to bring down the rebellious minority régime;

2. *Strongly condemns* the policies of the Governments, particularly those of Portugal and South Africa, which, in violation of the relevant resolutions of the United Nations and contrary to their specific obligations under Article 25 of the Charter of the United Nations, continue to collaborate with the illegal racist minority

[32]Cf. *AFR, 1972*, p. 393.
[33]Cf. same, p. 398.
[34]*AFR, 1971*, pp. 428-9.
[35]Cf. same, *1972*, p. 405.

régime in its racialist and repressive domination of the people of Zimbabwe, and calls upon those Governments to cease forthwith all such collaboration;

3. *Condemns* all violations of the mandatory sanctions imposed by the Security Council, as well as the failure of certain Member States to enforce those sanctions strictly, as being contrary to the obligations assumed by them under Article 25 of the Charter;

4. *Condemns* the continued importation by the Government of the United States of America of chrome and nickel from Southern Rhodesia (Zimbabwe) in contravention of the provisions of the relevant Security Council resolutions and contrary to the specific obligations assumed by that Government under Article 25 of the Charter, and calls upon the Government of the United States to terminate forthwith all such importation and to observe faithfully and without exception the provisions of the relevant United Nations resolutions;

5. *Requests* all Governments:

(*a*) To take stringent enforcement measures to ensure strict compliance by all individuals, associations and bodies corporate under their jurisdiction with the sanctions imposed by the Security Council and to ensure the complete discontinuance by them of any form of collaboration with the illegal régime;

(*b*) To take effective steps to prevent or discourage the emigration to Southern Rhodesia (Zimbabwe) of any individuals or groups of individuals under their jurisdiction;

6. *Further requests* all Governments to refrain from taking any action which might confer a semblance of legitimacy on the illegal racist minority régime and, in particular, calls upon the Government of the United States to take the necessary steps to put an end to the operation and activities within the United States of Air Rhodesia, the Rhodesian National Tourist Board and the Rhodesian Information Office, or any other activities which contravene the aims and purposes of the sanctions imposed by the Security Council;

7. *Considers* that, in view of the further deterioration of the situation resulting from the intensified repressive measures taken by the illegal racist minority régime against the people of Zimbabwe and with a view to putting an end to the illegal régime, the scope of sanctions against the régime must be widened to include all the measures envisaged under Article 41 of the Charter,[36] and

[36]Article 41 of the U.N. Charter states that measures not involving the use of armed force which may be invoked by the Security Council "may include complete or partial interruption of economic relations and of rail, sea, air, postal, telegraphic, radio, and other means of communication, and the severance of diplomatic relations."

accordingly invites the Security Council to consider taking the necessary measures in that regard and, in particular, calling upon all States to take effective steps aimed, *inter alia*, at:

(*a*) The unconditional confiscation of all shipments to and from Southern Rhodesia (Zimbabwe);

(*b*) The nullification of all insurance policies covering such shipments;

(*c*) The invalidation of passports and other documents for travel to Southern Rhodesia (Zimbabwe);

8. *Further draws the attention* of the Security Council, having regard to their persistent refusal to carry out the mandatory decisions of the Council, to the need, as a matter of priority, to consider imposing sanctions against Portugal and South Africa;

9. *Appeals* to those permanent members of the Security Council whose negative votes on various proposals relating to the question have continued to obstruct the effective and faithful discharge by the Council of its responsibilities under the relevant provisions of the Charter in this regard to reconsider their negative attitude with a view to the elimination forthwith of the threat to international peace and security resulting from the critical situation in Southern Rhodesia (Zimbabwe);

10. *Requests* the Special Committee[37] to follow the implementation of the present resolution.

(83) Convention on the Prevention and Punishment of Crimes Against Internationally Protected Persons, Including Diplomatic Agents, adopted by the General Assembly December 14, 1973.

(a) General Assembly Resolution 3166 (XXVIII), December 14, 1973, with text of the Convention.[38]

Convention on the Prevention and Punishment of Crimes against Internationally Protected Persons, including Diplomatic Agents

The General Assembly,

Considering that the codification and progressive development

[37]Special Committee on the Situation with regard to the Implementation of the Declaration on the Granting of Independence to Colonial Countries and Peoples (Committee of 24).

[38]Text from General Assembly, *Official Records: 28th Session, Supplement No. 30* (A/9030), pp. 146-9; adopted without objection.

of international law contributes to the implementation of the purposes and principles set forth in Articles 1 and 2 of the Charter of the United Nations,

Recalling that in response to the request made in General Assembly resolution 2780 (XXVI) of 3 December 1971, the International Law Commission, at its twenty-fourth session, studied the question of the protection and inviolability of diplomatic agents and other persons entitled to special protection under international law and prepared draft articles on the prevention and punishment of crimes against such persons,[39]

Having considered the draft articles and also the comments and observations thereon submitted by States, specialized agencies and other intergovernmental organizations[40] in response to the invitation extended by the General Assembly in its resolution 2926 (XXVII) of 28 November 1972,

Convinced of the importance of securing international agreement on appropriate and effective measures for the prevention and punishment of crimes against diplomatic agents and other internationally protected persons in view of the serious threat to the maintenance and promotion of friendly relations and co-operation among States created by the commission of such crimes,

Having elaborated for that purpose the provisions contained in the Convention annexed hereto,

1. *Adopts* the Convention on the Prevention and Punishment of Crimes against Internationally Protected Persons, including Diplomatic Agents, annexed to the present resolution;

2. *Re-emphasizes* the great importance of the rules of international law concerning the inviolability of and special protection to be afforded to internationally protected persons and the obligations of States in relation thereto;

3. *Considers* that the annexed Convention will enable States to carry out their obligations more effectively;

4. *Recognizes also* that the provisions of the annexed Convention could not in any way prejudice the exercise of the legitimate right to self-determination and independence, in accordance with the purposes and principles of the Charter of the United Nations and the Declaration on Principles of International Law concerning Friendly Relations and Co-operation among States in accordance with the Charter of the United Nations,[41] by peoples struggling against colonialism, alien domination, foreign occupation, racial discrimination and *apartheid*;

5. *Invites* States to become parties to the annexed Convention;

[39]For background and detailed references see *AFR, 1972*, p. 489.
[40]U.N. document A/9127 and Add.1.; for background cf. *AFR, 1972*, p. 510.
[41]Resolution 2625 (XXV), Oct. 24, 1970.

6. *Decides* that the present resolution, whose provisions are related to the annexed Convention, shall always be published together with it.

ANNEX

Convention on the Prevention and Punishment of Crimes against Internationally Protected Persons, including Diplomatic Agents

The States Parties to this Convention,

Having in mind the purposes and principles of the Charter of the United Nations concerning the maintenance of international peace and the promotion of friendly relations and co-operation among States,

Considering that crimes against diplomatic agents and other internationally protected persons jeopardizing the safety of these persons create a serious threat to the maintenance of normal international relations which are necessary for co-operation among States,

Believing that the commission of such crimes is a matter of grave concern to the international community,

Convinced that there is an urgent need to adopt appropriate and effective measures for the prevention and punishment of such crimes,

Have agreed as follows:

Article 1

For the purposes of this Convention:

1. "Internationally protected person" means:

(*a*) A Head of State, including any member of a collegial body performing the functions of a Head of State under the constitution of the State concerned, a Head of Government or a Minister for Foreign Affairs, whenever any such person is in a foreign State, as well as members of his family who accompany him;

(*b*) Any representative or official of a State or any official or other agent of an international organization of an intergovernmental character who, at the time when and in the place where a crime against him, his official premises, his private accommodation or his means of transport is committed, is entitled pursuant to international law to special protection from any attack on his person, freedom or dignity, as well as members of his family forming part of his household;

2. "Alleged offender" means a person as to whom there is suf-

ficient evidence to determine *prima facie* that he has committed or participated in one or more of the crimes set forth in article 2.

Article 2

1. The intentional commission of:

(*a*) A murder, kidnapping or other attack upon the person or liberty of an internationally protected person;

(*b*) A violent attack upon the official premises, the private accommodation or the means of transport of an internationally protected person likely to endanger his person or liberty;

(*c*) A threat to commit any such attack;

(*d*) An attempt to commit any such attack; and

(*e*) An act constituting participation as an accomplice in any such attack

shall be made by each State Party a crime under its internal law.

2. Each State Party shall make these crimes punishable by appropriate penalties which take into account their grave nature.

3. Paragraphs 1 and 2 of this article in no way derogate from the obligations of States Parties under international law to take all appropriate measures to prevent other attacks on the person, freedom or dignity of an internationally protected person.

Article 3

1. Each State Party shall take such measures as may be necessary to establish its jurisdiction over the crimes set forth in article 2 in the following cases:

(*a*) When the crime is committed in the territory of that State or on board a ship or aircraft registered in that State;

(*b*) When the alleged offender is a national of that State;

(*c*) When the crime is committed against an internationally protected person as defined in article 1 who enjoys his status as such by virtue of functions which he exercises on behalf of that State.

2. Each State Party shall likewise take such measures as may be necessary to establish its jurisdiction over these crimes in cases where the alleged offender is present in its territory and it does not extradite him pursuant to article 8 to any of the States mentioned in paragraph 1 of this article.

3. This Convention does not exclude any criminal jurisdiction exercised in accordance with internal law.

Article 4

States Parties shall co-operate in the prevention of the crimes set forth in article 2, particularly by:

(*a*) Taking all practicable measures to prevent preparations in their respective territories for the commission of those crimes within or outside their territories;

(*b*) Exchanging information and co-ordinating the taking of administrative and other measures as appropriate to prevent the commission of those crimes.

Article 5

1. The State Party in which any of the crimes set forth in article 2 has been committed shall, if it has reason to believe that an alleged offender has fled from its territory, communicate to all other States concerned, directly or through the Secretary-General of the United Nations, all the pertinent facts regarding the crime committed and all available information regarding the identity of the alleged offender.

2. Whenever any of the crimes set forth in article 2 has been committed against an internationally protected person, any State Party which has information concerning the victim and the circumstances of the crime shall endeavour to transmit it, under the conditions provided for in its internal law, fully and promptly to the State Party on whose behalf he was exercising his functions.

Article 6

1. Upon being satisfied that the circumstances so warrant, the State Party in whose territory the alleged offender is present shall take the appropriate measures under its internal law so as to ensure his presence for the purpose of prosecution or extradition. Such measures shall be notified without delay directly or through the Secretary-General of the United Nations to:

(*a*) The State where the crime was committed;

(*b*) The State or States of which the alleged offender is a national or, if he is a stateless person, in whose territory he permanently resides;

(*c*) The State or States of which the internationally protected person concerned is a national or on whose behalf he was exercising his functions;

(*d*) All other States concerned; and

(*e*) The international organization of which the internationally protected person concerned is an official or an agent.

2. Any person regarding whom the measures referred to in paragraph 1 of this article are being taken shall be entitled:

(*a*) To communicate without delay with the nearest appropriate representative of the State of which he is a national or which is otherwise entitled to protect his rights or, if he is a stateless person, which he requests and which is willing to protect his rights; and

(*b*) To be visited by a representative of that State.

Article 7

The State Party in whose territory the alleged offender is present shall, if it does not extradite him, submit, without exception whatsoever and without undue delay, the case to its competent authorities for the purpose of prosecution, through proceedings in accordance with the laws of that State.

Article 8

1. To the extent that the crimes set forth in article 2 are not listed as extraditable offences in any extradition treaty existing between States Parties, they shall be deemed to be included as such therein. States Parties undertake to include those crimes as extraditable offences in every future extradition treaty to be concluded between them.

2. If a State Party which makes extradition conditional on the existence of a treaty receives a request for extradition from another State Party with which it has no extradition treaty, it may, if it decides to extradite, consider this Convention as the legal basis for extradition in respect of those crimes. Extradition shall be subject to the procedural provisions and the other conditions of the law of the requested State.

3. States Parties which do not make extradition conditional on the existence of a treaty shall recognize those crimes as extraditable offences between themselves subject to the procedural provisions and the other conditions of the law of the requested State.

4. Each of the crimes shall be treated, for the purpose of extradition between States Parties, as if it had been committed not only in the place in which it occurred but also in the territories of the States required to establish their jurisdiction in accordance with paragraph 1 of article 3.

Article 9

Any person regarding whom proceedings are being carried out in connexion with any of the crimes set forth in article 2 shall be guaranteed fair treatment at all stages of the proceedings.

Article 10

1. States Parties shall afford one another the greatest measure of assistance in connexion with criminal proceedings brought in respect of the crimes set forth in article 2, including the supply of all evidence at their disposal necessary for the proceedings.

2. The provisions of paragraph 1 of this article shall not affect obligations concerning mutual judicial assistance embodied in any other treaty.

Article 11

The State Party where an alleged offender is prosecuted shall communicate the final outcome of the proceedings to the Secretary-General of the United Nations, who shall transmit the information to the other States Parties.

Article 12

The provisions of this Convention shall not affect the application of the Treaties on Asylum, in force at the date of the adoption of this Convention, as between the States which are parties to those Treaties; but a State Party to this Convention may not invoke those Treaties with respect to another State Party to this Convention which is not a party to those Treaties.

Article 13

1. Any dispute between two or more States Parties concerning the interpretation or application of this Convention which is not settled by negotiation shall, at the request of one of them, be submitted to arbitration. If within six months from the date of the request for arbitration the parties are unable to agree on the organization of the arbitration, any one of those parties may refer the dispute to the International Court of Justice by request in conformity with the Statute of the Court.

2. Each State Party may at the time of signature or ratification of this Convention or accession thereto declare that it does not consider itself bound by paragraph 1 of this article. The other States Parties shall not be bound by paragraph 1 of this article with respect to any State Party which has made such a reservation.

3. Any State Party which has made a reservation in accordance with paragraph 2 of this article may at any time withdraw that reservation by notification to the Secretary-General of the United Nations.

Article 14

This Convention shall be open for signature by all States, until 31 December 1974 at United Nations Headquarters in New York.

Article 15

This Convention is subject to ratification. The instruments of ratification shall be deposited with the Secretary-General of the United Nations.

Article 16

This Convention shall remain open for accession by any State. The instruments of accession shall be deposited with the Secretary-General of the United Nations.

Article 17

1. This Convention shall enter into force on the thirtieth day following the date of deposit of the twenty-second instrument of ratification or accession with the Secretary-General of the United Nations.[42]

2. For each State ratifying or acceding to the Convention after the deposit of the twenty-second instrument of ratification or accession, the Convention shall enter into force on the thirtieth day after deposit by such State of its instrument of ratification or accession.

---

[42]Twelve states had deposited instruments of ratification or accession as of Dec. 31, 1975.

Article 18

1. Any State Party may denounce this Convention by written notification to the Secretary-General of the United Nations.

2. Denunciation shall take effect six months following the date on which notification is received by the Secretary-General of the United Nations.

Article 19

The Secretary-General of the United Nations shall inform all States, *inter alia*:

(*a*) Of signatures to this Convention, of the deposit of instruments of ratification or accession in accordance with articles 14, 15 and 16 and of notifications made under article 18;

(*b*) Of the date on which this Convention will enter into force in accordance with article 17.

Article 20

The original of this Convention, of which the Chinese, English, French, Russian and Spanish texts are equally authentic, shall be deposited with the Secretary-General of the United Nations, who shall send certified copies thereof to all States.

IN WITNESS WHEREOF the undersigned, being duly authorized thereto by their respective Governments, have signed this Convention, opened for signature at New York on 14 December 1973.

(b) Views of the United States: Statement by Ambassador Bennett in Plenary Session, December 14, 1973.[43]

This Assembly can justly be proud of having successfully completed its work on this important convention.[44]

A debt of gratitude is owed to the International Law Commission. The Commission produced the excellent draft which was the basis of the Assembly's work and which by its excellence greatly facilitated our task. Since work of the highest caliber is what we can routinely expect from the Commission by now, it is worth noting

[43]USUN Press Release 134, Dec. 14; text from *Bulletin*, vol. 70 (1974), pp. 89-91.
[44]Document 83a.

that the Commission produced this draft at a single session in response to the request of the Assembly.

This effort which the Assembly has brought to fruition was in response to an urgent need. The long-established principle of the inviolability of diplomatic agents was being threatened by random acts of violence in various parts of the world. The continued effectiveness of diplomatic channels, the means by which states communicate with one another, has been jeopardized. Although the legal obligation to protect these persons was never questioned, the mechanism for international cooperation to insure that perpetrators of serious attacks against such persons are brought to justice, no matter to where they may flee, was lacking.

The Assembly here and now declares to the world that under no circumstances may a diplomat be attacked with impunity. In addition, the convention sets up a valuable legal mechanism which requires submission for prosecution or extradition of persons alleged to have committed serious crimes against diplomats. This mechanism is similar to that employed in the field of interference with civil aviation—specifically in the Hague (Hijacking) and Montreal (Sabotage) Conventions.[45] Indeed, many of the provisions of the new convention have been modeled on provisions of the Hague and Montreal Conventions. While the new convention in several cases makes drafting improvements or refinements, these are intended simply to clarify the intention of the previous conventions.

Paragraph 2 of article 1 defines the term "alleged offender." The definition, while couched in apparently technical language, must of course be read more broadly so it can be applied by the various legal systems. We shall regard it as incorporating the standard applied in determining whether there are sufficient grounds for extradition in accordance with normal extradition practice.

Article 2 of the convention defines the crimes covered. The Legal Committee decided to cover serious crimes, as was the initial intention of the International Law Commission. Subparagraph 1(a) has been clarified so that instead of referring to "violent attack" it refers to "murder, kidnapping or other attack." Obviously, the words "other attack" mean attacks of a similar serious nature to those expressly mentioned—murder and kidnapping. Covering threats, attempts, and accessoryship is appropriate because of the

[45]Convention for the Suppression of Unlawful Seizure of Aircraft, done at The Hague Dec. 16, 1970 and entered into force Oct. 14, 1971 (TIAS 7192; 22 UST 1641; text in *Documents, 1970*, pp. 350-55); Convention for the Suppression of Unlawful Acts Against the Safety of Civil Aviation, done at Montreal Sept. 23,1971 and entered into force Jan. 26, 1973 (TIAS 7570; 24 UST 565; text in *AFR, 1971*, pp. 548-55).

initial seriousness of the acts covered under subparagraphs (a) and (b) of paragraph 1.

The crimes covered in paragraph 1 of article 2 are those to which reference is made throughout the convention by the phrase "the crimes set forth in Article 2." Paragraph 3 of article 2 does not add to the crimes covered by the convention but merely states a basic fact that would be true whether or not this paragraph were included in the convention.

Together with articles 1, 2, and 3, articles 6, 7, and 8 join to form the basic mechanism of the convention. This mechanism is obviously central to the object and purpose of the convention, and without it the convention could not operate effectively.

Article 6 establishes the obligation upon states parties to insure the continued presence for the purpose of prosecution or extradition of an alleged offender when he is on the territory of that state party. The phrase "upon being satisfied that the circumstances so warrant" merely reflects the fact that before a state may take action it must know of the presence of the alleged offender in its territory.

The obligation in article 7 is clearly stated to be "without exception whatsoever." It forms a central part of the mechanism of the convention.

Several articles in the convention deal with cooperation among states in the prevention and punishment of the covered crimes. These are articles 4, 5, 6, 10, and 11. Article 4 deals with taking all practicable measures to prevent preparation for the commission of the covered crimes. The United States understands this obligation to refer to doing the utmost to prevent attempts to commit such crimes or conspiracy to commit such crimes. Article 10 is notable in that it substantially improves the prospects for proper presentation of cases when prosecutions are conducted outside the territory of the state party in whose territory the crime was committed. In such cases assistance in connection with the criminal proceedings, as well as the supply of all evidence at the disposal of other states parties, including witnesses who are willing or can be convinced to attend proceedings in another state, will be necessary for the mechanism of the convention to operate successfully.

Article 12 is a compromise article which was the result of a difficult negotiation. While the United States does not see the need for such an article in this convention, we recognize that there are some other countries that believe it essential that such an article be included. This having been said, we worked cooperatively with those countries to draft an article that is limited in its scope and clear in its language. The article states that this convention shall not affect the application of treaties on asylum in force as between parties to those treaties *inter se*. That is to say, even if the alleged offender is present on the territory of one party to such a treaty and the state on the territory of which the crime has taken place is also a party to such a treaty, if the internationally protected person attacked exercised his functions on behalf of a state not party to such a treaty or the alleged offender was a national of a state not party to such a treaty, the state where the alleged offender is present may not invoke that treaty with respect to the non-party state. Thus, the non-party state can hold the state where the alleged offender is present to its obligations under article 7 and may, if it wishes, request extradition under article 8.

The United States would- have preferred a stronger dispute-settlement provision than the one contained in article 13. The U.S. delegation made proposals to this end during the negotiations. However, many countries preferred to follow the model of the Hague and Montreal Conventions. Nonetheless, we are gratified that minor technical improvements have been made in paragraph 1 of article 13, which we consider reflect more precisely the intention of the drafters of the provisions in the Hague and Montreal Conventions.

We are also pleased that an acceptable compromise has been arrived at with regard to the final clauses which permits the widest possible adherence to the convention without placing the Secretary General in an impossible position.

Since the Assembly did such excellent work in completing the convention, we were pleased to vote in favor of the resolution which constitutes the formal act of adoption of the convention. Such a resolution constitutes the procedural step by which the international community, whether operating in the context of the General Assembly or a diplomatic conference specially convened for the purpose, concludes its legislative actions. While this resolution contains some paragraphs which we would not have considered necessary, we nevertheless see no particular harm in their inclusion since they do not purport to impinge—and of course cannot impinge—upon the convention. One such paragraph restated propositions we were all pleased to accept in the authoritative Friendly Relations Declaration at the 25th session.[46] It is perhaps always useful to recognize fundamental human rights, including the legitimate exercise of the right of self-determination in accordance with the charter.

Regarding the injunction in paragraph 6 of the resolution to the United Nations to publish the resolution in conjunction with the convention, we consider that this requires the convention to be

[46]Cf. above at note 41.

published as part of the United Nations volumes of resolutions of the General Assembly; in addition, the idea of including the resolution in the treaty series for information purposes could be regarded as useful in that those referring to the treaty series can conveniently have ready access to the resolution.

The convention will be opened for signature today, and my government has begun the necessary review of the final text in order to enable us to sign it before the end of the year.[47] We hope a number of others will do likewise.

The convention would not have been possible without the positive cooperation of all regional groups. Such cooperation was forthcoming, and as a result this Assembly has a major positive achievement.

(84) Conference on the Law of the Sea: General Assembly Resolution 3067 (XXVIII), November 16, 1973.[48]

Reservation exclusively for peaceful purposes of the sea-bed and the ocean floor, and the subsoil thereof, underlying the high seas beyond the limits of present national jurisdiction and use of their resources in the interests of mankind, and convening of the Third United Nations Conference on the Law of the Sea

The General Assembly,

Recalling its resolutions 2467 (XXIII) of 21 December 1968, 2750 (XXV) of 17 December 1970, 2881 (XXVI) of 21 December 1971 and 3029 (XXVII) of 18 December 1972,[49]

Having considered the report of the Committee on the Peaceful Uses of the Sea-Bed and the Ocean Floor beyond the Limits of National Jurisdiction on the work of its sessions in 1973,[50]

Recalling in particular paragraph 2 of resolution 2750 C (XXV),

Considering that the Committee has accomplished, as far as possible, within the limits of its mandate, the work which the General Assembly entrusted to it for the preparation of the Third

---

[47]Cf. above at note 22.

[48]Text from General Assembly, *Official Records: Supplement No. 30* (A/9030), pp. 13-14; adopted without objection.

[49]Cf. *AFR, 1972*, p. 479.

[50]General Assembly, *Official Records: 28th Session, Supplement No. 21* (A/9021 and Corr.1 and 3).

United Nations Conference on the Law of the Sea, and that it is necessary to proceed to the immediate inauguration of the Conference in 1973 and the convening of a substantive session in 1974, in order to carry out the negotiations and other work required to complete the drafting and adoption of articles for a comprehensive convention on the law of the sea,

Recalling further its resolutions 2480 (XXIII) of 21 December 1968, 2539 (XXIV) of 11 December 1969, 2736 (XXV) of 17 December 1970 and 3009 (XXVII) of 18 December 1972 concerning the composition of the Secretariat, as well as the general dispositions on the same matter recommended by the Fifth Committee and adopted by the General Assembly at its twenty-sixth and twenty-seventh sessions,

1. *Expresses its appreciation* to the Committee on the Peaceful Uses of the Sea-Bed and the Ocean Floor beyond the Limits of National Jurisdiction on the work it has done in preparing for the Third United Nations Conference on the Law of the Sea;

2. *Confirms* its decision in paragraph 3 of resolution 3029 A (XXVII) and decides to convene the first session of the Third United Nations Conference on the Law of the Sea in New York from 3 to 14 December 1973 inclusive for the purpose of dealing with matters relating to the organization of the Conference, including the election of officers, the adoption of the agenda and the rules of procedure of the Conference, the establishment of subsidiary organs and the allocation of work to these organs and any other purpose within the scope of paragraph 3 below;

3. *Decides* that the mandate of the Conference shall be to adopt a convention dealing with all matters relating to the law of the sea, taking into account the subject-matter listed in paragraph 2 of General Assembly resolution 2750 C (XXV) and the list of subjects and issues relating to the law of the sea formally approved on 18 August 1972 by the Committee on the Peaceful Uses of the Sea-Bed and the Ocean Floor beyond the Limits of National Jurisdiction[51] and bearing in mind that the problems of ocean space are closely interrelated and need to be considered as a whole;

4. *Decides* to convene the second session of the Conference, for the purpose of dealing with the substantive work of the Conference, for a period of ten weeks from 20 June to 29 August 1974 at Caracas and, if necessary, to convene not later than 1975 any subsequent session or sessions as may be decided upon by the Conference and approved by the General Assembly, bearing in mind that the Government of Austria has offered Vienna as the site for the Conference in 1975;

[51]General Assembly, *Official Records: 27th Session, Supplement No. 21* (A/8721 and Corr.1), para. 23.

5. *Invites* the Conference to make such arrangements as it may deem necessary to facilitate its work;

6. *Refers* to the Conference the reports of the Committee on the Peaceful Uses of the Sea-Bed and the Ocean Floor beyond the Limits of National Jurisdiction on its work and all other relevant documentation of the General Assembly and the Committee;

7. *Decides*, having regard to the desirability of achieving universality of participation in the Conference, to request the Secretary-General to invite, in full compliance with General Assembly resolution 2758 (XXVI) of 25 October 1971, States Members of the United Nations or members of specialized agencies or the International Atomic Energy Agency and States parties to the Statute of the International Court of Justice as well as the following States to participate in the Conference: Republic of Guinea-Bissau and Democratic Republic of Viet-Nam;

8. *Requests* the Secretary-General:

(*a*) To invite to the Conference intergovernmental and non-governmental organizations in accordance with paragraphs 8 and 9 of resolution 3029 A (XXVII);

(*b*) To invite the United Nations Council for Namibia to participate in the Conference;

(*c*) To provide summary records in accordance with paragraph 10 of resolution 3029 A (XXVII);

9. *Decides* that the Secretary-General of the United Nations shall be the Secretary-General of the Conference and authorizes him to appoint a special representative to act on his behalf and to make such arrangements—including recruitment of necessary staff, taking into account the principle of equitable geographical representation—and to provide such facilities as may be necessary for the efficient and continuous servicing of the Conference, utilizing to the fullest extent possible the resources at his disposal;

10. *Requests* the Secretary-General to prepare appropriate draft rules of procedure for the Conference, taking into account the views expressed in the Committee on the Peaceful Uses of the Sea-Bed and the Ocean Floor beyond the Limits of National Jurisdiction and in the General Assembly, and to circulate the draft rules of procedure in time for consideration and approval at the organizational session of the Conference;

11. *Invites* States participating in the Conference to submit their proposals, including draft articles, on the substantive subject-matter of the Conference to the Secretary-General by 1 February 1974 and requests the Secretary-General to circulate the replies received by him before the second session with a view to expediting the work of the Conference;

12. *Decides* that the provisions of paragraph 11 above shall not preclude any State participating in the Conference from submitting proposals, including draft articles, at any stage of the Conference, in accordance with the procedure adopted by the Conference, .provided that States which have already submitted any proposals and draft articles need not resubmit them;

13. *Dissolves* the Committee on the Peaceful Uses of the Sea-Bed and the Ocean Floor beyond the Limits of National Jurisdiction as from the inauguration of the Conference.

29. GENEVA CONFERENCE ON THE MIDDLE EAST

The closing weeks of the U.N. Assembly overlapped the period of intensive preparation for the Mideast peace negotiations, "under appropriate auspices," that had been envisaged in Security Council Resolution 338 of October 22, 1973.[1] "Appropriate auspices," as had been understood at the time and was confirmed by Secretary Kissinger at his November 21 news conference,[2] meant essentially the United States and the Soviet Union. Soviet-American sponsorship of the forthcoming negotiations, an outgrowth of Secretary Kissinger's October visit to the U.S.S.R., would obviously tend to relegate the United Nations—hitherto the central element in Mideast peacemaking efforts—to a more or less "symbolic" background role. Israel, with its ingrained mistrust of the United Nations, would presumably have consented to no other arrangement, although the Arab states seemed willing to accord a larger role to an institution among whose members they counted many supporters.

This exercise of diplomatic leadership by the two superpowers was also viewed with reserve by other U.N. member states. At a private meeting of the Security Council on December 15, the ten nonpermanent Council members cosponsored and then adopted—without support from any of the five permanent members—a resolution expressing hope for the success of the conference and voicing confidence that the Secretary-General would "play a full role" and would actually preside if the parties so desired.[3] The United States and the U.S.S.R., however, remained unmoved by this appeal and advised the Secretary-General on December 18 that they themselves proposed to act as cochairmen of the conference,

---

[1]Document 59b.
[2]Cf. Chapter 26 at note 13.
[3]Resolution 344 (1973), Dec. 15, 1973, adopted by a vote of 10-0-4 (U.S.) with China not participating; details in *UN Monthly Chronicle*, vol. 11 (Jan. 1974), pp. 20-21, and *U.S. Participation, 1973*, p. 11.

although they hoped the United Nations would provide the necessary facilities and that Mr. Waldheim would act as "convener" of the conference and preside at its opening session on December 21.[4]

To persuade the Mideast combatants to attend a U.N.-sponsored peace conference was even now a task of some complexity. Though Israel had long insisted on the necessity of direct negotiations with its Arab adversaries, it now had ample reason for misgivings about the concessions that would surely be demanded by its adversaries and quite probably by friends as well. Secretary Kissinger himself had implied as much in telling his November 21 news conference that Israel would have to recognize the impossibility of "a purely military solution to the problems of the Middle East."[5] In spite of its natural reservations, however, Israel's dependence on American good will provided a powerful incentive to cooperate, especially in light of the $2.2 billion in emergency assistance proposed by President Nixon,[6] which was now about to be voted on in Congress. Approved by the House of Representatives on December 11, this large allotment[7] won final Senate approval by a 66 to 9 vote on December 20, one day before the scheduled opening of the Geneva conference.

Even more serious difficulties could be anticipated on the side of the Arab countries, whose basic attitude still exhibited traces of the 1967 formula of "No peace with Israel, no negotiation with Israel, no recognition of Israel and maintenance of the rights of the Palestinian people in their nation."[8] In spite of widespread acceptance of the U.N. resolutions, and in spite of Egypt's apparent swing toward cooperation with the United States, it would not be easy for any of the Arab belligerents to go to Geneva at a time when feeling against Israel and the West was still running high and when Israel, after having occupied still more territory at the expense of Egypt and Syria, continued to cling to all its gains and to disregard the Security Council's order to pull back to the October 22 ceasefire line in the Suez area.

It was primarily to prevent these difficulties from congealing

---

[4]U.N. document S/11161, Dec. 18, in Security Council, *Official Records: 28th Year, Supplement for Oct., Nov. and Dec. 1973*, pp. 272-3.
[5]*Bulletin*, vol. 69 (1973), p. 705.
[6]Document 58.
[7]Emergency Security Assistance Act of 1973 (Public Law 93-199), Dec. 26, 1973, funded by Foreign Assistance and Related Programs Appropriation Act, 1974 (Public Law 93-240), Jan. 2, 1974; for details see *Senate Foreign Relations Committee History, 1973-4*, pp. 48-53.
[8]Khartoum declaration, Sept. 1, 1967, quoted in *The United States in World Affairs, 1967*, p. 122.

beyond reversal in advance of the proposed conference that Secretary Kissinger had begun a second flying visit to the Middle East immediately following his December 12 address to the Pilgrims in London.[9] Beginning this time with a stopover in Algiers, the Secretary of State appears to have somewhat mollified the sentiments of President Boumediene and to have laid a foundation for the resumption of U.S.-Algerian diplomatic relations some eleven months later. Continuing to Cairo for further conferences on December 13-14, Dr. Kissinger found himself in agreement with President Sadat that military disengagement must be accorded highest priority in the coming negotiations. In Riyadh, on December 14-15, he made some further headway in dissolving the reserve of the late King Faisal, but was still unable to win that monarch's promise to lift the oil embargo.

Another limited success was achieved by the Secretary's December 15 visit to Damascus, where President Hafez al-Assad proved unexpectedly communicative but refused to promise Syrian participation in the forthcoming conference. In Jordan, the Secretary of State had better luck, and nonbelligerent Lebanon also promised its good will. Israel, where Dr. Kissinger completed the Middle Eastern phase of his trip on December 16-17, signified general concurrence in American plans—but only on the understanding that its sensitivities regarding the Palestinians must be respected, and that nothing could be done about disengagement until after its parliamentary election on December 31.

The three-day interval remaining before the Geneva conference left time for the cultivation of two European governments whose good will was valued in Washington in spite of their undemocratic outlook and international unpopularity. In Lisbon, on December 17-18, the Secretary of State conferred "in a markedly friendly atmosphere" with the leading figures in the Portuguese regime of Prime Minister Marcelo Caetano, already nearing the end of a tenure that would be cut short some four months later in a coup by dissident military officers. An even warmer atmosphere, marked by "the greatest cordiality and understanding," prevailed in Madrid as the Secretary conferred on December 18-19 with 81-year-old Chief of State Francisco Franco and such pillars of his regime as Admiral Luis Carrero Blanco, the President of the Government, and Prince Juan Carlos de Borbón, the Chief of State-designate.[10] By a gruesome coincidence, Admiral Carrero Blanco, who had been regarded as the predestined heavyweight of any post-Franco

[9]Document 83. For details of the trip see especially Kalb, *Kissinger*, pp. 518-29, and Edward R. F. Sheehan in *Foreign Policy*, No. 22 (Spring 1976), pp. 25-30. Cf. also note 6 to Chapter 22.
[10]Lisbon and Madrid communiqués, in *Bulletin*, vol. 70 (1974), p. 26.

regime, was assassinated in Madrid the following morning as Secretary Kissinger prepared for what was to be another fruitless meeting in Paris with Le Duc Tho, his long-time Vietnamese antagonist and fellow Nobel Prize winner.

Violence seemed once again to be gaining the ascendant in these pre-Christmas days. On December 17, in what was described as the worst and most brutal massacre yet carried out by Palestinian Arab terrorists, a Pan American airliner about to take off from Rome for Beirut and Tehran was fire-bombed and incinerated, killing 32 passengers and an airport worker and injuring at least 40. In an operation apparently unsanctioned by any recognized Palestinian organization, the same five terrorists also killed an Italian hostage in the course of a hijacking and escape attempt that ended with their surrender and disappearance in Kuwait.[11] Such atrocities, said a shocked President Nixon, not only underlined the need for more effective measures for the protection of international air travel but were bound to "delay the day when peace and justice may return to the Middle East."[12]

For Israel, the incident offered further vindication of its insistence that it would in no circumstances join in any negotiations in which the Palestine Liberation Organization was a party. On December 20, the very day before the Geneva conference, Secretary Kissinger is said to have furnished the Israelis a secret "memorandum of understanding" guaranteeing that the membership of the conference would not be increased—in other words, that the PLO would not be admitted—without the consent of the original parties.[13]

Egypt, Israel, Jordan, the U.S.S.R., and the United States were the five "interested parties" whose Foreign Ministers sat down with Secretary-General Waldheim as the "Peace Conference on the Middle East" officially opened in Geneva's Palais des Nations on the morning of December 21. Syria, in spite of pressure from both Egypt and Jordan, had ultimately declined to attend; and the Israeli Government, in announcing its own attendance, again had made a point of its unwillingness to deal with any "terrorist organizations . . . whose declared aim is the destruction of the State of Israel." In spite of such reservations, however, Mr. Waldheim pointed out in his opening statement that the conference represented "a unique opportunity to come to grips with a most difficult, dangerous and complex international problem." Unless the opportunity was seized, the Secretary-General added, "the

[11]*Keesing's*, p. 26312.
[12]*Presidential Documents*, vol. 9 (1973), p. 1470.
[13]Sheehan, *loc. cit.*, p. 31.

world will inevitably be confronted once again with a dangerous and highly explosive situation in the Middle East.''[14]

But though a meeting of several interested parties around a conference table undoubtedly represented an achievement of some importance, it left untouched the substantive disagreements that had foiled all previous peacemaking efforts over the past six years. Soviet Foreign Minister Gromyko, speaking immediately after the Secretary-General, insisted once again on his government's support for the core elements of the Arab position: Israeli withdrawal "from all the territories occupied in 1967"; the safeguarding of the "legitimate rights" of "the Arab people of Palestine"; and Palestinian participation in the settlement of the Palestine problem. Disclaiming any Soviet hostility to Israel as such, Gromyko urged Israel to confirm "with deeds" its readiness for "an honest and mutually acceptable settlement." "The urgent and top priority task now," he added, in what was considered a conciliatory gesture to the United States, "is to solve the problem of an effective disengagement of forces."[15]

That Gromyko's general approach should be welcomed by the Arab representatives, and rejected by Israel, was a foregone conclusion. Secretary Kissinger, in his own address to the conference (Document 85a), avoided sweeping formulas and concentrated on the virtues of the "step-by-step" approach traditionally favored by the United States. The ultimate goal, the Secretary emphasized, was the full implementation of Security Council Resolution 242 of November 22, 1967; but "we must understand what can realistically be accomplished at any given moment," he cautioned. Like his Soviet counterpart, the American Secretary of State emphasized that the most immediate problem was the completion of the disengagement process initiated at Kilometer 101, and its extension to the Jordanian and Syrian fronts, in order to provide "a . . . base for the lessening of tensions and the negotiation of further steps toward peace."

Having recognized the prime importance of the disengagement process, the conference found itself with little more to do except to pronounce a blessing on the disengagement negotiations and establish some sort of continuing machinery to oversee them. At a second, closed session of the conference on the morning of December 22, the participants decided to establish a "military working group" which would "start discussing forthwith the disengagement of forces" and report its findings and recommendations to the con-

[14]*Keesing's*, p. 26317; Waldheim statement in U.N. document S/11169, Dec. 24, in *Official Records, loc. cit.*, pp. 276-7.
[15]*Soviet News*, No. 5719 (1973), pp. 533-4.

ference. To receive the reports of this and any other working groups that might be established, it was further decided that the conference itself would continue on an ambassadorial level, but would stand ready to reconvene in Geneva at Foreign Ministers' level "as needed in the light of developments."[16]

"We have completed the first stage of the conference and have achieved substantially what we came here to do," said Secretary Kissinger as he left for Washington that evening (Document 85b). "We have settled the procedural and organizational questions. Next week we expect that disengagement talks between Israel and Egypt may start[17] and we hope that other groups of this kind can be organized shortly afterwards. Of course, the road to peace in the Middle East will be long and sometimes painful. But . . . to have brought together the parties in the Middle East for the first time is an achievement of which first of all the parties should be proud, then the United Nations and all those who could play a role in it."

(85)   Opening Sessions of the Conference, December 21-22, 1973.

(a)   Statement of Secretary Kissinger to the Conference, December 21, 1973.[18]

Mr. Secretary General, distinguished Foreign Ministers, delegates: As one of the cochairmen of this conference, let me express my gratitude to the United Nations and to you personally for providing such excellent facilities for the conference, for convening it, and for doing us all the honor of presiding at this historic moment.

We are convened here at a moment of historic opportunity for the cause of peace in the Middle East and for the cause of peace in the world. For the first time in a generation the peoples of the Middle East are sitting together to turn their talents to the challenge of a lasting peace.

All of us must have the wisdom to grasp this moment—to break the shackles of the past and to create at last a new hope for the future.

Two months ago what we now refer to as the fourth Arab-Israeli war was coming to an end. Today there is the respite of an im-

---

[16]Waldheim statement, Dec. 22, in U.N. document S/11169, loc. cit., p. 276.

[17]Egyptian and Israeli military negotiators met in Geneva under Gen. Siilasvuo's chairmanship on Dec. 26 and 28 (Keesing's, p. 26318).

[18]Department of State Press Release 469, Dec. 22; text from Bulletin, vol. 70 (1974), pp. 21-4.

perfect cease-fire, but the shadow of war still hangs over the Middle East. Either we begin today the process of correcting the conditions which produced that conflict, or we doom untold tens of thousands to travail, sorrow, and further inconclusive bloodshed.

When the history of our era is written, it will speak not of a series of Arab-Israeli wars but of one war broken by periods of uneasy armistices and temporary cease-fires. That war has already lasted 25 years. Whether future histories will call this the era of the 25-year Arab-Israeli war, or the 30-year war, or the 50-year war, rests in large measure in our hands. And above all, it rests in the hands of the Israeli and Arab governments, not only those whose distinguished representatives are seated around this table but also those who are absent and who we all hope will join us soon.

We are challenged by emotions so deeply felt—by causes so passionately believed and pursued—that the tragic march from cataclysm to cataclysm, each more costly and indecisive than the last, sometimes seems preordained. Yet our presence here today, in itself a momentous accomplishment, is a symbol of rejection of this fatalistic view. Respect for the forces of history does not mean blind submission to those forces.

There is an Arab saying, *Elli Fat Mat*, which means that the past is dead. Let us resolve here today that we will overcome the legacy of hatred and suffering. Let us overcome old myths with new hope. Let us make the Middle East worthy of the messages of hope and reconciliation that have been carried forward from its stark soil by three great religions.

Today there is hope for the future, for the conflict is no longer looked upon entirely in terms of irreconcilable absolutes. The passionate ideologies of the past have, in part at least, been replaced by a recognition that all the peoples concerned have earned, by their sacrifice, a long period of peace.

From two recent trips through the Middle East I have the impression that people on both sides have had enough of bloodshed. No further proof of heroism is necessary; no military point remains to be made. The Middle East—so often the source of mankind's inspiration—is challenged to another act of hope and reconciliation, significant not only for its own peoples but for all mankind.

What does each side seek? Both answer with a single word: peace. But peace has of course a concrete meaning for each. One side seeks the recovery of sovereignty and the redress of grievances suffered by a displaced people. The other seeks security and recognition of its legitimacy as a nation. The common goal of peace must surely be broad enough to embrace all these aspirations.

For the United States, our objective is such a peace.

I cannot promise success, but I can promise dedication. I cannot guarantee a smooth journey toward our goal. I can assure you of an unswerving quest for justice.

The United States will make a determined and unflagging effort.

President Nixon has sent me here because for five years he has endeavored to build a new structure of international peace in which ties with old friends are strengthened and new and constructive relationships replace distrust and confrontation with adversaries.

But world peace remains tenuous and incomplete so long as the Middle East is in perpetual crisis. Its turmoil is a threat to the hopes of all of us in this room.

It is time to end it.

The question is not whether there must be peace. The question is: How do we achieve it? What can we do here to launch new beginnings?

First, this conference must speak with a clear and unequivocal voice: The cease-fire called for by the Security Council must be scrupulously adhered to by all concerned. Prior to last October, the United States did all it could to prevent a new outbreak of fighting. But we failed because frustration could no longer be contained.

After the fighting began, we, in concert with the Soviet Union, helped bring an end to the hostilities by sponsoring a number of resolutions in the Security Council. The six-point agreement[19] of November 11 consolidated the cease-fire. It helped create the minimal conditions necessary for carrying forward our efforts here. All these resolutions and agreements must be strictly implemented.

But regardless of these steps, we recognize that the cease-fire remains fragile and tentative. The United States is concerned over the evidence of increased military preparedness in recent days. A renewal of hostilities would be both foolhardy and dangerous. We urge all concerned to refrain from the use of force and to give our efforts here the chance they deserve.

Second, we must understand what can realistically be accomplished at any given moment.

The separation of military forces is certainly the most immediate problem. Disengagement of military forces would help to reduce the danger of a new military outbreak; it would begin the process of building confidence between the two sides.

Based on intensive consultations with the leaders of the Middle East, including many in this room today, I believe that the first work of this conference should be to achieve early agreement on the separation of military forces and that such an agreement is possible.

[19]Document 74.

Serious discussions have already taken place between the military representatives of Egypt and Israel at kilometer 101. It is important to build promptly on the progress achieved there. And on the Jordanian and Syrian fronts, a comparable base for the lessening of tensions and the negotiation of further steps toward peace must be found. Progress toward peace should include all the parties concerned.

Third, the disengagement of forces is an essential first step—a consolidation of the cease-fire and a bridge to the "peaceful and accepted settlement" called for in Security Council Resolution 242.[20] Our final objective is the implementation in all its parts of Resolution 242. This goal has the full support of the United States.

Peace must bring a new relationship among the nations of the Middle East—a relationship that will not only put an end to the state of war which has persisted for the last quarter of a century but will also permit the peoples of the Middle East to live together in harmony and safety. It must replace the reality of mistrust with a new reality of promise and hope. It must include concrete measures that make war less likely.

A peace agreement must include these elements, among others: withdrawals, recognized frontiers, security arrangements, guarantees, a settlement of the legitimate interests of the Palestinians, and a recognition that Jerusalem contains places considered holy by three great religions.

Peace will require that we relate the imperative of withdrawals to the necessities of security, the requirement of guarantees to the sovereignty of the parties, the hopes of the displaced to the realities now existing.

Fourth, we believe there must be realistic negotiations between the parties. Resolution 338[21] provides just such a process. It is on the parties that the primary responsibility rests. The United States intends to help facilitate these talks in every feasible way, to encourage moderation and the spirit of accommodation. We are prepared to make concrete suggestions to either side if this will help promote practical progress. But we must always remember that while a Middle East settlement is in the interest of us all, it is the people of the area that must live with the results. It must, in the final analysis, be acceptable to them.

Peace, in short, cannot last unless it rests on the consent of the parties concerned. The wisest of realists are those who understand the power of a moral consensus. There is a measure of safety in power to prevent aggression, but there is greater security still in

---

[20] *Documents, 1967*, pp. 169-70.
[21] Document 59b.

arrangements considered so just that no one wishes to overthrow them.

As we open this conference we take a momentous step. We are challenging a history of missed opportunities, of mutual fear and bottomless distrust. Our backdrop is a war that has brought anguish and pain, death and destruction; a war that has been costly to both sides; that has brought neither victory nor defeat; that reflected the failure of all our past efforts at peaceful solutions.

Mr. Secretary General, fellow delegates, President Nixon has sent me here with the purpose of affirming America's commitment to a just and lasting peace.

We do not embark on this task with false expectations. We do not pretend that there are easy answers. A problem that has defied solution for a generation does not yield to simple remedies.

In all efforts for peace the overriding problem is to relate the sense of individual justice to the common good. The great tragedies of history occur not when right confronts wrong, but when two rights face each other.

The problems of the Middle East today have such a character. There is justice on all sides, but there is a greater justice still in finding a truth which merges all aspirations in the realization of a common humanity. It was a Jewish sage [Hillel] who, speaking for all mankind, expressed this problem well: "If I am not for myself who is for me, but if I am for myself alone who am I?"

Fellow delegates, in the months ahead we will examine many problems. We will discuss many expedients. We will know success—and I daresay we shall experience deadlock and despair.

But let us always keep in mind our final goal:

We can exhaust ourselves in maneuvers, or we can remember that this is the first real chance for peace the Middle East has had in three decades.

We can concentrate on our resentments, or we can be motivated by the consciousness that this opportunity, once past, will not return.

We can emphasize the very real causes of distrust, or we can remember that if we succeed our children will thank us for what they have been spared.

We can make propaganda, or we can try to make progress.

The American attitude is clear. We know we are starting on a journey whose outcome is uncertain and whose progress will be painful. We are conscious that we need wisdom and patience and good will. But we know, too, that the agony of three decades must be overcome and that somehow we have to muster the insight and courage to put an end to the conflict between peoples who have so often ennobled mankind.

So we are here to spare no effort in the quest of a lasting peace in the Middle East, a task which is as worthy as it may be agonizing. In the words of the poet:

> "Pain that cannot forget
> falls drop by drop
> upon the heart
> until in our despair
> there comes wisdom
> through the awful
> grace of God."

(b) Remarks by Secretary Kissinger on leaving Geneva, December 22, 1973.[22]

As I go back to the United States to report to President Nixon, I leave with nourished hope. We have completed the first stage of the conference and have achieved substantially what we came here to do.

We have settled the procedural and organizational questions. Next week we expect that disengagement talks between Israel and Egypt may start and we hope that other groups of this kind can be organized shortly afterwards.

Of course, the road to peace in the Middle East will be long and sometimes painful. But at this holiday season to have brought together the parties in the Middle East for the first time is an achievement of which first of all the parties should be proud, then the United Nations and all those who could play a role in it.

I would like to thank the Secretary-General of the United Nations and the United Nations for the splendid arrangements that they made. I would particularly like to thank the Swiss Government for the efficiency, courtesy and attention they paid us all.

I wish you a Merry Christmas and a Happy New Year.

[22]Department of State Press Release 476, Dec. 28.

30. INTO THE UNKNOWN

The lack of fireworks at the Geneva conference was reassuring to American spirits at a time when a sense of encouragement was badly needed. Yet the return of the Middle East problem to conventional diplomatic channels was far from closing the lid upon the box of troubles that had flown open with the outbreak of hostilities on October 6. Politically, economically, and, above all, emotionally, the world as a whole was by now experiencing an upheaval that was all the more terrifying because it was utterly without precedent and there appeared to be no way of charting the likely course of events, let alone measuring the damage.

At least one segment of the problem was, however, already being subjected to cool analysis in the authoritative *Economic Outlook* published by the Organization for Economic Cooperation and Development (OECD). Two months after the October increase in petroleum prices, the OECD economists were able to detect premonitory signs of what would soon become known as the world recession of the mid-1970s. "The economic situation in the OECD countries is a very troubled one," the Paris-based organization reported in mid-December. "Inflation is continuing at an extremely high rate and the current restrictions on the supply of oil threaten to check economic growth in many countries and cause considerable dislocation of ordinary life. . . . Our countries are suffering from a psychological shock, with adverse effects on business and consumer confidence, somewhat similar to that following the strong action taken by the United States in August 1971."[1]

". . . It is now clear," the OECD added, "that the oil restrictions, unless quickly removed, will reduce the rate of growth below normal and may even cause a fall in output and employment in certain countries." Yet prospects for a quick removal of the oil restric-

[1] "Highlights from OECD Economic Outlook, December 1973," *OECD Observer*, No. 67 (Dec. 1973), pp. 19-21. For the U.S. action of Aug. 1971 cf. *AFR, 1971*, pp. 576-82.

tions still looked mediocre at best, in spite of Secretary Kissinger's diplomatic efforts and veiled reference to possible "countermeasures."[2] The oil exporting countries, after decades of what to them had appeared as pitiless exploitation by international companies and consumer nations, had at length become aware of their own strength and were clearly determined to use it to the full. Even as the Middle East conference was breaking up in Geneva, the OPEC countries in Tehran were preparing to boost the posted price of crude petroleum once again, this time from $5.11 to $11.651 per barrel.[3]

Nor did the outcome of the Geneva conference suffice to procure the sheathing of the "oil weapon" that had been drawn by Arab oil-producing countries at the height of the October War. Meeting in Kuwait on December 24-25, the Arab Oil Ministers declared themselves unwilling "to allow any economic disaster for any nation or group of nations," and announced that the flow of oil to Western Europe and Japan would be partially restored. At the same time, however, as already noted, they reaffirmed the politically inspired embargo on petroleum shipments to the United States and the Netherlands. The participants in the Kuwait meeting, said Saudi Arabia's Petroleum Minister, Ahmad Zaki al-Yamani, had been favorably impressed by "the gradual changes which started to show in American public opinion" with respect to the Arab-Israeli problem, and wished success to the American Government in its search for "an equitable peaceful solution."[4]

Sheik Zaki's implied suggestion that American public support for Israel was cooling seemed hardly to be borne out by Congress' recent approval of a full $2.2 billion in extra security assistance for that country.[5] Yet some refocusing of American attitudes regarding the Middle East would not be altogether surprising at a time when so many familiar landmarks, there as elsewhere, had been undermined by events that until lately would have been thought inconceivable. Even the shaken relationship between the American people and their own government had been further impaired by recent Watergate developments, among them the discovery of serious gaps, one of eighteen and one-half minutes' duration, in the tape-recorded evidence reluctantly yielded by the White House. Nor could the standing of the American presidency be much enhanced by Mr. Nixon's release of masses of private financial data in a

[2]Cf. Chapter 25 after note 13.
[3]Cf. Chapter 24 at note 13.
[4]*New York Times*, Dec. 26, 1973; cf. Chapter 24 at note 12.
[5]Cf. Chapter 29 at note 7.

vain attempt to disprove alleged irregularities and reestablish national confidence in "the integrity of the President."[6]

If President Nixon's personal position by now appeared to be disintegrating beyond recovery, his most publicized diplomatic achievement—the new relationship with Moscow—seemed also to be heading into turbulent waters. The October crisis in the Middle East had not provided an altogether convincing demonstration of the benefits of détente; nor did the American Congress seem willing to surrender its belief that the U.S.S.R. should earn its right to any American economic concessions by lifting its restrictions on Jewish emigration. As already noted, the pending Trade Reform Act, as reported in October by the House Ways and Means Committee, had flouted administration advice by barring the extension of non-discriminatory tariff treatment—though not of credits or guarantees—to any Communist country that restricted freedom of emigration.[7]

In spite of the threat of a presidential veto, this provision was now subjected to further reinforcement with the acceptance by the House of Representatives, by a vote of 319 to 80, of an amendment declaring such countries to be ineligible also for participation in any U.S. Government program extending credits or credit guarantees or investment guarantees. Passed on December 11 by a House vote of 272 to 140, the bill then went to the Senate, which was to retain the essence of the House-imposed restrictions in the legislation that was ultimately signed by President Ford—but declared unacceptable by the Soviet Government—at the beginning of 1975.[8]

These manifold uncertainties increased the difficulty of Secretary Kissinger's task in trying to provide his year-end news conference with a coherent survey of recent foreign policy highlights and prospective trends. In a lengthy statement **(Document 86)** that rigorously shunned all reference to recent domestic matters, the Secretary once again described the "basic architectural design" the Nixon administration had been seeking to implement in all its foreign policy initiatives. "I would like to stress again," Dr. Kissinger cautioned, "that the basic conviction of the administration is that the task that we have set ourselves cannot be completed in one administration or in one decade, because the international system that has grown up over many decades is fundamentally altered and the new international system will take many

---

[6] *Presidential Documents*, vol. 9 (1973), p. 1411.

[7] Cf. Chapter 21 at note 9.

[8] Trade Act of 1974 (Public Law 93-618), Jan. 3, 1975; for details cf. *AFR, 1972*, pp. 129-30.

years to construct. But its ultimate objective must be to contribute to the peace and to the well-being of all mankind.''

The goal would remain constant, however much the conditions of the game had changed.

(86) *Foreign Policy Highlights of 1973: News conference statement by Secretary Kissinger, December 27, 1973.*[9]

Secretary Kissinger: Ladies and gentlemen, I thought the way to give this conference some focus is for me to make a brief summary of the highlights of this year's foreign policy as we see it and some attempt of projecting it into the future.

First, let me begin with the event that started the year, which was of course the peace in Viet-Nam, and then let me go from there to the general design of the foreign policy and how the various pieces—how we attempted to fit the various pieces together.

The year began with ending the most divisive, the most difficult, the most agonizing war in American history—certainly the most divisive and agonizing foreign war in American history.

Throughout the four years of President Nixon's first term, the basic debate had been on the terms by which the war should be ended. And the fundamental condition that the United States had set was that we would not end the war by overthrowing the government with which we had been allied but that we were prepared to withdraw our forces and to leave the evolution of events in Indochina to the Indochinese.

At the beginning of January, last year, we achieved a settlement[10] which permitted the disengagement of American forces, which left the political resolution of the political future of Viet-Nam to be decided by negotiation among the Vietnamese parties, and which returned the American prisoners. It did not settle all the issues that had produced the conflict in the first place, a war that was partly a foreign invasion from the outside and partly civil war; an area that had been rent by conflict for 30 years could not possibly go from war to peace immediately or painlessly or perhaps at all.

We had defined the American role as permitting an evolution that left the destiny of the area in the hands of the people concerned. We had hoped—if you remember the speech of the President and my press conference[11]—we had hoped that the end of the war in Viet-Nam would permit also the beginning of an era of

---

[9]Department of State Press Release 472, Dec. 27; text from *Bulletin*, vol. 70 (1974), pp. 45-50.
[10]Document 5.
[11]Documents 3-4.

national reconciliation in this country. And much of the agony of the previous years had been assumed to be overcome by the fact that both those who had opposed the manner of conducting the war and those who had wanted to bring it to a conclusion along the lines that were achieved could agree now that there was a need to turn to more positive tasks.

For a variety of reasons, other issues arose that did not make this entirely possible. But the war in Viet-Nam is no longer—and the war in Indochina—is no longer a divisive national issue; and as far as the administration is concerned, it will, as I have pointed out in my last press conference,[12] heed the expressions of the Congress and stay true to the principles that it has consistently pursued.

In any event, with the war in Viet-Nam ended, the major focus of our foreign policy attention could turn to the design of the structure of peace that has been the President's principal goal since he came into office.

In its first phase, this meant that the United States had to reduce many of its overextended commitments and that the United States had to disengage gradually from any foreign involvement and, above all, that the United States should evoke a sense of responsibility for their own sake in many areas of the world. This was the so-called Nixon doctrine which characterized the first two or three years of the President's first term.

It was the prelude to the initiatives toward China and the détente with the Soviet Union that were to lay the basis for a fundamental realignment of the postwar period which had been based on a rigid division between opposing hostile blocs.

So, by the time the second term of the President started, we faced an international situation in which the basic assumptions of the immediate postwar period had been substantially altered. The rigid hostility between the Communist world and the non-Communist world had been altered first by the divisions within the Communist world itself and by the amelioration of relations between the Soviet Union and the United States, as well as the People's Republic of China and the United States.

Europe and Japan had gained strength and political self-confidence. The economic system that had been created in the immediate postwar period had become fluid and was in need of redesigning. So the great task before this administration, as it will be before its successors, has been to construct an international system based on a sense of justice so that its participants would have a stake in maintaining it, with a sufficient balance of power so that no nation or group of nations would be dependent entirely on

[12]Press conference of Dec. 6, in *Bulletin*, vol. 69 (1973), pp. 758-9 and 761-2.

the good will of its neighbors, and based on a sense of participation so that all nations could share in the positive aspirations.

This has been the basic architectural design that cannot possibly be completed in any one administration, and the work which must continue in future administrations. And when we speak of institutionalizing foreign policy, we do not mean that designated committees would carry out specific tasks, but that the basic goals of the long term are accepted by a sufficient consensus in America so that the future security of this country does not depend entirely on the vagaries of the political process.

Détente With Communist Countries

Now let me be more specific, and let me talk in various categories. Let me begin first with East-West relations. Our policy toward both the Soviet Union and the People's Republic of China has been characterized as a policy of détente. And it is the characteristic of policies that become more or less accepted that the benefits are taken for granted and that some of the difficulties that were overlooked in the beginning become more and more apparent.

Let me explain what we understand by détente. We do not say that détente is based on the compatibility of domestic systems. We recognize that the values and ideology of both the Soviet Union and the People's Republic of China are opposed and sometimes hostile to ours. We do not say that there are no conflicting national interests. We do say that there is a fundamental change in the international environment compared to any other previous period, a change which was expressed by President Eisenhower more than 20 years ago when he said, "There is no longer any alternative to peace." Under conditions of nuclear plenty, the decision to engage in general war involves consequences of such magnitude that no responsible statesman can base his policy on the constant threat of such a holocaust and every leader with a responsibility for these weapons must set himself the task of bringing about conditions which reduce the possibility of such a war to a minimum and, indeed, over any extended period of time reduce this possibility to zero.

So we do not say that we approve of the domestic evolution of the Soviet Union or of other Communist countries with which we are attempting to coexist. Nor do we accept that détente can be used for military expansion or for threatening weaker countries or for undermining our traditional friendships. But we do make a conscious effort to set up rules of conduct and to establish a certain interconnection of interests and, above all, to establish communications between the top leaders and between officials at every level that make it possible in times of crisis to reduce the danger of accident or miscalculation.

This has been our policy with the Soviet Union, and it is the policy we have pursued as well with the People's Republic of China.

With respect to the Soviet Union, it has led us into a series of negotiations on the limitations of strategic arms, on mutual and balanced force reductions (MBFR), on European security, on such measures as the agreement for the prevention of nuclear war[13]—into extended exchanges between the President and General Secretary Brezhnev designed to lay the basis for a more civil discourse.

This does not preclude that this relationship can break down.

Ideology, long-established relations, as well as the internal logic of certain areas such as the Middle East, can produce tensions and indeed can produce explosions that, whether or not they are fostered by the two superpowers, may bring them into conflict with each other.

Nor is it foreordained that the behavior of the two protagonists necessarily lives up to the principles that they declare. In those cases, as happened at one phase during the Middle East crisis, the United States will maintain its commitments and will defend its international position and the position of its friends.

But we will not be easily deflected from the course of seeking a relaxation of tension—a course which proved itself even in tension periods and a course which modern technology will impose on any administration even if we should be prevented from carrying out all the measures by different opinions about what should be the purposes of détente—such as the degree to which we should attempt to use our foreign policy to affect the domestic structure of other countries.

With respect to the People's Republic of China, we have established Liaison Offices in each other's capitals[14] that are performing many of the functions that are normally carried out by embassies. We have had two visits by myself to Peking[15] and also a substantial expansion of economic and other exchanges.

So we believe that with respect to the two great Communist countries, we are on a course which is in the interests of all of mankind and which is essential for the long-term prospects of peace.

[13]Document 32b.
[14]Document 12.
[15]Documents 11 and 75.

Relations With Atlantic Nations and Japan

In our relations with our friends in Europe, the year has been disappointing. It had been our intention, in what we called perhaps too rashly "the Year of Europe," to affirm that the important measures in foreign policy were not confined to relations with adversaries but that traditional friends could also seize the opportunities of the future. We intended in our various initiatives to lay to rest concerns about the possibilities of a condominium between the United States and particularly the Soviet Union. We attempted to emphasize that the very successes of the Atlantic alliance had created a new situation which required a new act of vision, and we invited Europe and Japan to participate with us in this task of construction.

Now there have been many debates about whether the tactics by which this objective was pursued were always ideal, and there were many comments about this or that initiative. And obviously, any senior official pursuing the policies of his government will always be convinced that the measures his administration took are correct, because otherwise he would not have taken them. But I do not believe that this is the key problem. There is one principal problem in our relations with, especially, Europe at this moment that only the Europeans can answer—all the other criticisms can be relatively easily taken care of—and that question is: What is to be the shape of the emerging unified Europe? Is this Europe to be organized on a basis which seeks its identity in exclusivity to our position—or at least in distance from the United States? Or is it prepared, while affirming its identity, to recognize that the opportunities of the future require Atlantic cooperation?

As far as the United States is concerned, we have given our answer. All of our proposals, however they were advanced, from the proposal of the Atlantic charter[16] to the proposal of the common approach to energy,[17] had one fundamental goal: to create a dialogue between ourselves and the Europeans in terms of the challenges that lay ahead of us and in terms of the common problems that needed to be solved.

That offer is still open. We believe that some progress was made in our recent talks in Europe, and we will continue both the work on the declarations with the European Community and with our NATO partners, as well as the work on the Energy Action Group.

But the United States is not concerned with developing some legal formula or with a document that responds to a single

[16]Document 21.
[17]Document 81.

initiative. The problem before us is whether the nations of the Atlantic area, as well as Japan, faced with self-evident problems that affect them all, can develop a common approach or whether they will consume themselves in the sort of rivalry that has destroyed other civilizations. I will have a word to say about that when I discuss the energy problem

As far as Japan is concerned, we believed that we were well underway to developing a new and mature partnership when the energy crisis diverted energies, diverted concerns, and when it created many temporary obstacles. But we believe that Japan should be an integral part of the relationship we are also attempting to develop with Europe and that Japan's importance and its growing strength and its political maturity entitle it to full consideration as an equal partner of the United States.

The Crisis in the Middle East

The most dramatic event of the year, of course, was the crisis in the Middle East. It is—it came upon us unexpectedly. We were not warned by any foreign government that there were any specific plans for an attack. The only warnings we received were general descriptions that the Middle East conflict—or that the tensions in the Middle East—might not be contained. And I have already described the kind of intelligence information that was available and which illustrated that facts are not self-explanatory, that one's preconceptions determine very importantly what interpretation is given to these facts.[18]

The war in the Middle East faced the United States with a number of profound issues. There was the commitment the United States has had through all postwar administrations to the security of Israel. It was our concern that another superpower not exploit the tensions in the area for its own advantage. There was our interest in maintaining a balanced relationship with the Arab countries. And there came to be, increasingly, the problem of the energy crisis.

Our policy had to go through several phases.

The first, during the military phase, was to bring—to contribute to a situation in which the postwar evolution would not be determined by military success primarily, especially by military success growing out of a surprise attack and achieved with Soviet arms.

And secondly, to conduct ourselves in such a manner that in the diplomacy that would follow the war, we would be able to talk to all of the parties involved—Arab as well as Israeli.

[18]Cf. news conference, Oct. 12, in *Bulletin*, vol. 69 (1973), pp. 534-7.

And thirdly, we had to conduct ourselves in such a way that the Middle East would not play the role of the Balkans in 1914, in which local rivalries produced a catastrophe from which Europe never recovered and in which, under contemporary conditions, if a general war occurred the world would never recover.

The result of these efforts was, first, the cease-fire of October 22;[19] then, the six-point agreement that was signed in early November;[20] and the Geneva Peace Conference which started last week.[21]

We are at the very beginning of what will be a slow and agonizing effort to reconcile objectives that in many respects seem contradictory. But as I have said repeatedly, and as the President has emphasized, the United States is committed to making a major effort to bring about a just and lasting peace in the Middle East that recognizes the security of all the countries in the Middle East as well as the legitimate aspirations of all of the peoples in the area.

We believe that the conference is well launched, and we hope that some progress can be made in the disengagement talks that are now going on between Egypt and Israel—and that could go on between Israel and the other Arab countries.

The Global Energy Problem

The Middle East—the war in the Middle East also brought to a head the energy crisis on a global basis. It brought it to a head, but it did not cause it.

The basic cause of the energy crisis is that demand for energy has been growing exponentially while the incentives for supply have not kept pace. And in these conditions, sooner or later, the energy-consuming countries would have come up against the situation where their demand far outstripped the possibilities of supply.

And therefore, it is the U.S. view that the long-term problem in the field of energy makes it essential that a worldwide cooperative effort between consumers, and between consumers and producers, be started so that we can deal with the challenges on a long-term basis and not have to improvise responses with every year.

In this respect, the energy crisis may be only a forerunner of similar difficulties in other areas—and this is why the United States supported the World Food Conference that has now been called for 1974.[22]

[19]Document 59b.
[20]Document 74.
[21]Document 85.
[22]Cf. Chapter 24 at note 7.

Tasks for the Future

These are some of the highlights of last year, and if one is to look ahead, one can see that the major task of building this international system remains to be done.

In East-West relations, in negotiations with the Soviet Union, we have before us the problem of SALT, and as I have pointed out repeatedly, no task is more urgent than to master the rapid technological change in which weapons may outstrip the capacity of political control.

And therefore the United States will make a determined effort to fulfill the promise that President Nixon and General Secretary Brezhnev made to each other to try to have an agreement on SALT in 1974.[23] It is a difficult assignment, because the first SALT agreement[24] dealt with quantitative change, the present negotiations deal with the problem of qualitative change, which is both technically and conceptually much more difficult.

And we will continue to pursue the negotiations on mutual force reductions and European security.

In relations with the People's Republic of China, we will continue the policy of normalization that was started and seek to accelerate it.

Our relations with Europe—the offer that we made in April and December still remains on the table, and we are prepared to discuss with our European allies those aspects of our consultative processes that they find difficult. We believe that the problem of fears of condominium cannot be settled by abstract declarations, but only by a confident cooperation in trying to devise a future that we can all believe in.

In the Middle East, we will strive for peace—based on justice and accepted by all of the parties. And we hope that the peace that has been so painfully achieved in Indochina can be preserved.

These are the major tasks that we have set ourselves, together with an initiative toward Latin America which will culminate in a Foreign Ministers meeting at the end of February in Mexico City, in which the Latin American Foreign Ministers have responded to an initiative by the United States last October that we should define together a new Western Hemisphere relationship.[25]

But I would like to stress again that the basic conviction of the administration is that the task that we have set ourselves cannot be completed in one administration or in one decade, because the in-

[23]Document 31b.
[24]Cf. Chapter 12 at note 9.
[25]Document 53.

ternational system that has grown up over many decades is fundamentally altered and the new international system will take many years to construct. But its ultimate objective must be to contribute to the peace and to the well-being of all mankind.

Now I'll be glad to answer your questions.[26]

---

[26]For remainder of the news conference see *Bulletin, loc. cit.*, pp. 50-56.

APPENDIX:
PRINCIPAL SOURCES

"AFR": *American Foreign Relations: A Documentary Record* (annual vols., 1971-   ). Continues the *"Documents"* series listed below. Volumes for 1971, 1972, and 1973 published for the Council on Foreign Relations by New York University Press (New York).

American Foreign Policy, 1950-1955: Basic Documents (Department of State Publication 6446; Washington: GPO, 1957, 2 vols.).

American Foreign Policy: Current Documents (Washington: GPO; annual vols. for 1956-67). The official documentary publication of the Department of State, now discontinued.

"Bulletin": *The Department of State Bulletin* (Washington: GPO, weekly). The official source for material of State Department origin appearing in this volume; contains also numerous documents originated by the White House and other governmental and international bodies.

"Documents": *Documents on American Foreign Relations* (annual vols., 1939-70). Volumes in this series were published prior to 1952 by Princeton University Press (Princeton, N.J.) for the World Peace Foundation; subsequent volumes were published for the Council on Foreign Relations by Harper & Brothers/Harper & Row (New York and Evanston) for 1952-66 and by Simon and Schuster (New York) for 1967-70. For continuation volumes see *"AFR"* above.

Documents on Disarmament (Washington: GPO; annual vols. for 1960-73). The most comprehensive collection of documents on disarmament and related topics, published annually by the U.S. Arms Control and Disarmament Agency.

IMF Survey (Washington: International Monetary Fund, semimonthly). The official bulletin of the International Monetary Fund.

International Legal Materials: Current Documents (Washington: American Society of International Law, bimonthly). Includes numerous documents of non-U.S. origin.

Kalb, Marvin and Bernard, *Kissinger* (Boston: Little, Brown and Company, 1974). A detailed account of the diplomacy of the Nixon administration from 1969 until early 1974.

"Keesing's": *Keesing's Contemporary Archives* (Bristol: Keesing's Publications, Ltd., weekly). A detailed review of current developments throughout the world.

The New York Times (New York: The New York Times Co., daily). Contains unofficial texts of numerous documents of international interest.

"Nixon Report, 1970": *U.S. Foreign Policy for the 1970's: A New Strategy for Peace—A Report to the Congress by Richard Nixon, President of the United States. February 18, 1970* (Washington: GPO, 1970, 160 p.). Text appears also in *Presidential Documents*, Feb. 23, 1970, pp. 194-239; *Public Papers, 1970*, pp. 116-90; and *Bulletin*, Mar. 9, 1970, pp. 273-332.

"Nixon Report, 1971": *U.S. Foreign Policy for the 1970's: Building for Peace—A Report to the Congress by Richard Nixon, President of the United States, February 25, 1971* (Washington: GPO, 1971, 235 p.). Text appears also in *Presidential Documents*, Mar. 1, 1971, pp. 305-77; *Public Papers, 1971*, pp. 219-345; and *Bulletin*, Mar. 22, 1971, pp. 341-432.

"Nixon Report, 1972": *U.S. Foreign Policy for the 1970's: The Emerging Structure of Peace—A Report to the Congress by Richard Nixon, President of the United States, February 9, 1972* (Washington: GPO, 1972, 215 p.). Text appears also in *Presidential Documents*, Feb. 14, 1972, pp. 235-411; *Public Papers, 1972*, pp. 194-346; and *Bulletin*, Mar. 13, 1972, pp. 311-418.

"Nixon Report, 1973": *U.S. Foreign Policy for the 1970's: Shaping a Durable Peace—A Report to the Congress by Richard Nixon, President of the United States, May 3, 1973* (Washington: GPO, 1973, 234 p.). Text appears also in *Presidential Documents*, May 14, 1973, pp. 455-653; *Public Papers, 1973*, pp. 348-518; and *Bulletin*, June 4, 1973, pp. 717-834.

"OAS Chronicle": *Chronicle of the OAS* (Washington: Secretariat of the Organization of American States, quarterly).

OECD Observer (Paris: OECD Information Service, bimonthly). The official review of the Organization for Economic Cooperation and Development.

"Presidential Documents": *Weekly Compilation of Presidential Documents* (Washington: GPO, weekly). The official source for White House materials reproduced in this volume. Much of the contents is republished in *Public Papers*, and many texts relating to foreign affairs appear also in the Department of State *Bulletin* and/or *Documents on Disarmament*.

Public Laws of the United States, cited in this volume by serial number and date of approval (e.g., Public Law 92-156, Nov. 17, 1971), are issued by the GPO in leaflet form and subsequently collected in the *United States Statutes at Large (Stat.)*.

"Public Papers": *Public Papers of the Presidents of the United States* (Washington: GPO, annual). Contains definitive texts of most presidential statements and some other material of White House origin, most of it previously published in *Presidential Documents*.

"Rogers Report, 1969-70": *United States Foreign Policy 1969-1970: A Report of the Secretary of State* (Department of State Publication 8575; Washington: GPO, 1971, 617 p.).

"Rogers Report, 1971": *United States Foreign Policy 1971: A Report of the Secretary of State* (Department of State Publication 8634; Washington: GPO, 1972, 604 p.).

"Rogers Report, 1972": *United States Foreign Policy 1972: A Report of the Secretary of State* (Department of State Publication 8699; Washington: GPO, 1973, 743 p.).

"Senate Foreign Relations Committee History, 1973-4": U.S. Senate, 93d Cong., *Legislative History of the Committee on Foreign Relations . . . January 3, 1973-December 20, 1974* (S. Rept. 94-37; Washington: GPO, 1975, 196 p.) Records congressional action on treaties and legislation considered by the Foreign Relations Committee during the 93d Congress in 1973-4.

Soviet News (London: Press Department of the Soviet Embassy, weekly). Includes unofficial texts or condensations of numerous documents of Soviet origin.

"TIAS": U.S. Department of State, *Treaties and Other International Acts Series* (Washington: GPO, published irregularly). This series presents the definitive texts of treaties and agreements to which the United States is a party, as authenticated by the Department of State. Issued in leaflet form under their individual serial numbers, items in this series are later republished with consecutive pagination in the official *United States Treaties and Other International Agreements* (UST) series, likewise published by the GPO on behalf of the Department of State.

United Nations General Assembly, *Official Records* (New York: United Nations). The *Official Records* of each session of the General Assembly include official texts of all resolutions adopted during the session as well as much related material. Unofficial texts are frequently printed in the *UN Monthly Chronicle* and other publications.

United Nations Security Council, *Official Records* (New York: United Nations). Includes official texts of all resolutions adopted by the Security Council, with much related material. Unofficial texts are frequently printed in the *UN Monthly Chronicle* and other publications.

The United States in World Affairs (annual vols., 1931-40, 1945-67, and 1970). The annual survey of U.S. foreign policy developments, published for the Council on Foreign Relations by Harper & Brothers/Harper and Row (New York and Evanston) from 1931 through 1966 and by Simon and Schuster (New York) for 1967 and 1970. Continued by the present series.

UN Monthly Chronicle (New York: United Nations Office of Public Information, monthly). The official account of current U.N. activities, with texts of major resolutions and other documents.

"U.S. Participation, 1973": *U.S. Participation in the U.N.:[28th] Report by the President to the Congress for the Year 1973* (H. Doc. 93-360; Washington: GPO, 1974, 272 p.) A detailed account covering all aspects of U.S. participation in the U.N. system.

"USUN Press Releases": Press releases of the U.S. Mission to the United Nations, as reprinted in the Department of State *Bulletin.*

The World This Year: Supplement to the Political Handbook and Atlas of the World (annual vols., 1971, 1972, and 1973). Condensed accounts of the organization and activities of governments and intergovernmental organizations, published for the Council on Foreign Relations by Simon and Schuster (New York).

Yearbook of the United Nations (New York: United Nations Office of Public Information). A comprehensive review of U.N. activities, issued annually.

INDEX

A

Afghanistan, 2, 230

Africa, 149-52, 208, 214-17, 497-8, 579-81; Newsom address, 152-61; Newsom statement on Sahel drought, 214-17; U.N. resolutions on Rhodesia, 580, 583-6

Agency for International Development (AID), Williams statement on food problems, 514-20

Agnew, Spiro T., 317; resignation of (Oct. 10), 3, 446, 482

AID, *see* Agency for International Development

Albania, 285

Algeria, 495, 605; *see also* Conference of Heads of State and Government of Nonaligned Countries

Allende Gossens, Salvador, 2, 118-19, 408-12

Alon, Yosef, 318

Amerasinghe, H.S., 582

Andreotti, Giulio, 180

Angola, 150, 151

Arab-Israeli conflict, 1-4, 163-8,· 317-34, 443-53, 529-31, 532-4, 603-8; Sisco address (May 7), 168-75; Nixon-Brezhnev communiqué (June 24, excerpt), 279

Discussion in U.N. Security Council (June-Aug.): Scali statement (June 14), 320-25; draft resolution (July 26), 325-6; Scali statement (same), 326-9; Scali statement on Israeli interception of Lebanese airliner (Aug. 14), 330-32; resolution condemning Israel (Aug. 15), 332-3; Scali statement (same), 333-4

Fourth Arab-Israeli war (Oct. 6 ff.): Kissinger address (Oct. 8), 443-42; Scali statement to Security Council (same), 453-5;

Nixon message on aid (Oct. 19), 455-7; Scali statement (Oct. 21), 457-9; first cease-fire resolution (Oct. 22), 459; second cease-fire resolution (Oct. 23), 459-60; Scali statement (same, excerpt), 460-61; Scali statement on Sadat request for U.S.-Soviet forces (Oct. 24), 461-3; Brezhnev message to Nixon, 449-50; Kissinger statement on U.S. military alert (Oct. 25, excerpts), 463-9; third cease-fire resolution (same), 469; resolution setting up UNEF (same), 469-70; Nixon statement (Oct. 26), 470-72; Waldheim report on UNEF (Oct. 27), 472-5; resolution approving Waldheim report (same), 475-6; Scali statement (same), 476-7; Jankowitsch statement (Nov. 2), 477-8; Scali statement (same), 478-9; Kissinger visit to Middle East (Nov. 5-9): 529-31, 532-4; letter to Waldheim on Egyptian-Israeli disengagement agreement (Nov. 9), 534-5; statement (Nov. 21), 537-9

Geneva conference (opened Dec. 21, 1973): background, 603-8; Kissinger statement (Dec. 21), 608-13; Kissinger remarks (Dec. 22), 613

Kissinger statement (Dec. 27, excerpt), 623-4

Arafat, Yasir, 166

Argentina, 2, 120-21, 408

Arias Navarro, Carlos, 2

Asian Development Bank (ADB), 497; Nixon message (Oct. 31), 510-14

al-Assad, Hafez, 605

Associated Press Editors, Kissinger address on "Year of Europe" (New York, Apr. 23), 181-9

Atlantic Declaration, *see* Europe, Western

Australia, 300, 373

B

Bahamas, Commonwealth of, 578

Belgium, 2, 91

Benites, Leopoldo, 416, 582

Bennett, W. Tapley, Jr., statement on Cambodia (excerpts), 545-50; on terrorism (Dec. 14), 594-8

Berlin, Quadripartite Agreement on (signed Berlin Sept. 3, 1971), 178, 238-9, 278, 565

Boumediene, Houari, 495, 605

Brandt, Willy, 180, 193

Brazil, 118, 193, 408

Brezhnev, Leonid I., 1, 3, 229, 286, 444, 553; visit to U.S. (June 18-25), 251-83; in Middle East crisis, 447-50

Bruce, David K.E., 77

Bulgaria, 286

Bunche, Ralph, 530

Bunker, Ellsworth, 412

Bush, George, 7

Butz, Earl L., 301

Byrd amendment, 151, 160, 579-80

Byrne, W. Matthew, Jr., 193, 195

C

Cabral, Amilcar, 150

Caetano, Marcelo, 605

Cambodia, 16-17, 18, 231, 255, 335-47, 372, 481, 541-3, 577; Nixon message rejecting "Cambodia Rider" (June 27), 340-41; Second Supplemental Appropriation Act (July 1, excerpt), 342-3; Joint Resolution (July 1, excerpts), 343; Nixon signature statement (same), 343-4; Rogers affidavit (Aug. 2, excerpt), 338-9; Nixon letter to Congress (Aug. 3), 344-5; Warren statement (Aug. 15), 345-7; Nixon address (New Orleans, Aug. 20, excerpt), 350; Nixon message on security assistance (Oct. 19), 455-7, 542-3; Bennett statement to U.N. General Assembly (Dec. 5, excerpts), 545-50

Cámpora, Héctor J., 120-21, 408

Canada, 17, 80, 230, 285

Carrero Blanco, Luis, 2, 605-6

Case, Clifford P., 336-7

Casey, William J., statement on energy situation, 217-24; address on development policy, 501-10

Castro, Fidel, 118, 495

CENTO, see Central Treaty Organization

Central Intelligence Agency (CIA), 7, 77; and Watergate, 193, 196-197; and Chile coup, 119, 408-12; and Middle East, 444

Central Treaty Organization (CENTO), 229-30; Council meeting (Tehran, June 10-11); Rogers statement (June 10), 231-4; communiqué (June 11), 234-6

Chiang Kai-shek, 76

Chile, 2, 118-19, 407; military coup in, 408-12; Kubisch statement, 412-15

China, People's Republic of (PRC), 3, 6, 16, 75-7, 302, 372, 532; Green address, 77-82; Kissinger visit (Feb. 15-19): joint communiqué (Feb. 22), 82-3; Kissinger statement (same), 83-6; Nixon statement on liaison office (Mar. 15), 86-7; Kissinger visit (Nov. 10-14): joint communiqué (Nov. 14), 535-7; Kissinger statement (Dec. 27, excerpt), 620-621

China, Republic of, 75-6, 300, 372, 532, 578

Chou En-lai, 76, 532

Church, Frank, 119, 336-7

Colby, William E., 409-10

Conference of Foreign Ministers of Latin America for Continental Cooperation (Bogotá, Nov. 14-16), 412

Conference of Heads of State and Government of Nonaligned Countries (Algiers, Sept. 5-9), 372, 495-6, 583

Conference of Tlatelolco (proposed), 412

Conference on Mutual Reduction of Forces and Armaments and Associated Measures in Central Europe (opened Vienna, Oct. 30), 178, 230, 285, 286-7, 420, 552-3; U.S.-Soviet communiqué (June 24, excerpt), 278-9; 19-nation communiqué (June 28), 290; Resor statement (Oct. 31), 557-63; NATO position, 237-8, 565-6

Conference on Security and Cooperation in Europe (opened Helsinki, July 3-5), 178, 229, 230, 285-6, 287-8; U.S.-Soviet communiqué (June 24, excerpt), 278; Rogers statement (July 25), 291-7; communiqué (July 7), 297-8; NATO position, 237, 238, 563-4

Congress (U.S.), and Indochina, 2, 4, 14, 255, 317, 336-40, 419-22; and economic policy, 92-3, 252-3, 421-4, 617; and Rhodesia, 151, 160, 579-80; and Kissinger confirmation, 351-2, 409, 419; and Chile, 119, 408-10; and troops in Western Europe, 178, 289, 420-21, 554; and détente, 421-24, 617
  Legislation:
  P.L. 93-50, July 1, Second Supplemental Appropriation Act, 1973: Nixon veto message (June 27), 340-42; text (excerpt), 342-3; Nixon signature statement (July 1), 343-4; Nixon letter to Congress (Aug. 3), 344-5; Warren statement (Aug. 15), 345-7
  P.L. 93-52, July 1, Joint Resolution Making Continuing Appropriations for FY 1974: text (excerpts), 343; Nixon signature statement (July 1), 343-4
  P.L. 93-126, Oct. 18, Department of State Appropriation Authorization Act of 1973: 336-7

P.L. 93-148, Nov. 7, War Powers Resolution: text, 485-90; Nixon veto message (Oct. 24), 490-94; White House statement on enactment of resolution (Nov. 7), 494

P.L. 93-155, Nov. 16, Department of Defense Appropriation Authorization Act, 1974: 421

P.L. 93-159, Nov. 27, Emergency Petroleum Allocation Act of 1973: Nixon address (Nov. 7), 520-28

P.L. 93-189, Dec. 17, Foreign Assistance Act of 1973: Nixon message (May 1), 210-14

P.L. 93-199, Dec. 26, Emergency Security Assistance Act of 1973: Nixon message (Oct. 19), 455-7, 604

P.L. 93-238, Jan. 2, 1974, Department of Defense Appropriation Act, 1974: 338, n. 10

P.L. 93-240, Jan. 2, 1974, Foreign Assistance and Related Programs Appropriation Act, 1974: 604

P.L. 93-373, Aug. 14, 1974, providing for increased U.S. participation in IDA: Nixon message (Oct. 31), 510-14

P.L. 93-537, Dec. 22, 1974, providing for increased U.S. participation in ADB: Nixon message (Oct. 31), 510-14

P.L. 93-618, Jan. 3, 1975, Trade Act of 1974: Nixon message (Apr. 10), 99-115; same (Sept. 10, excerpt), 425-7; Nixon statement (Oct. 4), 432-3

Connally, John B., 7

Convention on the Prevention and Punishment of Crimes Against Internationally Protected Persons, Including Diplomatic Agents (adopted Dec. 14, 1973), *see* Terrorism, U.N. Convention on

Cox, Archibald, 3, 196, 302, 446, 484

Cuba, 118, 122-6, 407, 412, 452; U.S.-Cuba memorandum on hijacking (accepted Feb. 15): text, 122-4; Rogers comments, 124-6

Cyprus, 167, 452

Czechoslovakia, 288-9

D

Daud, Muhammad, 2

Davis, Nathaniel, 409

Dean, John W., 3rd, 6, 192, 193, 252, 255, 446

Defense (U.S.), 7, 350, 420-21; Nixon address (Norfolk, Va., May 19), 200-207; same (New Orleans, Aug. 30, excerpt), 350; Nixon message (Sept. 10, excerpt), 428-30

Denmark, 91, 177, 286

Dent, Frederick B., 301

Disarmament: SALT, 251, 253-4; U.S.-Soviet agreement on negotiating principles (signed Washington, June 21): Kissinger statement, 256-61; text, 262-3; U.S.-Soviet nuclear war prevention agreement (signed Washington, June 22): Kissinger statement, 263-4; text, 264-9; Kissinger statement (June 25, excerpt), 269-73; U.S.-Soviet communiqué (released June 25, excerpt), 275-6; Kissinger statement (Dec. 27, excerpt), 625
    Discussion in U.N. General Assembly, 578-9; see also Mutual and Balanced Force Reduction

Drinan, Robert F., 302

E

Eagleton, Thomas F., 336, 337

East-West trade, 92-3

Eberle, William D., 379

Economic and financial affairs, 7, 89-93, 207-10, 256, 379-83; second devaluation of the dollar, 94-9; trade and development, 99-115, 495-7, 501-14, 583; OECD, 224-7, 556, 615-16, GATT, 383-94; IBRD/IMF, 394-406

Ecuador, 407, 582

Egypt, 320; resumption of ties with U.S., 530; see also Arab-Israeli conflict

Ehrlichman, John D., 3, 7, 193, 195, 446

Ellsberg, Daniel, 193, 195, 196

Energy crisis, 1, 208-9, 383, 443, 498-501, 555-6; Casey statement, 217-24; OECD communiqué (Paris, June 6, excerpt), 226-8; Nixon message (Sept. 10, excerpt), 427-8; Nixon address (Nov. 7), 520-28; Kissinger address (London, Dec. 12, excerpt), 572-5; Kissinger statement (Dec. 27, excerpt), 624

Ervin, Sam J., Jr., 3, 192, 252

Ethiopia, 152, 208

Europe, détente in, 1, 92, 177-80, 230, 285-98; Kissinger address (Apr. 23, excerpt), 187-9; U.S.-Soviet communiqué (June 24, excerpt), 277-9; Kissinger address (Oct. 8, excerpt), 437; Kissinger statement (Dec. 27, excerpt), 620-21

Europe, Eastern, 286-9; U.S.-Soviet communiqué (June 24, excerpt), 277-9

Europe, Western, 177-80, 230, 299, 352-4, 551-7; issue of U.S. troops, 289, 420-21, 551-7; proposed Atlantic declaration, 1, 3, 179-80, 230, 289, 299, 352-3; Kissinger address (New York, Apr.

23), 181-9, 554; Nixon remarks on foreign policy report (May 1, excerpt), 199; Kissinger statement (Sept. 26, excerpt), 367-9; and Middle East crisis, 551-2, 553, 555-7; Kissinger address (London, Dec. 12), 566-75; Kissinger statement (Dec. 27, excerpt), 622-3

European Communities/European Economic Community (EEC), 91, 180, 379, 380; enlargement, 177; proposed declaration (Sept. 11), 353-4; Kissinger statement (Sept. 26, excerpt), 368; statement on Middle East (Nov. 6), 553; meeting with Kissinger (Dec. 11), 554-5; summit meeting (Copenhagen, Dec. 14-15), 556

European Security Conference, *see* Conference on Security and Cooperation in Europe

F

Fahmy, Ismail, 530

Faisal, King, 530, 605

Federal Bureau of Investigation (FBI), 192, 195

Fielding, Lewis J., 193, 196

Finland, 285, 291, 452; European Security Conference in Helsinki, 291-8

Food and Agriculture Organization (FAO), 498, 581

Food shortages, 208, 497-8; Newsom statement, 214-17; Kissinger address (Sept. 24, excerpt), 364-5; Williams statement, 514-20

Ford, Gerald R., statement on Chile (Sept. 16, 1974), 410; succeeds Agnew (Dec. 6, 1973), 446; declaration with Tanaka (Tokyo, Nov. 20, 1974), 556-7; signs Trade Act of 1974 (Jan. 3, 1974), 617; message on terrorism convention (Nov. 13, 1975), 581

Foreign aid program (U.S.), 207-8, 496, 497, 543; Nixon message (May 1), 210-14; Nixon foreign policy report (May 3, excerpt), 200; Nixon message (Sept. 10, excerpt), 430-31

France, 3, 91, 180, 287, 300, 373

Franco, Francisco, 2, 605-6

Fulbright, J. William, 351

G

el-Gamasy, Mohamed, 531

Gandhi, Indira, 495

Garrastazú Médici, Emílio, 408

GATT, *see* General Agreement on Tariffs and Trade

Geisel, Ernesto, 408

General Agreement on Tariffs and Trade (GATT), 92, 379-81; meeting of Contracting Parties (Tokyo, Sept. 12-14): Shultz statement (Sept. 12), 94-9; "Declaration of Tokyo" (adopted Sept. 14), 391-4

Generalized trade preferences, 93, 117, 207, 496-7; Nixon message (Apr. 10, excerpt), 102-3; OECD communiqué (Paris, June 6, excerpt), 226

Geneva Conference on the Middle East (opened Dec. 21, 1973), *see* Arab-Israeli conflict

German Democratic Republic, 578; U.S.-Soviet communiqué (June 24, excerpt), 278

Germany, Federal Republic of, 91, 180, 578; U.S.-Soviet communiqué (June 24, excerpt), 278

Giscard d'Estaing, Valéry, 91, 180, 381

Godley, G. McMurtrie, 420

Gray, L. Patrick, 3rd, 192

Greece, 2, 286

Green, Marshall, 420; address on China, 77-82

Gromyko, Andrei A., 287-8, 607

Guinea, 150

Guinea-Bissau (Portuguese Guinea), 150, 580

H

Habbash, George, 319

Haile Selassie I, 152

Haldeman, H.R., 3, 7, 193, 252, 446

Halperin, Morton H., 195

Heath, Edward, 180

Helms, Richard, 7, 409

Helsinki conference, *see* Conference on Security and Cooperation in Europe

Holtzman, Elizabeth, 339, 340

Hoover, J. Edgar, 192

Huang Chen, 77

Humphrey, Hubert H., 484, 579

Hungary, 17, 286, 288, 445

Hunt, E. Howard, Jr., 193

I

IBRD, *see* International Bank for Reconstruction and Development

Iceland, Nixon meeting with Pompidou (May 31-June 1), 180

IDA, *see* International Development Association

IMF, *see* International Monetary Fund

India, 229, 495

Indochina, 2, 3, 5, 13-74, 230-31, 302, 335-47, 371-7, 541-3; Paris peace settlement, 20-52; International Conference on Vietnam, 54-63; cease-fire violations, 67-74, 374-5, 543-5; U.S. aid to, 208, 213-14; congressional action ending U.S. combat in, 335-47; *see also* Vietnam conflict

Indonesia, 17, 381

Inter-American Economic and Social Council (IA-ECOSOC), 117-18, 120, 145; Eighth annual meeting (Bogotá, Jan. 20-Feb. 9): Nixon message (Feb. 1), 121-2

Inter American Press Association, Nixon address (Oct. 31, 1969), 93, 117

International Bank for Reconstruction and Development (IBRD), 210, 381-3; annual meeting (Nairobi, Sept. 24-28): Shultz statement (Sept. 25), 396-406

International Civil Aviation Organization (ICAO), 166

International Conference on Vietnam (Paris, Feb. 26-Mar. 2, 1973), *see* Vietnam conflict

International Court of Justice (ICJ), 300

International Development Association (IDA), 382, 497; Shultz statement (Nairobi, Sept. 25, excerpt), 404; Nixon message (Oct. 31), 510-14

International Energy Agency (Nov. 15, 1974), 556

International Monetary Fund (IMF), 89-90, 91, 210, 381-3; annual meeting (Nairobi, Sept. 24-28): Wardhana report (Sept. 24), 394-6; Shultz statement (Sept. 25), 396-406

International Telephone and Telegraph Corporation (ITT), and Chile, 119, 120

Ioannides, Dimitrios, 2

Iran, 7, 230, 409, 446, 531

Iraq, 444

Ireland, 91, 177

Israel, 605; *see also* Arab-Israeli conflict

Italy, 2, 91, 180, 286

J

Jackson, Henry M., 93, 421-2, 449

Jackson-Mills-Vanik amendment, 93, 421, 423

Jamaica, 403

Jankowitsch, Peter, statement on Arab-Israeli war (Nov. 2), 477-8

Japan, 1, 4, 16, 75, 90, 299-316, 532; Nixon foreign policy report (May 3, excerpt), 199; meeting of Joint United States-Japan Committee on Trade and Economic Affairs (Tokyo, July 16-17): Rogers statement (July 16), 303-12; Nixon-Tanaka meeting (July 31-Aug. 1): joint communiqué (Aug. 1), 312-16; and Europe (Kissinger address, Apr. 23), 179, 367-9; Kissinger visit, 532; statement on Middle East (Nov. 22), 553; Kissinger statement (Dec. 27, excerpt), 622-3; Ford-Tanaka declaration (Tokyo, Nov. 20, 1974), 557-8

Jarring, Gunnar V., 164

Javits, Jacob K., 451

Jaworski, Leon, 23, 483-4

Jobert, Michel, 180, 554

Johnson, Lyndon B., 5, 151, 288; death of (Nixon address, Jan. 23, excerpt), 23

Jordan, 444; *see also* Arab-Israeli conflict

Juan Carlos de Borbón, 605

K

Kennedy, John F., 179, 288

Kennedy, Robert F., 166

Kim Il Sung, 300

Kissinger, Henry A., 2, 195-6, 317, 336, 349-52; statement on Vietnam agreement (Jan. 24), 23-8; visit to Hanoi (Feb. 10-13): joint communiqué (Feb. 14), 52-4; visit to China (Feb. 15-19): joint communiqué (Feb. 22), 82-3; statement (same), 83-6; address on "Year of Europe" (New York, Apr. 23), 181-9; visit to Moscow (May 4-9), 199, 251; statement reaffirming Vietnam agreement (Paris, June 13), 247-9; on SALT negotiating principles (June 21), 256-61; on nuclear war prevention agreement (June 22),

263-4; on Brezhnev visit (San Clemente, June 25), 269-73; nomination as Secretary of State: Nixon announcement (San Clemente, Aug. 22), 354-5; statement on same (same, Aug. 23), 356-9; statement on Chilean coup (Sept. 17), 409-10; address to U.N. (Sept. 24), 359-66; statement on current matters (New York, Sept. 26, excerpt), 366-70; letter on Byrd amendment (Oct. 3), 579; toast to Latin American ambassadors (New York, Oct. 5), 415-17; Nobel Prize award, 423, 606; address to Pacem In Terris conference (Oct. 8), 433-42; visit to Moscow (Oct. 20-21), 447, 448; statement on Middle East military alert (Oct. 25, excerpts), 463-8; visit to Middle East (Nov. 5-9), 529-31, 532-4; letter to Waldheim on Egyptian-Israeli disengagement (Nov. 9), 534-5; visit to China (Nov. 10-14): joint communiqué (Nov. 14), 535-7; statement on Middle East (Nov. 21), 537-9, 603; on Indochina (same), 541; on Watergate and foreign policy (Dec. 6), 3-4; address on U.S. and Europe (London, Dec. 12), 566-75; trips to Middle East (Dec. 13-17), 605; to Portugal and Spain (Dec. 21), 605-6; statement at Geneva Conference (Dec. 21), 608-13; remarks (Dec. 22), 613; statement on 1973 highlights (Dec. 27), 618-26

Kleindienst, Richard G., 193, 446

Korea, Democratic People's Republic of (DPRK), 300

Korea, Republic of (ROK), 300, 301, 302, 532

Kosygin, A.N., 447

Krogh, Egil, Jr., 196

Kubisch, Jack B., statement on Chile, 412-15

Kuwait, 446

L

Laird, Melvin R., 7

Laos, 16, 18, 231, 335, 338, 371-2; protocol on restoring peace and reconciliation (signed Sept. 14): U.S. statement (Sept. 14), 374; Nixon letter to Souvanna Phouma (same), 376

Latin America, 2, 93, 117-21, 407-12; relations with Cuba, 122-6; with Panama, 126-39; the OAS, 139-48; with Chile, 412-15; Kissinger toast (New York, Oct. 5), 415-17; see also organizational and country entries

Lebanon, 420; see also Arab-Israeli conflict

Le Duc Tho, see Tho, Le Duc

Libya, 499; see also Arab-Israeli conflict; Energy crisis

Liddy, G. Gordon, 193

Long Boret, 339
Lon Nol, 339
Luxembourg, 91, 286

M

Magruder, Jeb Stuart, 192, 252
Malik, Yakov A., 445, 451
Mansfield, Mike, 178, 420
Mao Tse-tung, 76, 77, 532
Marcos, Ferdinand E., 373
McCord, James W., Jr., 192
McGovern, George S., 5, 352
McNamara, Robert S., 382
Meir, Golda, 166, 530
Micronesia, *see* Trust Territory of the Pacific Islands
Middle East, 1, 2, 3, 4, 163-8, 208-9, 317-20, 529-31, 532-4, 582-3;
    Sisco address (May 7), 168-75; Nixon-Brezhnev communiqué
    (June 24, excerpt), 279; 4th Arab-Israeli war, 423, 443-79; U.S.
    military alert, 450-52, 463-9; Kissinger visit (Nov. 5-9), 529-31,
    532-5, 537-9; Geneva conference, 603-13; Kissinger statement
    (Dec. 27, excerpt), 623-4; *see also* Arab-Israeli conflict; CEN-
    TO; Energy crisis; and organizational and topical entries
Mills, Wilbur, 93, 421, 423
Mitchell, John N., 192, 195, 252
Moore, George C., 166
Morocco, 530
Morse, C. Jeremy, 381
Mozambique, 150, 151
Muhammad Zahir Shah, 2
Mutual and Balanced Force Reduction (MBFR), 286-7; NATO
    position, 237-8; U.S.-Soviet communiqué (June 24, excerpt),
    278-9; preparatory consultations (Vienna, Jan. 31-June 28):
    communiqué, 290; *see also* Conference on Mutual Reduction of
    Forces and Armaments and Associated Measures in Central
    Europe

N

Namibia, 149, 152, 580-81; Newsom address (excerpt), 166
National Security Council (NSC), 7, 191, 195, 350, 450

Netherlands, 91, 286, 446, 500, 616

Newsom, David D., address on Africa, 152-61; statement on Sahel drought, 214-17; on Byrd amendment, 579

New York Times, 196, 353, 450, 484

New Zealand, 300, 373

Nguyen Van Thieu, *see* Thieu, Nguyen Van

Nixon Doctrine, 5, 76, 299

Nixon, Richard M., 1, 4, 5-8, 93, 191-7, 410, 483-4
    Messages and communications to Congress: on trade reform (Apr. 10), 99-115; on energy crisis (Apr. 18), 209; on foreign aid (May 1), 210-14; on rejection of "Cambodia Rider" (June 27), 340-41; on Cambodia cutoff (Aug. 3), 344-5; on national legislative goals (Sept. 10, excerpts), 424-32; on aid to Israel and Cambodia (Oct. 19), 455-7, 542, 616; on veto of war powers resolution (Oct. 24), 490-94; on funds for IDA and ADB (Oct. 31), 510-514
    Other addresses, communications and remarks: letter to Thieu (Jan. 5), 19-20; second inaugural (Jan. 20), 8-12; on Vietnam peace agreement (Jan. 23), 20-23; message to IA-ECOSOC (Feb. 1), 121-2; on liaison office in Peking (Mar. 15), 86-7; joint statement with Thieu (San Clemente, Apr. 3). 63-7; on Watergate break-in (Apr. 17), 192; same (Apr. 30), 193; same (May 22), 196-7; on 4th annual foreign policy report (May 3), 197-200; on Armed Forces Day (Norfolk, Va., May 19), 200-207; meeting with Pompidou (Reykjavik, May 31-June 1), 180; joint statement with Brezhnev (June 24), 273-83; signature statement on bills ending combat in Indochina (July 1), 343-4; joint statement with Tanaka (Aug. 1), 312-16; on defense policy (New Orleans, Aug. 20, excerpt), 350; on Rogers resignation and nomination of Kissinger (San Clemente, Aug. 22), 354-5; on GATT meeting (Sept. 8, excerpt), 380; letter to Souvanna Phouma (Sept. 14), 376; on Kissinger visit to Far East (Oct. 3), 529; on trade reform (Oct. 4), 432-3; exchange with Brezhnev (Oct. 24-5), 449-50; on Middle East (Oct. 26), 470-72; on energy crisis (Nov. 7), 520-28; on Middle East terrorism (Dec. 17), 606
    See also Watergate scandals

Noel, Cleo A., Jr., 166

North Atlantic Treaty Organization (NATO), 178, 230, 286, 289, 353, 551, 553-4; Council meeting (Copenhagen, June 14-15): communiqué, 236-8; Kissinger statement (Sept. 26, excerpt), 368-9; Council meeting (Brussels, Dec. 10-11): communiqué, 563-6; Council meeting (Ottawa, June 18-19, 1974): "Declaration on Atlantic Relations," 556

Norway, 91, 286

Nuclear war prevention agreement (Agreement on the Prevention of Nuclear War, signed Washington, June 22, 1973): Kissinger statement (June 22), 263-6; text, 266-9

O

OECD, *see* Organization for Economic Cooperation and Development

Ohira, Masayoshi, 301

Oil embargo, 163, 446, 452, 498-501, 530, 533-4, 577, 605, 615-17; Nixon address (Nov. 7, excerpt), 528; and Western Europe, 551, 553, 555-6; *see also* Energy crisis

Organization for Economic Cooperation and Development (OECD), 209-10, 615-16; Council meeting (Paris, June 6-8): communiqué, 224-7; report on world economy (Dec.), 615-16; establishment of International Energy Agency (Nov. 15, 1974), 556

Organization of American States (OAS), 118, 120, 407-8; Third Regular General Assembly Session (Washington, Apr. 4-15): Rogers statement (Apr. 6), 139-48; *see also* Inter-American Economic and Social Council

Organization of Arab Petroleum Exporting Countries (OAPEC), 499

Organization of Petroleum Exporting Countries (OPEC), 208-9, 499-501, 616

Overseas Development Council, Casey address, 501-10

P

Pacem in Terris Conference, Kissinger address (October 8), 433-42

Pakistan, 229, 373, 531; *see also* Central Treaty Organization

Palestine Liberation Organization (PLO), *see* Arab-Israeli conflict

Panama, 118-20, 407, 412; U.N. Security Council meetings (Mar. 15-21): Scali statement (Mar. 20), 126-34; draft resolution (Mar. 21), 134-6; Scali statement (same), 136-9

Papadopoulos, George, 2

Park Chung Hee, 300, 301

"Pentagon Papers," 193, 195

Perón, Isabel Martínez de, 408
Perón, Juan D., 2, 120-21; death of, 408
Persian Gulf, 446
Pinochet Ugarte, Augusto, 408
Peru, 407
Philippines, 373
Poland, 17, 92, 288, 422
Pompidou, Georges, 180, 209, 551, 554
Popular Front for the Liberation of Palestine (PFLP), 319
Portugal, 445, 551, 605; see also Portuguese African territories
Portuguese African territories, 150; Newsom address (excerpt), 160
Portuguese Guinea, see Guinea-Bissau

R

Rabasa, Emilio O., 411
Resor, Stanley H., statement on MBFR (Vienna, Oct. 31), 557-63
Rhodesia, see Southern Rhodesia
Richardson, Elliot L., 3, 7, 193, 336, 446-7
Rogers, William P., 2, 7; statement to conference on Vietnam (Paris, Feb. 26), 54-8; comments on U.S.-Cuba hijacking agreement (Feb. 15), 124-6; statement to OAS (Apr. 6), 139-48; visit to Latin America (May 12-18), 120, 229, 407; statement to CENTO (Tehran, June 10), 231-4; to CSCE (Helsinki, July 5), 291-7; visit to Czechoslovakia (July 8-9), 288-9; on U.S.-Japanese relations (Tokyo, July 16), 303-12; visit to South Korea (July 16-18), 301; affidavit on Cambodia (Aug. 2, excerpt), 338-9; letter of resignation (Aug. 16, excerpt), 350; Nixon announcement on same (San Clemente, Aug. 22), 354-5; Kissinger statement (same, Aug. 23, excerpt), 356
Romania, 286, 288
Ruckelshaus, William D., 3, 447
Rush, Kenneth, 373
Russo, Anthony J., 193

S

al-Sadat, Anwar, 320, 444, 449-50, 529, 605
SALT (Strategic Arms Limitation Talks), see Disarmament

Saudi Arabia, 320, 605; *see also* Arab-Israeli conflict; Energy crisis

Scali, John A., 7, 579; U.N. Security Council meetings in Panama (Mar. 15-21): statements on U.S. views (Mar. 20), 126-34; same (Mar. 21), 136-9

Statements on Middle East (June 14), 320-25; same (July 26), 326-9; same (Aug. 14), 330-32; same (Aug. 15), 333-4

Council meetings on 4th Arab-Israeli war (Oct. 8-Nov. 2): statements on U.N. responsibilities (Oct. 8), 453-5; on U.N. cease-fire resolution (Oct. 21), 457-9; on same (Oct. 23, excerpt), 460-61; on request for U.S.-Soviet forces (Oct. 24), 461-3; on third cease-fire resolution (Oct. 25), 469; on UNEF (Oct. 27), 476-8; on same (Nov. 2), 478-9

Schlesinger, James R., 7, 193n.

Schneider, René, 410

Scott, Hugh, 337

Sea, law of the, 581-2; Rogers statement (Apr. 6, excerpt), 142-3; U.N. General Assembly resolution (Nov. 16), 598-601; *see also* Third U.N. Conference on the Law of the Sea

SEATO, *see* South-East Asia Treaty Organization

Segretti, Donald H., 194-5

Sharon, Ariel, 445, 448

Sharp, Mitchell, 17

Shultz, George P., 180, 209, 301; statements on dollar devaluation (Feb. 12), 94-9; to GATT (Tokyo, Sept. 12), 383-91; to IBRD/IMF (Nairobi, Sept. 25), 396-406

Sihanouk, Norodom, 17, 231, 336, 339, 372, 542

Siilasvuo, Ensio, 452, 531

Sirhan, Sirhan B., 166

Sirica, John J., 6, 190-92, 483

Smithsonian Agreement (1971), 89, 90, 92, 379, 380

Souphanouvong, Prince, 16, 371

South Africa, 149, 150-51, 580-81; Newsom address (excerpt), 160

South-East Asia Treaty Organization (SEATO), 373-4; 18th annual meeting (New York, Sept. 28): press statement, 376-7

Southern Rhodesia (Zimbabwe), 149-50, 150-52, 579-80; Newsom address (excerpt), 160; U.N. General Assembly resolution, 583-6

South West Africa, *see* Namibia

Souvanna Phouma, 16, 371-2; letter from Nixon (Sept. 14), 376

Spain, 2, 605-6

Sri Lanka (Ceylon), 582

Stans, Maurice, 195

Stein, Herbert, 301

Stoessel, Walter J., 354

State Department (U.S.), 168, 191, 349, 483; Rogers resignation and Kissinger nomination: Nixon announcement (San Clemente, Aug. 22), 354-5; Kissinger statement (same, Aug. 23), 356-9

Strategic Arms Limitation Talks (SALT), *see* Disarmament

Sudan, 152, 166-7

Sweden, 91, 194

Syria, 320; *see also* Arab-Israeli conflict

T

Tack, Juan Antonio, 412

Taiwan, *see* China, Republic of

Tanaka, Kakuei, 4, 301, 302; statement with Nixon (Aug. 1), 312-16; declaration with Ford (Nov. 20, 1974), 557-8

Teng Hsiao-ping, 532

Terrorism, 2, 164-7, 317-20, 581; Rogers statement (Apr. 6, excerpt), 143-4; U.N. General Assembly resolution (Dec. 14), 586-8; text of convention on, 588-94; Bennett statement (same), 594-8; Nixon statement (Dec. 17, excerpt), 606; *see also* Arab-Israeli conflict

Terrorism, U.N. Convention on (adopted Dec. 14, 1973): resolution, 586-8; text, 588-94

Thailand, 2, 16, 373

Thanom Kittikachorn, 373

Thieu, Nguyen Van, 13-14, 18; letter from Nixon (Jan. 5), 19-20; communiqué with Nixon (San Clemente, Apr. 3), 63-7

Third U.N. Conference on the Law of the Sea, General Assembly resolution (Nov. 16), 598-601; first session (New York, Dec. 3-15), 581-2; *see also* Sea, law of the

Tho, Le Duc, 13, 15, 18, 229, 231, 423, 606

Time, 192, 484

Tito, Josip Broz, 445

Torrijos Herrera, Omar, 118, 119

Trade Act of 1974, 380, 421-2, 617; Nixon message (Apr. 10),

99-115; Nixon foreign policy report (May 3, excerpt), 199; Nixon message (Sept. 10, excerpt), 425-7; Nixon statement (Oct. 4), 432-3; Kissinger address (Oct. 8, excerpt), 439

Trust Territory of the Pacific Islands (Micronesia), 300

Tunisia, 530

Turkey, 286; *see also* Central Treaty Organization

U

Union of Soviet Socialist Republics (U.S.S.R.), 1, 92-3, 251-6, 320, 349, 553, 617; Brezhnev visit to U.S. (June 18-25): Kissinger statement on agreement on SALT negotiating principles (June 21), 256-61; text (signed Washington, June 21), 262-3; Kissinger statement on nuclear war prevention agreement (June 22), 263-4; text (signed Washington, June 22), 264-9; Kissinger review of visit (San Clemente, June 25), 269-73; U.S.-Soviet communiqué (released June 25), 273-83

    Kissinger address (Oct. 8, excerpt), 439-40; Kissinger statement (Dec. 27, excerpt), 620-21

    See also Arab-Israeli conflict; Berlin; Brezhnev; Disarmament; Europe, détente in

United Kingdom, 90, 91, 177, 180, 447; fuel emergency, 555-6; Kissinger address (London, Dec. 12), 566-75, 605

United Nations, *see* following entries

U.N. Commission on the Unification and Rehabilitation of Korea (UNCURK), 578

U.N. Committee on the Peaceful Uses of the Seabed, 582

U.N. Conference on the Law of the Sea, *see* Third U.N. Conference on the Law of the Sea

U.N. Economic and Social Council (ECOSOC), 498, 581

U.N. Emergency Force (UNEF), *see* Arab-Israeli conflict

U.N. General Assembly (28th Session, Sept. 18-Dec. 18, Sept. 16, 1974): 577-83; Kissinger address (Sept. 24), 359-66; admission of new members, 578; budget, 578; Korea, 578; disarmament, 578-9; colonial issues, 579-81; proposed World Food Conference, 581; Middle East, 582-3; special session on development, 583

    Resolutions and statements on Cambodia, 545-50; on Southern Rhodesia, 583-6; on terrorism, 586-98; on law of the sea, 598-601

    Resolutions by number: 3067 (XXVIII), Nov. 16, on law of the sea conference, 598-601; 3116 (XXVIII), Dec. 12, condemning U.S. policy on Rhodesia, 583-6; 3166 (XXVIII), Dec. 14, adopting terrorism convention, 586-8

U.N. Peacekeeping Force in Cyprus (UNFICYP), 452

U.N. Security Council, meetings in Panama (Mar. 15-21), 126-39; and Southern Rhodesia, 150-51; and Namibia, 152, 161; and Portuguese African Territories, 151, 161; and Middle East, 163, 167-8, 320-34, 453-5, 457-63, 469-70, 472-9

 Resolutions by number: 337 (1973), Aug. 15, condemning Israel for seizing Lebanese airliner, 332-3; 338 (1973), Oct. 22, calling for a cease-fire in the Middle East, 459; 339 (1973), Oct. 23, calling for an immediate cease-fire in the Middle East, 459-60; 340 (1973), Oct. 25, calling for a cease-fire and emergency force, 469-70; 341 (1973), Oct. 27, establishing UNEF, 475-6

U.N. Truce Supervision Organization (UNTSO), 448, 452

U.N. Trusteeship Council, 300

United States, *see* appropriate topical, organizational and personal entries

V

Vanik, Charles A., 93, 421-2

Vázquez Carrizosa, Alfredo, 411

Vesco, Robert, 195

Veterans of Foreign Wars, Nixon address to, 350

Vietnam conflict, 5, 76, 230-31, 335-40, 371-4, 541-3; Nixon letter to Thieu (Jan. 5), 19-20; Nixon address on peace agreement (Jan. 23), 20-23; Kissinger statement (Jan. 24), 23-8; text of peace agreement (signed Paris, Jan. 27), 39-52; Kissinger visit to Hanoi (Feb. 10-13): joint communiqué (Feb. 14), 52-4

 International Conference on Vietnam (Paris, Feb. 26-Mar. 2): Rogers statement (Feb. 26), 54-8; "Act of Paris" (signed Mar. 2), 58-63

 Thieu visit to Nixon (San Clemente, Apr. 2-3), 63-7; U.S. note on cease-fire violations (Apr. 20), 67-74; Nixon foreign policy report (May 3, excerpt), 198-9; joint communiqué reaffirming Paris agreements (signed Paris, June 13), 239-46; Kissinger statement (same, excerpt), 247-9

 Joint U.S.-Soviet communiqué (June 24, excerpt), 277; U.S. note on airfield construction (Sept. 10), 374-5; U.S. note admonishing DRV (Oct. 26), 543-5; Kissinger news conference (Nov. 21, excerpt), 541; Kissinger statement (Dec. 27, excerpt), 618-19

Vietnam, Democratic Republic of (DRV), issue of U.S. aid to, 14-15, 335; Kissinger visit (Feb. 10-13), joint communiqué (Feb. 14), 52-4; U.S. note on airfield construction (Sept. 10), 374-5; U.S. note of admonition (Oct. 26), 543-5

Vietnam, Republic of, Nixon letter to Thieu (Jan. 5), 19-20; Nixon-Thieu communiqué (San Clemente, Apr. 3), 63-7

W

Waldheim, Kurt, report on Namibia, 152, 161; on Israeli attack on Libyan airliner, 166; on Middle East, 167-8, 317, 448; on UNEF (Oct. 27), 472-5; letter from Kissinger on Egypt-Israel disengagement (Nov. 9), 534-5; at Geneva Conference on Middle East (Dec. 21), 606-7

Wardhana, Ali, 381; report on monetary reform (Nairobi, Sept. 24), 394-6

War powers of the President, 419, 481-94; war powers resolution (passed by Senate Oct. 10; by House Oct. 12): text, 484-90; Nixon veto message (Oct. 24), 490-94; White House statement on enactment (Nov. 7), 494

Warren, Gerald L., statement on Cambodia (Aug. 15), 345-7

Warsaw Pact, 178, 286, 289

Watergate scandals, 1, 3-4, 6, 191-7, 251-2, 255, 301-2, 446-7, 616-17

Williams, Maurice J., statement on food shortages, 514-20

Witteveen, H. Johannes, 382

Y

Yaariv, Aharon, 531

"Year of Europe," see Europe, Western

Young, David R., 193

Yugoslavia, 92, 422, 445, 495

Z

Zablocki, Clement J., 482

Zaki al-Yamani, Sheik Ahmad, 616

Zambia, 150, 151

Zimbabwe, see Southern Rhodesia

Richard P. Stebbins graduated from Harvard with highest honors in English, returning to earn his M.A. and Ph.D. in modern history at a period when America's post-World War I isolationism was breaking down under the stress of developments in Europe and Asia. After teaching briefly at Harvard, Radcliffe, and Northeastern, he embarked on a career of research and writing with a year's membership in the Institute for Advanced Study as a Fellow of the Social Science Research Council; wartime service as a foreign affairs analyst in the Office of Strategic Services; and direction of political research on various European areas under the Department of State. He has also held a Guggenheim Fellowship and is co-author of a number of books on literary and musical subjects. Appointed editor of THE UNITED STATES IN WORLD AFFAIRS in 1949, he authored seventeen volumes in that standard series, becoming a Senior Research Fellow of the Council on Foreign Relations and supervising the preparation of numerous volumes in the Council's other annual series, DOCUMENTS ON AMERICAN FOREIGN RELATIONS and POLITICAL HANDBOOK AND ATLAS OF THE WORLD/THE WORLD THIS YEAR.

Elaine P. Adam received her bachelor's degree in political science at Goucher College and served as an analyst with the foreign language division of the Army Signal Corps during World War II. Since 1952 she has worked in various capacities on the annual publications of the Council on Foreign Relations and has developed a particularly strong association with the documentary series.